HARDPRESS
.NET

ISBN: 9781313541275

Published by:
HardPress Publishing
8345 NW 66TH ST #2561
MIAMI FL 33166-2626

Email: info@hardpress.net
Web: http://www.hardpress.net

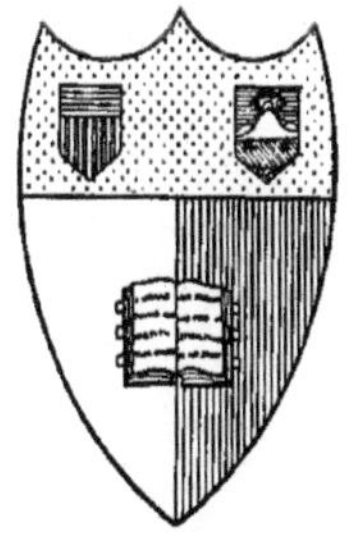

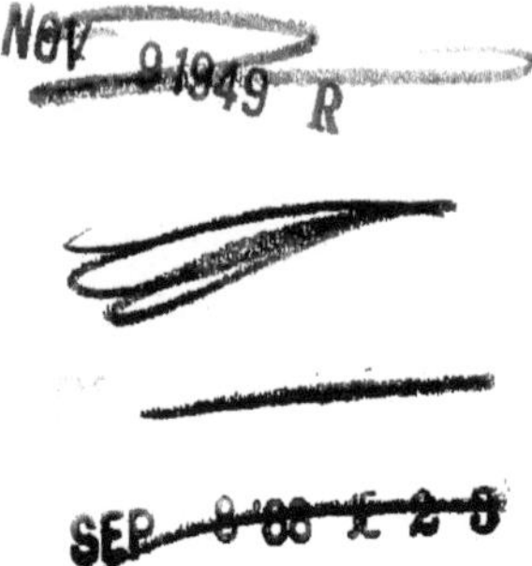

PUBLICATIONS OF THE UNIVERSITY OF MANCHESTER

HISTORICAL SERIES

No. XXX

# FREEDOM AFTER EJECTION

Published by the University of Manchester at
THE UNIVERSITY PRESS (H. M. McKECHNIE, Secretary)
12 LIME GROVE, OXFORD ROAD, MANCHESTER

LONGMANS, GREEN & CO.
LONDON: 39 Paternoster Row
NEW YORK: 443-449 Fourth Avenue and Thirtieth Street
CHICAGO: Prairie Avenue and Twenty-fifth Street
BOMBAY: Hornby Road
CALCUTTA: 6 Old Court House Street
MADRAS: 167 Mount Road

# FREEDOM AFTER EJECTION

## A REVIEW (1690–1692) OF PRESBYTERIAN AND CONGREGATIONAL NONCONFORMITY IN ENGLAND AND WALES

EDITED BY

ALEXANDER GORDON, M.A.

SOMETIME LECTURER IN ECCLESIASTICAL HISTORY IN THE UNIVERSITY OF MANCHESTER

*COLLIGITE QUAE SUPERAVERUNT FRAGMENTA NE PEREANT. COLLEGERUNT ERGO*

MANCHESTER:

AT THE UNIVERSITY PRESS

12 Lime Grove, Oxford Road

LONGMANS, GREEN & CO.

London, New York, Bombay, etc.

1917

PUBLICATIONS OF THE UNIVERSITY OF MANCHE[illegible]

No. CXIV

# PREFACE

THE Manuscript here for the first time printed, and reproduced *verbatim et literatim*, is fully described, pp. 170 *sqq*. The circumstances of its discovery and appreciation are detailed p. 171.

The thanks of the public are especially due to the Presbyterian Board of London, under whose sanction, and at whose desire, this document, of great historical interest and value, has been permitted to see the light. Still further thanks are due for the grant of unrestricted access to the Minutes of the Board, from its inception in 1690. Without a full use of the data furnished by these Minutes, much of the information given in the Commentary and Index could not have been supplied, and no effective annotation of the Manuscript could have been attempted.

The list of Authorities consulted will be found pp. 192-7. Detailed references are not given; not merely because they would unduly swell the matter of the Index, but further, because experience has shown that those who are concerned to test statements made are usually willing to examine sources for themselves. Among the Authorities, no indebtedness is greater, in regard to the education of Divines, than to the comprehensive works of Foster (for Oxford) and Venn (for Cambridge); and, in regard to the Indulgences of 1672, to the comprehensive work of Rev. Prof. George Lyon Turner; though, in regard to both these departments of inquiry, the present writer has long been engaged in original research.

Individual and very grateful thanks are due to Mr. George Harold Clennell, Book-keeper of the Presbyterian Board; to Rev. Francis Henry

Jones, and Rev. Robert Travers Herford, successively Librarians of Dr. Williams' Library; to Mr. H. M. McKechnie, of the Manchester University Press; and to Mr. Ernest Axon, Rev. Dr. Benjamin Nightingale, and Rev. Prof. George Lyon Turner, each of whom has done me the favour of going through the proofs of the Index, to the great advantage of the result.

To have attained the accuracy for which he has striven, and for which he will continue to toil, the present writer makes no futile claim. *Me laborantem adjuva, candide lector.*

A. G.

BELFAST, 1917.

# TYPOGRAPHY

ALL words and sentences printed in italic represent words and sentences scored out in ink (mostly very lightly) in the original, and easily deciphered.

All words and sentences, chiefly in margins, printed in smaller type, represent words and sentences deciphered from shorthand, respecting which see p. 173.

# THE MANUSCRIPT

| [2] | London & in and about y[e] Same— |
|---|---|
| [Mi]nisters y[t] [ar]e not fixed [to] particular [C]ongregac̃ons | |
| [M[r]] Alexander | M[r] Cornish's Chaplaine, has an euening Lecture at M[r] Turners |
| [M]r Barker | In Petty ffrance. poor. |
| [M]r Barham | In White ffryars, very aged and very poor |
| M[r] Barton | Chaplain to Rich[d] Hampden Esq[r] has a Lecture at M[r] Lobbs and at m[r] ffords |
| M[r] Burnet | A Scotchman, at M[r] Parsons in green Dragon Court in Cow:lane hath an euening Lectures at M[r] Quicks |
| M[r] Beerman | Preacheth at Wapping or thereabouts |
| M[r] Cawthorn | In Iuin Street |
| M[r] Coven | poor |
| M[r] Dowly | At Bird, in hand alley, in cheapside |
| M[r] Dod | May be heard of at his Son's an apprentice to M[r] Dentham in y[e] postern, is about to leaue Horn Ch : |
| M[r] Doolittle | With his father in St. John's. |
| M[r] Farlough | In hatten Garden if in towne |

| | |
|---|---|
| | is very poor |
| Mr Flauell | in New Street ^ neere mr Lobbs meeting house |
| Mr Finch | Preacheth at Mortlack |
| Mr Glascock | The Lady Wimbletons Chaplain, on ye Strand |
| [Mr Gle]ddall | Att mr Hodgkins in Doue Court in old ffish street |
| [Mr H]arris | In Prince's Street by ye Exchange. |
| [Mr H]orsman | Att ye white Cross in ye Poultry |
| [Mr] Hill | Att ye Lady Irbi's, west Minster, Chaplain and Tutor |
| [Mr] Hocker | At Edmondton Dadm De Luna's Chaplain |
| Mr James | Att ye Chirurgeons armes in Bartholomew Square old-street |
| Mr Jackson | Att Edmonton |
| Mr Jennings | Chaplaine to Madam Gould at Clapham |
| Mr Kempster | Neere Anthony's Church. |
| Mr King | Att ye Bell and Dragon, in Grace Church Street |
| [M]r Kentish | Juor on Pigghill neer Billingsgate hath a fortnights Lords day euening Lecture. |
| Mr Keeling | Att ye hand, in Thames Street neere Billings gate |
| Mr Lorimer | A Scotchman, at Mr Stones an Apothecary in Thames Street neere ye old Swan. |
| Mr Layton | Came lately from Nottinghamshire |
| Mr Lamb | Att his Brothers an Oyleman neere ye Spittall |
| Mr Mortimer | A Scotchman at in Long lane inclineable to goe into ye Countrey |
| Mr Merrill | Att ye Lady Cheekes in Chelsey, Chaplain and Tutor |
| Mr Mottershed | Att Clapham, hath a great Estate now entering upon preaching |

| | | |
|---|---|---|
| [M$^r$] Moor | Att a Scriveners in y$^e$ middle of Bucklersbury | |
| [M$^r$] Moreland | Assists his Brother in his School. at *hackl* hackney | |
| [M$^r$] Morland | Companion Holworthy Esq$^r$ at Hackney. | |

[3]

## Bedford

Ministers that haue a competent Supply.

## London, & in and about y$^e$ Same

| Ministers y$^t$ are not fixed to particular Congregations | | |
|---|---|---|
| M$^r$ Nabs | Att mr Wilkinsons, in maide Lane in St Mary Oueries | |
| M$^r$ Nesbet | *Att* Neere Rope-makers Alley, in Little moor fields, an euening Lords day Lecture at M$^r$ Williams, now w$^{th}$ D$^r$ Chauncey | |
| M$^r$ Porter | In Powells Alley, ag$^t$ the new Artillery ground | |
| M$^r$ Reynolds Iuo$^r$ | Att y$^e$ hand and pen in Swan-Alley in St John-Street an euening Lecture at M$^r$ Lobbs, and m$^r$ Fords | |
| M$^r$ Rogers | Att Hoxton, a fortnightly euening Lecture at Crosby Square | |
| M$^r$ Benoni Row | Att y$^e$ end of Grays-Inn Lane next y$^e$ fields | Going to Settle at Epsom |
| M$^r$ Rood | Att Hackney. Qu: whether hee preaches in y$^e$ Compter. | |
| M$^r$ Rathband | Att high-gate | |
| M$^r$ Roberts | Neere Salisbury-Street in Rotherith | |
| M$^r$ Stancliff | Neere Cruched ffryars Church | |

| | |
|---|---|
| Mr Starr | Att his Sons, an Apothecary on little-tower hill |
| Mr Stackhouse | In ye old Artillery preacheth wth mr Cockain |
| Mr Sanders | Neere Hicks-hall |
| Mr Terry | Att Newington |
| | *Ministers that Want Some Assistance* |
| Mr Thorowgood | In Anns Lane Westminster preaches at Woollwitch |
| Mr Thornly | Chaplain, to Sr Wm Ashhurst |
| Mr Troughton | Att Clapham, teaches School and preaches occasionally |
| Mr Trail | Preacheth wth mr Cole |
| Mr Vnik | Att Darlston in hackney, preacheth to a few in his own house |
| Mr Woodcock | Preacheth onley in his own house at Hackney— |
| Mr Wickens | Preacheth at Newington-green |
| Mr White | Preacheth wth mr Bragg |
| Mr Webb | Att Hackney past preaching, and is very poor |
| Mr Weeks | Att ye white-Cross in ye Poultry Reader |
| Mr Jo: Marshall | Mr John Quicks, wants Support in his preparitory Studies to ye ministry |

---

| | |
|---|---|
| Fran: ffreeman<br>Jno ffoxton<br>Roger Griffith<br>Benj: Pyke<br>Jno Earle<br>Charles Owen<br>Wm Holman<br>Sam: Brookes<br>Sam: Bourne<br>Honorate Superiori | Youths educated att Bednall Greene |
| Pike<br>Pool<br>Keith | Youths educated by mr Doolittle |

| [4] | Bedford | |
|---|---|---|
| Ministers that haue a Competent Supply | Places where there may be Oportunity of Seruis were there a Minister | |
| Ministers y$^{t}$ may want a Supply | Persons Quallified for the Ministry | M$^{r}$. Cockaye |
| Person contributing | | |

| [5] | Bedford | |
|---|---|---|
| Places y$^{t}$ haue had & where there may be opportunity of Religious assemblyes | Persons that may be Seruisable in the Ministry | M$^{r}$ Cockayne |
| S$^{t}$ Neotts | Want a minister can raise 80 *l* per annum | |
| Persons qualified for y$^{e}$ Ministry and not yet fixed | | |
| Persons qualifying for y$^{e}$ Min$^{r}$y | Persons contributing | |
| Proposalls | | |

| [6] Ministers yt haue a Competent Supply | Berks | Dr Samson and Mr Cockerell |
| --- | --- | --- |
| | has 4 or 500 hearers ye people considerably rich | —— —— |
| Mr *Juice* Duce | Att Reading has a very large Congregation | |
| Mr Hump: Gunter | Of Stanford preaches Sometimes at his own house gratis and all other times at Buckland | |
| Mr Hardy | Att Newbury has 1000 people as some say, has 50 *l* pr annū | |
| Mr Merriman | A young man preacheth att Newbury in ye afternoon | |
| Mr Tho: Dawson | Att Abington, has a great people, a comfortable Supply, has of his own | |
| | Att Hungerford | |
| Mr Smith | Att New Windsor and Eaton | |
| Mr Wm Brice | Sr Robert Pies Chaplaine Supplys Buckland by turnes wth mr Gunter | |
| Ministers yt may want supply. | | |
| | Solesly, Wantage and Heyburne very poore, good Schollar & man | |
| Richd Mr Comyn | Att *Cheseley* is low in ye world, hath a Competent Congregation but a very inconsiderable allowance, a good preacher and deserves incouragmt. hath ·7· children. | |
| *Mr Humph: Gunter.* | *Of Stanford preaches Sometimes at his own house Gratis and att all other times att Buckland* | |

| | | |
|---|---|---|
| *W$^{m}$ M$^{r}$ Brice*<br><br>put this in the upper column | *S$^{r}$ Robert Pyes Chaplaine Supplies Buckland by turns w$^{th}$ m$^{r}$ Gunter but haue neither of them any maintenance but what S$^{r}$ Robert gives them out of his own pockett.* | |
| M$^{r}$ Cheesman a blind man att East Ilsly | At Wantage where hee has about 25 *l* p$^{r}$ annum and a dwelling house—too Small a maintenance hee haueing a wife and a Son and 2 daughters where of one is blind, a Small people and hee very poore | |
| *M$^{r}$ Tho: Gilbert & M$^{r}$ Henry Cornish* | *At Oxon*<br>*att Stanton Harcourt* } *Two Superannuated ministers worthy men and very low in y$^{e}$ world.* | |
| M$^{r}$ Ja: Prince | Att Ockingham, has a fixed Congregation, has but 10 *l* p añ̄ñ a Londoner born about 60 years old they allow very Little | |
| M$^{r}$ John Brice | Att Maydenhead, has 200 hearers, not 20 *l* a year | |
| M$^{r}$ Meddowes | Att Bucklbury and Bradford, about 200 auditors, 2 children and about 20 *l* p$^{r}$ anū | |
| M$^{r}$ Nabbs | Att Binfield hath 30 *l* p$^{r}$ annum y$^{e}$ people poor & not able to continue without assistance | |
| m$^{r}$ Moor | Att Hungerford has but a Small maintenance can allow noe more but 17 *l* p$^{r}$ annum, desire assistance | |
| Persons contributing | | |

[7]

| | | |
|---|---|---|
| Places y$^{t}$ had and where there may be oportunity of Religious Assemblys | | D$^{r}$ Samson and M$^{r}$ Cockerell |

| | | |
|---|---|---|
| Market Ilseley | About Seuen miles from Abington from whence m^r Tho Cheesman lately remoued to Wantage. where hee had a Small Auditory and not aboue 10 *l* p^r añn. | |
| Beechill | The people there haue prevailed w^th one M^r Jn^o Edwards to reside amongst them. but y^e poverty of his hearers is Such y^t they cannot allow *him* a maintenance for himselfe and his family, desire Some assistance See this case fully in N^o 93 | see alsoe N^o 70 in y^e 2^d yeare. can but raise 14 *l* per anū : |
| Binfeild | M^r Nabbs is theire hath · 15 · *l* p Anñ was an Ejected minister—frō West Chester, | |
| Persons qualifyed for y^e Ministry & not yet fixed | | |
| Persons qualifying for the Ministry. | | |
| Proposalls | | |

| [8] Ministers that haue a Competent Supply | Bucks | Mr Mead and Dr Samson |
|---|---|---|
| Mr Sam: Clark Ejected | has 200 auditors Att Aylesbury, hath a fixed Congregation, ye maintenance is bare 20 *l* per annum. Ejected and soe remaines | |
| Mr Swinhow Ejected | Att Princes Risborough, preaches to a number of people in as hee has done in ye most difficult times his own house an aged man has Some estate | see mr Swinnows case stated by himselfe No 165:— |
| Mr Archibald Hamilton and *Ejected* young | Att Wycombe, a Scotchman, the maintenance promised was 26 *l* now falls Short . . ye first yt Sett up a meeting in yt towne, by mr Taylers advice and procurement | |
| Mr Sam: Smith Ejected | Att Eaton by Windsor a fixed congregation ye maintenance 30 *l* p annum | |
| Ministers yt may want a Supply. | | |
| Mr Jno Nott ejected | Att Woburne, a Small meeting. while ye Lord Whartons ^family^ is there his Chaplaine preaches to them. when absent Mr Nott has about 14 or 15 *l* p annum, preaches in my Ld Whartons chappell to a very small number | gone into Oxfordshire |

| | | |
|---|---|---|
| M$^{r}$ W$^{m}$ Alsop Ejected | Att Beaconsfield, very ancient his maintenance is about 15 *l* a yeare has about 20 *l* p$^{r}$ annum as p$^{r}$ N$^{o}$ 79 | |
| now att Barnett — m$^{r}$ Geo Swinnow | See his own case represented by himselfe with his Sons Letter to y$^{e}$ Board to y$^{e}$ Same purpose | |
| [9] | **Bucks** | |
| Places y$^{t}$ had and where there may be oportunity of Religious Assemblyes | | M$^{r}$ Mead and D$^{r}$ Samson |
| At Wendover | Was a meeting for about a quarter of a year where m$^{r}$ Not (M$^{r}$ Hampdens Chaplaine) preach'd once a day, till m$^{r}$ Hampden remoued his family to London, since w$^{ch}$ time hee has placed a publick minister there | |
| Winslow | A markett towne they haue Subscribed £10 :—per annum towards the maintenance of a Minister, and desire Some assistance, there is noe meeting neer them except of y$^{e}$ Anabaptists— | |
| Persons qualifyed for y$^{e}$ Ministry & not yet fixed— | | |
| Persons qualifying for y$^{e}$ Ministry | | |
| Proposalls | | |

| [10] Ministers y$^{t}$ haue a Competent Supply | Cambridge |
|---|---|
| M$^{r}$ Tho: Taylor Congregationall | In Cambridge maintenance 40 *l* p$^{r}$ an̄ they stand in need of an Assistant, and propose to raise 20 *l* p$^{r}$ An̄ towards his maintenance, and desire an allowance of 20 *l* p$^{r}$ An̄ more for some time see alsoe N$^{o}$ 57 & 58 |
| M$^{r}$ Josiah Chorley Presbiterian | Resides in Cambridge preaching y$^{e}$ Lecture, and his Course on y$^{e}$ Lords dayes. The Congregation is Supplyed on y$^{e}$ Lords dayes by |
| M$^{r}$ Steph: Scandrett M$^{r}$ Robert Billio & m$^{r}$ Fran: Williams | in their Courses, they allow 20s. p̱ diem for y$^{e}$ Lords dayes and about 13 *l* p̱ An̄ for the Lecture, they desire Some assistance towards y$^{e}$ Lecture. |
| M$^{r}$ Holcroft | Ejected, w$^{th}$ one part of his people, on y$^{e}$ South of Cambridge hath with him but one minister viz$^{t}$ |
| M$^{r}$ Harris | And wants another, the allowance for all is 40 *l* p$^{r}$ An̄ |
| M$^{r}$ W$^{m}$ Payn Sen$^{r}$ | Att Linton euery other Lords day a Considerable meeting they allow him 10s p$^{r}$ Diem,—is inclinable to sett up a fixed Congregation |

| | | |
|---|---|---|
| | at a convenient distance from sundry places | and desires Some assistance ye people being poor |
| Mr Flemming | At Soam and Burwell, they like his preaching well but desire a Con- man gregational *mall*, able to raise 30 *l* pr an̄— | |
| Ministers yt may want Supply | | |
| Mr Bradshaw | Att Wivlingham, ejected from thence his allowance this yeare was but fifty shillings. | |
| Mr Birchall | Att Sutton in ye Isle of Ely an ejected minister, no allow— but mans meat and hors-meat while hee workes. his own Estate when his boarding is paid but £4 : 10 dureing life | |
| w Mr Cadwell ^ | Of Swaffham a pious and Learned man of an infirm body, disabled from much publick Sevice has a wife and 5 children needs assistance | |
| *Mr Hunt* | *Of Oxfo Cambridge the Son of an ejected* | |
| Persons contributing | | |
| [11] Places that had & where there may be oportunity of Religious Assemblies | Cambridge | Mr Mead and Dr Samson |

| | |
|---|---|
| March & Strettam in y$^{e}$ Isle of Ely | Is a people y$^{t}$ doe meet but haue noe minister would be willing to allow 20 *l* p$^{r}$ An̄ |
| In y$^{e}$ City of Ely | Is a people willing to hear but haue noe minister, haue need of an able Minister and a man of courage, willing to contribute what they can to Such an one. |
| Wisbich | A considerable *people* place, noe minister, one greatly desired, hope to make 20 *l* p$^{r}$ An̄, need an able man and a Stout Anti-Arminian |
| Foardham | They are willing to give about 12 *l* p$^{r}$ anū, to haue y$^{e}$ Gospell preached there on y$^{e}$ Lords day by whom they can gett, haueing hitherto had it only on the week-day. |
| Catlige | They haue had a Lecture once a fortnight are willing to give 10 *l* p$^{r}$ annum, towards preaching on the Sabbath. M$^{r}$ Wright of Ousden is willing to Sitt down w$^{th}$ y$^{m}$ if hee had a competent incouragment. |
| Persons qualifyed for y$^{e}$. Ministry and not fixed | Icleton, Thriplo, Taft, Orwell, Gransden } These places haue agreed to haue y$^{e}$ Gospel preached to each of them once in 3 weekes on y$^{e}$ Lords dayes by m$^{r}$ Harris and m$^{r}$ Hunt by turnes, att 10$^{s}$ each a day. M$^{r}$ Hunt wants bookes, neither can hee nor M$^{r}$ Cawdwell Supply themselues |
| *M$^{r}$ Swaffham* *M$^{r}$ Cawdwell* | Att Swaffham *a pious and learned man of an infirm body, disabled from much publick Service, has a wife and 5 Children, needs Assistance* |

| | |
|---|---|
| Mr Hunt | The Son of an Ejected minister deceased, educated for ye ministry, keeps a School in Cambridge, hath of late begun to preach. preacheth at Seuerall places |
| Burwell & Some | Great Townes, there is a worthy man Mr fflemming a Scotch-man that hath by turnes preached to them, but ye people are many of such od opinions, that hee is discouraged and about to leave them, they give him little |
| Swaffham | Mr Rant there is ye chiefe incourager of mr Cawdwell, who hath a—wife and 5 if not 6 Small children and wanteth bookes |
| Soham or ffordham | Where mr ffleming has beene minister for a considerable time but has lately beene called to a Pastorall charge in Holland and has accepted it, they haue introduced one Doughty a Mechanick desire Some assistance to incourage a Lawfull Ministry |
| Persons qualifying for the Ministry | |
| mr Hunt | Brother to mr Wm Hunt of Cambridge, a very hopefull young wants Some assistance for ye perfecting of his Studies |
| Proposalls | Mr Oaks assistant to mr Taylor being remoued by death, the people begg assistance in Sending them a fitt person as soone as possible, and Such a one as may be an honour to ye Gospell, expect 20 *l* pr annū |

| [12] Ministers that haue a competent Supply | Chester | Mr Dan: Williams |
|---|---|---|
| Mr Coape | chappell<br>Att Haslington ∧ neere Nantwich in comfortable circumstances | |
| Mr Mosely | Att Rugely Chappell these two are aged Ministers | |
| Mr Joseph Eyton | Att *Congleton* Maxfield | |
| Mr Jones | Att Congleton. | |
| Mr Bryam | Att or neere Stopford. | |
| Mr Sam: Lawrence | Att Nantwych. | |
| Mr Tho: Kynnston | Att Knutsford. | |
| Mr Aynsworth | Att Whitly Chappell. | |
| Mr Latham | Neere ffrodsham | |
| Mr Stringer | Att Peever. | |
| Mr Holland | Towards Congleton. | |
| Mr Birch | ffather and Son fixed comfortably in ye vpper part of ye County | |
| Mr Lea | Att Vpton in Worrall, hath a fine congregation | |
| Mr Henry | *Att Broad Oak, a constant meeting on Lords days for all ordinances* | |
| | *Att Whittchurch. Hanmer and Vpton and else where in ye neighbourhood are monthly Lectures kept up* | |
| *Mr Fra: Tallent mr Jno Bryan and mr David Jones* | *Att Salop.* | |

| | | |
|---|---|---|
| *Mr Woodhouse and mr Doughty* | *Att Sheriff Hales. Shropshire* | |
| *Mr John Nevit* | *Att or neere Bridgnorth.* | |
| *Mr And: Barnett* | *Neere Oswestree* | |
| 1691 | | |
| mr Irlam | Of Congleton, cannot Subsist vpon his present allowance, ye people can give noe more than they doe, ye meeting like to fall if hee remove, has met wth more opposition than usuall. | |
| Ministers that want Supply | | |
| *Mr Sam: Tayler* | *Liues and preaches att Wem, hath a great charge of children lost by the fire there Some yeares agoe.* | |
| *mr James Owen* | *Att Oswestree, haueing ye Welch Tongue, unwearyed in his labours, receives little Recompence. in Salop* | |
| *Mr Finlow* | *Neere Acham, is aged and poore. in Shropshire Salop* | |
| Persons Contributing | | |
| Mr Henry of Chester | Likely to doe Somewhat | |
| [13] | Chester | |
| Places yt had and where there may be oportunity for Religious assemblies | | Mr Dan Williams |

| | |
|---|---|
| Persons qualifyed for y^e Ministry and not fixed | |
| M^r John Wilson | Late Chaplaine to madam Crew att Vtkinton hath beene very usefull, and still might be if employed and incouraged |
| Persons qualifying for y^e Ministry | |
| M^r Barker | A young man not yet ordained, is beginning a haruest and Promiseth well—About Wellaston & Brembro |
| Richard Edge | A young man intending for the ministry — well inclined but want some help and incouragm^t that way |
| John Lewis | (who hath y^e Welch tongue) D^o |
| James Thomson | A young man |
| these three belong to Shropshire | |
| Proposalls— | If anything can be communicated it might perhaps be best imployed by Setting up a moveable Lecture in Such circumstances and carryed on by Such hands as shall be thought to stand in most need of encouragment |

| [14] Ministers y[t] haue a Competent Supply | Cornwall |
|---|---|
| *Joseph* John Mr ∧ Sherwood | Att Errisey (his licenced place) his maintenance Solely from Eresy 16 *l* p[r] annũ preacheth a Lecture att Market Jew once a fortnight gratis |
| Mr Lewis ffacy | Penrin and Att ∧ Falmouth 1 *l* 6 p[r]) |
| *Mr Jos: Halsey* | Att Marthir. noe fixed maintenance had last year 9.19:6 y[e] yeare before 5:10: |
| *Mr Roger ∧ ank Flammick* | Att s[t] Inoder. Subscrip: 19 p[r] annũ, hee rec[d] last year but 6 *l*: |
| Mr Jon[a] ∧ Wills | Att S[t] Hellens. his maintenance Scanty |
| Mr Jn[o] Tutching | Att *Foy* Fowy has 24 *l* p[r] annum as p[r] N[o] 81 |
| *Mr Tho: Hancock* | *At Looe.* |
| Mr Sam: Martyn | Att Liskard neuer had a meeting before. |
| Ministers y[t] may want Supply | |
| Mr Tho' Hancock | Att Looe, but 7 *l* p[r] annum from y[e] people |
| Mr Tingcomb | Att Callington, has but 15 *l* p[r] anũ, neuer had a meeting before |
| Mr Tho: Trevethick | Preacheth in his own house in S[t] Eball where severall of the Neighbourhood resort, but hath noe maintenance |

| | | |
|---|---|---|
| M^r Jos: Halsey | At Marthir noe fixed maintenance had last year but £9 : 19 : 6, y^e year before £5 : 10 | |
| M^r Roger Flammank | Att S^t Indoer Subscriptions £19 :– p^r annū, hee rec^d y^e last year but £6: | |
| m^r John Cowbridge | | |
| see the other side | | |
| Persons Contributing | | |

[15]

## Cornwall

| | | |
|---|---|---|
| Places y^t had or where there may be oportunity of Religious Assemblies | | M^r How and M^r Hughes |
| Lancaston | | |
| Hartston | | |
| Penryn | | |
| Pordstow | | |
| Landrake | | |
| S^t Germaines | There was a meeting dureing y^e life of m^r Creswell | |
| Saltash | all these places where meetings were and cease for want of mn^rs | |
| Penzance<br>S^t Iues and Mazarion | Join for a minister m^r Quick informes theire may be a great congregation raised of about 3 or 4000 people | |
| Kenwin<br>Truro. Bodman<br>Laslithiel S^t Tossell<br>Redruth<br>S^t Colomb<br>Tintagoll<br>Camerford | Markett Townes where neuer weere meetings see more, at large in N^o 81 | |

| | |
|---|---|
| Stratton | Desires a minister |
| *Persons qualifyed for ye ministry and not fixed* | |
| *St Germans* | *By Plym there was one dureing the life of old mr Creswell* |
| Saltash | |
| Lancack | |
| Fowes | Where there might be opportunities of Religious assemblies |
| Pudstow | |
| Markett Jew | |
| Helstone | |
| Ministers qualifyed and not fixed | Mr John Cowbridg has noe fixed congregation, but preacheth to a few att St Maws where he *resorts* resides, some few of the meaner sort *resoft* resort to him, to whom he preacheth gratis |
| Persons qualifying for the Ministry | |
| Proposalls. | |

| [16] Ministers that haue a competent Supply | Cumberland | |
|---|---|---|
| m$^{r}$ Geõ: Larkham | aged aboue 60 a wife and 3 or 4 At Cockermouth, hath Wife, ∧ Children most dispossed of hath 30 *l* ꝑ Añ̄ and Some little Estate of his Owne see more 121 | has but 40$^{s}$ p$^{r}$ q$^{r}$ as p$^{r}$ N$^{o}$ 105 |
| m$^{r}$ Geõ: Nicholson | Hudlesbough At Kirk Oswald, A wife . 3 . or 4 . Children, hath a litle Estate his Congregation Contribute £30. ꝑ Añ̄ liues w$^{th}$out want | |
| m$^{r}$ Simon Atkinson | At Cawthwaite preacheth in his own howse hath a competent Estate | see his request in N$^{o}$ 74 y$^{e}$ Second year 1692: |
| | The 3 aboue mentioned ministers as m$^{r}$ *Robison* Robinson writes are poore and haue not aboue 10 *l* or 12 *l* p$^{r}$ añ̄u | |
| M$^{r}$ Geo: Larkham | has about eight pounds p$^{r}$ anū from his people, for preaching a Lecture weekly at Cockermouth, Supposed to haue 10 *l* p$^{r}$. annum., yet not certaine his reall estate 7 *l* or 8 *l* p$^{r}$ annum | |
| M$^{r}$ Simon Atkinson att Hescott. aged 68 | Refuseth to haue any thing from his people, taketh his share when any comes from London, hath a reall estate nigh 20 *l* p$^{r}$ an̄ū | hee now Sojourns att Cowthaate see his case by himselfe N$^{o}$ 127 |

| | | |
|---|---|---|
| Mr Geo: Nicholson att *hill Hiellossould* Hudlesbrough in Kirk oswald | hath alwayes had 20 *l* pr annum from his people, some reall estate of his own but not much. and a house and Some Land wch ye ch: bought for their minister, his estate a water-Mill wth ground to ye vallue of 8 *l* pr añ: | his people offer att 20 *l* pr anū: but for 30 years past haue not done it : |
| Ministers yt may want A Supply | Mr Bull att Carlile came a month since from Lond: 9r ye 12 : 90: | |
| | Penruddock *Att Keswick* | |
| mr Anto Sleigh about 56 yeares of age see his case No 127 | At ∧ Thelkeld, A Congregation, hath not aboue £5. p Añn Some yeares not aboue. 40s, his wife when dyed left him Money wth wch & manageing a farm liueth pretty well | |
| | A congregation on the borders of Engld wch were before a bad people now Seriously Attend and haue a Scotch man for whome they raise 15 or 20 *l* newCastle sent them 10 *l* p Añn | |
| | the aboue mentioned mr Antho: aged 60 yeares Sleigh ∧ has continued among his people (under many hardships, fineings, imprisonments, exiles) euer Since ye remouall of Dr Gilpin at ye restauration of C: ye 2nd. All his people can doe will not amount to aboue 6 *l* pr Añ. are affraid of his remouall by death, being infirme, and therefore concerned for ye future See alsoe No 105 | |
| Mr Geo: Dawes ∧ | at Kirkoswald<br>Near Penrith, has not aboue 10 *l* or 12 *l* pr anū | his allowance from his people is 13 *l* pr anū: see more No 127: |

| | | |
|---|---|---|
| Mr Bland | Near ye Same place in ye Same circumstances | |
| Mr Geo: Benson att Kellet | Neere Lancaster aged 70 yeares in ye Same circumstances<br>has but 7 *l* pr annum as pr No 111 See his case further Stated in No: 14o: 1691 & considered | |
| Persons Contributing | | |
| [17]<br>Places that had and where there may be opertuity of Religious Assemblys— | Cumberland | Mr Stretton and Mr Nisbett |
| × *Twedmouth* | *had a fixed Congregation & pastor they raised him 40 l p Ann he is gonn for Scotland* | These in Northumberland by mistake put heere |
| × *Milborn grang'* | *Had Mr Leuer they raised him £28 p Ann, latley dead* | |
| × *Hexham* | *Hath beene Endeauoring to get a preacher, can raise 30 l p Ann there be Some Anabaptists among them* | |
| × Brampton | mr Story. preached a while but hath giuen Ouer | ×They have got a young man to preach to them, but haue little to give him, they expect help |
| Carlile | Hath Some Dissenters but no Minister can be got | ××Mr Bull lately come to Carlile |
| Penrith | Do | |
| Att Keswick | There was a Church of wch mr Cane was Pastor but ye graue and ye | |

| | |
|---|---|
| | Ch: of England haue Swallowed up all y^e^ members but one or two. |
| Att Whitehaven | They are laying out themselues to gett a minister |
| Carlile | M Dan: Bull designes to reside there among a poor inconsiderable number of people, to carry on y^e^ work of the Gospell but without some assistance, they must Starue him from amongst them, they desire their case may be considered |
| Persons qualified for the Ministry but not fixed | |
| Persons qualifying for the Ministry | |
| Proposalls. | Some Serious young men to be Sent, and to Set Vp Itenerant Preachers, for Ministers is the great Want |

| [18] Ministers y[t] haue a Competent Supply | Derby |
|---|---|
| m[r] Benj: Robison | Preacheth one part of the day att Repton and y[e] other part att ffinderne hath 30 *l* p[r] annum or thereabout |
| m[r] Dan: Shelmadine | An aged ejected minister preaches at Seuerall places |
| M[r] Tim: Fox | An aged Ejected minister preaches at Seuerall places |
| M[r] Rob[t] Meseby | Att in y[e] hundred of the high Peak, is very rich, and as yet childless, who carryeth his labours into other Counties, where he is considered for them |
| M[r] Woodhouse | Att Melborne has noe want of Supply |
| M[r] Abra: Crumpton | Att Darby has noe need of Supply |
| *M[r] W[m] Bagshaw* | |
| M[r] Rob[t] Moore | |
| M[r] John Barrett | |
| M[r] Sam: Ogden | |
| M[r] Rob[t] Seddon | |
| M[r] Ogle | |
| M[r] Rob[t] Ferne | |
| M[r] John Oldfield | |
| Ministers y[t] a Supply | |

| | |
|---|---|
| M^r^ Rich^d^ Chantry sen^r^ | Att Hartshorne an aged ejected minister hath 9 children who haue all Some part of their dependence on him is afflicted with a great lameness and not able to goe without helpe, preacheth 3 Sabbaths in y^e^ month, y^e^ people poore not able to allow more then 4 *l* odd mony p^r^ quarter, of w^ch^ M^r^ Tym: Cox hath a ¼ part |
| M^r^ John Bennett at Littleover | An aged ejected minister *preaches euery 4h Sabbath att Hartshorne* these two ought to be put in the upper column |
| *M^r^ Dan: Shelmadine* | *An aged ejected minister, has noe fixed Congregation.* |
| *M^r^ Tim: Fox* | *An aged ejected minister, preaches once a m^o^ at Hartshorn* |
| M^r^ Keniston | Att Choulton about 4 miles from Manchester eastward has for tract of time kept up a meeting there, M^r^ Newcomen gives him a very good Caracter, y^e^ people frequent his ministry, and receive much benefitt by him, they are poor and soe is hee, and wants things necessary. |
| M^r^ W^m^ Bagshaw aged 63. | Supplyes Tidswell, ^Chimley, Ashford,^ Chawseworth ^Middleton, Chelmarcon^ and Hucklow has not aboue 12 *l* p^r^ annū: See more at large in n^o^. 8 and N^o^ 86 & 87 has a considerable Estate, see his own acc^t^ in N^o^. 103 |
| Persons contributing | |
| M^r^ Dan: Denton | |
| M^r^ Isaac Robinson | |

| | | |
|---|---|---|
| Mr Horne<br>Mr Peach<br>*Mr Chantry Juor*<br>mr Wilson | | |
| [19] Places yt had and where there may be oportunitys of Religious assemblys | Derby | Mr Cockerell Mr Rapier & Mr Coape |
| Att Middleton | The Vpholders are very mean in ye world hearers are about 200 | |
| Belper | The people there but able to raise 13 *l* pr annū soe there wants to. make up 28 *l* pr annū (ye least a minister can Subsist on in this County ye Sume of—15 *l*. £15 | |
| Chelmarton see No 103 | | |
| | aboue 8 *l*: 17 s | |
| Hollington | Not able to raise for constant Supply haue need of . . . £10 | |
| Alvaston | Stands in need of assistance at least . . . . £10 | can raise 17 : 10 : 8 |
| Aston | Stands in need of pr annum £10 | |
| Harrington | Stands in need pr annū of . £10 | |
| Hognaston | hath need of pr annū . . £10 | |
| Ilston | hath need of pr annū . . £13 | |
| Longdales and Rosson | Cannot raise aboue 6 *l* pr annum soe yt they stand in need of see more at large in No-84- £22 | |
| | £100 | |

| | |
|---|---|
| Cawdwell | There is preaching but once or twice a month for want of a maintenance. |
| Belper and Headge | Have had publick meetings (since *pu* liberty was first granted) supported by charitable contributions w$^{ch}$ now failes and of themselues are not able to raise aboue 13 *l* p$^{r}$ annum. see alsoe N$^{o}$ 116 |
| | Att Hartington is a meeting sett up where there is very great want of preaching, and very little livelyhood for a minister. |
| Persons qualifyed for y$^{e}$ Ministry and not fixed | M$^{r}$ Chantry has bread one Son a nonconformist minister who is expected daily from London |
| Duffield | The meeting there is in danger to goe downe, m$^{r}$ Henry Coape being dead who did contribute to y$^{e}$ Support of y$^{e}$ Gospell in that place. Decem$^{r}$ y$^{e}$ 7$^{th}$ 1691 |
| Persons qualifying for y$^{e}$ Ministry | |
| | M$^{r}$ Hughes son of m$^{r}$ Stephen Hughes soe well known for his piety and charity &c y$^{e}$ youth is hopefull & well disposed his mother y$^{e}$ widow is poor: entred already in Southwales |
| | M$^{r}$ Stubs brought up att Ashburn Schoole, of good parts and learning and very religiously inclined. under y$^{e}$ tuition of m$^{r}$ Woodhouse his friends not able to maintaine him, one hath contributed to him who cannot any longer continue his contribution |

| | |
|---|---|
| | Richard Peach brought up att Ashburn Schoole a youth of Laudable parts and learning and piously disposed, hath few relations and these very poor S J.G is dead who did contribute towards his maintenance att Schoole |
| *Mr Robt Ferne*<br>*Mr Jno Oldfield*<br>*Mr Dan: Denton*<br>*Mr Isaac Robison*<br>*Mr Horne*<br>*Mr Peach*<br>*Mr Chantry juor*<br>*Mr Wilson* | young ministers in this County preaching and not conforming<br>These should haue beene entred in ye *upper* aboue colume |
| Proposalls | |

| [20] Ministers y[t] haue a Competent Supply | Devon |
|---|---|
| M[r] Toogood | Att Axminster. |
| M[r] Edwards m[r] Blake & m[r] Sandors | Att Honiton. |
| M[r] Sam: Tapper | Att Limston. |
| M[r] Bernard Starre | Att Topsham. |
| M[r] Gaylard m[r] Hoppin m[r] Trose. Hallet. Atkins Ashwood [& Collins | Att Exon. |
| | Att St Mary Otteny M[r] Robert Carrill att Crediton. |
| M[r] Saundors, Saunderwick Moore & Bartlett | Att Tiverton. |
| M[r] Benj: Hooper | Att Dauerton. |
| M[r] Peard & Hanmer | Att Barnstaple. |
| M[r] Wood & Bowden | Att Biddiford |
| *M[r] Hen: Berry* | *Att Torrington a numerous people* |
| M[r] Hen: Flammick | At Tarystock. |
| M[r] Larkham | Att Shepistor. has not aboue 10 *l* per annum needs encouragm[t] |

| | | |
|---|---|---|
| M$^r$ Sherwill & Harding | Att Plimmouth. | |
| M$^r$ Horsham | Att Stoake. | |
| M$^r$ Edm$^d$ Toozer | Att Kingsbridge. | |
| M$^r$ Galpine Sen$^r$ | Att Tottnas. | |
| M$^r$ Jn$^o$ Galpine Juo$^r$ | Att Tauerton. | |
| M$^r$ Peirce & Palk | Att Ashburton. | |
| M$^r$ Flavell | Att Dartmouth. | |
| M$^r$ Withers | Att Lupton in Brixham. | |
| M$^r$ Will: Yea | Att Nawton Bushell. | |
| M$^r$ Soreton | Att Powdram. Except y$^e$ great townes y$^e$ maintenance of the other is not aboue 20 *l* p$^r$ Añ and of Some not Soe much. | |
| Ministers y$^t$ may want a Supply | | |
| M$^r$ Hart | Att Chimly, y$^e$ people very poore | |
| M$^r$ Hunt | At Southmorton, y$^e$ people poore | |
| M$^r$ Simmons | Att Appledore, y$^e$ people poore | |
| M$^r$ Taylor | At Holiworthy, y$^e$ people very poore | |
| M$^r$ Chapham | Att Oakhampton, y$^e$ people very poore | |
| M$^r$ Bart$^o$ Yeo | Att Jacobstow the people poore | |
| M$^r$ Searle | Att Plimpton y$^e$ people very poore | |
| M$^r$ Crompton | Att Exeter. an aged man and very poor | M$^r$ How |
| M$^r$ Jn$^o$ Berry | Att has a numerous family noe estate att all | M$^r$ How |
| M$^r$ Hen: Berry | Att Torrington, a numerous people but very poor | M$^r$ How |
| M$^r$ Burdwood | Att Dartmouth, very poor. as p$^r$ m$^r$ Hows acc$^t$ | |
| m$^r$ Knight | Ancient and infirm not able to goe abroad to preach | |

| | | |
|---|---|---|
| mr Baikaller<br>Persons contributing. | | |
| **[21]**<br>Places yt had or where there may be opportunity of Religious assemblies | Deuon | Mr How and Mr Hughes |
| h<br>Nortmontton<br>^<br>Morchard<br>Ilfarcomb.<br>Hatherbay<br>Bory Tracy<br>Moretowne<br>Collampton<br>*San* Shanghbrook | All places where meetings are kept up but noe fixt minister for want of maintenance Supplyed by Some of ye Itinerants | |
| Cudleigh and Chagford | Meeting deserted for poverty and noe minister—market townes. | |
| Modbury | That Country needs one | |
| Persons qualifyed for ye Ministry and not fixed | | |
| a<br>Mr Pulmer | | |
| *Mr Jno Berry.* | *has a numerous family of Children noe estate at all.* | |
| Mr Binmore | | |
| *Mr Crompton.* | *an Antient man & very poor. Exeter.* | |
| *Mr Knight.* | *an ancient infirm man and not able to goe abroad to preach.* | |

| | |
|---|---|
| *M^r^ Burdwood.* | |
| M^r^ Mortimer | |
| M^r^ Wood. | |
| M^r^ Edwards. | |
| *M^r^ Baikaller* | |
| M^r^ Balstar | |
| M^r^ Powell | all ministers unsettled and Itinerant preachers. |
| M^r^ Jn^o^ Paget | desires some allowance for a yeare y^e^ better to accomplish him for his Studies |
| Persons qualifying for the Ministry | M^r^ Galpine's Son. whom he intends for y^e^ ministry and desires Some assistance that way |
| Proposalls | |

| [22] Ministers y$^{t}$ have a Competent Supply | Dorset | M$^{r}$ Jn$^{o}$ Jurin |
|---|---|---|
| M$^{r}$ Short | Att Lime an Ejected Minister has a Compet maintenance | |
| M$^{r}$ Fenner | about Att Weymouth *Ej* has *betweene* £30 *& 40 l* but a great family of a wife and 6 or seven young children | |
| M$^{r}$ Clerke | Att Warham and Poole has 30 *l* p$^{r}$ ann a wife with 4 children, preacheth often 4 or 5 times a week | |
| M$^{r}$ Stone | d Att Blanford has neere 40 *l* p$^{r}$ an$\bar{n}$ | |
| M$^{r}$ Sprint | Att Stawbridge has about 50 *l* per an$\bar{n}$ | |
| M$^{r}$ Crane | Att Bemister & Netherbury | |
| M$^{r}$ Banger | Att Sherbourn | |
| M$^{r}$ Churchill | Att Dorchester | |
| M$^{r}$ Clifford | Att Crambourn | |
| M$^{r}$ King and M$^{r}$ Damer | Ejected, their circumstances not mentioned | |
| Ministers y$^{t}$ may want Supply | | |
| M$^{r}$ Downe | At Bridport an ejected Minister, has but a Small maintenance | |
| M$^{r}$ Eastman | Att Shaffton D$^{o}$— has not aboue 4 *5 or 6 l* p annum | |
| M$^{r}$ Moor | Preaches 3 or 4 times a month, att 8$^{s}$ p$^{r}$ day but very poor and in debt at Milborne Port | |
| M$^{r}$ Hopkins | Preacheth ∧ once in a fortnight ∧ at 10$^{s}$ p$^{r}$ time or 8$^{s}$ but is poor | |
| M$^{r}$ Fenner | Att Weymouth, has about 30 *l* p$^{r}$ annum but a great family. m$^{r}$ | |

| | | |
|---|---|---|
| | Taylor of Pinnars hall contributed to him formerly. | |
| M Clerk | Att Warham and Poole, contributed to by m$^{r}$ Cokayn | |
| Persons Contributing | | |
| [23] Places y$^{t}$ had or where there may be oportunityes of Religious Assemblies | Dorset | M$^{r}$ Jn$^{o}$ Jurin and M$^{r}$ Mayo |
| Sturmister, Winbourn, Beere & Winfruit | Where there would be a numerous auditory if meanes could be found to afford a maintenance | |
| Persons qualifyed for y$^{e}$ ministry and not fixed | | |
| Persons qualifying for the ministry. | | |
| M$^{r}$ Damer | Son to m$^{r}$ Damer before mentioned preacheth | |
| m$^{r}$ Tho: Rowe | The Son of m$^{r}$ Thomas Rowe a non-conforming Minister deceased, hath beene w$^{th}$ m$^{r}$ Tho: Rowe of London four yeares, y$^{e}$ widow his mother is not able any Longer to maintaine hinn, Some assistance is desired. June y$^{e}$ 1$^{o}$: 91 | |
| Proposalls | to consider m$^{r}$ Downe the people not likeing | |

| [24] Ministers y$^{t}$ haue A competent Supply | Durham | |
|---|---|---|
| D$^{r}$ Long | At Darlington. A congregation Setled, well prouided for | |
| m$^{r}$ Jn$^{o}$ Thompson | At Stockton. D$^{o}$ being a pious young man | |
| m$^{r}$ ^Tim Manloue | At Durham. D$^{o}$ formerly a preacher in Derbysh: a young man of great hopes, and usefullness, an encouraging auditory, but its feared little else | |
| | D$^{r}$ ^Geo Long is in low circumstances, one of very considerable abilities<br>These are all in this County and 30 miles about as D$^{r}$ L informes. | |
| Ministers y$^{t}$ may Want A Supply | | |
| Persons Contributing | | |
| [25] Places y$^{t}$ had & where there may be Oppertunity of Religious Assemblies | Durham | M$^{r}$ Stretton and M$^{r}$ Nisbett |
| Darlington | Are desirous of one m$^{r}$ W$^{m}$ Pell now at Boston in y$^{e}$ County of Lincoln, but want some help to give him a competent maintenance, one | |

| | |
|---|---|
| | Nickolson a D^r^ of Physick is very willing to encourage them as farr as hee can, see y^e^ case further, w^th^ y^e^ caracter of y^e^ s^d^ m^r^ Pell N° 38: 1691 |
| Persons qualified for y^e^ Ministry & not fixed | |
| Persons qualifying for y^e^ Ministry | |
| Propossalls | |

| [26] Ministers yt haue a competent Supply | Essex |
|---|---|
| Mr Gidly | Att Albrough Hatch. has Some 200 hearers Estate of his own and pr añ 30 *l* ∧ |
| Mr Rand Ejected | Att Baddow parva has by Subscription pr anũ 40 |
| Mr R. Taylor Ejected | Att Barbing Sm. Mark, has a good keeps a coach estate of his owne ∧ |
| Mr Kyltly Ejected | Att Bilerekay Mark has a good estate of his owne 300 hearers |
| Mr Bugby | Att Braintrey mark, Subscriptions Sufficient & a good Estate |
| Mr ∧ Wm Rawlinson | Att Brackstead, has a good Estate of his own, & Supports divers meetings att his own charge. has 200 hearers, a rich widdower |
| *Dr Hen: Wilkinson Ejectd -ed* | |
| Mr Clark | *Att Castle Honingham* Att Clider-ditch, an Estate & per annũ 26 *l* 60 pound pr annum |
| Mr Rogers | Att Chelmsford, good Subscriptions ∧ & a large estate of his own |
| Mr Allen | Att Chissel Clare *Clare at Clare att Stanborn* aged |
| Mr Hauers Juor | Att *Clare* ∧ *Stamburn has a fixed Ch: 20 pr añ of his own* |
| Mr Legg<br>Mr ffairfax<br>Mr ffowkes<br>Mr Gilson | Att Colchester a Burrough well provided for |

| | | |
|---|---|---|
| | Mr Brinsly att Barfield hath 10s pr Day, & ye like for others the parish church there | |
| Mr Porter Mr Biggin with Divers others | Att White Colne preach in ye parish church *above* haue 6 or 7s a day raised out of the tythes, | they expect some help from London |
| Mr Gouge Ejected | Att Coggeslal mark Some Estate of his own & 40 *l* Subscrip pr an̄ | |
| Mr Ellison Ejected tt | Att Coggslall, is very aged, sd to be Superanuated. | |
| Mr Stopp Ejected | Att Harwich. a Burrough Subscriptions pr annum 30 *l* | |
| Mr Warren Ejected | Att Hatfield mark Small Contribution. Some wt of his own | |
| Mr Scanderet Ejected | Att Hannerick mark, preacheth att Camb̄ once a month. | |
| Mr Billio Juor | Att Malden a Burrough has by Subscription pr an̄n 40 *l* | |
| Mr Day. | Att Oldenbury Inn. | |
| Mr Tyro. | Att Onger mark has by Subscrip- a worthy man but poor tions per annum 20 *l* ∧ see more in 88 ye Lady Rich—200 heares but poor | |
| Mr Hauers ∧ senr Ejected | Att Stamborn. a fixed Ch: allow: 20 *l* pr an̄u & estate of his own 12 *l* pr annum | |
| Mr Porter. | Att Stebbing. | |
| Mr Small Ejected | Att *Bishops Storford* ∧ Hatfield well provided for 300 heares little from them | |
| Mr Pateman Do | Stratfor le bow well provided for has an estate people give nothing | |
| M Pane sen Do | Att Thackstead *meeting considerable* | |
| | Att ye fforrest side well provided for, a considerable meeting | |

| | | |
|---|---|---|
| Ministers that want a Supply | *M$^{r}$ Pane Juo$^{r}$ att Saffron waldon mark* | |
| | Waltham Stow. Supplyed by divers from London maintained by some Gen$^{t}$ dwells in a little cottage and in debt | |
| | *M$^{r}$ Chadsly att Yeldham parva aged twixt 60 & 70 a worthy man* | |
| *D$^{r}$ Hen. Wilkinson* | *Att Castle Honingham Supperanuated & poore Ejected* | |
| M$^{r}$ Dent. Ejected Collier | Att Epping mark 20 *l* Subscriptions, little of his own | see m$^{r}$ Dents case in N$^{o}$ 96 |
| M$^{r}$ *Chollger.* Ejected | At Halstead mark. Subscrip: uncertaine, a large but poor people and little of his owne. 30 *l* p$^{r}$ annū: 600 heares many children not disposed of | |
| M$^{r}$ Dod Sen$^{r}$ Ejected | Att horn Church. a small and poor not aboue 100 hearers nor aboue 15 *l* or 20 *l* p$^{r}$ anū people ∧ little of his own has by Subscriptions per annum 12 *l*—of his own, 200 *l* his estate less than of that in all | |
| ri<br>M$^{r}$ B*u*mstead | Att Brent wood mark Some Subscrip: what uncertaine | |
| M$^{r}$ Lukin Ejected | Att Machin. Supported by y$^{e}$ family<br>a<br>of y$^{e}$ Massums Chaplaine | put this in the upper column |
| Giles<br>M$^{r}$ ∧ ffirmin Ejected | Att Redgwell little of his own getts Somewhat by practice of physick has Subscriptions per annum 12 *l* | |
| M$^{r}$ Whitston | Att Rumford. Ejected, aged poor and noe constant meeting | |
| M$^{r}$ Dod Juo$^{r}$ | Att. Wethersfield has by Subscriptions per annum 20 *l* | |

| | | |
|---|---|---|
| Mr Edmd Taylor Ejected | kept up by him and 3 others Att Witham, ∧ aged, hath Somewt of they give 5s pr day his own ∧ ye people poor | |
| Mr ffoxton | Preaches Sometimes at Witham brought up by charity under mr Doolittle, is but poor | is chosen their pastour desires some assistance |
| Mr Chadsley | Of Yeldam parva hath noe Congregation, his estate only a little Cottage in wch hee dwells, and in debt. | |
| *Mr Collier* | *At Halstead known to some in London, his people poore* | |
| Mr Pain Juor | Att Saffron Walden ꝑ Doct. Chancey & mr Cockayne 12 *l* ꝑ Añ | |
| Persons Contributing | | |
| [27] Places yt had, or where there may be opportunity of Religious assemblies | Essex | *Mr Faldoe and* Dr Samson mr Mather |
| Brackted | Not able to allow ye ministers yt preach to them aboue 5s pr day | |
| urn Bramham (*ram* in italics) | Where mr Rawllingson has Sett up a new meeting for whom mr Brand has promised 5 *l* per annum. ye air is bad | |
| Reyleigh | Where mr Rawllingson has begun a meeting, tis a small market Towne a known papist in ye Church. seuen adjacent ꝑishes without preaching. one mrs English offers to give any minister 12 monthes boarding No 39 | see also No 109 |

| | | |
|---|---|---|
| Vivenho. 3 miles from Colchester | Kept up their meeting almost constantly in ye worst of times, a small but zealous people, their allowance is but 6 or 7$^{s}$ pr day see N° 109 N° 39 | see alsoe N° 120 see alsoe N° 151 |
| Tiptry, or Messing | Where is one Crab a baptist an Ignorant fellow does much hurt if any maintenance could be had a minister might doe much good is likely to be a very large meeting and a very dark corner | |
| Bures | A large Village noe meeting neere | |
| Stebbing and Hedingham | | |
| Att Withamstow | Is a meeting kept up by combination by some from Lond | |
| Witham | Where m$^{r}$ ffoxton is about to Settle, auditors about 4 or 500 of the poorer sort, are not able to raise much if anything aboue 20 *l* p$^{r}$ anū | |
| Onger | A dark corner. m$^{r}$ Paget through m$^{r}$ Rowes meanes was prevailed w$^{th}$ to come among them, whose labours are well approved, they promised him 30 *l* per annum, but y$^{e}$ performance less than 20 *l* | |
| Ministers qualifyed for y$^{e}$ Min$^{r}$y and not fixed | Sibbe Hedinghame. Much pestered w$^{th}$ Quakers and Arminian Anabaptists, desire a minister, and some present maintenance | 1691 |
| *M$^{r}$ ffelsted* M$^{r}$ Porter of ffelstead | In this County a very worthy young man is willing to go to Reyleigh if any thing considerable will be allowed for his maintenance The people have giuen him a call to Settle among them, hee is willing to comply if hee may be incouraged | |

| | | |
|---|---|---|
| Mr Rands Son | brought up by mr Cradock, not yet fixed but preacheth up and down with good acceptance, liues wth his father at Baddow | |
| Brentwood 1691 | desire £5: per annum for ye Support of ye Lecture | 1691 |
| Hornchurch | From wch place mr Dod was necessitated to remove (after three yeares continuance among them) the people not being able to give him a maintenance, pray for some Supply, otherwise they must remaine (as they now are) destitute of a minister | |
| Childeitch | near Brentwood, haue had ye Gospell among them for many yeares, haue hitherto raised very little aboue 20 *l* per anū for their Minister who has a wife & 4 Small children has spent some of his Estate among them rather than remove &c | 91 |
| Persons qualifying for ye Minry | | |
| Mr Scandret Juor | Son to mr Scandret of Hannerick | |
| Proposalls | | |

| [28] Ministers $y^t$ haue a competent Supply | Gloucester |
|---|---|
| $M^r$ Sheal *Cong:* | Of Marchfield has about 20 *l* $p^r$ annum |
| $M^r$ Old ^h am. *Presb:* | Att his circumstances not yet known |
| $M^r$ Conway *D°* | Att Malmsbury, has about 20 *l* $p^r$ annum |
| *$M^r$ Andrew Tippett D°* | Att att Painswick, has about 20 *l* $p^r$ annum |
| $M^r$ Hen: Collet: *Cong:* | Att Burton on $y^e$ water, preaches freely |
| $M^r$ Davison: *Cong:* | Att Cambden has about 26 *l* $p^r$ annum |
| $M^r$ James Forbes: *D°* | Att Glocester, has about 30 *l* $p^r$ añ |
| $M^r$ Dancie | Of Stappleton } Their circumstances not mentioned |
| *$M^r$ Axtell* | *In Wootton under hedge* } |
| $M^r$ Beebie | Of Cirencester |
| $M^r$ Head $w^{th}$ $m^r$ Collet | Supply Burton, Cleave, Bizly, Cos Pawn where there are considerable meetings, who need noe Supply |
| Ministers that want Supply | |
| $M^r$ Tho: Worden | Att Nailsworth, has Scarce 15 *l* $p^r$ annũ: 30 of *his* the members in $y^e$ late persecution broke off from *his* $y^t$ Society, his contributers |

| | | |
|---|---|---|
| | being poor weavers or sheeremen, and haueing ∧ [little or] noe trade, he desires assistance | |
| M$^{r}$ Becket *Cong:* goeing to fix att Winchomb & Cleeve | Att Strowd, y$^{e}$ people poore not able to raise aboue 10 *l* p$^{r}$ an̄ | |
| | There are 2 nonconformists widdows att Ross 12 miles from Glocester both poor, their name, Smith. Father and Son were Ministers, and y$^{r}$ widdows are gracious persons, if they might haue a Small token, it would be very refreshing to them | |
| m$^{r}$ Andrew Tippett | Att Painsw[ick]*orth* has about 20 *l* per annum is much in debt | |
| m$^{r}$ Axell | Of wooton under hedge an itinerant preacher, hath 6 children and is poore see more largely in N$^{o}$ 147 | |
| m$^{r}$ Billinsley 1691 | Of in y$^{e}$ fforest of Deane is quite come off from y$^{e}$ Church of England, with about 200 of his parish, who haue Sett up a meeting for him in y$^{e}$ parish, they haue Subscribed 16 *l* or 17 *l* per annum, desire Some assistance | |
| Persons contributing | | |
| [29] Places y$^{t}$ had or where there may be oportunity of Religious assemblies | Gloucester | M$^{r}$ Meade |

| | |
|---|---|
| At Tuexbery | There was a Congregation, now none but Anabaptists, there might be a great opportunity for Service if a Lecture of able men could be Settled among them can raise but 20 *l* per anum |
| At Winchomb and cleeve to unite | Was a Congregation dissolved by the departure of m[r] Helms from them many good Still in those parts but poor |
| Att Little Horn | In Beeslie Parish is a new meeting, very poor give nothing, there may be a great opportunity for service there |
| Att Cleeve | Is a new meeting once a fortnight, poor, can give nothing there is a willing people to hear. |
| Att Berklie | A new meeting once a fortnight, give 10[s] a time |
| Att Cam | A new meeting, give 10[s] a time |
| Att Ranger | A new meeting give 10[s] a time |
| Att Wootton, under hedg | A new meeting, give 8[s], poor, great opportunity for Service |
| Cam, *and Wooton* | Allows 10[s] p[r] Sabbatum |
| Elverton | Allows 10[s] p[r] Sabbatum |
| Colford alias Couer | In y[e] fforest of Deane, y[e] meeting there is somthing considerable, supplyed by divers as they can be procured by some honest persons there, but want some assistance to carry on y[e] work. |
| Ministers qualifyed for the Ministers and not fixed | |
| M[r] Drew | |
| *M[r] Head* | |

| | |
|---|---|
| *Mr Collet*<br>mr Hancock<br>Mr Hodges.<br>Tuller<br>Mr Billingsley<br>Ministers qualifying for ye Ministry | Itinerent preachers |
| Mr Jno Drew<br>mr Richd Billinslie | Both of them teach school |
| | Mr James fforbes has 3 young men wth him Students in Phylosophie and Divinity *very* poor |
| Proposalls | The ministers of Somersetshire, Wiltshire and Glocestershire haue of late Sett up an association, and if it be desired the minutes of what hath beene and what shall be from time to time transacted among them will be Sent they.<br>haue already agreed upon an accommodation betweene Presb: and Congr: Ministers<br>and there haue beene talks of raising a fund among them. but trading Soe dead, taxes so high, and ye poverty of professors soe great that it greatly discourages. |

| | |
|---|---|
| [30] Ministers y$^{t}$ haue a competent Supply | Hereford |
| M$^{r}$ Edw$^{d}$ Primerose<br>M$^{r}$ Jn$^{o}$ Weaver<br>M$^{r}$ Jn$^{o}$ Barston<br>*M$^{r}$ Anth: Collier*<br>M$^{r}$ Jn$^{o}$ Drew<br>M$^{r}$ Sam: Phillips<br>M$^{r}$ Tho: Collins<br>M$^{r}$ W$^{m}$ Woodward. | Their principall Support is from their owne Estates. w$^{ch}$ yet are inconsiderable |
| Ministers that want Supply | |
| M$^{r}$ Anth: Collier | of Ross most<br>^ Stands in *worst* need of Supplys |
| Persons contributing | |
| [31] Att Longtowne | Is a meeting house lately erected but no minister they can raise 10 *l* per anū towards the maintenance of a Minister they desire help from London, alsoe they desire a minister y$^{t}$ may be fitt for y$^{e}$ place, and y$^{t}$ that preach in Welch as well as English |
| *Aberganvie*<br>Abergaueney | Where there is a great auditory but most of Anabaptists and their |

preachers are of that perswasion & possessed of the meeting place: they earnestly desire a minister of another perswasion and some allowance

Persons qualifying for y^e^ Ministry

Andrew
D^r^ Barnett haueing lost 30 *l* p^r^ annum in land, his son being dead has the charge of his poor widdow and Six small children cast upon him besides two of his own sons yett unprovided for, one of them being fitted for y^e^ university, is willing hee go to Glasco but is not able, and therefore beggs assistance

| [32] [Mi]nisters that [h]aue a competent Supply | Hertford |
|---|---|
| Mr Grew *Grue* | At St Albans a Burrough has 40 *l* or 50 *l* Subscriptions and some Estate of his owne, has 300 auditors: 50 communicants |
| Mr Hamilton | Att Theobalds Some Subscriptions and an estate |
| Mr Masters | att ye same place |
| Mr Waite | Att Chest-hunt Do |
| Mr Small | Att Bishop Storford a market towne, |
| Mr Warren | is wth ye Lady Barrington, wt hee and Mr Warren haue from ye church is uncertaine |
| | & Sissiphen, has a great people |
| [M]r Hussey | Att Hitchin ^ a market-towne, maintained by Subscrip. |
| [Mr] Hayworth | Att Hertford ye County-towne, hath some what by Subscriptions, and somewt from Hitchin where hee doth Sometimes preach |
| Mr Forester a Scotchman | Att Ware a Market-towne, maintained by Subscriptions |
| | Att Barkamstead neere Ware, maintained by one Mr Mayo a gentleman |
| . . . *Benson* | *Att Buntingford, educated by mr Doolittle* |
| Mr Hughes | Of Barnett, educated at Geneva |
| [M]r Allen | Att Barly, or thereabout, a Scotchman |
| [M]r Ottway | Lives att Cheshunt, where hee has Some estate and preacheth thereabout as att Enfield, Theobalds &c |

| | | |
|---|---|---|
| Mr Warren | Att Bp Storford euery other Lords day, ye other day being Supplyed as ye people can gett help | |
| [Mr] Carter | Att hide-hall wth Sr Robert Josselyn preaches at divers places, a bachelor<br>Mr Green, neer Hogsdon where he preacheth sometimes, is a rich bachelor was fellow of P.H | |
| [Mi]nisters yt [wa]nt Supply | | |
| | Buntingford | |
| [Mr] Benson | At ∧ Hodsdon a Small market towne, is poor and has but a Small maintenance educated by mr Doolittle | removed into Kent |
| [M]r Hocker | Att Barnett a market towne, ye people poor, has some Subscriptions | |
| [M]r Wilson | Att Hitchin, not able to raise aboue 10 *l* pr annū | |
| [33] Places that had or where there may be oportunity of Religious assemblies | Hertford | |
| Royston | A market towne. | |
| Balduck | A market towne | |
| Bigsworth | A market towne. | |
| Hatfield | A market towne. | |
| Watford, and Kickmansworth | Where there is only a meeting of Antipædobaptists | |
| Barkhamstead | A market towne. | |
| Buningford | A market towne, would haue a great meeting if Constantly Supplyed hath now only Some casuall helps | |
| *Hitchin* | Puckerage | |

| | | |
|---|---|---|
| [34] | | |
| [35] Places y$^{t}$ had or where there may be oportunity of Religious assemblies | Hertford | M$^{r}$ Faldoe and D$^{r}$ Samson |
| Buntingford | Who much desire a minister may be sent down to them (M$^{r}$ Benson being gone) the meeting will be Scattered w$^{th}$out Speedy Supply, their utmost Subscriptions am$^{o}$ to 23 *l* p$^{r}$ anū to make up which 16 persons haue out of their deep poverty drawn 32$^{s}$ p$^{r}$ annū i:e. 6d. a quarter each. | |
| 1691 Puckridge | By y$^{e}$ zeal and diligence of a godly man, conversing w$^{th}$ y$^{e}$ people, and bringing good Ministers Sometimes to preach among them, it hath pleased God to raise vp a considerable meeting of about 300 Auditors, they haue desired m$^{r}$ Bellio to come to them, w$^{ch}$ he has yeelded to, they can raise betweene 20 *l* & 30 *l* per annum. | |
| Persons qualifyed for y$^{e}$ Min$^{r}$y and not fixed | | |
| Persons qualifying for y$^{e}$ Min$^{r}$y | | |
| Proposalls | | |

| | | |
|---|---|---|
| [36] Ministers y$^{t}$ haue a competent Supply | Huntingdon | |
| M$^{r}$ Doue | Ejected from Layton, liueing at Kimbleton, preaches nowhere | |
| M$^{r}$ Lawton | Who euer Since his ejection has given himselfe up to y$^{e}$ Study and practice of Physick | |
| M$^{r}$ Josias Charters & M$^{r}$ Robert Billio | Att S$^{t}$ Iues, ingaged in their course at Cambridge are allowed 20$^{s}$ p$^{r}$ Sabbath and 10$^{s}$ p$^{r}$ fast | |
| Ministers that want Supply | | |
| *M$^{r}$ Simon King* | | |
| Persons contributing | | |
| [37] Places y$^{t}$ had or where there may be opportunity of Religious Assemblies | Huntingdon | M$^{r}$ Williams |
| Huntingdon Towne | A Lecture has been attempted, and happily begunn by m$^{r}$ Sheppard, who has lately withdrawn from the prelaticall partie, desire y$^{t}$ an annuall Sume m$^{a}$y be allowed for y$^{e}$ Support of the said Lecture | |

| | |
|---|---|
| S$^{t}$ Ives | They desire some assistance towards y$^{e}$ inlarging of their meeting house |
| Persons quali- ed fy*ing* for y$^{e}$ Min$^{r}$y and not fixed | |
| Persons quali- fying for y$^{e}$ Ministry | |
| Proposalls | |

| [38] Ministers y$^{t}$ haue a competent Supply | Kent | |
|---|---|---|
| M$^{r}$ Jaques | At Rochester a Scotchman about 500 auditors allowance about 60 *l* p$^{r}$ annum | |
| M$^{r}$ Parrot | Att Maidstone, about 700 auditors, 60 *l* p$^{r}$ annum | |
| M$^{r}$ French | Att Stapleherst, 30 *l* p$^{r}$ annum, about 300 auditors | |
| M$^{r}$ Bernard | Att Crane brooke 30 *l* p$^{r}$ annũ, hee is rich | |
| M$^{r}$ Batey | Att Feversham about 300 auditors, at *Cat* Canterbury 700 has 50 *l* p$^{r}$ annum, one weeke at Fever: & another at Canterbury | |
| M$^{r}$ Starr | At Dover, 700 auditors, 50 *l* p$^{r}$ annum | |
| M$^{r}$ Learner | Att Deale, has 3 or 400 auditors and 40 *l* p$^{r}$ an$\bar{\text{nu}}$ | |
| M$^{r}$ James | Att Ashford, 300 auditors 36 *l* p$^{r}$ annum | |
| M$^{r}$ Godman | Att Deptford 500 auditors has 40 *l* p$^{r}$ annum | |
| **Ministers that want a Supply** | | |
| M$^{r}$ Bush | Att Leige Castle a poor man about 200 auditors 20 *l* p$^{r}$ a$\bar{\text{n}}$. | |
| M$^{r}$ Den | Att Goudherst, a poor man, a wife & Severall children has but 20 *l* p$^{r}$ annum | fixed now at Eppin |
| M$^{r}$ Harrison | Att Canterbury, 2 or 300 auditors 20 *l* p$^{r}$ annum | remoued frõ Canterbury |

| | | |
|---|---|---|
| M$^{r}$ Prig | Att Eltam who is soe overwhelmed with Melancholly y$^{t}$ hee cannot be prevailed with to preach, though to y$^{e}$ Smallest number of hearers, and by this is forgotten of many who otherwise might be helpfull to him. nor will he make known his wants, though he had not a morsell to eate. the Lady Mohun and y$^{e}$ L: Clinton do both recommend him | |
| Persons contributing | | |
| [39] Places y$^{t}$ had or where may be opportunity of Religious assemblies *19* 1690 / 1 | Kent | M$^{r}$ Brand and D$^{r}$ Samson |
| Att Goudhurst | Some Serious Christians of the poorer Sort haue Struggled hard to keep up a meeting of 4 or 500 poor people, haue strained beyond their ability, and are Sinking under y$^{e}$ fear they must Lett it fall, and craue assistance | |
| Att Tunbridg. wells | Some haue taken a meeting house, are willing to help (but are not able wholly) to maintaine a minister, craue assistance, being a place of great consequence. | |
| Att Sevenock can raise 20 *l* p$^{r}$ anū auditors 100 very poor and Westcum | Some few haue with much difficulty kept up a fortnightly meeting by Seuerall ministers. they desire to gett a fixed Minister for themselues to preach at each place euery other Lords day. | |

| | | |
|---|---|---|
| Sandwich | Is vacant has 400 auditors | |
| 1691 Staplehurst | Haue long enjoyed ye Gospell, under ye Labours of seuerall Reverend Ministers. mr French their present has 5 Children Pastour ∧ was in 1684 plundred of all his goods, and Suffered 6 months imprisonmt. ye number of hearers 300. contributions at ye highest 33 *l*: now 7 *l* or 8 *l* is likely to goe off. presented augt 24° 1691 | |
| Town-Malling | mr Smith is now removing from thence. cannot raise above 20 *l* pr annum it is a populous place, remote from any meeting, the publick minister weak and Scandalous, even in ye account of his own, could one be settled among them tis hoped they might in a short time be able to maintaine a minister at their own charge, mr Thorogood proposed to fix there | 1691 |
| Persons qualifyed for ye Ministry and not fixed | | |
| Persons ~~fa~~ qualifying for the Ministry | | |
| Thomas Cullen at Maidstone | A young Studt Grandson to mr Perrot ye Minister, mr Perrot brought him vp to Schoole Learning, his father being dead and ye mother not able to provide for hinn. hee is willing to goe to Scotland, and help is desired for his maintenance there | |
| mr John Scoones | Of Staplehurst *in Ke* See his case at large in No 10—1691— | |
| Proposalls | | |

| [40] Ministers yt haue a Competent Supply | Lancaster |
| --- | --- |
| Peter Aspinwall | In Warrington Town, has 3 or 400 hearers, requires noe Sallery, has an Estate, preaches freely |
| Mr Sam:l Angier *John Hartley* | Att Toxteth Park, assistant to Mr Richardson at Liverpoole has 75 *l* pr annum and an estate Mackerfield a deserving young man |
| Wm Birchall *John Hartley* | Att Ashton, ∧ 150 hearers has 20 *l* pr an̄n̄ |
| Mr James Bradshaw | Att Rainford Chappell 200 hearers 10 *l* pr an̄n̄ū *has some estate of his own, by ye death of a neer Relation* deserves Some incouragment |
| Mr Ja: Naylor | Att St Ellins Chappell 400 hearers and some estate 30 *l* pr an̄ū ∧ |
| Mr Nath: Heywood | In Ormskirk towne 250 hearers 30 *l* pr anū |
| Mr Richardson | Att Liverpoole 400 hearers 75 *l* betweene him and Mr Angier as above<br>put these two together when you enter in the fair county book |
| mr Tho: Crompton | Att ye Loe juxta Liverpoole 2 or 300 hearers has 14 *l* pr annum, Some Estate by his wife |
| Mr Wm Aspinwall | Att Shierstead ∧ chappell has 14 *l* pr annum, and 4 *l* pr an̄ū given by Sr John Thomson |
| mr John Carrington | Att Lancaster, lately call'd and and an estate of his own ordain'd to ye Ministry. 20 *l* pr an̄ū |

| | | |
|---|---|---|
| M$^{r}$ Baldwin | Att Eccles neer Manchester, lately Settled there | |
| M$^{r}$ Pendlebury | Att Rachdale (w$^{th}$ an assistant) every other Lords day, and y$^{e}$ other day amongst his old people at Holcom. has 20 *l* p$^{r}$ añ̄ū att R: and Som Little at y$^{e}$ other place | M$^{r}$ Wtwth |
| M$^{r}$ John Walker | Att Rivington, turned out 24 aug$^{t}$ from Newton Chappel hath a plentifull temporall estate | |
| Ministers y$^{t}$ may want a supply | M$^{r}$ Robert Constantine y$^{e}$ ancientest that is alive of the outed Min$^{rs}$, hee was Minister of Oldam, hath a meeting of what Survive of his people, hath a little estate of his own, | |
| | M$^{r}$ Robert Eaton, hath a Congregation in Prestwich parish, the people not ungratefull and hath an estate | |
| | *Liverpoole* | |
| *M$^{r}$ Sam: Angier* | *Att Toxteth Park: neer Manchester has not aboue 10 l or 12 l p$^{r}$ añ: is assistant at Toxteth Park Liverpoole has 75 l p$^{r}$* | |
| | they want help | |
| John Hartley | Att Burton Wood 50 or 60 hearers 14 *l* p$^{r}$ annū | |
| | Croft in winwick parish has a good estate } | |
| Tho: Risley | Att *Culcheth*, 100 or 150 hearers 10 *l* p$^{r}$ annū } | |
| Tho: Collins a young man | Att Leigh in Little Wooton, *if* is lately come, yet his Stay must be Short without Some aide, and if this meeting failes y$^{e}$ countrey for 9 or 10 miles Long and 5 or 6 miles broad is utterly destitute. Severall of 50 years old and Some on dying beds haue told | |

| | |
|---|---|
| | m^r Crompton, they never heard any thing of the Gospell before hee came among them. |
| Persons Contributing | M^r Thomas Key, Att Walton Chappell two Lords dayes and else where the other dayes, an able minister, painfull, very poor, has lately beene very Sick & Scarce recovered |
| | Mr Valentine att Blakely neer Manchester y^e people willing but poor and there is need of help |
| | Mr Tyrer—about Heywood in Bury parish they want help |
| 1691 M^r Jn^o Hartley | Of Ashton in Mackerfield, a deserving Young man, their contributions cannot maintaine him, and hee must be forced to leaue them if some Supply from hence be not giuen |

| [41] Ministers y^t haue a Supply | Lancashire |
|---|---|
| M^r Henry ffinch | Att Birch Chappell, where in y^e former Liberty hee continued 11 years and *conti* is now there, the allowance in considerable, y^e charge of his horse will goe a great way in his allowance from the people, yet complains not |
| M^r John Lever | Att Bolton, a considerable Congregation, a Small estate and some allowance from y^e people. |
| M^r Crompton | Att Cockey Chappell euery other L^ds day, has an estate of his own and some allowance from the people |
| M^r Thomas Jolley | Outed from altam in Blakburne hundred, hath Since laboured in those parts and continues soe to doe, hath an estate and some very little help from y^e people |
| M^r Charles Sagar | Outed for nonconformity from head m^r of Blakburne School, Since has laboured in y^e work in those parts, and so doth still in severall places has an estate and Small charge and Some Small allowance |
| M^r Henry Newcome | Outed att Manchester, has continued w^th y^t people euer since, and has a Congregation there now |
| M^r Wood | Att Chowbent, was outed there, but gott in againe, and has continued there euer Since |
| M^r John Parr | Att Elswick Chappell 2 dayes. and at Euston the other two, has but small allowance, yet wants not. |
| M^r John Chorlton | Assistant to m^r Newcome att Manchester |
| M^r Nath: Scholes | Att Newton Chappell neer Manchester |
| M^r Whitworth | Att Rochdale assistant to m^r Pendlebury and preaches euery other Lords day att Cockey Chappell has allowance att both places, and Some estate of his own |

| | |
|---|---|
| Mr Alured | Att Horrige Chappell |
| Mr Whaley | Att Hin^d^ley Chappell a very hopeful useful man |
| Mr Saml Eaton | Son to mr Robert Eaton a pious learned young minister att present assistant to his father |

[42]

| [43] Places y$^{t}$ had & where there may be oportunities of Religious assemblies | Lancaster | M$^{r}$ Rapier & M$^{r}$ Williams |
|---|---|---|
| Choleton and Blakeley | Haue Striven to haue Settled ministers but are not able to doe any thing towards a necessary maintenance | |
| The ffilde Country | Is a field white for y$^{e}$ harvest and noe provision for a minister among them. if a competent allowance could be had for one to goe among them, it might be of great concerne to many Soules | 20 *l* p$^{r}$ anū would encourage to provide a man to goe among them |
| Att Tottle bank and Broughton Tower | In Fourness Fells Supplyed by noe Minister, call out to you, for one at least, for whose maintenance they'l collect 20 *l* p$^{r}$ annū besides Severall Legacyes, some in monys, some in land bequeathed towards a ministers maintenance. &c see more att large in N$^{o}$ 111 | See also Col Sawrys request on this account N$^{o}$ 111 |
| Teatham Chappell | Whereunto m$^{r}$ Carrington has gott m$^{r}$ Sawry a dissenting Shoolmaster and licenced for Dissenters worship, Supplyed by m$^{r}$ Anderton and m$^{r}$ Taylor Candidates for y$^{e}$ ministry, the maintenance (besides the Schoolm$^{rs}$ Settled Salary) is but 7 *l* p$^{r}$ anū promised by y$^{e}$ people, by y$^{e}$ Smallness of w$^{ch}$ | |

| | |
|---|---|
| | maintenance the meeting is like to fall, and if it should what a ruine would it be to y$^{e}$ vastly numerous poor people y$^{t}$ flock thither—see N° 111 |
| Att Bispham<br>Persons qualifyed for y$^{e}$ ministry and not fixed | A Congregation, constantly very numerous, Sometimes near or aboue 1000, one hundred of the hearers are Wealthy, yet haue noe fixt minister there, noe joint contributions, insomuch y$^{t}$ even y$^{e}$ Lectures there are like to fall unless you retrieve them see more—N° 111 |
| — — — — | |
| | Blakeburne hundred, it is judged very desirable that provision be made at least for one Minister there to assist M$^{r}$ Jolley and m$^{r}$ Sagar (M$^{r}$ Whaley a 3$^{d}$ being about to remove) |
| | Chorlton hath had a meeting place, the min$^{r}$ forced away for want of Subsistance, but they are Settling a min$^{r}$ and must have help if any can be had |
| | Preston Lecture cannot be kept up w$^{th}$ out help |
| Persons qualifying for the Ministry | |
| M$^{r}$ Roger Anderton & M$^{r}$ Tho: Taylor | Candidates for y$^{e}$ ministry Supply Teatham Chappell |
| James Taylor | has beene a year w$^{th}$ m$^{r}$ Frankland, but his father is very poor and cannot goe on to maintaine him |

there his father lives att Preston, mr Frankland would give him his tutorage (see alsoe No. 69 ye 2d yeare)

Proposalls

| [44] Ministers that haue a competent Supply | Leicester |
|---|---|
| — — — — | Supplyed by mr Jno Sheffield mr Richd Southwell and mr Jno Southwell |
| *Mr Wm Cross as I Suppose. vide no 26* | Att Stoak Golding is a meeting ∧ ye burden of wch doth almost wholly lye upon Mr Davile, and is too heavy for his Estate, they desire some assistance. |
| Mr Edmd Spencer | Att Leicester allowed 30 *l* pr Añn 7 or 800 heares aged 60 yeares |
| Mr Math: Clarke | Att Harborow allowed 30 *l* pr Añ |
| | *aged 60 yeares* |
| Mr Clark Juor | Att Harborow ∧ allowed 20 *l* pr Añu 30 *l* as pr 82 divided betweene him & his Son. . 5 or 600 attenders |
| Mr Jno Woodhouse | Att Diseworth. allowed 40 *l* pr annum |
| Mr Jno Sheffield | Att Temple Hall allowed 24 *l* pr annum |
| Mr Peter Dewly | Att Lutterworth, allowed 20 *l* pr annum |
| Mr Peregrine Phillips | Att Loseby, allowed 15 *l* besides his allowance from Pinnars hall, educated att Cambridg *aged 35* |
| Mr Jno St Nicholas | Att Burbage |
| *Mr Joseph Lee* | *Att Calthorp* |
| Mr Pike | Att Direworth in ye Roome of mr Smith deceased, allowance is said to be 50 *l* pr annum, a very great auditory. |

| | |
|---|---|
| Mr Jno Jennings | Att Langton, allowed but 5 *l* pr annū. as pr No 35. has 400 auditors, is not ingaged as pastour has noe maintenance, as pr No 82—has a good Estate. |
| Mr Peter Dowely | Att Lutterworth, has £28: per annum |
| Ministers that want a Supply | |
| | Hinkley |
| *Mr Southwell* | Att *ffinkly* has a populous Congregation, generally consists of ye lowest of ye people, though a markett towne yet are not able to raise above 20 *l* pr annum |
| Mr Wm Cross | At Loughborrow allowed 10 *l* pr annum 150 or 200 audit once a month a Lecture at notting: another Do at Leicester 10*s*, both places per day |
| Mr Saml Shaw | At Ashby-de-la Zouch noe allowance, teaches a publick School there, preaches in his School aged 50 yeares |
| *Mr John Jennings* att Dadlington | *Att Langton allowed but 5 l pr annum 400 hearers is not engaged as pastor, has no maintenance* |
| Mr Richd Southwell | Att Braddon allowed but 12 *l* pr Anū<br>Att templehall, severall young children 16 *l* pr annū 200 hearers. |
| Mr Jno Sheffield and Mr Richd Southwell | 13<br>Att Appleby allowed *15* pr annū ^ supplies a service at Stoke Davile (?) full 35 old pastour at Dudley in Worcester and may be left out now |
| Mr Mich: Mathews | Att Swedeland allowed 15 *l* pr annum |
| Mr Jos: Lee | Att Calthorp in a necessitous condition as per his own account in No 131 |

| Persons contributing<br><br>[45]<br>Places y$^{t}$ had or where there may be opportunity of Religious assemblies | Leicester | M$^{r}$ Meade *and* M$^{r}$ Alsop and D$^{r}$ Samson |
|---|---|---|
| At Melton Mowbray | There may be opportunity of publick Service | |
| Hinkley | A Congregation to w$^{ch}$ m$^{r}$ Watts preached, but since his death they haue yet noe man except aged M$^{r}$ S$^{t}$ Nicholas who doth what hee can gratis. they offer to raise 25 *l* p$^{r}$ annum. | |
| Lutterworth | Where there had never before beene any Settled meeting, in those parts. they gott an old barn to meet in. m$^{r}$ Lee preached there for a little time. hee falling into weakness, the meeting fell as to constancy of helps. at last among others one m$^{r}$ Dowley was Sent for, and continued to visit them for 2 yeares, though hee liued 20 miles Distant from them, in w$^{ch}$ time hee found a very great blessing vpon his ministry. hee is now desirous to fix among them. and that w$^{ch}$ weighed most with hinn, was the remembrance of m$^{r}$ John Wickliffe—being minister of that place. desire Some assistance. raise 7 *l* a quarter but feare the continuance of that | |

| | |
|---|---|
| Stoakgolding 1691 | The utmost they can raise is 12[l]: 10[s]: p[r] annum, and y[e] burden of that lies almost wholly vpon one m[r] Davile of y[e] Same towne, whose estate is but 60 *l* per añ |
| Persons qualifyed for y[e] ministry and not fixed | |
| Persons qualifying for the Ministry | M[r] Southall has one Son grown up and bred by m[r] Woodhouse for y[e] ministry |
| Proposalls | |

| [46] Ministers y$^{t}$ haue a Competent Supply | Lincoln | |
|---|---|---|
| M$^{r}$ Rastrick | Att Spalding, of a Con: turned a Non: Con. 30 *l* p$^{r}$ $\overline{\text{anu}}$ | Thankes but at pr.$^{t}$ neads not |
| M$^{r}$ Pell | Att Boston, has 2 or 300 auditors in y$^{e}$ afternoone they raise him about 60 *l* p$^{r}$ annum, but begin to be weary of Soe much, Since y$^{e}$ death of Some of y$^{e}$ better sort | |
| M$^{r}$ Modwitt | Att Stamford removed, to Tooting in Surry | |
| Ministers that want a Supply<br>— — — — | | |
| M$^{r}$ Drake | Att Lincoln— ‸an aged man‸ has not aboue 10 *l* or 12 *l* p$^{r}$ annum see his case more fully in N$^{o}$ 68 | |
| *M$^{r}$ Mat: Coats*<br>I know not whether this man be a minister or no<br>enter it on the other side | *Att Gainsbrough, needs a Supply, it being a convenient place for a Minister to settle in* | |
| M$^{r}$ Britton | Att Sleeford, has about 5$^{s}$ a Lords day | |
| Persons contributing | | |

| [47]<br>Places y$^{t}$ had or where there may be oportunity of | Lincoln | D$^{r}$ Samson and M$^{r}$ Rapier |
|---|---|---|

| | |
|---|---|
| Religious assemblies | they want a minister, propose to raise 10 *l* p$^{r}$ anū and Some thing *e* — from other towns about them |
| Att Gains-brough | ∧ There is a meeting at m$^{r}$ M: Coates house; needs Supply being a convenient place for a Minister to Settle in |
| Att Gedley Holbeach &c | Betweene Boston and Lin, a very heathenish place are desirous of a minister, will raise 40 *l* p$^{r}$ annum or more |
| Stamford | Want a Minister, can raise 40 *l* per anū see alsoe the case further stated in N$^{o}$ 13—1691 and considered |
| Grantham | Desire Some assistance towards Setting up a Lecture there |
| 1691 | The people of Grantam haue prevailed w$^{th}$ m$^{r}$ Drake and m$^{r}$ Scoffin to preach there once a fortnight, w$^{ch}$ is euery other Thursday. m$^{r}$ Drake began y$^{e}$ 30$^{th}$ of July last past, they desire y$^{t}$ the money promised may be sent them |
| Persons qualifyed for y$^{e}$ ministry not fixed | —Telney, not able to raise aboue 10 *l* per annum, are in hopes to be Supplyed w$^{th}$ a minister out of Yorkshire educated by m$^{r}$ Frankland, |
| Persons qualifying for y$^{e}$ Min$^{r}$y | |
| Proposalls. | |

| [48] Ministers yt haue a competent Supply | Middlesex |
|---|---|
| Mr Math: Mead & Mr Lawrence | Att Stepney |
| Mr Hodges | Att Bednall greene |
| Dr Wm Bates and mr Woodcock | Att Hackney |
| Mr Vnick | Att Dalston |
| Mr Starkey | Att Newington |
| Mr Jackson | Att Totnam |
| Mr Masters | Att Enfield |
| Mr Chantrey | Att Southgate |
| Mr Hocker | Att Barnett |
| Mr Rathband | Att High-gate |
| Mr Lobb | Att Hamstead |
| Mr Pemberton | Att Hammersmith removed |
| Mr Goodwin | Att Pinner |
| Mr Webb | Att Hackney, his low estate in ye world fully Stated see alsoe No 143 |
| Ministers that want a Supply | |
| Persons contributing | |

| [49] Places y[t] had or where there may be opportunities of religious assemblies | Middlesex | M[r] Jurin |
|---|---|---|
| Att Brainford | *Weree* Were m[r] Jackson and m[r] Dogeridge | |
| Att Stains | M[r] Mills Supplys and others as they can gett them | |
| Att Vxbridge | | |
| Att Colebrook | Ministers occasionally | |
| Att Acton | None | |
| Persons qualifyed for y[e] ministry & not fixed | | |
| Persons qualifying for y[e] Min[r]y | | |
| Proposalls | | |

| [50] Ministers y[t] haue A competent Supply | Norfolk | |
|---|---|---|
| m[r]. Hannot | At Yarmouth, a great Congregation hath £100 p Añ | |
| m[r]. Wright | Assistant a Young man hath £50 p Añ | |
| Jn[o]. Collinges | At Norwich, hath a Congregation & £56 p Añ | |
| Benj̃: Snowden | D[o] | |
| m[r] Finch | At Norwich, pator of a Congregation*all* & Assistant £130 | |
| m[r]. Green | At Tunstead, hath about £50 | |
| m[r] Say | At Guestwick. D[o] | |
| m[r] Bedbank | At Denton. Know not what he hath | |
| m[r] Purt | At Windham, hath not lesse then £50 | |
| m[r] Amirant | At Northrepps, hath £40. and helpt a little | |
| m[r] Lucas | At Norwich, preacheth a lecture may get £40 | |
| Enoch Wooyard | D[o]. if not worse | |
| Ministers y[t] may Want Supply— | | |
| m[r]. Williamson | At Lynn. hath. £30. p Añ provided for | |
| Thõ. Worth | At East Ruston, preacheth constantly to a poore people, hath 5[s] y[e] Lords day frõ a good Getlewoman | see also N[o]. 64 in y[e] Second yeare |
| Jn[o]. Hasbert | At East Deerham, newly Erected his meeting, £30 | |

| | | |
|---|---|---|
| Persons Contributing | | |
| m$^{r}$. Smith | Likely to doe Some what | |
| [51] Places that had & where may be an Opertunity for Religious Assembly's | **Norfolk** | D$^{r}$ Bates and M$^{r}$ Hartley |
| Southwatsam | Discontinewed but not certayn of it | |
| Northwatsam | Fit to raise a congregation in, Supplyed by Seuerall | |
| Derham | D$^{o}$. m$^{r}$. Hasbert is doeing it | |
| Persons Qualified for the Ministry not fixed | | |
| m$^{r}$ King | He was breed Wp at London w$^{th}$ m$^{r}$ Morton | |
| m$^{r}$. Steward | At present out of y$^{e}$ County, at Debenham aged about. 22 | |
| Persons Qualefing for the Ministry | | |
| One | 15. yeares Old teaching. 20. Children latine | |
| A ministers Son | 14. yeares Old. 4. yeare moore will doe his bussines | |
| Proposalls | Ministers cannot liue und$^{r}$. £50. p Ann̄ like Ministers. 200 *l* p Ann̄ will Supply it to y$^{e}$. 13. Congregations & keepe. 6. Children at Education proposalls for Education | |

| [52] Ministers y[t] have a Competent Supply | Northampton | |
|---|---|---|
| M[r] Jn[o] Maydwell | of Kettering Sen[r] has 20 *l* p[r] annum | |
| M[r] Strickland Negus | of Geddington past his work through age | |
| M[r] Dandy | Of great Okeley | |
| M[r] John Courtman Sen[r] | of Thorpe. | |
| M[r] Rich[d] Davis. | of Rowell has 30 *l* p[r] annum | |
| M[r] W[m] Sheppard | Att. Oundle has about 30 *l*: per annū | |
| M[r] Blore | Of Northampton | |
| M[r] Harding Dead— | Of Northampton, nothing but y[e] rent of y[e] meetinghouse p[d] by the Church | |
| M[r] ffowler | Of Crick | |
| *M[r] Worth sen[r]* | Of the Same place } preach principally in Warwickshire | considered in Warwickshere |
| *M[r] Worth jno[r]* | Son to y[e] aboue named } preach principally in Warwickshire | |
| M[r] Wills | Of Spratton | |
| m[r] Harrison | Att Portersperry, the people there haue under taken to provide him a maintenance. | |
| Ministers y[t] may want Supply | | |
| M[r] Simon King | Att Peterborough a Lecture *noe* ∧ very Small maintenance. well known to m[r] Baxter | |
| M[r] Math: Clarke | Att Ashley has but about 10 *l* p[r] annū | Lestershere |

| | | |
|---|---|---|
| mr Strickland Negus | Of Geddington, past his work throug age | |
| Persons contributing | | |
| [53] Places that had and where may be an oportunity of Religious Assemblyes | Northampton | Mr Alsop<br>Mr Cockerell &<br>Mr Rapier |
| Wellingborow<br>Geddington<br>Thorpe Waterfield<br>Creaton<br>Wellford<br>Daintree<br>Sibbertoft<br>Cranford | mr King gone Downe is Setling a congregation where they will raise him 30 *l* p Ann to Stay hath a wife. 1. Child & more Comeing if doth Settle must remoue his goods from Norfolks *mr Alsop*<br>Congregations formerly now discontinued if they had Ministers, there is a likelyhood of great Good. | Ordered mr King £10 p An |
| Brigstock<br>Bugbrooke<br>Peterborough<br>Warmington<br>Tocester | Places where there may be opportunity of publick Service | |
| Potters Perry | where mr Harrison is fixing desire Some assistance to wards repairing their meeting house | |
| *Persons qualifyed for ye ministry* | | |
| *Wolv* 1691<br>Wolverhampton<br>augt 24°:. | A great towne, they first began wth a week day Lecture & allowed 5s pr diem. afterwards they raised ye Lecture and mett vpon ye Sabbath dayes, and Chose one mr Greenwood for whom they raised £20: | |

| | |
|---|---|
| | for one yeare,. Seuerall of the contributors *inhabitants* haueing removed their habitations y^e^ 20 *l* is reduced to 12 *l* and out of that y^e^ rent of their meeting house is paid. soe like to be destitute w^th^ out some Supply |
| Persons qualifying for y^e^ ministry. | |
| M^r^ Math: Orlebar | of Polebrooke |
| M^r^ Chapman | of Gilsborow a Schoolmaster |
| M^r^ Jn^o^ Shuttlewood | Of Creaton |
| Mr. Tho: Wykes | Of Welford resident at present in London |
| M^r^ Tho: Loftus | of Thorpe Waterfeild, wants Education |
| Proposalls | |

| [54] Ministers that haue a competent supply | Northumberland | |
|---|---|---|
| m$^{r}$ Rich$^{d}$ Gilpin<br>m$^{r}$ Gill | At Newcastle they haue a meeting howse uery larg and alwayes full and are well prouided for. | |
| m$^{r}$ Luke Oagle | At Berwick. he hath a great congregation, | |
| m$^{r}$ James Jaffray | At Hexham, he was of the Church of England but dissatisfyed & willing to Joyne w$^{th}$ Dissenters, able to be an Itenerant, wher he is they be part Anabaptistes hath. £30 p Anñ | |
| Ministers that may want, Supply | | |
| m$^{r}$ Blunt | At Harlow, A Setled Congregation, hath. £25. p Anñ w$^{ch}$ is all he hath to liue on, he & his Wife | |
| m$^{r}$ Jn$^{o}$ Lomax | At Sheeles. his hearers Seamen hath about 16 *l* p Anñ keeps an Apothecarys Shop, his mother Supplys him w$^{th}$ part of her Joynture, hath a wife &. 3. Children see also N$^{o}$ 10 ʌ | v his mother is now dead soe y$^{t}$ his chief Support w$^{ch}$ hee had from her joynture is gone |
| Tho: Daws | At Austin moore, A young man & Maryed, hath. 17 *l* p Anñ | |
| M$^{r}$ Tho: Wilson | Neer Newcastle, very poor, he has nothing from his people, disabled from preaching by the Stone | |

| | | |
|---|---|---|
| Mrs Agnes Wilson<br>enter this on the other side like the persons that are qualifying for the ministry | Near Newcastle, a pious woman, whose Estate is not aboue 20 *l* pr anū: hath taken into her care ye Son of Mr Davice (a Non-conformist deceased) who is now fitting for ye ministry, humbly beggs some assistance in order to defray ye Charges of the sd young mans education | |
| Mr Blunt | Att Horsley near Newcastle is very poor and aged has not aboue 10 *l* or 12 *l* pr an̄. | |
| Persons Contributing | | |
| [55] Places that had Religious Assemblys—& where there may be oppertunity of Seruis | Northumberland | Mr Stretton and Mr Nisbett |
| Eatall | Gabl Semple, a Scoth man Preacheth there where he hath £60. p Ann̄ now is returning home | |
| Branton | James Noble, hath. £40. ye Same circumstance | |
| Hull Abby | Jno. Dizart. Do. hath £30 | |
| Little Harle | Robt. Willson. Do. hath £25 | |
| North Tine | Wm Thompson. Do. hath little & Uncertaine | |
| Twedmouth | A Scotch man, returned, a fixt Congregation, £40. p Ann̄ | |
| Milborn grang | mr Leuer, latly dead he had £28. p Ān̄n̄ | |
| Twedmouth | had a fixed Congregation and pastor they raised him 40 *l* pr ann̄, hee is gone for Scotland | |
| Milborn grang | had Mr Lever who is lately dead, they raised him 28 *l* pr an̄ | |

| | |
|---|---|
| Hexham | Hath beene endeavouring to get a preacher, can raise 30 *l* p[r] an̄n̄: there be some Anabaptists among them |
| Persons Qualifyed for the Ministry & not fixed | |
| Persons qualifying for the Ministry | |

| [56] Ministers yt haue a Competent Supply | Nottingham | |
|---|---|---|
| mr Jn° Whitlock | One of ye ministers of ye Presbyterian meeting in Nottingham preaches there once euery other Lords day has 14s pr day | |
| Mr Wm Reinolds | Vnder ye Same circumstances in ye Same place | |
| Mr Jn° Barrett | Liues at Sandyacre in Derbyshire preaches euery other Lords day to ye Presbyterian meeting in nottingham has ye Same allowance. | |
| Mr Jn° Ryther | Pastor of the Congregation ^all^ church in Nottingham | |
| Mr Jn° Billingsley | Att Selston and at places neere adjoyning, is promised 30 *l* pr annū yett doubtfull. they could raise 20 *l* pr annū. if 10 *l* could be added might be a meanes to ingage his aboade and labours among ym | |
| Mr Jn° Whitlock Juor | Lives in Nottingham, preaches 2 Lords dayes in 12 wth Mr Barrett and one Lords day in 12 wth mr Ryther and at other places | |
| Mr Saml Crumpton | Att Blidworth, preacheth there Sometimes, there being a meeting euery other Lords day, allowance 10s pr day, and in other places | considered out of ye ffund. |

| | | |
|---|---|---|
| Mr Dickenson | Minister of a Ch: of Congregationall Dissenters att Sutton, all his allowance comes short of 20 *l* pr annū | |
| Mr Eleazar Heywood | Liues wth mr Richd Taylor present high Sherriff of Nottinghamshire, keeps a meeting in his house, hath frequently other ministers on Lords dayes and allows 20s pr Sabbath | |
| Ministers that may want a Supply | | |
| Mr Jno Leighton | fformerly Vicar of Hucknall upwards of 67 yeares, has noe constant people or place hee preacheth in, hee is very poore, his wife uery much discomposed in her head and mind, now in London for cure at his charge of 5s pr week. | |
| Mr Tho: Rose | Liueing at Adbolton neere nottingham, very poore, noe constant people or preaching place, is lame, and has lately gott a further hurt and lameness, wch disables him for going abroad | see alsoe No 126 |
| Mr Jackson | Of Bleasbey, is very poore, little encouragmt ye people about him very poore | no fixed place |
| Mr Saml Coates | Att Mansfield, preaches there one Lds day in a mo 8s pr day, could 10 *l* a yeare be added ye meeting would be held up constantly for want whereof hee is forced to preach in other places | on condition to keepe the metting Constant 8 *l* p Ann̄ |
| mr John Billingsley | Att Selston as above, see his case as tated by himselfe in No 173 | |
| Persons contributing | | |

| | | |
|---|---|---|
| [57] Places yt had or where there may be an opportunity of Religious assemblies | Nottingham | Dr Bates |
| The Vale and ye Northclay | Two of ye Darkest places in ye County a minister there is much desired by mr Ryther | |
| E. Ratford | The people desier a Setled Minister can raise £12 p An̄n̄—They being well inclined and doe there Wt-most | |
| Persons qualifyed for the Ministry and not fixed | | |
| Mr Pigott | A young man, newly entred, preaches Sometimes att Worksop, Sometimes at or about Retford, allowance very little | |
| Persons qualifying for ye Ministry— | | |
| Proposalls— | | |

| [58] Ministers that haue a Competent Supply Froysier | Oxford |
|---|---|
| r | |
| m$^{r}$ Jer: Froyse | Att Henley has a large Congregation has 40 *l* p Añ̄ |
| m$^{r}$ Hen: Cornish | Aged 80 yeares yet in his masters Service at Bisister 30 *l* |
| m$^{r}$ Wheatley | Somewhat aged and infirme yet in att Milton Service *at Coomb b 20 & 30 l* betweene 20 and 30 pound a year |
| M$^{r}$ Oldfield | Att Oxford has from y$^{e}$ people 16 *l* p$^{r}$ anū and from Lond 50 *l* |
| M$^{r}$ Stockden | Att Banbury has about 50 *l* p$^{r}$ annum |
| M$^{r}$ Baley | Att Chipping Norton has 40 *l* p$^{r}$ annum |
| M$^{r}$ Wh | |
| Ministers y$^{t}$ may want a Supply | |
| m$^{r}$ Gilbert | neere 80 years old under many infirmities, disabled |
| M$^{r}$ Sanders | Att Coomb has betweene 20 & 30 *l* p$^{r}$ annum |
| m$^{r}$ Jn$^{o}$ Nott | At Tame has newly Sett up a constant meeting, y$^{e}$ people as yet cannot promise 15 *l* p$^{r}$ anū, see his case at Large in. . N$^{o}$ 92 |
| Persons contributing | Oxfordshire for Religion and good workes too barren to yeild contri- |

| | | |
|---|---|---|
| | buters to gospell propogation—other than those who beare their shares cheerfully in their Sallerys aboue Specifyed. | |
| [59] Places that had or where there may be opportunities of Religious assemblies— | Oxford<br>*Rutland* | Mr How and Mr Meade |
| Witney | There mr Hubert deceased formerly pastour, now mr Cornish preacheth once a fortnight on ye week dayes sometimes on ye Lords day in a friends house ; recompence Small. but must now recede | |
| Watlington & Tame and Dodington | Are other townes capeable, but Questionable whether Dodington mr Wheatleys place and Milton 2 miles apart ^ might not join and meet alternis vicibus in both places<br>Seuerall considerations offered wherein it would be a great inconvenience to joyne Daddington and Milton together | |
| Persons qualifyed for the Ministry and not fixed | | |
| Persons qualifying for ye Minry | | |
| Proposalls— | | |

| | Rutland | |
|---|---|---|
| [60] Ministers that haue a competent Supply<br>Ministers y^t may want a Supply | | |
| M^r Rob^t Ekyns | At Okeham, hath a Settled congregation administers all ordinances, has been there 17 yeares. has a wife & five Children, a numerous auditory, yet are able to raise not aboue 5 or 6 pounds p^r an̄ū for his maintenance<br>3 or 4 pound p^r annum as p^r N° 82<br>see alsoe m^r Thomas Woodcocks certificate | |
| Persons Contributing— | | |

| | Rutland | |
|---|---|---|
| [61] Places y^t had or where there may be opportunity of Religious Assemblies | | M^r Alsop M^r Woodcock & D^r Samson |
| Persons qualifyed for y^e ministry & not yet fixed.<br>Persons qualifying for y^e Ministry | | |
| Proposalls | | |

| [62] Ministers y[t] haue a competent Supply | Salop | |
|---|---|---|
| M[r] David Jones | Att Salop. though he be a minister to a Congregation there, yet hath y[e] Welch tongue—in Shrewsbury | |
| M[r] Fra: Tallent & m[r] Jn[o] Bryan | At Shrewsbury a Considerable Congregation | |
| M[r] Jn[o] Nevitt | Att Bridgnorth | |
| M[r] Jn[o] Woodhouse | Att Sherifthayles preaches to his pupils and Some few neighbours but neuer was a publick minister | |
| M[r] Henry | Att Broad Oake a constant meeting for all Ordinances | |
| M[r] Doughty | Att Sheriffhayles | |
| m[r] And: Barnett | At Oswestree | |
| *M[r] Sam Beresford* entered on y[e] other side | *Sometimes att S[r] Tho: Wilbrahams, an eminent Minister has left off preaching except very rarely for m[r] Woodhouse* | |
| Ministers y[t] may want Supply | | |
| M[r] Charles Edwards | An ejeted minister liues vpon a Farm, which hee now puts up, is inclineable to betake himselfe to his ministry if a maintenance could be had for him. Hee hath y[e] Welch tongue | if gives him Selfe Vp to the Ministry £8 p Anū |
| *M[r] James Owen* | *Att Oswestree haueing y[e] Welch tongue unwearyed in his labours receives little recompence.* | |

| | | |
|---|---|---|
| m$^{r}$ Sam: Taylor | Att Wem has a great charge of Children lost by the fire there, maintenance next to nothing | |
| M$^{r}$ Finlow | Neere Acham an ejected Minister aged & poore | |
| M$^{r}$ Bury | An ejected minister has noe encouragm$^{t}$ to preach y$^{e}$ Gospell | on |
| M$^{r}$ Jn: Wood neuer in any place except y$^{e}$ Colledge | Sometimes one of y$^{e}$ Sen$^{r}$ Fellows of Magdalene Colledge Cambridge eminent for learning, a pious person who w$^{th}$ y$^{e}$ 3 last mentioned stand in great need of reliefe | on condition he Attends y$^{e}$ Ministry £6 |
| m$^{r}$ David Jones | of Salop, some assistance is desired for him as p$^{r}$ N$^{o}$ 37: Sep$^{t}$ 23. 1691 | |
| Persons Contributing | | |
| [63] Places that had and where there may be oportunities of Religious assemblies— | Salop | M$^{r}$ Williams |
| | One part of the county (w$^{ch}$ lies betweene Shrewsbury and Ludlow neuer had any one to preach to them w$^{ch}$ has greatly troubled M$^{r}$ Tallant and m$^{r}$ Bryan. if incouragment may be had they will See it Supplyed | |
| Oldbury Village | three miles from Hales Owen the parish Church out of w$^{ch}$ m$^{r}$ Edward Paston was Ejected in 62: the inhabitants of Oldbury in former dayes procured liberty to build a Chappell, and endowed it w$^{th}$ about £6:—per anū: the people raise about 10 *l* or 12 *l* per annum more, and they are Supplyed every | |

| | |
|---|---|
| | Lords day w$^{ch}$ goes very hard with with them. request help to Support y$^{t}$ meeting |
| Wombridge 1691 | A parish, in y$^{e}$ Church whereof y$^{e}$ meeting is kept, y$^{e}$ people generally are poor Colliers, there is but Seven Nobles a year belongs to it, a peculiar where y$^{e}$ Bishop has noe power to visit, noe Ministers reside within Seuen miles of the place, y$^{e}$ Subscribers not able to bear y$^{e}$ charge y$^{e}$ chief whereof are mentioned in y$^{e}$ Letter |
| Persons qualifyed for y$^{e}$ ministry and not fixed— | |
| M$^{r}$ Sam$^{l}$ Beresford | Sometimes at S$^{r}$ Tho: Wilbrahams an eminent Minister has left off preaching except very rarely for m$^{r}$ Woodhouse |
| Persons qualifying for y$^{e}$ Ministry | |
| M$^{r}$ Owen | Son to m$^{r}$ James Owen of Oswestree, now w$^{th}$ m$^{r}$ Karr, is willing hee should Settle in Denbighshire if a maintenance may be had |
| Theodore West :macott | The son of a Deceased Dissenting Min$^{r}$, the widdow has 9 children all of them disposed of, this Son has beene some monthes with m$^{r}$ Woodhouse, very hopefull, of pregn$^{t}$ parts, y$^{e}$ Widow desires some assistance towards his education in Vniversitie Learning. No: 16: 1691 |
| Proposalls— | |

| [64] Ministers yt haue a competent Supply | Somerset | |
|---|---|---|
| Mr Butler | Att Frary, | Settled Pastors in ye Eastern Division. |
| Mr Bartlett & Mr Gardner | Att Yeovill. | |
| Mr Young | Att Stanton. | |
| Mr Cumming | Att Shepton: | |
| Mr Chandler | Att Colefort | |
| Mr Bishop | Att Charleton. | |
| Mr Harford & Mr Warren | Att Taunton | Settled Pastors in the Western Division |
| Mr Safford | Att Bicknoller & Tolland | |
| Mr Moor | Att Bridgwater | |
| Mr Marshall | Att Illminster | |
| Mr Kerring | Att Hillbishops | |
| Mr Pitts | Att Chard | |
| Mr Pinny | Att Brookhorne | |
| Mr Bush | Att Langport | |
| Mr Winny<br>Mr Weekes<br>Mr Sinclare<br>Mr Noble | Preach constantly in ye City of Bristoll | |
| Mr Thomas & Mr Barnes | Teach School in ye City preach abroad | |
| **Ministers yt may want a Supply** | | |
| Mr Davenish | Att Welleton. | Disabled from preaching |
| Mr Beckaller | Att Chard, | |

| | | |
|---|---|---|
| M$^{r}$ Glanvill | Att Taunton | |
| M$^{r}$ Batt | Att Taunton. } | |
| M$^{r}$ Chadwick | Att Dulverton. } Very infirm | |
| M$^{r}$ Turner | Att Crickett } | |
| M$^{r}$ Chadwick | Who preacheth Some times at Dulverton has no temporall Estate, Severall children to care for, taken off from his ministeriall Labours, by reason of more than ordinary bodily weakness, under w$^{ch}$ hee has laboured almost this 12 monthes. | |
| Persons contributing | | |
| [63] Places y$^{t}$ had or where there may be opportunity of Religious assemblies | Somerset | D$^{r}$ Chauncey & M$^{r}$ Rabdor |
| — — — — | | |
| E.D. | | |
| euery Sabbath Froom. Supplyed by | M$^{r}$ Albin, Phillips, Bartlett, Rossiter, Tidcombe 15$^{s}$ p$^{r}$ Sab | Winsham by m$^{r}$ Pinny, Ball, Turner att 5$^{s}$ p$^{r}$ Sabbatum |
| Hengrove, Supplyed by | M$^{r}$ Albin, Hopkins, Butler, Cumming Tidcomb. 10$^{s}$ p$^{r}$ Diem | |
| Wincanton. Supplyed | M$^{r}$ Albin, Hopkins Tidcombe 8$^{s}$ p$^{r}$ Sabbatum | |
| Gallington. by | M$^{r}$ Bartlett, Hopkins, Tidcombe, 10$^{s}$ p$^{r}$ Sabbatum | |
| Martlock by | M$^{r}$ Budd, Light, Bishop, Gatchell. . 6$^{s}$ p$^{r}$ Sab | |
| Seymonsford,by | M$^{r}$ Rossiter, Phillips, Flower, Gough 8$^{s}$ p$^{r}$ Sab | |
| Once a fortnight Bath by | M$^{r}$ *Cleere* reese, Daimey, Bourne, Barnes. 10$^{s}$ p$^{r}$ Sab | |
| Ingleshombe. by | M$^{r}$ Phillips, Cleere, Barnes. 10$^{s}$ p$^{r}$ Sabb | |
| *W: D$^{n}$* Coome. by | M$^{r}$ C*leere* reese . . . . . 10$^{s}$ p$^{r}$ Sab. | |

| | |
|---|---|
| once, a month. | Mr Woodcock, 10s pr Sabbatum |
| Wedmore by | |
| Croscombe by | Mr Chandler, Tidcombe 10s pr Sabbatum |
| Milborn-port by | Mr Hopkins, . . . . . 00 pr Sabbatum. |
| W: Dn<br>once a *mo* day } | |
| Wilscombe by | e<br>Mr Tayler, Toole, Woodcock att<br>∧<br>10s pr Sabbatum |
| Wellington by | Mr Batt., warren att . . . . 10s pr Sabbatum |
| Dulverton by | Jos.<br>Mr ∧ Chadwick, Tooel—att . . . *oo* 8s pr Sabbatum— |
| Persons qualifyed for ye ministry and not yet fixed: EDn s f | Pitminster, by Mr Warren, Blake, att Sabbatum 10s pr Diem<br>Hatch. by Mr Harford, Gatchel, att 8s pr Sabbatum<br>Lambrooke, by Mr Budd, Light att 6s pr Sabbatum |
| Mr *Cleere* Creese | Petherton—by Mr Gardner, Light att 7s pr Sabbatum once a fortnight} |
| Mr Abin | Stoackgursie by mr Woodcock at 10s pr Sab |
| Mr Phillips | Creech. by mr Adams: Deacon att 7s 6d pr Sab |
| Mr Rossiter | Broomvill, by mr Deacon, uncertaine |
| Mr Hopkins | Broadway, by mr Robt Pinny, Gatchel 5s pr Sab |
| Mr Tidcombe | These are itinerant preachers and Supply severall places as aboue |
| ......................<br>W: Dn<br>...................... | Bathe. see its case Stated in No 12—1691—considered— |
| Mr Taylor<br>Mr Woodcock<br>Mr Blake | |

| | |
|---|---|
| Mr Deacon<br>Mr Adams<br>Mr Gatchell.<br>Mr Tooell<br>Mr Budd.<br>Mr Light<br>Mr Gilling.<br>Mr Walsh | Itinerant preachers and Supply severall places as aboue |
| Persons qualifying for ye ministry | |
| Mr Jos: Chadwick's son . . | hee desires on behalfe of his son yt Some Supply may be afforded towards ye Education of his Son for ye ministry |
| Proposalls | |

[66]

| | |
|---|---|
| Glastonbury | There is a meeting only once a fortnight ye people being very poore cannot raise above 5 *l* per annum att present towards ye incouragment of a minister mr Adams (who has Some estate of his own) is willing to Settle among them provided they could raise him 30 *l* pr annum |
| Wilscombe | A considerable markett towne, is a meeting Supplyed by 3 Seuerall minrs in their turnes (vizt mr Christopher Taylor mr Richard Tooell, mr Josiah Woodcock) living 7 or 8 miles distant. they haue (by the charitable contribution of others) built a meeting place (not wholly paid for) hearers 4 or 500 most from places adjacent (the townes people being generally enemies to it) those that haue for some time afforded assistance haue withdrawn it. the meeting in danger of falling if not Supported by other charitable hands. |
| Dulverton | A poor people, haue beene embodyed ever since ye Ejectment. 2 or 300 auditors, but two persons yt contribute and about 5 or 6 farmers in ye countrey. |

kept up by three ministers m^r^ John Berry of Barnstable m^r^ Richard Tooell of Dulverton, and m^r^ Sam: Smith of South Molton they allow 8^s^ per Sabbath but this proueth soe hard that they are forced to haue a vacancie once in two monthes, else y^e^ Stock would not hold out.

| [67] Ministers y^t haue a Competent Supply | Stafford | |
|---|---|---|
| — — — | | |
| M^r Rich^d Hilton ejected | Maintaines a Lecture att Wassall, hath little assistance though is many able men in the towne ∧ minister of *Bromwich* Bromwich. | |
| *M^r W^m ffincher* | *Minister of Wednesbury* | all these are able to goe abroad euery Lords day 4. 5. or 6 miles for 9 or 7^s p^r day and horse hire paid out of it |
| *M^r Tho: Baldwin* | *Of Clent.* | |
| *M^r W^m Turton* | *Of Rowley* | |
| *M^r W^m Grace* | *Of Shenston* | |
| M^r Tho: Miles | Of Litchfield | |
| M^r Tho: Bladen | Of Alrewas. | |
| M^r Rich^d Channtry | Of Weeford. | |
| M^r Nath: Mansfield | Of Armitage. | |
| M^r Rich^d Swinfyn | Of Maves on Ridwar. | |
| M^r Tim: ffox | Of Drayton Bassett. | |
| M^r Rock | Of Mayfield *all these* ∧ aged and dark and preacheth not yet has 30 *l* p^r annum | |
| | Dudley well Settled | |
| M^r Southall | Att *Burton upon Trent, has* 50 *l p^r anū allowance* | |
| M^r Pike | Att Burton upon Trent—has 50 *l* p^r annum allowance | |
| M^r Myrrald | Att Utoxcester, who as others goes to other places—his people haue hired a meeting house att Longdoles | |

at $2^{l}:2^{s}:6^{d}$ p$^{r}$ annum haue mett with great opposition, but haue conquered their enemies, and are in hopes of haueing the greatest countrey meeting in all those parts if m$^{r}$ Merrald be incouraged to Stay among them, his wife keeps a Semstris's Shop in Uttoxcester, without w$^{ch}$ hee could not Subsist, see this case att large in . N° 71

Ministers y$^{t}$ may want a Supply

— — —

Eject

M$^{r}$ Eccleshall — At Sedgley where hee was minister hath little.

M$^{r}$ Grace, ejected — At Shenston, is blind and Indigent, can goe noe where to preach

M$^{r}$ Cony—91 — his condition is very Low, his very bed was Seized from under him, for his very bread y$^{t}$ hee has to keep him aliue, most of his helpers are dead, his Daughter as helpless as himselfe through poverty, hee is past preaching through age and other infirmities.

Persons contributing

[68] Places y$^{t}$ had or where there may be opportunity of Religious assemblies

## Stafford

M$^{r}$ Williams

---

Litchfield — is a Lecture, and allow 10$^{s}$ p$^{r}$ day, but it is but once a fortnight.

| | | |
|---|---|---|
| | would bring it to once a week . but . can not | |
| Tamworth | Is a Lecture euery fortnight, they allow $8^{s}$ but its feared will faile without help | |
| In Longdon | They haue a Lecture once in $y^{e}$ month their allowance is 5 or $6^{s}$. yet haue a Lecture euery Lords day | |
| In Thorny Lanes | Neer Uttoxcester they haue had a constant Lecture euer since the ejection. And Since Liberty was first indulged they haue endeavoured to bring it to Uttoxcester, hoping seuerall of the towne might be brought in, but they are disappointed, and discord arriseth, betwixt those of the towne and those of $y^{e}$ Countrey, though $y^{e}$ Country is the greater number, and they would Sett it up in Thorny Lanes againe but want assistance. | $m^{r}$ Wood hath $preach^{d}$ among them & is well liked they haue found out Merbrock Chapell $w^{ch}$ is 14. mile frõ Vxeter & 8 mile frõ any other would haue 8·or·10*l* work for an Other ꝑ Morris |
| The Moorlands and some part of Derbyshire Peak | A part of a countrey 16 or 20 miles distant from East to West, and about soe many from South to north, one of the barrenest *part* and darkest corners in England as to $y^{e}$ meanes of Grace, it is humbly desired it may be considered, see $y^{e}$ case att large in N° 84 and 85 | |
| Persons qualifyed for $y^{e}$ ministry & not yet fixed | | |
| | Seabridge $w^{th}$ in a mile of New Castle are designing to Sett up a meeting can but raise 16 *l* $p^{r}$ annũ : desire help See $y^{e}$ case more fully | |
| Wolverhampton | A great towne began their meeting $w^{th}$ a week-day Lecture and raised | |

5[s] a day, afterward they *rais* ceased their weekly Lecture & mett on Sabboth dayes, and chose one m[r] Dan: Greenwood for their Minister, whom they allowed 20 *l* per annum, but Seuerall of their contributers removing their habitations their 20 *l* is reduced to 12 *l* per annum & out of y[t] the Rent of y[e] meeting-house is to p[d] & are like to be destitute without some assistance.

m[r] Greenwood is gone from them for want of a Subsistance they desire an augmentation of 10 *l* per annum lesse will not do

Persons qualifying for y[e] Min[r]y

Proposalls

| [69] Ministers y[t] haue a Competent Supply | Southampton | |
|---|---|---|
| M[r] Nath: Robison | At Southampton—hath Some Estate of his own and 30 *l* p[r] anū | |
| M[r] Weaver | Of Crundaile has a good Estate of his owne, alwayes refused any recompence from y[e] people laid down by reason of persecution | |
| M[r] Sam: Sprint | Preacheth att Andover and Winton, has a Small estate of his own, and a low ministeriall maintenance —16 *l* p[r] anū | att winchester 16 *l* p[r] att Andover |
| M[r] Sam: Tomlyns Sen[r] | Preaches att Andover and Whitchurch. hath some competent Estate of his own, and but a Small ministerial maintenance | 30 *l* p[r] at Whitchurch 16 *l* p[r] |
| M[r] Chandler | Of Faram hath a competent maintenance £30 p[r] anū has many children and its hard with him though 30 *l* p[r] anum | |
| M[r] Earle | Att Gosport has a Competent maintenance promised has 40 *l* p[r] annum as p[r] N° 106 | |
| M[r] Wells | Att Nuport in y[e] Isle of Wight has a Small Estate of his own, and a low allowance from y[e] people 20 *l* p[r] anū as p[r] N° 106 | |
| M[r] Martin | Of Newport has a Competent Estate of his own | |
| M[r] W[m] Lee | Of the Isle of White, hath a Competent Estate & 30 *l* p[r] an̄ | |

| Ministers that may want Supply | | |
|---|---|---|
| | An ancient and learned man as any in y$^{e}$ County 70 yeares old and has a wife and children not disposed of as p$^{r}$ N$^{o}$ 106 | |
| m$^{r}$ Tho: Warren | Att Rumsey has but a poor maintenance 16 *l* p$^{r}$ anū | |
| m$^{r}$ John Hooke | Of Batingstocke has very little if any thing of his own Estate, and but Small recompence of his labours from ye people there | × hee lives w$^{th}$ y$^{e}$ L: Hook ye people of Batingstoak are desirous hee should fix with them |
| M$^{r}$ Clearke | Att Portsmouth hath but little of his owne, and noe great maintenance from the people. 20 *l* p$^{r}$ anū | |
| M$^{r}$ Rob$^{t}$ Whitekar | Att Froddingbudge, hath but a Small maintenance and but very little of his own & hath beene a Sufferer has a wife and severall children } 30 *l* | |
| M$^{r}$ Fowles | Att Southwick preacheth at Petersfield and hath but a Small Estate of his own, and a low recompence for his labours | |
| M$^{r}$ Nicoletts | Of Havant hath a Small maintenance | |
| M$^{r}$ Jn$^{o}$ Tomlyns Juo$^{r}$ | Of Alton hath some Estate of his own but not Sufficient to maintaine him, his allowance Small 20 *l* p$^{r}$ anū a young man, has many children, and goes hard with him | |
| [70] Places y$^{t}$ had or where there may be oportunity of Religious Assemblies | Southampton | M$^{r}$ Jurin |

| | |
|---|---|
| Kingsclere they go to Newbury as p^r^ N° 106 | 5 Miles from Newbury has beene a good meeting but m^r^ Auery Sometimes minister there being dead, are destitute. at times y^e^ gifted men of y^e^ Anabaptists preach, but haue promised to desist when a Minister is Settled there |
| Dounton Limington ∧ Christchurch and Ringwood | haue noe Settled Ministers for y^e^ present. att Limington the maintenance is Small. att y^e^ 2 other places they can raise at each place about 30 *l* p^r^ annum. att Ringwood £32 p^r^ anū |
| Winton and Whitchurch see N 154 | There is preaching but one *a* Lords day in a fortnight because they can make up but a Small maintenance, and ministers are Scarce |
| Alsford | A meeting might be raised if a minister were Sent thither |
| Limington | There might be a greater meeting if there were a Settled Minister and a Competent maintenance |
| Sutton | There might be a meeting Sometimes and in other Villages in y^e^ Countrey on y^e^ week dayes if ministers had, any Supports |
| Petersfield Odiam | No meeting being able to raise little or nothing see N° 154:—an acc^t^ of Whitchurch and Peterfield—see also N° 155:— |
| Havant | They want a minister are able to raise 50 *l* or 60 *l* p^r^ anū |

| [71] Ministers yt haue a competent Supply | Suffolk |
|---|---|
| Mr Cradock | Att St. Edmunds has a large Estate |
| Mr Milway | Att Bury ∧ Cong. There is another congregation Supplyed by Severall ministers, provided for 50 *l* pr an they allow 50 *l* |
| Mr ∧ Jno Fairfax | Att Ipswich ∧ every other Lords day or oftener, and a Lecture every fortnight, they are able to provide. |
| Mr Langston & mr Harris Supply the other Congregation att Ipswich— | Mr ffairfax is alsoe each other Lords day att Needham markett, and a constant weekly Lecture, has from ye town, though wth much difficulty 20 *l* pr anū. poor |
| Mr Sam: Petto | 10 Children and 2 his wife has Att Sudbury, able to provide *Seuerall* child: estate uncertaine No 129 they allow 45 *l* pr an̄ |
| Mr Tho: Steward | Att Deberham has 30 *l* pr anū a Single man very young |
| Mr Bidbanck | Att Woodbridge, able to provide 50 *l* pr anū |
| Mr Saml Manning | Att Wallpoole, Do |
| *Mr Jno Manning* | Att Peasevall. Do very little estate if any a wife and diverse children |
| | Att Framlington, able to provide |
| Mr Smith | Att Wrentham able to provide a good estate |
| Mr Francis Crow | Att Clare, they ∧ offered to allow him 25 *l* pr anū in money & 5 *l* otherwise but |

| | | |
|---|---|---|
| | not<br>he would ∧ stay, soe they are destitute | |
| Mr Wm Folkes and Mr Jno Meadowes ×× | mr ffolkes is disabled has some estate and children chargable<br>Their circumstances not related ××<br>hath a large estate | |
| *mr Jno Langston*<br>mr Fra Keeling.<br>mr Ja: Vortier<br>*& mr Harris* | Mr<br>*Do* Keeling a Single man . 24 yeares old Chaplaine to a Gentlewoman<br>mr Jam: Volier, aged about 60: noe wife, som children, temporall estate 20 *l* pr anū: by reason of Sickness has lost his opportunity of preaching once | a month at Bungay |
| | Mr. Wright has a wife by whom hee has Some temporall estate not much . a Chaplaine. | |
| Ministers yt want Supply<br>—— —— | | |
| mr Jno Fairfax aged 67 yeares | Att Needham Market, ye people very poore, and cannot but with great difficulty and doing beyond their ability raise 20 *l* per annum. preacheth a weekly Lecture, and more than one third part of ye Sabboths througout ye year Supplyes other places, they craue Some assistance. and ye rather because there is no other assembly Supplyed by Non: Con ministers wthin Six miles of it a wife & 4 children aged 66 yeares—10 *l* pr anū<br>a further request for mr Fairfax Nº 114 | mr Slauter desiers Some thing may be Alowed mr Fairfax That Soe a person may be constant |

| | | |
|---|---|---|
| Mr Ja: Waller | Att Hunston, preaches a weekly Lecture, allowance 3 *l* or 4 *l* pr annum, a great concourse of people aged 55: a wife and 3 children: one at Cambridge 5 *l* pr anŭ temporall estate Supplyes alsoe by turnes att Ipswich. | |
| ×Mr Tobias Legg | Supplys by turnes att Ipswich aged 64: very infirm wth ye gout. Some little temporall estate a wife & 6. or 7 children | ×has 10s per day in his turne at E: Bregholt |
| Mr Jno Sasheild | Att Badwell, a poor place has an estate of 40 *l* pr annū has a wife & 4 or 5 children see also 129 | |
| Mr Steph: Scandarett aged 56 yeares | Att Haverill, a poor place see alsoe No 129 | |
| mr Plumstead | Noe Estate a Single man att Wrentham 30 *l* pr anū | |
| mr Salcald | Some Estate, a wife and divers children att Walsham in ye Willows, hath not att most above 10 *l* per annum maintenance poor ancient and infirm | |
| mr Hen: Williamson | Of Southwold by the Sea, ye people being much decayed in their trade by the present warr, altho' they doe their utmost willingly, are not able to raise above 20 *l* per annum, if hee be unable to preach hee receives nothing for ye day, because the maintenance is raised by collections att ye meetings, hath a Quartan Ague, 3 or 4 small children, his wife has a hectic fever, want money to discharge the Apothecaryes bill. see No 152 see alsoe No 43 in 1691 | |

| | | |
|---|---|---|
| m$^{r}$ Jn$^{o}$ Manning | Of Sibton, very aged yet preaches every Lords day, the people much impoverished not able to raise 15 *l* per annum, his wife 12 *l* p$^{r}$ annum has expended 70 *l* on account of his Son, and borrowed money see N$^{o}$ 152 see alsoe | N$^{o}$ 43 in 1691 |
| [72] Places y$^{t}$ had and where there may be oportunity of Religious assemblies | Suffolk | D$^{r}$ Samson & M$^{r}$ Jurin |
| Hadley | A market Towne an ill Minister in y$^{e}$ publick no meeting neere it, for 5 miles round, exceeding poor, if a good Min$^{r}$ were Settled there, great good might be done | |
| Att Neiland | A meeting Supplyed by Severall ministers as they can procure them, whom they allow 10$^{s}$ p$^{r}$ Sabbath | see alsoe N$^{o}$ 162 : & 179 |
| East Bergholt | Supplyed after y$^{e}$ Same manner, a poor towne | |
| Att Beccles | Their Pastor is lately dead y$^{e}$ meeting kept up by a combination. | allow 50 *l* |
| Watsfield | Supplyed by Severall, on w$^{t}$ terms not known D$^{o}$ | allow 50 *l* |
| Ai | A large towne, well peopled, but noe good preaching in it or about it see alsoe N$^{o}$ 157 | |
| Lanham | A large towne, noe meeting in it, or neere, but pretty good preaching in y$^{e}$ church at present | *m$^{r}$ Williamson maintenance small* |

| | | |
|---|---|---|
| Southwold | Noe meeting in it, and but once a fortnight or month in y^e^ Church, y^e^ town but poor and not very populous | m^r^ Williamson the maintenance small |
| Bungay | A very poor towne, lately burnt can scarse raise 15 *l* p^r^ anū maintained by 4 or 5 ordinary men only for publick good assistance desirable | lately burnt down see N° 162: |
| Long Melford | Is a populous place, affords (w^th^ adjacent townes) a great Congregation, can give 25 or 30 *l* p^r^ anū, wants a minister, desired M^r^ Wright. to Settle among them but hee inclines rather to Catlige in Cambridgsh: | |
| Debenham | Allow 10^s^ p^r^ day | |
| *Nayland* | *A meeting kept up by combination allow 10^s^ a day* | |
| Palgraue | | |
| Syleham | | |
| Kittle Barson | Occasionally | |
| Newmarkett | Maintenance very deficient | |
| About Glensford | A Lecture very desirable | |
| Hargraue and Barrow | Att both these townes, there are Some honest people y^t^ would gladly haue an honest able preacher to come now and then to instruct them, if they knew how to incourage him see N° 160 | |
| Bacton 1691 | A dark corner of y^e^ countrey, where providence hath opened a door for y^e^ Gospell to be preached, y^e^ people are very poor not able to raise aboue 12 *l* per annum see N° 19:—in 1691 | |
| Harlestone | Desire y^e^ Same fauour in Supporting y^e^ Gospell as is given to Bungay and Ai, godlyness formerly flour- | |

| | |
|---|---|
| | h<br>ised there, but now there is great<br>^<br>profanness. but two that are of any ability to carry on such a work. they doe something one L^ds day in a fortnight but desire —N° 35: 1691 it euery L^ds day— |
| John Goodchild | Proposed May y^e 23° 1692 by m^r Jn° Langstone, as a young Student See more at large in N° 75 :— |

| [73] Ministers y[t] have a Competent Supply | Surrey |
|---|---|
| M[r] Jn[o] Wood | Att Dorking, hee gives noe account of his circumstances. |
| M[r] W[m] Bicknell | Att ffarnham, ejected 62. aged 56, has 5 children, about 200 auditors, and would be greater were it not y[e] Bishops seat, his maintenance for his work and house (where y[e] meeting is constantly kept) 10[s] p[r] Lords day and no more |
| M[r] John Chester & *M[r] Jn[o] Farroll* | Att Guildford, m[r] Chester Supplys 3 dayes of y[e] month and M[r] ffarroll (aged 70 yeares) Supplys y[e] fourth, auditors near 400. y[e] maintenance exceeds not 10[s] p[r] Lords day, y[e] people desire m[r] Chester wholly to Supply them, but will nott unless y[e] maintenance be increased. |
| Ministers y[t] want a Supply | |
| M[r] Sam:[l] Hall aged 28 :— | Att Godalming, where some meane persons haue Sett up a meeting, and the Charge lying upon a few is too heavy |
| M[r] James Waters | his maintenance is 10[s] p[r] Lords day Att Reigate has but at most from his people 14 *l* p[r] anū see his case at large in |
| M[r] Fish | Att Okley. his incouragm[t] is not much |

| | | |
|---|---|---|
| Mr Lobb | Att Horley, his encouragmt very little more than Mr Waters | |
| Mr ffisher. | about darkinge. Mr Meade. | |
| Mr ffarroll. | at Guildford. (as aboue.) | |
| mr Robt Fish—1691 | Of Oakley, hath about 50 communicants, very poore, doe not contribute aboue 12 *l* per annum in Such things as the Countrey affords, but little or no money, is possessed of an Estate of 20 *l* per annum, but incumbred with debts. aged 56 yeares, has a wife and 7 children to maintaine— | |
| [74] Places yt had or where there may be an opportunity of Religious assemblies | Surrey | Mr Mayo |
| — — — | | |
| *Godalming* | *Some mean persons haue sett up a meeting* | |
| Att Billott, or att Waltham on ye Thames Att Cranly or Att Ewhurst— | If a meeting could be Sett up in any of these places its probable there would be a considerable number of hearers | |
| Frimly | A parish where mr Bures resided many yeares and constant preached now destitute of a Settled Ministry only for want of maintenance, ye people are a thirsty people for ye word, it is to be wished, yt an | |

| | |
|---|---|
| | augmentation of 20 *l* p^r^ annū were given to that people, and y^t^ m^r^ Farroll would sitt down with them |
| Young Students | |
| M^r^ Lee | Vnder y^e^ Instruction of m^r^ Tho: Rowe, whose father being disabled by the warrs, can noe longer maintaine him there, but must be forced to putt him to some other employment, if some supply be not given him |

| [75] Ministers yt haue a Competent Supply | Sussex |
|---|---|
| Mr Troughton | Att Arundell a maior towne, a young man well reported of, a considerable Congregation, has 20 *l* pr añ as saith N° 30 has 25 *l* by the yeare, need assistance |
| Mr Benj Chandler | East<br>Att ∧ Greensted and Hapsfield has himselfe given an account of his assistance needfull circumstances to Dr Annesley ∧ |
| | a country village for a time needs a Settled minister |
| Mr Mortimer | Att Lindfield, ∧ an aged Nonconformist, his hearers of the meaner Sort, has 30 *l* pr annum |
| Mr Hallet<br>Hallet | Att Petworth, a worthy ejected minr 25 *l* pr anũ the highest maintenance is 30 *l* pr annum as by N° 69 |
| Mr Fish.<br>Mr Whiston<br>Mr Newton.<br>*Mr Bennet*<br>Mr Lob. Juor | Ejected ministers Mr Newton—<br>Att Lewes the shire towne, has a congregation, ye maintenance competent |
| Mr Bennet Juor | Chaplaine to mrs Becher at mayfield, but exercising his ministry among the people of the place |
| Tho<br>Mr ∧ Hammond | Att Framfield, Walldown & Warbleton, lately a conformist, but now throwing aside his Conformity |

| | | |
|---|---|---|
| Mr John Harrison | Of Ashling near Chichester, noe certaine knowledg of his State | |
| Mr John Hamper | Of Salvington, exerciseth his ministry noe where, few places need it more than where hee dwells. | |
| Mr Jos: Whishton | Att Lewes, has a Congregation, his maintenance competent | |
| Mr Tho: Goldham | Att Burwash, keeps a Grammar School, preacheth gratis occasionally | |
| Mr Jno Buck | Att Chichester has a Congregation, ye maintenance Supposed compt | |
| Mr Jno Crouch | Of Lewes, preacheth occasionally —his circumstances not known Supposed to be competent | |
| Mr John Mills | Of Helingleigh, preacheth gratis at Seuerall places, is worthy of Some Settled place and Encouragment | |
| Ministers yt want Supply— | Mr Wm Tirry ^e—Att Hasting, a place of great opposition 40 *l* pr annum—not too much for ye minister to receive, but more then ye people can raise by one halfe, particular concerne for this place is desired by Tho: Barnard. | |
| Mr Geo: Whitemarsh may preach occasionally att Shoreham: in great necessity | Att Brighthelmstone, has a numerous Congregation consisting of 400 auditors, ye people very poore, not aboue 20 *l* pr annū and yt like to decrease not aboue 16 per annum. used to raise a great maintenance | |
| Mr Merner | Att Medhurst in ye west part of ye County, an ancient Nonconformist, to whom an Additionall Supply would be wellcome has 20 *l* pr annum | an aged mother that he keepes and nothing else to liue vpon see No 46 in 1691 |

| | | |
|---|---|---|
| M$^{r}$ Joseph Bennet | Att Burwash, has a Small Cchool, preacheth at Some Stated times att Helingleigh, maintenance Small and uncertaine | |
| M$^{r}$ Joseph Bricknell | Att Lewes keepes a Grammar School, has little Encouragm$^{t}$ aged preacheth Occationaly in Lewis | |
| 1691<br>m$^{r}$ Tho: Hammond | Att Framfield about eight miles from Lewis, lately a Conformist, travells 3 or 4 miles on a Lords day to preach and Sometimes Six miles, the people (though their hearts are inlarged), yet not able to maintaine a minister to fix w$^{th}$ them, hee has nine children, cannot Subsist w$^{th}$ out some assistance, allowed 10 *l* per annum Aug$^{t}$ 31° 1691 | |
| [76] Places y$^{t}$ had or where there may be oportunity of Religious assemblies | Sussex | M$^{r}$ Meade & M$^{r}$ Cockerell |
| h<br>Horsam<br>^<br>*fforsum*<br>whoever is placed here had need of peculiar qualifycations. | A Markett towne at present destitute of any fixed minis$^{r}$ could one be sent among them its hoped there might be a considerable congregation, but y$^{e}$ contributions at least at present would be very Small, might be beneficiall to neighbouring places. | |

| | | |
|---|---|---|
| Stenning and Thaikham not aboue 5 miles distant | Where could a Minister be fixed its hoped much good might be done. one minister might Supply both. | see alsoe y$^{e}$ case of Stenning stated and represented in N$^{o}$ 174:— |
| Thecomb the same as above | And Stenning as aboue. both places offer 20 *l* p$^{r}$ annū | |
| Att Seaford, Bishopston, Alsiston, Lullington | The remotest of w$^{ch}$ places are 3 miles Distant, destitute of a minister cannot well raise 20 *l* p$^{r}$ annum. a minister placed there might occasionally try to give enterance to y$^{e}$ Gospell at Bourne, to a people who are strangers to these things. | |
| 1691 Stenning & Thacum | Labour under great feares of loosing y$^{e}$ Gospell, desire Something considerable towards y$^{e}$ maintenance of a Minister being uncapable of giving any competent maintenance | |
| Medhurst | M$^{r}$ Merner being dead, are destitute of a Minister desire a Minister and Some assistance, not being able to raise aboue 18 *l* or 20 *l* per annum at most | |
| Persons qualifyed for y$^{e}$ ministry and not fixed | Hastings and Battle a meeting alternatly sett up by m$^{r}$ Tho: Barnard hee has beene there $\frac{3}{4}$ of a year: another meeting is att Seaford and sonee other places neare, cannot raise aboue 11 *l* per annum, he desires assistance towards y$^{e}$ Support of the Gospell in these places | |
| M$^{r}$ Joseph Bennett Juo$^{r}$ | Is in a private family at y$^{e}$ towne of Mayfield, and sometimes preacheth there, is very fitt for more publick and constant employm$^{t}$ | |

| | |
|---|---|
| Proposalls | Very good Service may be done in Sussex by a cautellous & prudent proposall of the removall of Some Ministers from places less proper, to those that are more proper for them |
| | M^r^ Jeakes who preached gratis at Rye is lately dead, its feared the Gospell will loose its little hold in y^t^ place |

| [77] Ministers yt haue a Competent Supply | Warwick | |
|---|---|---|
| *Mr Tho: Taylor Congregationall* | *In Cambridge, has 40 l pr anū: they Sand in need of an Assistant and propose to raise 20 l pr anū and desire an allowance of 20 l more for some time* | |
| *Mr Josiah Chorley* | | |
| Dr Long | Of Coventry well maintained | |
| Mr Fincher and Mr Baldwin | Att Birmingham, of one Congregation well provided for. each of them 30 *l* pr annum | |
| Mr Turton | Att Birmingham of another Congregation well provided for | |
| Mr Sanders a junior | Att Bedworth neere coventry, provided for by his people | |
| Mr John Porter *Alcester* | Supplys 2 Lords dayes in a month att Stratford upon Avon | |
| Mr Heycock | Att Alcester whose people doe what they can but feare ye continuance of Subscriptions, desire Some help | |
| *Stratford upon Avon* Mr Porter | Att Stratford upon Avon, the fewness of those that are capable of contributing makes their provision small some additionall Supply may be requisite | put this on the other side |
| Mr Vincent | Chaplain to ye Lady Rouse provided for Sufficiently | |
| | Mr Porter desires yt 10 *l* or 20 *l* may be allowed to make his meeting place convenient, and hopes they shall haue noe further need, ye cold aire and other inconveniencies pinch them. | |
| Mr Showell | | |
| Mr John Bunn | | |

| Ministers yt want Supply | | |
|---|---|---|
| | Mr Showel, ye only minister left in Coventry Since ye death of Dr Grace and mr Bryan hee is infirm deafish, and unacceptable to many of the most judicious hearers, who are very numerous, said to be in all, in ye city and from ye Country 1500 | |
| | in ye Same place, there is another company joyned in ye Congr: way of whom mr John Bunn (a very worthy and Learned man) is pastor, but soe infirm yt he cannot come amongst them, liueing out of town two or three miles, and very poor and few | |
| | —— —— —— —— | |
| Mr JnoSingleton | has preached constantly since ye first Liberty Jacobi 2di Att Stretton a Small Village where some conversion work is wrought, ye people poor allow but 10 *l* pr annum and yt not certain much of his time taken up by another imploy to Supply yt defect hee is well provided for as by No. 50 | |
| Mr Wright | of Knole parish, very aged, almost dark, has noe people, is capeable ing of doe ∧ little and meritts charity | |
| Mr Sanders | hath a Settled poor people in and about Bedworth their number about 40 or 50. preaches Sometimes in other places for ye increase of his poor maintenance | |
| Mr Worth Senr<br>Mr Worth. Juor | An aged and poor non: Con. hath bred up his Son to ye ministry, they both Live in Northamptonshire, but upon ye borders of Warwickshire they principally ex- | alowed £10. |

| | | |
|---|---|---|
| | ercise their ministry, viz$^{t}$ at Rugby, Sowtham and other townes thereabout | |
| Persons contributing | | |
| [78] Places that had or where there may be opportunity of Religious Assemblies | Warwick | M$^{r}$ Faldoe D$^{r}$ Samson and M$^{r}$ Jurin |
| Coventry and Stretton under ffosse | There is an ancient Small people almost lost for want of a pastour, who haue giuen m$^{r}$ John Singleton a Call, to Support whom has divided his labours betweene them and Stretton 5 miles distant. from these hee hath 20 *l* p$^{r}$ annum. is willing to giue up either if a Supply may be had for the other see a further account of Stretton in N$^{o}$ 178 | |
| Att Blewlake neer Knole. and at Small:heath neere Birmingham | are two very considerable Lectures on y$^{e}$ week day carryed on by Severall ministers w$^{ch}$ are maintained by the Countrey | |
| Warwick | A great towne, it is desired y$^{t}$ Some care may be taken about it. were there a minister in it (thõ its doubted little would be done at present for his maintenance) there might be Some hopes of doing much Service. | |
| Stratford vpon Avon | A great Towne haue disbursed above 10 *l* in equipping their meeting place, the meeting increaseth notwithstanding y$^{e}$ greatest opposition | |

| | |
|---|---|
| | is made to it. m^r Porter Supplys it two Lords dayes in a month, they can but raise 15 *l* p^r anū and y^t lies hard upon 3 or 4 who are willing to doe w^t they can they earnest desire help, see the case more fully in their petition |
| Moseley Chapell by Birmingham | They have gott y^e Chapell lycenced for Dissenters, craue some assistance without w^ch y^e work is like to fall |
| Sutton Colefield 1691. | Haue kept vp their meeting in y^e darkest times, haue no Settled minister, allow 7^s per diem, but few y^t contribute to this work and Some of grown poor, not able to raise 10 *l* per anū: are willing to carry on y^e work, but not able to provide a Min^r for euery Lords day, promise to give an account of their contributions if they may be encouraged. |
| Birmingham Ashton | Desire some assistance to keep vp their meeting w^th out which it is like to fall, a willing and numerous auditory |

| | | |
|---|---|---|
| [80] | ## Westmorland | |
| Ministers y$^{t}$ haue A competent Supply | | |
| m$^{r}$ Benson | Neare Burton, hath a Congregation | |
| m$^{r}$ Darnley | At Kendall, for the present hath a considerable Company he is a young man, hath 23 *l* p Ann̄ they want a Metting house | |
| Ministers that may want, Supply | | |
| Persons contributing | | |
| [81] Places that had & where may be Opertunitys of Religious Assemblys | 1690 :— Westmorland | M$^{r}$ Rich$^{d}$ Stretton & M$^{r}$ Nisbett |
| About Russendaile | m$^{r}$ Punchion, is Sending Thether (a hopefull young man) there will be a competent prouision made for him<br>want of a competent liueleyhood may Discourage him | aboue 20 *l* p$^{r}$ annū besides 5 *l* p$^{r}$ anū given him by the L$^{d}$ Wharton |
| 5 Miles. W. of Kendall | there is a Well inclined people that long after means, but destitute | |
| 1691— | | |
| *Milthorp* | and places adjacent, far remote from any meetings of Nonconformists, haue liued long under a careless | |
| Milthrop | Ministry, are like to perish for | |

lack of knowledge desire Some allowance may be afforded to them to incourage Some awakening Ministers to come in their turns once a month. -aug[t]- y[e] 24[o]: 1691

Persons qualified for the Ministry & not fixed

Persons Qualifying for the Ministry

Proposalls

| [82] Ministers y[t] haue a competent Supply | Wilts |
|---|---|
| M[r] Haddesley | Att Salisbury has about 40 *l* per annum |
| M[r] Crofts | Att Alton hath a Considerable estate |
| M[r] Pemberton | Att Marlebrough hath 60 *l* p[r] annum dead |
| M[r] Gough | Att y[e] Devizes *he* and Brook hath some Estate & 30 *l* p[r] an: |
| M[r] fflower | Preacheth once a month at y[e] Devizes and one at Chepenham and one at Causam and at other places hath some Estate |
| M[r] South | Of Hunnett has a pretty good Estate of his own |
| M[r] Clifford | Preaches at Severall places, is Supposed to have but an ordinary maintenance |
| *M[r] Bourne* | *Att Colne* |
| *M[r] Conway* | *Att Malmsbury* |
| Ministers that may want Supply | |
| *M[r] Moore* | *Att hungerford has but a small maintenance* |
| M[r] Clifford | Preaches at Seuerall places has but an ordinary maintenance |
| Bourne. | Att Colne has not aboue 10 *l* p[r] anum, has many Children. D[r] Annesley |
| Conway. | Att Malmsbury is very poor. D[r] Annesly |

| | | |
|---|---|---|
| m$^{r}$ Jon$^{a}$ Rashley | Itinerant, who has near 20 years lived obscurly in a little towne called Lydyard about 10 miles from Marlbrough about $\frac{5}{m}$ agoe he removed and now dwells in a Cottage of 20$^{s}$ per annum has not had above 12 *l* per annum for preaching for soe many yeares. see his case in 92: | |
| Persons Contributing | | |
| [83] Places that had & *have* where there may be oportunities of Religious assemblys | Wilts | M$^{r}$ Mayo and M$^{r}$ Powell |
| Warminster, Brook & Seimours Court | Are Supplyed by seuerall Ministers | |
| Brinkworth | Not well able to keep up and maintaine a constant Ministry *wih* without some assistance, there is no Nonconformist meeting but w$^{t}$ is amongst them from Abergaynie to Glocester, w$^{ch}$ is 30 miles | |
| Person qualifyed for y$^{e}$ ministry and not fixed. | | |
| Persons qualifying for y$^{e}$ ministry | | |

| | |
|---|---|
| m^r Dangerfield | Att Marlebrough, willing to be ordained m^r Pemberton y^e minister there giues him a good character. |
| Stephen James | The Son of a poore man a Shoemaker in Colne, who is not able to allow him above ^ 5 *l* per annum the Conformists would haue Mantained him at Oxon if they could haue perswaded him to be entred there, hee is a very diligent pregnant hopefull youth and well inclined, above 16 yeares of age. |
| Proposalls | |

| [84] Ministers that haue a Competent Supply | Worcester |
|---|---|
| Mr Tho: Baldwin | Att Kiderminster hath an estate of his owne & Contrib |
| Mr Badland | Att Worcester has an estate and Contribution |
| | In |
| Mr Dan: Higgs | *Att* Bromsgroue parish hath an Estate & Contrib |
| Mr Spilsbury | Att Bromsgroue hath a Competencie |
| Mr Jno South-well | Att Dudley where hee is pastour, preaches elsewhere |
| Ministers that may want a Supply | |
| Jno<br>Mr ∧ Ward | Att Parshor, a Single man. has not aboue 5 *l* pr anū from ye peope, and |
| *Mr Blackmoore* | one Gentlewoman gives him his dyett |
| Mr Blackmore | In Worcester, Mr Badland who preacheth there being very ancient and almost past his labours, tis thought fitt yt Mr Blackmore be incouraged to continue there for ye upholding of the *mini* Gospell in that place, as by mr Hows advice |

| | | |
|---|---|---|
| Mr Daniel Higgs and mr Jno Higgs— | See there state fully represented under their own hands April ye 16 : 1691 Mr Dan: is considered in Southwales | |
| [85] Places yt had and where there may be opportunity of Religious assemblies | Worcester | Mr How |
| Eversham towne | A Considerable congregation of people of ye town and Country when there is a minister to preach. few able or forward to contribute to their maintenance | |
| Vpton upon Seuern | A Markett towne where would be a good auditory but want a minister<br>From Euesham as aboue, mr Jno Saffield requests assistance in sending them a Minister, and somewt towards his maintenance. | |
| Ministers qualifyed and not fixed | | |
| Mr Peter Peyton | Of Kiderminster who also practiseth physick | |
| Mr Blackmore | of Worcester | These preach at Seuerall places as they are desired and haue oportunity. haue noe estate of theire |
| Mr Tym: Greenwood | of Bewdley | |
| Mrs Edwd & Henry Osland | Neere Bewdley | |

| | | |
|---|---|---|
| Mr Wm Willetts | Neere Kiderminster | own ye most allowed them for preaching is ten shillings a day in many places not so much. and for preaching on week dayes Seldom any thing. |

| [86] | Yorkesheir West Riding | Mr Stretton |
|---|---|---|
| Ministers yt haue a competent Supply | | |
| | Formerly | |
| Mr Heywood | ∧ Att Coley Chappell neere halifax hath short of 20 *l* yet wants nothing. not now. at *Alverthorp Atter thorp* Northouram | |
| Mr Jonas Wakerhouse | Formerly Vicar at Bradford where hee is of use liues comfortably | |
| Mr Thomas Johnson | Att Criggleston neere Wakefield aged 61. liues on his own estate | |
| *Mr Prime*× | Of Sheffield trauels up and down to preach in Seuerall places | |
| Mr Tho: Sharp | Whom god hath Signally owned at Leeds | |
| *Mr Jos: Dawson*× | Att Morley, a gracious man of great use aged 56 | |
| Mr Isseb | Att neere Wakefield liues retired aged 62 | |
| mr Richd Frankland | Att Rawthmell, trains up young ministers. aged. 60 | |
| Mr Nathan Denton | Att Bolton vpon Dern preaching abroad at Sundry places | |
| Of ye younger sort | These 9 aboue mentioned were ejected in ye yeare 62, and so remaine | |
| Mr Tho: Whitaker | Living at Leeds. brought up wth mr ffrankland *Congregationall* | |
| Mr Tho: Elskon | Pastor of a Ch: at Topliff. Trained up wth mr ffrankland | |

| | |
|---|---|
| Mr John· Holdsworth | Liueing att Spen. preaches in Seuerall places. mr Franklands Schollar |
| Mr David Noble | Pastour of a Ch: att Heckmondwyke |
| Mr *Baxter* | Of Sheffield, came out of Lancashire about ye yeare 62 |
| Mr Math: Smith | Liveing in Hallifax parish, brought up under mr Ward, of great use |
| Mr Abra: Dawson | Capt Gills Chaplaine, preaches at Stannington Chap: Frankland scholar |
| Mr Richd Thorp | Of Hopton-hall hath a considerable estate yet preaches in his house |
| James<br>*Mr* ^ *Wright* | *Of Attercliff neere Sheffield, preaches at Seuerall places* |
| Mr Jona Wright | Preacheth att one of mr ffranklands Schollars, hopefull |
| Mr Denton Juor | Son to mr Denton, liues with his father and preacheth at Seuerall places |
| Mr Nat. Prieskly | Preacheth once a month for mr Heywood, mr Franklands Schollars |
| Mr Sagar | Preacheth at Aterthorp & Pontefract. mr ffranklands Scollar |
| Mr Kay | Of Gummershall that preacheth for mr Dawson |
| Mr Kershaw | In Crauen |
| Ministers yt may want Supply | Mr Tinothy Jolley pastor of a church att Sheffield one of Mr Franklands Schol: |
| Mr Wm Hawden an ejected minister in 62 | Formerly parson at Bradsworth aged 72 usefull in promoting good, as praying, conferring, not soe capeable of preaching, being defectiue in his Sight, hath little but what friends Supply wth |
| Mr Richard White *Whike* hurst ejected 62 | Att Lidgek in Bradford Dale hath a gathered church but little maintenance |

| | |
|---|---|
| Mr Rich: Prime | Of Shefield, travels up and down to preach in severall places |
| Mr Jos: Dawson | Att Morley, a gracious man of great use aged 56 |
| Mr Baxter | Of Sheffield, came out of Lancashire about ye year 62 |
| Mr Cornelius Tod | |
| Mr Shaw | |
| Mr Th: Wayte | |
| mr James Wright | At Attercliff. his condition extreamly necessitous, labours abundantly, hath about 12 *l* per annum, three small children himselfe very infirm, haueing almost lost ye Sight of both eyes |
| Persons contributing | |

| [87] Places y^t^ had and where there may be oportunity of Religious Assemblies | Yorkesheire | M^r^ Stretton & |
|---|---|---|
| Topliff alias Wood: Church | haue continued a church above 45 yeares, in former times they obtained an augmentation from Authority of 50 *l* per annum, w^ch^ is gone to Supply Deanes and Chapters. and 30 *l* Subscription from y^e^ church. of late yeares through the death of most of their aged and principall members they cannot raise aboue 20 *l* per annum and feare y^e^ continuance of that | |
| Ealand 1691 | near Hallifax, a meeting twice a month, being wholly carryed on by *b* m^r^ John Brooksbanke, desire some Supply y^t^ it may be euery Lords day. many reasons urged on this account attested by 5 Ministers of the County | |
| | There is a meeting one Lords day in a month at y^e^ house of one John Armitage a Blacksmith of Lidget in within y^e^ pish of Kirk-burton, a man truely gracious, where m^r^ O· Heywood hath Administred y^e^ Lords Supper three times to about 30 persons, desire some Supply y^t^ they may haue a Minister oftner | |

| | | |
|---|---|---|
| Clifford 1691 | A dark & Ignorant part of y^e Countrey, not able to raise aboue 5 *l* per annum amongst those y^t are able to doe any thing | |
| Persons qualifyed for y^e Ministry and not fixed | | |
| M^r Gill | Brought up with m^r ffrankland, lately begun to preach not Settled | |
| M^r Piggott | D^o unsettled | |
| Persons qualifying for y^e ministry | | |
| Jeremiah Gill | Son to widdow Gill very poor, has beene w^th m^r Jollie for Some time, a good Schollar, has pregnant parts, and a choice Spirit, has exercised 3 or 4 times to great satisfaction, wants some further Supply to compleat his Studies, and for bookes. | 22 y^r |
| Emanuel Dewsnop | his father a poor clothier is willing to Strain himselfe for one year more, y^e youth is a good chool Scholar, capeable Studious, and graciously disposed. | D^o |
| Rich^d Woolhouse | Son to m^r Anthony Woolhouse of Dublin, who has greatly Suffered in the late troubles, has a numerous family the youth is euery way hopefull, these young men are w^th m^r Jollie, is forced to teach a few petties to Supply him in his Studies w^ch hinders his *f* proficiency | D^o |
| Proposalls | | |

| | | |
|---|---|---|
| John Kings Son of Sheffield | One John King a poor Cuttler in Sheffield has a hopefull Son almost ripe for Academical Studies, y[t] w[th] Some assistance might make a usefull instrum[t]. | 17 |

| | | |
|---|---|---|
| [88] Ministers that haue A competent Supply | Yorkeshire. North Riding | |
| Rich$^{d}$ Frank-land | At Crauen A meeting in his howse & Teacheth youthes | |
| Nich$^{o}$ Kirshaw | At Pasture howse, A young man, A numerous Congregation | |
| Ministers that may Want Supply | | |
| Persons Con-tributing | | |
| [89] Places that had & where there may be Oper-tunity of Religious Assemblyes | Yorkeshire North Riding | M$^{r}$ Stretton |
| Ellingthorp | The Lady Brooks Chappell, m$^{r}$ Tod of Healey, m$^{r}$ Ward of York, she getts to Supply the Lords day by turnes, but desiers a fixed Minist$^{r}$ | |
| 3 Miles. E. from North Alerton | m$^{r}$ Frankland Sometimes Sends Young Ministers to preach they Very much desier to haue one fixed among them | |
| Winterburne | Desireous of the Word and Many people come in | |
| Tosside | D$^{o}$ | |
| Starbottom | D$^{o}$ | |

| Burham | D$^{o}$ m$^{r}$ Whaley often imployed w$^{th}$ great Successe |
|---|---|
| Selby | Where m$^{r}$ Ward preaches once in 3 weekes has a considerable number of people, but are not able to maintaine a minister of themselues |
| York City | There is only one meeting Incouragers very Barren, where m$^{r}$: ward preaches 3 Lords dayes in y$^{e}$ month |
| Rulston | |
| Persons Qualified for the Ministry & not Fixed | Slait Burn |
| | Hawton |
| | Rotheram |
| | Caue |
| | Holderness—see m$^{r}$ Charls account in N$^{o}$—153— |
| | Pontefract |
| | Fishlake and y$^{e}$ adjacent townes are Some very Serious people not able to bear y$^{e}$ charge of the work, desire Some assistance for continuing the Gospell in soe necessitous a place, one m$^{r}$ Perkins their minister as I suppose |
| Persons qualifying for y$^{e}$ Ministry | |
| m$^{r}$ Owen<br>m$^{r}$ Baddie | Best known to m$^{r}$ Stretton, they be uery hopefull |
| Thō: Binson, John Tayler, Jā: Mitchill<br>Thō: Dickinson, and Jn$^{o}$ Gorwood | With m$^{r}$ Franckland, there Relations are able to doe little for them and are much put to it in what they do, haueing gott little Supply from Others, exept Dickson & those feared |
| Spink and Dauis | Two poore Youthes frõ NewCastle, Taken Care of |

| | |
|---|---|
| m$^{r}$ Dawson<br>m$^{r}$ Baxter | Sons of Ministers who haue Seuerall Children neither of them complayn much tho their burthen may be great Enough. |
| Proposalls | That an anuall Stipend might be Sett apart w$^{th}$ respect to places that want it. by those in the Ministry & by Young men much blessed worke might be done for poore Soules, Or if could preuaill w$^{th}$ the .K. & Q. that any p$^{t}$ of the Pention Setled by .Q. E. on Itenerary Preachers in y$^{e}$ Northern Counties might be. Imployed this Way |

| | | |
|---|---|---|
| [90] Ministers that haue a Competent Supply | **Yorkeshire East Riding** | |
| S. Charles | At Kingston sup Hull Ejected in 1662 | |
| Richd. Astley | At. Do | |
| mr Foster | At. Beuerley | |
| mr Mitchell | At Cottingham, a young man | |
| mr Shaw | At Swanland | |
| mr Baiock | At South-caue formerly a Conformist | |
| Jno Humphryes | At Bridlington Say's-he-came out of Oxfordsheire. NB. | |
| Ministers that Want Supply | 2 . or . 3 . of the aboue poorely ·pro-uided for | |
| Persons Contributing | | |

| | | |
|---|---|---|
| [91] Places that had & wheire their may be Opertunity of Religious Assembly's | **Yorkeshire East Riding** | Mr Stretton |
| Holdernes | A Gentlewoman of a larg Estate desiers helpe, haue sent to mr Seddon | |
| The Closes 1691 | mr Joseph Dawson Minister, has had a very little recompence for his great paines, has 6 sons now grown vp to be disposed of abroad, | |

four whereof hee designes for y^e^ Ministry, one whereof is a godly usefull Minister, another w^th^ m^r^ Frankland. and y^e^ two youngest at home ready to be sent abroad for University learning

Swaledale — Where a worthy person, this last Summer at his own charge has built a meeting place (w^ch^ is certifyed at y^e^ Quarter Sessions for y^e^ County, hee will settle 10 *l* per annum for y^e^ future, and nothing by any body else, there is a numerous Auditory, most of them poor Miners, m^r^ Holland a young man unmarryed, educated by m^r^ Frankland Settles among them who has given him a very good caracter

1691 Persons Qualified for y^e^ Ministry — Hartford — near Richmond, desire some assistance, if it were but 5 *l* or 6 *l* per annum

Stentliffe} — In y^e^ parish of Betley near Leeds and Wakefield, the Auditory numerous. but of the poorer sort, can raise noe more than 18 *l* per annum, their Minister pays 40^s^ rent for his house earnestly begg some assistance, see their case N° 41. 1691

Kirksandall — Distant from Doncaster three little miles, Seuerall Countrey townes within a Mile of it, some less. viz^t^ Armthorpe, Long Sandall, Barnby Dun, and Hatfield 2 miles. the Assemby increaseth & would considerablely if constantly Supplyed. Madam Rokeby (who has laid out her Selfe beyond her ability to

| | |
|---|---|
| | Sett up a Lecture) has gott her house Registred for a Meeting place for a Congregation of Protestant Dissenters. |
| Persons qualifying for the Ministry | |
| Proposalls | |

| | | |
|---|---|---|
| 92] Ministers that want Supply | North Wales. q$^{t}$ Flint, Denbigh, Carnaruan, Ile Anglesey Merioneth, Mongomery | M$^{r}$ Williams |
| | **CARNARVONSHIRE** | |
| M$^{r}$ Dan: Phillipps | *Lately ordained preacheth in 2 or 3 places in y$^{t}$ County and some times in Merionethshire, his congregation poore and small* | |
| | **MERIONETHSHIRE** | |
| M$^{r}$ Hugh Owen | *Preacheth in 3 or 4 assemblies in y$^{t}$ County, and as many in Mountgomeryshire. chosen pastor to y$^{t}$ Congregation y$^{t}$ was formerly under m$^{r}$ Hen: Williams inspection* | |
| | *Att Bala and some other parts are great meetings, cannot be Supplyed aboue 4 times a year and some of them not soe often* | |
| | **DENBIGHSHIRE** | |
| M$^{r}$ John Owen of Wrexham | *Hath a numerous people but most of them poor, as all y$^{e}$ Welch Congregations are* | |
| | *Att Ruthin is a Lecture once a month supplyed by m$^{r}$ James Owen, where there is a Serious people, they call for y$^{e}$ Lords Supper but not yet administred for want of a minister* | |

| | Salop | |
|---|---|---|
| Mr Charles Edwards | *An ejected ministry liued formerly on a farme is now inclineable to undertake ye ministry if a maintenance could be had for him. hath ye welch tongue* | |
| [93] | North Wales | Mr Williams<br>Mr Griffith |

| | | |
|---|---|---|
| [94] Ministers that haue a Competent Supply | South Wales { Radnor, Brecknock, Cardigan, Pembrook, Carmarden, Glamorgan, Monmouth. | |
| Mr Watkin Jones<br>in stead of John Powell | Pastor of the Church att Mynyddislwyn in Monmouthshire liues upon a Small estate of Seuen or 8 *l* pr annum, and receiues nothing from his people receiues some Small pittance for helping mr Powell | |
| Mr Dauid Richards dead | Pastor of the Church at Merthyr in Glamorganshire hath not beene yet burthensom to his poore Congregation | Dead Morgan Wms & Roger Wms:— |
| VMr Saml Jones | Pastor of the Church at Kildeydy in Glam·shire Do 3 Children | 2·maryed teachth Lerning |
| Mr Rice Prythro*ck* | Att Aberllynvy in Brecknockshire hath some allowance did keepe Scholle had. 80 or 100. Scholers. and hath betakẽ him Selfe to ye ministry being Called by the Church of wch mr J Loyds Father is a member | |
| Vmr Owen Davies | Carmarthenshire. Pastor of a people at Pall hath. 4 *l* p Anñ frõ his father is a Widdower hath. children grown up | |
| Mal: Jones<br>Ministers that want Supply | | |

| | | |
|---|---|---|
| M$^r$ Jn$^o$ Powell | Pastor of the Church at Newport in Munmouthshire an aged and Sickly man, low in y$^e$ world. liues upon a small farm upon y$^e$ Rack rent *receiues from his people about* of 8 *l* p$^r$ annum | |
| assistant to m$^r$ Powell<br>M$^r$ Barnes ∧ | Receiues some Small pittance for helping m$^r$ Powell | |
| Dan<br>V M$^r$ ∧ Higgs<br>of long good service in his stead | Att Swansey in Glamorganshire, aged and infirme, hee and his John Higgs Son ∧ who assists him haue Some Small allowance | he is gone to Wost$^r$sher |
| V M$^r$ Peregrine Phillips<br>who as good does in his stead | Att Dredgmanhill in Pembrookshire liues on rack rent receiues from his people 8 *l* p$^r$ annum, w$^n$ y$^e$ yeares and providence fauours them, otherwise less. wiffe, & Children no Estate holds a farme | |
| M$^r$ Jn$^o$ Thomas & m$^r$ Tho: Bynon | Att Rhoseygilwen in Pembrook-sh: y$^e$ former has 4 *l* p$^r$ anū, has not rec$^d$ aboue 10$^s$ from his people last yeare, the Latter hath 2 *l* p$^r$ añ and hath not rec$^d$ aboue 10$^s$ | Bynon hath many Child and poore |
| V M$^r$ John James | Att Cryglas in Carmarthenshire hath free hould 6 *l* p$^r$ añ and hath not rec$^d$ aboue 20$^s$ from his Congregation, it being newly raised | |
| V M$^r$ Dauid Penry | Att Kanedy in Carmarthenshire has 6 *l* p$^r$ anū dureing the nonage of his Children hee receiues noe constant sume but some pittance w$^n$ they are able. | |
| V M$^r$ W$^m$ Evans | Att Penkader in Carmarthen-sh. hath 5$^l$: 10$^s$ by his wife dureing her life, teacheth a small private | |

| | | |
|---|---|---|
| | schoole. has not recd from ye Congregations aboue 15s in two yeares time no Children<br>Pen Carreg | |
| Mr Dauid Jones | Att *Kellans* in Cardiganshire | |
| Mr Dauid Edwards | Att Pen Carreg in Cardiganshire assistant to mr Dauid Jones aboue said | *Dead* |
| Mr Hamar. | Pastor of a church in Radnorshiere liues well on his Estate | |
| Mr Robt Thomas Dead.<br>a godly old man | Pastor of a church att Langyfelach, Glamor: | hath an Estate |
| [95] Places yt had or where there may be opportunity of Religious assemblys | South Wales | Mr Griffith and Mr Stretton mr Williams |
| Carmathansheire | Jenkin Thomas Called thether teacheth a Schoole<br>Lewis Dauis. Called to the ministry at prety well to liue | |
| Monmouth should be in Gloucestershire— | That great populous towne has no meeting in it but at Conard 4 miles Distant, and there generally one day in the month they haue none, there are in yt place a Serious people but very poore, desire some assistance if it were but 5 *l*: if a meeting were Sett up in Munmouth it would quickly maintaine it Selfe. 9r ye: 16th 1691 | |
| Persons qualifyed for the Ministry and not fixed | | |

| | | |
|---|---|---|
| Mr Malachy Jones | In the welch part of Herefordshire | |
| Mr John Jones & Mr Morgan Howell | Ancient usefull men yt assist in ye work of the Gospell in Cardiganshire | morgan Howell aged uery poore |
| Mr Wm Lloyd | A blind man but sound in the faith and usefull in instructing publickly | |
| Persons qualyfying for ye Minry | | |
| Mr Jenkin Thomas<br>Mr Dauid Lewis<br>*Wm Lloyd* | in Carmarthenshire preach constantly and are upon their probation for the Ministry | Dauid Lewis liveth wth his father who hath Some free hould |
| Mr Anth: Thomas | A poore young man | |
| Mr Dauid Jones | Keepeth a Schoole uery poore | |
| Mr Lewis Dauis | In Glamorganshire constantly preach and are upon their probation for the Ministry | |
| Mr John Harvys | A wery poore man wth mr Samll Jones perfecting in Loggick | |
| *Mr Jno Harvys*<br>Morgan Williams<br>Stephen Hughes ye Son of a minrs widdow<br>Morgan Dauis | hopefull young men that are poore and now in a way of Education for the Ministry with Mr Samuel Jones. Pembrookshire | |
| Mr Lewis Prytheroh<br>Evan Phillips<br>Rice James | In Brecknockshire in ye way of Education for the Ministry | |

| | | |
|---|---|---|
| [96] Ministers y[t] haue a Competent Supply | Hantshire | M[r] Jurin |
| Ministers that want Supply | | |
| Person contributing | | |
| [97] Places y[t] had and where there may be opportunity of Religious assemblys | Hantshire | M[r] Jurin |
| Kingscleere | *5 miles from Newbury has beene a good Meeting, but m[r] Auery sometimes Minister there being dead, are destitute, at times the gifted men of y[e] Anabaptists preach, haue promised to desist when a Minister is Settled there.* | |
| Persons qualifyed for y[e] ministry & not fixed | | |
| Persons qualifying for y[e] ministry | | |
| Proposalls— | | |

| [98] Ministers y[t] haue a Competent Supply — — — | North Wales q[r] | Flint, Denbigh, Carnarvan Isle Anglesey Merionith Montgomery. | |
|---|---|---|---|
| M[r] Hugh Owen | Chosen pastor to y[e] Congregation y[t] was formerly under m[r] Henry Williams inspection, and preaches in 3 or 4 places in (y[t] County viz[t]) Merionethshire, and as many in Mount-Gomeryshire | | |
| M[r] John ~~*Owen*~~ Evans | Of Wrexham, hath a numerous people but most of them poore as all y[e] Welch Congregations are. | | |
| James Owen | | | Salop |
| Ministers y[t] want Supply— | | | |
| M[r] Dan: Phillips | Lately ordained preaches to 2 or 3 places in Carnarvanshire, and Sometimes in Merionithshire, his Congregation poor and Small | | |
| M[r] Turner, M[r] Jn[o] Williams, M[r] Ryn[d] Wilson — itinerant | preach at Seuerall places up and down Seuerall Counties | | |
| m[r] Sam: Turner. Novem: 23.—1691— | Of Wrexham. Some Supply is requested for him as p[r] N[o] 37 | | |

| Persons contributing | | |
|---|---|---|
| [99] Pla.. y$^{e}$ had or where there may be opportunity of Religious assemblies | | |
| Att Bela and some other parts | In merionithshire are great meetings, yet cannot be Supplyed aboue 4 times a yeare and Some of them not so often | |
| Att Ruthin | In Denbighshire is a Lecture once a month supplyed by m$^{r}$ James Owen, there is a Serious people, they call for y$^{e}$ Lords Supper, but is not yet administred for want of a Minister | |
| Denbigh—1691 | hath for many yeares liued in great darkness, of Late a Lecture has beene Sett up by a good Minister without any incouragm$^{t}$ God has so succeeded his Labours y$^{t}$ y$^{e}$ people desire a Settled Ministry, they cannot raise aboue 7 *l* per annum, w$^{ch}$ y$^{e}$ Gen$^{t}$ that intends to Settle among them cannot Subsist on, hee desires only 15 *l* per annum | |
| Persons qualifyed for y$^{e}$ ministry and not fixed.— | | |
| Persons qualifying for y$^{e}$ ministry | | |
| — — — | | |

| | |
|---|---|
| Tho<br>Mr ^ Davis— | a young minister of good ministeriall abilities Stretton no lack |
| Mr Jno Lewis | wth mr Henry and wth mr James Owen this winter |
| Proposalls | |

# COMMENTARY

## THE HAPPY UNION

In a tractate of 21st May 1645, "Independency Not Gods Ordinance," the author, John Bastwick, M.D., discriminates between "the Presbyterian Government Dependent" and "the Presbyterian Government Independent." The former, or Dependent, type may be illustrated by the Presbyterianism of Scotland, and by the kindred and derivative (though not identical) Presbyterianism of Ireland. The latter, or Independent, type belongs to England. A strict autonomy of "particular churches" associated only for mutual counsel and advice, was the basis of the Presbyterianism of Thomas Cartwright and William Bradshaw. Cartwright might have liked to invest the associations with jurisdiction, if authorised to do so by law; in fact they never were so invested. Bradshaw maintained, in theory as well as practice, the independence of congregations, while organising them internally on the Presbyterian plan, the worshippers delegating their spiritual government to an oligarchy of pastor and elders. This independence, indeed, has constantly been the characteristic of English Presbyterianism, save during the short-lived and imperfectly achieved Parliamentary experiment, 1646–1660; an experiment which has no exact reproduction in any modern organism. The modern and admirable organisation (primarily of the Scottish element) under the name of the Presbyterian Church of England bears little resemblance to it.

The Parliamentary Presbyterianism (adopted, for political reasons, as an international compact), while an exotic novelty, departed from the Scottish model in more important respects than the mere nomenclature of offices. In England, under the Parliamentary system, the Presbytery was the Eldership of a particular parish (*Scottice*, kirk-session), for the congregations were strictly parochial. The Classis (*Scottice*, presbytery), called also Classical Presbytery, consisting of representatives of a group of parishes, gave great numerical preponderance to the representatives of the Laity; each parish deputing, along with its clergyman (rarely two clergymen), two, three, or four lay elders. In Scotland (as in Ireland) the principle of an equal number of clergy and laity was adopted in all courts above the kirk-session. This was the principle; in fact, owing to collegiate charges and representatives of Universities (not fully balanced by the representation of certain borough councils), the clergy in Scotland gained, in the higher courts, a slight numerical preponderance. In England, above the Classis, was the Provincial Assembly (*Scottice*, Synod) consisting of delegates from several Classes; a court which came into actual existence only in the provinces of London and Lancashire. Delegates from the Provincial Assemblies were to constitute the National Assembly; a court which never came into existence at all. Had it done so, it would not have been (like the Scottish General Assembly) a court of final appeal; for Parliament reserved the final appeal to itself. It should be added that no subscription was required, save to the Solemn League and Covenant of 1643, which defined the attitude of its signatories towards popery and prelacy; nor was this subscription always exacted. As regards doctrine, the condition of a man's faith was determined not by the scratch of a pen, but by the judgment of the Classis, which took into careful consideration each individual case. As is well known, the Parliamentary attempt to set up Classes throughout the Kingdom, in spite of Ordinances to this effect, proved abortive. In many counties, as in Cheshire, there were no Presbyterian Classes. In Worcestershire from 1652, under Baxter's powerful guidance, and in other counties, unions of clergy alone, holding various theories of church government, met as advisory bodies, claiming no jurisdiction. Further, both in Lancashire and in Yorkshire, Presbyterians made serious attempts to find room in their organisation for Congregationals.

On the eve of the Restoration (1660) the Presbyterian Classes disappeared altogether. No attempt was ever made to revive them, even by those who still judged them to be theoretically desirable. By 1704, as Calamy assures us, the only considerable person of that judgment was Daniel Williams, D.D., who did not, however, deem it expedient to make then any move in that direction. Close at hand, at the time of the Restoration and later, was the example of the Friends, for constructing and maintaining, in the worst of times, a graduated constitution of great strength. This example the Presbyterians did not make the smallest attempt to follow. Reasons for this may be given. Many of the Nonconforming clergy, though involved *pro tempore* in the Parliamentary Presbyterianism, had acquired a liking for Baxter's "rectoral" theory, which made the clergyman the spiritual master of his parish. To speak of Baxter as a Presbyterian, as some do, is to ignore not only this fact, but also his resolution "never to oppose" the claim for bishops "superiour in degree to presbyters." Hence he never joined in an ordination. Again many of the Nonconforming magnates rightly judged that their influence in the particular congregation was liable to be overruled in larger organisations. Giles Firmin, in *Weighty Questions*, 1692, p. 23, speaks of "one or two Gentlemen of *Purse*, *Piety* and *Parts* that stick close to the Minister and awe the People." The main strength of Friends lay in a democratic cohesion of the lower classes; while to the general body of Nonconformists the retention of the upper ranks, from whom continued support and co-operation were to be looked for, seemed a prime necessity.

Hence, after Ejection (1662) there was Presbyterian organisation only in particular congregations; never anything in the nature of Classical or Synodical courts. All congregations were now autonomous, all were non-parochial. Presbyterians could no longer object to the Congregational polity of "gathered churches," being themselves reduced to this expedient. Some specialities of internal organisation remained. Having, in their congregations, "presbyteries" (*i.e.* elderships, according to the English, which is also, as a rule, the Continental, acceptation of the term) they were entitled to describe themselves as Presbyterians, if they chose to do so. The points of difference were not enough to preclude plans of co-operation between Presbyterians and Congregationals, in view of their common distress, and in pursuit of the evangelical aims which all alike held supreme.

Reasons may be given for the preference shown for the term Presbyterian on the part of men who attempted neither Classical nor Synodical organisation. Most of them had taken part in the Parliamentary Presbyterianism, and it was natural to retain the name, expressing as it did the validity of ordination by presbyters. The term Independent, suitable enough as indicative of their actual ecclesiastical position, carried with it a political connotation, pointing to the fall of the monarchy, against which Presbyterians had protested. Calamy, in 1704, while frankly acknowledging that his own ideal of ecclesiastical polity might be construed as "a meer Independent Scheme," yet neither adopts the term for himself, nor in his accounts of the Ejected does he even apply it to Congregationals. Further, the term Presbyterian was significant as a verbal repudiation of the condition of chaos into which ecclesiastical matters had fallen, on the failure of the Parliamentary experiment. Some national organisation of religion was certainly the general desire. A modified Episcopacy, on Ussher's model, would have satisfied many, if not most. Baxter thought that comparatively few would have stood out against it.

The Episcopal returns of 1669 report a lecture at Hackney held in concert by Peter Sterry, M.A., Thomas Watson, M.A., William Bates, D.D. (who ranked as Presbyterians), Philip Nye, M.A., George Griffith, M.A., Thomas Brookes, and John Owen, D.D. (who ranked as Congregationals). Accordingly, during the royal Indulgence of 1672, "when the Nonconformists had some rest," a Tuesday morning lecture was established by London merchants at Pinners' Hall, Old Broad Street, the meeting place of a Congregational church. Of the six divines first chosen to lecture in rotation, Thomas Manton, D.D., William Bates, D.D., and William Jenkyn, M.A., were licensed under Indulgence as Presbyterian; John Collins, M.A., as Congregational; John Owen, D.D., whose license is not extant, was then the recognised leader of the Congregationals; Richard Baxter, who had never belonged to either party, was licensed simply as Nonconformist. This Lecture still exists. It testifies to interdenominational co-operation for over twenty years, till 1694. Since then it has been exclusively Congregational; for, after the expulsion of Daniel Williams from the Merchants' Lecture by a majority of its supporters, the other Presbyterian lecturers, Bates, Howe and Alsop, seceded (7th Nov. 1694) to form a new Tuesday morning Lecture at Salters' Hall, supported by the older section of original subscribers. In vain did John Howe do his utmost to smooth matters down, proposing that the two sets of Lectures should "alternate in both Places, which would take away all appearance of dissension."

A further project for common action "between the Brethren of the Presbyterian and Congregational Persuasion in Matters of Discipline" had been checked "by the Persecution raised against them in the year 1682." The idea was renewed on the appearance (1687) of James II.'s specious "Declaration of Liberty of Conscience" and again dropped. In their Address to William III. on his accession, the Dissenting Ministers of London prayed him "to establish a firm Union of your Protestant Subjects in the Matters of Religion, by making the Rule of Christianity to be the Rule of Conformity." William's very brief reply could hardly have been anticipated, a polite promise "whatsoever is in my Power, shall be employed for obtaining a Union among you."

The Toleration of 1689, granted (on terms) to Protestant Dissenters without further denominational label, led to closer measures of co-operation. To assume that London was leader in this respect is to misapprehend the strength and spread of a movement for union, general throughout the country. Action was soonest taken in the South; Lancashire came in late, and at a time when the brief duration of the London union was obviously reaching its term, so that while the stimulus of the London example doubtless had its effect, the potent force was in the sense of common duty and common need. A valuable record in the manuscript (see p. 47) tells us that already by 1690 the Ministers of Somersetshire, Wiltshire, and Gloucestershire had for some time agreed upon an accommodation between Presbyterians and Congregationals, and had offered inspection of their Minutes for London use. They had even projected a Common Fund.

In London the first measure to be adopted was the institution (1690) of a Common Fund, of which more anon. Then, on the initiation of John Howe, M.A., a Presbyterian, came a scheme for the amalgamation of the Presbyterian and Congregational ministries (but the ministries only). These were henceforth to drop their dividing names, and act together simply as "United Brethren." For this amalgamation a precedent widely known was to be found in Baxter's Worcestershire Agreement of May 1652 (see p. 152). There was an earlier precedent of the same kind, not in England but in Ireland, which would appeal to some of the happiest memories of John Howe. In 1626 John Ridge, B.A., an Oxford man, Episcopal and Puritan Vicar of Antrim, established in that town a monthly conference of clergy from the counties of Antrim and Down, without reference to theories of church government, relying on counsel and suasion, and not claiming jurisdiction. Even so stout a Presbyterian as John Livingstone, M.A., bears his testimony that the deliberations of the Antrim Meeting were "sometimes as profitable as either presbyteries or synods." In Ireland, the Antrim Meeting was the precursor of the movement against subscription promoted by John Abernethy's famous sermon, "Religious Obedience founded on Personal Persuasion" (1720). This was at once attacked by John Malcome, who disclaimed "putting personal persuasion in the room of a church Government" and denounced the Non-subscribers as "our Modern New Lights," an expression which originally referred not to doctrine but to discipline. Of the Antrim Meeting, which bore such far-reaching consequences, Howe was a member from 1671 to 1675, and at Antrim he wrote his best-known work, *The Living Temple* (1675).

The "Heads of Agreement," drawn up mainly by Howe, were accepted by "above fourscore" ministers, including all those in and about

London, except three Congregationals—Thomas Cole, Nathanael Mather and Richard Taylor. These objected to union with those Nonconformists who (like Baxter) were "for Sacramental Communion with the Church of England." The amalgamation, known as the "Happy Union," was inaugurated in the spacious Stepney Meeting-House on 6th April 1691, when its Congregational pastor, Matthew Mead, preached his famous sermon, "Two Sticks made One" (Ezek. xxxvii. 19). In May the "Heads" were published by Thomas Cockerill and John Dunton (see p. 163). Briefly, to sum their main points, they provided that congregations, in choosing their ministers, should consult neighbouring pastors, whose concurrence in ordinations was "ordinarily requisite"; that "in order to concord" and in difficult cases, synods (of undefined composition) be held, as consultative bodies, to whose advice weight should be given ; and that the orthodoxy of churches be ascertained by owning the doctrinal part of the Thirty-nine Articles, or of the Westminster Confession, or of its Larger Catechism, or of its Shorter Catechism, or of the Savoy Confession, to be agreeable to the Scriptures "the only Rule of Faith and Practice."

## Breach of the Union

Hardly had the Union been effected when, in May 1692, a theological controversy (on Justification) arose as a sequel to the publication (1690) of ancient and posthumous sermons by Tobias Crisp, D.D. Crisp had been forty-seven years dead when these sermons saw the light. A number of ministers vouched for the authenticity of these remains, and hence were currently supposed to be in accord with the views expressed in them. With protests and repudiations a wrangle began. The pith of the controversy was the subtle question whether, in the order of grace, repentance or faith precedes. In this dispute the protagonists were Daniel Williams, afterwards D.D., whose ecclesiastical preference was for a synodical Presbyterianism (though he had never in fact participated in an organisation of that kind, and had recently stood as candidate against Nathanael Mather for a Congregational charge) and Isaac Chauncy, M.A., L.C.P., Congregational in judgment. Open warfare was initiated by Williams' "Gospel Truth," 1692. The terms Antinomian and Neonomian did duty as the main weapons of offence. Though Williams and Chauncy, with their respective friends, signed an "Agreement in Doctrine" on 16th Dec. 1692, the controversy continued for some years unabated. The Congregationals, with few exceptions, began to withdraw (1693) from the Meetings of the United Brethren.

Similarly, in 1693 (probably in July) the rupture began seriously to affect the relations of that inner circle of Ministers and laymen on whom rested the responsibility of the management of the Common Fund. Details are wanting, for the Minutes between 26th June 1693 and 5th Feb. 1694/5 have not been transcribed. Evidently this was a period of which it was thought best to leave no record. Yet the work of the Fund went on. Chauncy (who left the Union on 17th Oct. 1692) had been absent from the Fund Board since 4th July in that year, but he resumed attendance on 20th March 1692/3. The last payment from it through a Congregational Minister (John James) was made on 31st Dec. 1694. A year later the Congregational Fund was established, 17th Dec. 1695. Its management was restricted to the Ministers and Messengers of Congregational Churches.

It is clear that, by the end of 1694, the "Happy Union" had, so far as London was concerned, perished beyond recall; though up to the end of 1696 efforts were still made to revive it. It did not, however, pass away before its "Heads of Agreement" (published in May 1691) had formed the basis of similar Unions throughout the country which continued their good work. Often known as Classes, these Unions, unlike the Presbyterian Classes, admitted no lay element, and were consultative and advisory bodies, claiming no jurisdiction, but exercising for a long period the function of ordination. One of these has maintained its existence to this day, the Exeter Assembly of Divines (1691) which has never admitted a lay element. Five others, now combined into one, survive with a modified constitution. The oldest of these five, the Cheshire Classis of United Brethren (1691) was, after the creation (1764) of a common Widows' Fund, amalgamated (1765) with the Lancashire Provincial Assembly (1693) originally distributed into four Classes (Manchester, Warrington, Bolton, and Northern) in which Presbyterian and Congregational Divines met together. This combination of five is now known as the Provincial Assembly of Presbyterian and Unitarian Ministers and Congregations in Lancashire and Cheshire; it was augmented in the last century (1856) by a system of lay delegates, "not exceeding three for each congregation." These only, and none of the existing County Unions (of Congregationals) can carry their lineage up to the days of the "Happy Union."

It is further to be remarked that the "fifty or sixty" London Ministers who (after the breach of Union by the withdrawal of Congregationals to a separate meeting at Pinners' Hall) kept up their meetings, in Dr. Annesley's Meeting-House at Little St. Helen's, did so still under the style and title of "The United Ministers." At least as late as 1698, they resented the application of the name Presbyterian to them by their former colleagues. They were unwilling to treat the "Happy Union" as dead. On the other hand, Stephen Lobb, a Congregational brother (who had been a member of the Union), misrepresented them or some of them, so says Vincent Alsop in 1697, as "inclining to the Unitarians." In support of his charge against Daniel Williams of Socinianising on the Atonement, Lobb had appealed to Anglican Divines, who, however, deemed Williams more orthodox than Lobb.

## The Common Fund

The Minutes of this Fund, now in the archives of the Presbyterian Board, open with the following historical statement, dated London, 1st July 1690:—

"The occasion and beginning of this vndertaking.

"When it pleased God to encline the hearts of our Rulers to permit ye religious Liberty of Dissenters by a Law, some persons (concern'd in this present worke) laid to heart ye great disadvantages which the Ministry of the Gospell was attended with in England and Wales, both by ye Poverty of Dissenting Ministers and the inability and backwardness of many places to afford them a meere Subsistance.

"They considered alsoe that many of the present Ministers (wonderfully preserved to this time) are aged, and therefore it was necessary to provide for a succession of fitt persons to propogate the Gospell when others were removed.

"By the importance of these considerations they were lead, to invite a considerable number of Ministers in and about the City of London to advise of some methods to obviate these difficulties, and as farr as the Law allowed to improve this Liberty to the best purposes.

"These Ministers judging a select number of Ministers might best contribute to these designes, did choose seven Ministers of the Presbiterian perswasion and ye Ministers commonly called Congregationall fixed on an equall number to assist in an affaire thus common to all, who desire the advancement of the Interest of our Blessed Lord.

"The Ministers thus appointed mett together and after seeking Councell of God, and many serious thoughts and Debates among themselves att last concluded.

"1—That some due course should be taken by way of Benevolence to relieve and assist such Ministers in more settled worke, as could not subsist without some addition to what their hearers contributed.

"2 ly—That Provision might be made for the preaching of the Gospell in some most convenient places where there are not as yett any fixed Ministers.

"3 ly—That what is thus contributed should be impartially applyed according to the Indigent circumstances and work of every such Minister.

"4 ly—That none might be admitted to a share in this supply as Ministers but such as are devoted to and exercised in the Ministry as their fixed and only Imployment with the approbation of other Ministers.

"5 ly—That some hopefull young men might be incouraged for y^e^ Ministry, and y^e^ sons of poor Dissenting Ministers (if equally capeable) might be preferred to all others.

"6 ly—That a number of private Gentlemen should be desired to concurr with the foreappointed Ministers in the procuring and disposall of the said Supply to the above described uses; w^ch^ Gentlemen were fixed on.

"By these steps this happy work was begunn, w:^ch^ 'tis hoped God will soe inlarge y^e^ hearts of the well-disposed to contribute to and attend with such a blessing, as may greatly advance the Kingdom of Christ, and give Posterity occasion

to adore the goodness of God in thus directing the minds of such as are ingaged therein."

From the fourth paragraph of this initial statement we may gather that the "considerable number of Ministers" originally invited to consider how "to improve this Liberty to the best purposes" belonged either exclusively or preponderantly to the "Presbiterian perswasion." Accordingly they chose seven Ministers of that class, and sought the co-operation of the "Ministers commonly called Congregationall," who selected other seven, to join in formulating a scheme for an object "common to all." Thus each denomination selected its own representatives, and while those of the "Presbiterian perswasion" constituted at that time the larger body, compared with those "commonly called Congregationall," an equality in representation was accorded.

The scheme arrived at by joint deliberation forms the next entry in the Minutes, and is given below. In its preamble the application of the term "Established" to the "Ministers and Meetings" of Dissenters anticipates the language of Lord Mansfield's famous judgment.

"Propositions agreed to by Voluntary consent of those of the Presbiterian and Congregationall perswasions both Ministers and Gentlemen for the better support of their Ministers and Meetings, as now allowed and Established by an Act of Parliament made the Twentyfourth of June One thousand six hundred eighty nine, in the first year of their Maj:^ties^ Reigne.

"1—That all things relating to the present affaire be put into a stated and Regular method vpon such a foot as may be generall, and as comprehensive as possible, with respect to all places in England and Wales.

"2 ly—That ye Managers of Ministers and Gentlemen appointed for this matter, may be fixed to a certaine number not exceeding fourteene Ministers and thirty Gentlemen, and upon y^e^ decease of any, the Vacancies to be filled up once a yeare, and their names to be inserted in the Entry-booke.

"3 ly—That seven of the said persons shall be a Quorum, whose orders and

Acts shall be valid; Three whereof Ministers and four private Gentlemen, or three private Gentlemen and four Ministers.

"4 ly—That the first Munday in every month att ten of the clocke is appointed for ye Constant meeting of the managers, and att other times as occasion shall offer.

"5 ly—That a President or Chair-man be agreed upon by the persons present as soon as a Quorum is come together.

"6 ly—That there be alwayes persons under the Denomination of a Treasurer, and in case of any ones decease, another to be chosen in his roome.

"7 ly—That one of the Treasurers be obliged to be present at every meeting.

"8 ly—That there be a person to be Writer or Book-keeper, under the Direction of the Treasurers, who shall be accountable for him.

"9 ly—That Books may be kept of all things done, and of all money rec:d and paid, viz,t a Booke of Entryes of all orders and transactions of the Generall managers, and such other Bookes as the Treasurers shall judge most proper & convenient.

"10 ly—That all Letters relating to this business be brought to the Booke-keeper, and put vpon a file.

"11 ly—That all persons that bring in any money doe note the time when they rec:d it and of whom, and the particular summe how much, which paper shall be signed by the same person, and put vpon a file.

"12 ly—That all the Minutes already taken be entered."

The second of these Propositions was amended on 4th Jan. 1691/2 by inserting "at least" before "once a yeare."

## MANAGERS OF THE FUND

The fourteen Ministers originally chosen as Managers of the Fund are here, for convenience, arranged alphabetically under their denominations:—

| *Presbyterian.* | *Congregational.* |
|---|---|
| Vincent Alsop. | Matthew Barker. |
| Samuel Annesley. | Isaac Chauncy. |
| William Bates. | George Cokayne. |
| John Howe. | John Faldo. |
| Richard Mayo. | George Griffith. |
| Richard Stretton. | Nathanael Mather. |
| Daniel Williams. | Matthew Mead. |

All these, except Williams, rank as Bartholomaeans, though Faldo (like Baxter) was unbeneficed at the Ejection of 1662. Annesley, Barker, and Griffith were septuagenarians. Faldo, in his fifty-seventh year, was the youngest of the Bartholomaean Managers, yet the first to die

(7th Feb. 1690/1); on 13th April 1691 his place was filled by Thomas Cole, M.A., a Bartholomaean and a Congregational, but (and this is noteworthy) he attended no meeting (see Index). After Cokayne's death (21st Nov. 1691) his successor in the ministry, John Nesbitt, born in the year before the Ejection, was appointed (9th May 1692) in his room; it had been ordered (14th Dec. 1691) that the choice of Cokayne's successor in the management "be left to the Brethren of that perswasion," but this order was rescinded at the next meeting (4th Jan. 1691/2); Nesbitt was co-opted by the Managers. Williams, it may be mentioned, was a minor in the year of Ejection; in that or the following year he was, according to his own statement, though under nineteen, "regularly admitted a preacher" (*i.e.* licensed, not yet ordained), being then with the Independents.

On 19th Dec. 1692 (breaking Prop. 2, above) six Ministers were added to the existing Managers, namely three Bartholomaeans:

Richard Fincher . John James Nathaniel Vincent

and three others, viz.:

Daniel Burgess Timothy Cruso John Shower.

On 6th March 1693 Vincent declined to act; accordingly on 3rd April Samuel Stancliff, a Bartholomaean, was appointed in his stead. At the same time Richard Taylor, a Bartholomaean, was appointed in the room of Cole, who had declined office; like Cole, he never attended. James and Taylor were Congregationals; all the others ranked with the Presbyterians, though Stancliff, according to Calamy, was "a man of no party," and of Fincher the same may be said. These names complete the list of Ministers appointed as Managers of the Fund, from its inception to the breach in 1693. Hence, when the breach occurred, the proportion of Presbyterian to Congregational, in the acting ministerial Managers, was no longer seven to seven as at first, but twelve to seven.

(No list of the "not exceeding thirty Gentlemen" is given; there seems to have been some difficulty in making up the number. The Minutes up to 1693 give the names of forty-one lay Managers, proposed or elected, nine of whom never attended.) The following, inasmuch as their names, or the names of those who replaced them, on death or resignation, or introduced their successors, occur in the list of the eighteen Gentlemen Managers selected on 5th Feb. 1694/5, after the Congregational withdrawal, may be presumed to rank with the Presbyterians:

Thomas Abney.
—— Ashhurst.
James Boddington.
Jarvis Byfield.
Henry Coape.
Thomas Cockerill.
—— Coward.
Thomas Cuddon,
Jarvis Disney.
Christopher Fowler.
Peter Hubland.
—— Jerrett.
John Jurin.
—— Kelsey.
Lucie Knightley.
William Nicholas.
Samuel Powell.
Theophilus Revell.
Thomas Rodbard.
Henry Sampson, M.D.
—— Waytes.

The following may be identified as Congregationals, inasmuch as their names (or names of those replacing them) occur in the Minutes of the Congregational Fund Board (projected on 25th Nov. and established on 17th Dec. 1695) as given in the *Transactions* (vol. v. No. 3) of the Congregational Historical Society:

George Boddington.
Jos: Bowles.
Joshua Brookes.
—— Coltman.
Bartholomew Gracedieu.
Thomas Hartley.
Thomas Owen.
—— Phillips.
Matthew Rapier.
Arthur Shallett.
Edward Underhill.

There is nothing to mark the denomination of the following:

Richard Bury.
Sir Humphrey Edwin.
George Hucheson.
Daniel Mercer.
Joseph Thomson.
Daniel Wight.
Anthony Wither.

For further particulars of these lay Managers, the Index may be consulted.

The four Treasurers chosen (14th July 1690) were Samuel Powell, Thomas Hartley, John Jurin, and Arthur Shallett. It seems safe to assume that there were two Treasurers from each Denomination. This is the ground for ranking Jurin (above) as Presbyterian. Hartley having resigned the Treasurership, George Boddington was elected (20th April 1691) to replace him, but declined (27th April) to act. On 30th Dec. 1695 George Boddington was appointed Treasurer of the Congregational Fund.

On 4th Aug. 1690, William Ashhurst was chosen Book-keeper, at a salary of £20 (subsequently doubled). A rent of £5 a year was paid to him for the room where the books were kept.

## Meetings of the Fund

The meetings of the Managers, and the examinations of Students, were held on the premises of Thomas Cockerill, who was paid £5 a year rent for the meeting-room; in addition £2 a year was distributed among his servants. Thomas Cockerill, a member of Annesley's congregation, was a publisher, mainly of Puritan and anti-Papal divinity, also of educational works. He was one of the two publishers of the "Heads of Agreement," 1691; the other being John Dunton, at the Black Raven in the Poultry (north side). Cockerill, says Dunton, "was always up to the ears among great persons and business . . . yet I will do my rival that justice, to say he was a very religious charitable man." He first appears in June 1672 as an agent for procuring some of the Indulgence licences of that year. In July 1674, we find him sharing premises with Robert Morden, cartographer, at the Atlas in Cornhill, near the Royal Exchange; from February 1678 till his death, he occupies premises at the Three Legs in the Poultry, over against the Stocks Market (now the Mansion House). Here, then, the Managers met.

Cockerill was a Manager of the reconstituted Fund (1695). The last meeting attended by him was on 18th May 1696; his decease occurred before 25th January 1696/7, when his successor was appointed.

The meetings, held for the most part weekly, on Mondays at 9 A.M., altered from 21st September 1691 to 10 A.M., were opened with prayer, not in those days a brief formality. At every meeting the President was a Minister, the first to preside being Matthew Mead. On 21st November 1692 it was "Ordered that noe Minister or Gentleman shall goe from this Board for y^e space of One hour after prayer without Leave from y^e Chairman."

## Contributions to the Fund

It must not be imagined that with this Fund the practice originated of subsidising from London the dissenting interest up and down the country. Very soon after 1662 we hear of such a Fund, of which William Jenkyn, M.A., was Treasurer. Further, the Minutes furnish abundant evidence both of private benefactions and of congregational collections previously devoted to this purpose. The object of the Fund was to induce concerted action, and to extend the scale of benefits. Individuals and congregations in London were accordingly invited to contribute their benefactions for administration through the Fund. Such contributions were in many cases earmarked, in whole or in part, for the benefit of particular ministers, congregations, missions, or students. Further contributions were invited from benevolent persons up and down the country.

### Subscribers to the Fund

It may be interesting to give in full the first Subscription List (which runs from 9th April 1690 to 16th June 1691), adding from the later lists, additional donors, to complete the period 1690–1692, and premising that the prefix "Mr," applied in the original lists both to Ministers and to laymen, is here omitted. As the prefix "Rev." nowhere occurs in the Minutes of this period (nor in later ones till the year 1711) names of Ministers are here given in the humbler italic type; their degrees, if known, and their Christian names, when not given in the Minutes, are here added. The prefix E is added to mark the Bartholomaeans; where the denomination is known, the denominational initial is appended in a smaller letter, as this was, just then, a minor matter. The sums, except where otherwise stated, are not mere donations but annual contributions promised.

| 1690 | | | £ | s. | d. |
|---|---|---|---|---|---|
| 9 Apr. | E | *Matthew Mead* c | 100 | | |
| ,, ,, | E | *Vincent Alsop*, M.A. p | 100 | | |
| ,, ,, | E | *John Howe*, M.A. p | 160 | | |
| ,, ,, | E | *Samuel Annesley*, D.D. p | 100 | | |
| 21 Apr. | E | *Richard Mayo*, p | 100 | | |
| ,, ,, | E | *John Faldo* c | 50 | | |
| 5 May | E | *Daniel Williams* p (D.D., 1709) | 50 | | |
| ,, ,, | E | *William Bates*, D.D. p | 50 | | |
| 5 May | E | *Richard Stretton*, M.A. p | 25 | | |
| ,, ,, | E | *Nathanael Mather*, M.A. c | 40 | | |
| 16 June | E | *Richard Fincher* c | 50 | | |
| 5 May | E | Henry Sampson, M.D. p | 50 | | |
| 23 June | | Matthew Rapier c | 40 | | |
| 29 July | | Sir Henry Ashhurst, Baronet p | 10 | | |
| ,, ,, | | Sir Thomas Lane Knt p | 10 | | |
| ,, ,, | | Thomas Foley, Esq. p | 5 | | |
| 1 Aug. | | Leonard Robinson, Esq. | 5 | | |
| 18 Aug. | | Thomas Owen Esq. "Coun: att Law" c | 10 | | |
| 8 Sep. | E | *George Griffith*, M.A. c | 50 | | |
| 15 Sep. | E | *Samuel Slater*, M.A. p | 100 | | |
| 29 Sep. | E | *John Quick*, M.A. p "in ready money" | 6 | 2 | 6 |
| ,, ,, | | "A friend July y^e^ 25" per E *Nathanael Mather* c | 50 | | |
| ,, ,, | E | *Isaac Chauncy*, M.A., L.C.P. c | 40 | | |
| 9 Oct. | | John Jurin p | 10 | | |

| 1690 | | | £ | s. | d. |
|---|---|---|---|---|---|
| 9 Oct. | | John Bridges p | 10 | | |
| 13 Oct. | | Philip Foley p | 10 | | |
| ,, ,, | E | *George Cokayne*, B.A. c | 100 | | |
| ,, ,, | E | *Richard Wavell*, B.A. c & | | | |
| | E | *Richard Taylor*, M.A. c "of Pinners Hall" | 80 | | |
| 23 Oct. | | *Edward Fenwick* | 5 | | |
| ,, ,, | | Peter & James Ducane p "in ready money" | 10 | | |
| 24 Oct. | | Gilbert Nelson | 5 | | |
| ,, ,, | | John Gardner | 10 | | |
| ,, ,, | | Samuel Howard | 15 | | |
| ,, ,, | | Thomas Abney p | 10 | | |
| 10 Nov. | | "Gift from a Friend" per Matthew Rapier c | 50 | | |
| 10 Nov. | | "Gift from a Citizen" per E *Richard Stretton* p | 2 | | |
| 17 ,, | E | *John James* c | 20 | | |
| ,, ,, | E | *Matthew Barker*, M.A. c | 80 | | |
| ,, ,, | E | *George Day*, M.A. p | 20 | | |
| 20 Nov. | | Daniel Mercer | 10 | | |
| 24 Nov. | | "Gift from a friend" per E *John James* c | 2 | 3 | 2 |
| 1 Dec. | | "recd from Mr Morgan Hinde" per E *Joseph Read*, B.A. p | 10 | | |
| ,, ,, | E | *Vincent Alsop*, M.A. p "an addition Subscrip." | 10 | | |
| 8 Dec. | E | *John Turner* p | 20 | | |
| 18 Dec. | | *Thomas Rowe* c "in ready money" | 10 | | |
| 22 Dec. | E | *Samuel Annesley* D.D. p "an additional Subsc$^{n}$" | 8 | | |
| ,, ,, | | *Daniel Williams* p "an additional Subscription" | 20 | | |
| ,, ,, | | Madam Bignall "by Mr. Matthew Raper" c | 5 | | |
| 29 Dec. | E | *John Quick*, M.A. p "in more ready money" | 3 | 17 | 6 |
| ,, ,, | E | *Matthew Sylvester* p | 30 | | |
| ,, ,, | E | *Edward Veal*, M.A. p | 10 | | |
| **1690/1** | | | | | |
| 5 Jan. | | *Edward Grace* c "of Clapham" | 25 | | |
| ,, ,, | E | *John Reynolds* p "in ready money" | 7 | 15 | 0 |
| 19 Jan. | | *Matthew* [*Samuel*] *Borfet* M.A. p | 22 | 10 | 0 |
| 2 Feb. | | Capt. Bowman c of Wapping | 1 | | |
| 9 Feb. | | *Timothy Cruso*, M.A. p (to begin Xmas 1690) | 20 | | |
| ,, ,, | | The Lady Priscilla Brookes p (promised donation) | 100 | | |
| ,, ,, | | Joshua Brookes c | 5 | | |
| 2 Mar. | | "A citizen" per E *Nathanael Mather*, M.A. c | 10 | | |
| ,, ,, | | "A Gen:$^{t}$ donation" per E *Nathanael Mather*, M.A. c | 2 | 10 | 0 |
| ,, ,, | | "Gift from a person" per E *William Bates* D.D. p | 5 | 7 | 6 |
| 9 Mar. | | *Nicholas Blakey*, M.A. p | 30 | | |
| **1691** | | | | | |
| 26 Mar. | | Peter Martell "a gift" | 5 | | |
| 27 April | | The collection Pinners' Hall | 120 | 1 | 4 |
| 1 May | | "Gift from a Gen$^{t}$" per E *Richard Stretton* M.A. p | 2 | | |

| | | £ | s. | d. |
|---|---|---|---|---|
| 1691 | | | | |
| 16 June | Mrs. Baker 𝔠 "a Gift" per Matthew Rapier . . | 3 | 5 | |
| 17 Aug. | John Carey per *Nicholas Blakey*, M.A. 𝔭 . . | 5 | | |
| " " | Peter Hussie per same . . . . . | 10 | | |
| 7 Sept. 𝕰 | *Daniel Burgess* 𝔭 . . . . . . | 40 | | |
| " " | Benjamin Williams, of Guildford, Surrey, a gift . | 10 | | |
| " " | ...........Booth (legacy) per Samuel Powell 𝔭 . | 50 | | |
| 14 Sept. | Roger Lock . . . . . . | 5 | | |
| " " | A Gent. in Yorks per 𝕰 *Richard Stretton*, M.A. 𝔭 a gift | 8 | | |
| " " | A Friend, per same . . . . . | 10 | | |
| " " | per same . . . . . . . | 5 | | |
| 5 Oct. | Francis Buyer per 𝕰 *Nathanael Mather* 𝔠 . . | 5 | | |
| 26 Oct. | A Gent:m per 𝕰 *Samuel Annesley* 𝔭 "a gift" . . | 50 | | |
| 30 Oct. 𝕰 | *Thomas Brand* 𝔭 . . . . . . | 20 | | |
| " " | *John Ker* 𝔭 . . . . . . . | 5 | | |
| 2 Nov. | Sir Humphrey Edwin . . . . . | 10 | | |
| " " | *John Shower* 𝔭 . . . . . . | 25 | | |
| 23 Nov. | *Robert Francklin* 𝔠 "a gift" . . . . . | 5 | 5 | |
| 5 Dec. | Bartholomew Gracedieu 𝔠 . . . . . | 10 | | |
| 14 Dec. 𝕰 | *Obadiah Hughes*, B.A. 𝔭 . . . . . | 12 | | |
| " " | John Gould . . . . . . . | 10 | | |
| 1691/2 | | | | |
| 4 Jan. | *Timothy Rogers*, M.A. 𝔭 and . . . . . | | | |
| " " | *Thomas Kentish*, jun. 𝔭 . . . . . | 17 | 16 | |
| " " | Richard Bury, Alderman (promised) . . . . | 5 | | |
| 15 Feb. | *Thomas Powell* 𝔭 . . . . . . | 5 | | |
| 7 Mar. 𝕰 | *William Bereman* 𝔠 𝕰 *Robert Bragge*, B.A. 𝔠 "a gift" | 10 | | |
| 1692 | | | | |
| 25 Apr. | Widow Newman 𝔠 gift, per 𝕰 *Isaac Chauncy*, M.A., L.C.P. 𝔠 | 5 | | |
| 30 May | Sir Patience Ward "gift" per 𝕰 *Richard Stretton*, M.A. 𝔭 | 10 | | |
| 6 July | Madam Martell 𝔭 . . . . . . | 5 | | |
| 3 Oct. | Daniel Wight senr . . . . . . | 10 | | |
| " " | Joseph Thomson 𝔭 . . . . . . | 10 | | |

This is hardly the subscription list one would have expected. It reveals the fact that to the personal zeal of Ejected divines was due, not merely the projection of a Common Fund, but also the financial equipment which made the project feasible. The dates show that the subscription list was opened nearly three months before the first meeting of Managers, who began their work with a subscription list before them amounting to £915, representing a much higher sum (perhaps thrice as much) in modern money; and more was coming in month by month. Seven of the Ejected subscribed sums ranging from £160 to £100, with a tendency to increase the amount; fifteen others, sums from £80 to £10, with the same tendency.

The highest lay subscription, £50, was from a physician, Henry Sampson, M.D., himself Ejected as a Nonconformist preacher, though never ordained; his subscription was reduced in the following year to £20 (raised again, later, to £30). A better example was shown by Matthew Rapier, who kept up his subscription of £40, and in 1691 paid £50. Knights and a baronet did not rise above £10, the minimum subscription from an Ejected divine.

So large are many of the clerical subscriptions, that one might be tempted to suppose them amounts for which these divines made themselves responsible, intending to obtain them from congregational collections, or from private friends. The list given above disposes of this interpretation. Throughout the Minutes, collections and gifts made through Ministers are kept quite distinct from their personal contributions. Nay, more, when funds were low, and pressing cases occurred, in several instances the Managers present, led by the Ministers, put their hands into their pockets and clubbed £1 a piece for the relief of some divine or student.

## Survey of Counties

On 14th July 1690 the Managers drew up a General Letter, to be sent to correspondents all over the country, asking information on the following points:

1. Names of survivors of the Ejected divines remaining Nonconformist; and of all others "under y[e] like Circumstances," whether Ministers or "disposed for y[e] Ministry."

2. List of settled Congregations; by what Ministers supplied; how maintained.

3. List of Religious assemblies discontinued; also of places where there might be opportunities of public service.

For collecting this information, and making report to the Managers of all matters from persons who give account of the state of their counties, the "Care of the several Counties in England and Wales" was (on 14th July 1690) committed to the following persons. Changes (given here in square brackets) when not otherwise dated, were made on 5th Sept. 1692.

Beds—𝕰 *G. Cokayne* 𝔠 [no appointment]
Berks—𝕰 H. Sampson 𝔭; T. Cockerill 𝔭 [Cockerill alone]
Bucks—𝕰 *M. Mead* 𝔠; 𝕰 H. Sampson 𝔭 [*Mead* alone]

Cambs—𝕰 *M. Mead* 𝖈
Chester—*D. Williams* 𝖕
Cornwall—𝕰 *J. Howe* 𝖕; 𝕰 *Obad. Hughes* 𝖕 [*Howe* alone]
Cumberland—𝕰 *R. Stretton* 𝖕; *J. Nesbitt* 𝖈 [*Stretton* alone]
Derby—T. Cockerill 𝖕; M. Rapier 𝖈; H. Coape 𝖕; [11 Jan. '92, T. Abney 𝖕 vice Coape decd; 3 Oct. '92, Abney alone]
Devon—𝕰 *J. Howe* 𝖕; 𝕰 *Obad. Hughes* 𝖕 [*Howe* alone]
Dorset—𝕰 *R. Mayo* 𝖕; J. Jurin 𝖕 [26 June '93, *Mayo* alone]
Durham—*J. Nesbitt* 𝖈 [no appointment]
Essex—𝕰 *J. Faldo* 𝖈; 𝕰 H. Sampson 𝖕 [no appointment]
Gloucester—𝕰 *M. Mead* 𝖈
Hants—J. Jurin 𝖕
Hereford—*D. Williams* 𝖕
Herts—𝕰 *J. Faldo* 𝖈; 𝕰 H. Sampson 𝖕 [no appointment]
Hunts—*D. Williams* 𝖕
Kent—𝕰 *T. Brand* 𝖕; 𝕰 H. Sampson 𝖕 [𝕰 *S. Annesley* 𝖕]
Lancs—*D. Williams* 𝖕; M. Rapier 𝖈 [*Williams* alone]
Leicester—𝕰 *M. Mead* 𝖈; 𝕰 *V. Alsop* 𝖕; 𝕰 H. Sampson 𝖕; M. Rapier 𝖈 [Sampson alone]
Lincoln—𝕰 H. Sampson 𝖕; M. Rapier 𝖈 [Sampson alone]
Middlesex—J. Jurin 𝖕
Norfolk—𝕰 *W. Bates* 𝖕; T. Hartley 𝖈 [no appointment]
Northants—𝕰 *V. Alsop* 𝖕; T. Cockerill 𝖕 [*Alsop* alone]
Northumberland—𝕰 *R. Stretton* 𝖕; *J. Nesbitt* 𝖈 [*Stretton* alone]
Notts—𝕰 *W. Bates* 𝖕 [no appointment]
Oxford—𝕰 *J. Howe* 𝖕; 𝕰 *M. Mead* 𝖈 [*Mead* alone]
Rutland—𝕰 *V. Alsop* 𝖕; 𝕰 H. Sampson 𝖕; 𝕰 *Thomas Woodcock*, M.A. 𝖕 [*Alsop* alone]
Salop—*D. Williams* 𝖕 [no appointment]
Somerset—𝕰 *I. Chauncy* 𝖈; T. Radbor 𝖕 [no appointment]
Stafford—*D. Williams* 𝖕
Suffolk—𝕰 H. Sampson 𝖕; J. Jurin 𝖕 [Jurin alone]
Surrey—𝕰 *R. Mayo* 𝖕
Sussex—𝕰 *M. Mead* 𝖈; T. Cockerill 𝖕 [𝕰 *S. Annesley* 𝖕; 3 Oct. '92 also W. Nicholas 𝖕]
Warwick—𝕰 *J. Faldo* 𝖈; 𝕰 H. Sampson 𝖕; J. Jurin 𝖕 [Jurin alone; 19 June '93, 𝕰 *Annesley* 𝖕 alone]
Westmorland—𝕰 *R. Stretton* 𝖕; *J. Nesbitt* 𝖈 [no appointment]
Wilts—𝕰 *R. Mayo* 𝖕; S. Powell 𝖕 [*Mayo* alone; 19 June '93, 𝕰 *D. Burgess* 𝖕 alone]
Worcester—𝕰 *J. Howe* 𝖕 [no appointment]
Yorks—𝕰 *R. Stretton* 𝖕
North Wales—*D. Williams* 𝖕
South Wales—𝕰 *G. Griffith* 𝖈 [*D. Williams* 𝖕]

## Collection of Statistics

With a view to the preparation of statistics, whether of resources, present claims, or future needs, resolutions were from time to time passed, as follows:

25th Aug. 1690.—"Ordered, y<sup>t</sup> a List of the Ministers names in and about y<sup>e</sup> City of London with the places of their aboad, be alwayes in readyness upon occasion."

✓ 22nd Sept. 1690.—"Ordered, that Dr. Samuel Annesley doe on Munday next bring in a List of all y<sup>e</sup> Ministers names in and about y<sup>e</sup> City of London y<sup>t</sup> have not stated Congregacons."

29th Sept. 1690.—"Ordered that the Book-keeper doe on Munday morning next bring in an Abstract of all such Dissenting Ministers in the Countrey (already returned) as want Subsisance."

6th Oct. 1690.—"Ordered, that it is desired, that a List of the names of such M<sup>r</sup>inisters in the Countrey, as receive any reliefe from the Ministers in London together w<sup>th</sup> what sume they receive Yearly or otherwise, be brought before the Managers."

"Ordered, that all such indigent Dissenting Ministers in the Countrey as receive any Contributions from any Congregations in this City, shall have the same allowance *of* out of this ffund, on Condition y<sup>t</sup> such Ministers as so contribute to them do bring into this ffund the Same Sume or more, and y<sup>t</sup> it shall be impartially applyed to the same persons as it used to be by the Contributors."

13th Oct. 1690.—"Ordered, that the Book-keeper doe on Munday next bring in a more perfect Abstract of all the Ministers names in each severall County of England & Wales whose cases are most necessitous."

3rd Nov. 1690.—"Ordered that those Ministers who have taken upon them the charge of the respective Counties in England and Wales, are desired to take an account what is allowed towards the Support of Indigent Dissenting Ministers in every County and that they signify the same to them."

17th Nov. 1690. "Ordered that all Ministers and Gentlemen concerned in this ffund that doe Contribute to the Education of Youth either in this City or in the Countrey doe on Munday next bring in their names; the Sume they Yearly contribute, the places where, and the persons names with whom they are educated."

"Ordered that the Book-keeper doe on Munday next bring in a distinct account of what money is allowed to every individuall Minister in every County apart by themselves, and that Ministers and Gentlemen that have undertaken for every such County doe take care that the said sumes allowed, be conveyed and paid to every such Minister."

"Ordered that the Abstract of the allowance to necessitous Dissenting Ministers in the severall Counties of England and Wales together with the severall sumes of money allowed for their support be Entred in this Booke, pursuant to an Order made this day for the same."

24th Nov. 1690.—"Ordered that all Gentlemen concerned in this Fund doe bring in an account in writing of what they pay or allow towards the Education of

Young men for the Ministry either in this City or in the Countrey, and that those that are present doe Communicate the same to those that are absent."

16th March 1690/1.—"Ordered that no Dissenting Ministers in or about the City of London shall have any allowance out of this Fond."

11th May 1691.—"Ordered that a Review be taken of the State of the severall Counties in England and Wales, of what Dissenting Ministers as well fixed as Itinerant, with their particular personall circumstances, are now resideing therein. As alsoe an account of ye Townes or places, wherein any meetings are, with what allowance is given to those that Supply them. And what young men there be yt are educated in Vniversity Learning."

29th Aug. 1692.—"Ordered that a Review be taken of all allowances made out of this ffund for the Yeare past, and that the Book-keeper doe on Munday next bring in an accompt of all the Ministers, places and young Students, with the particular Sums allowed to them, and yt those Ministers and Gentlemen yt have the charge of the Seuerall Counties in England and Wales doe make a Returne vpon, or before the first Munday in October next Ensueing."

The "accompt" and "Returne," here ordered, were brought in on 5th Sept., and entered on the Minutes. The "Returne" is a mere list of changes in those appointed to take charge of the several counties.

How far the previous orders for the preparation of detailed information were actually carried out it is impossible to say. The Minutes only record the reception and scrutiny of one of these lists (ordered on 13th Oct. 1690). It may indeed be inferred that the Book-keeper did bring in the "Abstract" ordered on 29th Sept. 1690; since on 13th Oct. following he was ordered to bring in "a more perfect Abstract." An Abstract of a different kind, namely of the allowances granted by the Fund, is specified in the third Order (above) of 17th Nov. 1690. Appended to the Minutes of that date, we find "The Abstract is as followeth." It is a list, arranged in counties, of those Ministers only to whom grants had been voted, with the amounts; in three cases the Book-keeper adds, later, a marginal intimation of the non-acceptance of the grant.

## The Manuscript

The Manuscript which is the subject of the present publication is no Abstract of this kind. It opens with a two-page list (an after-addition in the Book-keeper's handwriting) of sixty not fixed London Ministers with their residences (and fourteen Students) such as was ordered on 22nd Sept. 1690. The order of 11th May 1691 for a "Review" does, however, very exactly describe the remaining contents of this Manuscript, which nevertheless cannot possibly have been drawn up subsequently to the date of that order (see p. 172).

After lying long neglected in the archives of the Presbyterian Board, this manuscript was brought to notice on 25th July 1912 by James Patrick Longstaff, D.Sc., while engaged in seeking materials for his "Short Account of the History of the Congregational Church, Romford, Essex," 1913. Public attention was called to the discovery in a valuable article by Rev. William George Tarrant, B.A., in the *Inquirer* newspaper of 26th Oct. 1912.

## Condition of the Manuscript

The Manuscript book consists of 46 leaves small folio, in a brown paper cover. Slight damage has been done to some parts of the left edge of the first leaf; otherwise the Manuscript is practically uninjured. Every page contains writing except the first and the last. In the printed transcript the figures in square brackets in the left margin indicate pages of the original, beginning with the second and omitting the last. That these pages reach the figure 99 is due to the following facts. A loose folio sheet written on three sides, relating to Herefordshire and Hertfordshire (paged 31-34 in the transcript) has been attached in its topographical place by a pin, still remaining. A loose leaf, similarly attached, relating to Lancashire (paged 41-42 in the transcript) is written on one side. These are of rather smaller size than the leaves of the book, and bear a different watermark. Lastly, there is a broad slip of paper (paged 66 in the transcript) written on one side, and still pinned on to the second of the pages relating to Somerset. The majority of the entries are followed by reference numbers, indicating the original sources from which the various items were condensed; *e.g.* "see his case at Large in No. 92." These earlier documents are not forthcoming. The references may be to pages in the "Bookes," or, more probably, to numbers on the files of the letters, specified in the Rules above (p. 160). When they are mere numerals, *e.g.* "No. 6," in the transcript, it has been thought that it would serve no useful purpose to reproduce these reference numbers in detail. When introduced by words, as above, it was necessary to give them, in order to complete the sense. A general account of them, in relation to each County, will be found in the Index.

## Date of the Manuscript

The Manuscript is neither all in one hand nor written all at one time. At least three distinct hands were employed upon it.

The plan of the Manuscript is indicated by headings (names of Counties) in the earliest handwriting. In a few Counties the same handwriting starts the detailed information given under these headings. Now this earliest handwriting was at work on the Manuscript in 1690. That it must have begun its work earlier than Oct. 1690 is obvious from the fact that a later hand (the Book-keeper's) records, as living at Willingham, Cambs., Nathanael Bradshaw, who died at St. Ives on 16th Oct. 1690. The Fund Minutes enable us to be more definite. In the upper corners of the folios of the Manuscript are added the names of the persons appointed (14th July 1690) to have "Care of the severall Counties." In no case (not even when, as in Norfolk, all the other matter is in the earliest handwriting) are these names in that handwriting. They are added by the Book-keeper. It follows that the earliest handwriting is anterior to 14th July 1690 (the date when these names were selected), yet not much anterior, since this earliest hand records Robert Lever (*d.* 1st July 1690) as "latly dead."

The handwriting next in date is that of William Ashhurst, the Book-keeper, who contributes the bulk of the matter contained. While the Willingham entry, above mentioned, proves that the Book-keeper's hand was at work on the MS. before 16th Oct. 1690, other entries show that his work on it was continued till after 6th April 1691, the date of solemnisation of the "Happy Union"; for at first he had, now and then, distinguished Ministers denominationally as "Presbiterian" and "Congregationall," or as P and C. Of these denominational signs some (not all) have subsequently been struck through, evidently owing to the effectuating of the "Happy Union."

Definite proof that additions to the Manuscript were made later than 1690 is afforded by the fact that some entries bear later dates. Some are dated 1691. This figure, of course, according to the old reckoning (used throughout the Minutes) would cover a date from 25th March 1691 up to and including 24th March 1691/2. Its presence, to mark additions, clearly shows that the main body of this composite document belongs to the year 1690, which then ended on 24th March 1690/1. The latest year date for additions is 1692. One of these 1692 additions can be more exactly dated by help of the Fund Minutes. It refers to Stephen James, a prospective student, at Calne, Wilts, whose case was favourably considered by the Board on 9th May 1692, and who subsequently pursued his studies under Matthew Warren at Taunton. The latest fully dated entry is 23rd May 1692, also referring to a student, John Goodchild, in Suffolk; the Minutes of that date assign him to Ipswich, where he studied under John Langston. This seems fairly good evidence that the Book-keeper's latest entries in the Manuscript were in preparation for the Midsummer distribution of 1692 (though the bare figure 1692 would cover a date up to 24th March 1692/3).

By the third hand (or hands) only occasional notes are added; they seem to be memoranda by the chairmen of meetings. These notes would of themselves suffice to prove that the Manuscript was a document in use by the Managers when making their grants for 1690. For we find the following entry: "Mr Sam$^{l}$ Coates Att Mansfield, preaches there one L$^{ds}$ day in a m$^{o}$: 8$^{s}$ pr day. could 10*l* a yeare be added y$^{e}$ meeting would be held up constantly for want whereof hee is forced to preach in other places." The added marginal note is this: "on condition to keepe the meeting Constant 8*l* p Ann." The Fund Minutes tell us of the grant of £8 per annum made to "Mr Samuel Coates att Mansfield" on 17th Nov. 1690, "on Condition y$^{t}$ the meeting there be kept up constant." They further report on 29th Dec. 1690 that "Mr Samuel Coats at Mainsfield in Nottinghamshire refuseth to accept of £8 per annum on the Condition it was allowed him." So again we read in the Manuscript: "Mr Rastrick, Att Spalding, of a Con: turned a Non: Con: 30*l* p$^{r}$ ann." The marginal note in the Manuscript adds: "Thankes but at p$^{r}$ neads not." This is explained by further reference to the Fund Minutes, which record that on 17th Nov. 1690 a grant of £5 per annum was made to "Mr Rastrick att Spalding"; but on 29th Dec. it was reported that he "refuseth to accept of £5 per annum haveing no need of it." Need overtook him later; on 1st May 1693 a gift of £5 was made to him, to be at once paid, "for his incouragment." This we learn from the Fund Minutes; the Manuscript has no date so late as this. Others of these marginalia can be proved by the Fund Minutes to belong to 1690.

## THE SHORTHAND NOTES

There are many deletions in the Manuscript, but no erasures. All the words, and parts of words, crossed out are easily read. They have accordingly been reproduced in the transcript, and will be found printed in italics. Wherever italics appear in the print, this is a sign that the parts so printed have been deleted in the original Manuscript.

Much more trouble was given by the work of deciphering the brief notes in shorthand. After trying, without success, during a couple of years, all the seventeenth-century systems whose printed alphabets were available, especially the collection by the late John Eglington Bailey,

F.S.A. (now in the Manchester Reference Library), and after applying to experts whose kind assistance was given freely but in vain, the solution came suddenly.

The shorthand is the one employed by Pepys in his famous Diary. A facsimile page of the Diary made this clear. Use was then made of the paper by John Eglington Bailey, read at the Manchester Literary Club in 1875, "On the Cipher of Pepys's Diary," proving that Pepys had employed the Tachygraphy of Thomas Shelton. This led to a renewed recourse to Shelton's Tachygraphy, in the edition of 1671. Further and most important aid was obtained from a tiny volume in 32mo bearing the following title:

> The Whole Book of Psalms in Meeter According to that most exact & Compendious method of Short Writing Composed by Thomas Shelton (Being his former hand) aproued by both Vniversities & learnt by many thousands — Sold by Tho: Cockerill at the three Leggs and Bible in the Poultrey
> T: Cross Sculpsit.

The date of this little volume (which has Shelton's portrait prefixed) is not clear. The *Dict. Nat. Biog.*, under Shelton, dates it "about 1660"; the British Museum catalogue has [1670?]; but Thomas Cockerill (probably a son of the Manager) did not remove from Amen Corner to the Three Legs and Bible in the Poultry, opposite Grocers' Hall, till June 1699. The metrical Psalms rendered in shorthand are those of Sternhold and Hopkins. The "former hand" distinguishes the Tachygraphy from Shelton's later and totally different system, Zeiglographia, which was the cipher employed by Sir Isaac Newton.

The Tachygraphy system seems easy to practise, for any one with a good memory; the decipherer's difficulty arises from the extraordinary number of arbitrary signs, and arbitrary combinations of the alphabet, with the close resemblance of many of them. Bailey says there are 314 different signs; the printed Tachygraphy does not give them all; Shelton made a living by teaching the art. The shorthand annotator of the Manuscript does not always follow either the instructions of the printed manual or the usage of Pepys or that of the metrical volume. For the preposition *in*, Pepys and the metrical volume use an arbitrary sign; in the Manuscript the word is spelled alphabetically—most persons might find it easier to write it so. Again in the Manuscript the same word is sometimes written in different ways; thus on p. 26 *column* is spelled alphabetically, but on p. 40 for the first syllable an arbitrary character is used. Without a context it is sometimes impossible to be sure of the right reading. Thus on p. 150 "no lack" might as easily be read "no Latin"; but, as Davis was a student under Woodhouse, this reading is inadmissible. These notes are apparently by more hands than one. Most of them are directions for the Book-keeper's guidance, perhaps in some cases written by himself. With the exception of one sign, queried on p. 67, and by no means clearly written, it is believed that all these notes have been properly deciphered. They yield very little information.

The shorthand notes are printed in smaller type; this small type invariably means shorthand.

## USE OF THE MANUSCRIPT

As already stated, the Manuscript is in the nature of a "Review," or Survey, undertaken in 1690, of the state of the several Counties in England and Wales, enumerating the Dissenting Ministers, whether settled or itinerant, noting their particular personal circumstances; stating the places at which meetings for worship were held, or might reasonably be begun, with the amount of financial support in each case; enumerating also the students who were being educated in "University learning." It was in use from 1690 to 1692. If then the order of 11th May 1691 for a Review was carried out (which there is nothing to show) this earlier document was not at once superseded by it. It was, at any rate, the Book-keeper's manual as late as 1692. Among a very few faintly legible and meaningless scribbles of words and figures on its original paper cover, is one in the top left-hand corner of the first outer page of the cover (possibly in the Book-keeper's handwriting) which it would be tempting to read as "Committee," and take as indicating the body by whom the record was employed. This, on a first scrutiny, seemed plausible. The true reading, however, is "a minute." Like the other scribbles, it is a mere exercise in trying the pen.

## GRANTS TO MINISTERS

Some statistics of Ministers and their need may be useful; the calculation is somewhat difficult, owing to inconsistent and duplicate entries. The following computation is offered with the assurance that it has been made, and revised, with minute care:

*London.*—Incidentally the names of 20 Ministers appear, who are well settled with congregations. Of the 60 Ministers named as not settled with congregations, 1 is returned "poor," 4 "very poor"; the (erased) heading, about want of assistance, belongs to Bedfordshire. Thomas Woodcock, M.A., was one of those who took no fees for preaching; and in Middlesex he is properly placed among the well-to-do. The Rules of the Fund prohibited grants to Ministers so long as they remained in London; but the "poor" and "very poor" above noted received sums of £2, £3, or £5, from an anonymous donation of £50 brought in by Matthew Rapier for special distribution.

*Bedfordshire.*—The Ministerial list is blank.

*Berkshire.*—Ministers with a competence, 4; in need, 12. Two of the latter were originally entered as having enough; one of them, Humphrey Gunter [*q.v.*], when preaching at his own house, took no fees.

*Buckinghamshire.*—Ministers with a competence, 4; in need 3. One of the latter was originally recorded as having enough.

*Cambridgeshire.*—Ministers with a competence, 9; in need, 4; not settled, 6.

*Cheshire.*—Ministers with a competence, 12; in need, 1; not settled, 1.

*Cornwall.*—Ministers with a competence, 5; in need, 5; not settled, 1.

*Cumberland.*—Ministers with a competence, 2 (actually 3 are so classed, but all are recorded as "poor," and one of them, George Larkham [*q.v.*], at once received a grant); in need, 6; not settled, 2.

*Derbyshire.*—Ministers with a competence, 14; in need, 3 (one was preaching in Lancashire); not settled, 9.

*Devon.*—Ministers with a competence, 35; in need, 13; not settled, 9.

*Dorset.*—Ministers with a competence, 9 (two are conjectural); in need, 6.

*Durham.*—Ministers with a competence, 3; in need, 0.

*Essex.*—Ministers with a competence, 26; in need, 16; not settled, 2.

*Gloucestershire.*—Ministers with a competence, 9; in need, 5; not settled, 3.

*Hampshire.*—Ministers with a competence, 9; in need, 7.

*Herefordshire.*—Ministers with a competence, 7; in need, 1.

*Hertfordshire.*—Ministers with a competence, 15; in need, 3.

*Huntingdonshire.*—Ministers with a competence, 4; in need, 0.

*Kent.*—Ministers with a competence, 8; in need, 3.

*Lancashire.*—Ministers with a competence, 30; in need, 4.

*Leicestershire.*—Ministers with a competence, 8; in need, 7.

*Lincolnshire.*—Ministers with a competence, 3; in need, 2.

*Middlesex.*—Ministers with a competence, 7; in need, 0; not settled, 1.

*Norfolk.*—Ministers with a competence, 12; in need, 3; not settled, 2.

*Northamptonshire.*—Ministers with a competence, 10; in need, 2.

*Northumberland.*—Ministers with a competence, 7; in need, 7.

*Nottinghamshire.*—Ministers with a competence, 8; in need, 5.

*Oxfordshire.*—Ministers with a competence, 6; in need, 3.

*Rutland.*—Ministers with a competence, 0; in need, 1.

*Shropshire.*—Ministers with a competence, 9; in need, 6; not settled, 1.

*Somerset.*—Ministers with a competence, 22; in need, 6; not settled, 17.

*Staffordshire.*—Ministers with a competence, 8; in need, 3; not settled, 1.

*Suffolk.*—Ministers with a competence, 13; in need, 8.

*Surrey.*—Ministers with a competence, 3; in need, 7.

*Sussex.*—Ministers with a competence, 17; in need, 5; not settled, 2.

*Warwickshire.*—Ministers with a competence, 10; in need, 4.

*Westmoreland.*—Ministers with a competence, 2; in need, 0.

*Wiltshire.*—Ministers with a competence, 6; in need, 4.

*Worcestershire.*—Ministers with a competence, 5; in need, 4; not settled, 5.

*Yorkshire, East Riding.*—Ministers with a competence, 5; in need, 2.

*Yorkshire, North Riding.*—Ministerial list blank.

*Yorkshire, West Riding.*—Ministers with a competence, 22; in need, 9; not settled, 2.

*North Wales.*—Ministers with a competence, 3; in need, 5.

*South Wales.*—Ministers with a competence, 6; in need, 13; not settled, 10.

Thus we have in the Manuscript a total of 759 names of Ministers, of whom 218 are without competent means of support, and 133 (many of these also needy) are not settled with congregations. Regarded as a return of the entire Ministry of the two denominations, this total is obviously incomplete. There is no full return for London, none at all for Bedfordshire and the North Riding; in other counties, known and important names are missing. Of those given, 380 are Bartholomaeans; all but 17 still in more or less active service.

Grants to Ministers begin at once in 1690. Incidentally the Manuscript furnishes two estimates of a Minister's minimum requirements in the matter of stipend. From Belper, Derb., £28 a year is reported as "y[e] least a minister can Subsist on in this County"; towards this the Belper Nonconformists could only raise £13 a year (p. 27). From Norfolk we get a higher estimate: "Ministers cannot liue und[r] £50 p Añ like Ministers." What the London Ministers were paid there is nothing to indicate. The highest stipends recorded in the Manuscript are in Norfolk. The Yarmouth Congregationals (who had some Presbyterians in their membership) paid to their Minister, James Hannot, £100 a year, and to his assistant, Samuel Wright, £50 a year. The Norwich Presbyterians paid to their Ministers, John Collinges, D.D., and Benjamin Snowden, £56 a year apiece; their Lecturer, John Lucas, "may get £40." The Norwich Congregationals paid to their Minister, Martin Fynch, and his Assistant, John Stackhouse, £130 between them (p. 74). Liverpool and Toxteth Park together raised £75 (p. 58). This is the highest sum recorded for Lancashire. At Birch Chapel, near Manchester, the stipend of Henry Finch is not specified, but it is significantly said that "y[e] charge of his horse will goe a great way in his allowance from the people, yet complains not" (p. 61). Etal, Northumberland, raised £60 a year. Several stipends reached £50 and £40; but the great majority are below, often much below, the Derbyshire notion of a minimum. Apparently the lowest and most uncertain stipend was that afforded to Anthony Sleigh at Threlkeld, Cumberland, whose people did all they could, but this did not amount to above £6 a year, or £5 a year, and some years not above 40s. (p. 22).

Fixed stipends were by no means universal. One is surprised to learn that even the rich Presbyterian flock at Nottingham paid their four Ministers, John Whitlock, William Reynolds, John Barrett, and John Whitlock *secundus*, by the piece, *i.e.* 14s. per service (p. 82). This was a high rate; the customary fee was 10s.; but we find 8s., 7s., 6s., and even 5s. What the Nottingham congregation actually spent on the ministry in the course of a year cannot be gathered from the record. There were two services on most Sundays, probably on all; then there were certainly week-day and Fast services in addition; for these neighbouring Ministers were often called in. The first three Ministers above named were engaged for one service every other Sunday; when not engaged at Nottingham they were often many miles away, preaching elsewhere at a lower rate.

A considerable number of Ministers had properties of their own, some of large extent; often they held land, freehold or tenanted, which they farmed. Many kept school; even some who were diligent in missionary preaching, late at night and in the early morn, were schoolmasters during the day. Among Baptists, some, as we know, were in trade, but the Manuscript records no case of this. A trader, in accordance with Rule 4 above, would not be entitled to a grant from the Fund, but school-keeping and tutoring, in needy cases, was with true wisdom regarded as falling properly within the scope of the Minister's "fixed and only Imployment." If cleanliness is "next to godliness," as John Wesley said, education is an integral part of religion, as neither the early Nonconformists nor John Wesley were backward in demonstrating. There were cases of men well-to-do (and some not well-to-do) preaching without fee, and taking pastoral charge without stipend. Apart from fees, there were "tokens," as missionary biographies such as Oliver Heywood's show, *i.e.* small presents, usually in money, sometimes in kind, given by persons who had profited by a discourse, and not always applied by the preacher to his own use. None of these are recorded in the Manuscript.

There is no record of a Manse; on the contrary, the Minister's dwelling-house was in many cases freely thrown open as the Meeting-place for the worship of the congregation. In one case, at Northampton, we read: "nothing but y$^{e}$ rent of y$^{e}$ meetinghouse p$^{d}$ by the Church"; this Meeting-house was the dwelling of the Minister, John Harding. On the other hand, some few Ministers were still living, as Chaplains and

Tutors, in the houses of Nonconformist gentry or of their widows, and conducting services on the premises of their patrons and elsewhere.

A glance at any page of the Manuscript is enough to bring home to us a clear view of the necessitous condition of the main bulk of the Nonconformist Ministry in the provinces, and the calls from every quarter upon the resources of the London Fund.

Coming to the question of grants, the earliest existing "Cash Book" of the Fund is labelled No. 3; it begins on 23rd Oct. 1693. Previously to this, the Minutes furnish sufficient records of moneys promised and paid, and full lists of persons and places aided, with the amounts awarded. The largest grant made was to Joshua Oldfield at Oxford, who before the organisation of the Fund had received £50 from London; he was now granted £34 a year, till his removal to Coventry in 1694. Thomas Barnes of Newport, Monm., and William Clerke of Poole, Dors., were granted £20 a year; Abel Collier, of Halstead, Essex, and Robert Ekins, of Oakham, Rutland, were granted £12 a year each. No other Ministerial grant exceeded £10 a year, and the grants were in some cases as low as £2 a year.

At the reconstruction in 1695, many of these grants were stopped; most of those retained were reduced in amount, and only two new grants were made. This was rendered inevitable by the failure of subscriptions, none coming from Congregationals, though in several cases grants were still made to Congregational Ministers. When, at the end of the year, the Congregational Fund was established, several cases occur of Congregational Ministers receiving grants from both Funds. The present writer's ancestor, Thomas Irlam [*q.v.*], was especially successful in drawing from both sources. It is clear that the breach of Union had an unfavourable effect on the generosity of the Nonconformist laity. The combined income of the two Funds was not equal to that of the original Fund before the division.

## Grants to Congregations

In a large number of cases, grants were not made to Ministers, but to localities; and this, even when there were Ministers actively engaged in the localities aided. These grants were of a missionary character; they are described as grants for the Propagation of the Gospel, and are often saddled with conditions as to maintenance of continuous Sunday services, or of Lectures, *i.e.* expository discourses conducted in series, frequently by a concert of Ministers.

The highest of these grants, which do not begin till 1691, was for "the Moorlands" of Staffordshire, £20 a year, increased to £30, as had been promised "if they think good to have another Minister." Next in amount come £18 a year for High Peak in Derbyshire, "per William Bagshaw"; and £13 a year for Lichfield, Staff., "on condition that they get a Minister." No others exceed £10 a year, nor are any less than £4.

Of these missionary grants the great majority were cut off in 1695, and most of those retained were reduced. There were, however, a few new grants made in 1695, namely £16 a year for Oxford; £8 for Ashburnham, Derb.; £6 each for Lavenham, Suff.; Nuneaton, Warw.; and Doncaster, Yorks; £4 for Bingley, Yorks; £2 for Lydgate, Yorks.

The estimated size of congregations in small places is often surprising. The entry for Bispham, Lancs, is so remarkable that we reproduce it here. Bispham, then a perpetual curacy, was no doubt a large parish, eight miles long and between one and two broad, yet its population in 1801 was only 727 (Blackpool has since come into being within its bounds). The Manuscript, however, records that "Att Bispham" there was in 1690 "A Congregation, constantly very numerous, Sometimes near or aboue 1000, one hundred of the hearers are Wealthy, yet haue noe fixt minister there, noe joint contributions, insomuch y[t] even y[e] Lectures there are like to fall unless you retrieve them." Notwithstanding this moving appeal, no grant was made. Clearly it was no part of the policy of the Fund Managers to supply free Gospel in order to save the pockets of wealthy Nonconformists. Perhaps at Bispham the condition of the parish church had something to do with the position of Nonconformity. Bispham tithe (£28 in 1867) furnished but a lean living; perpetual curates seem to have made no long stay; we find Robert Wayte perpetual curate in 1689, Thomas Rikay in 1691, Thomas Sellom in 1692. Again, nothing was given to Penzance and St. Ives, Cornwall, though John Quick, B.A., intimated that a congregation of "about 3 or 4000 people" might be raised; the Fund Managers evidently thinking that so large a mass might be expected to provide for itself, if in earnest.

### Grants to Students

Order was made at the meeting of the Fund on 17th Nov. 1690 that "all Ministers and Gentlemen concerned in this ffund that doe Contribute to the Education of Youth either in this City or in the Countrey . . bring in their names, the Sume they Yearly contribute, the places where, and the persons names with whom they are educated."

A week later, on 24th Nov. 1690, it was "Ordered that all Gentlemen concerned in this Fund doe bring in an account in writing of what they pay or allow toward the Education of Young men for the ministry either in this City or in the Countrey, and that those that are present doe Communicate the same to those that are absent."

The Minutes show that this, with more or less regularity, was done.

The total number of Students for the Ministry mentioned in the Manuscript is 82, thus distributed: London, 14; Cambridgeshire, 1; Cheshire, 1; Derbyshire, 3; Devon, 1; Dorset, 2; Essex, 1; Gloucestershire, 5; Herefordshire, 1; Kent, 2; Lancashire, 3; Leicestershire, 1; Norfolk, 2; Northamptonshire, 5; Northumberland, 1; Shropshire, 5; Somerset, 1; Suffolk, 1; Surrey, 1; Wiltshire, 2; Yorkshire, 15; North Wales, 2; South Wales, 12.

The cautious care taken in examining into all cases proposed for relief, as exemplified in this Manuscript, and in the Fund Minutes, is nowhere more conspicuous than in the supervision of Students, and the consideration shown for them. Their career was watched, and certificates were given to them. Lads intending for the ministry were not helped by the Fund till they had acquired at school or privately some command of Latin; on 19th Oct. 1691 a Yorkshire lad, William Bowler, was reported "destitute of Grammar Learning, and therefore not capable of any Supply from this Fund."

Already on 29th Sept. 1690 it was "Ordered y$^{t}$ a Committee be appointed to examine y$^{e}$ young men that at present are, or for the future shall be maintained out of the publick Supply—and y$^{t}$ all persons concerned in this affaire, have liberty to be present, Ordered y$^{t}$ the Committee appointed for the examination of young men doe consist of Five Ministers, and that three of them shall make a quorum." The first five appointed were Griffith, Alsop, Howe, Annesley, and Mayo, one Congregational to four Presbyterians.

When it became necessary to reduce grants through shortness of funds, the grants to Students were, with the rarest exceptions, kept at the full rate originally granted. The largest sum paid (in two cases) to a Student was £25; but this, though paid through the Fund, was in one case partly made up by sums contributed for the purpose by friendly Ministers (no unusual circumstance), and in the other case was wholly the contribution of an individual Minister for the benefit of a personal protégé. A few Students received £20 a year, a few received £14, but as a rule £10 was the highest figure, while £2 was the lowest. Evidently the question of private means was minutely considered, as also was the question of the need of money for the purchase of books.

It should further be mentioned that Tutors of Academies are known to have remitted fees in the case of poor Students, charging only for board; and even making gifts toward their support, to be administered through the Fund. Living under the Tutor's roof was an integral part of the educational system, which depended largely for its effect on the discipline of the house, the share in its devotions, the recourse to its library, and the constant use of Latin, not only in the lecture-room, but in prayer, singing, and converse, save at certain specified hours of the evening. Singing in Latin was sometimes varied by singing Psalms in Greek, and even, in the case of at least one Academy, by actually singing the Psalms in the original Hebrew. After migrating from one Academy to another in England or Wales (led by the fame of a Tutor in some special branch of divinity, science, or philosophy, or attracted by the excellence of his library), the Student in many cases proceeded for further class instruction to Glasgow, Utrecht, or Leiden. Graduation was rare.

It will be observed that the name of a foreigner, Honorate Superiori, possibly a convert, appears (p. 4) at the end of the list of Students under education at Bethnal Green. On 13th April 1691 the Fund made to John White, "formerly a Romish priest," a grant of £5 in aid of his studies.

Many of the Students whose names appear in the Manuscript, or in the Minutes, rendered in after life good service to the religious interests of Nonconformity. Josiah Hort, named in the Minutes, achieved insignificance as an Irish Archbishop, and is best known as the last magnate who ate his dinner from a wooden trencher. Three only, in the period we are considering, stand out conspicuous in the world's estimate, though for very different reasons. They, too, are not mentioned in the Manuscript, we derive our information from the Fund Minutes. One of these is Edmund Calamy, who as "Student at Vtericht, Holland," was voted £10 a year on 2nd March 1690/1. Another, described in the Fund Minutes of 15th Feb. 1691/2 as "Mr John Toland a young student [M.A. Edin. 1690], resideing at present in or near this City," was granted a bursary of £8 per annum "towards the perfecting of his Studies att Vtricht or Leiden, in Holland, to be paid when [he] is fixed in his Studies at either of y^e said places." Sir Leslie Stephen says (*Dict. Nat. Biog.*) that Toland "spent two years at Leyden"; his name does not occur in the Leiden "Album Studiosorum." The Fund Minutes record two payments (12th Dec. 1692 and 19th June 1693) each of £8, to "John Toland att Vtricht in Holland." His name does not occur in the

Utrecht "Album Studiosorum"; but from the general absence of their names, at both of these Universities, it would appear that few of the Nonconformist students were matriculated, or entered for the regular course of studies. The third, a name greater than either Calamy or Toland, is Isaac Watts, who, as a Student under Thomas Rowe, was paid a bursary of £8 for the year ending 24th June 1693.

## TWO FUNDS

On the history, still somewhat obscure, of the breach in the "Happy Union," less light than might have been expected is thrown by the proceedings at the Board of the Common Fund. Officially the Board was independent of the Union, which neither Mather nor Cole had joined. One would certainly gather that by the middle of 1693 a crisis of some kind had been reached at the Board. Appended to the Minutes of 26th June, a memorandum specifies fifteen items of unpaid subscriptions, amounting to £279 : 5s. Between this date and 4th Sept. no meeting of the Managers was held. This is proved by the fact that the record of the meeting of 4th Sept. is headed "The fourth Year," which year really began in July. Following this heading is the name of Richard Mayo as presiding at the Meeting, then come seven pencil lines intended for the names of Ministers present, with three for names of Laymen; but no names are filled in, nor do any Minutes follow—merely blank leaves to the end of this first volume of the Minutes, though the Cash Book shows that work was being carried on. The next Minute Book opens with 5th Feb. 1694/5, on which date the Fund was reconstituted; without, however, introducing any denominational term to qualify in any way the expression "Dissenting Ministers." Howe presided at the first meeting of the reconstituted Fund. Except Fincher, who was now dead, all the Presbyterian Ministers who had been Managers of the Common Fund were continued as Managers, but none of the Congregational Ministers.

The Congregational Fund, as already stated, was not established till 17th Dec. 1695. Its constitution, curiously enough, was more in accordance with Presbyterian ideas of lay representation than that of its predecessor, at either stage. On the Congregational Fund Board, each congregation was represented by appointing, along with its Minister (in one case two Ministers), two of its lay members.

It is probable that, synchronously with the establishment (1695) of the Congregational Fund, the older and Common Fund was distinguished, in general parlance, though not in official language, as Presbyterian. Yet, as already stated, it certainly did not confine its grants to those claiming or adopting the name Presbyterian. Many grants to Congregationals (even when receiving from the other Fund) are entered in its Minutes. One of the most interesting of these entries is the grant in 1714 to Robert Trail, M.A., then in need; for Trail had not only been an uncompromising theological opponent of Daniel Williams, but was a Manager of the Congregational Fund.

The earliest official use of the term Presbyterian, for the older Fund, which has come under the present writer's notice is on 14th March 1771, when its title is given (in the Minutes) as "The Fund for Propagating the Gospel and Support of Poor Ministers in the Country commonly called the Presbyterian Fund." The accounts of the Treasurer, Robert Cooke, retain this tentative title till 1784. On 9th July 1784 his successor in the Treasurership, John Warren, uses for the first time the title "The Presbyterian Fund for the relief of Poor Ministers and Students."

## Richard Davis

On one matter, perhaps of more moment in regard to the breach of Union than has been usually or fully realised, the proceedings of the original Fund do shed a little light. In Calamy's "Abridgement," 1713, p. 512, under the year 1692, we read that "The Dissenters had this Year a troublesome affair with one Mr Richard Davis, of Rothwel in Northamptonshire: And at length the United Ministers published to the World their Sense concerning some of his erroneous Doctrines and irregular Practices, in these Words." The Testimony, which follows, nearly fills three octavo pages. Calamy does not specify either its exact date, or the means adopted for its publication. Nor does he tell us whether it was a unanimous declaration; though he implies this, by placing it anterior to the outbreak of "Animosity and Contention about Doctrinal matters" among the United Ministers, owing to the Crispian controversy above mentioned (p. 156). Unfortunately this cannot be checked by reference to the Minutes of the United Ministers, which do not appear to be extant; they are frequently referred to in pamphlets of the period. Yet it is clear at the outset, and will become clearer as we proceed, that Calamy, though right as to the year, is wrong as to the relative date of the Testimony. Davis's "Truth and Innocency Vindicated" was licensed for the press on 4th Nov. 1692. His case had then been before "the Dissenting Ministers of London," but he was as yet under no censure from them. It appears probable that the Testimony, like the "Agreement in Doctrine" of 16th Dec. 1692 (above, p. 156), was one of the measures by which it was hoped to reduce the Crispian controversy then raging.

Richard Davis (1658–10 Sept. 1714), a native of Cardiganshire and there educated, was a grammar-school master in London, and a member of Thomas Cole's Congregational church, when on 20th Feb. 1689 he was unanimously chosen pastor of the Congregational church at Rothwell, Northants (pronounced, and often spelled Rowell), on Cole's recommendation. Cole, it may be remembered, did not join the Union. Though elected a Manager of the Common Fund, he never attended, nor did he contribute to it. To Davis's ordination, on 7th March 1689, neighbouring Ministers were invited; but, learning that he was to be ordained by the Elders of his own church, "several of the neighbouring Ministers withdrew" (Matthias Maurice, "Monuments of Mercy," 1729, p. 65). Subsequently Davis was accused of Antinomianism in doctrine, of rebaptizing such as had received Anglican baptism, and of "sending forth Preachers unfit for the Ministry." As is not unusual in periods of religious excitement, his ministry was for a time attended with "hysterical fits" among some of his women hearers. The United Ministers, in their Testimony, which touches on these points, declare "that he never was, nor is by us esteemed, of the Number of the United Brethren."

In our Manuscript, the only reference to Davis is under the Northamptonshire "Ministers y[t] have a Competent Supply," where we find "Mr Rich[d] Davis. Of Rowell has 30*l* p[r]annum." What further we learn from the Common Fund Minutes is the following. On 13th Oct. 1690 two grants, of £1 : 5s. each, were allocated to "Mr Davis of Rowell" to be paid (with others) through Isaac Chauncy and George Cokayne respectively. Among the others are grants, amounting to £3, to William Paine, jun., of Saffron Walden, Essex, to whom, according to our Manuscript, Chauncy and Cokayne paid £12 per annum. Reckoning Davis's grants as also quarterly allowances, he was receiving from London £10 a year. It is clear that Chauncy and Cokayne had been in the habit of making these grants, prior to the creation of the Common Fund, and now earmarked their subscriptions to the same effect (Cokayne had become a subscriber on the same day; Chauncy a fortnight before). This is confirmed by the fact that these special grants are not entered in the Abstract of 17th Nov. 1690 (see p. 170).

No further grant to Davis is mentioned in the Minutes. On 4th Jan.

1691/2 orders were given "that noe allowance shall from henceforth be granted by this Board to m[r] Davis of Rowell in Northamptonshire"; also "that m[r] Nisbetts people be desired to grant noe such allowance to y[e] said Davis, and that m[r] Mathew Raper do signifie y[e] same to them." At this meeting Chauncy was present; Nesbitt, the successor of Cokayne, deceased, was not yet a Manager. Lastly, after the reconstruction of the Fund, it was on 8th June 1696 "Ordered That £5:— per annum be allowed to m[r] Millway to Commence from the 25th of December Last past, upon this account that hee hath done great Service against m[r] Davis and his pernicious Doctrine." In the list of payments (6th July 1696) that to Milway is placed under Lancashire, which must be an error. It is indeed one of several insertions, not by the Book-keeper, but made after the list had been drawn up; it runs thus: "To m[r] Milway a present Supply by m[r] Alsop-5- -." Thomas Milway was Congregational Minister at Coggeshall, Essex, licensed there 22nd July 1672; at Bury St. Edmunds (1674–92); finally, from 1693, at Kettering, where he was buried on 3rd April 1697. Thus for about four years he had been one of Davis's nearest neighbours.

Davis was no friend to the Union. He had been present at one of its meetings, about the time of its formation. Several months later he had received a letter from the United Ministers, with enquiries about his faith and practice; he had replied fully, but received no response. It is not impossible that the nature of his reply was the cause of his being dropped by the Common Fund Board (not by the United Ministers) in Jan. 1692, when the Managers did their best to stop further grants to him from another source (see above). In May 1692, Davis, being in London, again waited on the United Ministers, who, so he says, treated him "very civilly"; though, at the close of the conference, Williams publicly stated that he had many things against him "in matters of faith" ("Truth and Innocency," pp. 37-8). In the course of the same month, Williams published his "Gospel Truth," 1692, with which the Crispian controversy entered on a more serious phase. Davis calls it a "plausible book," and regards it (probably with much truth) as "lashing" at him "over the Shoulders of Dr Crisp" (*ibid.* p. 6). To "second it" came out "a virulent Pamphlet." This was "A Plain and Just Account of a Most Horrid and Dismal Plague, Begun at Rowell, By Mr P. Rehakosht &c," 1692. Almost certainly its author was John King, Congregational Minister at Wellingborough, Northamptonshire (best known for his later friendship with Doddridge). "Upon the heels" of this lively and contemptuous pamphlet, brimful of local gossip about Davis, his preaching, and his preachers, came what Davis calls "the Ketterin-Inquisition"; a commission (including Williams) from the London United Ministers, which sat at Kettering, with Henry Godman, of Deptford, a Bartholomaean and Congregational, as Moderator. This commission examined witnesses respecting Davis's teaching. The Testimony issued by the United Ministers (later than 4th Nov. 1692) was obviously the result of the evidence thus gleaned. It is remarkable that Williams, in his controversial writings, makes no reference to Davis, save in a "Postscript" (1698) to his "Gospel Truth," where he says of certain Congregational Ministers, that "their pulpits entertain, and they patronise, such as Mr Davies, Mr Jacob &c." Williams does not even take the trouble to spell his compatriot's name correctly. Joseph Jacob (1667–1722) was an eccentric preacher, originally a Quaker.

That Davis exercised a powerful influence in stirring up Congregationals to break the London Union cannot be denied, nor may it be ignored that other than doctrinal considerations contributed to the permanence of the breach. "We evidently perceived," says Davis, "their design was to hook away Judgment from a particular Church of Christ, and fix it in a Presbyterian Classis" (*ibid.* p. 40). Surmises and suspicions of this kind, originating partly, if not chiefly, in personal jealousies, did much to maintain the breach of Union, originally effected by the unfruitful controversy on the precedence to be assigned to repentance over faith, or faith over repentance, a controversy which wore itself out by 1698.

There was further, as the career of Davis demonstrates, an inevitable conflict between the staid methods of the older school, and the urgency of the rampant revivalist. Davis, like Crisp, was by his friends admitted to be a man of incautious speech; yet there was a freshness, if rashness, in some of his off-hand interpretations of Scripture, a vein of mysticism in his piety, an unconventional missionary spirit in his enterprises, disturbing to the settled ways of existing Nonconformity. At the same time, like John Wesley, he kept a strict disciplinary hold upon his adherents. All this, combined with a very robust belief in himself, while rendering him obnoxious to many learned divines, attached to his cause a popular following and attracted imitators. It soon became evident that the Congregationals in the London Union must either withdraw from the new alliance, or dissociate themselves from what seemed a promising movement within their own borders. They took the former course.

## Conclusion

Interest of a very unusual kind attaches to the picture which we are now enabled to form, the picture of Nonconformity rejoicing in "y[e] religious Liberty of Dissenters by a Law." We are accustomed to contemplate the Ejected, as we see them in Calamy's pages, men for the most part in their strenuous prime, yet reduced by the stroke of one fatal day to the sorrows of the outcast. Towering among them rises the gaunt and giant figure of Richard Baxter, the first to eject himself, with a call to the consciences of his brethren, who soon follow him, twenty-five hundred strong. Some fall back; the pinch of outlawry is too severe. Some leave the ministry for experiments in trade, in medicine, or in law. Eighteen hundred resolute men cannot forget their ordination vows; preach the Gospel they will, no power can make them afraid. Hence we behold them struggling with poverty, writhing under accumulating penal laws, succumbing to miseries that shorten life, yet never beaten out of their steadfast purpose. A gleam of indulgence just enables us to descry them as they emerge once more into the light of active service. Then darkness falls; they seem to belong to ancient history, and Puritanism to be a tale that is told. Yet the solicitude of James II. for the restoration of Roman Catholicism warns us that they still exist. A summary religious census, presented to that monarch on 3rd May 1688, estimates the total of Protestant Dissenters at 108,678 souls.

A year later, to these Nonconforming souls comes the dawn of religious freedom under the provisions of the Toleration Act. So we find, in villages as well as in towns, gatherings of poor people, who sometimes surprise us by amounting to hundreds in obscure places, craving the services of a ministry now at length set free. By help of the late-found Manuscript, elucidated by the Minutes of the body for whose use it was framed, we are introduced to a new and clear view of the residue of the Ejected. A glorious residue indeed it is. Passed away into the shadows are many famous leaders of religion and of learning. Alleine, Ambrose, Bridge, Caryl, Gale, the Goodwins, Jenkyn, Manton, Nye, Owen, Poole, Spurstowe, Tuckney,—these and their like are no more than gracious memories, when the muster-roll of the Bartholomaeans is called in 1689. Baxter survives in widowed loneliness, still plies his keen and ever-busy quill, and still can sometimes crawl to the Meeting-house a few doors from his lodging.

Yet the vision before us is neither of the gone nor of the going. It is a fair and shining vision of old men, with young hearts and never-dying hope, springing into fresh and beneficent activity as the sunlight of freedom beams upon their path, resolute to find new opportunities for Gospel enterprise, willing for the moment to sink minor differences in the enthusiasm of a common cause, strong in the co-operation of a younger race of divines, who amid constant hindrance and persecution had devoted themselves to the service of the Gospel, carrying forward a labour of love, hallowed to them by the sacrifices of their fathers. The guiding spirit in this bright advance toward agreement and co-operation is the genius of that "truly great man," John Howe, under whose suasive and skilful planning, men so differently constituted as Annesley and Mead, Chauncy and Williams, were brought into a larger brotherhood and, for the time being, drawn to work together.

If we must say that the conjunction was only for a time, we must also say that such episodes, rare and brief, are the beauty-spots of ecclesiastical history. No doubt there are features of pathos in the picture to which our eyes are directed. It is not possible to scan unmoved the touching list of London Ministers "not fixed to particular congregations." Some will never again be thus fixed; they are the broken-down veterans swept from many quarters into London as to a city of refuge, needing the charity of the benevolent, yet ready, nay, anxious to render, while they may, such service as their failing strength permits. Sprinkled among them in the list are stalwarts of ripe years, whose powers will soon find fit scenes of further labour, and young men on their promotion, whose permanent sphere of work has not yet been reached. In these seasoned standard-bearers and these brave beginners are latent the forces which will build the future of English Nonconformity.

A deeper pathos attaches to the very essence of the story we have endeavoured to recall. It is a story of Presbyterians and Congregationals (with little to distinguish them, when calmly viewed by the outside spectator) and of none else. Puritan strength has not detached itself from Puritan scruples. With Baptists there is no alliance; for their inclusion there is no desire. Mentioned, however, in the Manuscript are the seven following Baptist divines: Edward Gatchell, Joshua Head, Joseph Maisters, Henry Williams, John Wilson, Reynold Wilson, Richard Young. Not improbably the repugnance was mutual. Some of the Baptist pastors just named did indeed admit Congregationals to church-membership; but the time for a concert of The Three Denominations was not yet. This inability to recognise a fellowship in great principles as entitled to dominate the situation, making room for many varieties of conscientious conviction, reacted unhappily on the Happy Union. We must deal with it tenderly, for it was the pathetic weakness of strong men. Yet it goes far to explain how it should come about that a controversy, turning on subtle theological minutiæ, produced in 1694, so far as London and its influence were concerned, an eclipse of the unifying statesmanship of John Howe.)

Nevertheless, as we review the events of the opening years of an emancipated Nonconformity, we may well thank God that there did come a respite from the supremacy of prejudice, salutary if short-lived, and even, perhaps, prophetic.

# INDEX

THE Annotated Index contains the name of every Person and Place recorded in the Manuscript, or mentioned in the Commentary.

In regard to Persons, there is no attempt to furnish complete biographies. The primary object is to identify the Persons whose names are given (often very imperfectly) in the Manuscript, and to present the main landmarks in the career of each. Further and fuller details must be sought in the authorities specified at the close of each item. Thus, except for special reasons, nothing is said of the marriages or descendants of the persons named or of their contributions to literature. "There is one thing," writes Calamy in 1702, "in which I have not been able in many cases to do Justice to these Worthy Men, and that is as to their Degrees." Particular attention is here given to the details of the education and University standing (if any) of the Ministers named; and to their preferments before Ejection, and occupations after Ejection. The full date of the earliest academic record, in which a name has been found, is given; of later entries, *e.g.* degrees, only the year-date is here supplied. With these limitations it will nevertheless be apparent that, in almost every case, something has been added, and something amended, as compared with the usual sources of information.

In regard to Places, it should be noted that where they happen to be livings from which clergy were Ejected, the names of the Ejected are given, accompanied by notices of their careers, even briefer than those relating to Persons named in the Manuscript, yet preserving the same general features. This applies also to the Universities of Oxford and Cambridge, but not to London. In these briefer notices, reference to Palmer may be understood, but is not given when the reference to Calamy is sufficient.

# AUTHORITIES

*A* = Album Studiosorum, Leiden, 1875.
*Ab* = A. Barber, A Church of the Ejectment, Stratford-on-Avon, 1912.
*Ac* = Atterbury's Epistolary Correspondence, 1787, iv. 453.
*Ad* = Account of the Discoveries in Scotland, 1685.
*Am* = J. Armstrong's Appendix to J. Martineau's Ordination, 1829.
*An* = Answer to Mr. Read's Case, 1682.
*Ap* = Appleton, Cyclopaedia of American Biography, 1888.
*As* = Adkins, Brief Records, Independent Denom., Southampton, 1836.
*At* = Arber, Term Catalogues, 1903–6.
*Ax* = E. Axon, Note on Chadkirk, 1910.
*Ay* = Allen, Hist. of Yorkshire, 1831.

*B* = Browne, Hist. Congr. Norf. and Suff., 1877.
*Ba* = G.E.C., Complete Baronetage, 1900–9.
*Bb* = Bogue and Bennett, Hist. of Dissenters, 1808–12.
*Bc* = Burke, Commoners, 1833–38, vol. iii.
*Bd* = Bryan Dale, Annals of Coggeshall, 1863.
*Be* = Besant, London in Time of the Stuarts, 1903.
*Bf* = Beesley, Hist. of Banbury, 1842.
*Bg* = Burke, Landed Gentry, 1914.
*Bh* = C. H. Beale, Old Meeting, Birmingham, 1882.
*Bi* = Bank Street, Bolton, Bicentenary, 1896.
*Bl* = Baines, Lancashire, ed. Harland and Herford; also ed. Crossley.
*B.M.* = British Museum Library.
*Bn* = Brand, Hist. Newcastle-on-Tyne, 1789.
*Bo* = Boase and Courtney, Bibliotheca Cornubiensis, 1874–82.
*Br* = Sparke, Parish Registers of Bolton, 1914.
*Bs* = C. Badham, Hist. of All Saints', Sudbury, 1852.
*Bt* = B. Bartlett, Hist. of Mancetter, 1791.
*Bw* = J. Bickerton Williams, Mem. of Matthew Henry, 1865.
*Bx* = Booker, Birch Chapel, 1859.
*By* = Booker, Blackley Chapel, 1854.

*C* = Calamy, Abridgement and Continuation, 1702, 1713, 1727.
*Ca* = Mr. Read's Case, 1682.
*Cb* = Calamy, Fun. Sermon for J. Bennet, 1726.
*Cc* = W. Cole, M.S. Athenae Cantab. (*B.M.*).

*Cd* = Calamy, Church and Dissenters compared as to Persecution, 1719.
*Ce* = Diary of James Clegg, 1899.
*Cf* = Congregational Fund Minutes, MS. (Mem. Hall, London).
*Cg* = Graduati Cantabrigienses, 1823.
*Ch* = MS. Minutes, Cheshire Classis (Trustees, Brook St. Chapel, Knutsford).
*Ci* = Moses Caston, Independency in Bristol, 1860.
*Ck* = W. Cole, MS. Hist. King's Coll., Camb. (*B.M.*).
*Cl* = Clark's Lives, 1688.
*Cm* = Calamy, Own Life, 1830 (has Index).
*Cn* = Coleman, Northants Independent Churches, 1853.
*Co* = Congregational Hist. Soc. Transactions, Oct. 1911.
*Cp* = Peile, Biog. Register, Christ's Coll., Camb., 1910–13.
*Cr* = *Christian Reformer.*
*Cs* = F. Collins, Register of Settrington, 1810.
*Cu* = *Christian Life and Unitarian Herald.*
*Cw* = F. L. Colvile, Worthies of Warwickshire, 1870.

*D* = Dictionary of National Biography.
*Db* = Graduates, Univ. of Dublin, 1869.
*Dc* = Doddridge Chapel, Northampton, 1896.
*De* = Derbysh. Archaeol. and Nat. Hist. Soc. Journal, 1880.
*Dg* = T. R. Grantham, Dorking Congregationalism, 1903.
*Dk* = T. W. Downing, Records of Knowle, 1914.
*Dn* = J. Dunkin, Hist. of Bicester, 1816.
*Do* = A Dreadful Oration, 1683 (skit on S. Lobb).
*Dq* = Don Quixot Redivivus [1673].
*Dr* = Dukinfield Chapel Register (*S.H.*).
*Ds* = J. S. Davies, Hist. of Southampton, 1883.
*Du* = J. Dunton, Life and Errors (1705) reprint, 1818.
*Dw* = Dugdale, Warwickshire, ed. Thomas.
*D.W.L.* = Dr. Williams' Library.
*Dy* = F. Drake's Eboracum, 1736.

*E* = Davids, Nonconformity in Essex, 1863.
*Ed* = Catalogue, Edinburgh Graduates, 1858.
*Ek* = E. D. P. Evans, Hist. New Meeting, Kidderminster, 1900.
*Em* = MS. Minutes, Exeter Assembly (*D.W.L.*).
*En* = Encyclopaedia Britannica, eleventh edition.
*Ev* = Evans' List, *i.e.* MS. Statistics of Dissent, 1715–29 (*D.W.L.*).

*F* = Foster, Alumni Oxon., Early Series.
*Fc* = MS. Minutes, Fourth London Classis (*D.W.L.*).
*Fl* = John Flavell's Remains, 1691.
*Fo* = W. C. Fowler, Memorials of the Chaunceys, 1858.
*Fp* = G. Fox, Park Lane Chapel, 1897.
*Fr* = List of R. Frankland's Students (in E. Latham's Preparation for Death, 1745).

*G* = Gardiner, Registers of Wadham Coll., 1889, etc.
*Ga* = A. Gordon, Dukinfield Chapel, 1896.

*Gb* = W. R. Clark-Lewis, Beaumont Street Church, Gainsborough, 1912.
*Gc* = Venn, Biog. Hist. Gonville and Caius Coll., 1897.
*Gd* = A. Gordon, Dob Lane Chapel, 1904.
*Gl* = Norman Glass, Hist. Indep. Church, Rothwell, 1871.
*Gm* = Munimenta Univ. Glasg., 1854.
*Go* = A. Gordon, Heads, Eng. Unitarian Hist., 1895.
*Gr* = Great and Good News to Ch. of Eng., 1700.

*H* = Hunter, Fam. Min. Gentium, 1894–5.
*Ha* = J. B. Marsh, Story of Harecourt, 1871.
*Hc* = Clutterbuck, Hist. Co. Hertford., 1815–27.
*He* = Hennessy, Nov. Repertorium Londin., 1898.
*Hh* = Hunter, Oliver Heywood, 1845.
*Hl* = Halley, Lancashire Nonconformity, 1869.
*Hn* = T. Hall, Apologia pro Ministerio Anglicano, 1658.
*Ho* = T. W. Horsfield, Sussex, 1835.
*Hp* = H. Pigot, Hadleigh, 1860.
*Hs* = R. T. Herford, Memorials, Stand Chapel, 1893.
*Ht* = Horsfall Turner, O. Heywood's Diaries, 1882–5.
*Hu* = Hutchins, Hist. of Dorset, 1861–73.
*Hw* = W. M. Harvey, Hundred of Willey, 1872–8.
*Hx* = John Watson, Hist. of Halifax, 1775.

*I* = Inscriptions in Bunhill Fields, 1717.
*It* = J. Horsfall Turner, Nonconformity in Idle, 1876.

*J* = T. Smith James, Hist. Litigation Presb. Chapels, 1867
*Je* = W. D. Jeremy, Presbyterian Fund, 1885.
*Jo* = Admissions to St. John's Coll., Camb., 1893.
*Jp* = Journal, Presb. Hist. Soc., England, May 1916.
*Jw* = J. Wonnacott, Hist. Morley Old Chapel, 1859.

*K* = Hasted, Kent, 1778–99.

*L* = True Acct. of Taking of Mr Lobb, 1683.
*La* = Lansdowne M.S. 459 (*B.M.*).
*Lc* = W. Lewis, Hist. Cong. Ch., Cockermouth, 1870.
*Ld* = Little London Directory, 1677 (reprint, 1863).
*Le* = Le Neve, Fasti, 1854.
*Lh* = T. W. Horsfield, Hist. of Lewes, 1824.
*Ll* = W. Lloyd, Hist. Barton St. Chapel, Gloucester, 1899.
*Lm* = R. Masters, Hist. Corpus Christi Coll., Camb., ed. Lamb, 1831.
*Ln* = J. Nichols, Leicestershire, 1790.
*Lo* = H. B. Wheatley, London Past and Present, 1891.
*Lr* = J. P. Longstaff, Hist. Cong. Ch., Romford, 1913.
*Ls* = Wm. Salt Library, Stafford, "Account of the Province of Canterbury, 1676" (Shropshire entries printed by W. G. D. Fletcher, 1891).
*Ly* = Lysons, Environs of London, 1792–1811.
*Lz* = Lysons, Parishes in Middlesex, 1800.

*M* = MS. Minutes in possession of Presb. Board (*D.W.L.*).
*Ma* = J. E. Manning, Hist. Upper Chapel, Sheffield, 1900.
*Mc* = Cotton Mather, Magnalia Christi Americana, 1702.
*Mh* = J. Murch, Presb. and G. B. Churches, West of Eng., 1835.
*Ml* = Maitland, London, 1756.
*Mn* = Manning, Surrey, 1804–14.
*Mo* = Mem. of R. Mayo, 1912.
*Mp* = J. O. Payne, Family of Malthus, 1890.
*Mr* = *Monthly Repository.*
*Ms* = Mensalia Sacra, 1693.
*Mu* = Munk, Roll of Coll. of Physicians, 1878.
*Mw* = D. Mayo, Fun. Sermon for J. Waters, 1725.
*My* = J. G. Miall, Congregationalism in Yorkshire, 1868.

*N* = B. Nightingale, Ejected of Cumberland, 1911.
*Na* = Nash, Worcestershire, 1781–99.
*Nb* = Blomefield, Norfolk, 1805–62.
*Nc* = Newcourt, Repertorium, 1708–10.
*Nh* = J. Nichols, Hist. Hinckley, 1813.
*Nk* = F. Nicholson and E. Axon, Nonconformity in Kendal, 1915.
*Nl* = B. Nightingale, Lancashire Nonconformity, 1890–3.
*Nm* = W. Money, Hist. of Newbury, 1905.
*Nn* = J. W. Robinson, Ministers at Alston Moor, 1909.
*No* = B. Carpenter, Presbyterianism in Nottingham, 1862.
*Np* = Bridges, Northamptonshire, 1791.
*Nq* = *Notes and Queries.*
*Nr* = Northowram Register, ed. J. Horsfall Turner, 1881.
*Nt* = B. Nightingale, Hist. Indep. Chapel, Tockholes, 1886.

*O* = W. J. Odgers, Hist. Plymouth Unitarian Congr., 1850.
*Oc* = Ormerod, Cheshire, 1882.
*Od* = W. Densham and J. Ogle, Cong. Churches of Dorset, 1999 (*sic*).
*Om* = J. M. Connell, Story of Old Meeting Ho. [Lewes], 1916.

*P* = Palmer, Nonconformists' Memorial, 2nd Edn., 1802–3.
*Pa* = S. Palmer, Defence of Dissenters' Education, 1703.
*Pc* = B. Poole, Hist. Coventry, 1870.
*Pd* = Peck, Desiderata Curiosa, 1779, p. 505.
*Pe* = G. E. C., Complete Peerage, 1888–98.
*Ph* = T. A. Walker, Admissions to Peterhouse, 1912.
*Pi* = G. Pickford, Hist. Congleton Unitarian Chapel, 1883.
*Pn* = J. S. Pearsall, Outlines Congregationalism, Andover, 1844.
*Po* = Polwhele, Hist. Devonshire, 1806.
*Pr* = Prince, Worthies of Devon, 1701.
*Ps* = T. Whitaker, Sermons (posthumous), 1712.
*Pu* = P. Cunningham, Handbook of London, 1850.
*Pw* = A. N. Palmer, Nonconformity of Wrexham, 1888.

*Q* = Journal, Friends' Hist. Society.

*R* = True Acct., Rye House Plot, 1685.
*Ra* = T. Reynold, Life of J. Ashwood, 1707.
*Rb* = W. Blazeby, Rotherham, 1906.
*Rc* = W. Richardson, South Cave Parish Registers, 1909.
*Re* = J. S. Reid, Hist. Presb. Ch., Ireland, 3rd edn., vol. ii. App. iii.
*Rg* = Rudder, Gloucestershire, 1779.
*Ri* = J. S. Reid, Hist. Presb. Congregations, Ireland, 1886.
*Rj* = Information from Rev. Rees Jenkin Jones, Aberdare.
*Rl* = H. D. Roberts, Hope Street Church, Liverpool, 1909.
*Rp* = A. Peel, Seconde Parte of a Register, 1915.
*Rq* = *Reliquary*, xvi. 75.
*Rr* = Registrum Regale, 1847.
*Rs* = T. Richmond, Hist. Nonconf. Stockton, 1856.
*Rt* = Rivington Chapel Bicentenary, 1903.
*Rw* = T. Rees, Prot. Nonconformity in Wales, 1883.
*Ry* = List of Conspirators, Rye House Plot, 1683.

*S* = W. A. Shaw, Knights of England, 1906.
*Sa* = R. B. Wheler, Hist. Stratford-upon-Avon [1806].
*Sb* = Summers, Congr. Churches, Berks, Bucks, So. Oxon., 1905.
*Sc* = Manchester Socinian Controversy, 1825 [ed. by J. Birt; List of Chapels, by R. Slate].
*Sd* = Surtees, Durham, 1806–40.
*Sf* = Hew Scott, Fasti Eccl. Scot., 1876–81.
*Sg* = J. L. Sibley, Graduates of Harvard, 1873, etc.
*S.H.* = Somerset House.
*Sh* = H. Sharpe, Addition, 1912, to Hist. Rosslyn Hill Congn., 1909.
*Si* = J. Sibree and M. Caston, Independency in Warwickshire, 1855.
*Sl* = Stow, Survey of London, ed. Strype, 1720.
*Sm* = J. Smith, Bibliotheca Anti-Quakeriana, 1873.
*Sp* = J. Stedman, Presbyterian Priestcraft, 1720.
*Sq* = W. Smith, Morley Ancient and Modern, 1886.
*Sr* = W. Smith, Registers of Topcliffe, 1888.
*Ss* = Steven, Hist. Scot. Ch., Rotterdam, 1832.
*St* = Stow, Survey of London, ed. Kingsford, 1908.
*Su* = E. Taylor, Suffolk Bartholomeans, 1840.
*Sw* = G. C. Moore Smith, Extracts, T. Woodcock's Papers, 1907.
*Sx* = W. A. Shaw, Manchester Classis, 1890–91.
*Sy* = W. A. Shaw, Bury Classis, 1896–8.

*T* = G. Lyon Turner, Original Records, Nonconformity, 1911–14.
*Tb* = Pishey Thompson, Boston, 1856.
*Tc* = Ball and Venn, Admissions, Trinity Coll., Camb., 1913.
*Td* = C. Twamley, MS. Hist. Wolverhampton St. Chapel, Dudley (*penes A. G.*).
*Th* = Thornbury, Old and New London, vol. ii. [1879].
*Ti* = J. Horsfall Turner, Nonconformity in Idle, 1876.
*To* = J. Toulmin, Historical View, 1814.
*Ts* = J. Toulmin, Mem. of S. Bourn, 1808.
*Tt* = J. Toulmin, Hist. of Taunton, ed. J. Savage, 1822.
*Tw* = W. Tong, Dedication to J. Warren's Fun. Serm. for J. Merrel, 1716.

*U* = Album Studiosorum, Utrecht, 1886.
*Uc* = Urwick, Cheshire, 1864.
*Ue* = *Unitarian Herald*, 5th Aug. 1887.
*Ug* = Grounds and Occasions of the Controversy concerning the Unity of God, 1698.
*Uh* = Urwick, Herts, 1884.
*Uw* = Urwick, Worcester, 1897.

*V* = Venn, Matriculations and Degrees, Cambridge, 1913.

*W* = Wilson, Dissenting Churches, London, 1808–14.
*Wa* = R. Wallace, in Hist. Chesterfield, 1839.
*Wb* = J. R. Wreford, Presb. Nonconformity, Birmingham, 1832.
*Wc* = Walker, Sufferings of the Clergy, 1714.
*We* = Wilson's MS. E. (*D.W.L.*).
*Wg* = E. L. Glew, Hist. Walsall, 1856.
*Wh* = J. Whitehead, Hist. Gravel Pit Chapel, Hackney, 1889.
*Wi* = T. Witherow, Hist. and Lit. Mem. of Presb., Ireland, 1879.
*Wj* = J. C. Wedgwood, Wedgwood Family, 1909.
*Wk* = E. R. Wharton, Whartons of Wharton Hall, 1898.
*Wl* = C. Wicksteed, Memory of the Just, Mill-Hill Chap., Leeds, 1849.
*Wm* = Tho. Whitaker, Sermons and Memoir, 1712.
*Wn* = W. T. Whitley, Baptists of North-West England, 1913.
*Wo* = Wood, Athenae Oxon., ed. Bliss, 1813–20.
*Wp* = W. Whitaker, Puritan Tradition at Hull, 1910.
*Wr* = Wimbish Parish Register.
*Ws* = J. Waddington, Surrey Congr. History, 1866.
*Wu* = A. L. Humphreys, Materials for Hist. of Wellington, Part iii., 1913.
*Ww* = W. Whiston, Memoirs, 1749.
*Wy* = J. Waylen, House of Cromwell, ed. J. G. Cromwell, 1897.
*Wz* = List of Queen's Scholars, Westminster, 1852.

*X* = MS. Extracts, by Rev. Dr. Nightingale, Preston, from records of Lancashire Quarter Sessions.

*Y* = B. Dale, Yorkshire Puritanism, 1910.

*Z* = J. Brownbill, Lancaster Jottings, iii. (Trans. Hist. Soc. Lanc. & Ches., 1915).

# INDEX

ABERGAVENNY ('Abergaveney,' 'Abergaynie'), Monm.; misplaced in Heref. Ejected here in 1660 was . . . Abbot. **C.** [48, 124]

ABERLLYNFI ('Aberllynvy'), then a parish, now a hamlet in Glasbury parish, Brec. [143]

ABERNETHY, JOHN, M.A. (19 O. 1680–Dec. 1740). **P.** Born at Brigh, Co. Tyrone. Son of John Abernethy (d. 1703), then Presbyterian Minister there. Educ. in arts at Glasgow (graduating M.A.) and in divinity at Edinburgh, and further in Dublin. Minister at Antrim, ordained 8 Aug. 1703. Removed to Wood Street, Dublin, in 1730. His sermon on "Religious Obedience" was delivered in Belfast on 9 D. 1719, at a meeting of the Belfast Society, founded (1705) for ministerial interchange of thought on sacred subjects.

John Abernethy, F.R.S. (3 Ap. 1764—28 Ap. 1831), the eminent London surgeon, was his grandson. (*Wi.*) [155]

ABINGDON ('Abington'). [68]

ABNEY, SIR THOMAS (Jan. 1639/40—6 F. 1722). **P.** Born at Willesley, Derbysh.; fourth son of James Abney, high sheriff of Derbyshire (1656). Educated at Loughborough. Member of the congregation of John Howe, M.A. [*q.v.*]. Knighted 2 N. 1693. Attended the meeting of Managers of the Common Fund on 3 N. 1690, but was not appointed Manager till 2 Mar. 1690/1, replacing . . . Waytes [*q.v.*]; appointed Correspondent for Derbyshire, 11 Jan. 1691/2, in room of Henry Coape [*q.v.*]; his last attendance was on 10 Oct. 1692; at midsummer, 1693, his subscription was in arrear; he was reappointed Manager in 1695, but did not attend. An original director (1694) of the Bank of England; Lord Mayor, 1700–1; M.P. for London, 1701–2. He it was who, on the death of James II., carried in face of much opposition an address to the Crown from the Common Council of London renouncing the Pretender, an example which "spirited the whole nation" and was followed by the Act for abjuring the Pretender. From 1712 he entertained as permanent guest Isaac Watts, D.D. [*q.v.*]; hence it has been inferred that his later leanings were toward the Congregationals; the facts stated in the funeral sermon by Jeremiah Smith disprove this. His daughter Sarah married Joseph Caryl, M.A. [*q.v.*]. His estate, Abney Park, Stoke Newington, was in part converted (1840) into a general cemetery. (*Cm. D. M.*) [162, 165, 168]

ACADEMIES. [182]

ACHAM. [16, 89] *See* Shropshire

ACTON. Ejected here was Thomas Elford, of St. Mary Hall, Oxford; matric. 13 Dec. 1633, aged 19; B.A., 1635; rector of West Monkton, Som., 1653; rector of Acton, 1657; ejected, 1660. (*C. F.*) [73]

ADAMS, TOBIAS (*fl.* 1660–92). **P.** Vicar of Wembden, Som.; ejected. Licensed 5 S. 1672, as "Pr. Teacher" in his house at Middlezoy, Som. (*C. P. T.*) [93, 94]

ADBOLTON. [83]

AI. [106, 107] *See* Suffolk

ALBIN, HENRY (20 June 1624—25 S. 1696). **P.** Born at Batcombe, Som. From Glastonbury Grammar School went to study at Oxford University, but apparently did not matriculate. Held from 1646(?) the sequestered rectory of West Camel, Som.; ejected, 1660; rector of Donyatt, Som.; ejected, 1662. Thereafter he lived in Batcombe parish. The Episc. Returns, 1669, report him as one of the preachers to 300 persons "At the house of Thomas Moore, Esq[r]" in Batcombe parish; also as one of the preachers to 300 persons at Glastonbury "In a Barne, belonging to John Austin, where a Pulpitt and seats are built." Licensed, 5 S. 1672, as "Pr. Teacher of Spar grave," where the house (licensed) of Thomas Moore was situated. In 1687 he became preacher in rotation at Frome Selwood, Shepton Mallet, Bruton, and Wincanton. (*C. D. P. T. Wc.*) [92, 93]

ALCESTER. Ejected here was Samuel Tickner, matric. at Peterhouse, Cambridge, 1644; B.A., 1645/6 (*V.*). *See* Joseph Porter. [117]

ALDBOROUGH ('Albrough') HATCH, chapelry in Ilford parish, Ess. [38]

ALDRED. *See* Alured

ALEXANDER, DANIEL (1660—3 Sept. 1709). **P.** Studied under Charles Morton and Edward Veal [*q.v.*] (one or both); Assistant to Samuel Slater, M.A. [*q.v.*], at Crosby Hall, Bishopsgate, 1693–1704. Minister at Armourers' Hall, Coleman Street, 1704, till death. Published

Funeral Sermon (Job v. 26) for Slater, 1704, 4to. (*W.*) [1]

ALLEINE, JOSEPH, B.A. (1633—17 Nov. 1668). **P.** Younger son of Tobias Alleine, Devizes, Wilts. Entered Ap. 1649 at Lincoln Coll., Oxford; removed to Corpus Christi Coll.; matric. 14 N. 1651; scholar, 1651; chaplain, 1653; B.A., 1653. Ordained by presbyters (1655) as assistant to George Newton, M.A., at St. Mary Magdalen's, Taunton, Som.; both were ejected, 1662. Suffered many imprisonments as a "conventicler." His posthumous "Alarme to Unconverted Sinners," 1672, still in print, is a classic of evangelical appeal. (*C. D. F. P.*) [188]

ALLEN, JOHN? **C.** In Feb. 1672/3 was granted "Licence to John Allen, Congr. Teachr., at the house of Elizabeth King of Radwell in Bedfordsh." Radwell is in Herts, though near the boundary; Barley, though at some distance, is in the same northern part of Herts. (*T.*) [50]

ALLEN . . . [38]

ALLINGTON ('Alton'), South Wilts. Allington is meant (*see* Crofts, John); not Alton Barnes, from the rectory of which was ejected, in 1662, Obadiah Wills (son of Richard, of Sherbourne, Dors.), of Exeter Coll., Oxford; matric. 8 July 1642, aged 17; M.A., 1649; Fellow of New Coll., 1649; licensed, 30 Apr. 1672, as Grāll Congr. Teacher, being then of Devizes (near Alton Barnes). Walker says he got hold of the chapelry of Alton Priors by informing against the incumbent; this chapelry now goes with Alton Barnes. (*C. F.*)

ALRESFORD ('Alsford'). Ejected here was . . . Taylor. (*C.*) [102]

ALREWAS. Ejected here was Thomas Bladen [*q.v.*] [96]

ALSFORD. [102] *See* Hampshire

ALSISTON. [115] *See* Sussex

ALSOP, VINCENT, M.A. (?) (1630—8 May 1703). **P.** Son of George Alsop, rector of Collingham, Notts. From Uppingham grammar school admitted sizar 13 S. 1647, aged 17, at St. John's Coll., Cambridge; matric., 1647/8; no record of graduation; described as M.A. Ordained as an Anglican deacon, he became assistant in the grammar school at Oakham, Rutland, where the vicar, Benjamin King (appointed 1646, resigned 1660), cured him of rollicking ways, and led him to receive Presbyterian ordination. He was appointed (1655?) rector of Wilby, Northants, succeeding Andrew Perne (*d.* Dec. 1654). Ejected, 1662, he preached, under penalties, at Oakham and Wellingborough, Northants. His repeated application for a licence for a room over the school at Wellingborough was not granted; on 13 May 1672 he was licensed as a Congr. Teacher in his house at Geddington, Northants, whither he had removed from Wellingborough. He succeeded Thomas Cawton, B.A. (*d.* 10 Apr. 1677), as Minister of the Presbyterian congregation in Tothill Street, Westminster. On the issue of James II.'s Declaration for Liberty of Conscience, he went far in his approaches to that monarch, who, however, had earned his gratitude by pardoning some "treasonable practices" of his son. In 1685 he succeeded William Jenkyn, M.A. [*q.v.*], as a Pinners' Hall Lecturer, resigning (1694) on the expulsion of Daniel Williams, D.D. [*q.v.*], and becoming a Salters' Hall Lecturer. An original Manager of the Common Fund, and a strong supporter of the Happy Union, his bluff and tart humour, chiefly under a thin veil of anonymity, enlivened controversy; of this the most notable specimen is his anonymous "Anti-Sozzo," 1675, in which he trounces William Sherlock, who had disparaged the theology of Nonconformist leaders. Living to a ripe age, Alsop retained "his spirits and his smartness" to the last. John Lacy, who in 1706 fell in with the French Prophets, was a wealthy member of his flock. (*C. D. Jo. P. T. V. W.*) [68, 77, 87, 154, 158, 160, 164, 165, 168, 181, 186]

ALSOP, WILLIAM (*fl.* 1660–93). Held the sequestered vicarage of Ilminster, Som.; ejected, 1660. The Episc. Returns, 1669, report him among preachers to 400 persons at various houses in and about West Monkton, Som.; also to 200 persons at the houses of Henry Henly, Esq., and John Bennett, Winsham, Som.; also to 40 persons at Aisholt, Som.; also to 180 persons at Broadway, Som. He was voted, 1690, a grant of £5 a year for Beaconsfield "if he stay." By 20 Ap. 1691, he had removed to Barnet, Herts, where he received an annual grant of £6, 1691–3. "He lived and died in or near London." (*C. M. P. T. Wc.*) [10]

ALSTON MOORE. [79]

ALTHAM ('Altam'), chapelry in Whalley parish, Lanc., now vicarage. Ejected here was Thomas Jollie [*q.v.*]. [61]

ALTON, Hants. [101]

ALTON. [103] *See* Wiltshire

ALURED, *i.e.* ALDRED, JEREMIAH (1661—26 Aug. 1729). **P.** Son of James Aldred (*d.* Jan. 1718/9) of Monton. Entered Frankland's Academy, 18 June 1680. Ordained at Attercliffe, 12 S.

1688, probably for Horwich Chapel, parish of Deane, which was recovered for Nonconformists through the influence of Lord Willoughby and by connivance of Richard Hatton, vicar of Deane from 1673. Horwich New Chapel was not built by Nonconformists till 1716. Aldred was in the Bolton Classis of United Ministers till 1699, when, on the death of Thomas Crompton [*q.v.*], he succeeded him at Monton. In 1706, 1708, and 1709, the Fund made a grant of £5 to "Mr. Alread at Ekles" (spelled also Alreed and Alred). (*Hh. M. Nk. Nl.*) [62]

ALVASTON. [27]

ALVERTHORPE ('Alverthorp,' 'Aterthorpe,' 'Attérthorp'). [129, 130]

AMBROSE, ISAAC, M.A. (May 1604–Jan. 1663/4). Born at Ormskirk, Lanc., where his father was vicar. Matric. 2 N. 1621 at Brasenose Coll., Oxford, aged 17; B.A., 1624/5; incorp. M.A. at Cambridge, 1631/2. Vicar of Castleton, Derb., 1627–1631; one of the four 'king's preachers' for Lancashire, 1631; vicar of Preston, Lanc., 1640; vicar of Garstang, Lanc., 1654; ejected, 1662. Buried at Preston, 25 Jan. Halley names him the most meditative Puritan of Lancashire. (*C. D. F. Hl. P.*) [188]

AMIRANT, *i.e.* AMYRAUT, CHRISTOPHER, B.A. (*fl.* 1660–90). **C.** Apparently son of Paul Amyraut, of German birth; ejected (1660?) from the sequestered rectory of Mundesley, Norf. Matric. at Jesus Coll., Cambridge, 1649; B.A., 1652/3. Vicar of New Buckenham, Norf.; ejected (1662). The Episc. Returns, 1669, report him as one of the preachers at Trunch, Norf. (*see* Green, John); also as preaching at Sidestrand, Norf., at the house of one Clarke, sometimes at Overstrand at the hall place belonging to Mrs. Reimes. Licensed, 10 June 1672, as "Congr. Teacher in Sam: Knights howse in Overstrand, Norfolk." In 1675 he was a member of the Congregational church at Guestwick, Norf. He succeeded John Lougher (*d.* 14 O. 1686) as pastor of the Congregational church at Southrepps, Norf. He probably lived at Northrepps. He died before 1697, when the Southrepps membership was transferred to Tunstead, Norf. (*B. C. P. T. V.*) [74]

ANABAPTISTS. [10, 23, 42, 46, 48, 79, 81, 102, 147]

ANDERTON, ROGER (*d.* Apr. 1705). **P.** Born near Bolton, Lanc. Entered Frankland's Academy at Rathmel, 3 May or 3 June 1684. Ordained, 7 June 1693, as Minister at Whitehaven. His name appears in trust-deed (12 Feb. 1694/5) of Chapel erected 1694 as "a chapel that shall be used, so long as the law will allow, by Protestant Dissenters from the Church of England, whether Presbyterian or Congregational, according to their way and persuasion." He received, 1696–1703, £4 a year for Whitehaven from the Fund. In 1704 he removed to Newcastle-on-Tyne. (*Cu.* (19 *Aug.* 1876), *Fr. Hh. Lf. M. Nk. Nr. Rl.*) [63, 64]

ANDOVER. [100]

ANGIER, SAMUEL (1659?–20 F. 1697/8). **C.** ? Son of John Angier, M.A., vicar of Deane, Lanc.; grandson of John Angier (1605–1677) of Denton; wife's nephew of Oliver Heywood [*q.v.*]. Entered Frankland's Academy, 24 Ap. 1676. Ordained 1 June 1687, at Oliver Heywood's house, probably for Toxteth Park, where he ministered in conjunction with Christopher Richardson [*q.v.*], who began work in Liverpool in that year. Angier seems to have ministered to the Congregational church, in succession to Michael Briscoe (*see* Crompton, Thomas), and as he married Briscoe's daughter he was probably assisting at Toxteth Park before ordination; Richardson ministered to the Presbyterians; both bodies used the same Chapel. In July 1689 Angier registered the New Chapel, Castle Hey, Liverpool, and Toxteth Park Chapel for Prot. Diss. worship. In 1697 the house of Mary Briscoe in Toxteth Park was similarly registered. He remained at Toxteth till death. (*Hh. Nk. Rl.* (needs correction), *Wl. X.*) [58, 59]

ANGLESEY. [141, 148]

ANN'S LANE, *i.e.* [Great] St. Anne's Lane, Great Peter Street, Westminster. Here Robert Herrick, the poet, sequestered from the vicarage of Dean Prior, Devon, lived as a layman from 1647 to the Revolution. Parallel with it was Little St. Anne's Lane. (*Lo.*) [4]

ANNESLEY, SAMUEL, D.C.L. (1620/1–31 Dec. 1696). **P.** Born at Kenilworth. Only child of John Anneley of Haseley, Warw., 'pleb.' This (confirmed by his funeral sermon) disposes of the statement that he was nephew of Arthur Annesley (1614–86), first Earl of Anglesey, son of Sir Francis Annesley of Newport Pagnell, Bucks, afterwards Viscount Valentia. From Coventry grammar school he matric. (as Anneley), 21 Oct. 1636, at Queen's Coll., Oxford, aged 15; B.A., 1639; D.C.L., 1648. Possibly ordained as Anglican deacon. Ordained in London by presbyters, 18 Dec. 1644, as chaplain to Robert Rich, Earl of

Warwick, Lord High Admiral, on board the *Globe*; later he was with Warwick during the expedition to Holland. In 1645 (?) he obtained the rectory of Cliffe-at-Hoo, Kent, sequestered from Griffith Higges, D.D.; this he resigned in 1657, becoming lecturer at St. Paul's Cathedral, and (1658) vicar of St. Giles', Cripplegate, to which he obtained, 23 Aug. 1660, a new (the third) presentation from Charles II. Ejected in 1662, he continued to preach. The Episc. Returns, 1669, report him as preaching to 800 Presbyterians "In Spittlefeilds at a New House built for that purpose, w[th] Pulpit & Seates." At the time of Indulgence, Annesley was a leader of the "Ducklings," whose influence was with the middle classes (*see* Bates, William). On 2 Apr. 1672, he was licensed as Presb. Teacher in the above building, "his owne howse in Spittle Fields." This is the meeting-house, "with three good galleries," later described as at or near Little St. Helen's (now St. Helen's Place). Here Annesley ministered till death; here the meetings of the Ministers in the Happy Union were held; and here the first Nonconformist public ordination was held, 22 June 1694 (*see* Reynolds, Thomas). Daniel Defoe was a member of his flock. Being a man of good estate, Annesley devoted a tenth of his income to charitable uses. He married a daughter of John White (known as 'Century White') and had a numerous family; asked how many, he estimated them at either two dozen or a quarter of a hundred; but only a son, Benjamin, and two daughters survived him. His daughter Elizabeth was the first wife of John Dunton [*q.v.*], his youngest daughter, Susanna, married Samuel Wesley, and had nineteen children, among them being John [*q.v.*] and Charles, the founders of Methodism. Annesley was a near relative of Thomas Fuller, the church historian and humorist. (*C. Cm. Cw. D. F. M. P. Pe. Rt. T. W.*) [112, 123, 157 (Meeting House), 160, 163, 164, 165, 166, 168, 169, 181, 189]

ANTHONY'S, *i.e.* St. Anthony's Church, in Budge Row (*budge* is lambskin, dressed with the wool outward). Stow gives St. Anthonie as the saint to whom the church was dedicated; Strype gives St. Anthonine, vulgarly St. Antlin. Hence the modern form St. Antholin. The church, rebuilt as an oval, by Wren, was taken down in Sept. 1874. (*Lo. Sl. St.*) [2]

ANTI-ARMINIAN. [13]

ANTINOMIAN. [156, 185]

ANTIPAEDOBAPTISTS. A curious expression, since *pais* does not imply infancy. All Baptists are Paedobaptists on occasion, though not Brephobaptists. [51]

ANTRIM. [155]

APPLEBY, Leic. [67]

APPLEDORE. [31]

ARMINIANS. [42]

ARMITAGE. Ejected here was Nathaniel Mansfield, M.A. [*q.v.*]. [96]

ARMITAGE, JOHN (1632—22 Apr. 1700). **P.** His house at Kirkburton, *i.e.* at Lydgate [*q.v.*] in Wooldale township, Kirkburton parish, Yorks, was licensed, 5 Sept. 1672, for Presbyterian worship. He married Mary Moorehouse on 21 July 1679. His house at "Waldale, Lydgate" (*see above*) was certified for Nonconformist worship on 31 July 1689. He was a special friend of Oliver Heywood [*q.v.*]. (*Hy. Nr. T.*) [132]

ARMTHORPE, Yorks, W.R. (misplaced in E.R.). [139]

ARTILLERY GROUND, the New, was laid out in 1641 in Upper Moorfields, being "the third great Field from *Moorgate* next to the six Windmills." It lies between Bunhill Row and Finsbury Square, with entrance in Chiswell Street. (*Lo. Sl.*) [3]

ARTILLERY GROUND, the Old, is now represented by Artillery Lane (which runs from the east side of Bishopsgate Without) and by Artillery Passage and Gun Street (which run North from Artillery Lane). Stow says the ground was formerly called Tasell Close, "for that there were Tasels [teasels] planted for the vse of Clothworkers"; thereafter it was let to the crossbow-makers for practice; at length, being walled, it was made an Artillery Yard or Garden for the Fraternity of Artillery, chartered by Henry VIII. (*Lo. Sl. St.*) [4]

ARUNDEL ('Arundell'). Ejected here was John Goldwire or Gouldwyer (from Surrey, pleb.), of All Souls' Coll., Oxford; matric., 2 Nov. 1621, aged 18; B.A., 1624; appointed rector of Milbrooke, Hants, 1646; vicar of Arundel, ejected, 1662; taught school with his son (*see below*), first at Broadlands, afterwards at Baddesley, both near Romsey, Hants; licensed, June 1672, as Pr. Teacher in a house at Romsey; *d.* 22 May 1696 in 88th year. (*C. F. T.*) John Goldwire, the son, matric. (pensioner) at Queen's Coll., Cambridge, 1647; entered (subs.) at New Inn Hall, Oxford, 20 June 1651; B.A., 21 June 1651; M.A., 1654; vicar of Felpham, Suss., ejected, 1662; lived latterly at Romsey, Hants, and preached there nineteen years (*d.* 9 Dec. 1713, aged 83). (*C. F. V.*) [112]

ASHBOURNE ('Ashburn'). [28, 29]

ASHBURNHAM. [180]

ASHBURTON. Ejected here was Joshua Bowden, of Exeter Coll., Oxford; matric., 1 Apr. 1642, aged 17; rem. to Magdalen Hall; M.A., 1648; Fellow of Wadham Coll., 1648; rector of Ashburton, 1661; ejected, 1662; conformed, and became vicar of Frampton, Dors., 1664; *d.* 1 July 1686. (*C. F. Hu.*) [31]

ASHBY-DE-LA-ZOUCH. [67]

ASHFORD, Derb. [26]

ASHFORD, Kent. Ejected here was Nicholas Prigg, M.A. [*q.v.*]. [55]

ASHHURST, *i.e.* ASHURST, SIR HENRY (8 Sept. 1645—13 Apr. 1711). **P.** Of Waterstock House, Oxon. Born in London. Eldest son of Henry Ashurst (1614 ?–Nov. 1680), merchant and Alderman, and himself a merchant of London. Father and sons were great friends of Richard Baxter [*q.v.*]. M.P. for Truro, 1681–95; created a baronet, 21 July 1688; appointed a Manager (1695) of the reconstituted Fund, but did not attend; M.P. for Wilton, Wilts, 1698–1702. Buried at Waterstock. (*Ba. D. M.*) [164]

ASHHURST, . . . **P.** Proposed as Manager by Daniel Williams [*q.v.*] on 29 July 1690; attended no meeting. In all probability this was William Ashhurst [*q.v.*], whose appointment as Book-keeper took place on 4 Aug. 1690. (*Cm. M.*) Other contemporaries of this surname were (*a*) Henry Ashurst, son of Sir William Ashurst [*q.v.*]; educ. (1686) under Samuel Cradock [*q.v.*]; became Town Clerk of London; (*b*) Henry Ashurst (*d.* 17 May 1732), studied (1691) at Utrecht; succeeded his father, Sir Henry Ashurst [*q.v.*], as baronet. (*Ba. D. M.*) [162]

ASHHURST, WILLIAM, the Book-keeper. (*M.*) [162, 169, 170, 172, 173, 175]

ASHHURST, *i.e.* ASHURST, SIR WILLIAM. Born in London. Second son of Henry Ashurst (1614 ?–1680). Knighted 31 Oct. 1689; Lord Mayor of London, 1693. He was not a contributor to the Fund. (*D. M. S.*) [4]

ASHLEY. The margination 'Lestershere' seems a confusion between this place and Ashby Magna (*see* Clarke, Matthew). [76]

ASHLING. [113]

ASHTON. [120] *See* Warwickshire

ASHTON IN MAKERFIELD ('Mackerfield'). Ejected here in 1662 was James Wood, perpetual curate in 1648; *d.* 10 Feb. 1666/7; father of James Wood [*q.v.*]. (*C. D. Nl.*) [58, 60]

ASHWOOD, JOHN (1657—22 S. 1706). **C.** Born at Axminster, Devon; son of Bartholomew Ashwood, B.A., ejected, 1662, from the rectory of Bickleigh and vicarage of Axminster, Devon. Educated under Theophilus Gale [*q.v.*] at Newington Green. Taught school at Axminster, then at Chard, Som. Removed, under pressure, to Haverland, Norf., and arranged to leave for America in Jan. 1683/4. Prevented by illness, he removed to Weston, parish of Combe St. Nicholas, Som., and thence to one of the Bucklands. He now had a call to Exeter, was ordained, and ministered there for ten years (1689–99 ?). On 26 June 1693 the Common Fund made him a grant of £2. Called to London, for about two years he preached in the morning at Hoxton, in the evening at Spitalfields, moving finally to a charge at Peckham, Surrey. His last sermon was on a visit in failing health to his former flock at Exeter. (*M. Ra.*) [30]

ASPINWALL, PETER, B.A. (1636–June 1696). **P.** Son of a clergyman. Matric. at Brasenose Coll., Oxford, 25 July 1655; B.A., 1658/9. Ejected from the living of Heaton [? Huyton] in Lancashire. Licensed, 16 May 1672, as "Pr. Teacher in the howse of John Robinson," Ashton-in-Makerfield, Lanc. In July 1689 he registered the house in Warrington of Laurence Eccleston for Prot. Diss. worship. (*Nl. T. X.*) [58]

ASPINWALL, WILLIAM, B.A. (*d.* 1703 ?). **P.** Born in Lancashire. Matric. at Magdalene Coll., Cambridge, 1654; B.A., 1657. Ordained by presbyters at Clayworth, Notts. Vicar of Maghull, Lanc., in 1648; vicar, 1655/6, of Mattersey, Notts; indicted, 1661, for not reading Common Prayer (Notts Co. Records); ejected, 1662. Took to farming at Thurnscoe, Yorks. Licensed, 1 May 1672, on petition of parishioners of Winwick, as "Pr. Teacher" in the "outhowesinge" of Richard Birchall in Winwick parish. For Shierstead (Sheerestead, Shierside, Shireshead) *see* Shire Head. The Common Fund granted him (1693) £6 a year for Sheerestead, reduced in 1695 to £4, and ending 25 Dec. 1702. (*C. D. Hh. M. Nl. P. V. X. Y.*) [58]

ASTLEY, RICHARD (1640–1696). **C.** Born near Manchester. Educ. at Manchester grammar school. His father meant him for trade, but was persuaded to send him to a university (not specified). He was not there long, seeing that, before 1660, his gifts as a preacher had obtained his appointment to Blackrod, then a chapelry in the parish of Bolton, Lanc., whence he was ejected. He went to Hull, where in 1669 he succeeded John Canne as pastor of the congregation afterwards meeting at Dagger Lane. Licensed, June 1672, as "Ind. Teacher in the howse of John Robinson in Kingston upon Hull." In this charge he remained till death. (*C. My. P. T. Y.*) [138]

ASTON, *juxta* Birmingham. [120]

ASTON UPON TRENT. Ejected here (1660) from the sequestered rectory was Thomas Palmer, of Magdalen Coll., Oxford, M.A. (1654), formerly rector of St. Laurence Pountney, London, rector here from 1646. (*C. F.*) [27]

ASTY, JOHN. *See* Minister's son

ATCHAM ('Acham'), had 9 Nonconformists in 1676. (*Ls.*) [16, 89]

ATERTHORP. [130] *See* Yorkshire, W. Riding

ATKINS, HENRY (28 D. 1679–1742 ?). **P.** [Probably related to Robert Atkins, M.A. (1628 ?–28 Mar. 1685), ejected from the rectory of St. John's, Exeter, and founder of the Bow Meeting congregation.] He became Minister of Puddington, Devon (ordained 16 Oct. 1701), and in April or May 1717 sounded the alarm of heresy in James Peirce's pulpit (*see* Hallett, Joseph). Subsequently he removed to Totnes, Devon, receiving, 1728–1742, £5 a year from the Fund. He was succeeded (1727) at Puddington by William Nation from Fowy, Corn. (*Em. Ev. J. M.*) [30]

ATKINSON, SIMON (1634 ?–Sept. 1694). **C.** Held the sequestered vicarage of Lazonby, Cumb., in Jan. 1645/6; authorised 8 Mar. 1645/6 to officiate in the chapelries in Crosthwaite parish, Cumb. Took the engagement (1649) of loyalty to the government without King or House of Lords. Ministered also from 1652 in the chapelry of Hesket-in-the-Forest, Cumb. Opposed Quakers. Ejected, 1660. The Episc. Returns, 1669, report him as one of the preachers to "Independents 60 or more" at Hesket, Lazonby, and Kirkoswald. Licensed, 29 May 1672, as Congr. Teacher in house of William Sanderson at Hesket. Presented for Nonconformity, 1671–7. Buried 6 S. 1694 at Calthwaite, Cumb., where he was reported "Pastour" on 9 May 1692. (*C. M. N. P. T.*) [2]

ATONEMENT. [158]

ATTERCLIFFE, then a chapelry in Sheffield parish, Yorks; now vicarage. [130, 131]

ATTERTHORP. [129] *See* Yorkshire, W. Riding

AUSTIN. [79] *See* Northumberland

AVERY, RICHARD, M.A. (*fl.* 1653–79). **P.** Of a Newbury family. Matric. 'serv.' at Wadham Coll., Oxford, 24 June 1653; demy, Magdalen Coll., 1656–9; B.A., 1656; M.A., 1659; Fellow, 1659–60. Ejected in 1660 from the sequestered vicarage of Kingsclere, Hants. Calamy speaks of him as "of this County" (Berks), adding "I cannot Learn where he was Ejected." The Episc. Returns, 1669, report a conventicle at Hursley, Hants, "Att the house of Mrs. Dorothy Cromwell [daughter of Richard Mayor, of Hursley] wife to Richard Cromwell the late Usurper," consisting of "Supposed Presbyterians 49 of which 24 are Parishioners the rest strangers some of the Parishon^rs^ men of Estates," the preacher being "M^r^ Avery, M^rs^ Cromwell's Chaplaine, who being demanded by w^t^ Authorithy he held that unlawfull Assembly, Answered that he was Authorised thereto by Jesus Christ, and That his Lady would beare them out in all their meetings." A petition signed by 20 parishioners of Kingsclere asked "y^t^ M^r^ Richard Averie Presbiterian pswation may be allowed to be theire Teacher." Licensed, 10 June 1672, as "Presb. Teacher in the howse of W^m^ Jones," Kingsclere. In 1678 he was excommunicated for Nonconformity; on 17 S. 1679 a warrant was issued for his arrest. He lived at Newbury, Berks.

His relative, Benjamin Avery, D.C.L. (*d.* 23 July 1764), left the Nonconformist Ministry in 1720, being a Non-subscriber at Salters' Hall (1719), and became a physician. He was Treasurer of Guy's Hospital, and secretary to the Dissenting Deputies from their appointment in 1732. (*C. D. F. P. T.*) [102]

AXMINSTER. Ejected (1662) from this rectory was Bartholomew Ashwood, of St. Alban Hall and Exeter Coll., Oxford; B.A., 1642; rector of Blickleigh, Devon; afterwards of Axminster; living at Axminster, 1665; licensed, 11 Apr. 1672, as Ind. Teacher; his house at Axminster licensed same day as "a Place of Meeting of the Independent way"; *d.* about 1680. His son was John Ashford [*q.v.*]. (*C. F. T.*) [30]

AXTELL, or AXELL. Axtell was a great Nonconformist name in Hertfordshire. (*Uh.*) [44, 45]

AYLESBURY. Ejected here in 1660 was John Luffe, M.A., son of John Luffe of Langford, Som., pleb.; matric. at New Inn Hall, Oxford, 20 June 1634, aged 16; B.A., 1637; M.A., 1639/40; held the sequestered rectories of Street and

Walton, Som., 1646; of Chew Magna, Som., 1647; later, the sequestered vicarage of Aylesbury, where, after ejection, he preached for the restored vicar till 1662; licensed, 16 May 1672, as general Presb. teacher of St. Mary Magdalene parish, Southwark. (*C. F. P. T.*) [9]

AYNSWORTH, *i.e.* AINSWORTH, RALPH, M.A. (*d.* May 1716). From Blackburn school went to Trinity Coll. Dublin (C. Innes, "Early Scotch Hist.," 1861); graduated M.A. Glasg. 1672. Succeeded the father of Thomas Kynaston [*q.v.*] at Whitley Chapel in Great Budworth parish, Chesh. Superseded by a Conformist, he removed to Brombro' in Wirral, and thence, 1704, to Rivington, where he died. From the Fund he received, 1705–15, £6 a year. His son Abraham was minister at Crook, 1726–30. (*Gm. M. Nk. Uc.*) [15]

BACTON. [107]

BADDIE, THOMAS (*d.* June 1729). 𝔓. Born in N. Wales. It appears that 'Badi is a familiar form of Madoc.' Entered Frankland's Academy, 23 Nov. 1689. On 26 Jan. 1690/1, when he was certificated by Richard Stretton [*q.v.*], he is described as of Wrexham. The Common Fund granted him, 1691–3, as Student, £14 a year; and, 1711–28, as Minister at Denbigh, N. Wales, £8 a year; reduced, 1723, to £6. He came in for some property. In the will of Daniel Williams, D.D. [*q.v.*], he is named a beneficiary "if he continues to preach in Denbigh." (*Ev. Fr. M. Nk. Pw. Rw.*) [136]

BADDOW, LITTLE. Ejected here was Thomas Gilson; from Dedham grammar school matric., sizar, at Emmanuel Coll., Cambridge, 1645; rem. to Magdalen Hall, Oxford, B.A., 1648; Fellow of Corpus Christi Coll., 1649; M.A., 1649/50; vicar of Little Baddow, after 1650; ejected, 1662; preaching at Brentwood, 1669; licensed, 2 May 1672, as Pr. Teacher in his house in Brentwood, Ess.; his house licensed, same date, as Pr. meeting-place; licensed, 16 July 1672, as Pr. Grāll, being of South Weald, Ess.; Minister at Ratcliff, London; died there, 1680 (before 6 May), aged 50. (*C. E. F. T. V.*) [38, 43]

BADLAND, THOMAS, B.A. (1634—5 May 1698). 𝔓. Born in Worcester. Matric. serviens, at Pembroke Coll., Oxford, 27 N. 1650; B.A., 1653. Ordained, 20 May 1657, by Wirksworth Classis, Derb. Incumbent (1656) of the chapelry (now vicarage) of Willenhall, Staff.; ejected, 1662. The Episc. Returns, 1669, report him as one of two preachers to "about 200 of all sorts, some people of good sufficiency" in St. Nicholas' parish, Worcester, "Att the houses of Mr Thomas Stirrup & Mr Thomas Smyth every second Sunday." Licensed, June 1672, as "Pr. Teacher in the howse of Wm. Cheatle in Worcester." His flock was organised as "a particular Church of Christ" in 1687. Chewning Blackmore [*q.v.*] was his assistant from 1688. Warmstree House was certified as their meeting-place, on 1 Oct. 1689. (*C. De. F. P. T. Uw.*) [126]

BADWELL ASH. [105]

BAGSHAW, WILLIAM (17 Jan. 1627/8–1 Ap. 1702), the 'Apostle of the Peak.' 𝔓. Born at Litton, parish of Tideswell, Derb. Admitted, 1646, at Corpus Christi Coll., Cambridge, but did not matriculate. Received episcopal ordination, and ministered three months at Warmhill Chapel, parish of Tideswell; removed to Attercliffe, Yorks, as chaplain to Sir John Bright and assistant to James Fisher (*bur.* 29 Jan. 1666/7) at Sheffield; received Presbyterian ordination at Chesterfield, 1 Jan. 1650/1, as vicar of Glossop, Derb.; ejected, 1662. Retired to his estate, Ford Hall, parish of Chapel-en-le-Frith, Derb. Licensed, 18 Ap. 1672, as "Presb. Teacher in any licensed place"; also, 9 May as Pr. Teacher in house of George Shirt, Chapel-en-le-Frith; also, 8 Aug. as Presbyt: Teacher at the house of William Garlicke, Dinting, Derbs.; and in Sept. as Pr. Teacher at Glossop, Derb. 'Chimley' is Chinley, 'Chawseworth' is Charlesworth; 'Chelmarcon' is Chelmorton; he preached also at Bradwell, near Hucklow, and Malcoffe, near Ford. Buried at Chapel-en-le-Frith. (*C. D. Lm. Ma. P. T. V. Y.*) [25, 26, 180]

BAIKALLER, *i.e.* BACKALLER, HENRY (1618—20 F. 1703/4). 𝔓. Son of John Backaller of Axminster, Devon, pleb.; matric. at New Inn Hall, Oxford, 6 Ap. 1638, aged 20; assistant at Woodland, Devon, later at Newbury, Berks, ejected 1662; preached afterwards in Woodland parish church by connivance; about 1689 took charge of a congregation at Shobrooke, Devon (formerly Shogbrooke, MS. 'Shanghbrook'), till his death. Calamy calls him "Mr Blacabler" and "William Blackaller" and confuses him with a namesake; *see* Beckaller. (*C. Em. F. P.*) [32, 33]

BAILEY, J. E. [173–4]

BAIOCK, or BAYOCK, JAMES (1649?–Sept. 1736). 𝔓. Son of James Bayock, barber, York. Admitted pensioner at St. John's Coll., Cambridge, 15 June 1667, aet. 18; did not matriculate. Conformed; but subsequently entered the Nonconformist ministry. The Common Fund granted him (1691–1711) £10 a year for North Cave, reduced (1695) to £8. He removed to West End Chapel, South Cave, where he trained students for the ministry, and there died. His Meeting-house was put in trust, 30 May 1730, "for such persons as are or shall be known or distinguished most commonly by the name of Presbyterians." He was buried (apparently behind his Meeting-house) on 29 Sept. 1736, "aged 90 or upwards. A Dissenting Minr. supposed to be the oldest minr. in England." (*C. Jo. M. My. Nr. P. Rc. V. Y.*) [138]

BAKER, MRS. ℭ. Her "gift" was through Matthew Rapier [*q.v.*]. (*M.*) [166]

BALA ('Bela'). [141, 143]

BALDOCK ('Balduck'). Ejected from lectureship here in 1662 was William Sherwin, of St. John's Coll., Cambridge; matric. sizar, 1624; rem. to Queens' Coll.; B.A., 1627/8; M.A., 1631; held the sequestered rectory of Wallington, Herts, ejected thence, 1660. (*C. Uh. V.*) [51]

BALDWIN, ROGER, M.A. (1624—9 June 1695). 𝔓. Son (fourth child) of William Baldwin (*d.* 1673) of Standishgate, Wigan, pewterer; baptized, 28 N. 1624, at Wigan. Matric. at Glasgow Univ., 1643; M.A., at Edinburgh Univ., 15 Ap. 1645. Incumbent (1646–7) of Ellenbrook Chapel, parish of Eccles; lecturer and vicar of St. Cuthbert's, Carlisle, 1648–9; lecturer at Penrith, Cumb., 1649, and held the sequestered vicarage, 1653; ejected, 1660; incumbent of Rainford Chapel, ejected, 1662. Took to farming at Chisnal Hall, Coppull, parish of Standish, Lanc.; searched for arms, 1665, and again in 1683. Licensed, 25 July 1672, as "a genall. Teacher" at Coppull, where, on 5 S. 1672, "A Roome built by Pr: for a Meeting Place" was licensed. Removed to Eccles, where Mr Rodgers' barn was registered in 1689. There are discrepancies as to the day of his death in June. (*C. Ed. F. N. Nl. P. T.*) [59]

BALDWIN, THOMAS (*d.* 30 Jan. 1692/3). 𝔓. Matric. at Queens' Coll., Cambridge, 1646; B.A., 1648/9; M.A., 1654. Vicar of Wolverley, Worc., and member of Baxter's Worcestershire Association; held the sequestered vicarage of Chadsley Corbet, Worc.; ejected, 1660/1. Richard Baxter [*q.v.*], when driven from Kidderminster (1660), desired that his flock should be "ruled by" Baldwin, Chadsley being about four miles off. Baldwin, after his ejection, ministered at Kidderminster, not preaching during church hours. The Five Mile Act drove him (1666) to Dudley for a time. Licensed, 10 Aug. 1672, as "Pr. Teach: att Kidderminster." He died in Kidderminster, and his funeral sermon, by the vicar, Richard White, B.D., was printed, but with his name given as Thomas Badland. (*C. Ed. Ek. P. T. Uw. V. Wc.*) [126]

BALDWIN, THOMAS, *secundus* (*fl.* 1660–1690). 𝔓. Son of Thomas Baldwin [*q.v.*]. Matric. at Queens' Coll., Cambridge, 1655. Ejected from the vicarage of Clent, Staff. The Episc. Returns, 1669, report him as one of the preachers at the house of William Bell, Birmingham. Licensed, 5 S. 1672, as "Presby" of Rowley Regis, Staff. He settled (before 1689) as colleague to William Fincher [*q.v.*] in Birmingham, and there died. (*Bh. C. P. T. V.*) [96, 117]

BALEY . . . ? Thomas Bailife or Bayly, who entered Frankland's Academy on 6 July or 1 Nov. 1670. (*Fr. Ht.*) [85]

BALL, WILLIAM, M.A. (*b.* 1624). ℭ. Son of John Ball, gent., of Ottery, Dev. Matric. at Exeter Coll., Oxford, 8 Dec. 1637, aged 13; B.A., 1641; M.A., 1648. Vicar of Winsham, Som.; ejected (1660 ?). Reported in the Episc. Returns, 1665, as teaching school at Dartmouth, "but not Licensed nor well affected." Reported in the Episc. Returns, 1669, as one of nine preachers to 200 persons at two houses in Winsham. He signed the address to the Crown from the Dartmouth Congregations under John Flavell [*q.v.*] thanking for the Indulgence of 1672. Calamy just mentions his name; the account in Palmer belongs to Nathanael Ball, M.A. (1623—8 Sept. 1681), ejected from the sequestered vicarage of Barley, Herts. (*C. F. P. T.*) [92]

BALSTAR, *i.e.* BALSTER, JOHN, B.A. (1640–1713/4). 𝔓. Son of Joseph Balster of Stoke Trister, Som., pleb. Matric. at Hart Hall, Oxford, 28 N. 1661, aged 21; B.A., 7 D. 1661. The Episc. Returns, 1669, report him as preaching with Richard Saunders [*q.v.*] at Uffculme, Devon. Licensed, 2 May 1672, as "a Pr. Teacher in the howse of Humphrey Bawden in the Parish of Uffculme." From 1693 to 1713 the Fund granted him £5 a year for Oakhampton, where he was succeeded by John Parr, ordained 20 July 1715. (*Ev. F. M. T.*) [33]

BANBURY. Ejected here was Samuel

Welles of Magdalen Hall; son of William, of Oxford; *b.* 18 Aug. 1614; matric., 11 May 1632, aged 17; rem. to New Coll.; B.A., 1633; returned to Magdalen Hall, M.A., 1636; kept school at Wandsworth; curate at Battersea, 1639–44; army chaplain, 1644; held the sequestered rectory of Remenham, Berks, 1646; vicar of Banbury, 1649; ejected, 1662; preaching at Westbury, Bucks, 1669; licensed, 20 Apr. 1672, as Presb. Teacher in a house at Banbury;. also, 10 May 1672, in his own house there or any other place. (*Bf. C. F. T.*) [85]

BANGER, JOSIAH, M.A. (*b.* 1627–Aug. 1691). **P.** Younger son of Bernard Banger, rector of Yarlington, Som. Matric. at Magdalen Coll., Oxford, 10 N. 1645, aged 18; clerk, 1647–53; Fellow, 1648; B.A., 1648/9; Fellow of Trinity Coll., 1651; M.A., 1651; kept some terms at Cambridge. Vicar of Broadhembury, Devon; ejected, 1662. Twice imprisoned under the Five Mile Act. The Episc. Returns, 1669, report him as preaching "Every Sunday & some weeke dayes" to "300 or above" Presbyterians at Lillington, Dors. (near Sherborne), where he had an estate; also "sometimes" to 50 or 60 persons at Hermitage, Dors., and at North Cheriton to 200 persons. Later he removed to Montacute, Som. He signed the address of thanks for Indulgence (1672) from Ministers of Dorset. Licensed, 22 May 1672, as "Presb. Teacher in the howse of Wm Wheadon at Whotley in the Parish of Winshã, Somersett." Removing to Sherborne, Dorset, he died there, and was buried at Lillington.

From 1714 to 1735 the Fund Minutes refer to Benard Banger (probably son of the above) living in Somerset, and supplying various places in Dorset, etc. (*C. Em. F. M. P. T.*) [34]

BAPTISM (ANGLICAN). [185]

BAPTISTS. [178, 189]

BARBING. [38] *See* Essex

BARDFIELD ('Barfield'), may be Great Bardfield, Little Bardfield, or Bardfield Saling. [39]

BARDON. [67]

BARHAM, ARTHUR, B.A. (22 N. 1618–6 Mar. 1692/3). **P.** Born at Buxted, Sussex. Matric. sizar at Trinity Coll., Cambridge, 1634; B.A., 1644/5. Had first a legal training, but on his father's death studied divinity. Lecturer at St. Olave's, Southwark. Presented (1652 ?) to St. Helen's, Lond., by Sir John Langham, his connection by marriage. Ejected, 1662; removed to Hackney; retired (1666) to Sussex; licensed, 13 May 1672, as Presb. Teacher in his own house, Hackney. Assiduous in daily conduct of worship. On withdrawal of Indulgence, heavily fined. Removed to a London lodging; soon after disabled (with loss of memory) by apoplectic fits. On 10 Nov. 1690 £5 was granted him as share of anonymous donation (£50), per Matthew Rapier. From 1691 lived with his son-in-law, John Clarke, bookseller (a noted publisher of Nonconformist sermons and pamphlets in the first quarter of the eighteenth century and later). (*C. P. T. Tc. V.*) [1]

BARKAMSTEAD. [50, 51] *See* Hertfordshire

BARKER, *i.e.* BAKER, JOHN (*fl.* 1635 ?–1691). **P.** [? Born, 1635, in Warwickshire. From Coventry grammar school admitted pensioner at Peterhouse, Cambridge, 2 July 1652, aged 17.] Ejected from vicarage of Chisleton, Wilts. Episcopal Returns, 1669, report him as living in the house of John Goddard, an excommunicate person, at Winterborne Monkton, Wilts, preaching there and at Avebury and Barkwick Bassett, Wilts. Removed to London. Licensed there, 11 Apr. 1672, as general Presb. Teacher, Whitecrosse Street. On 10 Nov. 1690 £3 was granted to "Mr Baker" as share of anonymous donation (£50), per Matthew Rapier; on 1 June 1691 £5 was voted to him, he then being at Folkestone, Kent. (*C. M. P. Ph. T.*) [1]

BARKER, MATTHEW, M.A. (1619 ?–25 March 1698). **C.** Born at Cransley, Northants. Matric. sizar at Trinity Coll., Cambridge, 1634; B.A., 1637/8; M.A., 1641. He first taught school at Banbury, Oxfordsh. Leaving on the outbreak of the Civil War, he repaired to London (1641). He ministered for some five years (from 1642 ?) at St. James', Garlickhithe, and then removed to the lectureship at Mortlake, Surrey. Seth Wood was appointed to the sequestered rectory of St. Leonard's, Eastcheap, in 1650, and resigned in 1660, when Barker, who appears to have been lecturer from 1650, succeeded him (the sequestered rector, Henry Roborough, being dead), but was soon ejected from the rectory for Elkana Downes, D.D., was appointed rector on 17 N. 1661. He appears to have held the lectureship till ejected in 1662. He was licensed (29 May 1672) as "Rob: Barter" (corrected in the receipt, 12 June) to be a Congr. Teacher in the house of James March, parish of St. Clement's, Eastcheap; he was himself living in Duke's Place, parish of St. James. Subsequently he was allowed joint use of the Meeting-house in Miles' Lane, Cannon Street, and remained in charge there till his death. He was the last of the Congregationals to remain in the Happy Union. John Short [*q.v.*] succeeded him at Miles' Lane. (*C. He. P. T. Tc. V. W. Wc.*) [160, 165]

BARKER, . . . The Fund granted him £4 a year in 1690, as a Student at Bromborough; he was not on the Students' list after Feb. 1691; but received the same sum, 19 Dec. 1692, as Minister at Bromborough, when he must have filled the interval between John Wilson [*q.v.*] and Richard Edge [*q.v.*]. Perhaps he is Mr. Barker who received £4 a year as Minister of Creaton, Northants, in 1699 and 1704–8. (*M.*) [17]

BARKING ('Barbing Sm. Mark,' *i.e.* Small Market). Ejected here (1662), and from his other livings, was the pluralist, Benjamin Way of Trinity Coll., Oxford; matric., 22 May 1647, aged 16; rem. to Corpus Christi Coll.; B.A., 1650/1; M.A., 1653; Fellow of Oriel Coll., 1653. Vicar of Barking, 1656; rector of Frome Billet and West Stafford, Dors., 27 Feb. 1660/1. Living at Dorchester, 1665, having taken the Oxford oath; licensed, 1 May 1672, as Congr. Teacher in Dorchester; Minister at Castle Green, Bristol, 1676; *d.* 9 Nov. 1680. (*C. E. F. Hu. T.*) [38]

BARLEY ('Barly'). Ejected here in 1660 was Nathaniel Ball, M.A. [*See* Royston.] [50]

BARNARD, THOMAS (*b.* 1643). **C.** Son of Richard Barnard (*d.* 1666), draper of Lewes. Attended a conventicle at South Malling on 29 May 1670. Began his ministry in 1673. Ordained at Glynde, Suss. (24 Feb. 1687/8), by Edward Newton [*q.v.*] and others. On 9 May 1692 the Common Fund voted him £10 a year for "preaching at Hastings, Catsfield and Seaford," Suss. Assisted Newton at Lewes from 1695. Bought the Meeting-house there in 1698, and retained it when, in 1701, the growing congregation led to the building of a new Meeting-house for Newton in Crown Lane. Minister at Lewes at the date of Evans' List (8 Nov. 1717), assisted from 1711 and succeeded by John Olive from Mayfield, Suss.; living in 1723. (*Ev. Lh. M. Om.*) [113, 115]

BARNBY DUN, otherwise Barnby-upon-Don, W.R. (misplaced in E.R.). [139]

BARNES, THOMAS (*d.* 1703 ?). **C.** Sent from the church of Allhallows the Great, Thames Street, London, to preach the Gospel in Wales. Held the sequestered vicarage of Magor, Monm.; ejected, 1660/1. When silenced was living in Caerleon, near Magor, pastor of the church known as Llanvaches, and meeting in neighbouring places. The Episc. Returns, 1669, report "Thomas Barnes, late of Magor and now of Bristoll," as one of the preachers to about 200 persons meeting at Caerleon, Magor, Llanvaches, and three other places. Licensed, 10 Aug. 1672, as "Ind[t] Teach[r] att the house of Walter Jones," Magor. The Common Fund voted him (1690–93) £20 a year for Newport, Monm. The Congregational Fund voted him £10 on 20 Apr. 1696. (*C. Cf. M. P. T. Wc.*) [91, 92, 144, 179]

BARNET ('Barnett'). Ejected here was Samuel Shaw, of St. John's Coll., Cambridge; matric. sizar, 1651; B.A., 1655/6; rector of Chipping Barnet, 8 Dec. 1658; ejected, 1662. (*C. Uh.*) [10, 50, 51, 72]

BARNETT, ANDREW (*fl.* 1649–1707). **P.** Born at Uppington, Shrops., youngest child of Humphrey Barnett (see *Gd.*), then vicar there. Subsizar at Trinity Coll., Cambridge, 5 S. 1646; did not graduate. Incumbent of the chapelry of Church Hulme, Ches.; ejected (1649) for not taking the engagement to the government "without king or house of lords." Rector of Roddington, Shrops.; ejected, 1662. Practised physic. Licensed, 13 May 1672, as Pr. Teacher in his house in Astbury parish, Chesh., *i.e.* at Congleton; his house (probably after a removal) was again licensed, Oct. 1672. In 1690 he was near Oswestry; in 1692 he was preaching at Baddiley, Chesh.; in 1695 he was "minister of the Gospel at Daventry"; from 1699 to 1707 he was again near Oswestry, receiving £2 a year from the Fund.

"D[r] Barnett's son" (whose Christian name is not given, but is so called to distinguish him from another Student, Josiah Barnett) had from the Common Fund a bursary of £10 at Glasgow (1691) and (1692–6) at the Academy of John Woodhouse [*q.v.*]. He did not matriculate at Glasgow. (*C. Cn. M. P. T. Tc. Uc. V.*) [16, 49, 88]

BARNSTAPLE. Ejected here was Nathaniel Mathor, M.A. [*q.v.*]. [30, 95]

BARRETT, JOHN, M.A. (1621—30 O. 1713). **P.** Matric. sizar at Clare Hall, Cambridge, 1646; B.A., 1649/50. Ordained, 19 O. 1652, by Wirksworth Classis, as vicar of Wymeswold, Leic.

Rector (1656) of St. Peter's, Nottingham; member of the Nottingham Classis (1656–60); ejected, 1662. Licensed, 30 Apr. 1672, as Pr. Teacher in his house at Sandiacre, Derb.; also, 2 May 1672, in house of Mrs. Margery Derry, Nottingham, a licence for the Spice Chamber having been refused. Ministered from 1687 till death as co-pastor to the congregation which built (1690–91) the High Pavement Chapel, Nottingham. (*C. No. P. T. V.*) [25, 82, 178]

BARRINGTON, LADY. Dorothy (*d.* 27 O. 1703), daughter of Sir William Lytton of Knebworth, Herts, married (1643) to Sir John Barrington, Bart. (*d.* 24 Mar. 1682/3), of Barrington Hall in Hatfield Broad Oak, Ess. (*Ba.*) [50]

BARROW. [107]

BARSTON, JOHN, B.A. (*d.* 1701). **P.** Matric. 'pleb.' at New Inn Hall, Oxford, 30 N. 1652; B.A., 1656. Curate at Ashton, parish of Eye, Heref. (or perhaps vicar of Ashton, Glou.), ejected. The Episc. Returns, 1669, report him as one of three preachers to 60 or 80 persons at "Kidmarly Dabitot," probably Croome D'Abetot, Worc. Licensed, June 1672, as "Pr. Teacher in the howse of Joan Hall," Ledbury, Heref. He is evidently also the "John Persons" and "John Parston," licensed, 30 S. 1672, for himself and howse at Colwall, Heref. Pr. He died Minister at Ledbury. (*C. F. P. T.*) [48]

BARTHOLOMAEANS. [160-61, 164, 177, 188]

BARTHOLOMEW, or ST. BARTHOLOMEW, SQUARE is approached by Henry Street, which runs from the North side of Old Street, St. Luke's. No 'Surgeons' Arms' is there to-day, but there is a well-known firm of surgical instrument-makers. (*Sl.*) [2]

BARTLETT, or BARTLET, JOHN, M.A. (*fl.* 1615–1690). **P.** Matric. at Magdalene Coll., Cambridge, 1615/6; B.A., 1619/20; Fellow; M.A., 1623. Minister of St. Thomas', near Exeter. Ejected from St. Mary's in the Moor, Exeter; reported in Episc. Returns, 1665, as living in Exeter but not conventicling. Licensed, 2 Apr. 1672, as "Presbyt. Teacher in any licenced place." He reached "a good old age"; he could not have been much short of 90 in 1690. (*C. P. T. V.*) [30]

BARTLETT, ROBERT (1632—7 June 1710). **C.** Born at Frampton, Dors.; educated at its grammar school. Lecturer (1652–4) at Salisbury; rector (1654) of Over Compton, Dors.; ordained there by presbyters; ejected, 1662. Removed to his small estate at Bradford Peverell, Dors., and (1666), in consequence of the Five Mile Act, to North Cadbury, Som. The Episc. Returns, 1669, report him as one of the preachers to 300 persons at Kingsbury, Som.; also as one of the preachers to 200 persons "At the house of Edward Sutton," North Cheriton, Som.; also as one of two preachers to 50 persons "At the house of Thomas Perry, señ," Holton, Som.; also to 70 or 80 Presbyterians "At the house of Henry Beaton," Over Compton; as well as to a "number uncertaine" at his own house, North Cadbury, Som. Licensed, 8 May 1672, as "a Congr. Teacher in the howse of James Hanne in Over Compton," and in June 1672 as "a Pr. Teacher in the howse of Wm Buckler at Warminster, Wilts." He signed, 10 May 1672, an address of thanks to the Crown for the Indulgence, from Nonconforming Ministers of Dorset. In 1689 he removed to Lower Compton. He can only have given occasional assistance at Tiverton, where his son Samuel, who predeceased him, was Minister. We find him in 1690 sharing the ministry at Yeovil, Som.; in 1700 he became pastor at Yeovil, but continued to divide his Sunday labours between Compton and Yeovil, where a new Meeting-house was built in 1704. At Yeovil a set of Baxter's "Practical Works" (1707) is lettered, evidently in error, as a gift (1708) to "Ed. Bartlett" and "on his decease to his successor in the ministry." (*C. Mh. Od. P. T.*) [30, 91, 92]

BARTON (*fl.* 1690–1700). **C.** "Mr Barton" is mentioned (9 D. 1700) as a Lecturer at Crosby Square. (*M.*) [1]. [? Nathan Barton, B.D. (*b.* 1626 ?). **C.** Son of Edmund Barton, incumbent of Brosley, Salop. Matric. at New Inn Hall, Oxford, 12 Dec. 1634, aged 18; B.A., 1638; M.A., 1641; B.D., 1649. Ejected from the vicarage of Cauldwell, Derb. Living at Cauldwell, dispossessed of lands, 1669. Described in Episcopal Returns, 1669, as "Captaine or Major Barton a souldier agt the King and a minister at the beginning of the warres who purchased some of the King's lands wch he hath lost & is highly Discontented," being then at Cauldwell. Wood's "Fasti" describes him as "a sturdy, zealous, and daily preacher of the blessed cause in the parliamentary army." Calamy merely enters his name (as Nathaniel). (*C. F. M. T. Wo.*)]

BASINGSTOKE ('Batingstocke,' 'Batingstoak'). [101]

BASTWICK, JOHN, M.D. (1593–Oct. 1654). 𝔓. Born at Writtle, Essex. Entered at Emmanuel Coll., Cambridge, 19 May 1614; matric. pensioner, 1614; but took no degree; graduated M.D. at Padua, and from 1623 practised as physician at Colchester, Essex. Fined £1000 and imprisoned for his "Flagellum Pontificis," 1634, an argument for Presbyterianism. Fined £5000, shorn of his ears in the pillory, and sentenced to life imprisonment for his "Letanie," 1637, denouncing bishops. Released by Parliament, Nov. 1640. Captain of the Leicester trained bands, 1642, taken prisoner, but soon at liberty. The House of Lords voted him £9000, which he does not seem to have received. (*D. V.*) [151]

BATES, WILLIAM, D.D. (Nov. 1625–14 July 1699). 𝔓. Son of William Bates of St. Mary Magdalene's parish, Bermondsey, Surrey, gent. Matric., 9 July 1641, at New Inn Hall, Oxford, aged 15. Removed to Emmanuel Coll. and thence to Queens' Coll., Cambridge; matric. pensioner, 1644; B.A., 1644/5; M.A., 1648; D.D., by royal mandate, 1661. Vicar of Tottenham; succeeded (1650) William Strong (*d.* June 1654) as vicar of St. Dunstan's-in-the West. In the negotiations for the Restoration he took an active part; in 1660 he was made a royal chaplain. He was one of the commissioners for the Savoy Conference (1661), and was offered the deanery of Lichfield. Ejected in 1662, he took the Oxford oath (1665) against endeavouring alteration in Church or State. At the time of Indulgence, Bates was a leader of the "Dons," whose influence was with the gentry; *see* Annesley, Samuel. On 8 May 1672 he was licensed as a general Presb. Teacher. He was one of the original six lecturers at Pinners' Hall, 1672, but withdrew (1694) on the expulsion of Daniel Williams [*q.v.*], and became a lecturer at Salters' Hall. He founded the Presbyterian congregation at Hackney, and died there. He was known as the 'silvertongued' preacher. (*C. D. F. P. Rt. T. V. W.*) [72, 75, 84, 154, 160, 164, 165, 168]

BATEY, . . . [55]

BATH. Ejected here was William Green, assistant master at the grammar school. (*C.*) [92, 93]

BATINGSTOCKE. [101] *See* Hampshire

BATLEY ('Betley'), W.R. (misplaced in E.R.) [139]

BATT, TIMOTHY, M.A. (30 N. 1613–July 1692). 𝔓. Son of Robert Batt, of Street, Som., pleb. Matric. at Wadham Coll., Oxford, 28 Jan. 1630/1, aged 17; rem. to Emmanuel Coll., Cambridge; matric. sizar, 1633; B.A., 1634/5; M.A., 1638; known in the university as 'silver-tongued Batt.' Chaplain to Sir Robert Pye [*q.v.*]. Ministered at Mimms, Midx., and Ilminster, Som.; and held the sequestered vicarage of Creech, Som.; ejected, 1660, when the old vicar, Henry Masters (to whom Batt "once gave a Suit of Clothes"), was restored. Incumbent of Ruishton chapelry, Som.; ejected, 1662. The Episc. Returns, 1669, report him as one of the preachers to 400 persons at various houses in West Monkton, Som., and places adjacent; also to 200 persons at Creech; also to 230 persons in St. Magdalen's parish, Taunton, "in a Barne . . . where a Pulpitt and seats are built"; also to 260 persons at various houses in Bridgwater, Som.; also to 300 persons at Glastonbury, Som. Licensed, 8 May 1672, as "Pr. teacher in the howses of John Norman & Daniel Lock in the Parish of Wellington, Somersett." He continued preaching at various places till within a few months of his death, though blind for more than two years. (*C. F. P. T. V. Wc.*) [92, 93]

BATTLE. [115]

BAXTER, NATHANIEL, M.A. (1632?–12 Sept. 1697). 𝔓. Born at Astle, a hamlet in Prestbury parish, Chesh. Matric. at Jesus Coll., Cambridge, 1653; B.A., 1656; M.A., 1660. Further prepared for the ministry by Henry Newcome [*q.v.*]. Vicar of St. Michael-on-Wyre, Lanc.; ejected, 1662. Chaplain to Sir William Middleton of Aldwark, near Rotherham, Yorks. For seventeen years (to 1682?) he preached by connivance in the unendowed donative of Beauchief Abbey, near Sheffield, reading the Common Prayer. After the Declaration for Liberty of Conscience (1687), he felt free to preach without using the Prayer-book, but declined any settled charge. He had removed to Sheffield, and died at Attercliffe. The Common Fund granted him, 1690–95, £4 a year. (*C. Hy. M. P. V. Y.*) [130, 131, 137]

BAXTER, RICHARD (12 Nov. 1615–8 Dec. 1691). Nonconformist. Born at Rowton, Salop; son of Richard Baxter, of Eaton Constantine, Salop, by Beatrice, dau. of Richard Adeney of Rowton. His early education was under incompetent schoolmasters, till he studied (1629–32) at the grammar school of Wroxeter, Salop, under John Owen, who advised against his going to Oxford, and sent him to read (1632–3) with Richard Wickstead (chaplain to the council at Ludlow Castle) who neglected him, and advised his going to court. A month at Whitehall was enough. Returning home, he found that Owen was dying, and took his place for three months. In 1634, after his mother's death, he read theology with Francis Garbet, vicar of Wroxeter. In 1638 he became master of Dudley grammar school, having been ordained by John Thornborough, bishop of Worcester (without imposition of hands, as Thornborough was disabled). In 1640 he was curate at Bridgnorth, Salop. On 5 Apr. 1640/1 he was appointed to the vicarage of Kidderminster, Worcestershire, sequestered from George Dance. Interrupted by the incidents of the Civil War, his nineteen years' ministry at Kidderminster was one of unparalleled influence in the town and county, indeed in the country at large. In church government he held that the Minister should rule the parish; in ordinations he took no part, holding that the Minister of this function should be distinct from the ordinary presbyter. His Worcestershire Agreement (May 1652) was the model for the Happy Union. Ejected in 1660, he came to London, was made a royal chaplain, and offered the bishopric of Hereford. He took an active part in the Savoy Conference (1661) for considering emendations of the Prayer-book. On 25 May 1662, three months before the fatal Bartholomew Day, he preached his farewell to Conformity, and retired to Acton, Middx. His licence, 27 Oct. 1672, allowed "Richard Baxter a Nonconforming Minister to teach in any licensed or allowed place." Charles II. in 1672 ordered him a pension of £100 a year, which Baxter declined. He was one of the original lecturers at Pinners' Hall. In the Meeting-house built for him in Oxendon Street (1676) by his wife, he preached but once before his arrest and imprisonment; his offer to cede it for Anglican use was accepted. The climax of his numerous persecutions was reached in his trial before Jeffreys (1685), which Macaulay has made famous. In the theological disputes of his day John Owen, D.D. [*q.v.*], was the great conservative force, Baxter the man of development. He calculated that of the Ejected, 1800 resumed their ministry as Nonconformists, a figure which has quite erroneously been taken as his estimate of the total number of Ejected. To the last he remained in communion with the Anglican church, and declined the pastorate of a congregation, but from 1687 he assisted, without pay, Matthew Sylvester [*q.v.*] at Rutland House, Charterhouse Yard. Baxter, like Wesley, clung to his churchmanship, and was principled against separation. His case bears some resemblance to that of von Döllinger, who never joined the Old Catholics, though he was their leading spirit, preferring to die an excommunicated member of the Catholic Church. (*C. Cm. D. En. Go. P. T.*) [76, 152, 153, 155, 156, 160, 188]

BAXTER, SAMUEL (1660—19 July 1740). **P.** Eldest son of Nathaniel Baxter [*q.v.*]. Entered Frankland's Academy, 6 Feb. 1687/8. On 26 Jan. 1690/1 he was certificated by Richard Stretton [*q.v.*], and on 2 Mar. 1690/1 the Common Fund awarded him a "gift" of £4 "for one halfe yeare." Minister at Attercliffe; ordained at Stand, Apr. 1694. Minister at Framlingham, Suff.; rem. to Lowestoft about 1698; rem. to Ipswich, 1701, and there ministered till death. He received £10 from the Fund in 1730. (*B. Fr. Hy. Nk. M.*) [137]

BEACONSFIELD. Ejected here (1660 ?) from the sequestered rectory was Hugh Butler, 'a solid, gravê divine'; he was here in 1654. (*C.*) [10]

BEAMINSTER ('Bemister'). [34]

BECCLES. Ejected here were (1) John Clark or Clerke; preached at Beccles from 1642; pastor of the Congregational church there, 29 July 1653; held the sequestered rectory of Beccles, 1655; ejected, 1660. (*B. C.*) (2) The pastor mentioned as "lately dead," viz. Robert Ottie, born in Great Yarmouth; had a grammar school education; was originally in his father's trade as boddice maker. He became curate to Clark at Beccles, 1655, and pastor of the Congregational church there, 12 Nov. 1656; ejected, 1660. Reported in the Episc. Returns, 1669, as one of the preachers to above 100 persons at Gillingham, Norf. A petition of ten parishioners of Beccles, Suff., asked for the use of the Guild Hall for his services, to which nineteen trustees of the Hall certified their consent. This was not granted, but Ottie was licensed, 9 May 1672, as "Indep. Teacher in his howse in Beccles"; also, 10 June 1672, as "Ind. Teacher in the howse of Thomas Plumstead," Beccles; a further request for licence for his preaching "in y^e^ house of M^r^ Edward Artis, in Beckles" was ignored. Ottie died about the end of April 1689. (*B. C. T.*) [106]

BECHER, MRS. Henry Becher was rector

of Mayfield, Sus., in 1561. Mayfield Place was the residence of the Baker family from 1617 till the latter part of the eighteenth century. (*D. Ho.*) [112]

BECKALLER, *i.e.* BACKALLER (known also as Batchelor), HENRY (1615 ?–1713). 𝔓. Curate of Woodland, Dev.; later, vicar of Combe St. Nicholas, Som. Ejected from the vicarage of Chideock, Dors. The Episc. Returns, 1669, report " Backaller " as one of the preachers to 200 persons " At the houses of Henry Henly Esq and John Bennett " in Winsham, Som. Licensed, 2 May 1672, being of Chard, Som., as general Presb. Teacher; also, 8 May 1672, as " Pr. Teacher " in house of Sarah Kerridge at Wootton Fitzpaine, Dors. He signed the thanks to the Crown by Dorset Ministers, 10 May 1672, his then residence being near Charmouth, Dors. For some time he preached by connivance in Woodland parish church, but was " disabled from preaching above 20 years before his death." Aaron Pitts [*q.v.*] preached for him out of charity. He was a member of the Exeter Assembly. The Common Fund granted him (1690) £6 a year, reduced (1695) to £4, raised (1699) to £5, and continued to 1713. He lived to be " almost 99 " or " wanted but a few months of being a hundred." He died " somewhere about Exeter " in 1713, when " he wanted but a few months of being an hundred years of age." He had sixteen children. (*C. F. M. Od. P. T.*) [91]

BECKET, WILLIAM (*fl.* 1660–91). ℭ. Originally a tradesman; no scholar. Ejected from the rectory of Compton Abdale, Glou. Licensed, 10 June 1672, " being of the Congregationall pswasion," for his house at Winchcombe, Glou. The Common Fund granted him (1690) £10 a year for Stroud; on 26 Jan. 1691 no more was to be paid him " as att Stroad." (*C. M. P. T.*) [45]

BEDBANK, *i.e.* BIDBANCKE, WILLIAM, M.A. (*d.* 7 Apr. 1692). ℭ. Matric. at Emmanuel Coll., Cambridge, 1650; B.A., 1654/5; M.A., 1659. Held the sequestered vicarage of Scottow, Norf.; ejected (1660) and was coadjutor (till 1676) with John Green [*q.v.*] in the ministry of the Congregational church at Tunstead, Norf. In the admission entry of his son George to St. John's Coll., Cambridge (17 May 1662), he is described as " William Bidbanke, gent." The Episc. Returns, 1669, report him as one of the preachers at Woodnorton and at Lammas, Norf. (*see* Finch, Martin). Licensed, 8 May 1672, as " Congr. Teacher in the howse of Rob. Primerose in Denton, Norfolk "; also, 10 June 1672, as " Congr. Teacher in the howse of Thomas Church at Lammas." In 1676 he was dismissed from Tunstead to be pastor of the Congregational church at Denton, Norf. He had a small estate. The wise church covenant drawn up by him runs thus: " We covenant and engage, by the assistance of the Spirit of God, to give up ourselves unto the Lord and unto his people, to walk together in all the ordinances of Christ, according to the order of the gospel, owning him as our head, Lord, and King." (*B. C. Jo. P. T. V.*) [74]

BEDFORDSHIRE. [3, 5, 167, 176, 177] The first headlines and deleted middle line (in the earliest handwriting) on p. 3 of the original Manuscript show that Bedfordshire was to have been begun there; but the Book-keeper utilised the page to continue the London list. Similarly on pp. 4, 5, the original headlines and middle lines appear, but the Book-keeper has superseded (yet not deleted) them, by his own arrangements.

The return seems to have come late; it is numbered 150. St. Neots, the only place specified, did not receive any grant (till 1720). Ebenezer Chandler, ℭ., of Bedford, was voted (2 N. 1691) £10 a year. (*M.*)

BEDNALL. *See* Bethnal

BEDWORTH. Ejected here was Dudley Rider or Ryder, son of Robert Ryder of Wisbech, Camb. (Burke, *Peerage*); of Magdalene Coll., Cambridge; matric. sizar, 1645/6; B.A., 1649/50; M.A., 1660; rector of Bedworth, ejected, 1662; he lost a good estate through an uncle's objection to his nonconformity; he removed to Weddington, War., till 1666; he was licensed, 16 May 1672, as Grāll Pr. Teacher; his house at Wolvey, War., was licensed, 22 May 1672, as Pr. Meeting Place; for some time he preached at King's Lynn; lastly he was chaplain to Sir Samuel Clark; *d.* about 1683. His elder son, Dudley, was father of an archbishop of Tuam; his younger son, Richard, was ancestor of the Earls of Harrowby. (*C. T. V.*) [117, 118]

BEEBIE, or BEEBEE, WILLIAM (*fl.* 1646–1690). 𝔓. Studied at Oxford, 1646 (not in Foster), then privately at home, and was ordained. Chaplain in Scotland to Col. Knight's regiment in Monck's army. Preached in Knight's house after the Restoration. Practised physic at Rowley Hall, near Bridgnorth,

Shrops. Licensed, Nov. 1672, as "Pr. to Teach at the house of Wm Ash" at Tideswell, Derb. Preached also at Gornal, Staff., and Stourbridge, Worc., and spent his last years as pastor at Cirencester, Glou. (*C. Mh. P. T.*) [44]

BEECHHILL. Grants were made of £4 a year from 1691. Subsequently grants were made (*e.g.* 1702) from the Congregational Fund. (*Cf. M.*) [8]

BEERE. [35] *See* Dorsetshire

BEERMAN, BEREMAN, or BEARMAN, *i.e.* BERMAN, WILLIAM (*d.* 7 Oct. 1703). **C.** In 1654 he was the rector of Gestingthorpe, Ess., on the presentation of John Sparrow (one of the translators of Jacob Boehme). Ejected (1662) from lectureship at St. Thomas, Southwark. His farewell sermon (Acts xx. 17-38) is in the London collection. Described in Episcopal Return of 1669 as "a Silkman" in Southwark. Preached with three others to 200 persons at a malthouse in St. Olave's. Licensed, 15 Apr. 1672, as assistant to Joseph Caryl, M.A., then preaching in house of Thomas Knight, merchant, Leadenhall Street, to the congregation which ultimately (1708) met at Bury Street, St. Mary Axe. Preached occasionally, to this and other congregations, while living in Hoxton Square. Declined to serve the congregation, then at Mark Lane, during vacancy caused by resignation (15 Apr. 1701) of Isaac Chauncy [*q.v.*]. Erected eight almshouses for women at Hoxton, adjacent to his residence. Left a large estate in trust for educational and charitable purposes. For his will, signed Berman, see *Co.*, Nov. 1916. (*C. La. P. T. W.*) [1, 166]

BEESLIE, BIZLY. [44, 46] *See* Gloucestershire

BELA. [141, 149] *See* Bala

BELLIO. [52] *See* Billio

BELPER. [27, 28, 177]

BEMISTER. [34] *See* Dorsetshire

BENNET, JOSEPH, B.A. (1627–1707). **P.** Born at Matching, Ess. Son of John Bennet, gent. Calamy makes him son of a clergyman who died young, leaving him to the care of an uncle, T. English, and connects him with Tonbridge grammar school. From Stafford grammar school he was admitted pensioner at St. John's Coll., Cambridge, 12 Sept. 1644, aet. 17; matric., 1645; B.A., 1649. Chaplain in the family of Sir John Wollaston, at Highgate. Curate or lecturer at Hooe, Suss., and later at Burwash, Suss.; rector (1658) of Brightling, Suss.; ejected, 1662. He remained in the parish twenty years, and took pupils. Licensed, 13 Apr. 1672, as "Presb. Teacher in his howse in Brightling." Later his congregation centred at Hellingly, Suss. In 1696 he removed from Burwash to Hastings, Suss., and there died. The Common Fund granted him, 1690–1704, £6 a year, reduced (1695) to £4, but raised again to £6 (1697). (*C. Jo. M. P. T. V.*) [112, 114]

BENNET, JOSEPH, *secundus* (1665—21 F. 1725/6). **P.** Born at Brightling, Suss. Son of Joseph Bennet [*q.v.*]. Educ. by Thomas Goldham [*q.v.*] and (before 1686) at the Academy of Charles Morton, Newington Green. Usher to Thomas Singleton, who, dismissed for Nonconformity from a mastership at Eton, kept school in London till after 1690. His chaplaincy at Mayfield (1690) probably followed the ushership. Preached as probationer at Stratford, Ess. Ordained, 22 June 1694, at the first public ordination of London Nonconformists since Ejection (*see* Reynolds, Thomas). Copastor at Newington Green till 1699, then pastor till 1708; assistant at the Old Jewry, 1708 till death. Chosen a Manager of the reconstituted Fund, 7 N. 1715, but only attended once (7 May 1716). Non-subscriber at Salters' Hall, 1719. He was then living in Hoxton Square. (*Cb. Cm. Ev. M. W.*) [112, 115]

BENNETT, JOHN, B.A. (*d.* May 1693). **P.** Born in London. Admitted sizar from Suffolk, 1648, at Corpus Christi Coll., Cambridge; matric., 1648; B.A., 1651/2; episcopally ordained. Held the vicarage of Whitwick, Leic.; ejected, 1662. Removed to London for about ten years. Licensed, June 1672, as Pr. Teacher in his house at Littleover, where he taught school. Died on a journey to London. He received (10 N. 1690) £2, as share of an anonymous donation of £50 presented through Matthew Rapier [*q.v.*].

His son, John, was studying (1692) in the Academy of John Woodhouse [*q.v.*], and was Minister (1703) at Potterspury, Northants. (*C. Lm. M. P. T. V.*) [26]

BENSON, GEORGE (1616?–1692). **C.** Son of George Benson, of Kendal, pleb.; matric., 3 June 1636, at Queen's Coll., Oxford, age 18; did not graduate. Vicar of Bridekirk, Cumb., 1649; ordained, 1651, as Teaching Elder of the Congregational church at Cockermouth, of which George Larkham [*q.v.*] was Pastor; ejected from Bridekirk, 31 O. 1660. Removed (1662) to Kendal, Westm., retaining till death his connection with the Cockermouth church. Licensed, 16 July 1672, as

"Pr." in his house at Kendal. In 1689 his house at Nether Kellet, Lanc., was certified as a Meeting-place for "Presbiterians." Burton is Burton-in-Kendal, 8 or 9 miles N. of Nether Kellet. The Common Fund granted him, 1690–92, £8 a year "att Kellett." His successor, Robert Waddington, was reported on 7 July 1692.

George Benson, D.D. (1 S. 1699—6 Apr. 1762), a leader of liberal Dissent in London, was his grandson. (*C. F. M. N. Nk. Nr. P. T.*) [23, 121]

BENSON, JOHN (*d.* 1738 ?). **P.** Son of John Benson (*d.* 1682). Ejected from the rectory of Little Leighs, Ess. He is mentioned in the Fund Minutes as being at Sandwich, Kent, on 13 June 1692. From 1695 to 1738 he received grants as Minister at Sandwich. Sandwich was vacant in 1739. (*C. M.*) [50, 51, 52]

BENSON. *See* Binson

BERE REGIS ('Be re'). Ejected here was Philip Lamb, son of Henry Lamb, Minister of Combe Abbas. Of Clare Hall, Cambridge; matric. sizar, 1641; B.A., 1646; vicar of Bere Regis and Kingston, 1649; ejected before 28 June 1662; living at Alton in 1665; licensed, 1 May 1672, as Congr. Teacher at East Morden, Dorset; his house there licensed same day as a Congr. Meeting-place; signed, 10 May, the Dorset thanks for Indulgence; rem. to London, 1673; Minister at Clapham, Surrey; *d.* there, 25 Mar. 1689, in 67th year. The Common Fund voted, 11 Jan. 1691/2, £14 a year for "preaching every Lord's Day" at Bere Regis and Searne [Cerne Abbas]. (*C. Hu. M. T. V.*) [35]

BERESFORD, BERISFORD, or BERRISFORD, SAMUEL, M.A. (*d.* Oct. 1697). Born in St. Alkmund's parish, Shrewsbury. From Shrewsbury school, proceeded to Cambridge University; matric. either at Magdalene Coll., 1634; or Queens', 1647. If of Magdalene, then B.A., 1637/8; M.A., 1641. If of Queen's, then B.A., 1651/2; M.A., 1655. Vicar of St. Werburgh's, Derby; ejected, 1662. Remained in Derby till removed (1666) by the Five Mile Act. The Episc. Returns, 1669, report him as one of the preachers at Little Ireton, Derb., to "200, 300 & 400 at a time every L[ds] day att the house of Colonell Saunders within a mile of S[r] John Carson's dwelling house, who (though a Justice of peace)—never went about to restrayne them." Licensed, 22 Apr. 1672, as "Pr. Teacher in his howse in Shrewsbury." Here for a time he kept school. He had skill as a physician, but attended only personal friends. Being well off, he preached gratuitously. Latterly he lived at Shifnal, Shrops., and died at Weston-under-Lizard, Staffs., the seat of Lady Wilbraham. (*Ba. C. P. T. V.*) [88, 90]

BERGHOLT, EAST ('Bregholt'). [105, 106]

BERKELEY ('Berklie'). In Evans' List the congregation appears as at Barkley or Newport (a village in Berkeley parish). [46]

BERKHAMPSTEAD ('Barkamstead'). [50, 51]

BERKSHIRE. [6, 167, 176]. Except the word Berks, and small additions, all is in the Book-keeper's hand. The returns are numbered from 5 to 132.

Abington is Abingdon.

Bradford is Bradfield [*q.v.*].

Cheseley (and Solesly) is Cholsey [*q.v.*].

Heyburne is East or West Hagbourne.

Ockingham, or Oakingham, is Wokingham [*q.v.*].

Stanford is Stanford-in-the-Vale (not Stanford Dingley).

BERNARD, . . . [55]. ? Barnard, Thomas [*q.v.*].

BERRY, HENRY (1625–Aug. 1694). **P.** Born at Castle-Combe, Wilts. Son of Henry Berry. From Wotton-under-Edge grammar school admitted sizar at Christ's Coll., Cambridge, 21 Mar. 1645/6, age 20; matric., 11 July 1646. Ejected from the rectory of Dulverton, Som. The Episc. Returns, 1669, report him as preaching, perhaps at Chard, Som., certainly as one of the preachers at Dulverton to 100 persons "At the houses of Richard Bishop, Robert Lucks, Thomas Ebbott, John Collard, Richard Escott, Richard Whitehaire," and at Brushford, Som., to 80 persons "At the house of John Newbery sen."; also perhaps at Wiveliscombe, Som.; probably also one of the preachers at Crediton, Devon., to "2 or 300" persons, "on Sundayes & other dayes." Licensed, 11 Apr. 1672, as of Crediton, "to be a Presb. Teacher in any allowed Place." Subsequently he preached at Torrington, and is there buried. The Common Fund paid him (1690) £5 for Torrington, and ordered (1 June 1691) that no more be paid him pending inquiry into his circumstances. (*C. Cp. Em. M. P. T. V.*) [30, 31]

BERRY, JOHN, M.A. (1631–Dec. 1704). **P.** Son of John Berry, rector of Georgeham, Devon. Matric. at Exeter Coll., Oxford, 9 Apr. 1647, aged 16; Fellow (dispossessed, 1648); rem. to Oriel Coll., M.A., 1653. Episcopally ordained. Vicar of Landkey, Devon; rector of East

Down, Devon, 1658; ejected, 1662. Signed the Devon Address, 22 Mar. 1671/2. Licensed, 18 Apr. 1672, being of Barnstaple, Devon, as "a Presb. Teacher in any licensed place"; his house at Crediton licensed 30 Apr. 1672. From 1690 the Common Fund granted him £5 a year for Barnstaple, raised to £6 in 1697. In 1704 he is described as "at Barnstable or Illfarcomb." This is some slight confirmation of Calamy's statement that from 1689 Ilfracombe and Puddington were the chief scenes of his labours. (*C. F. M. P. T.*) [31, 32, 95]

BERWICK-UPON-TWEED. Ejected here was duke Ogle ('Oagle'), M.A. [*q.v.*]. [79]

BETHNAL ('Bednall') GREEN. In Stow's Survay (1598) we find "Blethenhal green now called Bednal-greene." Stow further says of Roger Niger or Le Noir—bishop of London from his consecration, 10 June 1229, till his death, 20 Sept. 1241—that he "dyed at his Mannor of Bishops hall, in the lordship and parish of Stebunheth" [Stepney]. Niger, like Thomas Brand [*q.v.*], was an Essex man, "of worthy life, excellently well learned, a notable Preacher, pleasant in talke, mild of countenance, and liberall at his table." The Bishop's Hall Academy, originally under Brand, with the able aid of John Ker [*q.v.*], was afterwards under John Short [*q.v.*]. Before this, one Walton, ejected from Westham, Ess., had a boarding-school, "first at Bishop's Hall, and afterwards at Bethnal Green," to which Calamy went in 1685. (*C. Cm. D. M. St.*) [4, 72, 182]

BETLEY. [139] *See* Yorkshire, W.R.

BEVERLEY. Ejected here was (not Joseph Wilson; *see* Hull) Samuel Ferris, vicar of St. Mary's, in succession to Wilson; ejected, 1660. (*Wp.*) [138]

BEWDLEY. [127]

BEYNON. *See* Bynon

BICESTER. Calamy gives Basnet or Barnet as ejected from this vicarage. John Byrde, B.A., was vicar from 15 Feb. 1604/5 till his death on 19 Sept. 1652, aged 77. His place may have been filled for a time by Samuel Basnett, M.A. (*see* Coventry). For the Meeting-house at Bicester in 1669, *see* Wheatley, Thomas. (*C. Dn. T.*) [85]

BICKNELL, WILLIAM, M.A. (*d.* Feb. 1696/7). 𝔓. Born at Farnham, Surr. Matric. 'pleb.' at Magdalen Hall, Oxford, 1 May 1651; B.A., 1655; M.A., 1657. Curate at Newport, I. of Wight; vicar of Portsea, Hants; ejected, 1662. He fixed his residence at Farnham, preaching there and at Alton, Hants. Licensed, June 1672, as "Pr. Teacher in the howse of Henry Matthew at Alton." From 1689 till death he was pastor at Farnham. (*C. F. P. T. Ws.*) [109]

BICKNOLLER. Ejected here was Thomas Safford, B.A. [*q.v.*]. [91]

BIDBANCK, GEORGE (1644—12 Jan. 1710/11). ℭ. Born at Denton, Norf. Son of William Bidbancke ('Bedbank') [*q.v.*]. From Bungay grammar school, admitted pensioner at St. John's Coll., Cambridge, 27 May 1662, age 18; did not matriculate. To Dec. 1672 belongs the entry "Licence George Bidbanke of Denton Congr Teachr Northamptonsh." This should be Norfolk (*see* Bedbank, *i.e.* Bidbanck, William, his father). Admitted member of the Congregational church, Yarmouth, 1 Apr. 1673; demitted, 7 N. 1689, on a call to the pastorate at Woodbridge, where a Meeting-house had just been built. From Michaelmas 1706 he was disabled by paralysis. (*B. Jo. T. V.*) [103]

BIDEFORD ('Biddiford'). Silenced here was William Bartlett (brother of John Bartlett [*q.v.*]); of New Inn Hall, Oxford; matric., 4 Nov. 1631, aged 21; held the sequestered rectory of Bideford, 25 July 1644; resigned, before 29 June 1647; living at Bideford, 1665; licensed, 2 Apr. 1672, as Congreg. Teacher in any allowed place; *d.* 1682; father of John Bartlett (*see* Fremington). (*C. F. T.*) [30]

BIGGIN, or BIGLEY, JOHN (*fl.* 1650–1700). 𝔓. Held (after 1650) the sequestered curacy of Colne White, Ess.; this being a donative, he continued in it without conforming. The Episc. Returns, 1669, report him as one of two preachers at Marks Tey, Ess.; also as preaching to "about 40 the basest sort of people" in Stoke-by-Nayland, Suff., "At the house of one Mrs Mary Groome." Licensed, 13 May 1672, being of Colne White, as "Grāll Pr. Teacher." John Biggin, *alias* Bigley, was still curate in 1700.

On 24 Aug. 1691 the case of a Student, "son of Mr. Biggen, Stebben (*i.e.* Stebbing), Essex," was considered; on 28 Sept. it was reported that the father had "noe need of Assistance towards ye education of his son." This son was John Biggin (1675—30 D. 1707), Presbyterian Minister at Bungay, Suff., from 1699. (*B. C. E. M. P. T.*) [39]

BIGNALL, MADAM. ℭ. [165]

BIGSWORTH. [51] *See* Hertfordshire

BILLERICAY ('Bilerekay'). [38]

BILLINGSGATE (derivation unknown), in Thames Street, was from 1559 an open space for landing or embarking fish, corn, salt stores, victuals, fruit (except grocery), and no other merchandise; from 10 May 1699 it was a free market for the sale of fish. (*Lo. Sl.*) [2]

BILLINGSLEY, JOHN (1657—2 May 1722). **P.** Born at Chesterfield, Derbs. Son of John Billingsley, M.A. (14 S. 1625—30 May 1684); ejected, 1662, from the vicarage of Chesterfield. Said to have studied, but did not matriculate at Trinity Coll., Cambridge. Educ. (1660–1668) under Edward Reyner, M.A. Ejected from the vicarage of St. Peter's at Arches, Lincoln., and under John Whitlock [*q.v.*], his uncle. Ordained, 1684, by his father and others. Preached first at Chesterfield; then at Sheffield; then, for seven years, at Selston, Notts, receiving £6 a year (1690–92) from the Common Fund; then, for ten years, at Kingston-on-Hull; colleague (1706 ?) to William Harris, D.D., at Poor Jewry Lane, Crutched Friars, London. A Non-subscriber at Salters' Hall, 1719. He suffered all his life from ill-health. (*C. M. No. P. Tc. V. W.*) [82, 83]

BILLINSLEY, *i.e.* BILLINGSLEY, NICHOLAS, B.A. (1633–Dec. 1709). **P.** Born at Faversham, Kent (baptized, 1 N. 1633); son of Nicholas Billingsley, M.A., master of Faversham school, and rector (1644–51) of Betteshanger, Kent. Matric. at Merton Coll., Oxford, 10 Mar. 1656/7; B.A., 1658. Vicar of Weobley, Heref.; ejected, 1662. Taught school at Abergavenny, Monm. Sir Edward Harley put him in the privileged chapelry of Blakeney, parish of Awre, Glou.; the vicarage of Awre he refused. He was several times suspended, and resigned, 1689. The Common Fund made him a gift of £10, 1692–1702, when he was in Gloucestershire; and again, 1704–5, when he was at Bristol, where he died. His congregation appears in Evans' List as "Blakeney near the Forest of Dean, P.," but he preached in various parts of Gloucestershire. He published three volumes of poems, 1657, 1658, 1667.

His younger son, Nicholas, was Minister at Ashwick, Som., in 1699, and received grants from the Fund till 1729. (*C. D. F. J. M. P. Rg.*) [45, 47]

BILLINSLIE, *i.e.* BILLINGSLEY, RICHARD (*b.* 1660). Elder son of Nicholas Billingsley [*q.v.*]. Matric. at St. Mary Hall, Oxford, 4 Mar. 1674/5, aged 14. Minister at Whitchurch, Hants, where he died before 1713. The Common Fund granted him £8 a year for Whitchurch, 1699–1703. (*F. M.*) [47]

BILLIO, JOSEPH (*fl.* 1687–1729). Son of Robert Billio [*q.v.*]. Minister at Maldon, Ess., from about 1687; where a Meeting-house was erected for him in St. Peter's parish. Living in 1729. (*E. Ev.*) [39]

BILLIO, ROBERT (1623—19 Apr. 1695). **P.** Born at Sible Hedingham, Ess. From the Castle Hedingham grammar school he proceeded to Trinity Coll., Cambridge, but did not matriculate. His early ministerial charges were at West Bergholt, Ess., and Hatfield Peverel, Ess. About 1658 he became rector of Wickham Bishops, Ess.; ejected, 1662. Settling with no congregation, he preached in various places. The Countess of Warwick befriended him and aided the education of his children. In Dec. 1664 he was preaching in the house of Jeffrey Meage, at Felstead, Ess. In 1668 he disputed publicly with Quakers. The Episc. Returns, 1669, describe him as of Scanbridge (? Cambridge) and as preaching at Kelvedon, Ess., Thaxted, Ess., and Aythorp Roding, Ess. Licensed, 22 July 1672, being of Stebbing, Ess., "to teach in any place Pr"; and on 10 Aug. he was licensed for a house in Hanningfield, Ess. He spent some time in Herts in the house of Israel Mayo [*q.v.*], who is probably the "godly man" mentioned in connection with Puckeridge, partly in Braughing parish, Herts. The house of John Brett at Braughing was certified (29 Apr. 1691) for Dissenting worship, by Robert Billio, preacher. In 1692 the Common Fund granted him £6 at Buntingford, Herts, for preaching at Puckeridge. He died at Bacton, Suff. His sons, Robert [*q.v.*] and Joseph [*q.v.*], and his grandsons, Robert and Joseph, were all in the Nonconformist ministry; but the two latter conformed, after 1720. (*C. E. M. P. T. Tc. Uh. V.*) [11, 52]

BILLIO, ROBERT, *secundus* (*d.* 5 May 1710). **P.** Son of Robert Billio (*supra*). Educated at the Academy of Samuel Cradock [*q.v.*]. Chaplain in the family of Sir Francis Bickley, Attleborough, Norf. Minister at Little Chishall, Ess. Fled to Holland, 1685. Minister at St. Ives, 1687. One of the witnesses against Richard Davis [*q.v.*] at Kettering in 1692. Removed, 1700, to Mare Street, Hackney, where he ministered till death. He attended, as a Manager of the Fund, 3 Mar. 1700—4 Feb. 1703/4. (*Gl. M. Wh.*) [53]

BILLOTT. [110] *See* Surrey

BINFIELD. [7, 8]

BINGLEY. [180]

BINMORE, RICHARD, M.A. (*b.* 1621). **P.**

Son of Bartholomew Bynmoore, of Bickington, Devon, pleb. Matric. at Exeter Coll., Oxford, 4 May 1638, aged 17; B.A., 1641–2; M.A., 1642. Appointed, 26 June 1646, to the sequestered rectory of Woodleigh-on-Avon, Devon; ejected, 1662, the surviving sequestered rector allowing him to keep the living in 1660. Arrested for preaching a funeral sermon (with the rector's leave) in his old church. On 30 Apr. 1672 he was licensed as "Pr. Teacher," and his house in Woodleigh, or Woodland, was licensed as a "Pr. Meeting Place." (*C. F. P. T. Wc.*) [32]

BINSON, THOMAS, *i.e.* BENSON, JOHN (*d.* 1720). Entered Frankland's Academy, 3 Apr. 1690. Minister in succession to Richard Whitehurst [*q.v.*], at Bridlington, E.R., where a Meeting-house was built in 1698, and a new Meeting-house (Zion Chapel) was built (1706 ?) and endowed by Matthew Yeates and Matthew Prudom, his grandson. Benson was buried on 2 May 1720. (*Fr. My. Nr.*) [136]

BIRCH, chapelry in Manchester parish (now rectory). Ejected here was Robert Birch, incumbent of the Chapel about 1651; ejected, 1662; preaching at Wilmslow, Ches., in 1669, at which time the Episc. Returns report "frequent and numerous Conventicles at Birch Chapel," chiefly of Independents; licensed, 30 Sept. 1672, as Indep[t] Teacher at Wilmslow; subsequently practised as physician and surgeon; *d.* 1693, at Grindlowe in Chorlton Row (now Chorlton-on-Medlock, Manchester). He was probably the father of Eliezer Birch [*q.v.*] who witnessed his will, and is certainly the person so designated in the Manuscript. Nonconformists regained possession of the Chapel for a time (*see* Henry Finch). (*Bx. C. Nl. T.*) [61, 177]

BIRCH, ELIEZER (*d.* 12 May 1717). **C.** Entered at Frankland's Academy, 9 Feb. 1676/7. Minister at Congleton, till 1688; Dean Row, 1688–1707; Great Yarmouth, 1707–10; Cross Street, Manchester, 1710 till death. In 1715 Cross Street Chapel was wrecked by the Jacobite mob. It was in his house at Dean Row that the Cheshire Classis (*see* p. 157) was formally constituted in June 1691. (*Fr. Nl. Uc.*)

BIRCHALL, or BURCHILL, WILLIAM, M.A. (*fl.* 1662–93). **P.** Sizar at Trinity Coll., Cambridge, 17 Mar. 1645/6; B.A., 1649; M.A., 1653. Rector of Wentworth, Cambs.; ejected thence, he lived at Wilsford, near by, and preached privately. Licensed, 29 May 1672, as Pr. Teacher in his house at Wentworth, Isle of Ely. From 1689 preached twice each Sunday at Sutton, Camb. The Fund made him (1690–3) a grant of £5 a year for Sutton. (*C. M. P. T. Tc. V.*) [12]

BIRCHALL, WILLIAM. **P.** A hitherto unknown predecessor of Thomas Blinstone (1673–1721), whose ministry at Park Lane began in 1697. Birchall's house in Ashton-in-Makerfield was registered July 1689. (*Fp. X.*) [58]

BIRD-IN-HAND ALLEY, now Bird-in-Hand Court, runs from the South side of Cheapside, between Nos. 76 and 77. [1]

BIRMINGHAM. Ejected here was Samuel Willes (born at Coventry) of Christ's Coll., Cambridge; matric. pensioner, 1627; B.A., 1630/1; M.A., 1634; rector or vicar of Croxall, Derb.; lecturer at Great St. Helen's, London; rector of St. Martin's, Birmingham, 6 Aug. 1646; ejected, 1660/1; preached at St. John's, Deritend, till driven from Birmingham; living and preaching at Hampton-in-Arden, War., in 1669; licensed, 1 May 1672, as Pr. Teacher in his house at Birmingham; his house licensed, same date, as Pr. Meeting-place; also licensed, 10 June 1672, as Pr. Teacher in his house at Whitley (a manor house with old chapel, two miles from Coventry, but in St. Michael's parish); the house licensed, same date, Presb.; also licensed, 22 July 1672, as Pr. Teacher at another house in Birmingham, licensed same date, Prb.; removed to his son in Shropshire; *d.* 14 May 1684, aet. 73. (*C. Dw. T. V.*) [117, 119, 120]

BISHOP, . . . ? Edward Bishop, who received £4 a year (1716–22) from the Fund as Minister at Up Ottery, Devon. (*M.*) [91, 92]

BISHOPS CLEEVE ('Cleave'). [44, 45]

BISHOPS HULL ('Hill bishops'). Ejected here was Nathaniel Charlton or Charleton, of Exeter Coll., Oxford, 1637; rem. to Queens' Coll., Cambridge; B.A., 1644/5; rector of Woodborough, Wilts, 1653; held the perpetual curacy of Bishops Hull; preaching in his own house at Bishops Hull, at Oake, Taunton Magdalen, and West Monkton, Som., in 1669; licensed, 17 Apr. 1672, to teach as Presbyt. in his house at Taunton; his house licensed, same date, as Presb. Meeting-place. (*C. F. T. V.*) [91]

BISHOPS STORTFORD ('Storford'). Ejected here was John Paine [? of New Inn Hall, Oxford; matric., 20 June 1634, aged 18; B.A., 1636; M.A., 1638/9]; held the sequestered vicarage of

Broxbourne, Herts, 1643–47; that of Sawbridgeworth, Herts, 1646–50; vicar of Bishops Stortford, 1650/1; ejected, 1662; licensed, 1 May 1672, as Teacher of Presbyterians in a house at Bishops Stortford; living there in 1684; his son Jonathan, grocer, *d.* there, 24 June 1681, aged 31. (*C. T. Uh.*) [39, 50, 51]

BISHOPSTONE ('Bishopston'). [115]

BISISTER. [85] *See* Oxfordshire

BISLEY ('Beeslie,' 'Bizly'). Ejected here was Richard Britton, of New Inn Hall, Oxford; matric. 16 Nov. 1632, aged 19; B.A., 1635; rector of Bisley, 1641; ejected, 1662; afterwards conformed. (*C. F.*) [44, 46]

BISPHAM. [64, 180]

BLACKBURN ('Blakburne'). Ejected here from headmastership of the grammar school was Charles Sagar [*q.v.*]. [61]

BLACKBURN ('Blakburne') HUNDRED. [61, 64]

BLACKLEY ('Blakely,' 'Bleakley'). Ejected here were (1) James Booker, curate [? of Emmanuel Coll., Cambridge; matric. sizar, 1654; B.A., 1654/5; Fellow; M.A., 1658], who afterwards conformed. (*By. C. V.*) (2) Thomas Holland; B.A., Edinburgh, 15 Apr. 1645; ord. by presbyters as Minister of Ringley Chapel, 15 Apr. 1647; removed to Blackley Chapel, 1654; ejected, 1662; licensed, 18 Nov. 1672, as Pr. Teach: in his own house in Oldham parish; his residence after ejection was at Newton Heath; and he was disabled from preaching "some years" before he died; he was buried at the Collegiate Church, Manchester, 28 Dec. 1674. (*C. Ed. Nl. T.*) [60, 63]

BLACKMORE, CHEWNING (1 Jan. 1662/3—2 Aug. 1737). **P.** Born at Islington. Only son of William Blackmore, M.A. (1618 ?–July 1684), ejected (1662) from the rectory of St. Peter's, Cornhill, by his first wife, Mary Chewning (*d.* Nov. 1678). He was at school (1672) at Writtle, Essex, under John Benson, M.A.; ejected from the vicarage of Little Leighs, Essex; afterwards at Newington Green (under Charles Morton, till 1685 ?); and at the Academy of John Woodhouse [*q.v.*]. Went to Oxford to prepare for the Ministry; did not matriculate. On leaving, Henry Cornish, D.D., gave him a testimonial (18 Apr. 1688) as a "spiritually accomplished" member of his flock. Became assistant (1688) to Thomas Badland [*q.v.*] at Worcester. The Common Fund voted him (1690) £8 a year for Worcester "on condition hee stay there." It was paid to him till 1693. He succeeded Badland as pastor, and refused, 1706/7, a call to London. The Angel Street Meeting-house was built for him (1708) and certified for Presbyterians. He was assisted (till 1719) by Jonathan Hand, and from 1720 by John Stokes. He appears to have been disabled for three years before his death. (*D. J. M. To. Uw.*) [126, 127]

BLACKPOOL. [180]

BLADEN, or BLADON, THOMAS (*fl.* 1655–1690). Matric. pensioner at Magdalene Coll., Cambridge, 1655; did not graduate. Vicar of Alrewas, Staff.; ejected, 1662. The Episc. Returns, 1669, report him as one of the preachers to "above 300" persons at various houses in Walsall, Staff. He lived many years in Birmingham, and died at Tamworth. (*C. P. T. V.*) [96]

BLAKBURNE. [61] *See* Lancashire

BLAKE, MALACHI (*b.* 1651—18 June 1705). **P.** Son of John Blake (1629–1682). He was one of three preachers at Honiton, in the back-house of William Clarke, chandler, from 1687; he was proposed as pastor, but superseded (after 1690) by Thomas Edwards [*q.v.*]. Lived at Blagdon, parish of Pitminster, Som. Itinerant preacher in Somerset. Died Minister of Wellington, Som.

His second son, Malachi (1687–1760), was Minister at Langport, Som. (1712–1717), and afterwards at Blandford Forum till death. (*D. Em. M. Mh. Wu.*) [30, 93]

BLAKELY, BLEAKLEY. [60, 63] *See* Lancashire

BLAKEY, NICHOLAS, M.A. (*d.* 1698). **P.** Born in Scotland. Graduated M.A. at Edinburgh, 15 Apr. 1652, as "Nicolaus Blaikie, minister verbi." Licensed, 2 Apr. 1672, as "a Presbyterian Teacher in a certaine Howse neare adjoining to Blackfryers Church." Minister of the Scots Church, Founders' Hall, Lothbury, from 1684 till death. (*Ed. T. W.*) [165, 166]

BLAND, . . . [23]

BLANDFORD FORUM. Ejected here was William Alleine of New Inn Hall, Oxford; matric., 4 Nov. 1631, aged 17; B.A., 1634; M.A., 1636/7; chaplain in London; thence to Ilchester, and afterwards Bristol; then, London again; vicar of Blandford, 1653; ejected, 1660; gathered a church at Blandford; removed to Bristol, and thence to Yeovil, Som.; *d.* there, Oct. 1677. (*C. F.*) [34]

BLEASBY ('Bleasbey'). Ejected here was John Jackson (*q.v.*]. [83]

BLEWLAKE, in Knowle parish, War.

[119] *See* Wright, James (1610–Dec. 1691)

BLIDWORTH. Ejected here was Thomas Rose [*q.v.*]. [82]

BLORE, *i.e.* BLOWER, SAMUEL, M.A. (*d.* 1701). **C.** Born at Loughborough, Leic. Matric. pleb. at Magdalen Coll., Oxford, 20 F. 1648/9; demy, 1648–52; B.A., 1651/2; Fellow, 1652–60; M.A., 1654. Lecturer at Woodstock, Oxf.; ejected, 1660. Licensed, 28 Oct. 1672, as "Congr. genall Teacher of Sudbury in Suffolk." Minister from 1674 (?) till 1695, of the Congregational church at Northampton. One of the witnesses against Richard Davis [*q.v.*] at Kettering in 1692. Removed to Abingdon, and there died. (*C. Cn. Dc. Gl. P. T.*) [76]

BLUNT, ROBERT (1624–1716). **C.** Admitted sizar at Trinity Coll., Cambridge, 2 July 1643; matric., 1643; Scholar, but did not graduate. Vicar of Kirkharle, Northumb.; ejected, 1662. Living at Alnwick, 1665, when presented for Nonconformity. Licensed, 8 May 1672; as "Pr. Teacher" in his own house at Alnwick, Northumb.; he had applied in vain for the Tolbooth at Alnwick. He was outlawed and fined after withdrawal of Indulgence. In 1682 he became Minister of the Congregational church at Horsley, Northumb., and continued to preach there till 1714, having James Atkinson as colleague. The Common Fund granted him (1690–93) £5 a year for Harlow, Northumb.; and (1705–11) £6 a year for Horsley. Harlow Hill and Horsley are both in Ovingham parish. (*C. J. M. P. T. Tc. V.*) [79, 80]

BODDINGTON, GEORGE. **C.** Member of the congregation of Nathanael Mather [*q.v.*]. Manager of the Common Fund from the first, and a very regular attendant; elected a Treasurer, 20 Apr. 1691, in place of Thomas Hartley [*q.v.*], but declined to act (27 Apr.); last attendance, 26 June 1693. Treasurer of the Congregational Fund from its formation (1695) till his retirement, 2 Feb. 1701/2, and one of its correspondents for Dorset and Gloucestershire. (*Cf. Co. M.*) [162]

BODDINGTON, JAMES. **P.** Appointed a Manager of the Common Fund, but attended no meeting, and resigned 8 Dec. 1690, owing to pressure of business. As his resignation was conveyed through John Jurin [*q.v.*] he is here assigned to the same denomination. There is nothing to show relationship to George Boddington [*q.v.*]; it is hardly likely that two brothers would be appointed. (*M.*) [162]

BODMIN ('Bodman'). [19]

BOLTON, Lanc. Ejected here were: (1) Richard Goodwin, of Emmanuel Coll., Cambridge; matric. sizar, 1632; B.A., 1635/6; M.A., 1639; ordained episcopally incumbent of Cockey Chapel, Lanc., 1640 (?); fled to Hull, 1645, thence to London, thence to Hargrave, Northants; assistant minister at Bolton, 20 May 1647; vicar of Bolton, 1657; ejected, 1662; licensed, 22 May 1672, as Pr. Teacher in a house at Bolton; *d.* 12 Dec. 1685, aged 72. (*Bi. C. T. V.*) (2) Robert Parke, bapt. at Bolton, 17 Aug. 1600; of Emmanuel Coll., Cambridge; matric. sizar, matric. pensioner, 1615; B.A., 1618/9; M.A., 1622; vicar of Bolton, 1625; resigned before Nov. 1630; Congregational Minister at Rotterdam, 1639; returned as lecturer to Bolton, 1649; vicar of Mortlake, Sur., 1656; rector of Lavant, Suss., 1658; Goswell lecturer at Bolton, 1660; ejected, 1660; bur. 25 Dec. 1668 at Bolton. (*Bi. Br. C. V.*) John Jaques, who afterwards conformed, was of Bolton-le-Sands. (*C. Sy.*) [61]

BOLTON CLASSIS. [157]

BOLTON-UPON-DEARNE ('Dern'). Ejected here was Nathan Denton, B.A. [*q.v.*]. [129]

BOOTH, . . . [166]

BORFET, MATTHEW, *i.e.* SAMUEL, M.A. (*fl.* 1650–1691). **P.** Scholar of King's Coll., Cambridge, 29 June 1650; matric. pensioner, 1650; B.A., 1653/4; Fellow and M.A., 1657. Rector of High Laver, Ess., 1657; resigned (1662 ?). For some time preached at Maidstone, Kent, as a Nonconformist. He was of Woolwich, Kent, when licensed, 22 July 1672, and of Finsbury, London, and also of Woolwich, when licensed, 10 Aug. 1672, as a general Presb. Teacher. Minister at Curriers' Hall, Cripplegate, 1685–91. In 1691 he was laid aside from work. (*C. Ck. M. P. T. V. W.*) [165]

BORY TRACY. [32] *See* Devonshire

BOSTON. Ejected here was Bankes Anderson, of Magdalene Coll., Cambridge; matric. pensioner, 1626; B.A., 1629/30; M.A., 1633; Mayor's chaplain at Boston, 1651; one of the Savoy Conference of Congregationals, 1658; ejected, 1662; *d.* Sept. 1668. (*C. Tb. V.*) [36, 70, 71]

BOURNE. [115] *See* Sussex

BOURNE, *i.e.* BOURN, SAMUEL (1648–4 Mar. 1718/9). **P.** Born at Derby; son of a clothier; nephew of Robert Seddon [*q.v.*]. Studied but did not matriculate at Emmanuel Coll., Cambridge; left, 1672, without degree, declining subscription. Taught school at Derby. Chaplain to Lady Hatton. Ordained by presbyters in London. Samuel Annesley [*q.v.*] sent him to Calne, Wilts, where he was pastor from 1679. The Common Fund granted him (1690) £8 a year for Calne, reduced (1695) to £6. The Calne congregation must have prospered under his ministry, since they were able to offer him a higher stipend than Bolton, if he would return to them. Bourn, however, succeeded Seddon in 1698 as Minister at Bolton, Lanc., was the first Minister of Bank Street Chapel (opened Oct. 1696), and there remained till death. The records of the Hulton Trust at Bolton, showing payments for his catechising there in the years 1696–99, prove conclusively that he had removed to Bolton, though the Fund payments for Calne were still made for those years to a person of the same name, probably Samuel Bourne (*fl.* 1691–1742) [*q.v.*].

Bourn's son, Samuel, and grandsons, Joseph and Samuel, were Nonconformist Ministers of distinction. (*Bi. D. M. Ts. V.*) [92, 123]

BOURNE, SAMUEL (*fl.* 1691–1742). 𝔓. Not son of Samuel Bourn [*supra*]. Received grants, 1691–92, as student at Bishop's Hall, Bethnal Green, with Thomas Brand [*q.v.*], and under the instruction of John Ker, M.D. [*q.v.*]; also 1692–95 at Bishop's Hall, under John Short [*q.v.*]. The payments for Calne from Midsummer 1696 to the end of 1699 were probably made to him. He was Minister at Epping, Essex, 1706–41, and perhaps earlier. The Common Fund granted him (1706) £5 a year for Epping. This was discontinued in 1722 "because of his having a good Estate and no Children." From Midsummer 1728 to Michaelmas of 1741 £7 a year was paid to him, and he received special grants on Nov. 1741 and 8 Nov. 1742. He was succeeded in 1742 by John Nettleton (Doddridge's brother-in-law). (*Ev. M.*) [4]

BOURTON ('Burton')-ON-THE-WATER. Ejected here was Anthony Palmer, of Balliol Coll., Oxford; matric., 3 Dec. 1634, aged 16; B.A., 1638; Fellow, 1640–49; M.A., 1641; rector of Bourton-on-the-Water, 1646; assistant commissioner for ejecting scandalous ministers, 1654; ejected, 1662. In 1664 he was living in Finsbury Fields, and preaching in Soper Lane and the Strand. The Episc. Returns, 1669, report him as preaching to 200 persons at Mill Lane; in 1672 he had a gathered church at the Glass House (Pinners' Hall). Licensed, 19 Apr. 1672, to preach in a house on London Bridge. Minister of Pinners' Hall Congregational church, London; *d.* 26 Jan. 1678/9. (*C. D.*) [44]

BOVEY TRACEY ('Bory Tracy'). [32]

BOWDEN, JOHN, or JONATHAN (*d.* 18 Mar. 1698/9). 𝔓. Ejected from the rectory of Littleham St. Swithin, Devon. The Episc. Returns, 1669, report him as one of the preachers to 100 persons "At the Barne of John Fisher, att Mr Button's barne, & att Mr Walter's house" in Batheaston, Som.; also as sole preacher to 100 persons "Att a Publiqe Inne" in Bath; further as one of the preachers to 300 persons "Att the Sheepe-house of Willm Clement señ & Willm Clement jun" in Dunkerton, Som. Licensed, 15 Apr. 1672, as general Presb. Teacher; he settled eventually as Minister in Bideford. (*C. P. T.*) [30]

BOWLER, WILLIAM. (*M.*) [181]

BOWLES, JOS: ℭ. Attended as Manager of the Common Fund, 20 Oct. 1690; last attendance, 10 Nov. 1690. Manager (1695) of the Congregational Fund, and one of its correspondents for Essex and Suffolk. Apparently he was the Captain Bowles who was Calamy's fellow-traveller to Holland in March 1687/8, and his subsequent acquaintance in London, where he was a leading member of the Congregational church in Ropemakers' Alley, Moorfields, under Walter Cross, M.A. He was "an everlasting talker" and "a great reader," who took pleasure in starting difficulties, being himself "a real Origenist, and, if such a thing was possible, an Arminian and an Antinomian both." When Calamy told him he was "doing the devil's work, by unsettling people," he replied "that he thought he rather did them a kindness by guarding them against taking their principles upon trust." (*Cf. Cm. M.*) [162]

BOWMAN, CAPT. ℭ. His "gift" came through John James (1626 ?–1696) [*q.v.*]. [165]

BRACKSTEAD, BRACKTED. [38, 41] *See* Essex

BRADDON. [67] *See* Leicestershire

BRADFIELD ('Bradford'). Ejected here was John Smith, who went to Ireland. [7]

BRADFORD. [129]

BRADFORD DALE. [130]

BRADSHAW, JAMES (1636–1702). 𝔓. Born at Hacken, parish of Bolton, Lanc. From Bolton grammar school, matric. 'ser.' at Corpus Christi Coll., Oxford, 13 May 1653. Took no degree, under the influence of his uncle, Holmes, a Northamptonshire divine. Ordained by the Fourth Lancashire Classis. Incumbent (1658) of Hindley Chapel, parish of Wigan; implicated in Sir George Booth's rising; ejected, 1662. Imprisoned for continuing to preach. Licensed, 1 May 1672, being at Hindley, as "Grall Pr. Teacher"; his house at Hindley was licensed 22 July 1672. On the quashing of Indulgence, he obtained possession of Rainford Chapel, parish of Prescot, Lanc. (it was registered on his application, 18 July 1689), and retained it till death by having one of the neighbouring clergy to read the Anglican service once or twice a year; he was also one of the Monday lecturers at Bolton, Lanc. His house at Rainford was licensed for public worship, 11 Oct. 1697. The Common Fund granted him (1690) £6 a year for Rainford Chapel; ended 25 D. 1701.

His son, Ebenezer, was Minister at Ramsgate, Kent. (*C. Cm. D. F. M. Nl. P. X.*) [58]

BRADSHAW, NATHANAEL, M.A. (29 May 1619—16 O. 1690). **P.** Born at Keddington Hall, Suff., son of Thomas Bradshaw, of Bradshaw, Lanc. Admitted pensioner at Trinity Coll., Cambridge, 14 Apr. 1637; matric., 1637; B.A., 1640/1; M.A., 1644; Fellow, 1645–47; not B.D. Rector of Willingham, Cambs.; he was there in 1654, and is thus characterised from a local point of view—"he preaches twice a day, but have been better served, little to edification"; ejected, 1662. Preached at various places, including Childerley, Cambs., and London. Licensed, Nov. 1672, as Presb. Teacher at his house in Hemingford, Hunts. In 1689, living then at St. Ives, Hunts, he resumed work at Willingham, "desiring no more than his diet from Saturday night till Monday morning, and his horse-hire from St. Ives," where he died. He was buried in the chancel at Willingham. A wicked story tells that when the sexton was digging the grave for Naylor, Bradshaw's successor as rector, nigh to Bradshaw's, a high churchman exclaimed, "Why do you bury him so near that fanatic?" Quoth an aged woman, "It can't affect them while they lie here, and they may be far enough off at the resurrection." (*C. La. P. T. Tc. V.*) [12, 172]

BRADSHAW, WILLIAM, M.A. (1571–May 1618). **P.** Born at Market Bosworth, Leic.; son of Nicholas Bradshaw, of a Lancashire family. Had his schooling at Worcester and Ashby-de-la-Zouch. Matric. sizar, at Emmanuel Coll., Cambridge, 1589; B.A., 1592/3; M.A., 1596. Tutor in family of Sir Thomas Leighton, governor of Guernsey, where he came under the influence of Thomas Cartwright [*q.v.*]. Appointed, 1599, one of the original Fellows of Sidney Sussex Coll., Cambridge. In July 1601, became lecturer at Chatham, Kent, but was suspended in May 1602. Tutor in the family of Alexander Redich, Newhall, near Stapenhill, Derbysh., and obtained licence to preach in the diocese of Coventry and Lichfield. Died of fever on a visit to Chelsea. His "English Puritanisme," 1605 (translated into Latin by William Ames, D.D.), gives his views on church government. (*D. V.*) [151]

BRADSWORTH. [130] *See* Yorkshire, W.R.

BRAGG, *i.e.* BRAGGE, ROBERT, B.A. (1627—14 Apr. 1704). **C.** Son of John Bragge, of Heychurch, Dorset, captain in the parliamentary army. Matric. as servitor, 9 Apr. 1647, at Wadham Coll., Oxford, aged 19; scholar, 1648; B.A., 1649; Fellow, 1650, being then of Colyton, Devon (where Foster erroneously makes him vicar). Left Cambridge, 1652, and gathered a church in Allhallows the Great, London, whence ejected (1660?) before 12 June 1662. The vestry of Cheshunt parish, Herts, petitioned, 12 Dec. 1660, that he might be continued their Minister. Reported in Episc. Returns, 1669, as preaching at Theobalds, Herts. Gathered a church in Pewterers' Hall, Lime Street, London, and ministered there till death; assisted by Ralph Venning (1620?–10 Mar. 1673), ejected from lectureship at St. Olave's, Southwark.

His son, Robert Bragge (1665—12 Feb. 1737/8), who studied at Utrecht (1691), was ordained, 1698, as pastor of Congr. church in Paved Alley, Lime Street, London, and was known as Eternal Bragge, from preaching for four months on Joseph's coat (Gen. xxxvii. 3). Subscriber at Salters' Hall, 1719. (*C. Cm. F. G. P. T. U.*) [4, 166]

BRAINFORD. [73] *See* Middlesex

BRAINTREE ('Braintrey'). Ejected here was John Argor, of Queens' Coll., Cambridge; matric. sizar, 1620; B.A., 1623/4; M.A., 1647; rector of Leighs, Ess., 1639; member of the Fourth Presb. Classis of Essex; vicar of Braintree after 1650; ejected, 1662; taught school at Braintree; licensed, 2 Apr. 1672, as Presbyterian Teacher at houses in Copford and Birch Magna, Ess.; his house at Copford licensed, Pr., 5 Sept. 1672; *d.* Dec. 1679, aged 77. *See* Wivenhoe. (*C. E. T. V.*) [38]

BRAMPTON. [23]

BRAND, THOMAS, B.A. (1635—1 Dec. 1691). 𝔓. Son and heir of Thomas Brand, rector of Leaden Roding, Essex. Schooling at Bishops Stortford, Herts. Matric., 24 June 1653, at Merton Coll., Oxford; B.A., 1660. Of the Inner Temple, 1656. Turned to the ministry under influence of Samuel Annesley, D.D. [*q.v.*]. Chaplain and tutor in family of the dowager Dame Bridget (23 Aug. 1626–Apr. 1706), widow of Sir Howland Roberts, Bart., at Glassenbury, parish of Cranbrook, Kent, preaching there and in the vicinity, and giving his salary in charity. Licensed, 20 Apr. 1672, as "Presb. Teacher in the Lady Roberts howse in Cranbrooke." On death (1674) of Daniel Poyntel (ejected from rectory of Staplehurst, but licensed, 10 Aug. and 30 Sept. 1672, as Presb. Teacher in house of Peter Burrens, Staplehurst, Kent), Brand removed to Staplehurst, and was ordained. Driven thence, he had many wanderings, settling at length at Bishop's Hall, near Bethnal Green [*q.v.*]. His former pupil, Jocelyne Roberts, Esq., lived at Bethnal Green. At Bishop's Hall, Brand conducted an Academy, assisted by John Ker, M.D. [*q.v.*]. His charities were unstinted; he built Meeting-houses, aided Ministers and students, gave away thousands of books and catechisms, and sold Bibles under cost, on condition they were not to be sold again. His estate was entailed, "but he would squeeze it as long as he lived." He married a widow; his children all died young. His estate came ultimately, by bequest, to John Disney, D.D., sometime Minister of Essex Street Chapel, Strand. (*C. D. F. Je. K. La. P. T.*) [41, 56, 166, 168]

BRANTON. [80]

BRAXTED. [38, 41]

BREACH OF UNION. [156, 183 *sqq.*]

BRECKNOCKSHIRE. [143, 146]

BREGHOLT, EAST. [105, 106] *See* Suffolk

BREMBRO. [17] *See* Cheshire

BRENTFORD ('Brainford'). [73]

BRENTWOOD. [40, 43]

BRICE, JOHN, B.A. (*fl.* 1650–1696). 𝔓. Son of William Brice [*q.v.*]; and matric. as cler. fil. at St. John's Coll., Oxford, 13 N. 1650; B.A., 1652. Ejected, 1662, from rectory of East Hampstead, Berks. Reported in Episc. Returns, 1669, as preaching with his father at Wraysbury and Colebrooke, Bucks. Licensed, 17 Apr. 1672, to be a Presb. Teacher "in his owne house & Francis Ligo's in Beckenham, Kent." In 1691 and 1692 received grant of £5 a year for Maidenhead. Living at Dover, 1696, when he granted a lease of property at Maidenhead. [It is not certain that all the above particulars refer to the same man.] (*C. F. M. P. Sm. T.*) [7]

BRICE, WILLIAM, M.A. (*fl.* 1620–92). 𝔓. Alumnus of Eton, 1620; Scholar of King's Coll., Cambridge, 1620; B.A., 1623/4; Fellow; M.A., 1627. Ejected, 1662, from rectory of Henley-on-Thames, Oxfordsh.; thereafter lived on his estate at Maidenhead, Berks; took no regular charge, but preached up and down the country. The Episc. Returns, 1669, report him as one of the preachers to "neere 100" persons in the parish of St. Helen's, Abingdon, Berks, holding "Sundry meetings at ye houses of Consolation Fox, Parlmt Army Capt. Abbettors are ye forenamed Army men; Fox, Stevenson, Peck; Mrs Hancock." Also "Brices both Fathr & sonne" are reported among 13 Teachers of 200 or 300 Presbyterians at Wraysbury and Colebrooke, Bucks. Licensed, 25 July 1672, as Presb. Teacher "in his howse at Maidenhead, Berks." After the death (23 Aug. 1691) of Humfrey Gunter [*q.v.*], Brice was in sole charge at Buckland, Berks; his place was frequently supplied by Calamy when at Oxford (1691–92), Squire Southby, of Carswell, near Faringdon, Berks, sending a man and horse to fetch Calamy on Saturday afternoons. Brice died at an advanced age (before 1696?). John Brice [*q.v.*] was his son. (*C. Cm. M. P. Rr. T. V.*) [6, 7]

BRICKNELL, JOSEPH. [? Bricknall, James, M.A. Calamy gives Samuel Bricknal, ejected from the rectory of Wiston, Suss. Licence was granted, 25 May 1672, to "James Bricknoll of Preston, Sussex, to be Grāll Pr. Teacher." James Bricknall was postmaster, 1649, at Merton Coll., Oxford; matric. 'ser.,' 22 N. 1650; B.A., 1652; M.A., 1655. The suggestion is that all these are one and the same person.] (*C. F. P. T.*) [114]

BRIDGE, WILLIAM, M.A. (1600?–12 Mar. 1670/1). ℭ. Born in Cambridgeshire. Entered Emmanuel Coll., Cambridge, aged 16; M.A., 1626, and Fellow. Lecturer at Colchester, Essex, 16 Apr. 1631; lecturer at St. George's, Tombland, Norwich, 1 Oct. 1632, and rector of St.

Peter's, Hungate, Norwich, till 1636, then silenced. Excommunicated, he fled to Holland and became teacher in the Congregational church at Rotterdam founded by Hugh Peters (June 1598—16 O. 1660). Renounced his Anglican orders and was ordained by Samuel Ward, B.D. (1577 ?–1639/40). Returning to England (1641), he constituted (1642) at Norwich a Congregational church, with which he removed (1643) to Great Yarmouth. Appointed (1643) a member of the Westminster Assembly, he held a London lectureship, and was a leader of the Dissenting Brethren. His Yarmouth flock met in the chancel of the parish church, from which they were ejected, 1661. Removing to Clapham, Surrey, he continued to preach there. (*B. C. D. P.*) [188]

BRIDGES, JOHN. Ɒ. Of Barton Seagrave, Northants; eldest son of Col. John Bridges of Alcester, Warw., Baxter's friend. He was a Manager (1695) of the reconstituted Fund. (*D. M.*) [165]

BRIDGNORTH. Ejected here was Andrew Tristram, born in Staffordshire. Matric. sizar at Emmanuel Coll., Cambridge, 1647; did not graduate. On 5 Nov. 1667 he was admitted an extra-licentiate of the College of Physicians. Licensed, 5 Sept. 1672, as Presb. Teacher at his own house in Bridgnorth. His son, Benjamin, was vicar of Fillongley, Warw., in 1704. (*C. F. Mu. P. T. V.*) [16, 88]

BRIDGWATER. Ejected here in 1662 was John Norman, of Exeter Coll., Oxford; son of Abraham, of Trusham, Dev.; matric. 16 Mar. 1637/8, aged 15; B.A., 1641; ord. by presbyters, vicar of Bridgwater, 1647; *d.* at Bristol, 1671 ?; Calamy understates his age as 40. (*C. F. Mh.*) [91]

BRIDLINGTON. Ejected from this rectory was William Lucke [? of Jesus Coll., Cambridge; matric. sizar, 1631; B.A., 1634/5; M.A., 1638]. Application was made in 1672 for licence to William Lucker, of Bridlington, to preach in the Court House there, or in any licensed place; no licence for the Court House was granted; on 16 May 1672 Wm. Lucker was licensed as Grāll Pr. Teacher; on 20 May 1672 the original application was amended by giving the name as William Lucke and dropping the Court House; in June a licence was made out for " The howse of Wm Luck to be a Pr. Teacher in his howse in Bridlington." (*C. T. V.*) [138]

BRIDPORT. Ejected here was John Eaton [? of Trinity Coll., Cambridge; matric. sizar, 1628; B.A., 1632/3]; rector of Bridport, 1650; ejected, 1660. Licensed, 16 Apr. 1672, as Congr. Teacher at a house in Temple Combe. Signs, as John Eatón, Address of thanks, 10 May 1672. (*C. Hu. T. V.*) [34]

BRIGHTHELMSTONE, now Brighton. Ejected from this vicarage was Robert Everenden, or Evernden, of Emmanuel Coll., Cambridge; matric. sizar, 1630; he was preaching in 1669 at Cranbrook, Kent, to 200 or 300 Presbyterians and Independents, and to about 200 persons at a house in Brighton. (*C. T. V.*) [113]

BRIGSTOCK. [77]

BRINKWORTH. Ejected here was John Hardinge (eldest son of John, D.D., Oxford), of Magdalen Coll., Oxford; matric., 25 Oct. 1616, aged 15; B.A., 1620; M.A., 1623; D.D., 1648; rector of Stoke-Pero, Som., 1623; vicar of Ashbury, Berks, 1621; rector of Brinkworth, about 1642; ejected, 1662; strong Presbyterian; his son, John, M.A., was ejected from Melksham, Wilts. (*C. F.*)

It seems clear that the passage, " there is no Nonconformist meeting but wt is amongst them from Abergaynie to Glocester, wch is 30 miles," is misplaced, and belongs to Colford [*q.v.*]. [124]

BRINSLEY, or BRINLEY, SAMUEL (1625–1695 ?). Ɒ. Son of Laurence Brinley, merchant, of Ironmonger Lane, London. Matric., 26 May 1642, age 16, at New Inn Hall, Oxford. Admitted pensioner at St. John's Coll., Cambridge, 20 Sept. 1644, aet. 20; matric., 1645; B.A., 1645/6; Fellow, 1647; M.A., 1649. Held, after 1650, the sequestered rectory of Alphamstone, Ess.; ejected, 1662. After ejection, lived " principally in and about London." Licensed, June 1672, being of Dedham, Ess., as " Grāll Pr. Teacher." ' Barfield ' may be Great Bardfield, Little Bardfield, or Bardfield Saling. (*C. E. F. Jo. P. T. V.*) [39]

BRISTOL. Ejected here were: (1) Thomas Ewins; originally a mechanic; pastor of Congregational church at Llanvaches; morning preacher at Christ Church; held also five lectureships; ejected, 1660; first pastor of a gathered church, which ultimately became Broadmead Baptist church, and so continued till his death, 26 Apr. 1670. (*C. P. T.*)

(2) Ralph Farmer; at Cambridge University in 1638; did not matriculate; held the sequestered vicarage of St. Nicholas; ejected, 1660; but became lecturer till ejected, 1662; a man of property; *d.* at Hanham, Glou., about 1669. His son Thomas, of Wadham

Coll., Oxford, *d.* 21 Nov. 1672, aged 17. (*C. F. V.*)

(3) Edward Hancock [*q.v.*].

(4) Matthew Hazard; ejected from St. Mary Redcliffe; rector of St. Ewen's, Bristol, ejected, 1662; preaching at Bristol in 1665. [? Nath. Hazard, of Queens' Coll., Cambridge; matric. sizar, 1615; B.A., 1619/20; M.A., 1623.] (*C. T. V.*)

(5) John Knowle or Knowles, of Magdalene Coll., Cambridge; matric. pensioner, 1620; B.A., 1623/4; rem. to St. Catherine's Hall; M.A. and Fellow, 1627; lecturer at Colchester, 1635–37; went to New England, 1639; returning, 1651, was lecturer in Bristol cathedral, 1652/3; ejected, 1660; lecturer at All Hallows, London, 1661; ejected, 1662; co-pastor (1672) to Presbyterian congregation in parish of St. Catherine-in-the-Tower; *d.* 10 Apr. 1685. (*C. D. V.*)

(6) John Paul, or Paule, of Jesus Coll., Oxford; matric., 30 Apr. 1624, aged 17; B.A., 1627; M.A., 1630; incorp. at Cambridge, 1632; held the sequestered rectory of St. George's, Botolph Lane, London; held the sequestered vicarage of St. James', Bristol, 1645; ejected, 1662; preaching in Bristol, 1665. (*C. F. T. V.*)

(7) William Thomas, B.A. [*q.v.*]. [91]

BRITTON, or BRITTAINE, THEOPHILUS (1634—12 S. 1706). Born at Brattleby, Linc. Son of Robert Brittaine, merchant, of Lincoln. From Lincoln grammar school, matric. sizar at St. John's Coll., Cambridge, 5 June 1651, aged 17; did not graduate. Ejected from the rectory of Brockleby, Linc.; kept school at Swinderby, Linc., and suffered imprisonment for it. Chaplain to Col. King of Ashby, Linc. Took a farm at Roxholme, near Sleaford, Linc., and had pupils. Under arrest (1683) on suspicion of complicity with the Monmouth rebellion. The Common Fund granted him £6 a year for Sleaford, from 1690 to June 1691, and then dropped it. He was disabled for five years before his death. (*C. Jo. M. P. V.*) [70]

BRIXHAM. Ejected here was John Kempster, M.A. [*q.v.*]. [31]

BROAD OAK ('Broad Oake'), in Malpas parish, Flint. [15, 88]

BROADWAY. [93]

BRODSWORTH. Ejected here was William Hawdon, B.A. [*q.v.*]. [130]

BROMBOROUGH. [17]

BROMSGROVE. Ejected here was John Spilsbury, M.A. [*q.v.*]. [126]

BROMWICH. [96] *See* Staffordshire

BROOK, a manor in Westbury parish, Wilts. [123, 124]

BROOK, or BROOKES, LADY. **P.** James Brook, Brooke, or Brookes (1594–1675), merchant of York, and twice its Lord Mayor (1651, 1661), bought Ellenthorpe Hall. He married Priscilla Jackson, who was living at Howgrave, Yorks, very old, at the end of 1691. The title Lady was commonly given, as a life-long honour, to the wife of a Lord Mayor of York, in accord with the old York saw: "My Lord is a Lord for a year and a day, But My Lady's My Lady for ever and aye." Lady Brook or Brookes built in 1658 a small but ornate chapel, near to Ellenthorpe Hall, and gave £500 as endowment. The chapel ranked as Presbyterian, but it is interesting to note that, before there was "a fixed Minister," the supplies paid by the foundress were a Presbyterian and a Congregational alternately.

Her only son, John Brook or Brookes, who died before her in 1691, was created a baronet as Sir John Brookes on 13 June 1676. Hence, to distinguish his mother from Lady Brookes, his wife and widow, the elder lady was called Lady Brook or Lady Priscilla Brookes. (*Ba. Dy. H. Hh. My.*) [135, 165]

BROOKES, or BROOKE, JOSHUA (1629–16 Jan. 1696/7). Merchant Taylor. Member of the congregation of George Griffith, M.A. [*q.v.*]. Attended as Manager of the Common Fund, 15 Sept. 1690; last attendance, 10 Oct. 1692. Manager (1695) of the Congregational Fund, and one of its correspondents for Yorkshire. He gave £5 a year (1695–96) to Nathan Denton [*q.v.*]. (*Cf. Co. M.*) [162, 165]

BROOKES, SAMUEL (*fl.* 1690–1706). **P.** Received grant of £10 (1690) as student with Thomas Brand [*q.v.*] at Bishop's Hall, Bethnal Green, under the instruction of John Ker, M.D. [*q.v.*]. Minister at Dorking, Surr., 1695–1706. Removed to London early in the reign of Anne, and died shortly after. Buried at Dorking. (*Dg. M.*) [4]

BROOKES, or BROOKS, THOMAS (1608–27 Sept. 1680). **C.** Matric. pensioner at Emmanuel Coll., Cambridge, 7 July 1625; did not graduate. Chaplain to Rainsborough, admiral of the parliamentary fleet, and to his son, Col. Thomas Rainsborough (*d.* Nov. 1648). He was a preacher (1648) at St. Thomas Apostle's, and chosen by the parishioners (1652/3) as rector of St. Mary Magdalene's, New Fish Street (a sequestered living). Here he gathered a Congregational church, and the parish petitioned against his proceedings. He describes himself (in

August 1660) as "Preacher of the word at Margaret's, New Fish Street, London, and Pastor of the Church of Christ meeting there." He was ejected in 1660. In 1666, after the Fire, he preached openly in London. On 22 July 1672 he was licensed as Congr. Teacher in the house of John Bagges, Lime Street, London. His sermons are still kept in print; some have been translated into Gaelic and Welsh. (*C. D. P. T. V. Wc.*) [154]

BROOKHORNE. [91] *See* Somerset

BROOKSBANKE, JOHN. His house "in Ealand in the vicaridge of Hallifax" was certified for Nonconformist worship on 19 July 1689. Nicolas Brooksbank of Elland (M.A., Christ's Coll., Cambridge, 1672), second son of John Brooksbank, "a Preacher," "but retired many years," died 25 July 1690, aged 43, and was buried at Elland. The Common Fund voted £6 a year for Elland on 4 Jan. 1692, but it was only paid for that year. Joseph Brooksbank, citizen of London (*d.* 11 June 1726), endowed the Meeting-house and a school at Elland. (*Cp. Hy. My. Nr.*) [132]

BROOMFIELD ('Broomvill'). [93]

BROUGHTON TOWER, in the parish of Broughton-in-Furness (or West Broughton). *See* Tottlebank. [63]

BRYAM, *i.e.* BYROM, JOHN (*d.* 9 Sept. 1709). Entered Frankland's Academy, 17 Mar. 1676/7. One of the founders (1691) of the Cheshire Classis (*see* p. 157), being then Minister of Stockport, his first charge; he left about 1697, was afterwards at Lydgate, and there died. (*Fr. Mc. Nr.*) [15]

BRYAN, JARVIS or GERVASE, M.A. (*d.* 27 Dec. 1689). **P.** Matric. at Emmanuel Coll., Cambridge, 1640; B.A., 1643/4; Fellow; M.A., 1647. Held the sequestered rectory of Old Swinford, Worc., 1654; ejected, 1662. Licensed, 25 July 1672, as "Pr. Teacher in his howse at Old Swinford." Later, lived at Birmingham; succeeded his brother, John Bryan, D.D. (*d.* 4 Mar. 1675/6), as Minister at Coventry, and died there. (*C. D. La. P. Si. T. V. Wc.*) [118]

BRYAN, JOHN, M.A. (1627—31 Aug. 1699). **P.** Eldest son of John Bryan, D.D. (*d.* 1676), ejected from the vicarage of Trinity, Coventry. Admitted pensioner at Emmanuel Coll., Cambridge, 10 Jan. 1643/4, aged 16; rem. to Peterhouse, 3 D. 1644; B.A., 1647; M.A., 1651. Vicar (1652) of Holy Cross, Shrewsbury; vicar (1659) of St. Chad's, Shrewsbury; ejected, 1662. Imprisoned for preaching, he removed (1666), under the Five Mile Act, to Shifnal, Shrops., visiting his Shrewsbury congregation by night. Licensed, 13 May 1672, as "Pr. Teacher in the howse of Charles Doughty in Salop." He preached also in the licensed house (10 June) of Elizabeth Hunt. Francis Tallents [*q.v.*] became his colleague (1674); their ministry was much disturbed till 1687. (*C. D. P. Ph. T. V.*) [15, 88, 89]

BUCK, JOHN. He is referred to in the Minutes (7 S. 1691) as "Mr Bucke of Sussex," and is asked to report about Steyning and Thakeham. He does not appear in Evans' Sussex List, 8 Nov. 1717. In Evans' Yorkshire List (communication not dated) John Buck appears as Minister at Idle, W. Riding. This John Buck removed to Bolton, Lanc., in 1729, and died 8 July 1750. (*Ev. It. M.*) [113]

BUCKINGHAMSHIRE. [9, 10, 167, 176]. All except the heading "Bucks" is in the handwriting of the Book-keeper. The returns are numbered from 11 to 56.

The only grant made was £5 a year to George Mills of Chafforn [Chalfont St. Giles], 4 Apr. 1692. (*M.*)

Eaton is Eton [*q.v.*].

Woburne is Wooburn.

BUCKLAND. [6, 7]

BUCKLEBURY ('Bucklbury'). Ejected here was one Smallwood; the Episc. Returns, 1669, report "Mr Smallwood" as one of the preachers to 40 Presbyterians at Bledlow, Bucks. (*C. P. T.*) [7]

BUCKLERSBURY. So called from the Bokerel or Buckerel family; Andrew Buckerel was Mayor from 1231 to 1236. From the time of the Elizabethan dramatists it was noted as a street of grocers and druggists. (*Lo.*) [3]

BUDD, THOMAS, M.A. (*b.* 1615). **P.** Matric. pleb. at Merton Coll., Oxford, 17 Jan. 1633/4, aged 18; B.A., 1633/4; M.A., 1636. Vicar of Montacute, Som., 1639; held the sequestered rectory of Kingsbury, Som., 1646; the former rector, William Piers, D.D. (*d.* Apr. 1682), received other preferment at the Restoration, hence Budd was probably not ejected till 1662. Licensed, 29 June 1672, being of Barrington, Som., as "Grāll Pr. Teacher." (*F. T. Wc.*) [92, 93, 94]

BUGBROOKE. [77]

BUGBY, ISAAC (*fl.* 1672–92). **C.** Licensed, 10 Aug. 1672, as "Cong: Teacher" at his house in Braintree, Ess. (*T.*) [38]

BULL, DANIEL, M.A. (*fl.* 1647–1690). **P.**

Matric. at Emmanuel Coll., Cambridge, 1647; B.A., 1649/50; Fellow of Christ's Coll., 1650–54; M.A., 1652; incorp. at Oxford, 11 July 1654. Held from 27 Sept. 1657 the sequestered rectory of Stoke Newington, Midx.; ejected, 1660, but continued as lecturer, residing at Newington Green; ejected, 1662. In 1664 he is reported as conventicling in Smithfield and the Minories. The Episc. Returns, 1669, report "Mr Bull" from London as a preacher to 60 or 70 at the house of Michael Hervey, J.P., Yetminster (?), Dorset. Licensed, 19 Apr. 1672, as "Presbyterian Teacher in his howse," and that of Mrs. Stock, widow, in Stoke Newington. Assistant (1676 ?) to John Howe [*q.v.*] at Haberdashers' Hall; dismissed, 1681, for adultery. His taking up work at Carlisle is a new fact, confirming the statement of his penitence. On 29 Dec. 1690 a grant of £10 a year was made from the Common Fund "towards the Propogation of the Gospell att Carlisle." Bull was not long at Carlisle, for in 1692 Daniel Jackson was "called to preach the Gospel" there. Bull died in London, "in his closet," probably before 1702, certainly by 1705, as his "last hours" were witnessed by Samuel Stancliff [*q.v.*]. (*C. Cp. D. F.* (*under* Ball), *M. N. P. T.*) [22, 23, 24]

BUMSTEAD (altered to Brimstead), WILLIAM, appears in the Fund Minutes as Brumstead and Bumpsted, receiving, from 1690, £6 a year for Brentwood, Ess., not renewed in 1695. He does not appear in Evans' List, 1716. (*Ev. M.*) [40]

BUNGAY. Ejected here was Samuel Malbon, of Harvard Coll., New England, for three years; rem. to New Inn Hall, Oxford; matric., 26 May 1651; B.A., 29 May 1651; rector of Bungay; ejected, 1660; became pastor of a church in Amsterdam. (*C. F.*) [104, 107]

BUNN, *i.e.* BOHUN or BOUN, JOHN (1628—23 Feb. 1691/2). **C.** Born at Coundon, Warw. (a manor in Trinity parish, Coventry), where his family, originally of Derbyshire (the pedigree goes back to the beginning of the 15th century), had been long settled. Son of Abraham Boun (1597–Nov. 1670) of Coundon, gent., by his second wife, Elizabeth, daur. and co-heiress of Simon Chambers of Finham, in Stoneleigh parish, Warw. Matric. ('Bourne') at Emmanuel Coll., Cambridge, 1644; did not graduate; bred to the law. Not an ejected divine, though Palmer, by a strange misplacement, makes him ejected at or near Settrington, Yorks (the ejected of Settrington was Alexander Metcalfe, who held the sequestered rectory from Sept. 1653 to near the end of 1661). Calamy knows him only (on the authority of William Tong) as living and preaching in Warwickshire. Among the State Papers Domestic is a letter by J. B. from Coventry, 8 Apr. 1664, calendared as by John Bryan, D.D., but evidently by Boun. It is in reply to John Johnson, of Alcester, who had sent to his acquaintance, J. B., "a very active man to good works," a copy of the "Narrative" of Polish Exiles, *i.e.* the section, then in Holland, of the Socinians expelled from Poland in 1662. Their theological complexion was kept in the background by their English friends. Boun was ready to help if recommendation were forthcoming from "less private hands," *e.g.* from such as "Mr Baxter, Mr Griffith, Drs Owen and Goodwyn." The "howse of John Boun in Coventry" was licensed, 9 May 1672, as a "Congr. Meeting Place." The application for Coventry licences, signed J. B., is by him. Later, Boun lived at Finham, in bad health (*see* Collier, Abel, and Saunders, Julius). His mural monument, on which he is named John Bohun, Esq., of Finham, is in Trinity Church, Coventry. He married (1) Anne, daur. of Martin Dallison, Esq., of London, by whom he had a son and daughter, who died in infancy; (2) Mary (1639–1708), daur. of Hugh Sowdon, a London merchant, and had by her one daughter, Mary, who married George Lucy, Esq., of Charlcote, Warw. (*C. Cs. Dw. P. Pc. Si. T. Tw.*) [117, 118]

BUNTINGFORD ('Buningford'). [50, 51, 52]

BURBAGE, chapelry in Aston Flamville parish, Leic. The Earls of Kent were lords of the manor of Burbage. [66]

BURDWOOD, JAMES (1637—21 Aug. 1693). **P.C.** Born at Yarnacombe, parish of West Allington, Devon. From Kingsbridge grammar school proceeded to Pembroke Coll., Oxford (not in *F.*). Ministered at Plympton St. Mary, Devon; lecturer at St. Petrock's, Dartmouth, Devon; ejected, 1662. Set up a Latin school at Dartmouth, where the Episc. Returns, 1665, report him as holding "private Meetings." Under pressure of the Five Mile Act, he removed (1666) to Batson, parish of Marlborough, Wilts, preaching in his house there; thence (1671) to Hicks Down, parish of Bigbury, Devon. Licensed, 22 Apr. 1672, "to be a Teacher to Presb. & Indep. in his howse called Hexdown in Bigbury." In 1678 he returned to Dartmouth; in 1682–3 he and his family were guests of Dr. Richard Burthogge at Bowden, near Totnes; he returned to Dartmouth disabled by calculus. The description "Ancient and infirm not able to goe abroad to preach" attached to John Knight [*q.v.*] must refer to Burdwood. From 1690 the Fund granted him £5 a year. Of his 17 children, 3 survived him. (*C. M. P. T.*) [31, 33]

BURES. [42]

BURES, RICHARD, B.A. (Nov. 1629—7 May 1697). Born at Northall, Midx., where his grandfather, Isaiah Bures, M.A. (*d.* 1610), had been vicar. Educ. at St. Paul's School, London. Calamy says he was of Christ Church, Oxford; he was scholar of University Coll., 1648; matric. 'gent,' 5 Jan. 1648/9; Fellow, 1649; M.A., 1650. Vicar of Stourmouth, Kent; ejected, 1662. He removed to Guildford, Surr., and while there was twice imprisoned for preaching; thence he removed to Farnborough, border of Hants and Surrey, and thence to Frimley, Surr. Licensed, 30 Apr. 1672, being of Frimley, as "Pr. Grãll Teacher"; his house licensed, six months later. About 1677 he removed to London without pastoral charge. In 1692 he succeeded John Turner (*d.* 1692 ?) [*q.v.*] at Leather Lane, Hatton Garden, and was succeeded there by Christopher Taylor [*q.v.*]. (*C. F. Ly. M. P. T. W. Ws.*) [110]

BURGESS, DANIEL (1645 — 26 Jan. 1712/3). **P.** Born at Staines, Middx. Son of Daniel Burgess, M.A. (1626–June 1679); ejected from the rectory of Collingbourn Ducis, Wilts. From Westminster school he entered as commoner at Magdalen Hall, Oxford, 1660; matric., 21 F. 1661/2, aged 15. He was a hard student, but the Uniformity Act dismissed him without a degree, as he could not conform; yet, as it did not deprive him of any status he had already attained, he is not called a Bartholomaean. Became chaplain to Foyl of Chute, Wilts, later to Smith of Tidworth, Wilts. In 1667 he went to Ireland with Roger Boyle, Earl of Orrery, lord president of Munster. The Episc. Returns, 1669, report him as preaching with his father to 30 or 40 persons at Richard Pike's house, Collingbourn Ducis. He was headmaster of the school founded by Orrery at Charleville, Co. Cork, and subsequently he was chaplain to Lady Mervin, near Dublin, and was ordained by Dublin presbyters. Visiting (1674) his father at Marlborough, Wilts, and preaching there, he was committed to Marlborough gaol. In 1685 he settled in London as Presbyterian Minister at Brydges Street, Covent Garden, moving (1695) to a Meeting-house in Russell Court, Drury Lane, and (1705) to a new Meeting-house in New Court, Carey Street, Drury Lane (wrecked in 1710 by the Sacheverell mob). His congregation included persons of rank; his pulpit fame was a tribute to his exuberant animation and pithy humour, the latter "medicinal, and restorative of spirits for nobler thoughts." Appointed (1692) a Manager of the Common Fund, he was reappointed at the reconstitution of the Fund (1695).

His son, Daniel Burgess, M.A. (*d.* F. 1747), who had been Secretary to the Princess of Wales, conceived the idea of the English *regium donum* (1723), which was paid through him. (*Cm. D. F. T. W.*) [161, 166, 168]

BURHAM. [136] *See* Yorkshire, W.R.

BURNET, *i.e.* BURNETT, ANDREW (*d.* 1707). **P.** He is mentioned, 2 Mar. 1695/6, as "Mr Burnett of Barbakin." The Barbican Presbyterian congregation "became extinct with him in the year 1707." (*M. W. We.*) [1]

BURNHAM ON CROUCH. [41]

BURTON IN KENDAL. [121]

BURTON, or BURTON ON YE WATER. [44] *See* Gloucestershire

BURTON UPON TRENT. Ejected here was Thomas Bakewell, of Lincoln Coll., Oxford; matric., 17 Apr. 1635, aged 16; B.A., 1638; M.A., 1641; ord. episcopally; rector of Rolleston, Staff.; ejected, 1661; lecturer at Burton; ejected, 1662; preaching at Burton in 1669; licensed, 13 May 1672, as Congr. Teacher in a house at Longdon, Staff.; also licensed, Sept. 1672, as Pr. at Tatenhill, Staff.; his house there licensed Pr. same date; he was "earnestly desired to go to London," but does not seem to have done so. (*C. F. T.*) [96]

BURTONWOOD ('Burton Wood'). Ejected here was Samuel Mather (13 May 1626—29 Oct. 1671); taken to New England by his father, Richard Mather, in 1635, he was educ. at Harvard Coll.; M.A., 1643, and Fellow (the first who had graduated there); chaplain of Magdalen Coll., Oxford, 1650; Minister at Leith (Scotland), 1653; incorp. at Trinity Coll., Dublin, and Fellow, 1654; ord. by presbyters, 5 Dec. 1656; preacher at St. Nicholas', Dublin; suspended, 1660; perpetual curate of Burton Wood, 1660/1; ejected, 1662; gathered a Congregational church at New Row, Dublin; *d.* 29 Dec. 1671. (*C. D.*) [54]

BURWASH. Ejected here was Thomas Goldham, M.A. [*q.v.*]. [113, 114]

BURWELL. Ejected here was . . . Cole, who afterwards conformed. (*C.*) [12, 14]

BURY, Lanc. [60]

BURY, EDWARD (1616—5 May 1700). 𝔓. Born in Worcestershire. Educ. at Coventry grammar school, and at Oxford (not matriculating). Walker says he was a tailor. Chaplain in a private family. Held (before 1654) the sequestered rectory of Great Bolas, Shrops.; ejected, 1662. Remained at Great Bolas till driven away (1666) by the Five Mile Act. Licensed, 22 July 1672, as "Pr. Teacher in the howse of Wm Smallwood Routon Towne [*i.e.* Ronton] Stafford." From the Common Fund he received £5 a year, 1690–92. He was blind some years before his death.

His son, Samuel (1663—10 Mar 1729/30), was Minister at Bury St. Edmunds (where the existing Chapel in Churchgate Street was built for him in 1711) and at Bristol. (*C. D. M. P. T. Wc.*) [89]

BURY, RICHARD. Alderman. He attended one meeting of Managers on 8 F. 1691/2. (*M.*) [162, 166]

BURY ST. EDMUNDS. Ejected here were (1) Nicholas Clagget, of Merton Coll., Oxford; B.A., 20 Oct. 1631; rem. to Magdalen Hall; M.A., 1634; vicar of Melbourne, Derb., 1636; lecturer of St. Mary's, Bury, for 18 years till ejected; *d.* 12 Sept. 1663. (*C. F.*) (2) Samuel Slater, M.A. [*q.v.*]. (3) Thomas Taylor, B.A. (*q.v.*]. [103, 186]

BUSH, JOHN (1632?—9 Mar. 1711/2). Born at Gillingham, Dors. From Gillingham grammar school matric. serv. at Queen's Coll., Oxford, 2 Oct. 1652; curate (in discharge of tutorial assistance) at Grittleton, Wilts, for Timothy Tully; chaplain to Col. Strode; vicar (1659?) of Hewish with Langport, Som., ejected, 1662. He opened a grammar school and his wife resumed a mercery business. The Episc. Returns, 1669, report him as one of the preachers to 300 persons at Kingsbury, Som.; also to 200 persons "At the house of Nathaniel Barnard," Fifehead, Som.; also to 300 persons at Martock, Som. Licensed, June 1672, as "Pr. Teacher in the howse of Rob: Bagnall," Keynsham, Som.; also, June 1672, as "Grāll Pr," of Langport, Som. He received, 1699–1706, £6 a year as Minister at Langport. (*C. F. M. P. T.*) [91]

BUSH, WILLIAM (*d.* 1740). 𝔓. The Common Fund made (12 Jan. 1690/1) a gift of £4 to "Mr. Bush at Leige Castle in Kent," *i.e.* Leeds Castle, Kent. On 9 April 1695 a gift of £5 was voted to "Mr Bush at Madestone in Kent" also "near Maidstone." A grant of £15 was made (4 May 1696) by the Congregational Fund to "Mr Bush of Feversham," *i.e.* Faversham, Kent. On 6 July 1696 a gift of £2 was made to "Mr William Bush att Feversham" by the older Fund; again, on 7 F. 1702/3, £5 was given to "Mr Bush of Kent," and the same in 1704. On 2 Apr. 1705 it was "Agreed that Feversham allowance be taken of Mr Bush being removed to Wapping." Evans' List gives him as Minister (I. has been altered to P.) at Broad Street, Wapping (where he succeeded Samuel Harris [*q.v.*]), his private address being "in Anchor and Hoop Alley, Wapping." On 5 Oct. 1730 £10 was granted to "Bush of Wapping." Bush was a Non-subscriber at Salters' Hall (1719), and died in 1740. (*Co. Ev. M. We.*) [55]

BUTLER, HENRY, M.A. (1624—24 Apr. 1696). ℭ. Born in Kent. Educ. at Cambridge, Mass.; M.A., 1651. After 11 or 12 years in New England, he ministered for a year or two at Dorchester, and then became vicar of Yeovil, Som.; ejected, 1662. The Episc. Returns, 1669, report him as one of the preachers to 300 persons at Kingsbury, Som.; also to 200 persons at White Lackington, Som.; also to 300 persons in Yeovil parish, and to 200 at North Cheriton, Som.; also to 300 at Martock, Som. Licensed, 25 May 1672, as Congr. Teacher at house of Elias Barnes, Yeovil, Som.; also, June 1672 (as Henry Butter), as "Grāll Pr." of "Lavington, Somerset" [*i.e.* Wilts]; also, 25 July 1672 (as Henry Butler), as "Congr. Teacher in the howse of Matthew Morris at Maiden Bradley, Wilts. He settled ultimately as pastor at Witham Friary, Som. (*C. Mh. Mc. P. T.*) [91, 92]

BUYER, or BYER, FRANCIS. Of the East India House. (*M.*) [166]

BYFIELD, JARVIS. 𝔓. Appointed a Manager of the Common Fund, but attended no meeting, and resigned on 8 Sept. 1690. As John Jurin [*q.v.*] was deputed to interview his proposed successor, he is assumed to be of the same denomination. (*M.*) [162]

BYFLEET. Ejected here was Samuel Scudamore (son of William, of London, gent.), of New Inn Hall, Oxford; matric., 4 Nov. 1631, aged 21; B.A., 1634; vicar of Epsom, 1637; rector of Byfleet, 1647; ejected, 1662. (*C. F.*) [110]

BYNON, *i.e.* BEYNON, THOMAS (*d.* June 1729). The Common Fund granted him, 1690–93, £6 a year for Rhoseygwylyn, Pemb. On 7 Apr. 1718 £8 a year was voted him "at Rhidlogin in Cardiganshr"; reduced (1723) to £6, this was paid to 1728, and same year an addition of £4 was given. From 1715 he was preaching at New Chapel, Newport, Pemb., and Trewen, Pemb., his private address being "at Rhyd-Logyn near Cardigan." (*Ev. M.*) [144]

BYRAM ('Burham'). [136] in Brotherton parish, W.R. (misplaced in N.R.)

BYROM. *See* Bryam

CALAMY, EDMUND, D.D. (5 April 1671—3 June 1732). **P.** Born in the parish of St. Mary Aldermanbury, London; only son of Edmund Calamy, M.A., ejected from the rectory of Moreton, Essex, and grandson of Edmund Calamy, B.D., ejected from the perpetual curacy of St. Mary Aldermanbury. After passing through four schools, the last being Merchant Taylors', he studied under Samuel Cradock [*q.v.*] and Thomas Doolittle [*q.v.*], at Utrecht (1688–91), and privately at Oxford. His settlements in the ministry were at Blackfriars (1692–5) as assistant to Matthew Sylvester [*q.v.*], at Hand Alley, Bishopsgate (1695–1703) as assistant to Daniel Williams [*q.v.*], and at Tothill Street, Westminster, 1703 till death (the congregation removed to Long Ditch, since called Princes Street, in 1719). He was a Salters' Hall lecturer from 1702; M.A. and D.D. of Edinburgh, D.D. of King's College, Aberdeen, and D.D. of Glasgow (1709). His great work was the "Abridgment" (1702) of the autobiography of Richard Baxter [*q.v.*] with an "Account" of the Ejected in chapter ix.; the second edition of the "Abridgement," 1713, expanded the "Account" into a separate volume; and a "Continuation" appeared in 1727, 2 vols. All these volumes by Calamy are perversely catalogued at the British Museum under Baxter; with equal perversity, "The Nonconformist's Memorial," 1775, and 1802–3, by Samuel Palmer, is there catalogued under Calamy. Calamy's "Historical Account of my own Life" was not published till 1829 (and 1830, with Index). The direct Calamy line, which included six successive Edmunds, expired with Michael Calamy of Exeter, on 3 Jan. 1876. (*D. Cong. Hist. Soc. Trans.*, Aug. 1914.) [152, 153, 154, 161, 182, 183, 184, 188]

CALLINGTON. [18]

CALNE ('Colne'). Ejected here was Thomas Jones. (*C.*) [123, 125, 172]

CALTHORP. [66, 67] *See* Leicestershire

CALTHWAITE ('Cawthwaite,' 'Cowthaate'). [21]

CAM. In Evans' List, Cam near Dursley. [46]

CAMBDEN. [44] *See* Gloucestershire

CAMBRIDGE. Ejected here from the University were:

(1) "Alcock, Fellow, Trinity." No Fellow of Trinity Coll. (or of any other) of this surname; William Alcock, of Trinity Coll., matric. sizar, 1647, did not graduate. (*C. Tc. V.*)

(2) "Alden, scholar, St. John's." Not found. (*C. P.*)

(3) George Barker, matric. pensioner at St. Catharine's Hall, 1645; B.A., 1648/9; Fellow; M.A., 1652; B.D., 1659; ejected, 1660; afterwards conformed and was rector of Danby, Yorks. (*C. V.*)

(4) John Bond, LL.D. Born at Chard, Som., 12 Apr. 1612; son of Dennis Bond; from school at Dorchester entered and matric. at St. Catharine's Hall, 1628; B.A., 1631/2; Fellow; M.A., 1635; LL.D., 1645/6; member of the Westminster Assembly, 1643; Master of the Savoy, 1645; Master of Trinity Hall, Mar. 1646; law professor at Gresham College, 1649; one of the expurgators, 1654; vice-chancellor of the University, 1658; ejected, 1660; retired to Dorset; died at Sandwich, Kent; buried at Steeple, Dorset, 30 July 1676. (*C. D. P. V.*)

(5) Robert Brinsley, M.A., M.D., matric. at Emmanuel Coll., 1653; B.A., 1656/7; Fellow; M.A., 1660; after ejection took M.D. at Leiden, and practised and held municipal office, 1681 and 1692, at Yarmouth, where his father, John Brinsley, M.A., of Emmanuel Coll. (*d.* 22 Jan. 1664/5, aged 64), had been minister. (*C. P. V.*)

(6) John Broadgate, B.D. Born in St. Foster's parish, Midx.; son of Giles Broadgate, merchant tailor; from Merchant Taylors' school entered sizar at St. John's Coll., 11 Feb. 1645/6, aet. 18; B.A., 1649/50; Fellow; M.A., 1653; B.D., 1660; after ejection conformed and went to Smyrna. (*C. Gc. Jo. V.*)

(7) John Castell, M.A., B.D. Born in London; entered Trinity Coll. as pensioner, 21 Sept. 1649; Scholar, 1651; B.A., 1653/4; M.A., 1658; B.D., 1685. [Not recorded as Fellow; if ejected, must have subsequently conformed.] (*C. P. Tc. V.*)

(8) Abraham Clifford, M.A., B.D.,

M.D.; matric. at Pembroke Hall (now College), 1646; B.A., 1649/50; M.A., 1653; B.D., 1660; ejected from the rectory of Quendon, Ess., 1662; studied medicine at Leiden; M.D., Oxford, 20 Dec. 1670, being secretary to the Prince of Orange; died in St. Sepulchre's parish, London, 1675. (*C. F. P. V.*)

(9) Samuel Corbin, M.A. Born in Worcestershire; admitted pensioner at Trinity Coll., 18 June 1648; Scholar, 1650; B.A., 1651/2; M.A., 1655; chaplain, 1655; ejected, 1660; the Episc. Returns, 1669, report him as preaching at Hadenham, Histons, Milton, Orwell, Over, and St. Michael's, Cambs; licensed, 8 May, as Congr. Teacher in Cambridge, and, June 1672, as Congr. Teacher in his house near Aldersgate, London. He assisted Francis Holcroft [*q.v.*]. (*C. P. T. Tc. V.*)

(10) William Crosseland, B.A. Born in Yorkshire; entered Trinity Coll. as subsizar, 19 N. 1655; Scholar, 1659; B.A., 1659/60 [no record of Fellowship]. (*C. P. Tc. V.*)

(11) John Davie, M.A. Matric. sizar at Trinity Coll., 1634/5; Scholar, 1638; B.A., 1638/9; Fellow, 1645; M.A., 1646; Junior Dean, 1649–50. Calamy, who calls him Davis, says he was known as Rabbi Davis. (*C. P. Tc. V.*)

(12) James Day [*q.v.*].

(13) William Dell, M.A. (*d.* 1664); matric. at Emmanuel Coll., 1623/4; B.A., 1627/8; M.A., 1631; secretary to Archbishop Laud; Master of Gonville and Caius Coll., 4 May 1649; ejected, 11 May 1660. Calamy calls him "a very unsettled man"; he refused to "allow any such distinction of Christians as Presbyterians and Independents"; he had sympathy with many of the positions of Friends. (*C. D. P. V.*)

(14) William Disney, M.A. Of the Lincolnshire family; entered Trinity Coll. as pensioner, 27 June 1638; Scholar, 1641; B.A., 1642/3; Fellow, 1645; M.A., 1646; Vicemaster, 1654–55. (*C. P. Tc. V.*)

(15) William Duncome, M.A. Matric. at King's Coll., 1648; B.A., 1651/2; M.A., 1655. (*C. P. V.*)

(16) Robert Ekyns [*q.v.*].

(17) Daniel Evans. Born at Monk Moor, near Shrewsbury; from the Shrewsbury grammar school proceeded to Jesus Coll.; not matric.; ejected, 1662; chaplain to Chancellor Smith of Norwich, two years, and then to Honywood of Hampstead; had a congregation at Woolwich, 1673–1689; removed to Bethnal Green; died there, July 1698, aged 58. (*C. P. V.*)

(18) William Green, M.A. Matric. at St. Catharine's Hall, 1645/6; B.A., 1648/9; Fellow; M.A., 1652; lic., 25 May 1672, at Fenny Stanton, Hunts, as general Presb. teacher. (*C. P. T. V.*)

(19) Alexander Greene, M.A. [*q.v.*].

(20) "Hayes, Fellow, Trinity." No Fellow of Trinity Coll. (or of any other, in that period) of this surname. Philemon Hayes, matric. pensioner at Clare Hall, 1657; B.A., 1660/1. (*C. Tc. V.*)

(21) Joseph Hill, M.A., B.D. Born, Oct. 1625, at Bramley, near Leeds; son of Joshua Hill, then Minister of Bramley Chapel; admitted pensioner of St. John's Coll., 20 Aug. 1646, but allowed seniority of a year; B.A., 1649; elected Fellow of Magdalene Coll., M.A., 1651; B.D., 1660; retired, 1662, to save ejection; entered Leiden University, 29 Mar. 1664; pastor of the Scots Church at Middeburg, Zeeland, 19 June 1667; banished from Zeeland, Charles II. offered him a bishopric; Minister of the English Presbyterian Church, Rotterdam, 13 Jan. 1678; died there, 5 Nov. 1707; Greek lexicographer. (*C. D. Jo. P. V.*)

(22) Francis Holcroft, M.A. [*q.v.*].

(23) Edmund Hough, M.A.; matric. at Jesus Coll., 1651; B.A., 1654/5; Fellow; M.A., 1658. Afterwards conformed and became rector of Thornton in Craven, Yorks, and (26 June 1689) vicar of Halifax, *d.* 1 Apr. 1691, in his 59th year. (*C. Hx. P. V.*)

(24) Edward Hulse, M.A. Born in Cheshire. Matric. at Emmanuel Coll., 1656; B.A., 1656/7; M.A., 1660; ejected soon after the Restoration. Entered at Leiden University, 4 July 1668, aged 32; M.D., Leiden; incorp. M.D. at Oxford, 20 Dec. 1670, being physician to the Prince of Orange; Fellow of the College of Physicians, 22 Dec. 1677; treasurer, 1704–9; died 3 Dec. 1711, in 81st year. (*C. F. Mu. P. V.*)

(25) John Hutchinson, B.A. Born, 15 Apr. 1638, in London. From Merchant Taylors and Eton he entered Trinity Coll. as subsizar, 13 Feb. 1654/5; Scholar, 1657; B.A., 1658/9; Fellow, 1659 [no record of M.A.]; ejected, 1660; helped Joseph Hill (*see above*) in lexicography; travelled in France and Italy; claimed a licence from the College of Physicians (not in Munk); practised at Hitchin, Herts; known as Doctor; member of Tyler Street, Hitchin, preached gratis at neighbouring places as a Congregational; removed to Clapham as physician

for two years; then kept boarding-school at Hackney nine years; died 9 Feb. 1714/5. (*C. P. Tc. V.*)

(26) James Illingworth, M.A., B.D. (*d.* Aug. 1693). Born in Lancashire. Matric. at Emmanuel Coll., 1645; B.A., 1648/9; Fellow; M.A., 1652; B.D., 1659; after ejection was chaplain to Philip Foley [*q.v.*] for several years; at his death he was chaplain to Elizabeth, daughter of Edward Milton of Weston under Lizard, Staff., and widow of Sir Thomas Wilbraham, Bart. (*d.* Aug. 1692). Buried at Weston under Lizard on 30 Aug. 1693. (*Ba. C. P. V.*)

(27) Thomas Lock. Born in London; entered Trinity Coll. as subsizar, 4 July 1657; Scholar, 1659; no degree; ejected, 1660; assisted Joseph Oddey (*below*), 1664; the Episc. Returns, 1669, report him as preaching at Meldreth and Orwell, Cambs; licensed, 8 May 1672, as Congr. Teacher at Meldreth; acted under Francis Holcroft [*q.v.*]. (*C. P. T. Tc. V.*)

(28) "Mathum, Fellow, St. John's." William Metham, M.A.; matric. at St. John's Coll., 1623; B.A., 1626/7; M.A., 1630; not Fellow. (*C. P. V.*)

(29) Edmund Moore, M.A. Born at Ditton, Cambs; from a school at Cambridge admitted pensioner at Trinity Coll., 15 Apr. 1650, aged 14; Scholar, 1651; B.A., 1653/4; Fellow, 1656; M.A., 1657; ejected, 1660 (?); chaplain to Serjeant Maynard; preached at East Sheen, Surrey; died May 1689. (*C. P. Tc. V.*)

(30) Thomas More, M.A.; matric. at Magdalene Coll., 1654; B.A., 1657/8; Fellow; M.A., 1661. (*C. P. V.*)

(31) William Moses, M.A. Born about 1623 in St. Saviour's parish, Southwark; son of John Moses, merchant tailor; admitted to Christ's Hospital, 28 Mar. 1632, aged 9; matric. at Pembroke Hall (now College), 1639; B.A., 1643/4; Fellow; M.A., 1647; Master, 1655; ejected, 1660; turned to law; counsel to East India Company; serjeant-at-law, 11 June 1688; died same year. (*C. D. P.*)

(32) Joseph Oddey, M.A. Born in Leeds. From its grammar school entered Trinity Coll. as subsizar, 9 May 1653; Scholar, 1655; B.A., 1656/7; Fellow, 1658; M.A., 1660; ejected here and from vicarage of Meldreth, Camb.; preacher, 1667, at Willingham, Cambs, acting in conjunction with Francis Holcroft [*q.v.*]; the Episc. Returns, 1669, report him as preaching at Hadenham, Histon, March, Milton, Oakington, Orwell, Over, Stow-cum-Quy and Willingham, Cambs; licensed with Holcroft, 8 May 1672, as Congregational Teacher in Cambridge; did much itinerant work; died 3 May 1687, buried at Oakington, Cambs. (*C. P. T. Tc. V.*)

(33) Augustine Plumsted [*q.v.*].

(34) Samuel Ponder, B.A. Born in Northants; entered Trinity Coll. as sizar, 17 June 1656; Scholar, 1659; B.A., 1659/60. (*C. P. Tc. V.*)

(35) John Pratt, M.A., M.D. Matric. at Emmanuel Coll., 1625; B.A., 1628/9; M.A., 1632; Lic. Med., 1639; M.D., 1645; Fellow of Trinity Coll., 1645; admitted Candidate of the College of Physicians, 22 Dec. 1649. (*C. P. Mu. Tc. V.*)

(36) John Ray, M.A., F.R.S. Born at Black Notley, near Braintree, Ess., 29 Nov. 1627; son of Roger Wray, blacksmith; from Braintree grammar school entered St. Catharine's Hall, 28 June 1644; migrated as subsizar to Trinity Coll., 21 Nov. 1646; B.A., 1647/8; Fellow, 1649; M.A., 1651; ord. deacon and priest, 23 Dec. 1660; ejected, 1662; remained an Anglican communicant; died at the Dewlands, Black Notley, 17 Jan. 1705/6. Calamy, referring to his labours as a naturalist, calls him "an extraordinary humanist." (*C. D. P. Tc. V.*)

(37) John Rayner, M.A. Son of Reyner of Lincoln; matric. at Emmanuel Coll., 1649; B.A., 1652/3; Fellow; M.A., 1656; ejected, 1662; practised medicine and died at Nottingham. (*C. P.*) ?John Rayner, son of Thomas Raynor, gent., who was extra-licentiate of the College of Physicians, 22 June 1710, being of Brotherton, Yorks. (*C. P. Mu.*)

(38) John Sadler, M.A. Born at Patcham, Suss., 18 Aug. 1615; son of the vicar there; matric. at Emmanuel Coll., 1631; B.A., 1634; M.A., 1638; Master, 1650; ejected, 1660; he had studied law at Lincoln's Inn; was Master in Chancery, 1644; Town Clerk of London, 1649–60; M.P. for Cambridge, 1653; M.P. for Great Yarmouth, 1658; retired to his manor of Warmwell, Dors., in 1662; died, April 1674. (*C. D. P. V.*)

(39) Henry Sampson, M.A. [*q.v.*].

(40) Thomas Senior, M.A., B.D. Born in London. From Westminster school, matric. at Trinity Coll., 1646; scholar, 1647; B.A., 1649/50; Fellow, 1650; M.A., 1653; B.D., 1660; licensed, 12 Apr. 1672 as Presb. Teacher in his house at Clapton; later was chaplain to Alderman Bewley at Hackney, and lecturer in the house of Alderman Ashhurst. (*C. P. T. Tc. V.*)

(41) Anthony Tuckney, D.D. [*q.v.*].
(42) Jonathan Tuckney. (*See* Tuckney, Anthony.)
(43) Willoughby West, M.A. Born in Lincolnshire; entered Trinity Coll. as subsizar, 18 Apr. 1650; scholar, 1651; B.A., 1653/4; Fellow, 1656; M.A., 1657, (*C. P. Tc. V.*)
(44) James Wheeler, M.A., son of James Wheeler, weaver of Colchester; matric. at Sidney Sussex Coll., 1644; B.A., 1647/8; removed to Gonville and Caius Coll.; M.A., 1651; junior Fellow, 1649; senior Fellow, 1650; President, 1660; ejected, Midsummer, 1661. (*C. Gc. P. V.*)
(45) Robert Whitaker, B.A. [*q.v.*].
(46) John Wildbore, M.A. Matric. at Sidney Sussex Coll., 1647/8; B.A., 1651; M.A., and Fellow of Clare Hall, 1655; "an unsettled man." (*C. P. V.*)
(47) John Wood, M.A. [*q.v.*]. [11, 12, 14, 53, 66, 89, 105, 117]

CAMBRIDGE, MAGDALENE COLLEGE. [89]

CAMBRIDGESHIRE. [11, 12, 107, 168, 176, 181] Except the heading 'Cambridge,' and a small addition, all is in the handwriting of the Book-keeper. The returns are numbered from 33 to 120.
Catlidge is now called Kirtling [*q.v.*].
Taft is Toft.

CAMELFORD ('Camerford'). [19]

CANE, *i.e.* CAVE, JAMES (*d.* 1694). **C.** Born at Banbury, Ox., son of Capt. Cave, brazier. Appointed, 3 N. 1652, incumbent of Thornthwaite, Newlands and St. John's, chapelries in Crosthwaite parish, Cumb.; ordained as a Preaching Presbyter, 16 O. 1656, by the Associated Ministers of Cumberland; appears (1657–1668) as Pastor of a Congregational church at Keswick; ejected from Thornthwaite, 1660. Perhaps he is "Mr Cane of Yorkshire" reported in Episc. Returns, 1669, as preaching to 40 or 50 "middle and meaner sort of people," at Westbury, Bucks. Licensed, 10 June 1672, as Pr. Teacher in the house of Mrs. Hannah Manley, widow, Daventry, Northants. Ultimately he removed to London. (*C. N. P. T.*) [23]

CANTERBURY. Ejected here were (1) Robert Beake, of Peterhouse, Cambridge; matric. pensioner, 1637; B.A., 1640/1; M.A., 1645; vicar of St. Stephen's, Hackington; ejected, 1662; preaching at Canterbury in 1669; licensed, 1 May 1672, as Pr. Teacher in a mansion at Canterbury; *d.* 31 Aug. 1679, aged about 59. (*C. T. V.*)
(2) John Durant (*b.* 1620) "once a wash-ball maker," lecturer at St. Peter's, Sandwich, 1642; ejected from the Cathedral; preaching at Canterbury in 1669; licensed, 2 Apr. 1672, as Congregational Teacher in Almirey Hall, outside Canterbury. (*C. T.*)
(3) John Player, of Clare Hall, Cambridge; matric. sizar 1612; B.A., 1615/6; M.A., 1619; incorp. at Oxford, 1619; vicar of Kennington, Kent, 1620; public preacher at the Cathedral, 1641 (?); ejected 1660. (*C. F. V.*)
(4) Francis Taylor, of Corpus Christi Coll., Cambridge; matric. pensioner, 1639; B.A., 1642/3; M.A., 1646; blinded by smallpox; rector of St. Alphage's, 1643 (?); ejected, 1660; preaching at Canterbury in 1669; licensed, 10 June 1672, as Pr. Teacher in a mansion at Canterbury; became Congregational. (*C. T. V.*)
(5) Thomas Ventris, of Corpus Christi Coll., Cambridge; matric. pensioner, 1628; B.A., 1630/1; M.A., 1634; ord. by archbishop Laud; curate in Canterbury; rector of St. Margaret's, 1638; ejected, 1662; preaching at Canterbury in 1669; licensed, 1 May 1672, as Congr. Teacher (in the same mansion as No. 1) at Canterbury; his age at death was about 72. (*C. R. T. V.*) [55]

CARDIGANSHIRE. [143, 145, 146, 185] Kellans is Cellan, otherwise Kellan.

CAREY, JOHN. [166]

CARLISLE ('Carlile'), Cumb. Ejected here was Comfort Starr [*q.v.*]. [22, 23, 24]

CARMARTHENSHIRE ('Carmarden,' 'Carmathan'). [143, 144, 145, 146]

CARNARVONSHIRE ('Carnarvan'). [141, 148]

CARRILL, *i.e.* CARRELL, ROBERT, M.A. (*d.* 20 May 1702). **P.** Matric. 'pleb.' at Exeter Coll., Oxford, 2 Apr. 1652; B.A., 1655; M.A., 1659. Held the sequestered (yet *see Wc.*) rectory of Uplowman, Devon; ejected, 1660. The Episc. Returns, 1669, report him as one of the preachers at Cullompton (*see* Saunders, Richard). Licensed, 1672, as "Mr Carle" to preach in Mrs. Mary Kendall's house at Cofton in Dawlish parish. About 1689 he settled at Crediton, where he was succeeded by Josiah Eveliegh, ordained there in 1702. (*C. Em. F. Mh. P. T.*) [30]

CARRINGTON, JOHN (1660–Mar. 1700/1). **P.** Born in Cheshire. Entered Frankland's Academy, 27 Mar. 1680. Ordained at Alverthorpe, 4 S. 1689, for Lancaster, where he had succeeded Robert Chaderton (*d.* Oct. 1687). Houses in Newland, near Ulverston and in Furness Fells were registered for worship, 4 Oct. 1692, on his application; also one at Hart Barrow, 10 July 1694; and another at Broughton in Furness, 1695. He was drawn into the case (1689) of Richard Dugdale, the supposed demoniac of Surey, near Clitheroe, which reflects little credit on the good sense of the Nonconformist divines concerned in it. He was presented in 1697 for performing a marriage. After his death an appeal was made (6 O. 1701) to the Fund for help to Lancaster, stating that "Mr Carrinton was their Ministr and haveing an Estate never ask't you for anything." Annual grants (usually of £8) were made to his successor, James Grimshaw. (*Hh. M. Nk. Nl. X.*) [58, 63]

CARSWELL, SOLOMON. *See* Creswell

CARTER, *i.e.* CATER, ANDREW, M.A. (*fl.* 1634–1700). **P.** Matric. sizar, at Queen's Coll., Cambridge, 1634; B.A. 1637/8; M.A., 1641. Held the sequestered rectory of Graveley-cum-Chisfield, Herts, 1654; ejected, 1662. Lived in the family of Sir Robert Jocelyn [*see* Josselyn] at Hide Hall, near Sawbridgeworth. Licensed, 1 May 1672, being "of ye perswasion comonly called Presbyterian . . . to teach in any place or places licenced." By will (26 June 1700), in which he is described as of St. Andrew's, Hertford, Cater left land the rent of which was to be employed in teaching four poor children of Sawbridgeworth to read, and then giving them a Bible, an Assembly's catechism, the catechisms of Joseph Allein and Thomas Vincent, and Joseph Flavell's "Exposition." This charity has long been lost. (*C. Lm. P. Uh. V. Wc.*) [51]

CARTWRIGHT, THOMAS, M.A. (1535?–27 Dec. 1603). **P.** Born at Royston, Herts. Entered as sizar at Clare Hall, Cambridge; matric. Nov. 1547; elected scholar, St. John's Coll., 5 Nov. 1550; removed, 1560, to Trinity Coll., Fellow of St. John's, 6 Apr. 1560; M.A., 1560; fellow of Trinity, Apr. 1562. Chaplain, 1565, to Adam Loftus, archbishop of Armagh; left Ireland, 1567. Lady Margaret professor at Cambridge, 1569; deprived Dec. 1570, and of his fellowship, Sept. 1571. Repaired to Geneva, returning Nov. 1572. In Dec. 1573, went to Heidelberg, thence to Antwerp to minister to the English church, thence to Middelburg in the same capacity. In 1576 visited the Channel Islands, and assisted in settling their church discipline on Presbyterian lines, subsequently returning to Antwerp as pastor. Appointed 1585 by Robert Dudley, earl of Leicester, master of his hospital at Warwick. Imprisoned in the Fleet, 1590. Died at Warwick. (*D. Uh.*) [151]

CARYL, JOSEPH, M.A. (1603?–1672/3). **C.** Born in London. Matric. 20 July 1621 (as Carrill) at Exeter Coll., Oxford, 'gent.', aged 17; B.A., 1624/5; M.A., 1627. Preacher at Lincoln's Inn, 1632–1647; member of the Westminster Assembly, 1643; rector of St. Magnus, London Bridge, 1645; from 7 D. 1646 member of the Fourth Presb. Classis of London, and one of its "Tryars of the Elders"; on 30 Apr. 1649 nominated as a delegate to the Provincial Assembly, but not elected; he did not attend again; one of Cromwell's Triers, 1653; ejected, 1662, but continued lecturer till Feb. 1663. The Episc. Returns, 1669, report him as preaching to 500 persons "At Mr Knight's house in Leaden hall Streete." On 13 Apr. 1672 he was licensed "to teach in the house of Thomas Knight Mercht in Leadenhall Street London. Congregationall." Here he founded the congregation which ultimately (1708) met in Duke's Place, Bury St., St. Mary Axe. He died in Bury Street; the date is variously given as 7 Feb., 25 Feb., and 10 March. He wrote 12 quarto vols., 1651–66 (reprinted in 2 vols., folio), on Job. (*C. D. F. Fc. P. T.*) [188]

CASTLE HEDINGHAM ('Honingham'), Ess. Silenced here (according to *C.*) was John Smith, previously ejected (1660) from the sequestered vicarage of Great Dunmow; according to *Nc.*, John Smith obtained the perpetual curacy here in 1664. (*C. E. Nc.*) [38, 40]

CATER. *See* Carter

CATLIGE. [13, 107] *See* Cambridgeshire

CATTHORPE. [66, 67]

CAULDWELL ('Cawdwell'); a chapelry in Stapenhill parish, Derb. Ejected here was Nathan Barton [*q.v.*] [28]

CAUSAM. [123] *See* Wiltshire

CAVE, JAMES. *See* Cane

CAVE, NORTH and SOUTH, Yorks, E.R. (misplaced in N.R.). [136, 138]

CAWDWELL. [28] *See* Derbyshire

CAWDWELL, THOMAS (*d.* Oct. 1724). **P.** The Fund granted him, for Swaffham Prior, Camb., £6 a year, 1690–1724, besides special gifts.

Contemporary with him was Thomas Cawdwell, jun., **P.** (probably his son), who received Fund grants, yearly and special, for Tolsbury, Essex, near Malden (where he lived), 1714–23, when he removed to Spaldwick, Hunts, near Wabridge Forest. He was probably the

Thomas Cawdwell who received Fund grants, yearly and many special, for Hatfield Broad Oak, Essex, 1732–51. [According to *E.*, Thomas Caudwell succeeded, at Hatfield Broad Oak, James Small, who removed in 1704, and George Wigget followed Caudwell. Wigget, however, is noted as already Minister at Hatfield Broad Oak on 3 Mar. 1706/7.] (*E. Ev. M.*) [12, 13, 14]

CAWTHORNE, or CAUTHON, JOSEPH, M.A. (*d.* 9 Mar. 1707). 𝔓. Came of a Stamford family. Admitted from Huntingdonshire, 1646, at Corpus Christi Coll. Cambridge; matric. 1647; B.A., 1650/1; M.A., 1654. Probably ordained episcopally. Rector of St. George's, Stamford, Linc., before 1658; ejected, 1662. Licensed, 10 June 1672, as Presb. Teacher in house of Humph. Reynolds, Stamford. On 10 Nov. 1690 he received £3 as share of anonymous donation (£50) per Matthew Rapier [*q.v.*]. Minister at Stoke Newington for several years till death. (*C. Lm. M. P. Rq. T. V. W. Wc.*) [1]

CAWTHWAITE. [21] *See* Cumberland

CELLAN ('Kellans'). [145]

CHADSLEY, ROBERT, B.A. (*d.* 1691). Matric. sizar, at Queen's Coll., Cambridge, 1635; B.A., 1637/8. Held the sequestered rectory of Faulkbourn, Ess. (1645–6); in 1654 he was holding the sequestered rectory of Little Yeldham, Ess.; ejected, 1662. The Common Fund granted him (1690) £6 a year for Yeldham; on 12 O. 1691 he was reported dead. (*C. E. La. M. P. V.*) [40, 41]

CHADWICK, JOSEPH, B.A. (*d.* 29 Jan. 1690/1). Matric. at Emmanuel Coll., Cambridge, 1651; B.A., 1654/5. Vicar of Winsford, Som., a college living; ejected, 1662. The Episc. Returns, 1669, report him as one of the preachers to 100 persons at various houses in Dulverton, Som., also at various houses in Bicknoller and Stogumber; also to 80 persons at houses in Wiveliscombe, Som. Licensed, 22 Apr. 1672, as "Grāll Pr. Teacher" in Cruwys Morchard parish, Devon. The Common Fund voted him, 1690, £6 a year for Dulverton; on 4 May 1691 £6 was added; on 15 June he was reported dead. For education of his son (whose Christian name is not given) no payment was made. (*C. Em. M. P. T.*) [92, 93, 94]

CHAGFORD. [32]

CHANDLER, BENJAMIN (*fl.* 1682–1729). 𝔓. In 1720 he is spoken of as "a pastor 38 years standing" and one who "has deserved well of the Ministry above these 30 Years." He was then Minister at Worth, near East Grinstead, Suss., living at Turner's Hill, hard by, and from 1699 to 1729 in receipt of yearly and special grants from the Presb. Fund. "The Apostles' Creed better than the Assembly's Catechism," 1720, by B. C., is ascribed to him, but can hardly be his; it shows learning and strength of argument, very ably directed in the interest of an uncompromising Arianism. His "Apology," 1720, for standing by his neighbour, Joseph Stedman, accused of perjury, does credit to his sense of fairness, but is a feeble production. (*M. Sp.*) [115]

CHANDLER, HENRY (*d.* 1719). Born at Taunton. Son of a tradesman. Educ. at Taunton grammar school and Doolittle's Academy. Ministered successively at Malmesbury, Wilts; Hungerford, Berks; and Coleford, Som.; lastly, for nineteen years, and till death, at Frog Lane, Bath; receiving, 1704–1718, £10 a year from the Fund. He died early in 1719. Father of Samuel Chandler, D.D. (1693—8 May 1766). (*Cm. Ev. J. Mh.*) [91, 93]

CHANDLER, SAMUEL (*fl.* 1667–1700). 𝔓. Son of Francis Chandler (*d.* May 1667), ejected, 1663, from the sequestered rectory of Thoydon Mount, Essex. On 22 F. 1698/9 he disputed against Baptists at Portsmouth. From the pastorate at Fareham, Hants, he removed (1700 ?) to that at Andover, Hants, where Jacob Ball was Minister from 1715. (*M. P.* ii. 221-2. *Pn.*) [100]

CHANTRY, or CHANTRYE, RICHARD, B.A. (1631—22 July 1694). 𝔓. Son of John Chantry, farmer, of Repton, Derb. Admitted sizar at St. John's Coll., Cambridge, 21 June 1649, aet. 18; B.A., 1652/3. Ordained 26 Mar. 1654/5, by Wirksworth Classis. Held the chapelry of Weeford, Staff.; ejected, 1662. Removing (1666) under the operation of the Five Mile Act, he took a small farm in Derbyshire. Licensed, 13 May 1672, as Pr. Teacher in his house at Smithsby, Derb. In 1690 he was of Hartshorne, Derb., and received, 1690–93, £8 a year from the Common Fund. He died at Hartshorne. (*C. De. Jo. P. T. V.*) [26, 28, 96]

CHANTRY, ROBERT (*fl.* 1690–1734). 𝔓. Son of Richard Chantry [*q.v.*]. In 1699 he received a Fund gift, £5, as Minister at Dedington, Oxon; from 1712 to 1734 he received Fund grants, yearly and special, as Minister at Staines, Midx., where he died. (*Ev. M. P.*) [27, 29, 72]

CHAPHAM, *i.e.* CHAPMAN, WILLIAM (*d.* 1738). 𝔓. Son of Samuel Chapman, ejected from the vicarage of Yoxford, Suff. Entered Frankland's Academy, 23 Aug. 1689. On 1 Feb. 1692 a grant of

£5 was made to him for Oakhampton, Devon; on 26 Sept. 1692 he is reported "removed to a place where y^e people are well able to mantaine him." This was Lower Rotherhithe, whence he removed (1703–7) to Bethnal Green, and there died. He was succeeded at Oakhampton by John Balstar [*q.v.*]. (*C. Ev. Fr. M. W. We.*) [31]

CHAPMAN, . . . [78] [Query, identical with the foregoing]

CHARD. [91]

CHARLES II. [22]

CHARLES, SAMUEL, M.A. (6 Sept. 1633—23 Dec. 1693). Born at Chesterfield, Derb. Matric. sizar, at Corpus Christi Coll., Cambridge, 1649; B.A., 1653/4; M.A., 1657. He had a share in correcting the transcripts of MSS. in his College library, used in preparing Sir R. Twysden's "Hist. Anglic. Scriptores X," 1652, fol. (*see* p. 2768 *verso*). Ordained 22 Aug. 1655, by Wirksworth Classis as rector of Kniveton, Derbs.; lived in the house of Sir John Gell, of Hopton. Vicar of Mickleover, Derbs. (1658?); ejected, 1662. The Episc. Returns, 1669, report him as "a Nonsubscriber" preaching to "about 70" persons in Findern, Derbs., "Att the house of John Cooke, a great encourager & maintain^r of them." Licensed, June 1672, as "Pr. Teacher in the howse of John Bromiley in Chesterfield, Derbs."; also, 10 Aug. 1672, his house at Belper, Derbs., was licensed for "Pr." worship. He preached also at Hollington, Derbs., and elsewhere; but made Kingston-on-Hull his headquarters, perhaps from 1673 (*My.*) or 1680 (*Wp.*), having a house in Myton Gate. He suffered imprisonment in 1682. Probably he ministered in Bowl Alley Lane, where a Meeting-house was built by Christopher Fawthorp before 1696. (*C. De. Lm. My. P. T. Wp.*) [136, 138]

CHARLESWORTH ('Chawseworth'). [26]

CHARLETON. [91] *See* Somerset

CHARTERS, JOSIAS. [53]

CHAUNCEY, *i.e.* CHAUNCY, ISAAC, M.A., L.C.P. (23 Aug. 1632—28 Feb. 1712/3). **C.** Born at Ware, Herts; eldest son of Charles Chauncy, afterwards president of Harvard. His father took him to New England, reaching Plymouth in Dec. 1637. He graduated at Harvard Coll. (B.A., 1651; M.A., 8 Aug. 1654), and there studied medicine and theology. There is no authority for Wilson's conjecture that he finished his studies in England. Returning thither, he obtained (before 1660) the rectory of Woodborough, Wilts. Ejected thence in 1662, he removed to Andover, Hants. The Episc. Returns, 1669, report him as "presented at the Assizes as a seditious person," and one of the preachers at Andover to 200 Presbyterians (*see* Sprint, Samuel). On 5 July 1669 he was admitted an Extra-Licenciate of the College of Physicians, London. On 1 May 1672 he was licensed on his own description as Presb. Teacher in his house at Easton Town (Crux Easton?), Hants. He, however, became pastor of the Andover Congregationals. Coming to London, he was admitted a Licenciate of the Coll. of Physicians on 30 Sept. 1680. Hence he is usually called Dr. Chauncy. In 1681–82 he was living in "Blew Boar Court, in ffriday Street." In Oct. 1687 he succeeded David Clarkson, B.D. (ejected from the cure of Mortlake, Surrey), as pastor of the Congregational church then meeting in the house of Dr. Clark, Mark Lane, London; having as coadjutor, Isaac Loeffs, M.A., ejected from the rectory of Shenley, Herts. Isaac Watts was his assistant from 1698 (and his successor). His part in the Crispian controversy is mentioned in the Introduction. His constant preaching on church order and discipline wore away his congregation; he resigned on 15 April 1701. Thereafter, till his death, he presided over the Academy in Tenter Alley, Moorfield, supported by the Congregational Fund. He practised as a physician during the whole of his career after ejection. His daughter, Elizabeth, was wife of John Nesbitt [*q.v.*]. (*C. Cm. D. Fo. Mu. P. Sg. T. W.*) [3, 41, 92, 156, 157, 160, 164, 166, 168, 185, 186, 189]

CHEAPSIDE. [1]

CHEEKE, LADY. Widow either of Thomas Cheek, of Pirgo, Essex, or of Hatton Cheek, both knighted on 11 May 1603. (*S.*) [2]

CHEESMAN, CHESEMAN, or CHESMAN, THOMAS, M.A. (*d.* 1710). **P.** Became blind in his fourth year from smallpox. Educ. at Tunbridge grammar school and Pembroke Coll., Oxford; M.A., 9 July 1656. Vicar of East Garston, Berks; ejected, 1662. Came to London and preached frequently, subsequently returning to Berks. His preaching there led to his excommunication, and fifteen weeks incarceration in Reading gaol. The Episc. Returns, 1669, report "Thomas Cheesman, an Excommunicate person" as one of the preachers at East Ilsley, otherwise Market Ilsley, Berks, "in a Barne of Thomas Cheesmans" to "Vulgar People from divers parishes"; also as one of the preachers at Wantage, Berks, to "a Conventicle every Sunday" of "Presbyterians 4 or 500" and many "Inhabitants of the towne." Licensed, 16 May 1672, as Presb. Teacher "in his howse in the Parish of East Ilsley, Berks." On 13 Jan. 1672/3 the house of John Chesman at Wantage, Pr., was licensed. From 1690 received a grant of £10 a year from the Common Fund for Wantage; reduced (1695) to £6; increased (1696) to £8; ended Midsummer 1710; from 1704 he was living at Ilsley, Berks. In 1698 and 1701 he received grants of £3 from the Congregational Fund. Collections were made at Newbury for his benefit in 1705 and 1707. (*C. Cf. F. M. P. Sm. T.*) [7, 8]

CHELMORTON ('Chelmarcon,' Chelmarton'). [26, 27]

CHELMSFORD. Ejected here was Mark Mott, of Queen's Coll., Cambridge; matric. pensioner, 1620; B.A., 1623/4; M.A., 1627; curate at Chelmsford before 1639; held the sequestered rectory, 1643; accused of severity to Brownists; ejected, 1660. (*C. E. V. Wc.*) [38]

CHELSEA. [2]

CHEPENHAM. [123] *See* Wiltshire

CHESELEY. [6] *See* Berkshire

CHESHIRE. [15, 16, 152, 168, 176, 181] Except the heading 'Chester' in the earliest handwriting, all is in the handwriting of the Book-keeper. All the returns are numbered 6, except a 1691 addition, numbered 4.

Brembro is Bromborough.

Maxfield is Macclesfield [*q.v.*].

Peever is Peover [*q.v.*].

Rugely is Ringhay [*q.v.*]; the name is also spelled Ringway, Ringay, Ringey and Ringley (this last has been misread by the Book-keeper).

Stopford is Stockport.

Wellaston is Willaston in Wirral, not the Willaston near Nantwich.

In response to the Proposalls, the Fund made a grant of £3 for propagation of the Gospel at "Rossett near Chester"; this village is partly in Denbighshire, partly in Flint.

CHESHIRE CLASSIS. [157]

CHESHUNT ('Chest-hunt'). Ejected here (1660) was John Yates, who held the sequestered vicarage of Cheshunt, 9 Apr. 1656; licensed, 1 May 1672, as Congr. Teacher in a house at Theobalds, Herts. *d.* Aug. 1679, aged nearly 100. (*C. T. Uh.*) [50]

CHESTER ('West Chester'). Ejected here were:

(1) William Cook; educ. by John Ball, an Oxford divine who kept school at Whitmore near Newcastle-under-Lyme, Staff.; chaplain of Wroxall (Abbey), Warw.; vicar of Ashby-de-la-Zouch, Leic.; vicar of St. Michael's, Chester, 1650; imprisoned, 1659, for complicity in Sir George Booth's rising; ejected, 1662; imprisoned, 1663, for preaching in his own house; retired, 1666, to Wirrall; licensed, 8 May 1672, as Pr. Teacher in Chester; also, 16 May 1672, as Congr. Teacher in Chester; died 4 July 1684, aged 72. (*C. P. T. Uc.*)

(2) John Glendole, M.A.; born in Warwickshire, pleb.; matric. at Christ Church Coll., Oxford, 22 Jan. 1618/9, aged 20; B.A., 1619/20; M.A., 1625; vicar of St. Oswald's, Chester, 1642; later, rector of St. Peter's, Chester; ejected, 1662; retired to Great Budworth, Ches., 1666; licensed, Sept. 1672, as Cong. Teacher in his house at Chester. (*C. F. P. T. Uc.*)

(3) Thomas Harrison, D.D.; born at Kingston-upon-Hull, Yorks; educ. in New England; chaplain to governor of Virginia; came to London; succeeded Thomas Goodwin, D.D., in the 'gathered church' at St. Dunstan's-in-the-East, 1650; removed to Wirrall, Chesh.; chaplain to Henry Cromwell in Ireland, 1657, and preacher at Christ Church Cathedral, Dublin, D.D., at Trinity Coll., Dublin; ejected, 1660 (though there was no Irish Act of Uniformity till 1667); preached in Chester Cathedral; ejected, 1662; returned to Dublin, 1670, as minister of Winetavern Street congregation; licensed, 5 Sept. 1672, as Indept. Teacher in Chester; Meeting-house in Cooke Street, Dublin, built for him, 1673; died 22 S. 1682, aged 63. (*Am. C. D. P. T.*)

(4) Peter Leigh, M.A., matric. at Emmanuel Coll., Cambridge, 1645; B.A., 1647/8; M.A., 1653; preached at Chester Cathedral before 1653; vicar of St. John's, Chester, 1658; ejected, 1662; retired to Knutsford; licensed, 9 Dec. 1672, to preach in his own house there; living in 1686. (*C. P. T. Uc. V.*) [8, 16]

CHESTER, JOHN (*d.* May 1696). **P.** [John Chester matric. as fellow-commoner at St. Catherine's Hall, Cambridge, 1641; another John Chester matric. as pensioner at Queen's Coll., Cambridge, 1647; neither graduated.] Held the sequestered rectory of Witherley, Leic.; ejected, 1660. Removed to London, where he assisted William Jenkyn [*q.v.*] till 1662. He was very active in the Plague year. The Episc. Returns, 1669, report him and another "both Presbyterians, who doe Chatechize and Administer the holy

Sacramt and marry & privately Baptize Children," officiating to "Presbyterians and Independts about 600 In Globe Alley in two large meeting-houses built on purpose, into wch the other small Conventicles empty themselves. The reasons they Alleage for their under practices are their Dissatisfaction with our Established worship, and His Maties permission and Toleration of them." Licensed, 13 Apr. 1672, as "Pr. Teacher in ye howse of [himself?] in Maide Lane, Southwark." Later he had a Meeting-house (1687–1694?) in Gravel Lane, Southwark. Being in ill-health, he removed (1690) to Guildford (to be near his son, a physician) and died there. (*C. M. P. T. V. W. We.*) [109]

CHICHESTER. Ejected here were (1) William Martin (son of Thomas, of Witney, Oxf.) of Merton Coll., Oxford; matric. pleb., 3 July 1635, aged 15; B.A., 1639; Fellow, 1642; M.A., 1648; rector of St. Peter's, Chichester; ejected, 1662; licensed, 30 Apr. 1672, a 'Wm Martaine,' as Pr. Teacher in a house at Kingston-by-Lewes, Suss. (where he was then living); *d.* 3 Aug. 1686, in 66th year; bur. at Witney. (*C. F. T.*)

(2) William Speed, of Magdalen Hall, Oxford; admitted, 27 May 1614; B.A., 1617/8; M.A., 1620; lecturer at Uxbridge, Midx.; rector of St. Pancras, Chichester, 1630; ejected, 1662. (*C. F.*) [113]

CHILDERDITCH ('Childeitch,' 'Cliderditch'), Ess. Ejected here was John Harvey, vicar, 1653; ejected, 1662. (*C. E.*) [38, 43]

CHIMLY. [31] *See* Devonshire

CHINLEY ('Chimley'). [26]

CHIPPENHAM ('Chepenham'). [123]

CHIPPING CAMPDEN ('Cambden') [44]

CHIPPING NORTON. Ejected here were (1) . . . Clark. (*C.*)
(2) Stephen Ford [*q.v.*]. [85]

CHISHALL ('Chissel'), LITTLE. [38] Ejected here was James Willet, of King's Coll., Cambridge; matric. pensioner, 1614; B.A., 1617/8; Fellow; M.A., 1621; rector of Little Chishall, 1622; member of the Ninth Presb. Classis of Essex; anticipated ejection by resigning, 13 June 1662. Walter Ball, ejected from Royston, was licensed here, 25 May 1672, as General Presb. Teacher. There was a Nonconformist congregation here in 1694. (*C. E. T.*) [38]

CHOLETON. [63] *See* Lancashire

CHOLSEY. Ejected here in 1662 was Richard Comyn, M.A. [*q.v.*]. [6]

CHORLEY, JOSIAH, M.A. (*d.* 1720). **D.** Second son of Henry Chorley, Preston, Lanc. Pensioner at Trinity Coll., Cambridge, 26 June 1669; did not graduate there. Succeeded John Collinges [*q.v.*] as one of the ministers of the Presb. congregation at Norwich; his first entry in its register being in Sept. 1691, his last, in Sept. 1719. His "Metrical Index to the Bible," 1711, has been twice reprinted. (*D. Ev. V.*) [11, 117]

CHORLTON ('Choulton,' 'Choleton'). Chapelry in Manchester parish, now the rectory of Chorlton-cum-Hardy. The Common Fund granted (1692) £5 a year for work here, reduced (1695) to £4. [26, 63, 64]

CHORLTON, JOHN (1666—16 May 1705). Born at Salford, Lanc. Entered Frankland's Academy, 4 Apr. 1682. Assistant (7 Aug. 1687) to Henry Newcome [*q.v.*] and his successor at Cross Street, Manchester. Ordained at Warrington, Jan. 1687/8. On the death of Richard Frankland [*q.v.*] he began, 21 Mar. 1699/1700, an Academy at Manchester; assisted both in this and in the congregation from 1700 by James Coningham, M.A. (1669/70–1 S. 1716), his successor. Buried at the Collegiate Church (now Cathedral). (*D. Ht. Nk.*) [61]

CHOULTON. [26] *See* Lancashire

CHOWBENT. Chapelry in Leigh parish, now called Atherton, and a vicarage. Ejected here in 1670 was James Wood [*q.v.*]. [61]

CHRISTCHURCH, Hants. Ejected here was John Warner, of Magdalen Hall, Oxford; matric. 9 Mar. 1631/2, aged 19; B.A., 1632; M.A., 1634/5; vicar of Bathford, Som., 1636; vicar of Christchurch, ejected, 1662 (?). (*C. F.*) [102]

CHULMLEIGH ('Chimly'). [31]

CHURCH OF ENGLAND. [24, 45, 79]

CHURCH (Parish). [41]

CHURCHILL, JOSHUA (*fl.* 1644–92). **C.** Matric. sizar, either at Queen's Coll., Cambridge, 1644, or at Emmanuel Coll., 1647/8; did not graduate. Ejected from the vicarage of Fordington, Dors. Imprisoned at Dorchester, 1663–4. The Episc. Returns, 1665, report him as "now Resident at Compton Valence," Dors. Those of 1669 report him as one of the preachers to "100 or 200 of ordinary Ranke most foreigners At Mr Thomas Graves and his sonnes house" in Donhead St. Andrew, Wilts; also as preaching, with William Benn, M.A., to "a constant conventicle" of 200 persons at Fordington. Licensed, 17 Apr. 1672, as "Congregationall Teacher in his owne howse in Dorchester & Benjamin Devenish's in Fordington." He signed the Address of thanks from Dorset Ministers, 10 May 1672. At Dorchester he assisted William Benn, M.A. (1600—22 Mar. 1680/1). **C.** Ejected from the rectory of All Saints, Dorchester, and succeeded him as Minister of the Friary (afterwards Pease Lane) congregation, now extinct. His death-date (before 1712) is unknown; the statement that Baruch Nowell (*d.* 1739), "the most disagreeable preacher" John Fox ever heard, succeeded him in 1689, is obviously incorrect. (*C. Mh. P. T. V.*) [34]

CIRENCESTER. Ejected here was Alexander Gregory, of Magdalen Coll., Oxford; matric. 16 June 1610, aged 16; B.A., 1614; M.A., 1617; vicar of Cirencester; ejected, 1662; removed, 1666, to Minchinhampton, Glou.; *d.* soon after. In 1672 a Presb. Congregation here under James Greenwood applied for licence of the Weavers' Hall. (*C. F. T.*) [44]

CLAPHAM. [2, 4]

CLARE. [38, 103]

CLARK, *i.e.* CLARKE, MATTHEW, *secundus* (2 F. 1664/5—27 Mar. 1726). **C.** Born at Leicester Forest. Son of Matthew Clarke [*q.v.*]. Educated by his father and at the Academy of John Woodhouse [*q.v.*], and under George Griffith [*q.v.*]. Assisted his father at Market Harborough from 1684. Minister at Sandwich, Kent, 1687–9. Ordained (1694 ?) as pastor of the Congregational church, Miles Lane, London. Elected a Pinners' Hall lecturer, 1697. Subscriber at Salters' Hall (1719), but refused to treat Non-subscribers as heretical. He was then living "in Three Tun-Court, over against Crouched-Friars-Church." (*D. Ev.*) [66]

CLARK, or CLARKE, SAMUEL, M.A. (12 N. 1626—24 F. 1701). **P.** Born at Shotwick, Ches. Eldest son of Samuel Clarke (10 O. 1599—25 D. 1683), the martyrologist, ejected from the cure of St. Bennet Fink, London. Matric. pensioner, at Pembroke Hall (now College), Cambridge, 1638; B.A., 1641/2; Fellow, 1644–51; M.A., 1648. Appointed, 26 S. 1645, one of the Tryers of the Elders for the Seventh London Classis. Rector of Grendon Underwood, Bucks, 1657; ejected, 1662. The Episc. Returns, 1669, report him as preaching apparently (the record is confused) at Cuddington, Bucks, "Sect not knowne"; also, with others, at Thame, Oxfordshire, to "About 200 Presbyterians, Anabaptists, etc. In y^e houses sometimes of John Burton, sometimes W^m Atkins, &c. This Meeting upon y^e appearing of the Justices is removed into Buckinghamshire." Licensed, 17 Apr. 1672, as a Presb. Teacher in house of Thomas Bryan, Leighton Buzzard, Beds. On 10 June, and again on 22 July, his house at Winchendon was licensed for Presb. worship. For a time he was chaplain to Lord Wharton, at Over Winchendon, Bucks. Ultimately he settled at High Wycombe, Bucks, and there died. He is best known as annotator (1690) of the Bible. (*C. Cc. D. P. T.*) [9]

CLARK, MR. It is impossible to say whether this is (1) Thomas Clarke, ejected, 1662, from the sequestered rectory of Stisted, Ess., and licensed, 22 July 1672, being of Great Dunmow, Ess., Congr.; or (2) Timothy Clarke, ejected from some position at Lindsell, Ess., and licensed, 5 S. 1672, of Rayne, Ess., Pr. Nothing more is known of either. Three of the name graduated B.A. at Cambridge in 1640/1, 1642/3 and 1654/5 respectively; two others of the name graduated M.A. at Cambridge in 1630 and 1646 respectively. (*E. T. V.*) [38]

CLARKE, MATTHEW, or MATHIAS, M.A. (1630 ?–1708 ?). **C.** Born in Shropshire; younger son of a clergyman of good family near Ludlow. From the Charterhouse and Westminster schools, entered at Trinity Coll., Cambridge, May 1648; matric. pensioner, 1651; B.A., 1651/2; minor Fellow, 1653; M.A., 1655; sublector, 1656. Chaplain to Col. Hacker's regiment in Scotland. Held, from 1657, the sequestered rectory of Narborough, Leic.; ejected, 1660. He had signed (1659) the protest against the royalist plans of Sir George Booth. Thrice imprisoned in Leicester gaol for conventicling. Lived at Leicester Forest till the Five Mile Act drove him (1666) to Stoke Golding, Leic. The Episc. Returns, 1669, report "Matthew Clarke gent." as preaching to "about 50 Presbyterians meaner sort" at Earl Shilton, Leic.; also, being of Stoke Golding, to a "great" number of persons at Barwell, Market Bosworth, Leic.; also as one of the preachers to "about 40 Presbyterians" at Hugglescote, Leic.; also as one of the preachers to about 40 of "all sects" at Ibstock, Leic.; also as one of the preachers to about 40 Presbyterians, Independents and Anabaptists at Sibstone, Leic.; also to about 200 persons at Stoke Golding, Leic.; also to about 200 Presbyterians at Great Bowden, Leic.; also as one of the preachers to about 100 Presbyterians at Market Harborough and St. Mary in Arden [*i.e.* Ashley], Leic.; also as one of the preachers to about 200

"Presbyterians & Independents held together" at Kibworth, Leic.; also as one of the preachers to about 50 "Presbyterians & Independents" at Theddingworth, Leic.; also as one of the preachers to about 100 "Presbyterians & Independ^ts" at Ashby magna, Leic.; also as one of the preachers to about 40 "Presbyterians & Independents" at Sapcote, Leic. Licensed, 29 May 1672, being of Market Harborough, as "Pr. Teacher"; also, 18 N. 1672, as "Pr. Teach: at y^e house of Tho: Johnson," Horninghold, Leic. From 1673 he maintained (with an interruption, 1683) a Congregational church at Market Harborough, preaching there in the afternoon, and at Ashley, Northants, in the morning. In the controversy about Richard Davis (p. 184) he acted as a man of peace. He began to learn Persian in his 67th year. Disabled at length from preaching, he went to live with his daughter, Mrs. Allen, at Norwich, and there died. (*C. D. P. T. V. Wc.*) [66, 76]

CLEARKE, *i.e.* CLARK, THOMAS (*d.* 1690). **P.** Held the (? sequestered) vicarage of Godshill, I. of Wight; ejected, 1662. Chaplain for ten years to Sir Anthony Irby (*see* Irby, Lady); chaplain (1675–80) to Sir Philip Harcourt, at Stanton Harcourt, Oxf., whose only son Simon, afterwards (1721) viscount Harcourt, married (1680) Clark's only daughter, Rebecca (*d.* 1687). Removing to Portsmouth, Hants, Clark followed John Hickes (left, 1681) as Minister of the congregation now meeting in High Street, Portsmouth, where his ministry ended in 1690. (*C. P. Pe. Wc.*) [101]

CLEAVE, or CLEEVE. [44, 45, 46] *See* Gloucestershire

CLEERE. [92] *See* Creese, Thomas

CLENT. [96] Ejected here was Thomas Baldwin, *secundus* [*q.v.*].

CLERKE, or CLARKE, WILLIAM (1649–23 Sept. 1722). **C.** Son of a Dorchester clothier. Educated under William Benn (1600—22 Mar. 1680/1); ejected (1662) from the rectory of All Saints', Dorchester. Pastor of the Congregational church, Wareham, 1670. Licensed, 10 June 1672, as "Congr. Teacher in the howse of Rebecca Hastings" at Winfrith Newburgh, Dors.; signed Address of thanks from Dorset Ministers, 10 May 1672. On 8 June 1691 the Common Fund granted him £20 a year for Poole (adding in Nov.) and Wareham; it was paid till 1693. He married a daughter of William Eastman [*q.v.*]. In June 1694 ground was bought on which a Meeting-house at Wareham was built. Here he ministered till death. (*J. M. Mh. Od. P. T.*) [34, 35, 179]

CLIDERDITCH. [38, 43] *See* Essex

CLIFFORD. [133]

CLIFFORD, SAMUEL, B.A. (1630—29 O. 1699). **P.** Born at Yarlington, Som., where his father, William Clifford, M.A., was then rector. From grammar schools at Frampton, Dors., and Salisbury, Wilts, matric. at Magdalen Hall, Oxford, 2 Apr. 1652; B.A., 1654. Succeeded his father as rector of East Knoyle, Wilts, 1655; resigned, 1660. The Episc. Returns, 1669, report him as one of the preachers at Donhead St. Andrews, Wilts (*see* Churchill, Joshua); also as one of the preachers to "4 or 500" persons "At y^e Barne of M^r Alexander Cray" in Horningsham, Wilts. Licensed, 1 May 1672, as "Pr. Teacher in his howse at Knogell," *i.e.* East Knoyle. From 1695 to 1699 the Fund granted him £6 a year for Malmesbury, Wilts, in succession to William Conway [*q.v.*], and from 1696, £5 a year also for East Knoyle and Chapmanslade, Wilts. He seems to have served several places from Cranborne, Dors., on the boundary of Wilts.

He was succeeded at East Knoyle and Chapmanslade by his son Samuel (*d.* 1726); educated by Thomas Doolittle [*q.v.*]. He received £5 a year (1699–1725) from the Fund.

The Minutes incorrectly place East Knoyle in Dorset. (*C. Cm. Ev. F. Hu. M. P. T.*) [34, 123]

CLINTON, LADY. **P.** Anne, daughter of John, second earl of Clare, married Edward Clinton, styled Lord Clinton, eldest son of Theophilus, earl of Lincoln; he died 1657. The widow (who remarried, Charles Bates) died in London, Oct. 1707, and was buried "in a presbiterian meeting-house yard." She was a member of Dr. Calamy's congregation. (*Cm. Pe.*) [56]

CLOSES, THE. A farmhouse in Spen Valley, in Birstall parish, Yorks, W.R. (misplaced in E.R.). [138] *See* Holdsworth, John

COAPE, HENRY (*d.* Dec. 1691). **P.** Appointed, 14 July 1690, as Correspondent for Derbyshire. Attended meetings of Managers from 25 Aug. 1690 to 6 July 1691. His death is reported in the Minutes of 11 Jan. 1691/2; *see also* notice of it, and of his connection with Duffield (p. 28). (*M.*) [27, 28, 162, 168]

COAPE, or COPE, JOSEPH, B.A. (1623–24 Aug. 1704). **P.** Son of Thomas Cope, of Charldon [Cauldon ?], Staff., pleb.

Matric. at New Inn Hall, Oxford, 7 Apr. 1642, aged 18; migrated to Cambridge; matric. pensioner at Jesus Coll., Cambridge, 1645/6; B.A., 1645/6. Held, from 1644, the sequestered vicarage of Sandbach, Ches.; ejected, 1662. Subsequently he preached about, in Cheshire, Shropshire and Staffordshire. The Episc. Returns, 1669, report him as one of the preachers to above 300 persons at houses in Walsall, Staff. Licensed, 30 Apr. 1672, as Pr. Teacher in Edw. Harrison's house, Eccleshall, Staff.; also, Jan. 1672/3, at the house of Christopher Hoford [Holford Hall] at Goosetrey, Ches. By connivance of the rector of Barthomley, with the consent of the owner of the building, he was allowed from 1689 till death to minister at Haslington Chapel (built by the Vernon family but not consecrated) in Barthomley parish, where Matthew Henry preached his funeral sermon. Cope was a member of the Cheshire Classis (*see* p. 157). (*C. F. P. T. Uc. V.*) [15]

COATES, SAMUEL (*d.* 1704). **P.** Son of Samuel Coates, M.A. (1614–1683); ejected from West Bridgford, Notts. He was at St. Catharine's Hall, Cambridge, 1679, but did not matriculate. Ordained, 1684, Minister of the Old Meeting-house, Mansfield, 1690–1704 (despite his refusal (1690) of a grant "on Condition yt the meeting there be kept up constant"). (*M. No. Y.*) [83, 173]

COATS, MATTHEW (*fl.* 1663–1701). **P.** A mercer at Gainsborough. Presented at the Consistory Court in 1663 and 1664. On 5 Sept. 1672, licence was granted for "The house of Matthew Coates of Gainsbrow in Lincolnsh Presb." On 12 July 1701 "Matthew Coats the elder, mercer," conveyed to certain trustees "that house or building lately erected in a place called the Ratton Row in Ganesburgh . . . now used and intended to be used as a Chappell or Meeting House as by the lawes of this Kingdome the same is now permitted and Authorised for such Protestant dissenters persons or people to meet, assemble and worshipp God in, or distinguished or goe under the names of Congregationall, Independents or Presbiterians with the ground whereon it stands." (*Gb. T.*) [70, 71]

COCKERILL, THOMAS. **P.** *See* p. 163. [6, 7, 27, 77, 114, 156, 162, 163, 167, 168]

COCKERILL, THOMAS, *secundus*. *See* p. 174. For the changes in the Cockerills' places of business, consult *At.*

COCKERMOUTH. Ejected here was George Larkham [*q.v.*]. [21]

COCKEY CHAPEL, in Middleton parish, now called Ainsworth, and a vicarage. Ejected here was John Lever [*q.v.*]. The building, however, came to be in use by Nonconformists (*see* Joseph Whitworth). [61]

COGGESHALL ('Coggeslal,' 'Coggslall'), Ess. Ejected here was John Sames; educ. in New England; held the sequestered vicarage of Kelvedon, Ess., 1647; succeeded John Owen, D.D. [*q.v.*], as vicar of Coggeshall, 1654; ejected, 1662; preaching at Coggeshall, 1669; licensed, 1 May 1672, as Congr. Teacher at Coggeshall; bur. 16 Dec. 1672. (*Bd. C. T.*) [39, 186]

COKAYNE, GEORGE, B.A. (1619/20—21 Nov. 1691). **C.** Of ancient family, son of John and Elizabeth Cokayne; baptized at Cople, Beds, 16 Jan. 1619/20. Educ. Sidney Coll., Cambridge; B.A., 1639/40. Held the sequestered rectory of St. Pancras, Soper Lane, London, before 1648 (also chaplain to Sir Bulstrode Whitelocke); ejected, 1660. Licensed, 16 May, and again 10 June 1672, as Congr. Teacher in his house, Redcross Street, parish of St. Giles', Cripplegate. Minister, from 1688 till death, in Redcross Street, possibly at Stocking-Weavers' Hall, where his body lay previous to burial, 27 Nov. 1691, in Bunhill Fields. He married Abigail Plott, and left issue. The congregation under his successor, John Nesbitt [*q.v.*], moved to Hare Court, Aldersgate Street (removed to Harecourt Chapel, Canonbury, 1857). (*C. D. Ha. P. Wc.*) [4, 5, 35, 41, 160, 161, 165, 167, 185, 186]

COLCHESTER. Ejected here were (1) Owen Stockton (31 May 1630—10 Sept. 1680) of Christ's Coll., Cambridge; matric. sizar, 1646; B.A., 1649/50; rem. to Gonville and Caius Coll.; Fellow, 1654; M.A., 1653; ord. by presbyters, 1655; town lecturer at Colchester, 1657; ejected, 1662; preaching in Colchester; rem. to Chattisham, Suff., 1665; preaching in Colchester and Ipswich, 1669; licensed, 16 Apr. 1672, as Presb. Teacher in Ipswich; also, 22 May 1672, as Ind. Teacher in Colchester; also, 22 July 1672, as Pr. Teacher in Hadleigh, Suff.; lived at Ipswich, preaching alternately there and at Colchester; *d.* 31 Aug. 1680; by will, founded a scholarship and fellowship at Gonville and Caius Coll. (*C. D. E. T. V.*) [38, 42] (2) Edward Warren, *alias* Sidling; matric. sizar at Pembroke Coll., Cambridge, 1638; B.A., 1641/2; M.A., 1646; vicar of St. Peter's, 1657; ejected (1662?); remained in Colchester, and practised physic; licensed, 17 Apr.

1672, as Presb. Teacher in his own and another house. (*C. E. T. V.*)

COLE, THOMAS, M.A. (1628 ?–16 Sept. 1697). **C.** Son of William Cole, gentleman, of London. From Westminster School he matric., 1 Feb. 1646/7, at Christ Church, Oxford, aged 18; B.A., 1649; M.A., 1651. John Locke entered under him as tutor in 1652; Principal of St. Mary Hall, 1656; incorp. M.A. at Cambridge, 1658. Ejected from his Principalship, 1660. Kept a philosophy school at Nettlebed, Oxf., of which James Bonnell (1653–1699), his pupil, complains as wanting in moral and religious supervision. Palmer wrongly states that Samuel Wesley "had been one of his pupils." Licensed, 22 Apr. 1672, as a Congr. Teacher at John Tyler's house and Alexander Bernard's barn, Henley-on-Thames; and on 16 May as the same at his house, Henley-on-Thames. In Feb. 1674 he was ordained at Cutlers' Hall, Cloak Lane, London, as pastor of the Congregational church, founded by Philip Nye, which subsequently, under Cole's ministry, removed to Tallow-Chandlers' Hall, Dowgate Hill, and again to Pinners' Hall. He did not join the Happy Union, and though elected (13 Apr. 1691) a Manager of the Common Fund, he never attended and declined to act. He was an original Manager of the Congregational Fund (1695), and one of its correspondents for Oxfordshire. He preached his last sermon 22 Aug. 1697. In the Crispian controversy he was zealous against the 'Neonomian' view. (*C. Co. D. F. M. P. T. W.*) [4, 156, 161, 183, 185]

COLEBROOK. [73] *See* Middlesex

COLEFORD ('Colford,' 'Couer,' 'Conard'; pronounced Covert) is in Newland parish, Glou. *See* Brinkworth and Monmouth. The Common Fund granted (1692) £6 a year, not renewed 1695. (*M. Rg.*) [46, 145]

COLEFORD ('Colefort'), Som. [91]

COLESBOURNE ('Cos Pawn'). [44]

COLEY, then a chapelry in Halifax parish, now vicarage. Ejected here was Oliver Heywood [*q.v.*]. [129]

COLLAMPTON. [32] *See* Devonshire

COLLET, HENRY (*fl.* 1660–1690). **C.** Perhaps ejected from rectory of Claydon, Suff. Licensed, 29 May 1672, as "Congr. Teacher" in his house in Tewkesbury, Glou. (*C. P. T.*) [44, 47]

COLLIER, ABEL, B.A. (1630—29 May 1695). **C.** Matric. 'ser.' at New Inn Hall, Oxford, 9 D. 1650; B.A., 1653. Ejected from the rectory of Nether Whitacre, Warw. Went into business in London. Licensed, 9 May 1672, as "Congr. Teacher in the howse of John Boun in Coventry." (*See* Bunn, *i.e.* Bohun, John). The Common Fund granted him, from 1690, £12 a year for Halstead. Buried in Bunhill Fields. (*F. M. P. Si. T.*) [40, 41, 179]

COLLIER, ANTHONY (*fl.* 1660–99). **P.** Held the sequestered rectory of Morton-on-Lugg, Heref.; ejected, 1660; vicar or curate of Morton Valence, Glou., also of Whitminster (*alias* Wheatenhurst), Glou.; ejected, 1662. Licensed, 20 Apr. 1672, as "Presb. Teacher in his howse in Rosse, Hereford." The Common Fund granted him (1690–99) £5 a year for Ross. (*C. M. P. T.*) [48]

COLLINGES, JOHN, D.D. (1623—18 Jan. 1690/1). **P.** Born at Boxted, Ess. He calls 1654 "the two and thirtieth year current of my age." Son of Edward Collens or Collins, M.A. Cantab. 1610. From Dedham grammar school, matric. at Emmanuel Coll., Cambridge, 1639; B.A., 1642/3; M.A., 1646; B.D., 1653; D.D., 1658. Chaplain (1644) to Isaac Wyncoll of Bures, Ess.; vicar (Sept. 1646) of St. Saviour's, Norwich; held (1653) the sequestered vicarage of St. Stephen's, Norwich; ejected, 1662. He had lived at Norwich as chaplain in the house of Sir John Hobart, bart. (*d.* 20 Apr. 1647), Chapelfield, and remained chaplain to his widow (*d.* 21 N. 1664). He was one of the Savoy Commissioners (1661) for considering revision of the Prayer-book. The Episc. Returns, 1669, report him as preaching, with Benjamin Snowden [*q.v.*], to "about 300 Presbyterians & Independents Att the house of John Barnham, hosier," in the parish of St. John's Maddermarket, Norwich. Licensed, 30 Apr. 1672, as "Pr. Teacher in Jonathan Wilson's howse in the Parish of St. Stephens, Norwich." The Norwich corporation leased (14 May 1672) to his congregation the East Granary (behind St. Andrew's Hall), which they kept till they erected (1689) a Meeting-house in the parish of St. George's Colegate. Collinges, though in other respects a bitter controversialist, was strongly for the union of Presbyterians and Congregationals; his funeral sermon was preached by Martin Finch [*q.v.*]. He spelled his name Collings, till his ejection. (*B. Ba. C. Cc. D. P. T. V.*) [74, 177]

COLLINS, JOHN, M.A. (1632—3 Dec. 1687). **C.** Son of Henry Collins, starchmaker. Sailed for New England with his father (whose conformity was certified by the rector of Stepney) in the 'Abigail' on 30 June 1635, being then aged 3 years. His father (who, according to Sibley, was Edward Collins) became a deacon of the Congregational church at Cambridge, Mass., and died 9 Apr. 1689, aged about 86. The son was B.A. of Harvard, and Fellow, 1649; M.A., 1652; incorp. M.A. at Cambridge, 1654. Preacher to the Scottish Council, 1655; accompanied General Monck from Scotland to London as chaplain. Silenced, 1662. The Episc. Returns, 1669, report him as one of the preachers in Bell Lane, Spitalfields. Licensed, 29 May 1672, as Congr. Teacher in house of James Best, Duke's Place, Aldgate, London. One of the six original Pinners' Hall lecturers, 1672. About the same time he succeeded Thomas Mallery, ejected from lectureships at St. Michael's, Crooked Lane, and St. Nicholas, Deptford, as pastor of the Congregational church in Paved Alley, Lime Street.

His son, John Collins (1673 ?–19 Mar. 1714/5), was co-pastor of the same church from 1698, and Pinners' Hall Lecturer from 1706. (*C. Cc. D. P. Sg. T.*) [154]

COLLINS, ROBERT, M.A. (1620 ?–6 Mar. 1697/8). **P.** Matric. 'gent.' at Exeter Coll., Oxford, 12 N. 1650; Fellow, 1652–5; B.A., 1653; chaplain, 1654; M.A., 1655. Rector of Talaton, Devon; ejected, 1662. Retired to his estate at Ottery St. Mary. Heavily fined for preaching in his own house, a handsome building near the church. The Episc. Returns, 1665, report him as keeping conventicles frequently, especially upon Sundays, but not arrested "for want of a Justice of Peace." The Episc. Returns, 1669, describe him as "a Non-Conformist minister," "a gent. of a good estate," preaching at his own house to "about 200 few gentry, but may (*sic*) tradesmen of good note." Licensed, 20 Apr. 1672, as "Presb. Teacher in his howse." Subsequent persecutions led him to sell his estate and drove him to Holland. Under Toleration he returned. He bequeathed £20 towards a new Meeting-house at Ottery St. Mary. He "lived to be near 80." (*C. Em. F. P. T.*) [30]

COLLINS, or COLLINGS, THOMAS (*fl.* 1690–1736). **P.** Had a grant from the Common Fund (reported 17 N. 1690) of £8 a year, "att Leigh in little Wootton." *See* Crompton, Thomas. On 2 Mar. 1691 a grant of £10 a year appears for him as student at "Vtericht, Holland"; this was renewed next year. For part of the first year he was fellow-student with Edmund Calamy [*q.v.*]. On 14 F. 1692/3, on the request of Mr. Thomas Collins and others, it was agreed by the justices that "a house at yᵉ end of Lord Street, Liverpool, belonging to Mʳ David Poole of yᵉ same, merchant" should "be sett apart for yᵉ exercise of religious worship . . . and the said Mʳ Thomas Collins is to be allowed to preach there." Poole, who came to Liverpool from Preston, was assessed (1708) for premises in Lord Street for a "chapelle." In or soon after 1718, Thomas Collins, apparently the same man, was Minister at Temple Combe, otherwise Combe Abbas, Som.; he received (1723–36) from the Fund a yearly grant of £6. (*Ev. M. Rl.*) [48, 59]

COLNBROOK ('Colebrook'). [73]

COLNE. [123, 125] *See* Wiltshire

COLTMAN, . . . **C.** Proposed as Manager, 29 July 1690, by Arthur Shallett [*q.v.*], and presumed to be of the same denomination; attended no meeting. (*M.*) [162]

COMBE LONGA ('Coomb'). [85]

COMMON FUND. [155, 157, 158 *sqq.*]

COMPTER, THE. The reference is probably to the Compter in the Poultry. There was another in Wood Street, each being a prison, belonging to one of the sheriffs of London, for all persons arrested within the City and Liberties. The Compter in Southwark was only for debt. (*Sl.*) [3]

COMYN, COMYNS, or CUMMYN, RICHARD (1617–1706 ?). **P.** Born at Durham. Son of Timothy Commyn, under-sheriff of Durham; admitted pensioner at St. John's Coll., Cambridge, 3 Apr. 1633, aet. 16; matric. 1633; did not graduate. Episcopally ordained Rector of Cholsey, Berks; ejected, 1662. Preached at Wallingford, Berks. Licensed, 15 May 1672, to teach in house of Austin Cooke, Wantage, Berks, Presbyterians; also, 30 S. 1672, as Presb. Teacher at his own house, Cholsey; at the same time the houses of Benjamin Jones and Mary Hans were licensed at Cholsey, both Pr. Comyn received (1691–96) a grant of £10 a year for Cholsey; and (1697–1705) £8 a year for the same. (*C. Jo. M. P. T. V.*) [6]

CONARD. [145] *See* Gloucestershire

CONGLETON. Ejected here was Thomas Brook; preacher at Congleton Chapel in Astbury parish; known as "bawling Brook"; ejected, 1660; preacher at Great Moreton Chapel, same parish; ejected, 1662; buried, 31 Aug. 1664, aged 72. (*C. P.*) [15, 16]

CONGREGATIONAL FUND. [157, 179, 183]

CONGREGATIONAL MINISTERS. [47, 179]

CONGREGATIONAL POLITY. [153]

CONSTANTINE, ROBERT, M.A. (1618/9–Dec. 1699). 𝔓. Third son of Thomas Constantine, rector of Taxal, Ches.; baptized, 14 Mar. 1618/9. From a Glossop school went (1636) to Glasgow Univ.; matric. 21 Apr. 1638. Preached first at Fairfield and Buxton, Derb.; presented by parishioners (3 N. 1647) to Oldham, a chapelry in Prestwich parish, Lanc.; removed, Oct. 1650, refusing the engagement of fidelity to the Commonwealth without king or house of Lords; accepted call to vicarage of Birstall, Yorks; reinstated at Oldham, Mar. 1654/5; ejected, 1662. Living in Salford, 1671. Licensed, 8 May 1672, on petition from inhabitants of Oldham, as "Pr. Teacher in the Barne of Rob: Wild [Wylde] of Heaside in the parish of Oldham." Later he lived and preached at Greenacres in the same parish. On his wife's death (29 Mar. 1695) he retired from duty to Manchester, and dying there was buried at Oldham on 14 or 16 D. 1699. The statement that in 1690 he was the "ancientest" of the then surviving Ejected, must be understood with reference to his own county. He was at that date not more than 71, and the junior of John St. Nicholas [*q.v.*] by not less than fourteen years. (*C. Gm. Nl. P. Y.*) [59]

CONWAY, WILLIAM (*fl.* 1657–93). 𝔓. Matric. 'ser.' at Magdalen Hall, Oxford, 18 Mar. 1657/8; ejected, 1660. He lived at Witney, Oxfordsh. The Episc. Returns, 1669, report him as one of the preachers at Coggs, Oxfordsh., along with Henry Cornish [*q.v.*] and others, to "about 100 Presbyterians & Independents In the howse of one Mr Blake of ye Fine Office — once & sometimes twice every Lord's Day." Licensed, 10 June 1672, as "Pr. Teacher in the Barne of Edw: Browne in the Parish of Westport in Marlebrough [*i.e.* Malmesbury], Wilts." The Common Fund granted him (1690–93) £6 a year for Malmesbury, Wilts, where he was succeeded (1695) by Samuel Clifford [*q.v.*]. (*C. M. P. T.*) [44, 123]

CONY, or CONEY, . . . (*fl.* 1660–92) [? Nathaniel Cony, matric. sizar, at St. John's Coll., Cambridge, 1629; B.A., 1632/3; M.A., 1636]. Ejected from the rectory of Broughton, Oxf. The Common Fund, on 4 Jan. 1691/2, granted £5 to "Mr Comy at [blank] in Staffordshire as a present assistance to him." (*C. M. P. V.*) [97]

COOKE, ROBERT. (*M.*) [184]

COOMB. [85] *See* Oxfordshire

COOME. [92] *See* Somerset

CORNHILL. [163]

CORNISH, HENRY, D.D. (1611 ?–18 D. 1698). 𝔓. Son of William Cornish, Ditchet, Som., pleb. Matric. at New Inn Hall, Oxford, 4 N. 1631, aged 20; B.A., 1634; M.A., 1636/7; B.D., 1648; D.D., 1649 (though he is said to have refused this degree). Held the sequestered rectory of St. Giles in the Fields, London, 1642/3–1647. Canon of Christ Church, Oxford, 1648; ejected, 1660. Chaplain to Sir Philip Harcourt at Stanton Harcourt, Oxfordsh. The Episc. Returns, 1669, report him as one of the preachers, along with William Conway [*q.v.*] and others, to "about 200 Presbyterians & Independents In the howse of one Mr Blake of ye Fine Office—once & sometimes twice every Lord's Day," at Coggs, Oxfordsh. Licensed, 18 Apr. 1672, at Stanton Harcourt, Pr.; again licensed, 29 June, as a general Presb. Teacher, of Stanton Harcourt; yet again, 10 Aug., as the same. He was ministering at Oxford in 1688. In 1690/1 he settled at Bicester. The Common Fund granted him, 1690–93, £10 a year at Bicester, where Cornish had "a small but intelligent and sober people, with whom he lived very lovingly." (*C. Cm. F. M. P. T. Wc.*) [7, 85, 86]

CORNISH, WILLIAM (*fl.* 1672–1690). 𝔓. Licensed, 17 Apr. 1672, "to teach" at the house of Sir Heneage Fetherston, bart., in Cow Lane, West Smithfield. In Oct. 1672 licence was granted for "The house of Wm Cornish of Henley upon Thames Bucks Pr." "Mr Cornish" received, 10 Nov. 1690, £3 from an anonymous donation of £50 made through Matthew Rapier [*q.v.*]. (*M. T.*) [1]

CORNWALL. [18, 19, 168, 176] Except the heading "Cornwall" in the earliest handwriting, all is in the handwriting of the Book-keeper. The returns are numbered 18 to 81. The Indulgence licences show that the statement "there never were meetings" at Bodmin, Lostwithiel and Redruth is erroneous.

Camerford is Camelford.

Fowes is Fowey.

Hartston. ? Error for Helstone.

Lancack is Lancast.

Lancaston is Launceston, not Lancast.

Laslithiel St is Lostwithiel (formerly Lestwithiel).

Marthir is Merther.

Mazarion is Marazion.

Pordstow (or Pudstow) is Padstow.

St. Eball is St. Eval.

St. Hellens is Haligan or Helligon, a

manor in St. Mabyn parish, seat of family of Silly; *see* Wills, Jonathan.

St. Inoder (or St. Indoer) is St. Enodor. Tossell is St. Austell.

CORSHAM (' Causam '). [123]

COS PAWN. [44] *See* Gloucestershire

COTTINGHAM. Ejected from this rectory in 1662 was Joseph Robinson [? of Sidney Sussex Coll., Cambridge; matric. pensioner, 1649; B.A., 1652/3; M.A., 1659]; *d.* soon after ejection. (*C. My. V.*) [138]

COUNTIES, SURVEY OF. [167-8]

COUNTY UNIONS (Congregational). [157]

COURTMAN, JOHN, M.A., B.D. (1627–9 F. 1691/2). **C.** Born at Sible Hedingham, Ess. Subsizar at Trinity Coll., Cambridge, 10 F. 1645/6; matric., 1646; Scholar, 1649; B.A., 1649/50; Fellow, 1650; M.A., 1653; B.D., 1660; university preacher. Rector of Thorpe Malsor, Northants. After 1662 he employed a curate, and preached privately in the house of John Mansell, Esq., the patron, ultimately resigning the living to his son John (*d.* 1719). Licensed, 25 May 1672, as " Congr. Teacher in the howse of John Mansell in Thorp Malsor." After resigning his living, he practised physic, and had a reputation for the treatment of the paralytic and insane. He was a man of ready wit. (*C. P. T. Tc. V.*) [76]

COVEN, STEPHEN (*fl.* 1655–1690). **C.** Originally a ship-joiner. Presented, 1655, to the sequestered rectory of Sandford Peverell, Devon. Ejected, 1660. Described in Episcopal Return, 1665, as " A Wandering Seditious Seminary " at Halberton, Devon; and again, same year, as one " who goes about from place to place teaching Sedition, but where his Constant abode is we cannot learne." Licensed, 9 May 1672, being at Grub Street, London; also 22 May 1672 as Congr. Teacher in houses of Thomas Ovey, Watlington, Oxon, and George Gooding in Latchford. On 10 Nov. 1690 £2 was paid to him as share of a £50 anonymous donation per Matthew Rapier. He published " The Militant Christian; or The Good Soldier of Jesus Christ, described," 1668 (a sermon on 2 Tim. ii. 3); reprinted, 1805, with title " The Dead Raised," and introduction by W. Batson, who claims to have corrected the original; he has corrected Alexander Severus into " Mr Alexander Severus." An abridgment, by R. Goadby, was published in 1781. (*C. M. P. T.*) [1]

COVENTRY. Ejected here were (1) Samuel Basnett (son of Thomas Basnett, mercer, Mayor of Coventry); of Emmanuel Coll., Cambridge; matric. pensioner, 1644; B.A., 1647/8; rem. to Oxford; Fellow of St. John's Coll., 1648; incorp. B.A., 1649; Fellow of All Souls' Coll., and M.A., 1649; incorp. M.A. at Cambridge, 1651; lecturer at St. Michael's on Sundays and at Holy Trinity on a week-day; gathered a Congregational church; ejected, 1662; removed to Atherstone, 1665; *d.* there in 1666. (*C. F. Pc. T. V.*)

(2) John Bryan, of Emmanuel Coll., Cambridge; matric. sizar, 1620; B.A., 1626/7; M.A., 1632; B.D., 1645; D.D., 1651; rector of Barford, War., 25 June 1632; vicar of Holy Trinity, 1644; ejected, 1662; preaching at Coleshill, War., 1669; licensed, 16 May 1672, as Pr. Teacher in a ' house ' in West Orchard, Coventry; trained up many ministers; *d.* 4 Mar. 1675/6. (*C. D. Dw. T. V.*)

(3) Obadiah Grew, D.D. *See* Grace

COVER. [46, 145] *See* Coleford, Glou.

COW LANE, now King Street, West Smithfield. Green Dragon Court was on its south-west side, not far from Snow Hill. (*Lo. Sl.*) [1]

COWARD, . . . **P.** [Probably William Coward (1648—28 Apr. 1738), founder of the educational Trust.] Attended no meeting; replaced, 2 Mar. 1690/1, by Theophilus Revell [*q.v.*]. As John Jurin [*q.v.*] was deputed to interview his proposed successor, it is assumed that Coward was of the same denomination. (*D. M.*) [162]

COWBRIDGE, or CAWBRIDGE, JOHN (*fl.* 1662–92). **P.** Ejected from the vicarage of St. Anthony, Corn. Chaplain to Hugh Boscawen. Licensed, 10 June 1672, and 20 June, as Teacher in the house of Widow Mary Trelawdwy or Trelawdry at Penryn, and signed the thanks from Cornish Ministers. St. Mawes, a village in the parish of St. Just-in-Roseland, returned two members to Parliament till 1832. In 1690 a grant of £8 a year was made to Cowbridge for St. Mawes " on condition hee fix there "; this was withdrawn, 27 June 1692, as he had not preached there for " several moneths." (*C. M. P. T.*) [19, 20]

COWTHAATE. [21] *See* Cumberland

CRAB, . . . [42] ? Nathanael Crab, who in 1689 represented the General Baptist church of Shad Thames, at the Particular Baptist Assembly (information from Rev. W. T. Whitley, LL.D.)

CRADOCK, SAMUEL, B.D. (1621—7 O. 1706). **P.** Born at Greetham, Rutland. Son of the rector of Thistleton, Rutl. Matric. pensioner at Emmanuel Coll., Cambridge, 1637; B.A., 1641; M.A., 1644 (incorp. at Oxford, 1649). Fellow, 1645; B.D., 1651. Rector of North Cadbury, Som., 1656; ejected, 1662. Shortly afterwards he became, under the will of a relative, owner of the estate of Geesings, parish of Wickhambrook, Suff. The Episc. Returns, 1669, report him as one of the preachers to a few Presbyterians at Chalfont St. Giles, Bucks, "in the house of M[rs] Fleetwood" (perhaps widow of George Fleetwood, the regicide). Licensed, 2 Apr. 1672, as "Presbyterian Teacher" at Geesings. Here for 24 years he ministered gratuitously, removing in 1696 to Bishops Stortford, Essex, preaching there, and becoming pastor of a church afterwards (and perhaps then) Congregational, at the neighbouring village of Stansted-Mountfitchet (meeting-house built about 1698). Prior to the Toleration Act he opened an Academy for philosophy and theology, holding that the graduation oath which debarred from prelecting outside the universities applied only to prelections for a degree. Calamy was his student (1686–8) in philosophy, along with Timothy Goodwin, afterwards archbishop of Cashel; his students included many sons of peers and gentry. He preached twice every Sunday till within a fortnight of his death in his 86th year. (*C. Cm. D. F. P. T. V.*) [43, 103]

CRANBORNE ('Cramborn'). [34]

CRANBROOK ('Crane brooke'). Ejected here was William Goodrich, of Gonvile and Caius Coll., Cambridge; matric. sizar, 1634; B.A., 1637; vicar of Cranbrook, 1646; ejected, 1662; preaching in his house at Hessett, Suff., in 1669; licensed, 10 June 1672, as Pr. Teacher at his house at Hessett; his house licensed, same month, Pr. (*C. K. T.*) [55]

CRANE, THOMAS, M.A. (1630–Aug. 1714). **P.** Born at Plymouth; son of a merchant. Matric. at Exeter Coll., Oxford, 15 F. 1648/9; rem. to Gloucester Hall; M.A., 1655. Assistant to Richard Allein, M.A.; ejected from the rectory of Batcomb, Som. Rector of Rampisham, Dorset; ejected, 1662. Settled at Beaminster, Dorset. Licensed, 8 May 1672, as "William Craine of Beaminster" to be "a Grãll Pr. Teacher"; and signed the Address of thanks from Dorset Ministers, 10 May 1672. He remained in charge of the Beaminster congregation till death. On 19 June 1693 the ministerial Managers of the Fund contributed £10 towards his present needs. (*C. F. M. Od. P. T.*) [34]

CRANFORD. Ejected from this rectory was Henry Searle, of Sidney Sussex Coll., Cambridge; matric. pensioner, 1633; B.A., 1636/7; M.A., 1640; licensed, 8 May 1672, as Pr. Teacher in Lady Pickering's house at Titchmarsh, Northants. (*C. T. V.*) [77]

CRANLEY or CRANLEIGH ('Cranly'). [110]

CRAVEN. A hilly district in the North of Yorkshire, W. Riding. [130, 135]

CREATON. [77, 78] Ejected from this vicarage was Richard Hooke, of New Inn Hall, Oxford; matric., 1 Feb. 1632/3, aged 19; B.A., 1635; incorp. at Christ's Coll., Cambridge; M.A., 1641; vicar of Desborough, Northants, 1646; vicar of Moulton, Northants, 1656; vicar of Rothersthorpe, Northants, 1661, etc.; ejected, 1662; retired to Northampton, his birthplace, where he had some estate; taught school; licensed, 13 May 1672, as Pr. Teacher in his house at Northampton; his house licensed, same date, as Pr. Meeting-place; *d.* 30 June 1679, aet. 67. (*C. F. N. P. T. V.*) The Common Fund granted (1691) £6 a year for Creaton, reduced (1695) to £5. (*M.*) [77, 78]

CREDITON. [30]

CREECH ST. MICHAEL. [93]

CREESE, THOMAS, B.A. (1623–1698?). **P.** Born in Somersetshire. Son of Morgan Creese of Widcombe, Som., pleb. Matric. at St. Alban's Hall, Oxford, 27 Mar. 1640, aged 17; rem. to Queen's Coll., Cambridge, B.A., 1644/5. Rector (1646) of Combe Hay, Som.; ejected, 1662. The Episc. Returns, 1669, report him as one of the preachers to 100 persons at Monckton Combe, Som.; also to 100 persons at Batheaston, Som.; also to 300 persons at Dunkerton, Som.; also to 200 persons at Cameley, Som., "In the parish church"; also to 300 persons at Glastonbury, Som. Licensed, July 1672, being of Dunkerton parish, as "gen[all] Presb: Teacher." Latterly he lived at Bath "and preached in all the obscure corners of the country." The Common Fund granted him, 1690, £6 a year for Bath and Coome (Monckton Combe), reduced, 1695, to £4 and continued till 1697. He died in his 76th year. (*C. Cm. F. M. P. T. V.*) [92]

CRESWELL, *i.e.* CARSWELL, SOLOMON, B.A. (1609–1698?). **P.** Born in Devonshire. Matric. pleb., 3 May 1629, at Exeter Coll., Oxford, aged 20; B.A., 1623/4. Held the sequestered rectory of Woodham Ferrers, Essex, which he resigned before May 1646 for the vicarage of St German's, Corn.; driven thence by the king's forces. Licensed, 22 Apr. 1672, as Presb. Teacher in his own house at St. German's. Preached there gratis till

within a fortnight of his death, when about 89. (*C. F. P. T. Wc.*) [19, 20]
CREWE, MADAM. Mary (July 1604–6 July 1690), second daughter and co-heiress of Sir John Done, Knight, of Utkinton Hall, Chesh., married (Dec. 1636) John Crewe, Esq. (*d.* 12 May 1670), second son of Sir Randle Crewe, Knight, of Crewe. She was born and died at Utkinton Hall. (*Oc.*) [17]
CREWKERNE (' Brookhorne '). [91]
CRICK. Ejected here was Stephen Fowler, M.A. [*q.v.*]. [76]
CRICKET (' Crickett '), MALHERBIE. Ejected here was John Turner, B.A. [*q.v.*].
CRICKET (' Crickett '), ST. THOMAS. Ejected from this vicarage was John Langdall, or Langdale, of King's Coll., Cambridge; matric. sizar, 1623; rem. to St. John's Coll.; B.A., 1626/7; preaching at Merriott, Wayford, Winsham, and other places, Som., in 1669; licensed, May 1672; also on 13 Jan. 1672/3, as Pr. Teach[r] in a house at Henton St. George. (*C. T. V.*) [92]
CRIGGLESTONE (' Criggleston '). [129]
CRIGLAS or CRICKLAS (' Cryglas '), in Abergwilly parish, Carm. [144]
CRISP, TOBIAS, B.D. (1600—27 Feb. 1642/3. Puritan. Born in Bread Street, London; third son of Ellis Crisp, Alderman and Sheriff of London, whose elder son, Nicholas (1599 ?–26 Feb. 1665/6), was knighted in 1641, and made a baronet in 1665. From Eton he entered Christ Coll., Cambridge; B.A., 1624; incorporated at Balliol Coll., Oxford, 1626/7; M.A., 1626/7 (incorporated at Cambridge, 1638); B.D., 1638. Said to have become D.D. Became rector of Newington, Surrey, 1627; rector of Brinkworth, Wilts, 1629. Driven from Brinkworth (Aug. 1642) by royalists, and retired to London. All his published sermons were posthumous; on the appearance of the first series, "Christ Alone Exalted," 1643, the Westminster Assembly wanted it burnt as heretical. His "Works," 1690, were collected by his son Samuel. His friends admitted his use of incautious language, but maintained his orthodoxy. (*D. F. V.*) [156, 186, 187]
CRISPIAN CONTROVERSY. [156, 184-6, 190]
CROFT, in the manor of Culcheth, Winwick parish. [59]
CROFTS, JOHN, M.A. (*b.* 1621). 𝔓. Son of Thomas Crofts, of Hornton, Oxf., pleb. Matric. at St. John's Coll., Oxford, 5 Apr. 1639, aged 18; rem. to Gloucester Hall, B.A., 1642/3; M.A., 1646. Rector of Mottiston, I. of Wight; ejected, 1662. The Episc. Returns, 1669, report him as "Chaplaine to M[rs] Lisle," and preacher to "Presbyterians 200 Of the meaner sort, who come most of them from Ringwood & out of Dorsetshire" in a conventicle at Ellingham, Hants, "kept at Moyles court, the house of M[rs] Lisle the Regicides wife," *i.e.* Alice (1614 ?–2 S. 1685), daughter and heiress of Sir White Beckenshaw, of Moyles Court, and second wife (1630) of John Lisle (1610 ?–11 Aug. 1664), who had been one of Cromwell's House of Lords; hence known as Lady Lisle, whose judicial murder was the crowning infamy of Jeffreys. Later he was chaplain to Frances (1621—17 Oct. 1691), daughter of Richard Whitehead of Tytherley, Hants, and second wife of Hon. Nathaniel Fiennes (1608 ?—16 D. 1669) of Newton Toney, Wilts, who had been one of Cromwell's House of Lords. Licensed, 8 May 1672, as "Congr. Teacher in the howse of John Girle in Newton Tone, Wilts"; also, 13 May 1672, as "Pr. Teacher in the howse of Fran: Fines in Newton Tony, Wilts." ' Alton ' is Allington, the parish next to Newton Toney. (*C. D. F. P. T.*) [123]
CROMPTON, JOHN (*d.* Aug. 1703). 𝔓. Candidate for the ministry; silenced, 1662. Licensed, Sept. 1672, being of 'Doulton,' Lanc., *i.e.* Bolton, as "Pr.", "to Teach at his house" there. He appears to have succeeded John Lever [*q.v.*] at Cockey Moor Chapel, parish of Middleton, in 1689. He was a member of the Provincial Meeting of United Ministers. (*Bb. C. Nl. T.*) [61]
CROMPTON, THOMAS (1635—2 Sept. 1699). 𝔓. Born at Great Lever, Lanc. From Manchester grammar school, matric. ' pleb.' at Brasenose Coll., Oxford, 5 Apr. 1650. Appears as Presbyterian Minister of Toxteth Park Chapel, 1657; where also services were held by Michael Briscoe (1589–Sept. 1685) of Trinity Coll., Dublin, Congregational. Neither was ejected, the building (now Unitarian, erected, 1618, by the inhabitants for Richard Mather (1590–1669), Congregational divine, founder of the famous New England family) being extra-parochial, extra-episcopal and held under lease from Caryll, Viscount Molyneux, a Roman Catholic. The Episc. Returns, 1669, report "Two Conventicles of Independents held in Toxteth Parke, the usuall number of each is betwixt 100 & 200 some of them husbandmen, oth[rs] merchants, w[th] severall sorts of Tradesmen." Crompton and Briscoe were licensed for Toxteth

Park in 1672; Crompton on 8 May "to preach att a meeting house built by the inhabitants for that purpose," on the application of "Gilbert Aspinwall of the [Inner] Temple, in the name and behalfe of all the rest"; Briscoe (wrongly called James) on 16 May (two licences) and again on 29 May, as General Congregational (also, in error, General Presbyterian), and as "Congr. Teacher in the Meeting House in Toxtell Parke." Crompton probably ceased to minister at Toxteth Park between Briscoe's death (1685) and the arrival (1687) of Christopher Richardson [*q.v.*], though he may still have lived there. His ministry at Loe, Lee, or Leigh, near Gateacre, Lanc., contemporary with that of Thomas Collins [*q.v.*], was precursor to the formation of the Gateacre congregation. He left for Eccles some time after the death (1695) of Roger Baldwin [*q.v.*]. The site of the Chapel at Monton was bought in 1697. Crompton died in Manchester. (*C. F. Nl. P. Rl.*) [58, 60, 61]

CROMPTON, WILLIAM, M.A. (13 Aug. 1633–July 1696). **P.** Born at Little Kimble, Bucks, where his father, William Crompton, M.A. (1600—5 Jan. 1641/2), was then preacher (afterwards lecturer at Barnstaple). From Merchant Taylors' school (1647) entered as student at Christ Church, Oxford, 1649; B.A., 1649/50; M.A., 1652. Vicar of Cullompton, Devon, 1658; ejected, 1662. The Episc. Returns, 1669, report him as one of the preachers to "nigh 500," "twice every Sunday," "cheife Abbettors are: Willm Sumpter a Capt under ye late Usurper, Christopher Clarke, merchant, James Hartnoll, Grocer, Anne Pullman. But most of ym are women & Children & men of noe esteeme." Licensed, 11 Apr. 1672, being of Exon, as "a Pr. Teacher in any licensed place." He was the founder of the Pound Square congregation, Cullompton, but for some years before his death he was disabled by a fistula in the breast. The Common Fund from 1690 granted him £8 a year, at Exeter, reduced in 1695 to £6, and paid till July 1696. (*C. Em. F. M. Mh. P. T.*) [31, 32]

CRONDALL. Ejected here was Humfrey Weaver, B.A. [*q.v.*]. [100]

CROSBY SQUARE is on the East side of Bishopsgate Street Within, between Nos. 34 and 36. The Square, occupying the site of most of the famous mansion known as Crosby Place, was not laid out till after the fire of 1674, which destroyed the mansion, with the exception of its noble Hall (used as a Presbyterian Meeting House till 1769, and now removed to Chelsea). (*Lo.*) [3]

CROSCOMBE. Ejected here was John Whiteborne, son of Alexander, of Milton Abbott, Dev.; of Christ Church Coll., Oxford; matric., 1 Sept. 1634, aged 18; rector of Croscombe, 1643, as B.A. (*C. F.*) [93]

CROSS, or CROSSE, WILLIAM (*d.* 1697). **P.** Born at Fringford, Oxon. Matric. 'pleb.', at Pembroke Coll., Oxford, 25 July 1655. Ordained by presbyters at Nottingham. Vicar of Attenborough, Notts; vicar of Beeston, Notts; ejected, 1662. Removed to Loughborough. The Episc. Returns, 1669, report him as one of the preachers to about 40 Presbyterians at Hugglescote, Leic.; also as one of two preachers to 20 persons at Bradmore, Notts, "At the house of Mr Robert Kirkby on Sundayes, morning & evening, in time of Divine Service." Licensed, 17 Apr. 1672, as "Presb. Teacher in the howse of Thomas Porter in Bingham, Notts"; also, 30 Apr. 1672, as "Pr. Teacher" in his house at Loughborough, Leic. He received £2 (10 N. 1690) from an anonymous donation received through Matthew Rapier [*q.v.*]. The Common Fund granted him (1690 to 1696) £10 a year for Loughborough, reduced (1695) to £8. On 4 S. 1697 he was reported dead, and payment made to Sanford, his successor at Loughborough. Calamy says he died pastor at Derby, evidently an error. (*C. F. M. P. T.*) [66, 67]

CROUCH, JOHN (*fl.* 1657–1690). **C.** Chorister, at Magdalen Coll., Oxford, 1657; matric. 'ser.', 31 July 1658; demy, 1659–60. Candidate (*i.e.* licensed to preach, but not ordained), in 1662. The Episc. Returns, 1669, report him as one of the preachers to "about 200" persons at houses in St. Edmund's parish, Salisbury, Wilts, also to "30 or 40 at most" at various houses in Allington and Newton Tony, Wilts. Licensed, 9 May 1672, being "Mr John Crouch the younger of Lewes," as "Congr. Teacher" in the back house of Mr. Thomas Fissenden, junior, Lewes, Suss. License was given, 10 June 1672, to "John Crouch Mr of Arts" as "Congr. Teacher" in "The meeting House in White's Ally, belonging to Mrs Holmes widow in Little More Fields, Criplegate, London." The M.A. seems a misdescription. Calamy says he sometimes resided in London; he never had pastoral charge. (*C. F. P. T.*) [113]

CROW, FRANCIS, M.A. (1627?–1692). **P.** Calamy says "he was of the family of Hughhead in Scotland, within six miles of Berwick." Perhaps this needs to be corrected to Haughhead, parish of Eckford, Roxburghsh. Crow was usher in the Berwick grammar-school. "Franciscus Craue, minister verbi" (apparently the same person), graduated M.A. at Edinburgh, 22 July 1647. Crow studied theology at Sedan, under Pierre du Moulin. "Francis Craw" had charge of a parish (name unknown) in the presbytery of Chirnside; he was convicted of irregular procedure, 8 D. 1653; in Feb. 1658, admitting immorality, he deserted his charge (Scott's *Fasti*, i. 453). Crow was ejected (1662) from the vicarage of Hundon, Suff. He remained for a time at Hundon, removing thence to Ovington, Ess. The Episc. Returns, 1669, report him as preaching at Rede, Suff., to a congregation "of the vulgar sort, but some of cōsiderable Quality"; also as one of the preachers to "2 or 300" persons in St. Mary's parish, Bury St. Edmunds. Licensed, 1 May 1672, as "Pr. Teacher in his howse in Ovington." Subsequently he preached in a Meeting-house in the adjacent parish of Clare, Suff., and once a month at Bury St. Edmunds. Under persecution he emigrated (1683), and in 1686 was at Port Royal, Jamaica, but came back, disappointed, in 1687. Refusing a London charge, he returned to Clare and there died of calculus. He published (1690) a tiny tract against astrology, of which his Jamaican associates had been too fond. (*B. C. D. Ed. Ms. P. T.*) [103]

CRUMPTON, *i.e.* CROMPTON, ABRAHAM (*d.* 1725). **P.** Son of John Crompton, M.A. (*d.* 9 Jan. 1668/9); ejected, 1662, from the vicarage of Arnold, Notts. Abraham Crompton, of Derby, also of Chorley Hall, Lanc., gave land on which was built (1725) the Meeting-house at Chorley. He is spoken of (29 D. 1727) as "of Derby, lately deceased." (*C. Nl. Ts.*) [25]

CRUMPTON, *i.e.* CROMPTON, SAMUEL (*fl.* 1690). **P.** Brother of Abraham Crompton [*q.v.*]. [82]

CRUNDAILE. [100] *See* Hampshire

CRUSO, TIMOTHY, M.A. (1656?–26 N. 1697). **P.** Born probably at Newington Green, Middx.; studied in the Academy at Newington of Charles Morton, M.A. (ejected from the rectory of Blisland, Cornw.), where Defoe was his fellow-student. He graduated M.A. at a Scottish University (not Edin., Glasg., or King's or Marischal, Aberdeen). Before 1688 he became Minister of the Presbyterian congregation at Crutched Friars, Mark Lane, London. He took no part in the Crispian controversy, was elected (1692) a Manager of the Common Fund, and after the exclusion of Daniel Williams, D.D. [*q.v.*], from the Pinners' Hall lecture, he was elected Lecturer (1694) in the room of John Howe, M.A. [*q.v.*]. He was not appointed a Manager on the reconstitution of the Fund (1695). He did not join the Congregationals, but his congregation, by a majority of one, chose as his successor Thomas Shepherd, Congregational; the election was overruled and William Harris, D.D. [*q.v.*], was appointed. (*D. M. W.*) [161, 165]

CRUTCHED FRIARS CHURCH is St. Olave's, Hart Street, at the entrance to Crutched Friars. It escaped the Great Fire, and was the parish church and burial-place of Samuel Pepys, the diarist. (*Lo. Sl.*) [3]

CRYGLAS. [144] *See* Criglas

CUDDON, THOMAS. **P.** Appointed a Manager on 13 Apr. 1691, in room of Jarvis Disney [*q.v.*]; as his appointment was intimated through John Jurin [*q.v.*] he is assumed to be of the same denomination; further, he was a Manager of the reconstituted Fund, 1695; his last attendance was on 8 June 1696. His name is also spelled Cudden and Cuddin. (*M.*) [162]

CUDLEIGH. [32] *See* Devonshire

CULCHETH. [59] *See* Croft

CULLEN, THOMAS (*fl.* 1692–96). A grant of £3 was made to him (1692) as a Student under John Woodhouse [*q.v.*], increased to £6 and continued to June 1696. (*M.*) [57]

CULLOMPTON ('Collampton'). Ejected here was William Crompton, M.A. [*q.v.*]. [32]

CUMBERLAND. [21, 23, 168, 176, 177] The returns for this county are largely in the earliest handwriting, the remainder are in that of the Book-keeper. The returns are numbered 1 to 128.

Cawthwaite or Cowthaate, is Calthwaite.

Hescott is Hesket in the Forest.

hill Hiellossould is probably Kirkoswald.

Hudlesbough or Hudlesbrough, is Huddleskeugh in Kirkoswald parish.

Thelkeld is Threlkeld.

Returns from Cumberland were among the first received, as indicated by numbers attached to the returns as filed. These show that the first returns from the various counties were received in the following order:

Cumberland, Durham, Northumberland, Westmorland.
Norfolk.
Yorkshire, N.R.
Yorkshire, E.R.
Berkshire.
Cheshire, Shropshire, North Wales.
Derbyshire.
Yorkshire, W.R.
Buckinghamshire.
Lancashire.
Dorset.
Essex.
Devonshire.
Wiltshire.
Oxfordshire.
Worcestershire.
Rutland.
Northamptonshire.
Leicestershire.
Nottinghamshire.
Huntingdonshire.
Sussex.
Herefordshire.
Cambridgeshire.
Warwickshire.
South Wales.
Hertfordshire.
Surrey.
Staffordshire.
Gloucestershire.
Lincolnshire.
Somerset.
Middlesex.
Bedfordshire

CUMMING, JOHN, M.A. (*d.* 1710). **P.** Minister at Bridgwater, and maintained an Academy there till death. (*Mh. W.*) [91, 92]

DADDINGTON. [86] *See* Oxfordshire

DADLINGTON. Chapelry in Hinckley parish, Leic.; now vicarage. [67]

DAIMEY, *i.e.* DAUNCY, THOMAS (*d.* 1702 ?). **P.** Licensed, 1 May 1672, as "Pr. Teacher in John Blackmore's howse in the Parish of Shelden, Devon." The Common Fund granted him (1690) £5 a year as Itinerant in Somerset; reduced, 1695–7, to £4; renewed, 1701, at £5; and continued to 1702. (*M. T.*) [44, 92]

DAINTREE. [77] *See* Northamptonshire

DALSTON. [72]

DAMER, EDWARD, B.A. (*b.* 1632). **C.** Born at Godmanston, Dors. Second son of John de Amory or Damer (*d.* 1675) of Godmanston; from whose sixth son, George, the Damers, Earls of Dorchester (1792–1808), descended. From Bridport grammar school admitted sizar (under Daniel Bull [*q.v.*]) at Christ's Coll., Cambridge, 1 July 1650, age 18; B.A., 1653. Chaplain to the Jersey garrison; held the sequestered rectory of Wyke Regis, Dors. (1652); ejected, 1660. Steward to Denzil, Lord Holles. Living in Dorchester, 1666, having complied with the Oxford Act. Licensed, 22 Apr. 1672, as "Congr. Teacher in the howse of John Binghā in the Parish of Stickland, Dorset"; signed the Address of thanks to the Crown from Dorset Ministers, 10 May 1672. He was then of Dorchester, and remained there till death. (*C. Cp. Hu. P. T. V.*) [34, 35]

DAMER, JOSEPH (1666—16 Aug. 1699). **C.** Son of Edward Damer [*q.v.*]. Minister at Ringwood, Hants; died at Pensford, Som. (*Hu. M.*) [35]

DANCIE, *i.e.* DAUNCY, THOMAS. (*See* Daimey.) [44, 92]

DANDY, FRANCIS, M.A. (*b.* 1619). **P.** Son of William Dandy of Lanreath, Cornw., pleb. Matric. at St. Alban's Hall, Oxford, 17 June 1636, aged 17; B.A., 1639; M.A., 1642. Chaplain to Sir William Fleetwood of Woodstock, Oxf.; afterwards to Col. Brooke of Great Oakley, Northants (with whose son he lived till death); vicar of Great Oakley; ejected, 1662. Licensed, 13 May 1672, as "Pr. Teacher" in the "mansion house of Mrs Margaret Brooke [widow of Col. Brooke] in Oakley Magna." Calamy calls him Thomas. (*C. F. P. T.*) [76]

DANGERFIELD, WILLIAM (*fl.* 1690–1717). **P.** Appears to have first settled at Bradford, Wilts; on 13 Dec. 1717 he was ministering at Trowbridge, Wilts, but living at Bradford. (*Ev. Mh.*) [125]

DARKINGE. [109, 110] *See* Surrey

DARLINGTON. Ejected here was . . . Parish, who afterwards conformed and held a living in Yorkshire. (*C.*) [316]

DARLSTON, *i.e.* DALSTON [*q.v.*]; another form was Dorleston. [4]

DARNLEY, *i.e.* DEARNILEY, WILLIAM (*d.* 28 May 1701). Entered Frankland's Academy ('Dearmerley'), 28 June 1687. He was at Kendal ('Darneily') till 1691 at least. Ordained at Knutsford, 27 S. 1692, as Minister of Ringhay Chapel, an unconsecrated donative chapel of ease in the parish of Bowdon, Ches. It was forcibly taken (1722 ?) from Nonconformists, who built Hale Chapel, 1723. Dearniley's early death was greatly lamented. (*Fr. Nk. Uh.*) [121]

DARTMOUTH. Ejected here were (1) James Burdwood [*q.v.*]; (2) John Flavell [*q.v.*]; (3) Allan Geere or Geare

(1622–Dec. 1662); born at Stoke Fleming, Devon; studied at Leiden, 1640–48; created M.A. at Oxford, 15 Apr. 1648; ord. by presbyters; perpetual curate of St. Benet's, Paul's Wharf, London, 1648–1654; chaplain at Woburn to the Earl of Bedford, 1654–6; vicar of St. Saviour's, Dartmouth, 1656; ejected, 1662. (*C. F.*) [31]

DAUNCY. *See* Daimey

DAVENISH, *i.e.* DEVENISH, JOHN, M.A. (*b.* 1614). 𝔓. Son of John Devenish, vicar of Bridgwater (1605–44). Matric. at Wadham Coll., Oxford, 4 N. 1631, aged 17; rem. to New Inn Hall, B.A., 1635; M.A., 1637/8. Held (1652) the sequestered vicarage of Weston Zoyland, Som.; ejected, 1662. Signed the Address of thanks for Indulgence from Dorset Ministers, 10 May 1672. Licensed, 5 Sept. 1672, as Presb. Teacher at Pulham, Dors. 'Welleton' is Wellington, Som. (*C. F. P. T. Wc.*) [91]

DAVENTRY. Ejected here was Timothy Dod (son of John Dod of Fawsley), of Emmanuel Coll., Cambridge; matric. pensioner, 1612; B.A., 1615/6; M.A., 1619; Minister, 1644–47, at St. Peter's, Eastcheap; ord. by presbyters, 1646, as afternoon lecturer at Daventry; after ejection, retired to Everdon, Northants; *d.* there, 12 Dec. 1665. (*C. Np. V.*) The Common Fund granted (1692) £6 a year for Daventry; reduced (1695) to £5. (*M.*) [77]

DAVERTON. [30] *See* Devonshire

DAVICE, or DAVIS, *i.e.* DAVIES, SAMUEL (*fl.* 1676–92). Son of John Davies (1626–96), ejected from the vicarage of Bywell St. Peter, Northum., whose six children were looked after by Richard Wilson, a gentleman of small estate. Samuel Davies entered Frankland's Academy on 3 Sept. 1689; and having been certificated, 26 Jan. 1690/1, by Richard Stretton [*q.v.*], was awarded (2 Mar. 1690/1) jointly with Thomas Dickenson [*q.v.*] a grant from the Common Fund at the rate of £8 a year "for one year & a halfe"; in Jan. 1691/2 the joint sum of £22 was paid to these two students, who seem to have been closely associated. (*C. Fr. M. P.*) [80, 136]

DAVIES, or DAVIS, OWEN. ℭ. Ordained pastor of the church worshipping in the Pâl (near Llandilo, Carm.) and neighbouring places, from 1688. The Common Fund voted him (28 S. 1691–19 June 1693) £4 a year for Swansea, Glam., the grant being transferred from Daniel Higgs [*q.v.*].

An Owen Davis was Congregational Minister at Mitcheldean, Glou., in 1715. (*Ev. M. Rw.*) [143]

DAVILE, *i.e.* DAVIL, DAVILL, or DAVELL, THOMAS, eldest son of Thomas Davil (1597–1684), ironmonger, of Stoke Golding, Leic., by his first wife, Elizabeth Smith, was buried at Stoke Golding on 3 N. 1714. In 1680 he or his father gave £105 towards a Free School at Stoke Golding. On 16 Aug. 1702, "Thomas Davill of Stoke, gent., did by indenture grant to Henry Firebrace, D.D., and others, an annuity or rent-charge of £3, 6s. to commence from his death (Nov. 3, 1714) and to be paid quarterly; in trust, to provide a sermon upon morality on April 11, yearly, from the Minister of this town, and other neighbouring Ministers (none to preach oftener than once in seven years), and to allow for the same 10s.; and to provide two Bibles, of the price of 7s. for two poor children of this town; and twelve penny loaves, yearly, for the poor; and two strong grey coats for two poor aged persons; and also six penny loaves, every Sunday morning, for six poor persons; Such annuity to be issuing out of a messuage, two closes with a lane, and one other close, called *The Kinge* to the said messuage belonging, and a meadow called *Licet meadow*, all lying in Aldwick in Staffordshire, then occupied by Joseph Rogers and John Smallwood." If Davil was really buried on the day he died, that is remarkable. Aldwick (Alrewich) is now Aldridge. Henry Firebrace (son of the well-known royalist of the same names), whose mother was Elizabeth, sister of Thomas Davil the grantor, was a Fellow of Trinity Coll., Cambridge.

Davil's son, the third Thomas Davil (1681—11 Apr. 1746), 𝔓., was ordained on 16 Sept. 1708, and received a Fund grant of £8 in 1710 for ministering at Loughborough and Sheepshead, Leic. In 1715, 1718, and apparently in 1729 he was ministering at Stoke Golding. His tombstone at Stoke Golding describes him as Thomas Davil, gent. (*D. Ev. M. Nh.*) [66, 67, 69]

DAVIS, LEWIS (*d.* 1712 ?). ℭ. Born probably at Llanedi, Carm., the place of his dwelling. Ordained, about 1693, as Minister of Mynyddbach, near Swansea, Glam., in succession to Robert Thomas [*q.v.*]. He was a zealous preacher over a wide district, which he worked with the help of ministerial coadjutors. His successor, David Thomas, was appointed in 1712. (*Rj.*) [145, 146]

DAVIS, MORGAN. As a student under

Samuel Jones, M.A. [*q.v.*], he was awarded (12 Dec. 1692) a yearly grant of £5. (*M.*) [146]

DAVIS, RICHARD (1658–1714). **C.** [76, 184 *sqq.*]

DAVIS, *i.e.* DAVIES, STEPHEN (*d.* 1739). **P.** Grandson of Hugh Davies of Wrexham, Denb. Daniel Williams [*q.v.*] in his will called Stephen 'cousin,' his father and Williams's mother being apparently brother and sister. Entered Frankland's Academy, 9 Apr. 1690. He was Minister at Banbury, Oxon. (1709 ?–1739 ?); a special grant was made him from the Fund in 1728. (*Fr. M.*) [136]

DAVIS, *i.e.* DAVIES, THOMAS (1666–20 Feb. 1723/4). **C.** Born near Llanybri, Carm. Member of the church under Stephen Hughes [*see under* Owen, James]. Educ. in the Academy of John Woodhouse [*q.v.*]. Succeeded (1691) Peregrine Phillips [*q.v.*] at Dredgmanhill, parish of Haverfordwest, Pemb., preaching also at Pembroke, Trefgarn, Pemb., and other places. The Common Fund transferred to him (28 S. 1691) the grant of £5 a year previously voted to Peregrine Phillips; and made him in 1718 a special grant of £10, doubtless owing to the state of his health, which compelled him, in 1720, to confine his services to Pembroke. During the whole of his ministry he kept a school. (*Ev. M. Rj.*) [150, 175]

DAVISON, WILLIAM, M.A. (*d.* 25 D. 1711). **C.** Matric. sizar at Trinity Coll., Cambridge, 1634; B.A., 1641/2; M.A., 1661. Rector of Notgrove, Glou.; ejected, 1662. Licensed, 10 June 1672, as "Congr. Teacher" in his house in Tewkesbury, Glou. Died Minister at Chipping Campden, Glou. (*C. P. T. Tc. V.*) [44]

DAWES, GEORGE. Nothing further is known of him. (*N.*) [22]

DAWS, THOMAS (*d.* Apr. 1703). **C.** "From teaching a few petty boyes and girls at Salkeld-yeats advanced to the profession of a Pastor" (Bp. Nicolson). Presented, 5 June and 3 July 1677, for acting as Reader at Renwick, Cumb., without licence. Minister (1687 ?) at Loning Head, near Garrigill, parish of Alston, Cumb. (but on the Northumberland border). Received (1698) grant of £4 from the Congregational Fund. Buried, as "Thomas Daws, clerk," at Kirkoswald, 28 Apr. 1703. Will of Thomas Dawes, clerk, of Kirkoswald, 1703, leaves £30, the interest to go to his successors, "who shall preach at the Meeting House lately erected at Lonninghead." He must not be confused with the Thomas (or John) Dawes who entered Frankland's Academy on 8 May 1690. (*Cf. N. Nn.*) [79]

DAWSON, ABRAHAM (7 May 1663—5 F. 1732/3). **P.** Eldest son of Joseph Dawson [*q.v.*]. Entered Frankland's Academy, 13 Apr. 1680. He preached his first sermon, 2 Jan. 1683/4; was ordained at Attercliffe, 11 Sept. 1688; and was Minister at Underbank Chapel, Stannington, West Riding, from about 1689, removing to Cottingham, East Riding, about 1696. There he ministered till his death. (*Fr. Ht. My. Nk. Nr.*) [130, 137]

DAWSON, JOSEPH, B.A. (1634 ?–26 June 1709). **P.** Eldest son of Abraham Dawson, clothier, of Morley, West Riding. Matric. gent. at University Coll., Oxford, 29 May 1652; pensioner at St. John's Coll., Cambridge, 26 Apr. 1653, aged over 18; B.A., 1656/7. Curate of Thornton Chapel, West Riding; ejected, 1662. The Episc. Returns, 1669, report him as one of the preachers to "neere 100" persons at Sowerby, Coley, etc., West Riding. Licensed, 16 May 1672, as "Pr. Teacher in his howse in the Parish of Hallifax"; also, 25 July 1672, as "Pr. Teacher att the house of y[e] sd Dawson att Bristell," *i.e.* Birstall, West Riding. Ordained by presbyters in Manchester, 29 O. 1672. In 1688 he became Minister at Morley, West Riding, where the Parsonage House, built in that year, was certified for worship on 11 July, the Old Chapel not being restored to Nonconformists till 1693. For the year 1696 his stipend was £24. He regularly exchanged with John Holdsworth [*q.v.*] at "The Closes," for which the Common Fund granted (1691) £8 a year, reduced (1695) to £5, and continued to Dawson, or one of his sons, till 1710. He had four sons in the ministry; the youngest, Eli, had six sons in the Nonconformist ministry; four of them afterwards conformed, the other two left the ministry. (*C. F. Hh. Jo. M. My. Nr. P. Sq. T. Y.*) [129, 130, 131, 138]

DAWSON, JOSEPH, *secundus* (14 Mar. 1666/7—15 Apr. 1739). **P.** A younger son of Joseph Dawson [*q.v.*]. Entered Frankland's Academy, 30 Sept. 1689. On 26 Jan. 1690/1 he was certificated by Richard Stretton [*q.v.*], and is then described as of Morley. The Common Fund granted him (1690/1–3) a bursary of £6 a year, increased to £10. Ordained at Rathmel, 7 June 1693. Preached in Yorkshire. His dwelling-house in Yorkshire Street, Rochdale, was registered for worship, 1698. Minister at Rochdale till death, receiving yearly Fund grants, £6 (1714–22) and £4 (1723–1738). (*Fr. Hh. Hy. M. Nk. Nr. X.*) [137]

DAWSON, THOMAS. Brother of Joseph Dawson, *secundus* [*q.v.*]. [6]

DAY, GEORGE, M.A. (*d.* 3 D. 1697). P. Matric. 28 Mar. 1655 at Hart Hall, Oxford, as 'pleb.'; B.A., 1657; M.A., 1660. Vicar of Wiveliscomb, Som., 1661; ejected, 1662. The Episc. Returns, 1669, report him as one of the preachers at Wiveliscomb to 80 persons at the houses of Joseph Stocker and John Day; also to 18 persons at Nether Stowey, Som.; further, as one of the preachers at Glastonbury, Som., to 300 persons "in a Barne, belonging to John Austin, where a Pulpitt and seats are built." On 30 Apr. 1672 "George Day of Wiveliscomb" was licensed as a general Presb. Teacher. Later he was Minister of a congregation at Ratcliff, Middx., where he died. (*C. F. P. T.*) [165]

DAY, JAMES (*fl.* 1660–90). C. Matric. at St. John's Coll., Cambridge, 1657; said to be ejected Student of Emmanuel Coll. Licensed, 8 May 1672, as "Congr. Teacher in a Place called the Kitchin in High Dike in the Town of March in the Isle of Ely"; also, 30 S. 1672, as "Cong: genall Teach:" at Oakington, Cambs. He eventually became pastor (1683) of a congregation at Wood Hall, parish of Arkesden, Ess. 'Oldenbury' is perhaps Hallingbury. (*C. E. P. T. V.*) [39]

DEACON, BALDWIN (*fl.* 1653–1729). P. Ordained by Presbyters. Matric. pleb. at Wadham Coll., Oxford, 24 June 1653. Rector of Beer Crocombe, Som., 1658–1661; appointed, 21 Apr. 1659, one of the Ministers at Wimborne Minster, Dors.; ejected, 1660. Licensed, 10 Aug. 1672, as "Pr. Teach," in the house of Philip Cornish, Kingston, Som. 'Broomvill' is Broomfield, Som., where he lived. He appears (1715) as Minister of Stogursey (otherwise Stoke Courcy), and Stowey, Som., removing thence to Stogumber, Som., receiving yearly Fund grants of £7 for Stogumber (1726–29).

Baldwin Deacon, junior, was Minister at Langport, Som., 1733–37, Wiveliscomb., Som., 1738–41, and Stowey, Som., 1742–48. (*Ev. F. Hu. M. P. T.*) [93, 94]

DEAL ('Deale'). Ejected here was Samuel Seliyard, of Trinity Coll., Cambridge; matric. pensioner, 1633; B.A., 1636/7; M.A., 1640; he succeeded Hezekiah or Ezechias King, M.A., in the rectory of Deal; ejected, 1662. (*C. K. V.*) Calamy (who rightly gives King as ejected from Foulmire rectory, Camb., in 1662) was 'informed' that he was ejected at Deal. King was of Christ Church Coll., Oxford; matric., 21 Feb. 1616/7, aged 16; B.A., 1619/20; M.A., 1622; incorp. at Cambridge, 1623; in London, 1624; rector of Deal, 1629; rector of Foulmire, Camb., 1646; ejected, 1662; living in parish of St. Michael, Cornhill, 1662–65; licensed, 8 May 1672, as Pr. Teacher in his house at Hornsey, Midx.; his house licensed, same date, as Pr. Meeting-place. (*C. F. T.*) [55]

DEAN ('Deane'), FOREST OF (Glou.). The place left blank is Blakeney chapelry in Awre parish. [45, 46] *See* Billinsley

DEARNILEY. *See* Darnley

DEBENHAM ('Deberham'). Ejected from this vicarage was John King, Congregational; took to farming; *d.* before 1670. (*C.*) [75, 103, 107]

DEDDINGTON. [86]

DEERHAM, DERHAM. [74] *See* Norfolk

DE LUNA, MADAM. [2]

DEN. [55] *See* Dent, Henry

DENBIGH. Ejected here was William Jones, *b.* in Merionethshire [? of Hart Hall, Oxford; matric., 8 Dec. 1615, aged 20; B.A., 1617; M.A., 1620; ? rector of Halford, War., 1617]; schoolmaster at Ruthin, Denb.; rector and vicar of Denbigh, 1648; ejected, 1662; removed 1666 to Plas Teg, Flint; licensed, 28 Oct. 1672, as Congr: Teacher in his house in Denbighsh.; removed to Hope, Flint; *d.* there, Feb. 1678/9, "in a good old age." (*C. F. T.*) The "Gent that intends to Settle" (1690) and had set up a lecture (1691) is probably Thomas Baddie [*q.v.*]. [149]

DENBIGHSHIRE. [141, 148, 149]

DENT, HENRY, M.A. (1632 ?–Mar. 1695). P. Born in Wales. From school at Salisbury, matric. 'ser.', at Wadham Coll., Oxford, 14 N. 1650; Scholar, 1649; B.A., 1652/3; M.A., 1655; Fellow, 1656. Curate at Salisbury; at Stanton Prior, Som.; and at Ramsbury, Wilts; silenced, 1662. Taught school. While still at Ramsbury, the Episc. Returns, 1669, report him as one of the preachers to "Presbyterians 600 ordinarily at least" in Newbury, Berks; also as one of the preachers, being "a Pention Scholemaster," to "about 60 or 70 Presbyterians" at Lambourn, Berks; also as one of six preachers to 50 or 60 Presbyterians in "a Conventicle very often, but not Constant" at Ramsbury. He was several times excommunicated. He appears to have removed (1690) from

Goudhurst, Kent, to Epping, Ess. The Common Fund granted him, 1690–93, £8 a year for Epping, and added £2 for 1692. (*C. F. M. P. Sm. T.*) [40, 55]

DENTHAM, . . . A layman in business. [1]

DENTON, Norf. Ejected here was Thomas Lawson, of St. Catharine's Hall, Cambridge; matric. sizar, 1633; B.A., 1636/7; M.A., 1640; Fellow of St. John's Coll., 1644; living at Doningland, 1649, when he joined the Congregational church at Norwich; rector of Denton, 1650/1, and pastor of Congregational church there, Apr. 1655; removed to Bury St. Edmunds, 1659; ejected at Denton, 1660; preaching at Bury, Rattlesdon, and Wattesfield in 1669; licensed, 17 Apr. 1672, as Ind. Teacher in his house at Norton, Suff. (*B. C. T. V.*) [74]

DENTON, DANIEL (*d.* 18 Feb. 1720/1). Son of Nathan Denton [*q.v.*]. Chaplain (1692) to Mr. Rich of Bull House, near Peniston, where a Meeting-house was built before 1692. He had a congregation of 200. (*Ev. My. Nr. Y.*) [26, 29, 130]

DENTON, NATHAN, B.A. (1634–Oct. 1720). **P.** Born in Bradfield chapelry, parish of Ecclesfield, West Riding. From Worsborough grammar school he proceeded to University College, Oxford; matric. 'ser.', 17 Mar. 1653/4; B.A., 1657. Taught grammar school at Cawthorne, West Riding, preaching at Cawthorne and High Hoyland alternately. Ordained (1658) by West Riding Classis as rector of High Hoyland; incumbent of Derwent Chapel, Derb.; perpetual curate of Bolton-upon-Dearne, West Riding; ejected, 1662. Remained in Bolton (except when driven away by the Five Mile Act), and for a year after ejection acted as lecturer in the parish church of Hickleton, West Riding. The Episc. Returns, 1669, report him as preaching to "Presbyterians 60 or 80 the Daughter of Sr John Jackson Mrs Everet" in Hickleton, "formerly at the house of Sr John Jackson, but now at the house of William Smyth." Licensed, 8 May 1672 as "Presb. Teacher in the howse of Silvanus Rich near Peniston," West Riding. Latterly he preached at Great Houghton, parish of Darfield (near Bolton), West Riding. The Common Fund granted him (1693 ?) £8 a year, reduced (1695) to £3, when Joshua Brookes [*q.v.*] gave him £5 a year; 1697 to 1711 the Fund granted him £6 a year, and on 14 Mar. 1719/20 made him a gift of £10, he being then at Bolton. He was buried on 13 Oct. 1720, having survived all the other Ejected, beneficed in 1662 (*C. D. F. M. My. Nr. P. T. Y.*) [129, 130]

DEPTFORD. According to Hasted, ejected here in 1662 was Thomas Mallory, of St. Catharine's Hall, Cambridge; matric. sizar, 1629/30; B.A., 1633/4; M.A., 1637; vicar of St. Nicholas', Deptford, 1644–59; lecturer at St. Michael's, Cornhill; certainly ejected thence in 1662. (*C. F. K. V.*) [55, 187]

DERBY ('Darby'). Ejected here were (1) Joseph Swetnam, of Magdalene Coll., Cambridge, M.A. (1627), vicar of All Saints', who (like Baxter) resigned before the Act took effect; his son, Thomas, of Derby, was licensed as a Presb., July 1672. (*C. V.*) (2) Luke Cranwell, born in Loughborough, of Christ's Coll. and Pembroke Hall, Cambridge, M.A. (1659), vicar of St. Peter's; licensed, 13 May 1672, as Pr. Teacher in Derby; *d.* 11 Nov. 1683. (*C. V. T.*) (3) Samuel Beresford, M.A. [*q.v.*]. [25]

DERBYSHIRE. [25, 27, 36, 98, 168, 176, 177, 180, 181.] Except the heading 'Derby,' all is in the Book-keeper's handwriting. The returns are numbered from 7 to 123. Annual grants were made as follows, from 1691: High Peak Hundred, £18; Belper and Heage, £10, reduced, 1695, to £8; Duffield, £5, increased, 1692, to £10, reduced, 1695, to £8; Hollington, £10, reduced, 1695, to £8; Alvaston, £10; Hognaston, £10; Ilston, £5. Ashburnham (? Ashbourne), 1695, £8.

Ashburn is Ashbourne.
Cawdwell is Cauldwell [*q.v.*].
Chawseworth is Charlesworth.
Chelmarcon is Chelmorton.
Chimley is Chinley.
Harrington is Hartington.
Ilston is Ilkeston.
Longdales is Longdoles.
Rosson is Roston.

DEREHAM ('Derham,' 'Deerham'), EAST. [74, 75]

DEVENISH. *See* Davenish

DEVIZES. [123]

DEVONSHIRE. [30, 32, 168, 176, 181.] Except the headings, 'Devon' and 'Deuon,' in the earliest handwriting, and the erased account of William Crompton, in another hand, all is in the handwriting of the Book-keeper, who has not read his materials correctly, and hence has several errors in personal and place names. All the returns but three are numbered 17; the others are 49 and 52.

Bory Tracy is Bovey Tracey.

Chimly is Chulmleigh.
Collampton is Cullompton [*q.v.*].
Cudleigh is Gidleigh.
Daverton is Thorverton, otherwise Thaverton.
Hatherbay is Hatherleigh.
Holiworthy is Holsworthy.
Limston is Lympstone.
Moretowne is Moreton Hampstead.
Nawton Bushell is Newton Bushel (now part of Newton Abbot).
Northmontton (or Northmoulton) is North Molton.
Oakhampton is Okehampton.
Plimpton is Plympton St. Mary.
Shanghbrook (for Shaughbrook) is Shobrooke (old spelling, Shogbrook).
Shepistor is Sheepstor.
Southmorton is South Molton.
St. Mary Otteny is Ottery St. Mary.
Tarystock is Tavistock.
Taverton is Thorverton, otherwise Thavorton

DEWLY. *See* Dowely

DEWSNOP, EMANUEL. The Common Fund voted him, 25 Apr. 1692, £5 for one year as Student under Timothy Jollie [*q.v.*]. (*M.*) [133]

DICKENSON, JOHN (*fl.* 1681–93). Entered Frankland's Academy, 23 June 1681. He received a Fund grant of £10 a year, 1690–93, for Sutton in Ashfield, Notts. He may be the Mr. John Dickenson of Gildersome, West Riding, who was buried 22 Aug. 1704. (*Fr. M. Nr.*) [83]

DICKINSON, DICKSON, *i.e.* DICKENSON, THOMAS (1670—26 D. 1743). Entered Frankland's Academy, 3 July 1689. *See* Davice, *i.e.* Davies, Samuel. Preached first at Gorton, Manchester, 1694–1702. Ordained at Stand, 29 Mar. 1694. Rem. to Northowram, West Riding, 1702, and there died. His continuation of Heywood's Register gives him a claim to the gratitude of biographers. (*Fr. Hy. M. Nr.*) [136]

DISEWORTH ('Direworth'). [66]

DISNEY, JARVIS, or GERVIS, *i.e.* GERVASE (8 Apr. 1641—3 Apr. 1691). 𝔓. Second son and heir of John Disney of Swinderby, Linc. He was elected Manager, 29 Sept. 1690, in the room of Jarvis Byfield [*q.v.*]. His last attendance was on 16 March 1690/1. (*Hu. M.*) [162]

DIZART, *i.e.* DYSART, JOHN, M.A. (1660 ?–1732). 𝔓. Educ. at Glasgow; M.A., 1680. Ordained, 1686, as Minister at Dalton, in Newburn parish, Northum. Hulne Abbey is in Alnwick parish. Admitted Minister of Langton, Berwicksh., 30 Apr. 1691; translated to Coldingham, Berwicksh., 24 July 1694, against the wish of the Episcopalian parishioners; installed by military force; for some time carried pistols with him to the pulpit. (*Sf.*) [80]

DOD, JOHN, M.A. (*fl.* 1646–91). Son of Nehemiah Dod, vicar of Coggeshall, Ess. Admitted to St. John's Coll., Cambridge, 17 Oct. 1646; incorp. at Oxford; Fellow of Corpus Christi Coll., 1648; M.A., 1649. Rector of Betteshanger, Kent, 9 N. 1660; ejected, 1662. To "M[r] Dod Sen[r] att Horne Church," Essex, the Common Fund, in 1690, granted £6 a year; on 8 June 1691 he was reported "removed from Hornchurch," and his grant was to be paid up to 24 June and no longer. (*F. M. P.*) [1, 40, 43]

DOD, ROBERT (1632 ?–9 Apr. 1695). 𝔓. Son of a clergyman. Matric. at Corpus Christi Coll., Oxford, 25 Mar. 1652. Rector of Inworth, Essex, 27 July 1660; ejected, 1662. Licensed, 10 June 1672, as Presb. Teacher in his house at Sible Hedingham, Essex, where he was preaching in 1669. After 1673, preached at Wethersfield, Essex, and other places. Tombstone at Wethersfield gives his death on 9 Apr. 1695, aged sixty-three years. Widow married Merrills and died 28 Dec. 1704. (*C. E. F. P. T. Wc.*) [40]

DODDRIDGE, PHILIP, D.D. (26 June 1702—20 Oct. 1751). ℭ. Born in London, twentieth child of Daniel Doddridge (*d.* 17 July 1715), oilman. After schools at Kingston-on-Thames and St. Albans, entered (Oct. 1719) the Academy of John Jennings (*d.* 1723), Congregational Minister at Kibworth, Leic., removed (1722) to Hinckley. The Fund, on the motion of Jeremiah Smith (*d.* 1723), chairman [Presb. Min. of Silver Street, London], on 3 Nov. 1718 "agreed that an Allowance of Ten Pounds be made to M[r] Peter Dodderidge a Candidate for the Ministry with M[r] [Samuel] Clark [or Clarke (1684–1750; Presb. Min.] of St Albans to commence from X[t]mas next." On 4 May 1719 the usual enquiry as to his proficiency was sent to Clark, signed by William Tong (1622–1727), Presb. Min. of Salters' Hall, London. On 4 Apr. 1720, on the motion of Arthur Martin, treasurer, it was "agreed that the Allowance be continued to M[r]. Phillip Dodderidge, upon his Removal from M[r]. Clark, at St. Albans, to M[r]. Jennins at Kibworth in Leicesters." On 10 Jan. 1720/1 the enquiry as to his proficiency was sent to Jennings; the grant was paid to Oct. 1722. Minister at Kibworth, 1723–9; Castle Hill, Northampton, 1729 till death. His famous Academy was opened at Market Harborough in July 1729, and removed in Dec. to Northampton. (*D. M.*) [186]

DODINGTON. [86] *See* Oxfordshire

DOGERIDGE, *i.e.* DODDRIDGE, JOHN, B.A. (1621–1689). **P.** Son of Philip Doddridge of Isleworth, Midx., gent. Matric. at New Inn Hall, Oxford, 22 Mar. 1638/9, aged 18; rem. to Pembroke Coll.; B.A., 10 N. 1642. Held the sequestered rectory of Shepperton, Midx.; ejected, 1660. His house at Twickenham, Midx., was licensed, "Pr.", 10 Aug. 1672; he was licensed, Sept. 1672, as "Pr. Teacher." He died suddenly; his funeral sermon was preached 8 S. 1689. Philip Doddridge, D.D. [*q.v.*], was his grandson. (*C. F. P. T. Wc.*) [72]

DONCASTER, W.R. (misplaced in E.R.) [139, 180]

DONHEAD, ST. MARY ('Hunnett'). [123]

DOOLITTLE, SAMUEL (1662 ?–10 Apr. 1717). **P.** Son of Thomas Doolittle, M.A. (*see below*); educated in his father's Academy at Islington. Assistant to his father at Mugwell [Monkwell] Street, and at the same time to John Turner at Leather Lane, Hatton Garden. Became Minister (1692 ?) at Reading, and there died; but was not Minister there in 1715. He published (1) "A Sermon [Is. xxix. 6] Occasioned by the Late Earthquake . . . Eighth of September, 1692. Preached to a Congregation in Reading," 1692; (2) "The Righteous Man's Hope at Death," 1693 (sermon [Prov. xiv. 32], after his mother's death in the previous December). (*D. Ev. W.*) [1]

DOOLITTLE, THOMAS, M.A. (1632 ?–24 May 1707). **P.** Third son of Anthony Doolittle, glover; born at Kidderminster, where, as a schoolboy, he heard Baxter preach his sermons published as "The Saints' Everlasting Rest." Admitted sizar, 7 June 1649, at Pembroke Coll., Cambridge, aged 17; B.A., 1652/3; M.A., 1656. Chosen (1653) rector of St. Alphage's, London Wall, by parishioners, and received presbyterian ordination; ejected, 1662. Held boarding school in Moorfields; then in Bunhill Fields; then (1665) at Woodford Bridge, Essex. In 1666 erected a wooden preaching-house in Bunhill Fields, and before 1669 (*vide* Episcopal Returns) a Meeting-house in Mugwell (now Monkwell) Street, "built of brick, with three galleries full of large pews; and thirty-eight large pews below, with locks and keys to them, besides benches and forms." This building, the first of the kind in London, if not in England, was taken possession of under royal authority and utilised as a Lord Mayor's Chapel. On 2 Apr. 1672 he obtained licence for it as "a certaine roome adjoining to ye dwelling-house of Thomas Doelitle in Mugwell Street" (the original licence is at Dr. Williams' Library). He lived, however, at Islington, where he now conducted an Academy for university learning. On the withdrawal of Indulgence he removed his Academy to Wimbledon, returning to Islington before 1680, but moved (1683) to Battersea, and thence to Clapham. From 1687 he was at St. John's Court, Clerkenwell. In 1689 he resumed his ministry at Mugwell Street, having successively as assistants, Thomas Vincent, M.A., ejected from St. Mary Magdalen's, Milk Street (who had helped in his school), John Mottershed [*q.v.*], Samuel Doolittle [*q.v.*], and Daniel Wilcox, who succeeded him. Among the students at Doolittle's Academy were Edmund Calamy, D.D., Thomas Emlyn, Matthew Henry, John Ker, M.D. [*q.v.*], and Thomas Rowe [*q.v.*]. (*C. D. P. T. V. W.*) [4, 41, 51]

DORCHESTER. Ejected here were (1) William Benn (Nov. 1600—22 Mar. 1680/1); from St. Bees grammar school, entered Queen's Coll., Oxford, as servitor; did not matriculate; rector of Wokingham, Berks; chaplain to Marchioness of Northampton; rector of All Saints', Dorchester, 1629; ejected, 1662; living at Maiden Newton, 1665; preaching at Fordington, 1669; licensed, 1 May 1672, as Congr. Teacher at Dorchester, where he died. (*C. T. Wo.*) (2) George Hammond (1620–Oct. 1705), Scholar and B.A. of Trinity Coll., Dublin; incorp. at Oxford, 12 Oct. 1639; of Exeter Coll.; M.A., 1641; rector of Mainhead, Devon, 1645, and vicar of Totnes; rector of Holy Trinity and St. Peter's, Dorchester, 1660; ejected, 1662; living in Dorchester, 1665, having taken the Oxford oath; licensed, 11 Apr. 1672, as Pr. Teacher in houses at Dorchester; preached also at Taunton from 1677 to 1685. (*C. F. Mu. T.*) [24]

DORKING ('darkinge'). [109, 110] *See* Edward Nabbs

DORSETSHIRE. [34, 35, 168, 176, 181]. Except the heading "Dorset" in the earliest handwriting, and two small items in other hands, all the returns are in the Book-keeper's handwriting. The returns are numbered 15, with one exception, 175.

Beare is Bere Regis [*q.v.*].

Bemister is Beaminster.

Crambourn is Cranborne.
Lime is Lyme Regis [*q.v.*].
Shaffton is Shaftesbury.
Stawbridge is Stalbridge.
Warham is Wareham.
Winbourn is Wimborne.
Winfruit is Winfrith Newburgh.

DOUGHTY, . . . [14]

DOUGHTY, SAMUEL, M.A. (*fl.* 1637–1718). 𝔓. Matric. sizar at Emmanuel Coll., Cambridge, 1637; B.A., 1640/1; M.A., 1644. Ejected from the rectory of Sibbeston, Leic.; licensed, Oct. 1672, to preach at his own house, Ashby-de-la-Zouch, Leic. "Mr Doughty" appears in the Minutes, 25 D. 1704 and 25 D. 1708, as the person through whom a grant for places in Shropshire was paid; on 3 Mar. 1717/8 he is reported as having for two years been unable to act through ill-health. (*C. M. P. T.*) [16, 88]

DOUNTON. [102] *See* Hampshire

DOVE, . . . [Many of this surname at both Universities.] His ejection is not recorded by Calamy. Layton is the vicarage of Leighton Bromswold, Hunts, of which Simon Gunter, a puritan, was vicar in 1654; Robert Guidott, M.A., was presented, 28 Apr. 1658. Guidott became rector of Little Barford, Beds., 1661; Dove may have succeeded him, or been his *locum tenens*, but his name is not in the parish register. (*F. Leighton registers. V.*) [53]

DOVE COURT, OLD FISH STREET. This street disappeared to make way for Queen Victoria Street (1867–71). Dove Court ran from its South side, near St. Nicholas Cole Abbey. Strype describes it as "a pretty handsome Place, adjoining to the *Labour in vain Yard.*" (*Lo. Ml. Sl.*) [2]

DOVER. Ejected here was Nathaniel Barry, son of John Barry, rector of Cottesmore, Rutl.; born there; from Dronfield school entered St. John's Coll., Cambridge; matric. pensioner, 1630/1, aged 15; vicar of St. Mary's, Dover, 1654/5; ejected, 1661; preaching at Dover in 1663 and 1669; licensed, 10 June 1672, as Pr. Teacher in an Outhouse at Dover; *d.* 1675. (*C. Jo. T. V.*) [55]

DOWELY, or DEWLY, *i.e.* DOWLEY, PETER (*fl.* 1690–1715). ℭ. One of the witnesses against Richard Davis [*q.v.*] at Kettering in 1692. He received (20 Apr. 1696) a grant of £4 from the Congregational Fund, and was still Minister at Lutterworth in 1715, and apparently till 1729. (*Cf. Ev. Gl.*) [66, 67, 68]

DOWLY, *i.e.* DOWLEY, RICHARD, B.A. (1623?–1702). 𝔓. Born in Berks, younger son of John Dowley, afterwards vicar of Alveston, Warwicksh. Matric. at All Souls' Coll., Oxford, 10 Oct. 1639, aged 16; grad. B.A. as demy of Magdalen, 1643. Completed his studies under John Bryan, D.D., at Coventry, but still retained connection with Oxford till Aug. 1648. Became chaplain to Sir T. Rous at Rous Lench, Worc. Was ordained by presbyters, and a member of Baxter's Worcestershire Association. From 1656 held the sequestered vicarage of Stoke Prior, Worc.; ejected, 1660. Assisted his uncle, incumbent of Elford, Staffs, till 1662; then silenced. Licensed, 18 Nov. 1672, for his own house at Orton West, Leic. Removed to London (1680?), taught school and preached occasionally, attending John Howe's ministry. Arrested and fined. From 1689 preached some time at Godalming, Surrey, but returned to London, infirm, to live with his children. Settled again at Godalming about 25 Mar. 1692. Died in London. (*C. D. F. M. P. T.*) [1]

DOWNE, RICHARD (*fl.* 1662–92). ℭ. Ordained by presbyters. Rector of Winterborne Monkton, Dors.; ejected, 1662. Retired to Bridport, Dors. Licensed, 1 May 1672, as "Congr. Teacher in the howse of John Golding in Bridport." His congregation then numbered about 100. Imprisoned in 1680. Calamy says he died in August 1687, an evident error. On 11 Jan. 1691/2 his case for a grant was set down to be "further considered" on 18 Jan., but there is no subsequent record of it. (*C. Ha. M. Mh. P. T.*) [34, 35]

DOWNTON ('Dounton'). [102]

DRAKE, MICHAEL, M.A. (1622–96). 𝔓. Born at Pikeley in Bradford parish, Yorks. Son of John Drake, yeoman. From private school at Halifax, matric. at Magdalene Coll., Cambridge, 1639; admitted sizar at St. John's Coll., 26 N. 1639, aet. 17; B.A., 1642/3; M.A., 1647. Preacher many years at Lincoln. Rector of Pickworth, Linc. (1645?); and member of the Folkingham Classis, also lecturer at Grantham; ejected, 1662. Removed to Fulbeck, Linc., preaching every Saturday evening in the house of John Disney at Lincoln. Licensed, 16 May 1672, as "Pr. Teacher in his howse in Fulbeck." Disney's house was licensed, 22 July, and again 5 Sept. 1672. Under arrest in 1685 on suspicion of complicity with Monmouth's rebellion. Removed (1687) to Lincoln, and maintained a congregation. The Common Fund granted him £8 a year from 1690 to

1696; also, for the Grantham Lecture (which he shared with William Scoffin [*q.v.*], £10 a year (1691–93). His son, Joshua, and grandson, Joshua, were successively vicars of Swinderby, 1692–1765. (*C. Jo. M. P. T. V. Y.*) [70, 71]

DRAYTON BASSETT. Ejected here was Timothy Fox [*q.v.*]. [96]

DREDGMANHILL, in Haverfordwest parish, Pem. [144]

DREW, JOHN (*d.* 1715). 𝔓. Minister of Ross, Heref., with Blakeney, Glou. He received for Blakeney a Fund grant of £5 a year, 1708–15. The appointment of Joseph Pyke, his successor, is noted on 6 F. 1715/6. (*Ev. M.*) [46, 47, 48]

DUBLIN. [133]

DUCANE, PETER and JAMES. 𝔓. The family was Presbyterian; memoirs of some of them are extant at a later date than this. [165]

DUCE, THOMAS, B.A. (1626–1706 ?), whom Calamy gives as Juice and Foster as Ince, was son of Richard Juce ['Ince'] of Worcester, pleb. matric. 5 D. 1642, at Exeter Coll., Oxford, aged 16; B.A., 1647. Ejected from St. Martin's, a living of £100 at Worcester. Kept school there till driven away (1666) by the Five Mile Act. Became Minister (1673 ?) at Reading, where he died between 1705 and 1707. (*C. F. P. Sm. Uw.*) [6]

DUDLEY. [67, 96, 126]

DUFFIELD. Ejected from this vicarage in 1662 was Roger Morrice or Morris, of St. Catharine's Hall, Cambridge; M.A., 1659; chaplain to Denzil, Lord Holles, and later to Sir John Maynard; vicar of Duffield, 1658; lived latterly at Leek Firth in Leek parish, Staff.; *d.* at Hoxton, 17 Jan. 1701/2, aet. 73; left for Students for the ministry, books and an endowment. He made a vast collection of ecclesiastical manuscripts, some of which are among the most valuable treasures of Dr. Williams' Library, including "The Seconde Part of a Register," edited (1915) by Albert Peel. (*C. Rp. V.*) [28]

DULVERTON. Ejected here was Henry Berry [*q.v.*]. [92, 93, 94, 95]

DUNTON, JOHN. 𝔓. (4 May 1659–1733). Son of John Dunton (*d.* 24 N. 1676), rector of Graffham, Hunts, who designed him for the Anglican ministry, the profession of his forefathers. Apprenticed (1673) to Thomas Parkhurst, a London bookseller. Married (3 Aug. 1682) Elizabeth, daughter of Samuel Annesley [*q.v.*]. His "Life and Errors" (1705) depicts an erratic career, and is full of curious information about laymen and divines connected in various ways with the printing and publishing business of his day. (*D.*) [156, 163]

DURHAM. Ejected here were (1) Jonathan Devereux, of Cambridge University [perhaps matric. sizar at Emmanuel Coll., 1626; more probably matric. pensioner at Christ's Coll., 1647; B.A., 1650/1; M.A., 1656]; perpetual curate of St. Nicholas, Durham; died soon after ejection. (*C. V.*) (2) Joseph Holdsworth; matric. pensioner at Magdalene Coll., Cambridge, 1625; B.A., 1629/30; vicar of St. Oswald's, Elvet; resigned, 1656, in hope of "some place in the South," but stayed on for a time; hence his ejection is doubtful; no successor is known till the appointment of John Wood, M.A., 1662. (*C. N. Sd. V.*) [36]

DURHAM COUNTY. [36, 163, 176] The headings and three returns, numbered 1, are in the earliest handwriting; the remainder (entries numbered 76; and 38 in 1691) are in the Book-keeper's handwriting. From Cumberland, Durham, and Northumberland came the earliest returns.

EALAND. [132] *See* Yorkshire, W. Riding

EARLE, JOHN, *i.e.* JABEZ, D.D. (1676 ?–29 May 1768). 𝔓. Received grants, 1691–92, as student with Thomas Brand [*q.v.*] at Bishop's Hall, Bethnal Green, under the instruction of John Ker, M.D. [*q.v.*]. Chaplain (1692) to Sir Thomas Roberts, at Glassenbury, Kent. Assistant (1699) to Thomas Reynolds [*q.v.*]. Ordained, 1699, at St. Albans. Succeeded (1706 ?) Francis Glascock [*q.v.*] at Drury Lane, Westminster, and removed the congregation (after 1729) to Hanover Street, Long Acre. One of the twenty-seven Presbyterian Subscribers at Salters' Hall, 1719. Elected (1723) a trustee of Dr. Williams' foundations. D.D. Edin. (1728); also D.D. of King's Coll., Aberdeen. Salters' Hall lecturer (1730). Retained his vigorous ministry till death, though many years blind. Thrice married. In 1715–29 he lived "at Mrs Willis's in Gilbert-street, Bloomsbury, near Montagu-house." (*D. Ev. We.*) [4]

EARLE, . . . [? John Earl, son of John Earl (1634 ?–20 Mar. 1669/70), ejected, 1662, from the vicarage of East Terring, Suss. The son was pastor of a church at Chichester, Sussex. (*C. P.*)] [100]

EASTBOURNE ('Bourne'). [115]

EASTMAN, WILLIAM (*fl.* 1660–1701). 𝔓. Ejected, 1660, from a sequestered living in Hants; ejected, 1662, from the rectory of Everley, Wilts. Removed to Salisbury, Wilts, and thence to Shaftesbury, Dors. Licensed, 17 Apr. 1672, being of Shaftesbury, as "Presb. Teacher in any allowed place." The Common Fund granted him £6 a year (1690–93) for Shaftesbury. According to *Od.* the first piece of church property (manse, etc.) was purchased "in his time," 1 Mar. 1700/1; his successor, Samuel Bates, was appointed "about 1703." (*C. M. Od. P. T.*) [34]

EATALL. [80] *See* Northumberland

EATON. [9] *See* Buckinghamshire

EATON, ROBERT, M.A. (1624?–Aug. 1701). 𝔓. Born at High Walton, Ches. Son of Thomas Eaton, and grandson of Robert Eaton, rector (1582–1621) of Grappenhall, Ches. Matric. pensioner at Christ's Coll., Cambridge, 10 Apr. 1646, age 22; did not graduate at Cambridge; after seven years there, migrated to All Souls Coll., Oxford, and graduated M.A., 15 July 1653. He first had some curacy or preferment in Essex. He held before 1658 the sequestered rectory of Walton-on-the-Hill, Lanc.; and is described as "parson of Walton" where his son Samuel [*q.v.*] was baptized (24 Jan. 1657/8) by Henry Finch [*q.v.*], the vicar. The Walton to which he went from Essex may have been his native place; certainly he became perpetual curate of the parochial chapel of Daresbury, where his family had property; the parish includes the townships of Over or Higher and Nether Walton. Ejected, 1662. Sir George Booth, whose royalist aims he (like Henry Finch [*q.v.*]) had favoured, now (1661) Baron Delamer, made him his chaplain at Dunham Massey, Ches. Licensed, 30 Apr. 1672, as "Pr. Teacher in his howse in Manchester." His house, then in Deansgate, was licensed same day as "a Pr. Meeting Place"; and there, on 29 Oct. 1672, was held the first Nonconformist ordination since 1660. He and his hearers were fined for a conventicle, 5 Oct. 1673, in the barn of William Walker, merchant of Whitefield. The Chapel at Stand, parish of Prestwich, was built for him in 1693 (registered, 20 June). In the same year the Lancashire Provincial Meeting of United Ministers was founded. Eaton was Moderator on 4 S. 1694. His residence at the time of his death was in Millgate, Manchester; he was buried at the Collegiate Church (now Cathedral), on 25 Aug. 1701. (*C. Cp. F. Hs. Nl. P. T. V. X.*) [59, 62]

EATON, SAMUEL (16 Jan. 1657/8—5 S. 1710). 𝔓. Second son of Robert Eaton [*q.v.*]. Matric. at St. Edmund Hall, Oxford, 17 Mar. 1672/3, aged 15. Assistant and successor to his father. Being married, he lived in Pool Fold, Manchester. Ordained at Macclesfield, 17 June 1700. Buried at the Collegiate Church (now Cathedral). (*F. Hs.*) [62]

ECCLES. Ejected here was Edmund Jones, bapt. 12 Sept. 1624; of St. John's Coll., Cambridge; matric. pensioner, 1645; B.A., 1649; rem. to Jesus Coll.; M.A., 1660; ord. 25 Jan. 1649/50 by presbyters as minister of Eccles, and succeeded his father, John Jones, as vicar in 1653; ejected, 1662; licensed, 1 May 1672, as Pr. Teacher in Outbuildings at Eccles; *d.* 2 May 1674, aged 49. (*C. Jo. Nl. T. V.*) [52]

ECCLESHALL, JOSEPH, B.A. (*fl.* 1650–1691). 𝔓. Matric. sizar at Emmanuel Coll., Cambridge, 1650; B.A., 1653/4. Left the University about 1654. Curate and then vicar of Sedgley, Staff.; ejected, 1662. Continued to live at Sedgley, till the Five Mile Act drove him (1666) to Kinver, Staff., whence he made night preaching visits to Sedgley. The Episc. Returns, 1669, report him as preaching to about 200 Presbyterians at his house in Sedgley; also as one of the preachers to near 1000 persons in the Leather Hall, Coventry (*see* Grace). Licensed, June 1672, as "Pr. Teacher in his howse in the Parish of Sedgley." (*C. P. T. V.*) [97]

EDGE, RICHARD (*fl.* 1690–93). Entered the Academy of John Woodhouse [*q.v.*], and received from the Common Fund (Feb. 1691) a gift of £4, and (Dec. 1692) a grant of £6 a year. He was ordained at Knutsford (27 S. 1692) as Minister of Bromborough, in succession to John Wilson [*q.v.*]; he left before Christmas 1693; apparently he served Bromborough as a Student. (*M. Uc.*) [17]

EDMONTON. [2]

EDUCATION. [178]

EDWARDS, CHARLES, B.A. (1628–1691?). 𝔓. Son of Robert Edwards of Llansilin, Denbighsh., pleb. Matric. as 'serv.' at All Souls Coll., Oxford, 9 Apr. 1644, aged 16; expelled (1648) from All Souls Coll., but elected scholar of Jesus Coll., 27 O. 1648; B.A., 1649. Sinecure rector of Llanrhaiadr-yn-Mochnant, Denbighsh.; preached as an Itinerant; ejected, 1662. Returned to Oxford, 1666, and began a remarkable career as author, in Welsh, Latin, and English, of works bearing on Welsh history and literature. Licensed, 10 Aug. 1672, as "gen^all^ Pr. Teach" at Oswestry, Shropsh. He rejected the repeated offer of £8 a year from the Common Fund (1690) if he would devote himself to the ministry; but was paid it for the first half of 1691. Calamy and Palmer ignore him; Rees just mentions his name. (*D. F. M. T.*) [88, 142]

EDWARDS, DAVID (1660—28 S. 1716). **C.** Born at Cellan, Card., son of David and grandson of Peter Edwards of Deri Odwyn. Educ. at some Academy, for he is described as "schr" (scholar) in Evans' List. Began to preach at Caeronen, Card., at the age of 20 (1680); ordained there, 1688. In addition to this ministry, he succeeded David Jones (*fl.* 1654–94) [*q.v.*] at Pencarreg, Card., and at Cilgwyn, Card., where and at other "5 or 6 places" he was ministering in 1715, when he was living "at Abermyrick" (Abermeurig). He was buried in Nantcwnlle churchyard, Card. (inscription). His widow, Jane (Bowen), died long after him at Carmarthen. (*Ev. Rj. Rw.*) [145]

EDWARDS, THOMAS (*fl.* 1690–1705). A young man from Wellington, Som., who succeeded Goswell of Exeter, one of the preachers at Honiton in the back-house of William Clarke, chandler, and became the first pastor of the congregation, superseding Malachi Blake [*q.v.*]. He divided the congregation; Clarke excluded him from his premises; his friends opened another place, but scandal arose and Edwards was deserted, the two parties uniting (1705) under John Ball (1665 ?—6 May 1745). He conformed, and became curate or rector of North Leigh, near Honiton. (*Mh.*) [30, 33]

EDWIN, SIR HUMPHREY (1642—14 Dec. 1707). Wool merchant; knighted, 18 N. 1687. Attended one meeting of Managers, 21 March 1692/3. His subscription was in arrear at Midsummer, 1693. Lord Mayor, 1697–98; gave great offence by attending Nonconformist worship on the afternoons of Sundays 31 O. and 7 N. 1697, in full civic state. There is conflict of testimony as to the Meeting-house; the evidence is in favour of Pinners' Hall; Salters' Hall is also mentioned, and attendance may have been given at each place. While his denomination is doubtful, he was probably at first Presbyterian, afterwards Congregational. He was not a Manager of the reconstituted Fund (1695) or of the Congregational Fund (1695). (*Cm. Co. D. M.*) [162, 166]

EKYNS, EKINS, or EIKINS, ROBERT, B.A. (*d.* Dec. 1716). **C.** Born in Northamptonshire; subsizar at Trinity Coll., Cambridge, 20 June 1655; matric., 1656; scholar, 1657; B.A., 1658/9. In 1660 he was Senior Bachelor and expecting a Fellowship. For six months he resisted an arbitrary order to conform or quit. Retiring in 1661, he thrice declined (1662) offers of preferment, and was disowned by his family. Licensed, 13 May 1672, as "Congr. Teacher in the howse of Eliz. Mutsoe in Twywell," Northants. His settlement at Oakham was in 1683. The Common Fund granted him, 1690–1715, £12 a year for Oakham Rutl., reduced (1695) to £10. He died Minister at Oakham. (*C. Ev. M. P. T. Tc. V.*) [87, 179]

ELBERTON ('Elverton'). Ejected here was . . . Hilton. [46]

ELIZABETH, QUEEN. [137]

ELLAND ('Ealand'). [132]

ELLENTHORPE ('Ellingthorp.'). [135]

ELLISON, *i.e.* ELLISTONE, MATTHEW (*d.* 1693). **P.** Born at Coggeshall, Ess. Matric. pensioner at Emmanuel Coll., Cambridge, 1642; did not graduate. Appointed, Sept. 1646, to the sequestered rectory of Stanford Rivers, Ess.; ejected, 1660. Removed to Little Coggeshall, Ess. Licensed, 13 May 1672, as "Pr. Teacher in his howse" at the Grange in Little Coggeshall. Buried at Markshall, Ess., 3 May 1693. (*C. E. P. T. V.*) [39]

ELSKON, *i.e.* ELSTON, THOMAS, M.A. (1651 ?–31 Mar. 1710). **C.** Entered Frankland's Academy, 6 July 1670, along with Thomas Whitaker [*q.v.*]; rem. with Whitaker to Edinburgh University; M.A., 1674. Preacher at Topcliffe, West Riding, 1675. Chaplain and tutor in family of Samuel Baker of Wattisfield, Suff. (1678 ?–1685). Pastor at Topcliffe, 1686; removed, 8 July 1709, to Chesterfield, where he died, 31 Mar. 1710, aged 50, and was buried, 3 Apr. 1710. Whitaker preached his funeral sermon at Topcliffe. The Common Fund granted (1692) £6 a year for Topcliffe, reduced (1695) to £4. (*B. Ed. Fr. M. My. Nk. Nr. Sr. Wm.*) [129]

ELSWICK, chapelry (building held and now rebuilt by Nonconformists) in St. Michael-on-Wyre parish. [61]

ELTHAM ('Eltam'). Ejected here, according to Calamy, was . . . . . Overton [? William Overton, of Trinity Coll., Oxford; matric., 30 Apr. 1619, aged 16; B.A., 1622; M.A., 1625; rector of Fringford, Oxf., 1635.] He held the sequestered vicarage of Eltham, 1646, but ceded it in 1658; there is no place for him in Hasted's list of vicars. (*C. F. K.*) [56]

ELVERTON. [46] *See* Gloucestershire

ELY. [13] Ejected here was William Sedgwick, M.A.; born in Bedfordshire; son of William Sedgwicke of London, gent.; matric. at Pembroke Coll., Oxford, 2 D. 1625, aged 15; B.A., 1628; M.A., 1631; incorp. at Cambridge, 1635; rector of Farnham, Ess., 1634; chaplain in parliamentary army, 1642–43; in 1644 became the chief preacher in Ely; known as "apostle of the Isle of Ely"; ejected, 1660; retired to Lewisham, Kent; conformed and became rector of Mattishall Burgh, Norf., 1663; died in London about 1669. He was a Puritan and mystic. (*C. D. F. P.*)

ELY, ISLE OF. [12, 43]

ENFIELD. [50, 72] Ejected here was Daniel Manning, of St. Catharine's Hall, Cambridge; matric. pensioner, 1645/6; B.A., 1649/50; rem. to Pembroke Hall; Fellow; M.A., 1653; vicar of Enfield, 6 May 1659; ejected, 1662; *bur.* at Enfield, 2 Mar. 1666/7. (*C. P. V.*)

ENGLAND. [22]

ENGLISCOMBE ('Ingleshombe'). [92]

ENGLISH, MRS. [41]

EPPING ('Eppin'). Ejected here was Thomas Harper, who afterwards conformed. (*C.*) [40, 45]

EPSOM. [3]

ERISEY ('Errisey,' 'Eresy'), manor in Grade parish, Corn. [18]

ESSEX. [38, 41, 168, 176, 181] Only the headings "Essex" are in the earliest handwriting; the remainder, with slight exceptions, is in the Book-keeper's handwriting. The returns are numbered from 16 to 151, and in 1691 from 18 to 50.

'Mark' following place-names is Market.

Barbing is Barking [*q.v.*].
Barfield is Bardfield [*q.v.*].
Brackstead, Brackted, is Braxted.
Chissel is Chishall, Little.
Castle Honingham is Castle Hedingham.
Cliderditch, Childeitch, is Childerditch.
Hannerick is Haverhill, Suff.
Machin is Matching.
Redgwell is Ridgewell [*q.v.*].
Reyleigh is Rayleigh [*q.v.*].
Rumford is Romford.
Vivenho is Wivenhoe [*q.v.*].
Withamstow is Walthamstow

ETAL. [80, 177]

ETON ('Eaton'). Ejected here were:

(1) John Bachelor, of Gloucester Hall, Oxford; matric., 4 July 1634, aged 18; B.A., 1636/7; M.A., 1640; Fellow of Eton, 1647; Vice-provost; ejected, 1660. (*C. F. Rr.*)

(2) John Boncle, Buncle or Bunckley, created M.A., Oxford, 22 Dec. 1652; master of Charterhouse school, 1653; Fellow, 18 Sept. 1655, and Headmaster; ejected, 1660. ? Master of Mercers' Chapel school in 1673. (*F. Rr.*)

(3) Thomas Goodwin, D.D. [*q.v.*].

(4) Paul Hobson, captain in the parliamentary army; chaplain at Eton College; ejected, 1660; an anti-Trinitarian Baptist. (*C. See* his writings.)

(5) Nicholas Lockyer, B.D., son of William Lockier of Glastonbury, Som., pleb.; matric. at New Inn Hall, Oxford, 4 Nov. 1631, aged 20; B.A., 1633; rem. to Cambridge, incorp. at Emmanuel Coll., 1635; M.A., 1636; B.D., 1654; Fellow of Eton Coll., 1649/50; chaplain to Protector Oliver; Provost, 1658/9; after ejection thence (1660), preacher at St. Pancras, Soper Lane, London; rector of St. Bennet, Sherchog; ejected thence, 1662; reported in Episcopal Returns, 1669, as one of the preachers in Bell Lane, Spitalfields; wealthy in landed property, he died at Woodford, Ess., 13 Mar. 1684/5. (*C. D. F. P. Rr. T.*)

(6) John Oxenbridge (30 Jan. 1608/9—28 Dec. 1674). Born at Daventry; of Lincoln Coll., Oxford; matric., 20 June 1623; B.A., 1624; M.A., 1627; preached in Bermuda; returned to England, 1641; Fellow of Eton College, 1652; ejected, 1660; preached at Berwick-on-Tweed; ejected, 1662; preached at Beverley, Yorks, 1664; went to West Indies and New England, 1669; *d.* at Boston, U.S.A. (*C. F. Rr.*)

(7) Richard Penwarden, of the Inner Temple, 1638, and of New Inn Hall, Oxford; M.A., 1648; Fellow of Eton College, 1650; ejected, 1662. (*C. F. Rr. Wp.*) [9]

EUXTON ('Euston'). Chapelry in Leyland parish, now vicarage. [61]

EVANS, JOHN (1629—16 July 1700). **C. B.** Born at Great Sutton, in Diddlebury parish, Shrops. Son of Matthew Evans, rector of Penegoes, Montg. Matric. at Balliol Coll., Oxford, 6 Mar. 1646/7, aged 18; expelled, 1648, by parliamentary visitors. Ordained priest at Brecon, 28 N. 1648, by Roger Mainwaring, bishop of St. David's. Ceasing to conform, he became one of the Itinerant preachers in Wales, and master of Dolgelly grammar school, subsequently (1657) of Oswestry grammar school on Cromwell's recommendation; ejected, 1660. Chosen pastor, 1668, of Congr. church, Wrexham. The Episc. Returns, 1669, report him as preaching with others at Llanfyllin and Llanfechan, Montg., and at Oswestry, Shrops. Licensed, 22 May 1672, as

"Congr. Teacher in the howse of Edw: Kenricke in Wrexham, Denbigh." Subsequently the Presbyterians joined his flock, and by 1689 the Baptists, Evans himself having adopted their views; in 1691 the Presbyterians withdrew. At p. 141 he is wrongly called John Owen.

His son, John Evans, D.D. (1680?–16 May 1730), who entered Frankland's Academy, 26 May 1697, assisted him before his death, and subsequently became the first Minister of the seceding Presbyterians (ordained, 18 Aug. 1702). He left for London in 1704, and became assistant and successor to Daniel Williams [*q.v.*]. In 1716 he was living "over against the Grate in Bishopsgate-street near Angel-Alley." He was D.D. both of Edinburgh and Glasgow. His collections for a history of Nonconformity are in Dr. Williams' Library, where is also the volume of statistical reports, from counties, of the Dissenting interest in England and Wales (1714–19), known as Evans' List. He was buried in Dr. Williams' vault in Bunhill Fields. (*C. D. Ev. F. Fr. Nk. P. T. Rw.*) [141, 148]

EVANS, WILLIAM (*d.* Jan. 1717/8). 𝕮. Described as "sch$^{r}$," *i.e.* equipped for the ministry (by Stephen Hughes). [*See* Owen, James.] From Pencadair he removed to Carmarthen, where in 1702 he followed Roger Griffith [*q.v.*] as Tutor, removing the Academy to Carmarthen, and conducting it, along with his ministry, till death. His Academy is specified in the will of Daniel Williams, D.D. [*q.v.*]. (*Ev. Rw.*) [144]

EVESHAM. ('Eversham'). Ejected here was George Hopkins (15 Apr. 1620—25 Mar. 1666), son of William, Bewdley, Worc.; of New Inn Hall, Oxford; matric., 2 Mar. 1637/8, aged 17; B.A., 1641; M.A., 1648; vicar of All Saints, Evesham; ejected, 1662; *d.* at Dumbleton, Glou. (*C. F.*) [127]

EWHURST. [110]

EXAMINATION OF STUDENTS. [181]

EXCHANGE, THE ROYAL. [2]

EXETER ('Exon'). Ejected here were:

(1) Robert Atkins, born at Chard, 1626; of Wadham Coll., Oxford; matric., 9 Apr. 1647, aged 18; Fellow, 1650–61; M.A., 1652; chaplain to Cromwell; rector of Theydon, Ess., 1653–57; preacher at St. Sidwells; afterwards at the Cathedral; ejected, 1660; vicar of St. John's Bowe, 1660; ejected, 1662; living at Exeter in 1665; preaching at Chard in 1669; licensed, 2 Apr. and 11 Apr. 1672, as Presbyt. Teacher in any licensed place; founder of Bow Meeting; *d.* 28 Mar. 1685; Henry Atkins [*q.v.*] was his son. (*C. F. T.*)

(2) John Bartlett, M.A. [*q.v.*].

(3) Mark Downe (younger brother of Thomas), of Queen's Coll., Cambridge; admitted sizar, 1629; M.A., 1635; rector of St. Petrock's; ejected, 1662; in London in 1664; living at Exeter, 1665; licensed, 30 Apr. 1672, as Pr.; *d.* Oct. 1680. (*C. T. V.*)

(4) Thomas Downe [? admitted sizar at St. John's Coll., Cambridge, 1598; M.A., 1605; incorp. at Oxford, 1605; another, of these names, was admitted sizar at St. John's Coll., Cambridge, 1625], rector of St. Edmund's and St. Mary Steps; ejected, 1662; *d.* 1666. (*C. F. V.*)

(5) Thomas Ford, born at Brixton, Devon; of Magdalen Hall, Oxford; matric., 23 June 1621, aged 16; M.A., 1627; rector of Aldwincle All Saints, Notts, 1637–47, with Oundle; member of the Westminster Assembly; preacher at the Cathedral and rector of St. Lawrence, Exeter; ejected, 1662; living at Exeter, 1665; licensed, 30 Apr. 1672, as general Pr. Teacher; *bur.* in St. Lawrence church, 28 Dec. 1676. (*C.* (wrong dates) *F. T.*)

(6) Alexander Hodge of Wadham Coll., Oxford; matric., 1651; M.A. and Fellow, 1654; incorp. at Cambridge, 1656; vicar of St. Thomas'; ejected, 1662; chaplain at Amsterdam, 1669, till death; *d.* Dec. 1689. (*C. F. V.*)

(7) Thomas Maule or Mall, of Pembroke Hall, Cambridge; M.A., 1653, and Fellow; preached in Cornwall, and later at the Cathedral; ejected, 1662; living in Exeter, 1665; preached at Cruse Morchard and Crediton, 1669; licensed, 16 Apr. 1672, as Congreg. Teacher at South Molton, Devon. (*C. T. V.*)

(8) Ferdinando Nicolls, of Magdalen Coll., Oxford; matric., 10 Nov. 1615, aged 17; M.A., 1621; rector of St. Mary Arches, 1634 (also vicar of Twickenham, Midx., 1645); ejected, 1662; *d.* 14 Dec. 1662. (*C. F.*)

(9) Thomas Powell, M.A. [*q.v.*].

(10) Lewis Stuckley, of Wadham Coll., Oxford; matric., 19 May 1637, aged 15; B.A., 1641; rector of Newton Ferrers, Devon, 1646; curate at Great Torrington and preacher at the Cathedral; ejected, 1662; preacher at Nether Exe, Cruse Morchard, and Crediton, Devon, 1669; minister of Congregational church at Exeter in 1672; licensed, 10 Aug. 1672, as Cong. Teacher at Crediton; *d.* at Bideford, July 1687. (*C. F. T.*)

(11) John Tickle, of New Inn Hall, Oxford; B.A., 27 June 1649; Fellow of

New Coll., 1649; chaplain of Christ Church Coll., 1650; M.A., 1651/2; ejected, 1662; preached at Abingdon, Berks, Barnstaple, Devon, and Exeter; living in Exeter, 1665; conformed, and became vicar of Withecombe, Devon, 1674–90; *d.* there, 30 June 1694. (*C. F. T.*) [30, 31, 32]

EXETER ASSEMBLY. [157]

EYE. Ejected here was Edward Barker, of Gonville and Caius Coll., Cambridge; matric. pensioner, 1637; B.A., 1640/1; from being a high Anglican, became Congregational; vicar of Eye; ejected, 1660; removed to Wrentham, Suff.; he died before 1679 (Calamy says in 1665, but he was preaching at Great Yarmouth in 1669). (*B. C. T. V.*) [106, 107]

EYTON, *i.e.* EATON, JOSEPH, M.D. (*fl.* 1655–1719). **P.** Born in Cheshire. Entered Frankland's Academy, 4 Apr. 1678; studied also, without matriculating, at Pembroke Hall, Cambridge; graduated M.D. at Leiden, 19 D. 1686, having entered there 9 Oct. 1685, aged 30. Ordained at Warrington, Jan. 1687/8. One of the founders (1691) of the Cheshire Classis (*see* p. 157), being then Minister of Macclesfield. He left the ministry in 1697, and practised medicine in Nottingham for a short time, removing to Colchester, and thence to London, where he was admitted a Licenciate of the College of Physicians, 25 June 1713. He was a Fund Manager, attending from 6 June 1715 till 2 Mar. 1718/9. Benjamin Grosvenor, D.D., dedicated to him his Essay on Health, 1716; the dedication reappears in the second edition, 1748, when Eaton, if living, was aged 93. (*Ht. M. Mu. Nk. No. Uc.*) [15]

FACY, LEWIS, B.A. (*d.* 1704?). **P.** Entered at New Inn Hall, Oxford, 25 July 1655; rem. to New Coll., B.A., 1658/9. Rector of Upton Helions, Devon, 1661; ejected, 1662. Licensed, 18 Apr. 1672, being of Werrington, Devon, as Presb. Teacher in any licensed place. The house of John Facy at Werrington was already licensed (13 Apr.) as a Presb. meeting-place. He was once imprisoned at Bodmin, and ministered to a congregation at Falmouth. In 1695–96 he received grants as successor to Roger Flamank [*q.v.*] at St. Enodor; and continued to receive grants (from 1701, for Falmouth) to the end of 1703; a successor, Jasper How, appears in 1704. (*C. F. M. P. T.*) [18]

FAIRCLOUGH. *See* Farlough.

FAIRFAX, JOHN, M.A. (1623—11 Aug. 1700). **P.** Second son of Benjamin Fairfax (1593–Jan. 1675/6), ejected from the vicarage of Rumburgh, Suff. Admitted from Norfolk, 1640, at Corpus Christi Coll., Cambridge; B.A. and Fellow, 1645; M.A., 1647; ejected from Fellowship for refusing the engagement (1649) of fidelity to the Commonwealth without king or house of lords. Rector of Barking-cum-Needham, Suff.; ejected, 1662. The Episc. Returns, 1669, report that at Dedham, Ess., "On y^e 16 of Septemb. last, upon y^e occasion of M^r Newcomen's death in Holl^d An Outragious Conventicle was kept, & dangerous words sayd to be there spoken by M^r Fairfax, late Minist^r of Barking in Suffolk." He was imprisoned at Bury St. Edmunds in 1671. Licensed, 10 June 1672, as "Pr. Teacher" in an out-house belonging to Widow Margaret Rozer at Needham Market, Suff. From 1680 he took charge of the Presbyterian congregation at Ipswich, in addition to that at Needham, and opened (26 Apr. 1700) the existing Meeting-house, St. Nicholas Street, Ipswich. He preached also at Colchester. In 1697 the Fund granted him £10 for Needham. He died at Barking. (*B.C.D.Lm.P.T.*) [38, 103, 104]

FALDO, JOHN (1634?–7 Feb. 1690/1). **C.** Studied at Cambridge; did not matriculate. An army chaplain under the Commonwealth, not beneficed in 1662. The Episc. Returns, 1669, report him as one of the preachers to a congregation of 200, in Chipping Barnet, Herts, "At a great Chamber hired by John Faldo." Four applications were made in 1672 for licence to him at Chipping Barnet "in a Roome in a Common yard in Wood Street adioyning to the house of M^r John Minshue Congr." On 13 May 1673 John Foldoe was licensed apparently as a general "Pr. Teacher"; on the same date "the howse of John Foldoe in Chipping Barnet" was licensed as a "Pr. Meeting Place." Unless, like others [*e.g.* Joseph Caryl], he changed his denomination, "Pr." is an error. The receipt for these licences (14 May) describes them as "M^r Foldoe for his person: & M^r Minshu's house in Chipping Barnet"; this answers to the 1669 statement that the Chamber was hired. Soon after, he had a controversy (1672–5) with William Penn. On the death (6 Aug. 1684) of Nathanael Partridge, he succeeded him as Minister of the Congregational church in Old Street Square, London; he removed it to Plaisterers'

Hall, Addle Street. He died on the eve of the Happy Union; John Quick, B.A. [*q.v.*], the Presbyterian preacher of his funeral sermon, speaking of him as "a man of singular moderation," and saying he had "an especial hand in the healing of our breaches," adds that "those two divided parties in this nation, that had been so for above forty years, are now once again united and become one, and we shall no more hear of those unhappy terms of distinction and separation, Presbyterian and Independent, but we shall be called, as the primitive church of Antioch, by his name who hath redeemed us, and anointed us with his holy spirit, even Christians." His inscribed tomb in Bunhill Fields places his death in his 57th year. (*C. P. Sm. T. W. We.*) [41, 52, 119, 160, 164, 168]

FALMOUTH. [18]

FAREHAM ('Faram'). [100]

FARLOUGH, *i.e.* FAIRCLOUGH, SAMUEL, M.A. (*d.* 31 Dec. 1691). **C.** Second son of Samuel Fairclough, ejected from Ketton, Suff. Educ. at Emmanuel Coll., Cambridge; matric. pensioner, 1644 (as Fairecloth); B.A., 1646/7; M.A., 1650; rem. to Gonville and Caius Coll., senior Fellow, 1650–6; Hebrew lecturer, 1651; Logic lecturer, 1658. Held the sequestered rectory of Houghton Conquest, Beds; ejected, 1660. Licensed 18 Nov. 1672, under name Fairecloth, as Congr. Teacher at Chippenham, Cambs. Buried at Heveningham, Suff. (*B. C. Gc. P. T. V. Wc.* Fun. Serm. (1692) by N. Parkhurst, vicar of Yoxford, Suff.) [1]

FARNHAM. Ejected here was Samuel Stileman, of St. Catherine's Hall, Cambridge; matric. sizar, 1643; B.A., 1646; M.A., 1652; incorp. at Oxford, 1657; vicar of Farnham, ejected, 1662; *d.* 1663. (*C. F. V.*) Farnham Castle is the chief residence of the bishops of Winchester; the bishop from 1687 to 1706 was Peter Mews, whose resistance to the unconstitutional action of James II., and whose leaning towards terms for the comprehension of Nonconformists, were well known. [109]

FARROLL, JOHN, M.A. (1623?–1702?). **P.** Son of George Farroll, M.A., ejected (1662) from the rectory of Worplesdon, Surr. Matric. at Magdalen Hall, Oxford, 11 O. 1639, aged 16; Fellow of Magdalen Coll., 1648; M.A., 1648. Held the sequestered vicarage of Selborne, Hants; resigned, 1660. He removed to Guildford, Surr., and kept a boarding-house for pupils at the grammar school. The Five Mile Act, 1666, drove him to Farnham, Surr. In 1669 he was imprisoned six months for preaching (14 June) at Godalming, Surr. Licensed, June 1672, as "Pr. Teacher in the howse of Rich: Collier," Farnham. He removed to West Horsley, Surr., and in 1687 returned to Guildford, preaching there and at Godalming and Farnham. The Common Fund offered him (1690) £8 a year "if he fix at Godalming." He was paid at the rate of £5 a year for Guildford up to Midsummer, 1691; on 23 N. 1691 the grant was withdrawn. His last move was to Lymington, Hants, where he died in his 80th year. (*C. F. M. P. T. Ws.*) [109, 110, 111]

FAST DAY SERVICES. [178]

FAVERSHAM ('Feversham,' 'Fever:'). Ejected here was Nathaniel Wilmot; rector of Faversham and vicar of Preston, Kent; ejected, 1662; preaching at Davington and Godmersham, Kent, also at Midhurst and Petworth, Suss., in 1699; licensed, 15 Apr. 1672, as Presb. Teacher in a house at Davington, Kent; finally he was Minister at Dover, where Comfort Starr, M.A. [*q.v.*], was his assistant; *d.* about 1690. (*C. K. T.*) [55]

FELSTEAD. Ejected here was Nathaniel Ranew, of Emmanuel Coll., Cambridge; matric. sizar, 1617; B.A., 1620/1; M.A., 1624; held the sequestered rectory of St. Andrew Hubbard, London; vicar of Felstead, 29 Feb. 1647/8; member of the Eleventh Presb. Classis of Essex; ejected, 1662; licensed, 30 Apr. 1672, as Pr. Teacher in a house at Billericay, Ess.; *d.* 1672, aged about 72. (*C. E. T. V.*) [42]

FENNER, JOHN (*d.* 1712?). **C.** On 8 June 1691 the Common Fund granted him £10 a year for Weymouth; discontinued, 1695. On 13 Apr. 1696 the Congregational Fund granted him £6 a year (subsequently increased to £10) for Weymouth. "Mr Taylor of Pinnars hall" must mean Richard Taylor [*q.v.*]; the pastor at Pinners' Hall was Richard Wavell [*q.v.*]. Premises in St. Nicholas Street, Weymouth, were bought by John Fenner, clerk, for £40 on 3 June 1703, and conveyed to trustees, on 18 Feb. 1705, for the use of successive Ministers of "the separate congregation of reformed Christians in Weymouth and Melcombe Regis, commonly called Dissenters." Fenner's pastorate ended in 1712. (*Cf. M. Od.*) [34]

FENWICK, EDWARD (*b.* 1624). Perhaps the Fenwick ejected from some post at King's Lynn. He subscribed to the Common Fund till 1692, increasing his contribution to £10. On 7 D. 1702 £3 was granted to "Mr Fenwick . . . 78 Years of age very poor." (*C. M.*) [165]

FERNE, ROBERT (1652—6 June 1727). **P.** Colleague to Thomas Ogle [*q.v.*] at Chesterfield till 1703. Minister at Wirksworth, Derb., till death. (*Ev. Wa.*) [25, 29]

FEVERSHAM. [55] *See* Kent

FILDE COUNTRY. [63] *See* Lancashire

FINCH, HENRY (1633—13 N. 1704). **P.** Born in Standish parish, Lanc.; baptized 8 S. 1633. From Wigan and Standish grammar schools, matric. 'serv.' at St. Mary Hall, Oxford, 26 N. 1650. Preached in the Fylde district, Lanc.; vicar (30 July 1654) of Walton-on-the-hill, Lanc. (in which parish was Liverpool); member of the Fifth Lancashire Classis; sequestered, 1659/60, owing to complicity with Sir George Booth's royalist plans; ejected, 1662. He retired to Warrington to his wife's relatives; the Five Mile Act drove him (1666) to Manchester (not then a corporate town), where he kept school; The Episc. Returns, 1669, report at Birch Chapel "frequent & numerous Conventicles, consisting cheifly of Independents." Licensed, 30 Apr. 1672, as "Grāll Pr. Teacher," and at the same time Birch Chapel, described as "A Private Oratory belonging to Thomas Birch Esqr of Birch-hall" was "licensed for a Congr. & Pr. Meeting Place." Finch's own house in Manchester was licensed, 10 June 1672, as "Pr. Meeting Place." He was imprisoned (1685) on suspicion of favouring the Monmouth rebellion, and an attempt made to put a conformist into Birch Chapel, of which Finch retained the use till 1697. He then preached at certified houses in Platt and Birch till a Chapel was built for him at Platt. He was a member of the Provincial Meeting of United Ministers (1693) and a contributor to the distressed nonjurors. (*C. D. F. Nl. P. T.*) [61, 177]

FINCH, or FYNCH, MARTIN (1628?–13 F. 1697/8). **C.** Born in Norfolk. Pensioner at Trinity Coll., Cambridge, 23 Jan. 1645/6; Scholar, 1647; did not graduate. Vicar of Tetney, Linc.; ejected, 1662. In 1668 he was one of three teachers to 300 Independents in the house of John Tofts, grocer, and other places, in St. Clement's parish, Norwich. The Episc. Returns, 1669, report him as one of the preachers to about 300 Independents "At the house of John Hooker, sometimes of Henry Brett, & sometimes of Richard Clements an excommunicate pson" at Woodnorton, Norf.; also at Oulton, Norf., "Sometimes at the house of Wm Bell sen sometimes of Willm Bell junr"; also to Independents "Att the house of Thomas Church junr Worsted-weaver, an excom̃unicate pson" at Lammas, Norf. Licensed, 10 June 1672, as "Congr. Teacher" at "A roome or roomes in ye mantion house of Nicolas Withers in ye Parish of St. Clements in ye City of Norwich." He left Norwich and was licensed, 5 Sep. 1672, as "Congr. Teacher" at Great Grimsby, Linc.; his house there was licensed, 10 Aug. and 5 Sept. 1672. He became pastor of the Congregational church in succession to John Cromwell (*d.* April 1685), meeting in the West Granary, behind St. Andrew's Hall. He removed his congregation to a Meeting-house (formerly a brew-house) in St. Edmund's parish; and thence to a building in St. Clement's parish (erected, 1693) as the New Meeting; now known as the Old Meeting.

His Assistant (co-pastor about 1690/1) was John Stackhouse (1648—14 S. 1707). (*B. C. D. P. T. Tc. V.*) [74, 177]

FINCH, PETER, M.A. (6 Oct. 1661—6 Oct. 1754). **P.** Son of Henry Finch [*q.v.*]. Entered (3 May 1678) the Academy of Richard Frankland, then at Natland, Westmorland; graduated (1680) M.A., Edin. Chaplain to William Ashurst, afterwards knighted. Minister at Norwich, 1691, till his death on the 93rd anniversary of his birth. Not related to Martin Finch [*q.v.*]. (*D.*) [2]

FINCHER, RICHARD, B.A. (*d.* 10 F. 1692/3). **P.** Probably son of John Fincher (*d.* 1663?, aged 80) of Shell Manor, parish of Himbleton, Worc. Matric. at Emmanuel Coll., Cambridge, 1647; B.A., 1650. Ejected from the rectory of St. Nicholas, Worcester, he opened a school. The Episc. Returns, 1669, report him as one of the preachers to "about 200 of all sorts, some people of good sufficiency Att the houses of Mr Thomas Stirrup & Mr Thomas Smyth every second Sunday" in the parish of St. Nicholas, Worc. Licence was applied for him as "Congreg: the house of Rich: Corenton in Worcester"; in June 1672 he was licensed as "a Congr. Teacher in the howse of Rich: Cornton in Worcester"; but the licence for the house is marked Pr. At the Revolution he was Minister of a Presbyterian congregation in Unicorn Yard, Southwark. He was "a man of peace, so far as ever he could go, without forsaking truth and holiness." He was chosen (19 Dec. 1692) a Manager of the Common Fund, and attended till within a month of his death. In the same year his congregation was augmented by some sixty seceders from the ministry of Nathaniel Vincent [q.v.]. (*C. Ek. M. P. T. W.*) [161, 164, 183]

FINCHER, WILLIAM (*fl.* 1660–1692). 𝔓. Born at Shell, parish of Himbleton, Worc. Younger brother of Richard Fincher [*q.v.*]. Had a liberal education (not matric. at Oxford or Cambridge). Ejected from the vicarage of Wednesbury, Staff. Preached at Gornall, in Sedgley parish, Staff., and elsewhere. The Episc. Returns, 1669, report him as one of three preachers to "2 or 300" persons "att the houses of Henry Hopkins & John Tunck" in Wednesbury; also to "above 300" at houses in Walsall, Staff.; and to "1 or 200" at houses in Darlaston, Staff.; perhaps he is also the "John Fineper" reported as preaching with Thomas Baldwin [*q.v.*] and another to "about 100" at the house of William Bell in Birmingham. Licensed, 22 July 1672, as "Pr. Teacher in his howse in Birminghã." Under persecution he took refuge near his native place, his sister having married Mence, a farmer at Himbleton, where he "often preached in the troublous times." He finally settled in Birmingham, earlier than William Turton [*q.v.*], who became his colleague, but, the congregation increasing, it was divided after 1689. Fincher's congregation, the oldest in Birmingham, was the one that afterwards (1692) built the New Meeting (now Church of the Messiah). He died in Birmingham, apparently about 1692. (*Bh. C. P. T.*) [96, 117]

FINDERN ('ffinderne'). [25]

FINLOW, or FINDLOWE, REGINALD, B.A. (*d.* 1713). 𝔓. Matric. at Jesus Coll., Cambridge, 1646; migrated to Clare Hall; B.A., 1649/50. Held the sequestered vicarage of Stottesdon, Shrops.; ejected. He preached about the country, and took a little farm. Licensed, 10 June 1672, as Pr. Teacher in his house at Cold Weston, Shrops., a long way from Atcham. He received from 1690 to 1712 grants of £40. At Christmas 1713 he is reported dead. (*C. M. P. T. V.*) [16, 89]

FIRMIN, GILES (1614–Apr. 1697). 𝔓. Born at Ipswich. Matric. pensioner at Emmanuel Coll., Cambridge, Dec. 1629; did not graduate; studied medicine. Went (1632) to New England with his father; practised medicine, and was ordained deacon of the First Church, Boston. Returning (1647), he was ordained by presbyters as vicar of Shalford, Ess. He actively promoted (1657) the Agreement of the Associated Ministers of Essex, on Baxter's Worcestershire model. Ejected, 1662, he retired to Ridgewell, Ess. Licensed, 11 Apr. 1672, as "Pr. Teacher at Thomas Bryons howse at Redgwell"; also, Dec. 1672, his own house at Ridgewell was licensed. In the Crispian controversy he wrote (1693) against the views of Richard Davis. (*C. D. E. P. T. V.*) [40, 153]

FISH, ROBERT, M.A. (*fl.* 1641–1705). 𝔓. Matric. pensioner at Clare Hall, Cambridge, 1641; rem. to Trinity Coll.; B.A. 1644/5; M.A., 1648; incorp. at Oxford, 14 Oct. 1648; Fellow of Magdalen Coll., Oxford, 1648. Held the sequestered rectory of Nuthurst, Suss.; ejected, 1662. The Episc. Returns, 1669, report him as one of the preachers at Arundell, Suss.; also to "about 200" at Brighton, Suss., apparently Presbyterians. Licensed, 11 Apr. 1672, as "Pr. Teacher in his howse in Ockley in Sussex" (corrected in a later entry to Surrey). Here he taught school. The Common Fund voted him (1690) £6 a year for Ockley; reduced (1695) to £5, and paid up to 1705. The Congregational Fund voted him £5 on 20 Apr. 1696. He declined a call to succeed Matthew Mead [*q.v.*] in 1699 at Stepney. He is said to have "died about his 70th year," but must have been nearer 80. (*C. F. M. P. T. V. Wc.*) [109, 110, 112]

FISHER, JAMES, M.A. (1605–1691). ℭ. Matric. at Emmanuel Coll., Cambridge, 1625; B.A., 1627/8; M.A., 1631. Held the sequestered rectory of Fetcham, Surr.; ejected, 1660. Kept school at Dorking, Surr. The Episc. Returns, 1669, report a conventicle of "Independ[ts] about 100" at his house in Dorking, but do not report him as one of their preachers. Licensed, 1 May 1672, as "Congr. Teacher in his howse" at Dorking. On the information of Matthew Mead [*q.v.*] the Common Fund voted him (1690) £8 a year, he then being "neere" Dorking; on 15 June 1691 he was reported dead. (*C. M. P. T. V. Wc. Ws.*) [110]

FISHLAKE, W.R. (misplaced in N.R.). [136]

FLAMMANK, *i.e.* FLAMANK, ROGER (1607?–1694?). 𝔓. Elder brother of Henry Flamank [*q.v.*]. Studied, without matriculating, at Cambridge. Held the sequestered vicarage of Sithney, Corn.; ejected, 1660. The Episc. Returns, 1665, report him living at St. Wendron, Corn., and "peaceable." Licensed, 9 May

1672, as "Pr. Teacher in his howse in Guendron"; signed the thanks from Cornish Ministers. Later he maintained a small congregation at Gourounsan, parish of St. Enodor, Corn. Lived to be 87, and ministered to the last. Grants of £6 a year were made to him for St. Enodor from the Common Fund from 1690; in 1695 the grant is made to Lewis Facy [*q.v*], his successor. (*C. M. P. T. V. Wc.*) [18, 19]

FLAMMICK, *i.e.* FLAMANK, HENRY (*d.* 8 May 1692). Studied at Cambridge, without matriculation. Chaplain to Sir Hardren Waller, at Pendennis Castle. Held the sequestered rectory of Lanivet, Corn.; ejected, 1660. Licensed, 30 Apr. 1672 (as 'Hammack'), to be Pr. Teacher, in the house of William 'Hammack' called 'Goonrowson,' *i.e.* Gounrounsan, parish of St. Enodor, Corn.; signed the thanks from Cornish Ministers, but strongly opposed James II.'s Declaration for Liberty of Conscience, 1687. Minister of Abbey Chapel, Tavistock, 1688–92. (*C. P. T. Wc.*) [30]

FLAVELL, JOHN (1630—26 June 1691). **C.** Born at Bromsgrove, Worc.; elder son of Richard Flavell, ejected (1660) from the sequestered rectory of Willersley, Glouc.; and brother of Phineas Flavell [*q.v.*]. Entered as servitor at University Coll., Oxford (date not given), but did not graduate. His tutor was William Woodward [*q.v.*]. Assistant, 27 Apr. 1650, to Walplate, at Diptford, Devon; ordained, 17 O. 1650, at Salisbury; succeeded Walplate in the rectory of Diptford; resigned it on appointment, 10 D. 1656, to the rectory (of inferior value) of St. Clement's, Townstall, mother church of Dartmouth; ejected, 1662. The Episc. Returns, 1665, report him as holding "private Meetings" at Dartmouth. Under stress of the Five Mile Act, he removed (1666) to Hudscott House in Slapton parish, preaching there at midnight. Licensed, 2 Apr. 1672, as "a Teacher of y^e Congregational way, in a Congregation in his owne house at Dartmouth" (for this, he and his congregation signed an address of thanks to the Crown); also, 18 Apr. 1672, as "a Congr. Teacher in any licensed place." Subsequent persecution drove him (1685) to London, where he declined two calls, returning in 1687 to Dartmouth, where a Meeting-house was built for him. He warmly engaged in the local union of Presbyterian and Congregational Ministers, and died suddenly at Exeter as Moderator of that body. His sermon, which should have been preached at Taunton, on 2 Sept. 1691, to "United Brethren, of Gloucester, Dorset, Somerset, and Devonshire," was published posthumously (1691). Buried at Dartmouth, 29 June 1691. (*C. D. F. Fl. P. T.*) [31]

FLAVELL, PHINEAS (*d.* 1725 ?). **C.** Younger son of Richard Flavell, ejected (1660) from the sequestered rectory of Willersley, Glouc.; and brother of John Flavell [*q.v.*]. Matric. at Magdalen Coll., Oxford, 21 Mar. 1658/9; chorister, 1659–60; did not graduate. Ejected, 1662. Chaplain to Edward, Lord Russell. Preached occasionally about London. On 10 Nov. 1690 £3 was paid him as share of anonymous donation (£50) per Matthew Rapier. He had a grant (1698) from the Congregational Fund. Died in Westminster a few years prior to 1729. He published "The Deceitful Heart try'd and cast," 1676, 8vo. (*C. Cf. F. M. P.*) [2]

FLEMMING, *i.e.* FLEMING, ROBERT, the younger (1660 ?–21 May 1716). **P.** Born at Cambuslang, Lanarksh. Educated in Holland; ordained there, 9 F. 1688. Removing to England, was chaplain in a private family about four years. Minister, 1692, of the English Presbyterian congregation, Leiden; succeeded his father, Robert Fleming (1630—25 July 1694) as Minister of the Scots Church, Rotterdam. From 1698 till death, Minister of the Scots Church, Founders' Hall, Lothbury; from 1702 a Salters' Hall Lecturer, in succession to Vincent Alsop [*q.v.*], resigned. Though a Scots Presbyterian, yet a pioneer (1705) in the matter of Non-subscription. He was living (1715–16) "at Homerton in Hackney." (*D. Ev.*) [12, 14]

FLINTSHIRE. [141, 148]

FLOWER, BENJAMIN (1626 ?–Aug. 1709). **P.** Born at Castle Combe, Wilts. Son of Roger Flower, B.A., ejected (1662) from the rectory of Castle Combe. From Wotton-under-Edge grammar school, admitted pensioner at Christ's Coll., Cambridge, 11 May 1646, age 19; matric. 11 July 1646. Held some post at Cardiff, Glam.; ejected, 1660; curate to his father at Castle Combe; ejected, 1662. Set up a school. The Episc. Returns, 1669, report him as preaching to "Meane ignorant people" at Castle Combe "in an Outhouse of James Organs"; also as one of the preachers to "about 200 Presbyterians" at Bradford, Wilts; also to "4 or 500" Presbyterians at Horningsham, Wilts; also to "about 200 or 300 Presbyterians Independents Anabaptists promiscuously" at Warminster, Wilts. Licensed, 30 Apr. 1672, as "Pr. Teacher in his howse in Chippenham, Wilts" (signed the thanks from Wilts Ministers). Here he was pastor till death, also of Devizes from 1693 to 10 Apr. 1709. (*C. Cp. F. P. T.*) [92, 123]

FOLEY, PHILIP (1653—20 June 1716). **P.** Of Prestwood Hall, Staff.; youngest son of Thomas Foley (2 D. 1617—1 O. 1677), of Witley Court, Worc. (*D. Na.*) [165]

FOLEY, THOMAS (*d.* 22 Jan. 1732/3). **P.** Of Witley Court, Worc.; studied at Utrecht (1691). M.P. for Stafford, 1695–1712; created 1 Jan. 1711/2, baron Foley of Kidderminster. (*Cm. D. Pe.*) [164]

FOLKES, WILLIAM, M.A. (*fl.* 1662–1690). **P.** Matric. sizar at St. Catharine's Hall, Cambridge, 1642; B.A., 1645/6; M.A., 1649. Ejected (1662) from the vicarage of All Saints, Sudbury, Suff. Retired to Wenham, Suff., where he had a small estate. The Episc. Returns, 1669, report him as one of the preachers to "2 or 300" persons in St. Mary's parish, Bury St. Edmunds. Licensed, 1 May 1672, being then of Great Cornard (about a mile from Sudbury) as "Pr. Teacher in John Clarkes howse in St Edmondsbury, & John Parish's in Sudbury." On the death of Owen Stockton (31 May 1630–31 Aug. 1680), ejected, 1662, from the town lectureship at Colchester, Ess., and subsequently preaching alternately at Ipswich and Colchester, Folkes succeeded him at Colchester, taking only £10 a year for horse hire. His disablement probably dated from the beginning of 1689, when John Meadows [*q.v.*] removed to Bury St. Edmunds, and Samuel Bury began work there in the other (*i.e.* Presbyterian) congregation. (*B. Bs. C. E. P. T. V.*) [38, 104]

FORBES, JAMES, M.A. (1630—31 May 1712). **C.** Of King's Coll., Aberdeen; M.A., 1648; incorp. at Oxford, 31 May 1654. Weekly preacher at Gloucester cathedral (Aug. 1654), where he gathered a church; ejected, 1660. A report of Jan. 1664 states that "Forbes now lives at Clapham as a Shoemaker." He suffered imprisonments. Licensed, 22 May 1672, as "Congr. Teacher in the howse of Samson Bacons in Glocester"; also Feb. 1672/3, as "Independt Teacher in the Barne of Charles Eliot of Stinchcomb," Glou. The Meeting-house in Barton Street, Gloucester, was built for him in 1699. He educated many students for the ministry, aided first by the Common Fund, afterwards by the Congregational Fund. The three students referred to (p. 47) were Thomas Willis, Josiah Hort [*q.v.*], and a son of George Seal [*q.v.*], all of whom received grants from the Common Fund in 1691. Forbes, a Calvinist of catholic temper, was a pioneer of the Happy Union (p. 155). (*C. F. Ll. Mh. P. T.*) [44, 47]

FORD, STEPHEN (*d.* 1694). **C.** Said to have studied at Oxford, but is not in Foster, and seems to have been in service to one of the heads of houses (probably Thankfull Owen, president (1650–60) of St. John's Coll.). He was ejected, 1660, from the sequestered vicarage of Chipping Norton, Oxfordsh. In the Episc. Returns, 1669, "one Ford, a servant to Thankful Owen" is reported as one of the preachers to a congregation of 100 "in Mill lane Att the malthouse of one Walker a Brewer" in the parish of St. Olave's, Southwark. Licence was issued, 2 Apr. 1672, to Stephen Ford as "a Teacher of the Congregationall way" in "A certain Howse or Roome near Miles lane [Cannon Street] London." Here he ministered till death, having in his old age Matthew Clarke (1664–1726) [*q.v.*], from May 1692, as co-pastor. (*C. P. T. W. Wc.*) [1, 3]

FORDHAM ('Foardham'). A grant of £10 a year was voted to "Soham or ffordham on condition a minister be fixed." As this was confirmed, 12 D 1692, presumably the condition was fulfilled. (*M.*) [13, 14]

FORDINGBRIDGE ('Froddingbudge'). Ejected in this neighbourhood was Richard Crossen or Crossing, of Exeter Coll., Oxford; matric., 12 Nov. 1650; B.A., 1653; Fellow, 1654–6; M.A., 1656; ord. by presbyters; held a sequestered living near Fordingbridge; ejected, 1660; in 1662, Seth Ward, bishop of Exeter, instituted him, without reordination, to the vicarages of Otterton and Kenton, Devon; *d.* 11 Jan. 1688/9. (*C. F.*) [101]

FORESTER, . . . Calamy mentions "Mr Forster" among the unbeneficed clergy, in and about London, silenced in 1662. Joseph Hussey [*q.v.*] preached at Ware on 16 June 1689 for "Mr Forster," then the settled Minister; he was succeeded in 1695 by Thomas Cotton. (*C. Uh.*) [50]

FOSTER, . . . **P.** According to Miall, he was Minister at Beverley in 1689. Richard Moulton was licensed as Pr. Teacher at Beverley in 1672; John Steere, Minister there, died in 1715. (*Ev. My. Nr. T.*) [138]

FOURNESS FELLS. [63] *See* Lancashire

FOWEY ('Fowy,' 'Fowes'; pronounced

Foy). Ejected here was John Tutchin [*q.v.*]. [18, 20]

FOWKES. *See* Folkes

FOWLER, CHRISTOPHER. **P.** Of Hackney. Elected a Manager, 9 May 1692, replacing Lucie Knightley, but never attended. As his appointment was conveyed through John Jurin [*q.v.*] he is assumed to be of the same denomination. (*M.*) [162]

FOWLER, STEPHEN, M.A. (*b.* 1625). **P.** Son of Richard Fowler of Sadbury, Glouc., pleb. Matric. at Lincoln Coll., Oxford, 10 D. 1641, aged 16; M.A., 1648/9. Held (1652) the sequestered rectory of Crick, Northants; ejected, 1662. He had lived in the neighbouring parish of Kilsby, where his sons, Stephen and Timothy, were born in 1659 and 1660. Licensed, May 1672, as "Psb" at his "now dwelling house in Killesby." Calamy, who confuses him (as others have done) with Samuel Fowler, brother to Edward Fowler, bishop of Gloucester, says he was called to Newbury, Berks, on the death of John Woodbridge (probably meaning Benjamin Woodbridge, *d.* 1 N. 1684), and died of hard study. He is not known to have left Northamptonshire. (*C. F. P. T. Wc.*) [76]

FOWLES, or FOWLE, HENRY, B.A. (*d.* 1719/20). **C.** Entered at Magdalen Hall, Oxford, 7 N. 1655; B.A., 1658. Schoolmaster in Sussex; ejected, 1662. Licensed, June 1672, as "Pr. Teacher in his howse in Arundell," Suss. In 1690 the Common Fund voted him, being at Southwick, Hants, £6 a year "on condition he continue at Peterfield"; this was paid till Midsummer 1692; shortly after this he removed to Deal, Kent, and ministered there till death. The Congregational Fund voted him a grant of £5 on 1 June 1696. (*C. Cf. F. J. M. P. T.*) [101]

FOX, TIMOTHY (1629–May 1710). **P.** Born at Birmingham. Son of Edward Foxe. From Aston grammar school admitted pensioner at Christ's Coll., Cambridge, 23 Mar. 1646/7, age 17; matric., 18 Mar. 1647/8; did not graduate. Studied under Billingsley at Birmingham. Appointed rector of Drayton, Staff., 4 F. 1650/1; ordained at Whitchurch, Shrops., by the Bradford North Classis; ejected, 1662. Removed to Derbyshire (1666) owing to the Five Mile Act, but imprisoned under it, May–Nov. 1684. Licensed, 25 May 1672, as Pr. Teacher in his house at Tickenhall, Derb. Some time after 1690 ministered regularly, gratis, to a congregation in his house at Cauldwell, Derb. He is referred to (p. 26) as "Mr Tym: Cox." On 4 May 1691 he was reported as preaching at Appleby, Leic., "one Sabbath in ye month." (*C. Cp. M. P. T.*) [25, 26, 96]

FOXTON, *i.e.* FOXON, JOHN (*d.* 26 Oct. 1723). **C.** Student at Bishop's Hall, Bethnal Green [*q.v.*], 1690; afterwards under William Paine [*q.v.*]. The Common Fund granted him, 1691–6, £5 a year for Witham; the Congregational Fund granted him (18 May 1696) £5 for perfecting his studies under Paine. Before 1703 ministered at East Bergholt, Suff., removing thence to Fareham, Hants. In 1706 succeeded Thomas Rowe [*q.v.*] at Girdlers' Hall, Basinghall Street, London, where David Jennings (afterwards D.D.) and Henry Francis were successively (from 1716) his assistants. He was a Pinners' Hall lecturer (1717) and subscriber at Salters' Hall, 1719. At that time he was living "in Bull-Hand-Court in Jewen Street." (*B. Cf. Ev. M. W.*) [4, 41, 42]

FRAMFIELD. Ejected from this vicarage was John Bushnell [? John Bushnall of Emmanuel Coll., Cambridge; matric. pensioner, 1640], a good mathematician. (*C. V.*) [112, 114]

FRAMLINGHAM ('Framlington'). Ejected here was Henry Sampson, M.D. [*q.v.*]. [103]

FRANCKLIN, ROBERT (*b.* 16 July 1630). **P.** Born in London. From the grammar school at Woodbridge, Suff., entered (1645) Jesus Coll., Cambridge; migrated to Queen's Coll; matric., 1647; did not graduate. Held (Aug. 1651) the sequestered rectory of Kirton, Suff.; later, the sequestered vicarage of Blythburgh, Suff.; finally, the sequestered vicarage of Westhall, Suff., of which he obtained legal possession (1658), but was ejected, 1662. Chaplain (1663) to Sir Samuel Barnardiston at Brightwell Hall, Suff. Imprisoned at Aylesbury, 1668; preaching to 100 persons in Blue Anchor Alley, 1669. Licensed, 11 Apr. 1672, as Presb. Teacher "in his howse in Blew Anchor Alley in White Cross Street," London. Much harassed till 1687. His Meeting-house was in Bunhill Fields. The funeral sermon for his widow is dated 1713. He was one of the authors of a very popular tract, "A Murderer Punished; and Pardoned," 1669. (*C. Cm. P. T. V.*) [166]

FRANKLAND, RICHARD, M.A. (1 N. 1630—1 O. 1698). **P.** Born at Rathmell, parish of Giggleswick, West Riding. Son of John Frankland. From Giggleswick grammar school (1640–48) admitted minor pensionary at Christ's Coll., Cambridge,

18 May 1648; B.A., 1651/2; M.A., 1655. Ordained by presbyters at Lanchester, Durh., 14 S. 1653. Chaplain to John Brook, at Ellenthorp Hall, Yorks (*see* Brookes, Lady Priscilla). Curate at Sedgfield, Durh. Designed for some post in Cromwell's Durham Coll., 1657. Vicar (1659) of Bishop Auckland, Durh.; ejected, 1662. Retired to Rathmell and there began his Academy ('Christ's College') in March 1670. Licensed, 22 July 1672, as "Pr. Teacher in his howse at Rushmilne." Under persecution, migrated with his Academy to Natland, near Kendal, Westmor. (1674); Calton Hall, parish of Kirkby Malham, in Craven, West Riding (1683); Hart Barrow, near Cartmell Fell, Lanc. (1685); Attercliffe, near Sheffield, West Riding (1686); Rathmell, 1689, till death, though still frequently prosecuted. The statement (p. 135), misplaced in North Riding, cannot be correct in regard to Frankland's residence, though it is possible that worship was still carried on at Calton Hall, the seat of the Lamberts, and that Frankland sometimes preached there. He was buried at Giggleswick. (*C. D. Kn. Nk. P. T. Y.*) [64, 65, 71, 129, 130, 133, 135, 136, 139]

FRARY. [91] *See* Somerset

FREEMAN, FRANCIS (*d.* 17 N. 1726). 𝔓. Received grants, 1691–2, as Student with Thos. Brand [*q.v.*] at Bishop's Hall, Bethnal Green, under the instruction of John Ker, M.D. [*q.v.*]. Minister at Tooting, Surrey, from 1696 till death. On 7 May 1711 the Fund voted him £1 as share of a bequest; on 3 N. 1712 a grant of £10 was made to him; repeated, 6 May 1717 and 2 D. 1717; £20 on 8 June 1719. On 3 Oct. 1720 he paid to the Fund an anonymous gift of £50. On 3 May 1725 a grant of £5 was made to him. He lived at Lower Tooting.

His son Samuel, educated under Henry Grove at Taunton with aid from the Fund, was Minister (1728–35) at Horley, Surrey. (*Ev. M. We.*) [4]

FRENCH, SAMUEL (*d.* 20 Aug. 1694). Son of a clergyman. Matric. at Christ Church, Oxford, 18 O. 1654. Vicar of Town Malling, Kent; ejected, 1662. Licensed, 1 July 1672, as "Pr. Teacher in the howse of Rich: Sighurst in Town Mallin." Imprisoned at Maidstone, 1684, under the Five Mile Act, and visited in gaol by friends from Staplehurst, to whom he became Minister till death. The Common Fund grant (1691) of £4 a year to Staplehurst was continued after his death. (*C. F. M. P. T.*) [55, 57]

FRIENDS, SOCIETY OF. [42, 152, 153]

FRIMLEY ('Frimly'). [110]

FRODDINGBUDGE. [101] *See* Hampshire

FRODSHAM. [15]

FROME ('Froom') SELWOOD. Ejected here in 1662 was John Humfrey (Jan. 1621–1719), son of William, of St. Albans; of Pembroke Coll., Oxford; matric., 22 Mar. 1638/9; B.A., 1641; M.A., 1647; ord. by presbyters, 1649; vicar of Frome Selwood, 1656; reordained, episcopally, without subscription, 1660, but renounced this ordination and destroyed the certificates [? licensed, June 1672, being of Kingsbury, Som., as Grāll Pr.; his house at Kingsbury licensed, 30 Sept. 1672]; came to London, and gathered a Congregational church, which met in Duke's Place (1700) and ultimately in Petticoat Lane; in controversy no party man, but an inveterate pamphleteer; survived all the Ejected except Nathan Denton, B.A. [*q.v.*]. (*C. D. F. T.*) [92]

FROYSIER, or FROYSELL, JEREMIAH (*fl.* 1672–91). 𝔓. [Richard Steel, in address prefixed to posthumous sermons, 1678, by Thomas Froysell, M.A. (1610 ?–1672 ?), ejected from the vicarage of Clun, Shrops., says he left six children, but gives no further particulars.] Licensed, 5 S. 1672, being of Garston, Herts, as "Pr. Teacher"; also, 30 S. 1672, as "Pr. Teacher at the house of John March," Garston, Herts. This is John Marsh (*d.* Sept. 1681), whose estate of Garston is near Watford. (*T. Uh.*) [85]

FULLER ('Tuller'), FRANCIS, M.A. (1637—21 July 1701). 𝔓. Younger son of John Fuller, vicar of Stebbing, Ess., and ejected (1660) from the sequestered rectory of St. Martin's, Pomeroy, Ironmonger Lane, London. Matric. pensioner at Queen's Coll., Cambridge, 1653; B.A. at Pembroke Coll., 1656; M.A. at Queen's, 1660/1; incorp. at Oxford, 14 July 1663. Curate at Warkworth, Northants; resigned as Nonconformist. Alternated between London and the West of England. Licensed, 30 S., also, 28 Oct., 1672, being of Bristol, as "genall Pr. Teacher." Died in London. (*C. F. P. T. V.*) [47]

FUND CONTRIBUTORS. [163 *sqq.*]

FUND MANAGERS. [160 *sqq.*]

FUND MEETINGS. [163]

FUND TREASURERS. [162]

FURNESS FELLS. [63]

FYLDE COUNTRY is the Western part of the hundred of Amounderness; the Common Fund granted (1691) £12 a year for work here; reduced (1695) to £10. (*M.*) [63]

G., S. I. *See* Peach, Richard

GAINSBOROUGH ('Gainsbrough'). [70, 71]

GALE, THEOPHILUS, M.A. (1628–1677/8). ℭ. Born at Kingsteinton, Devon; son of the vicar, Theophilus Gale, D.D. Entered a commoner at Magdalen Hall, Oxford, 1647; demy of Magdalen Coll., 1648–50; B.A., 1649; Fellow, 1650; M.A., 1652; incorp. at Cambridge, 1656; preacher at Winchester Cathedral, 1657; ejected from this and Fellowship, 1660. Tutor (1660–66) to sons of Philip, fourth Baron Wharton, at Quainton, Bucks, and Caen, Normandy. In 1666 opened an Academy at Newington Green, acting also as assistant and eventually successor to John Rowe (1626—12 O. 1677), whose congregation met in St. Andrew's parish, Holborn. His great work, "The Court of the Gentiles" (1669–78), traces all European languages to Hebrew, and the entire culture of pagan antiquity to Hebrew tradition. (*C. D. F. P. W.*) [188]

GALLINGTON. [92] *See* Somerset

GALPINE, JOHN, B.A. (*d.* 2 Sept. 1698). 𝔓. Matric. 'pleb.' at Exeter Coll., Oxford, 25 July 1655; rem. to New Inn Hall; B.A., 1658. He was the fourth holder in succession of the sequestered vicarage of Yarcombe, Devon; ejected, 1660; served the chapelry of Ashpriors, Som.; ejected, 1662. The Episc. Returns, 1669, report him as one of the preachers to 42 persons "At the houses of William Doble, Thomas Proctor als Matthewes, Robert Hucker & John Slape" in Thurlbear, Som.; also as one of the preachers to 60 persons "At the houses of Robert Selleck & Skinner" in Lydeard St. Lawrence, Som.; also as one of the preachers to 400 persons at eleven houses in West Monkton, Som.; also as one of the preachers to an uncertain number "At the house of one Harnham" in Oake, Som.; also as one of the preachers to 200 persons "At the houses of Henry Henly Esq^r & John Bennett" in Winsham, Som.; also to 20 persons at Stoke St. Mary, Som., in the houses of the same persons as at Thurlbear, above; also as one of two preachers to 60 persons "At the houses of M^r Edward Blake & M^r Edward Brampton" in Dunster, Som.; also as sole preacher to an uncertain number "At the hoase of George Skinner" in Brompton-Ralph, Som.; also as one of the preachers to an uncertain number at six houses in Bicknoller and Stogumber, Som.; also as one of the preachers to 80 persons "At the houses of Joseph Stocker and John Day" in Wiveliscombe, Som.; also as sole preacher to an uncertain number "At the house of Elizabeth Burnoll" in Harford, Som.; also as one of two preachers to 40 persons "At the houses of Lancellott Ceely and John Musgrove" in Holford, Som.; also as one of the preachers to 260 persons at eight houses in Bridgwater, Som.; lastly as one of the preachers to 90 persons at four houses in North Petherton, Som.; this long list testifies to nothing out of the common on the preacher's part, but only to the vigilance of informers. Licensed, 20 Apr. 1672, as "Presb. Teacher in the howse of Rob: Sellerke in the Parish of Laurence Liddiard, Somerset." In 1689 he settled at Totnes, and there died. (*Em. F. P. T. Wc.*) [31, 33]

GALPINE, JOHN, *secundus* (*d.* 24 Nov. 1712). 𝔓. (*Em.*) [31, 33]

GARDNER, JOHN (*b.* 1624). 𝔓. Born in Somerset. Son of John Gardner. Matric. at New Inn Hall, Oxford, 9 July 1641, aged 17. Held (after 1653) the sequestered rectory of Staplegrove, Som.; ejected, 1662. The Episc. Returns, 1669, report him as one of the preachers to 400 persons at West Monkton, Wellington, and Buckland, Som.; also to 60 persons "At the houses of John Gardner & George Bindon" in Staplegrove; also to many persons at Oake, Som.; also to 260 persons at various houses in Bridgwater, Som. Licensed, 19 Apr. 1672, being of Bridgwater, as "Pr. Teacher in any licensed place." He was pastor at Bridgwater, 1676–9. His connection with Yeovil is a new fact. (*C. F. Mh. P. T. Wc.*) [91, 93]

GARDNER, JOHN. [165]

GATCHELL, EDWARD (*fl.* 1672–1690). 𝔅. Two licences, without date of issue, but evidently belonging to 30 S. 1672, run thus: "The house of Edw^d Gatchell of Pitminster Som^rset Pr. Licence to y^e said Gatchell to Teach att his house abovesd^d Anab:^t" (*T.*) [92, 93, 94, 189]

GAYLARD, ROBERT, B.A. (*d.* 14 Feb. 1697). 𝔓. Matric. at St. John's Coll., Oxford, 27 F. 1650/1; B.A., 1653. Held the perpetual curacy of Ide (pron. Ede), Devon; ejected, 1662. Retired to Exeter. Signed the thanks of Devon Ministers, 22 Mar. 1672. Licensed, 11 Apr. 1672, being of Exeter, as "a Grāll Pr. Teacher." Minister of Bow Meeting, Exeter, in conjunction with Robert Atkins [*q.v.*] and John Hoppin [*q.v.*]. (*C. Em. F. Mh. P. T.*) [30]

GEDDINGTON. Ejected from this vicarage was Thomas Elborowe, who afterwards conformed. Son of John Elborowe, farmer, of Haselbeech, Northants; from Peterborough school entered St. John's Coll., Cambridge; matric. sizar, 30 Apr. 1639, age nearly 17; B.A., 1642/3; *d.* 15 Apr. 1675. (*C. Jo. V.*) [76, 77]

GEDNEY ('Gedley'). [71]

GENEVA. [50]

GIDLEIGH ('Cudleigh'). [32]

GIDLY, *i.e.* GIDLEIGH, JOHN, M.A. (*d.* Sept. 1711). 𝔓. Matric. at Exeter Coll., Oxford, 'gent.', 17 Mar. 1653/4; B.A., 1657; M.A., 1660. Episcopally ordained. Lived on his estate at Exeter, and occasionally preached; silenced, 1662. Licensed, 20 Apr. 1672, being of Exeter, as "Presb. Teacher in any licensed place." Settled eventually at Great Marlow, Bucks, and there died. He received Fund grants of £4 a year for Great Marlow, 1703–9. (*C. Em. F. P. T.*) [38]

GILBERT, THOMAS, B.D. (1613—15 July 1694). ℭ. Son of William Gilbert, of Prees, Shropsh., pleb. Matric. at St. Edmund Hall, Oxford, 13 N. 1629, aged 16; B.A., 1633; M.A., 1638; B.D., 1648; Chaplain of Magdalen Coll., 1656–1660. Vicar of Nash, Monm., 1635; vicar of St. Lawrence, Reading, 1647–50; vicar of Over Winchendon, Bucks, and rector of Edgmond, Shrops., 1649; ejected from Edgmond, 1660, from Winchendon, 1662. He published a tract, 'Vindiciae supremi Dei Dominii,' 1655, dedicated to Cromwell, in which, though a strong Calvinist, he maintained against John Owen, D.D. [*q.v.*], that pardon is possible without a satisfaction; he also held that all sins, past, present, and to come, were pardoned at once (posthumous tract of 1695, which had been approved by Owen). The Episc. Returns, 1669, report him as one of several preachers to 80 persons at Whitchurch, Shrops. Retiring to Oxford, he was licensed, 30 Apr. 1672, as a general Congr. Teacher. In 1687 he opened a Meeting-house in St. Peter's parish. On 10 Nov. 1690 he received £3 from an anonymous donation of £50 through Matthew Rapier [*q.v.*]. The Common Fund granted him (1690–93) £8 a year. In 1691–92 (when Calamy enjoyed his society at Oxford) he attended alternately at the Anglican and Presbyterian services. He was famed as a writer of epitaphs, including those for Thomas Goodwin, D.D. [*q.v.*], and John Owen, D.D. (*C. Cm. D. F. M. P. Sm. T.*) [7, 85]

GILL, CAPTAIN, *i.e.* COLONEL JOHN GILL of Carhouse, near Rotherham, a friend of Oliver Heywood [*q.v.*], who often mentions him in his diaries from 1678. In 1692 he was High Sheriff of Yorkshire. Heywood waited on him at the York Assizes in March of that year. (*Dy. Hh. Ht.*) [130]

GILL, JEREMIAH (1668–Jan. 1708/9). ℭ. Entered Frankland's Academy, 10 Jan. 1686/7. Lived (1689–97) with Timothy Jollie [*q.v.*] as his pupil and, subsequently, assistant. On 23 Feb. 1690/1 the Fund awarded him a 'gift' of £5 "if he give himself to the ministry." On 4 May 1691 he was certificated as having finished his course of studies. In 1691 he was preaching at Pontefract. In 1697 he became Minister of the Hull congregation afterwards meeting in Dagger Lane. In 1698 he was ordained, and a new Meeting-house built. Being in bad health, he went for change of air to York, and there died, about 23 Jan. 1708/9, aged 40 years.

His son, Jeremiah (*d.* 1758), educated under Timothy Jollie [*q.v.*], was Minister at Fulwood, West Riding. His grandson, Jeremiah (*d.* 1796), was Minister at Gainsborough, Linc. (*Fr. Ht. M. Ma. My. Nk. Nr. Ps. Wm.*) [133]

GILL, JOSEPH (*fl.* 1672–1694). ℭ. Licensed, 25 July 1672, being "of Stockton upon Tine," *i.e.* Tees, Northumb., as "Grāll Congr. Teacher." He had ceased to be assistant to Richard Gilpin [*q.v.*] by 1694 (*see* Pell, William). (*T.*) [79]

GILL, WIDOW. [133]

GILLING, ISAAC (1662—20-21 Aug. 1725). 𝔓. Born at Stogumber, Som.; elder son of Richard Gilling, baker. Educ. in the Academy at Taunton of George Hammond, M.A.; ejected from the rectories of Holy Trinity and St. Peter's, Dorchester. Ordained, 25 Aug. 1687, at Lyme, Dors., being then curate of Barrington with St. Mary's, Seavington, Som. Ceasing to conform, he became usher in Axminster grammar school, and preacher to Congregationals; thereafter pastor of the Presbyterian congregation at Silverton, Devon; and finally of that at Newton Abbot (or Newton Bushel) in Wolborough parish, Devon, in succession to William Yeo, M.A. [*q.v.*]. Gilling was scribe of the Exeter Assembly till 1718; a nonsubscriber in 1719, he was excluded from the Assembly and deserted by the majority of his flock. (*D. Ev.*) [94]

GILPIN, RICHARD, M.D. (1625—13 F. 1699/1700). 𝔓. Born at Strickland-Kettle, parish of Kendal, Westm.; baptized, 23 Oct. 1625. Second son of

Isaac Gilpin. Educ. at Edinburgh university; M.A., 30 July 1646. After preaching at Lambeth; as assistant to John Wilkins (afterwards bishop of Chester) at the Savoy; and at Durham Cathedral; he obtained (1652) the sequestered rectory of Greystoke, Cumb., and organised his parish on the Congregational model, though he would have preferred the Presbyterian (not adopted in Cumberland). In Aug. 1653 he was a founder of the voluntary association of Cumberland and Westmorland Ministers. Cromwell appointed him visitor to his projected college at Durham (1657). At the Restoration he declined the See of Carlisle, resigned Greystoke (2 F. 1660/1), and retired to his manor of Scaleby Castle, Cumb., preaching in the large hall. In 1662 he removed to Newcastle-on-Tyne, where the Episc. Returns, 1669, report him as one of "four Ringleaders & Speakers." Licence was made out, 16 Apr. 1672, for him as "Presb. Teacher in a Place called the Moothall in Castle garth, Newcastle," but this was "not approved nor given out"; but licence was given him, 13 May 1672, under the name of 'John Gilpin,' as "Pr. Grall Teacher." His house, Scaleby Castle, was licensed 5 Sept. 1672. He graduated M.D. at Leiden, 6 July 1676, and had much repute as a physician, in addition to his fame as a preacher at Newcastle, till death. (*C. D. N. P. T. Wc.*) [22, 79]

GILSBOROW. [78] *See* Northamptonshire

GILSON, DANIEL (1657 ?–8 F. 1727/8). **P.** Son of Thomas Gilson (*see* Barking). First Minister at St. Helen's Lane, Colchester. (*E.*) [38]

GLAMORGANSHIRE. [143, 144, 145, 146]

GLANVILL, JOHN, B.A. (1630 or 1631–1693 ?). John Glanvill, aged 16, son of John Glanvill of Honiton, Devon, gent., and John Glanvill, aged 15, son of Richard Glanvill, of Honiton, Devon, gent., matric. together at Exeter Coll., Oxford, 16 D. 1646; B.A., together, 15 June 1650. One of these two was curate at St. James', Taunton; ejected, 1662. The Episc. Returns, 1669, report him as one of the preachers to 42 persons at Thrulbere, Som.; also to 400 persons at various houses in West Munkton, Som., and places adjacent; also to 120 persons in St. James's parish, Taunton, Som.; also to 20 persons at Stoke St. Mary, Som. Licensed, 20 Apr. 1672, as "Presb. Teacher in his howse," St. James's parish, Taunton. Here he continued to preach till death. (*C. F. P. T.*) [92]

GLASCOCK, FRANCIS (*d.* 1706 ?). **P.** Read lectures privately to some of Charles Morton's former pupils, after 1685. Minister at Drury Lane, Westminster. Attended as a Manager of the reconstituted Fund on 7 D. 1702. Chosen, 1705, a lecturer at Pinners' Hall, though a Presbyterian, in succession to Thomas Rowe. In 1706 Glascock was succeeded by John Collins, *secundus* (*see* Collins, John, M.A.). After his death, Robert Trail, M.A. [*q.v.*], published, "Some Propositions Concerning The Two Covenants: Whether the Gospel be a New Law; and Repentance be a Condition of Justification. By the late . . . Francis Glascock," 1708. This is against the positions of Daniel Williams, D.D. [*q.v.*]. Trail, in his Preface (8 Apr. 1708), emphasises the fact that "Mr Glascock was a Presbyterian." (*M. W.*) [2]

GLASGOW ('Glasco'). [49, 182]

GLASTONBURY. Ejected here was Samuel Winney [*q.v.*]. [94]

[? GLE]DDALL, *i.e.* probably GLEDHILL, JOHN (1661—10 Dec. 1727). **C.** Born at Norland, parish of Halifax, Yorks. Entered Frankland's Academy, 1 O. 1679. Preacher at Moorfield, Yorks. Member of the Congregational church at Topcliffe, W.R., 1691. Minister at Moor Lane, Colchester, from Dec. 1693 (dismissed from Topcliffe to this charge, 15 July 1694) till death. Died at Colchester. (*Fr. Fun. Serm. by John Barker,* 1728; *My.*) [2]

GLEMSFORD ('Glensford'). [107]

GLOUCESTER ('Glocester'). Ejected here was James Forbes, M.A. [*q.v.*]. Calamy inserts here Increase Mather, D.D. (1639—23 Aug. 1723), though admitting that he was not one of the ejected; he left Gloucester before the Restoration; it was in Guernsey that, refusing to conform, he declined a benefice, and returned to New England. (*C. D.*) [44, 45, 124]

GLOUCESTERSHIRE. [44, 45, 47, 145, 155, 168, 176, 181] Only the headings "Gloucester" are in the earliest handwriting; the remainder in that of the Book-keeper. The returns are numbered from 59 to 147 (most of them 61) and 45 in 1691.

Beeslie or Bizly is Bisley [*q.v.*].

Burton, or Burton on the water, is Bourton on the Water [*q.v.*].

Cambden is Chipping Campden.

Cleave or Cleeve is Bishops Cleeve.

Colford is Coleford.

Cos Pawn is Colesbourne.

Elverton is Elberton [*q.v.*].

Ranger is Rangeworth.

Tuexbery is Tewkesbury [*q.v.*].

Wooton under hedge is Wotton under Edge [*q.v.*].

GODALMING. [109, 110]

GODMAN, HENRY, B.A. (1630—29 Jan. 1702/3). C. Born at Lewes, Suss. From Merchant Taylors' School, London, admitted pensioner at Peterhouse, Cambridge, 17 Apr. 1647, aged 17; B.A., 1650/1. Held the sequestered rectory of Rodmell, Suss.; ejected, 1660, though the former rector, Thomas Crundy, died in 1651. Lived in London; preached at South Malling, Lewes, 29 May 1670, when his hearers were heavily fined. Licensed, 2 Apr. 1672, as "Teacher of the Congregationall way in Upper Deptford." Licence was also granted, 19 Apr. 1672, for the house of John Savage on London Bridge as a "Congregationall Meeting place"; the application for this had mentioned Godman as the preacher. He died in charge at Deptford, having been pastor there for 29 years. (*C. Lh. P. Ph. T. V. We.*) [55, 187]

GOLDHAM, THOMAS, M.A. (*fl.* 1640–1690). P. Matric. at Emmanuel Coll., Cambridge, 1640; B.A., 1643/4; M.A., 1647. Ejected from the vicarage of Burwash, Suss. Licensed, 30 Apr. 1672, as "Pr. Teacher in his howse at Burwash." He died before 1715. (*C. Ev. P. T. V.*) [113]

GOMERSAL ('Gummersball'). Then a township in Birstall parish, now vicarage. [130]

GOODCHILD, JOHN (*d.* 1711?). C. The Common Fund voted him (26 June 1693), as a Student under John Langston [*q.v.*], £8 a year "when the Fund can bear it." In 1704; being then, with his wife and three sisters, among those attending the Congregational church at Green Yard, Ipswich, he was invited to the pastorate of the Congregational church, Yarmouth, but declined as "neither fit nor willing." His wife was a widow before March 1711, when she became a member of the Ipswich church. (*B. M.*) [108, 172]

GOODWIN, JOHN, M.A. (1594–1665). C. Born in Norfolk. Matric. sizar at Queen's Coll., Cambridge, 1612; B.A., 1615/6; Fellow, 1617; M.A., 1619. After preaching in various places, came to London, 1632, and became vicar (1633) of St. Stephen's, Coleman Street. He now inclined to Congregationalism, was practically an Arminian, and soon a republican. Ejected, 1645, he set up a Congregational church in Coleman Street, regaining the use of the church, 1649–57; yet in 1654 he is returned as holding the rectory of East Barnet. (*La.*) Thomas Firmin (June 1632—20 D. 1697), the philanthropic Unitarian, was one of his hearers, and took down his sermons in shorthand. He translated (1648) part of the "Stratagemata Satanae" of the broadly tolerant Acontius, but went beyond him, maintaining that error in fundamentals may be innocent, and would have men "call more for light and less for fire from heaven." Even denial of the Trinity he will not treat as "damnable heresy," for orthodoxy is a doctrine of inference. Obtaining indemnity at the Restoration, he kept up his Coleman Street flock. After 1662 he fled to Leigh, Ess. (see his letters to his wife, Sarah, in S.P. Dom., 1663, 1664), and died (in Essex?) during the plague year; buried in London on 3 Sept. He was an indefatigable writer. (*Cc. D. V.*) [188]

GOODWIN, THOMAS, D.D. (5 O. 1600–23 F. 1679/80). C. Born at Rollesby, Norf. Entered Christ's Coll., Cambridge, 25 Aug. 1613; matric. pensioner, 1614; B.A., 1616; removed to Catherine Hall, 1619; M.A., 1620; Fellow; B.D., 1630. Lecturer at Trinity Church, Cambridge, 1628; vicar, 1632. On becoming Congregational, resigned, 1634, and removed to London. Fled to Holland, 1639, and became pastor of the English church at Arnheim. Returning (1640) to London, he gathered a church in the parish of St. Dunstan's-in-the-East. Covenanted member of the Westminster Assembly, 1643, and a leader of the Dissenting Brethren. Had a gathered church at St. Michael's, Crooked Lane (1648), but the Fourth Presb. Classis would not permit him to celebrate the Lord's Supper there. Chaplain to the Council of State, 1649. President of Magdalen Coll., Oxford, 1650 (where also he had a gathered church; *see* Howe, John), and D.D., 1653. One of the leaders at the Savoy Conference (1658) when the Westminster Confession was revised on Congregational principles. Fellow of Eton College, 1658/9. Ejected, 18 May 1660. Formed in London the Congregational church, afterwards removed to Fetter Lane. Licensed, 2 Apr. 1672, "to be a Teacher of the Congregationall way in his owne howse in Cripplegate parish." From his habit of wearing two double skull-caps, he was lampooned as "Dr Nine-caps." He "prayed with his hatt on and sitting." Buried in Bunhill Fields, with epitaph by Thomas Gilbert [*q.v.*]. (*D. F. Fc. Rr. Sw. T. V. W.*) [188]

GOODWIN, THOMAS, *secundus* (1650 ?–1716 ?). 𝕮. Son of Thomas Goodwin, D.D. [*q.v.*]. Educated in England and Holland. Evening lecturer (1678) at a coffee-house in Exchange Alley, London. Travelled in Europe (1683–July 1684), and then became colleague to Stephen Lobb [*q.v.*] at Fetter Lane. Minister after Lobb's death (1699) at Pinner, Midx., where he had an estate, and maintained an Academy for training Ministers. Strongly against Daniel Williams [*q.v.*] in the Crispian controversy. (*D. We.*) [72]

GORWOOD, JOHN (*d.* 1720). Born in Yorkshire. Entered Frankland's Academy, 3 June 1688. The Fund granted him (2 Mar. 1690/1) a 'gift' of £4 "for one halfe yeare." He had grants of £10 (1691–2) as a Student in Scotland, and in 1693 "for necessities." During his ministry he had a £5 grant (1706/7), "being very infirm" (? at Revesby, Lincs); a £10 grant (1711), being "lately minister of Boston" and "very distressed"; also, in 1713/4, at Hull. In 1715 he is reported disabled; a grant of £10 was made him (1718/9) in an illness from which he made no recovery. He was "of Hull, a Min^r" when he died, and his burial was on 2 or 3 May 1720. (*Fr. Ht. M. Nk. Nr.*) [136]

GOSPORT. [100]

GOUDHURST ('Goudherst'). Ejected here was Edward Bright [? of Clare Hall, Cambridge; matric. pensioner, 1617; B.A., 1620/1; M.A., 1624]; vicar of Goudhurst, 1639; ejected, 1662; described as a silkman at the Golden Fleece, Lombard Street, 1669; preaching at Goudhurst and Marden, Kent, in 1669; persons who knew his wife's gift of tongue were of opinion "that it fell out very well, that he was pretty thick of hearing." (*C. K. T. V.*) [55, 56]

GOUGE, ROBERT (1631 ?–Oct. 1705). 𝕮. Born at Great Yarmouth, Norf.; son of Robert Gooch. From Bungay grammar school, Suff., admitted minor pensionary at Christ's Coll., Cambridge, 11 Mar. 1646/7, in 17th year. Master of the grammar school and preacher at one of the churches in Maldon, Ess. Rector, 1652, of St. Helen's, Ipswich, where he had a gathered church; ejected, 1662. Continued in Ipswich till he succeeded John Sames (*d.* Dec. 1672) as pastor at Coggeshall, Ess. The Fund Minutes report him (2 N. 1691) as having £50 a year and some estate. Hence an allowance of £5 a year formerly made to him by Matthew Barker [*q.v.*] was discontinued. Calamy says "a decay of his Intellectuals through Age gave him his *Quietus*."

His son, Thomas (1665?–8 Jan. 1700/1), of Amsterdam and London, a famous preacher, was chosen a Pinners' Hall lecturer in place of Daniel Williams, excluded 1694. (*C. D. M. P.*) [39]

GOUGH, WILLIAM, B.A. (1627 ?–1693 ?). 𝕻. Eldest son of Edward Gough, rector of Great Cheverell, Wilts. Matric. at Queens' Coll., Cambridge, 1645/6: B.A., 1647/8. Taught school and preached without benefice at Warminster, Wilts; rector of Inkpen, Berks; ejected, 1662. Removed in 1666 to Earlstoke, Wilts, and lived there till two years before his death. Licensed, 13 May 1672, as "Pr. Teacher in his own howse in Stoke, Wilts," *i.e.* Earl Stoke, between Warminster and Devizes. Signed the thanks from Wilts Ministers. Declined, on Protestant grounds, to present Address of thanks to James II. at Bath in 1687. Pastor both at Devizes and at Brook in Westbury parish, Wilts, and lecturer in turn at Salisbury. Succeeded Matthew Pemberton [*q.v.*] as pastor at Marlborough, Wilts. He was aged 66 at death.

His son, Strickland Gough (*d.* 1718), assistant Minister at Lewin's Mead, Bristol, 1699–1708, and after dismissal thence, assistant Minister at Tucker Street, Bristol, 1710–17, was father of Strickland Gough (*secundus*), author of "An Enquiry into the Causes of the Decay of the Dissenting Interest," 1730, who conformed soon after, and was living in 1751. (*C. Ci. D. Mh. P. T.*) [92, 123]

GOULD, JOHN. 𝕮. Probably son of Madam Gould [*q.v.*]. [166]

GOULD, MADAM. 𝕮. Widow of John Gould, Esq. (1616–1679), of Clapham, Surrey (one of the Agents for obtaining Indulgences in 1672), whose former wife, Honoria, died in 1661. (*Ly. Pr. T.*) [2]

GRACE, EDWARD (*d.* 1714 ?). 𝕮. Minister at Clapham, 1690 ?–1714 ? Moses Lowman (1680—3 May 1752) was his assistant from 1710, and ordained pastor in 1714. Manager (1696) of the Congregational Fund. (*Cf. Ev. We.*) [165]

GRACE, *i.e.* GREW, OBADIAH, D.D. (1 N. 1607—22 O. 1689). 𝕻. Born at Atherstone, Warw.; third son of Francis Grew, a layman of good estate. From tuition under an uncle at Reading, he entered Balliol Coll., Oxford, 1624; B.A., 1628/9; M.A., 1632 (1635 ?); B.D. and D.D., 1651. Master of Atherstone grammar school, 1632; vicar of St. Michael's, Coventry, 1642; member of the Kenilworth Classis; ejected, 1662. He was strongly against the execution of Charles I. He resumed his ministry at Coventry in 1665, was driven away (1666) by the Five Mile Act; yet the Episc. Returns, 1669, report a conventicle at Coventry held by him and others. Licensed, 30 Apr. 1672, as "Pr. Teacher in the howses of Edmund Kirton, John Basnet & Thomas Jessen in Coventry." From this time he maintained his ministry (with gaps due to imprisonment) till his death. The Leather Hall (St. Nicholas' Hall, West Orchard) was fitted up as a Meeting-house for him in 1687. He married (1637) the widowed mother of Henry Sampson, M.D. [*q.v.*]. (*Bt. C. D. F. Hn. P. Si. T.*) [117, 118, 119, 179]

GRACE, WILLIAM, M.A. (*d.* 1699). P. Matric. sizar at Clare Hall, Cambridge, 1627; B.A., 1629/30; M.A., 1633. [?Held (after 1644) the sequestered rectory of Rearsby, Leic.] Vicar of Shenston, Staff.; ejected, 1662. He took a farm in Staffordshire, but was compelled by the Five Mile Act to leave it in 1666. [?The Episc. Returns, 1669, report him as preaching to "about 20 Presbyterians" at Rearsby.] Licensed, 10 June 1672, as "Pr. Teacher" at "the howse of John Panell in Rugely," Staff. It seems probable that the Rearsby rector and the Shenston vicar were father and son. Both were nearly related to Archbishop Sheldon, who ultimately took care of two of the rector's children. The Common Fund granted (1690) £5 a year to Grace at Shenston, continued to Sept. 1699. (*C. M. P. T. V. Wc.*) [96, 97]

GRACECHURCH STREET. Stow calls it Grassestreete, Strype calls it Grass Church Street. These names come from the parish church of St. Benet (demolished 1867) "called Grasse Church," says Stow, "of the Herbe market there kept"—an unlikely story, since the church in 1181–1204 appears as St. Benedict de Garcherche, and the market was not a herb-market, but from the time of Edward I. was the City corn-market, also for cheese and malt. The street was often called Gracious Street, especially by Quakers. (George Fox died in White Hart Court, on the west side, near the top.) The adaptation, Gracechurch Street, has survived as its modern name. (*Lo. Sl. St.*) [2]

GRACEDIEU, BARTHOLOMEW. C. Member of the congregation of Matthew Mead [*q.v.*]. Attended as Manager of the Common Fund, 20 Oct. 1690; last attendance, 2 Jan. 1692/3; his subscription was in arrear at Midsummer, 1693. Manager (1695) of the Congregational Fund. (*Cf. Co. M.*) [162, 166]

GRANSDEN, LITTLE. [13]

GRANTHAM ('Grantam'). Ejected here were (1) John Starkey, M.A. [*q.v.*]; (2) Henry Vaughan, M.A. [? of Wadham Coll. Oxford; M.A., 6 July 1652]; vicar of Grantham; ejected, 1662; licensed, 8 May 1672, being of Spitalfields, as Grāll Pr. Teacher; went twice to the Bermudas, and there died. (*C. F. T.*) [71]

GRANTS to Ministers [175-9]; to Congregations [179-80]; to Students [180-83]

GRAY'S INN LANE ran in a north-westerly direction from Holborn to the Hampstead Road. Its lower portion, from Holborn to Euston Road, is now known as Gray's Inn Road. (*Lo. Sl.*) [3]

GREEK. [182]

GREEN, *i.e.* GREENE, ALEXANDER, M.A. Matric. at Pembroke Hall (now College), Cambridge, 1646; B.A., 1647/8; Fellow; M.A., 1651. (*C. P. V.*) [51]

GREEN, JOHN, B.A. (1629?–17 Feb. 1709/10). C. Born at Cambridge. Son of John Greene. From a Cambridge school admitted sizar at Christ's Coll., Cambridge, 6 Jan. 1646/7, aet. 17; B.A., 1650/1. John Green, 'Scoller,' was admitted as member of the Congregational church, Yarmouth, on 4 O. 1655; becoming vicar of Tunstead, Norf., he was dismissed, 26 Apr. 1659, to the Congregational church in that parish; ejected (1660?). The Episc. Returns, 1669, report him as preaching at Tunstead "Att one Christopher Applebyes"; also as one of the preachers to "40 or 50 Presbyterians & Independ[ts] Att the house of Robert Wright & sometimes of John Gogle" at Trunch, Norf.; also as one of the preachers "all laymen," to "sometimes 60 sometimes 100 Independents Att the house of Jeoffery Dallison" at Fritton, Norf. Licensed, 10 May 1672, as Teacher "in the house of William Newson in Dickleburgh County Norfolke, Congregationall"; also, 10 June 1672, as "Congr. Teacher in Edm. Bells howse at Dilham, Norf."; also, 9 D. 1672, as "Congr̄. Teach[r] at his owne house in Tunstead." His church book begins (1680) with seven members. From 1697 to 1707 he preached both at Tunstead and at Bradfield, Norf. Residing latterly at North Walsham, Norf., he preached only at Bradfield. (*B. Cp. T. V.*) [72]

GREEN DRAGON COURT. [1] *See* Cow Lane

GREENSTEAD, EAST. [112] *See* Sussex

GREENWOD, TYM: *i.e.* GREENWOOD,

TIMOTHY (*fl.* 1690-1749). **P.** Minister at Duffield, Derb., 1703-49, receiving from the Fund £8 a year; reduced to £6 from 1723, when the main duty seems to have fallen on Richard Rogerson, his colleague, and latterly on Samuel Statham, his successor. (*Ev. M.*) [127]

GREENWOOD, DANIEL (*fl.* 1690-1736). **P.** Educ. under John Woodhouse [*q.v.*]. His lecture at Wolverhampton is not otherwise known. Minister at Stamford, Lincs, 1697-1701, with yearly grant of £6 from the Fund; at the Old Meeting House, Birmingham, 1702-1730; colleague there to William Turton [*q.v.*], and also preaching at West Bromwich, Staff., for which he received from the Fund £5 a year, 1713-15; on Turton's death he became responsible also for Oldbury, Staff., receiving from the Fund for it, from 1723, £5 a year, which he shared, 1723-32, with his assistant, Edward Brodhurst (1691—21 July 1730), who had been his successor at Stamford, and was "in needy Circumstances." It is curious that though Brodhurst died in 1730 (he was buried at St. Philip's, Birmingham, on 24 July 1730), his name is given in the Minutes as sharing the Fund grant with Greenwood till 1732. In 1732 Daniel Mattock (who had also begun his ministry at Stamford) became sole Minister at the Old Meeting House, Birmingham, and Greenwood sole Minister at Oldbury till 1736. (*Bh. Ev. M. N. To. Wb.*) [77, 99]

GREW, JONATHAN, M.A. (1626-1711). **P.** Born at Atherstone, Warw.; eldest son of Jonathan Grew (*d.* 1646), eldest son of Francis Grew (*see* Grace). Matric. sizar, at Pembroke Hall, Cambridge, 1646; B.A., 1649/50; M.A., 1655. Curate to his uncle's stepson, Henry Sampson [*q.v.*], at Framlingham, Suff.; ejected, 1660. Tutor in the family of Lady Hales, first at Coventry, afterwards at Caldecote Hall, Warw. Bishop Hacket offered him (1662) a prebend at Lichfield and the rectory of Caldecote. He kept school at Newington Green. He began work at St. Albans (perhaps serving it at first from London) much earlier than Urwick supposed. The Meeting-house in Dagnal Lane was built in 1697, and Grew ministered in it till death. On 8 Jan. 1710/1 the Fund voted him a grant of £7, to which Benjamin Grosvenor added £3. He was buried in the Abbey, close by the shrine of St. Alban. (*C. D. P. Uk. V.*) [50]

GREW, OBADIAH. *See* Grace

GRIFFITH, GEORGE, M.A. (1619-1691). **C.** Born in Montgomerysh. Was in service before entering at Magdalen Hall, Oxford; matric., 2 Nov. 1638, aged 19; B.A., 1642. Removed to Emmanuel Coll., Cambridge; M.A., 1645. Appointed, 6 June 1648, in the place of the ejected preacher at the Charter House, London. Held also a week-day lecture at St. Bartholomew's-by-the-Exchange. Appointed, 20 March 1654, one of Cromwell's "triers." He was scribe to the conference of Congregational Ministers at the Savoy (Oct. 1658) to revise the Westminster Confession in their sense. Ejected, 1660. Signed the declaration, Jan. 1661, against the Fifth-monarchy rising under Thomas Venner. Preached at various places in London, 1663-64. In 1666, after the Fire, preached openly in London. Licensed, 22 Apr. 1672, as Congr. Teacher in his own house, Addle Street, Wood Street, London. In or before 1682 his congregation met in Girdlers' Hall, Basinghall Street. In 1683 he was under suspicion of complicity with the Rye House plot. His death was reported to the Fund Managers on 14 Dec. 1691. (*C. F. M. P. T. W.*) [142, 145, 154, 160, 164, 168, 181]

GRIFFITH, ROGER (*d.* Oct. 1708). Received grants, 1691-2, as Student at first with Thomas Brand [*q.v.*] at Bishop's Hall, Bethnal Green [*q.v.*], and under the instruction of John Ker, M.D. [*q.v.*]; and, 1693, for study at Utrecht. Became Minister at Abergavenny, Monm. On the death, 7 Sept. 1697, of Samuel Jones, M.A. [*q.v.*], Griffith succeeded him as Tutor, removing the Academy to Abergavenny. In Dec. 1698, having then five pupils, he was "inclined to conformity." In 1702 he gave up the Academy, conformed, and by the interest of Robert Harley (afterwards first earl of Oxford) became rector of New Radnor (1706) and Archdeacon of Brecon. His death (according to the parish register of New Radnor) occurred "soon after" 10 Oct. 1708, his daughter Margaret having been baptized "about" that time. (*C.* (under John Weaver [*q.v.*]) *Ch.* (1852) *Je. M. Information from Rev. O. G. Owen.*) [4]

GRINSTEAD, EAST. Ejected from this vicarage in 1662 was Christopher Snell, of Queens' Coll., Cambridge; matric. sizar, 1642; B.A., 1644/5; preaching to Independents at his house in East Grinstead, 1669; licensed, 13 May 1672, as Pr. Teacher in his house at East Grinstead; his house licensed, same date. (*C. T. V.*) [112]

GUESTWICK. Ejected here was John Hooker, of Magdalen Coll., Oxford;

clerk, 1653–58; B.A., 23 July 1653; M.A., 1655; held the vicarage of Guestwick; ejected, 1662; living at Woodnorton, Norf., 1669. (*C. F. T.*) [74]

GUILDFORD. Ejected here was John Manship (son of Samuel, of Locking, Som.), of Brasenose Coll., Oxford; matric. pleb., 9 Dec. 1631, aged 18; B.A., 1633/4; rem. to Lincoln Coll.; M.A., 1640/1; vicar of Compton-Dando, Som., 1643; rector of Guildford, ejected, 1662; admitted an extra-licenciate of the College of Physicians, 5 June 1663; preached as well as practised medicine at Guildford; licensed, 25 May 1672, as Pr. Teacher in his house there; his house licensed, same date, as Presb. meeting-place. His son John was Fellow of Corpus Christi Coll., Oxford; M.A., 1683/4; M.B., 1687/8. (*C. F. Mu. T.*) [109, 110]

GUILSBOROUGH. There was here an endowed grammar school, also a writing school. (*Np.*) [78]

GUMMERSHALL. [130] *See* Yorkshire, W.R.

GUNTER, HUMFREY, M.A. (*d.* 23 Aug. 1691). Born in Berkshire. Matric. as gent. at Merton Coll., Oxford, 25 N. 1653; rem. to Magdalen Coll.; B.A., 1656/7; M.A., 1659, and Fellow. An oriental scholar. Ejected, 1662, from his Fellowship. The Episc. Returns, 1669, report him as preaching "at Major Dunch his house," Pusey, Berks, to "Many from severall parishes Dunch afores[d] cheife abbett[r]"; Gunter "lives in Dunches house." He was tutor in private families in Berks and Oxfordshire; but "never ceased to preach twice every Lord's day." His denomination is not stated, but he was "of moderate principles." (*C. F. P. T. Y.*) [6, 7, 176]

HACKNEY. Ejected here were (1) Ezekiel Hopkins (3 Dec. 1634—19 June 1690) of Magdalen Coll., Oxford; matric. 'serv.', 19 Nov. 1650; B.A., 1653; M.A., 1656; lecturer at Hackney; ejected 1662 (?); conformed; lecturer at St. Edmund's, Lombard Street, and St. Mary, Woolnoth; rector of St. Mary Arches, Exeter, 1666; chaplain to Lord Robartes, Lord Lieutenant of Ireland, 1669; archdeacon of Waterford, prebendary of St. Patrick's, Dublin, 1669; dean of Raphoe, bishop of Raphoe, 1671; D.D. (T.C.D.), bishop of Derry, 1681; lecturer of St. Mary Aldermanbury, 8 Sept. 1689; *d.* 19 June 1690. (*C. D. F.*). (2) William Spurstowe, D.D. [*q.v.*]. [3, 4, 72, 154]

HADDESLEY, JOHN, M.A. (1624—11 June 1699). 𝔓. Born at Ware, Herts. Matric. as John Headsley, sizar, at Corpus Christi Coll., Cambridge, 1640; B.A., 1643/4; M.A., 1647. Rector of Poole, Dors., 1647; ejected, 1650, for refusing to obey Cromwell's order for a Thanksgiving day; imprisoned, 1653, and expelled from Poole; had £30: 16s. allowed him out of Lord Digby's estate. Chaplain to Sir Thomas Trenchard. Rector of Rockbourne, Hants (donative); ejected, 1662. Remained at Rockbourne, and is reported in Episc. Returns, 1669, as one of three preachers at Fordingbridge, Hants, to "Presbyterians seldome lesse than 200; sometimes above 300 middle sort of people, consisting most of women and Children who come from the neighbo[r] pishes; & out of Wilts & Dorsetshire." Signed the thanks of Wilts Ministers. Licensed, 20 Apr. 1672, as "Pr. Teacher in Anthony Cooke & Stephen Hasketts howse in New Sarū." From this date he ministered at Salisbury till death, though once imprisoned, and for several months absent, his Meeting-house having been wrecked (1686) by a mob. He was a Baxterian in sentiment. (*C. Hu. Lm. P. T.*) [123]

HADLEIGH ('Hadley'). The rector of whom unfavourable opinion is given was Charles Trumbull, D.C.L. (*d.* 4 Jan. 1723/4, aged 78); who had been chaplain to Archbishop Sancroft (*d.* 24 Nov. 1693), and attended his death-bed. As a Non-juror, Trumbull was deprived in 1691, and the living given to Zachariah Fiske, M.A. (*d.* Sept. 1708), rector of Cockfield, Suff.; but as long as Fiske lived he gave all the Hadleigh emoluments to Trumbull, who continued to officiate at baptisms, marriages, and burials, the common prayer being read by Thomas Fiske, curate. (*Hp.*) [106]

HAGBOURNE. [6]

HALESOWEN ('Hales Owen'), formerly partly in Shropshire; now wholly in Worcestershire. Ejected here in 1660 was Edward Paston, M.A. [*q.v.*]. In 1676 there were 4 Nonconformists here. (*Ls.*) [89]

HALIFAX ('Hallifax'). Ejected here was Ely Bentley (Aug. 1652—31 July 1675), *b.* at Sowerby; of Trinity Coll., Cambridge; admitted, subsizar, 26 Apr. 1647; matric. 1647; Scholar, 1650; B.A., 1650/1; Fellow, 1651; M.A., 1654; curate at Halifax; vicar, 1657; ejected, 1662; licensed, 5 Sept. 1672, to teach in his house at Halifax, Presb (*C. T. Tc. V.*) [130, 132]

HALIGAN, or HELLIGON ('St. Hellens'). [18]

HALL, SAMUEL (*b.* 1662). **C.** The Common Fund in 1690 voted him £6 a year for Godalming "in case he continue there".; this was paid up to June 1691. On 6 June 1692 £10 a year was voted to Godalming where Richard Dowley, B.A. [*q.v.*], had "lately settled"; this was paid for two years.

It is probable that this Samuel Hall was the son and namesake of Samuel Hall, ejected from the vicarage of Barlaston, Staff.; if so, he was ordained in Feb. 1692/3, and was ministering at Tiverton, Devon, in 1716. (*C. Ev. M.*) [109]

HALLET, *i.e.* HALLETT, JOSEPH (4 N. 1656–1722). **P.** Son of Joseph Hallett (1628 ?–14 Mar. 1688/9); ejected (1660) from the sequestered rectory of Chiselborough, Som. Educated by his father. Ordained, 1683. Became assistant (1687) to his father at James's Meeting, Exeter, continuing as assistant to George Trosse [*q.v.*], and becoming pastor in 1713, in which year James Peirce (1674 ?–30 Mar. 1726) became his colleague. From 1690 Hallett conducted an important Academy at Exeter, for the education of Ministers and laymen. His most distinguished students were Peter King (1669—22 July 1734), afterwards Lord Chancellor, and James Foster (16 S. 1697—5 N. 1753), who, according to Pope, was competent to "excel Ten Metropolitans in preaching well." The germs of heresy were brought into the Academy in 1710 by the assistant tutor, Hallett's son, Joseph Hallett (1691 ?–2 Apr. 1744), with the result of provoking in 1716 the Exeter controversy, and producing in 1719 the Salters' Hall schism. Hallett and Peirce were excluded from James's Meeting on 6 Mar. 1719; on 27 Dec. the Mint Meeting, built for their use, was opened. The Academy was closed in 1720. Hallett's address was "By Southgate," Exeter. (*D. Ev. Mh.*) [30]

HALLET, THOMAS, B.A. (1627—1 F. 1707/8). **P.** [? Son of John Hallet, M.A., rector of Pendomer, Som.; matric. at Trinity Coll., Oxford, 25 July 1655; B.A., 1658/9.] Rector of Street, Suss.; ejected (1662 ?). The Episc. Returns, 1669, report him as one of the preachers to "about 200" persons at Brighton, Suss.; also to "above 200 many of good estate" at Westmeston, Suss. Licensed, 10 June 1672, as "Presbiterian" for the house of Thomas Hurst, Wivelisfield. Presented for conventicling, 1675. He was many years pastor at Petworth; while there, in 1706, he received £4 from the Fund. He died at Lewes. (*C. F. M. P. T.*) [112]

HALSEY, JOSEPH, M.A. (1626—1 O. 1711). **P.** Born in Leicestershire. Subsizar at Trinity Coll., Cambridge, 23 Apr. 1645; matric. 1645; Scholar, 1647; B.A., 1648/9; Fellow, 1649–53; M.A., 1652; tutor, 1652–53. Chaplain to Hugh Boscawen, Esq., Tregavethan, and rector of St. Michael Penkevil, Corn.; ejected, 1662. On the Five Mile Act, removed (1666) to Philleigh, Corn., and thence to Merther, Corn., to be nearer Tregavethan, where he preached in Boscawen's house as well as in his own, as long as he lived. The Episc. Returns, 1665, report him as living at St. Michael Penkevil "in y<sup>e</sup> parsonage house there which he renteth of y<sup>e</sup> present Incumbent and is peaceable and Quiet." Signed the thanks of Cornish Ministers. Licensed, 22 May 1672, as Presb. Teacher in the house of Thomas Harvey at Nancarrow in the parish of St. Michael Penkevil. He kept also a boarding school, to which neighbouring gentry sent their sons. Received grant of £5 a year (increased to £6), 1690–1710, for Merther. (*C. M. P. T. Tc. V.*) [18, 19]

HALSTEAD. Ejected here was William Sparrow, either of Gonville and Caius Coll., Cambridge; matric. pensioner, 1640; B.A., 1643/4; M.A., 1647; or of Queens' Coll.; matric. pensioner, 1646; B.A., 1649/50; M.A., 1653; held the sequestered vicarage of Halstead before 1650; ejected, 1662. (*C. E. V.*) [40, 41, 179]

HAMAR, *i.e.* HANMER, JOHN (*fl.* 1660–1690). **C.** Born in Radnorshire. Salaried by the Commissioners as Itinerant preacher in Radnorshire and Brecknockshire; ejected, 1660. Licensed, Nov. 1672, as "Congr. Teacher," being "of Llanbister," Radn. Many years Minister at Cellan, Card.; retired thence to his estate at Llanbister, but continued preaching till death. (*C. P. T.*) [145]

HAMILTON, ARCHIBALD (*fl.* 1690). He was not the first to set up a meeting at High Wycombe (*see* Swinhow, George). Licences were issued for John Ritch, Congr. (22 May 1672), and for Thomas Taylor, Bapt. (June 1672), at High Wycombe. The latter is possibly the M<sup>r</sup> Tayler referred to, and the meaning may be that this was the first meeting after Toleration. If the reference be to a London Minister, it is probably to Christopher Taylor [*q.v.*], who was familiar with Scottish divines. (*T.*) [9, 50]

HAMMERSMITH. [72]

HAMMOND, THOMAS (*fl.* 1690–1720). The Common Fund voted him (31 Aug.

1691) £10 a year for Framfield, Suss.; this was paid up to 1720. (*M.*) [112, 114]

HAMPDEN, RICHARD (1631–Dec. 1695). **P.** Second son of John Hampden, the patriot, by his first wife, Elizabeth Symeon; was bapt. 13 Oct. 1631. He voted for offering the crown to Cromwell, was strongly Presbyterian, and befriended Ejected Ministers. He took a leading part in opposition to the succession of the Duke of York to the crown, and in 1689 was chairman of the committee of the whole House which declared the throne vacant. In 1689 he was appointed privy councillor, and became chancellor of the exchequer (1690–94). Neither peerage nor pension would he accept, preferring to "die a country gentleman of ancient family." (*D.*) [1, 10]

HAMPER, JOHN (*fl.* 1660–90). Ejected from the rectory of Selsey, Suss. (*C. P.*) [113]

HAMPSHIRE. [100, 101, 147, 168, 176] Except the headings "Southampton" in the earliest handwriting all is in the Book-keeper's hand; the "Hantshire" pages are entirely so. Most of the returns are numbered 19; four run from 106 to 155.

Alsford is Alresford [*q.v.*].
Batingstocke is Basingstoke.
Crundaile is Crondall [*q.v.*].
Dounton is Downton.
Froddingbudge is Fordingbridge [*q.v.*].
Limington is Lymington.
Ramsey is Romsey [*q.v.*].
Winton is Winchester [*q.v.*].

HAMPSTEAD ('Hamstead'). Ejected here was John Sprint, elder brother of Samuel Sprint [*q.v.*]. Of Pembroke Coll., Oxford; matric. 26 Nov. 1624, aged 18; rem. to Brasenose Coll.; B.A., 1628; rem. to Christ Church Coll.; M.A., 1631; perpetual curate of Hampstead, 17 Dec. 1633; ejected, 1662; *d.* 1692. (*C. D. F. P.*) [72]

HANCOCK, EDWARD (*fl.* 1659–90). **P.** [? of Oriel Coll., Oxford; matric. 30 Apr. 1619, aged 17; B.A., 1622.] Held the sequestered rectory of St. Philip and St. James, Bristol, 1659; ejected, 1662. Preaching at various places in London, 1664. Owner of considerable property at Horfield, Glou. The Episc. Returns, 1669, report him as one of the preachers to 100 persons at the house of Francis Poole, Monckton Combe, Som.; also as one of the preachers to 100 persons at barns and a house in Batheaston, Som.; also as one of the preachers to "500 at least" in a barn at Beckington, Som.; also as one of the preachers to 300 at a sheep-house in Dunkerton, Som.; also to a conventicle "by stealth," at Yatton, Wilts; also as one of three preachers in rotation to 300 or 400 at Charlton, Wilts. Licensed, 16 May 1672, being of Horfield, as "Grāll Pr. Teacher"; also, 30 S. 1672, as "Pr. Teacher at yᵉ house of Sam̄: Wallington at the Headborough of Wotton undredg," Glou. He died at Horfield.

His son, Edward, was B.C.L., Oxon., 1691. (*C. F. P. T.*) [47]

HANCOCK, THOMAS (*d.* 1706?). **P.** Said to have been a tanner. Held the sequestered vicarage of St. Winnow, Corn.; ejected, 1660. Continued preaching thereabout. Signed the thanks of Cornish Ministers. Licensed, 10 or 20 June 1672, as Presbyterian, to teach in his house, parish of Morval, Corn.; the house was licensed, 22 July. From 1687 he maintained a congregation at East Looe, parish of St. Martin, two miles from Morval, and received annual grants (£10, reduced 1695 to £6) from 1690 to end of 1705. (*C. M. P. T. Wc.*) [18]

HANMER. [15]

HANMER, JOHN, M.A. (1642—19 July 1707). **P.** Born at Bideford, Devon. Son of Jonathan Hanmer, M.A. (1605?–18 D. 1687); ejected (1662) from the vicarage of Bishops-Tawton, Devon, and lectureship of Barnstaple. From Barnstaple grammar school admitted pensioner at St. John's Coll., Cambridge, 30 June 1659, aet. 17; matric., 1659; graduated, by favour, without subscription, according to his father's letter (*C.*), date not given, degree not entered (*Cg.*). Removed to London, and after serving chaplaincies with Sir T. Hooke, Tangier Park, Hants, and Squire Elford, Bickham, Devon, settled with his father at Barnstaple. He began to preach in 1668, but was not ordained till 1682 (privately, by presbyters), after which he entered on a stated ministry at Barnstaple. His sentiments were Baxterian; his conjunction with Oliver Peard [*q.v.*] was an instance of 'happy union.' (*C. Jo. P. V.*) [30]

HANMER, JOHN. *See* Hamar

HANNERICK. [39, 43] *See* Essex

HANNOT, JAMES (*d.* 7 June 1704). **C.** Educ. in the Academy of Charles Morton, at Newington Green. Admitted member of Yarmouth Congregational church, Oct. 1679, and made assistant Minister; ordained pastor, 12 June 1688, by Congregational and Presbyterian Ministers; assisted (1690) by Samuel Wright [*q.v.*]. (*B.*) [74, 177]

HANTSHIRE. *See* Hampshire
HAPPY UNION. [1, 156, 158, 172, 183, 190]
HAPSFIELD. [112] *See* Sussex
HARBORROW. [66] *See* Leicestershire.
HARDING, JOHN, M.A. (*d.* 1690?). **P.** Son of John Hardinge, D.D. (*b.* 1601); ejected from the rectory of Brinkworth, Wilts. Matric. at Magdalen Coll., Oxford, 20 Feb. 1648/9; B.A., 1649/50; M.A., 1652. Vicar of Ambrosden, Oxf. (1655), and of Melksham, Wilts (1658); ejected from both, 1662. Licensed, 9 D. 1672, as "Pr: Teacher at his owne house in Northampton Towne." (*C. F. P. T.*) [76, 178]
HARDING, NATHANIEL (22 Mar. 1655–Feb. 1743/4). **C.** Born in Ireland; son of Nicodemus Harding, Presbyterian Minister at Bandon, Co. Cork (from 1679 till after 1701). Educated at the Dublin Academy under John Ker [*q.v.*]. Left Ireland "by accident" in 1688, and, landing at Dartmouth, was kindly received by John Flavel [*q.v.*]. On the death of Nathan Jacob (1629–1690), ejected from the vicarage of Ugborough, Devon, Flavel recommended Harding as Minister to the congregation founded by Thomas Martyn, ejected from a lectureship at St. Andrew's, Plymouth. For this congregation the Treville Street Meeting-house was built. Harding (ordained, 27 Aug. 1690) took part against Arianism in the Exeter controversy (1719). He had as assistants Henry Brett (1707–23), Joseph Cock (1721–31), and (1731) Henry Moore (*d.* 1762) from South Molton, who succeeded him, and ultimately became an Arian. Harding is the subject of a caustic character-sketch by John Fox (10 May 1693—3 S. 1747); (see *D.*). (*Em. Ev. M. O.*) [31]
HARDY, SAMUEL, B.A. (1636—6 Mar. 1690/1). **P.** Born at Frampton, Dorset. Matric. as servitor at Wadham Coll., Oxford, 1 Apr. 1656; B.A., 1659; qualified for M.A., but dismissed, without that degree, for Nonconformity. Incumbent of Charminster, Dorset (1662?–1667), a peculiar belonging to the Trenchard family, exempt from episcopal jurisdiction. Incumbent of Poole, Dorset, 1667, a donative, whence ejected, 23 Aug. 1682. Incumbent of Badsly (? North Baddesley, Hants), 1682–4. Chaplain to Esquire Heal, at Overy Hatch, Essex (1684–6). Thereafter at Newbury, where he died. (*C. F. P.*) [6]
HARFORD, EMANUEL (1641—8 Aug. 1706). **P.** Entered, pleb., at Exeter Coll., Oxford, 15 June 1657. Taught school. Ejected, 1662, from the chapelry of Upton Noble, Som. The Episc. Returns, 1669, report him as one of the preachers ('Emanuel Harvey') to 42 persons at various houses in Thrulbere, Som.; also ('Mr Hartford') to 400 persons at various houses in West Munkton and places adjacent; also to 230 persons at various houses in St. Mary Magdalen's parish, Taunton, Som.; also at various houses in Bicknoller and Stogumber, Som.; also ('Mr Hanford') at houses in Crowcombe, Som.; also ('Mr Halford') at various houses in Bridgwater, Som. Licensed, 1 May 1672, as "Pr. Teacher in the howse of Thomas Prockter," Stoke Hill, parish of Stoke St. Mary, Som. In 1687 he became co-pastor at Paul's Meeting, Taunton, with Matthew Warren [*q.v.*]. (*C. F. Mh. P. T. Tt.*) [91, 93]
HARGRAVE. [107]
HARLE, LITTLE, a township in Kirkwhelpington parish, Northumb. [80]
HARLESTON ('Harlestone'). [107]
HARLOW HILL, in Ovingham parish. [99]
HARRINGTON. [27] *See* Derbyshire
HARRIS, . . . [? Francis Harris, ejected from the cure of Deerhurst, Glouc.; licensed, 10 June 1672, as "Congr. Teacher in his howse at Painswick," Glouc. "Harris of Bristol" is mentioned, 1714, as one of the preachers at Wrington, Som.] (*C. M. P. T.*) [11, 13, 103, 104]
HARRIS, SAMUEL (*d.* 1738). **P.** Minister of a Congregational church at Canterbury about 1691. Became Minister about 1697 of the Presbyterian congregation in Broad Street, Wapping; owing to some dispute he left (before 1705) to form a Presbyterian congregation in Mill Yard, Goodman's Fields. He was assisted, 1707–10, by John Lewis [*q.v.*], who left for the Congregational church, Red Cross Street; and from 1711 by John Shuttlewood [*q.v.*]. Harris was a subscriber at Salters' Hall (1719). He was disabled long before his death, and from 1728 had Jenkin Lewis (*d.* 1751?), Congregational, a son of his former assistant, as colleague. Hence in Evans' List the denomination of Mill Yard is changed from P. to I. (*Ev. We.*) [2]
HARRISON, JOHN (*fl.* 1660–90). **P.** [Ten persons of these names matriculated at Cambridge between 1627 and 1656; seven of them graduated.] Ejected from the sequestered rectory of Warblington, Hants; licensed, 29 June 1672, as "Presb. Teacher in the howse of Thomas Bayly in

Havant," Hants. (*C. Lm. P. T. Tc. V. Wc.*) [113]

HARRISON, MICHAEL (*d.* Jan. 1726/7). **P.** Vicar of Caversfield, Oxf. Calamy preached at a monthly fast in his church (some time between July 1691 and March 1692) when Harrison was from home "gathering a congregation of Dissenters about Potterspury, designing to quit the Church and settle among them." He probably removed to Potterspury in 1692, bringing a pulpit with him, and fitting up a barn as a Meeting-house; Calamy preached at its opening. Harrison left at the end of 1702. In 1709 he removed to St. Ives, Hunts, and there died. The Common Fund granted him, 1695–1702, £8 a year for Potterspury. From 1714 he took part in a Lecture "near Huntingdon," supported by the Fund. He received grants of £6 a year (reduced later to £4) for St. Ives, from Midsummer 1718 till 1727. (*Cm. Cn. Ev. M.*) [76, 77]

HARRISON, THOMAS (?) (*fl.* 1690–1717). **P.** The Fund offer of £10 a year for Town Malling, Kent, was transferred, 1 F. 1692, to Harrison, owing to the death of Nicholas Thorowgood [*q.v.*]. Payment was made for Town Malling till 1699, without mention of Harrison. In 1706 Alexander Bertram was appointed to Town Malling. There is a trace of Harrison (1715–17) at Goudhurst, Kent, to which William Whittaker was appointed, 2 D. 1717. He is perhaps the Thomas Harrison who conformed after 1720. (*Cm. Ev. M.*) [55]

HART, THOMAS (*d.* 1695). [? of Pembroke Coll., Cambridge; matric. sizar, 1637; B.A., 1640/1.] For Chulmleigh he received £5 a year, from 1690, from the Common Fund, and on 1 July 1695 was reported dead. (*M. V.*) [31]

HARTFIELD ('Hapsfield'). [112]

HARTFORTH ('Hartford'), Yorks, N.R. (misplaced in E.R.). [139]

HARTINGTON ('Harrington'). [27, 28]

HARTLEY, JOHN, M.A. (*d.* 1724). **P.** M.A., Edinburgh, 29 Mar. 1688, as Anglo-Hybernus. Ordained, 27 Sept. 1692. The Common Fund granted him (1690) £4 a year for Burtonwood (four miles North of Warrington). From 1691 he is described as "at or near Ashton" in Makerfield; grant increased (1692) to £8; reduced (1695) to £6; ending 25 Dec. 1702. Minister at Ashby-de-la-Zouch, Leic., and author of anonymous "Vindication of Presbyterian Ordination," 1714, and "Defence," 1716. (*Ed. Ev. M.*) [58, 59, 60]

HARTLEY, THOMAS. **C.** Elected a Treasurer of the Common Fund, and a Correspondent for Norfolk, 14 July 1690, and attended regularly; resigned the Treasurership on or before 20 Apr. 1691 [*see* Boddington, George]; last attendance, 26 June 1693. (*M.*) [75, 162, 168]

HARTSHORN ('Hartshorne'). [26]

HARTSKON. [19] *See* Cornwall

HARVYS, JOHN. John Harris, **C.**, from Carmarthenshire, was first Minister at the Chapel (built 1694) in Penmaen, Monm., and for a time extremely popular; ultimately he was dismissed for insobriety. (*Rj.*)

John Harries was Minister at Glynyrefail, parish of Cilycwm, Carm., in 1715. (*Ev.*) [146]

HARWICH. [39]

HASBERT, or HASBART, JOHN, B.A. (*fl.* 1660–1690). **C.** Admitted from Norwich, 1655, at Corpus Christi Coll., Cambridge; matric. sizar, 1656; B.A., 1659. Ejected from some position at Norwich; a rousing preacher. Licence is noted in Feb. 1673 for "the house of John Walker of Eastdearham in Norfolk Congr." Nothing is known of a Meeting-house there before 1812; the "meeting" was probably the Congregational church connected with Mattishall, four miles from East Dereham. (*B. C. Lm. P. T. V.*) [74, 75]

HASLINGTON CHAPEL. [15] *See* Coape, Joseph

HASTINGS ('Hasting'). [113, 115]

HATCH. [93]

HATFIELD, Herts. [39, 51]

HATFIELD, W.R. (misplaced in E.R.). [139]

HATFIELD BROAD OAK. Ejected here was John Warren, M.A. [*q.v.*]. [39]

HATHERLEIGH ('Hatherbay'). [32]

HATTON GARDEN, according to Strype, "is a very large place now, containing several Streets: *Viz. Hatton street, Charles street, Cross street,* and *Kirby street* . . . very gracefully built, and well inhabited by Gentry; especially *Hatton street,* which is spacious, and in a strait Line comes out of *Holbourn,* and runs Northwards to *Hatton Wall*"; this street is what is now called Hatton Garden. (*Sl.*) [1]

HAVANT. [101, 102]

HAVERHILL ('Hannerick,' 'Haverill'). Ejected here was Stephen Scandrett or Scandaret, M.A. [*q.v.*]. [39, 43, 105]

HAVERS, or HAVER, HENRY, B.A. (*b.* 1620). **P.** Born in Essex, of good family. Matric. sizar, at St. Catharine's

Hall, Cambridge, 1637; B.A., 1641/2. In 1647 he was rector of Chipping Ongar, Ess., and member of the Sixth or Ongar Classis; held (1648–50) the sequestered rectory of Fifield, Ess.; chaplain to the earl of Warwick; ordained in London by presbyters as rector (1651 ?) of Stambourne, Ess., without taking the engagement (1649) of fidelity to the commonwealth without king or house of lords; ejected, 1662. Never left Stambourne, even under the Five Mile Act. The Episc. Returns, 1669, report him as preaching at Stambourne. Licensed, 16 Apr. 1672, as "Presb. Teacher in Grey Friers in Nicholas Parish, Ipswich," here he co-operated with Owen Stockton (*d.* 10 S. 1680), silenced at Colchester, Ess.; also licensed, 2 May 1672, as "Pr. Teacher at his howse in Stamborn." He was living in 1705, and died before 1713.

He was succeeded at Stambourne by Henry Havers (*secundus*) [*q.v.*]. (*B. C. E. Ev. P. T.*) [39]

HAVERS, HENRY, *secundus* (*d.* 1723). 𝔓. Son of Henry Havers, B.A. [*q.v.*], whom he succeeded at Stambourne. He was himself succeeded there by his nephew, Henry Havers, *tertius*. Clare is in Suffolk, where probably he assisted Francis Crow [*q.v.*]. (*E. Ev.*) [38]

HAWDEN, WILLIAM, B.A. (1618 ?–26 Aug. 1699). 𝔓. Born at Holbeck, near Leeds. Matric. at Pembroke Coll., Cambridge, 1635; B.A., 1638/9. Vicar of Brodsworth, West Riding; ejected, 1662. Remained at Brodsworth till the operation (1666) of the Five Mile Act removed him to Sherburn, West Riding. The Episc. Returns, 1669, report him as one of five preachers to "60 Presbyterians & Independents" at the house of John Wordsworth of Swaith, West Riding. Licensed, 2 May 1672, as "Pr. Teacher at the Whitehowse in Sherborne, Yorkeshire"; also, 9 May 1672, as "Presb. Teacher in his howse in Sherborne, Yorkeshire." In 1691 he took part in the movement for extending the Happy Union to Yorkshire. He was imprisoned in 1685 during the scare of Monmouth's rebellion. The Common Fund granted him (from 11 Jan. 1691/2) £4 a year; he was then at Wakefield; from June 1693 till his death his address is given "near Hallifax." He became quite blind. He died at Wakefield, and was buried, 28 Mar. 1699, at Morley, West Riding, where his tombstone remains. This gives his age as 88, so does Calamy, whose informant was Oliver Heywood, yet Heywood's register gives his age as 84; the age given in the MS. is more likely to be right, hence he would be 81 at death. (*C. M. My. Nr. P. Sr. T. V. Y.*) [130]

HAWTON. [136] *See* Yorkshire, N.R.

HAYWORTH, *i.e.* HAWORTH, WILLIAM, M.A. (*d.* Jan. 1702/3). ℭ. Born at Preston, Lanc. Son of Lawrence Haworth. From Sedbergh grammar school admitted sizar at St. John's Coll., Cambridge, 24 Aug. 1652, age not given; matric., 1653; migrated to Christ's Coll.; B.A., 1655/6; M.A., 1660. Vicar of St. Peter's, St. Albans, 1658; ejected, 1662. Removed to Hertford. Preached (1669) to Baptists at St. Albans and Hitchin. Pastor, 1673, of the Congregational church, Hertford; died there. In the Crispian controversy he sided with Richard Davis [*q.v.*]. (*C. Jo. P. T. Uh. V.*) [50]

HEAD, JOSHUA (*fl.* 1660–1715). 𝔅. Ejected from some unknown place in Gloucestershire. Licensed, 29 May 1672, as "Congr. Teacher in his howse in Cleeve," *i.e.* Bishop's Cleeve, Glou. Preached also at Bourton-on-the-water, Glou., and was Baptist Minister there in 1715. (*C. Ev. P. T.*) [44, 46, 189]

HEADS OF AGREEMENT. [155, 156, 157]

HEAGE ('Headge'). [28]

HEALAUGH ('Healey'). [135]

HEBREW. [182]

HECKMONDWIKE ('Heckmondwyke'), then a village in Birstall parish, Yorks, now market town and vicarage. [130]

HEDINGHAM. [42] *See* Sible Hedingham

HELLINGLY ('Helingleigh'). Ejected from this vicarage was John Stone [? of Harvard Coll., New England; B.A., 1653; incorp. at Cambridge, 1655; Fellow of Pembroke Coll.; M.A., 1657]; licensed, Dec. 1672, as Pr. Teacher at a house in Waldron, Suss.; also, Jan. 1672/3, as Pr. Teacher at the house of Lady Boswell, Sevenoaks, Kent [*i.e.* Margaret (Bosville) who inherited the manor of Braborne, Sevenoaks, became widow of Sir William Boswell, who died 1649, and died herself 1692, aged 88]; perhaps at Blandford, Dors. [*q.v.*], in 1690. (*C. K. Mc. T. V.*) [113]

HELMS, *i.e.* HELME, CARNSEW (*fl.* 1622–1690). ℭ. Son of William Helme of Eldersfield, Worc., pleb. Matric. at Exeter Coll., Oxford, 16 Dec. 1641, aged 19. Vicar of Winchcombe, Glou., before 1651. Though Walker, without evidence, says he had been a "lewd soldier" and was an intruder, very active in replacing royalist clergy by parliamentarians, yet at his settlement in Winchcombe he had the general repute of a fair-minded and moderate man, a follower of Baxter. This is clear from the introductory matter to his often-published "Disputation" on church matters, at Winchcombe, 9 Nov. 1653, with Clement Barksdale (Nov. 1609–Jan. 1687–8), then chaplain to Lord Sudeley at Sudeley Castle, Glou. Ejected, 1662. Calamy, who calls him Camshaw Helms or Helmes, says he "came to London and was Pastor to Mr Feake's people." Christopher Feake (*fl.* 1645–1660), a Fifth Monarchy man who became a Baptist, was probably dead by 1662; Helme may have succeeded him. He was certainly preaching in White's Alley, Little Moorfields, in 1669. (*C. D. F. P. T. Wc.*) [46]

HELSTONE ('Hartston'). [19, 20]

HENGROVE. [92] *See* Somerset

HENLEY-ON-THAMES. Ejected here was William Brice, M.A. [*q.v.*]. [85]

HENRY, MATTHEW (18 O. 1662—22 June 1714). **P.** Born at Broad Oak, Flint; second son of Philip Henry [*q.v.*]. Entered (1680) the academy of Thomas Doolittle [*q.v.*]. Admitted at Gray's Inn, 1685. On 9 May 1687 he was ordained by presbyters in London, and began his ministry at Chester. One of the founders of the Cheshire Classis (*see* p. 157). A Meeting-house was erected for him (1700) in Crook Lane; a gallery was added (1706) to accommodate Independents. Daniel Williams [*q.v.*] named him as a trustee of his foundations, but he did not live to enter on the trust. Removed to the ministry of Mare Street, Hackney, 1712. Died on a visit to Nantwich, and buried in Trinity Church, Chester. His "Exposition of the Old and New Testament," 1708–10, has not been superseded for practical uses. He was elected a Fund Manager on 4 Jan. 1711/2, though his stated ministry at Hackney did not begin till 18 May following. At his death the Hackney congregation was divided, one section being under John Barker, the other under George Smyth. (*Cm. D. M.*) [16, 150]

HENRY, PHILIP, M.A. (24 Aug. 1631–24 June 1696). **P.** Eldest son of John Henry, keeper of the orchard at Whitehall. From Westminster school entered Christ Church, Oxford, 15 D. 1647; B.A., 1650/1; M.A., 1652. Preacher at Worthenbury Chapel, Flint., from 1655; ordained by presbyters, 1657; ejected, 1661. Settled at Broad Oak, Flint., his wife's property. Under the Five Mile Act removed (1666) to Whitchurch, Shrops. The Episc. Returns, 1669, report him as one of four preachers to 80 persons at Whitchurch. Licensed, 30 Apr. 1672, as "Pr. Teacher in his howse [Broad Oak] in the Parish of Malpas." Several times imprisoned. In 1689 he was for comprehension, or for toleration without subscription; there were points in the articles which "without a candid interpretation would somewhat scruple mee, so would the Bible its. strictly taken & in the letter, in those places which seem contradictory, were it not for such an interpretation." To trace their descent from Philip Henry is a matter of especial pride, both among Anglicans and Nonconformists in this country and America. *See* S. Lawrence, "Descendants of Philip Henry," 1844; also S. L. Swanwick and J. E. Jones, "Descendants of Rev. Philip Henry," 1899 (limited to two branches). (*C. D. F. P. T.*) [15, 88]

HENSTRIDGE ('Hengrove'). [92]

HEREFORDSHIRE. [48, 146, 168, 171, 176, 181] Only the heading "Hereford" is in the earliest handwriting; the rest in that of the Book-keeper. The returns are numbered from 32 to 139

HERTFORD. Ejected here was Jeremiah Burwell (1624—11 Feb. 1667/8) of Emmanuel Coll., Cambridge; matric. pensioner, 1644; B.A., 1647/8; M.A., 1651; rector of St. Andrew's, Hertford, in 1650; ejected, 1660; *d.* at Codicote, Ess. (*C. Uh. V.*) [50]

HERTFORDSHIRE. [50, 51, 52, 168, 171, 176] Only the third heading "Hertford" is in the earliest handwriting; the rest, with slight exception, is in that of the Book-keeper. The returns are numbered from 43 to 122.

Barkamstead is Berkampstead.

Bigsworth, a market town, cannot be Biddesworth, a manor in Kimpton parish; it is probably Rickmansworth.

Hodsdon, Hogsdon is Hoddesdon.

Kickmansworth is Rickmansworth.

The following Ministers in Herts, not named in the Manuscript, received grants from the Common Fund: (1) Mr. Squire, a necessitous Dissenting Minister near St. Albans; £5 grant (1692). (*M.*) (2) William Terry, £5 grant (1692) for Hitchin; he came from Hastings, was pastor (1649–99) at Back Street, Hitchin; removed to Kettering. (*M. Uh.*)

HESKET ('Hescott') in the Forest. [21]

HEXHAM. [23, 79, 81]

HEYBURNE. [6] *See* Berkshire

HEYCOCK, . . . [117]

HEYWOOD. [60]

HEYWOOD, ELEAZAR, *i.e.* ELIEZER

(18 Apr. 1657—20 May 1730). **P.** Second son of Oliver Heywood [*q.v.*]. Entered Frankland's Academy, 26 May 1674. Ordained at Attercliffe, 21 Apr. 1687. Minister (1691) at Wallingwells, Notts; afterwards at Dronfield, Derbs., and there buried. From 1709 he received Fund grants for Dronfield (£6; reduced, 1723, to £5). (*Fr. Ht. M.*) [83]

HEYWOOD, NATHANIEL, M.A. (6 June 1659—26 O. 1704). **P.** Born at Ormskirk. Eldest son of Nathaniel Heywood (16 S. 1633—16 D. 1677); ejected from Ormskirk vicarage; and nephew of Oliver Heywood [*q.v.*]. Entered Frankland's Academy, 25 Apr. 1677. Graduated M.A. at Edinburgh, 1680. Chaplain to one Dickins in Staffordshire. Ordained at Attercliffe, 1 June 1687, for Ormskirk, where a Meeting-house was built for him and registered 1 May 1693. The dwelling-house of Mrs. Elizabeth Heywood was registered 19 Apr. 1697 (and that of Mary Heywood, widow, in Aughton Street, in 1708/9). His ministerial career was broken by ill-health. (*D. Ed. Fr. Nk. Nl. X. Y.*) [58]

HEYWOOD, OLIVER, B.A. (March 1629/30—4 May 1702). **P.** Born at Little Lever, Lanc.; baptized 15 March. Third son of Richard Heywood. From Bolton grammar school and other schools, matric. pensioner (as Hewood) at Trinity Coll., Cambridge, 1646; entered, on residence, 9 July 1647; B.A., 1650. Incumbent of Coley Chapel, West Riding, 26 N. 1650; ordained, 4 Aug. 1652, by Bury Classis; ejected and excommunicated, 1662. By 1655 he had removed his residence to Northowram (near Coley) in Halifax parish; in 1665 he was living at Coley Hall, but returned to Northowram. He was much persecuted for conventicling, as he undertook the work of itinerant evangelising in the North. The Episc. Returns, 1669, report him as one of the preachers to "neere 100" at Sowerby and Coley; also at a house in Otley, West Riding; also to a "very numerous" audience at Morley, West Riding. Licensed, 20 Apr. 1672, as "Presb. Teacher in his owne howse in the Parish of Hallifax." He was probably then living at Coley Hall, as one of the applications for his licence describes him as "at Coley Chappell in y[e] parrish of Halifax." He was licensed, 25 July 1672, as Pr. Teacher in the house of John Butterworth at Halifax. On 29 O. 1672 he took part in an ordination at Manchester, the first held by Presbyterians in the North. His Meeting-house at Northowram was opened 8 July 1688. He built also a school at Northowram, of which David Hartley, an Oxford scholar, and father of the philosopher, was the first master from 5 Oct. 1693. Heywood was the main instrument in extending the 'Happy Union' (2 Sept. 1691) to Yorkshire. (*C. D. P. T. V. Y.*) [129, 130, 132, 178]

HICKS' HALL, in St. John's Street, Clerkenwell, was built (1612) at a cost of £900, as a session-house for the Middlesex magistrates, by Sir Baptist Hicks, one of them; the building stood till 1779. Hicks was a wealthy mercer in St. Pancras Lane, Cheapside; knighted on 24 July 1603, he maintained (1607) his right to keep a shop in London after knighthood. In many ways a public benefactor, he rendered important financial services to the Crown. He was created a baronet, 1 July 1620; was M.P. for Tavistock, 1620–23; for Tewkesbury, 1624–26, and March to May 1628; on 5 May 1628 he was created Baron Hicks and Viscount Campden. He died 18 Oct. 1629, aged 78. (*Pe. St.*) [4]

HIDE HALL (now Hyde Hall) in Sawbridgeworth parish, Herts, seat of the Earl of Roden. [51]

HIELLOSSOULD. [22] *See* Cumberland

HIGGS, DANIEL, B.A. (*d.* Sept. 1691). **C.** Born at Chadwick in Bromsgrove parish, Worc. Matric. pleb., at Magdalen Hall, Oxford, 29 Jan. 1648/9; B.A., 1651. Held the sequestered rectory of Rhossily, Glam.; ejected, 1660/1; rector of Port Eynon, 1661; ejected, 1662. His father refused him assistance unless he conformed. The Episc. Returns, 1665, report him removed out of St. David's diocese. Licensed, 17 Apr. 1672, as "Congr. Teacher at his howse in Swanzey," Glam.; application for the school-house in Swansea was not granted. There was a break in his Swansea ministry owing to ill-health, during which he taught "academical learning" at Chadwick. He returned to Swansea, but was soon compelled (1690) to leave again. The Common Fund voted him (16 Feb. 1690) £4 a year for Swansea; but on 28 Sept. 1691, Higgs having died at Chadwick, it was transferred to Owen Davies [*q.v.*]. (*C F. M. P. T. Wc.*) [126, 127, 144]

HIGGS, JOHN (*d.* 1728 ?). **C.** Son of Daniel Higgs, B.A. [*q.v.*]. Probably educated by his father, whom he assisted at Swansea; he cannot have been his successor, this being Owen Davies [*q.v.*]. According to *Cr.* (1852), he was Minister at Evesham, Worc. *Cr.* says there is an epitaph (not detailed) in All Saints' church, Evesham, dating the death of John Higgs in Sept. 1728, and that of his wife in Oct. 1728. No such epitaph is recorded in W. Tindal's "Hist. of Evesham," 1794, or is now extant; nor does the register of All Saints', Evesham, record the burial in 1728 of John, Thomas, or Daniel Higgs. The Fund Minutes record grants of £8 a year to Thomas Higgs, at Evesham, 1695–96, and to Mr. Higgs, in Worcestershire, 1697–99; of £7 to Mr. Higgs of Evesham, 1700; of £6 to the same (name sometimes spelled Higs), 1701–15, and to Daniel Higgs, Evesham, 1716–22; of £5 to the same, 1723–28, the transfer of the grant to Francis Blackmore being made on 2 Dec. 1728. It seems clear that all these grants were made to the same person; it is conceivable that he had two Christian names, or adopted his father's name; Thomas may have been a misreading of Jno. Evans' List (1715) also gives Daniel Higgs as the Evesham Minister, marks him Presbyterian, and places his death in Oct. 1728. (*Cr. Ev. M.*) [127, 144]

HIGH PEAK. [25, 180]

HIGHGATE ('High-gate'). [3, 72]

HILL, JOSEPH (11 Oct. 1667—21 Jan. 1728/9). **P.** Born at Salisbury. From the Salisbury grammar school he entered Charles Morton's Academy at Newington Green; removing (1686) to that of John Sprint, near Andover, Hants, and (1687) studied in London under Richard Stretton, M.A. [*q.v.*], and Francis Glascock [*q.v.*]. Stretton recommended him as chaplain to Lady Irby [*q.v.*], with whom he lived nearly seven years. He was ordained, 22 June 1694, with Thomas Reynolds [*q.v.*], and ministered to a Presb. congregation in Swallow Street, Westminster. In 1699 he became Minister of the English Presbyterian church at Rotterdam, returning in 1717 to succeed James Coningham, M.A., at Haberdashers' Hall, Staining Lane, Cheapside, where he settled, 16 Feb. 1717/8, and remained till death. He was a subscriber, in 1719, at Salters' Hall. He attended as a Fund Manager from 4 Jan. 1719/20 to 4 O. 1725. (*Cm. D. M. Ss. W.*) [2]

HILLBISHOPS. [91] *See* Somerset

HILTON, RICHARD, B.A. (1625 ?–1706 ?). **P.** Son of Richard Hilton of Bloxham, Oxf., pleb. Matric. at Christ Church, Oxford, 9 Apr. 1641, aged 16; B.A., 1644. Vicar of West Bromwich, Staff.; ejected, 1662. The Episc. Returns, 1669, report him as one of the preachers to above 300 persons at Walsall "at the houses of M^rs Pearson, M^r Fowler & M^r Eves." Licensed, Nov. 1673, being of West Bromwich, as "Pr. Teacher." Chaplain to Philip Foley [*q.v.*]. Lived many years at Walsall and there died. On 4 Mar. 1705/6 he was reported to the Fund Board as "old above 80" and having John Godly as assistant; a grant of £6 was made, and received by Godly, who was at Walsall till 1729. (*C. F. P. M. T.*) [96]

HINCKLEY ('Hinkley'). Ejected here was Thomas Leadbetter, of Christ's Coll., Cambridge; matric. pensioner, 1647/8; B.A., 1651; M.A., 1656; chaplain to Lady Wimbledon [*q.v.*]; curate or lecturer at Hinckley, in 1659; ejected, 1662; rem. to Nantwich, Ches. (his native county); licensed, 16 Apr. 1672, as Presb. Teacher at his house in Sandbach parish, Ches.; his house, licensed same date as Presb. meeting-place, was at Armitage (or Hermitage), where he had a good estate; he became Minister of a congregation in Wirral, and *d.* there, 4 Nov. 1679, aged 52. (*C. T. V.*) [67, 68]

HINDE, MORGAN. **P.** [165]

HINDLEY, chapelry in Wigan parish, now vicarage. Ejected here was James Bradshaw [*q.v.*]. [62]

HITCHIN. [50, 51]

HOCKER, WILLIAM (1663—12 Dec. 1721). **P.** Born at Trelill, near Wardbridge, Cornwall. Schooling under Joseph Halsey [*q.v.*]; university learning under Charles Morton, M.A., at Newington Green. Returned to Cornwall. Removed to Edmonton (1690) as chaplain; while there, was ordained to pastoral charge of "a small people of his own forming." The Common Fund voted him (1690) £6 a year for Barnet, Herts, but this was transferred (1691) to William Alsop [*q.v.*]; a Fund gift of £10 was made to him, 7 May 1716. After 30 years at Edmonton, returned to London (1720) and assisted Samuel Powfret, at Gravel Lane, Houndsditch. "He was concerned and desirous to have his Name seen among those that had subscrib'd the great Article that relates to the Doctrine of the ever blessed Trinity." (*Ev. M. W. Fun. Serm. by T. Reynolds*, 1722.) [2, 51, 72]

HODDESDON. [51]

HODGES, JOHN (*fl.* 1662–1690). **C.** [? John Hodges, matric. 'ser.', at Wadham Coll., Oxford, 2 July 1658; rem. to Magdalen Hall; B.A., 1661/2.] Ejected from St. Katherine's in the Tower. The Episc. Returns, 1669, report a conventicle of Independents in "Bednall greene, at a house lately fitted for y^e purpose." John Hodges was licensed, Sept. 1672, as "Congr Teach" in the "house of Rich Ward of Bethnall Green." (*C. F. P. T.*) [72]

HODGES, WILLIAM, B.A. (*b.* 1631). **P.** Son of Thomas Hodges (? vicar of Radbourne, War.). Matric. 'serv.', at Trinity Coll., Oxford, 15 Dec. 1647, aged 16; demy Magdalen Coll., 1650–53; B.A., 1650/1. Perpetual curate of Leonard Stanley, Glou.; ejected, 1662. Licensed, 16 July, as "Pr. Teacher in the howse of Widow Hodges," Shipton Moigne, Glou. Subsequently he lived at Wotton-under-Edge, Glou., close by. (*C. F. P. T.*) [47]

HODGKIN, or HODGKINS. Probably a layman. [2]

HODSDON. [51] *See* Hertfordshire

HOGNASTON. Ejected from the perpetual curacy was Jonathan Staniforth, of Magdalene and Christ's Coll., Cambridge; M.A., 1654; licensed, 22 July 1672, as Pr. Teacher in Derby; his house in Derby licensed, 5 Sept. 1672, Pres.; also licensed, 30 Sept. 1672, as Pr. Teacher at a house in Chaddesdon. (*C. T. V.*) [27]

HOGSDON. [51] *See* Hertfordshire

HOLBEACH. [71]

HOLCOMBE ('Holcom'). [59]

HOLCROFT, FRANCIS, M.A. (1629?–6 Jan. 1692/3). **C.** Son of Sir Henry Holcroft, of West Ham, London (knighted 1 May 1622). Matric. at Clare Hall, Cambridge, 1647 (chamber-fellow with Archbishop Tillotson, then an Independent); B.A., 1650; Fellow; M.A., 1654. Preached for some years at Litlington, Cambs. About 1655 became vicar of Bassingbourne, Cambs; ejected, 1662; imprisoned, 1663, for preaching, and said to have been kept nearly twelve years in Cambridge gaol, the gaoler letting him out at night to preach. The Episc. Returns, 1669, report him as one of several preachers (1) at Hugglescote, Leic., to about 40 Presbyterians; (2) at Willingham, Cambs, in various houses, to "usually about 100. All very meane, Except some few yeomen men. And many of them come from other places, and goe from place to place to Conventicles"; (3) at Histon, Cambs, to "Independ^ts. About 30. Of y^e middle & mean^r sort, Most women & mayds"; (4) at Over, Cambs, to about 100 "Fanatiques" of "Meane condition," and "not 20 of this pish"; (5) at Stow-cum-Quy, in the house of Henry Bostock, carpenter, to "sometimes neere 100. From other Parishes halfe at least. Mean^r & poorer sort most of them: yet some strang^rs come amongst y^m that are wealthy"; (6) at Haddenham, Cambs, to "Fanatiques. About 60. Of meane condition. Most women"; (7) six months previously at Widow [of Richard Petit] Elizabeth Petit's, in St. Michael's parish, Cambridge, to "about 100 Meane sort & inconsiderable persons." Licensed, 8 May 1672, along with Joseph Oddey (*d.* 1689) as Congr. Teachers in the house of Job Hall, Bridge Street, Cambridge. He was again imprisoned in London, when Tillotson showed him much kindness. Oddey's death and Holcroft's ill-health led to a partition of their flock, Thomas Taylor [*q.v.*] taking charge of the northern portion, at Green Street. Holcroft died at Thriplow, Cambs, and was buried at Oakington, Cambs. (*C. Cc.* (calls him Holdcroft), *D. P. S. T. V.*) [11]

HOLDERNESS ('Holdernes'), E.R. (also misplaced in N.R.). [136, 138]

HOLDSWORTH, JOHN (*d.* 15 D. 1711). **P.** Born at Birstal. [? Son of Josiah Holdsworth (1638–1685); son of John, clothier, of Wakefield; admitted sizar at St. John's Coll., Cambridge, 9 Apr. 1655, aet. 17; B.A., 1658/9; chaplain to Sir Richard Houghton, of Houghton Tower, Lanc.; set up a meeting in Heckmondwyke in 1672. (*C. Jo. V.*)] Admitted at Christ's Coll., Cambridge, 30 June 1671; did not matriculate. Entered Frankland's Academy, 20 F. 1672/3; lack of means cut short his education, and he taught school. From 1677, at least, he preached to the Cleckheaton congregation in Spen Valley, meeting at "the Closes" farmhouse. Ordained at Alverthorpe, 4 S. 1689. Regularly exchanged with Joseph Dawson [*q.v.*] and John Ray [*q.v.* under Kay]. In 1710 the first Meeting-house (known as the Red Chapel) was built at Cleckheaton. Holdsworth received £5 from the Fund in 1711. He was buried (18 D. 1711) at Birstall. (*Fr. Hh. M. My. Nk. Nr. V.*) [130]

HOLIWORTHY. [31] *See* Devonshire

HOLLAND. [14]

HOLLAND, JOHN (*d.* 19 N. 1732). **P.** Entered Frankland's Academy, 15 Oct. 1688. Ordained at Rathmell, 7 June 1693, as Minister in Swaledale, East Riding, at a Meeting-house adjoining Smarber Hall (built by Lord Wharton); he had ministered there from 8 Oct. 1691. Removed (1722) to Alfreton, Derbs., and there died. From 1723 he received £5 a year for Alfreton from the Fund. He was succeeded there by another John

Holland. (*Ev. Fr. Hh. Ht. M. My. Nk. Nr.*) [139]

HOLLAND, ROBERT (1650 ?–1705). **C.** Associated with the pastor (Robert Bury) in the ministry at Allostock, Chesh., some time after 2 March 1689/90; a founder (1691) of the Cheshire Classis (*see* p. 157). The existing chapel at Allostock was built in his time. "Mr Holland of Cheshiere" was granted (1696) £10 from the Congregational Fund; grants also were made to his son as a student under Timothy Jollie [*q.v.*] at Attercliffe. (*Cf. Uc.*) [15]

HOLLINGTON. [27]

HOLMAN, WILLIAM (*fl.* 1690–91). Received grants (1691) as student with Thomas Brand [*q.v.*] at Bishop's Hall, Bethnal Green [*q.v.*], under the instruction of John Ker, M.D. [*q.v.*]. (*M.*) [4]

HOLSWORTHY ('Holiworthy'). Ejected here was Humphrey Sanders, of Oriel Coll., Oxford; matric. 6 Dec. 1622, aged 17; B.A., 1625/6; M.A., 1628; rector of Stubton, Lincs, 1630; rector of Holsworthy, 1632; prebendary of Exeter, 1635; moderator of the Exeter Assembly, 12 May 1658; ejected, 1662; living at Clawton, 1665; brother of Richard Sanders [*q.v.*]. (*C. F. T.*) [31]

HOLWORTHY, MATTHEW (*bapt.* 27 Mar. 1674). Son and heir of Sir Matthew Holworthy, Knt. (*bur.* 23 O. 1678), by his wife Susanna (*bur.* 21 May 1690). Married Eliza, daur. of Dr. James Desborowe, a descendant of Cromwell. (*Ly.*) [3]

HONITON. Ejected here was Francis Soreton [*q.v.*]. [30]

HOOK, L: Elizabeth (*d.* 1708 ?), daur. of Sir William Thompson, Knt., and widow of Sir Thomas Hooke, bart. (*d.* 1678), of Tangier Park, parish of Wootton, Hants. (*Ba.*) [101]

HOOKE, *i.e.* HOOK, JOHN, B.A. (1634–1710). Son of William Hook, M.A. (1600—21 Mar. 1677/8), sometime Master of the Savoy. He went with his father to New England (1640 ?), but returned before him. Matric. at Magdalen Coll., Oxford, 27 N. 1652; B.A., 1654. Rector of Kingsworthy, Hants; ejected (1662 ?). In 1663 he was made chaplain of the Savoy Hospital by Henry Killigrew, D.D. (11 F. 1612/3—14 Mar. 1699/1700), whom he succeeded as Master in 1700; the hospital was dissolved in 1702, at which time Hook was Minister at Basingstoke, where he continued to preach, though blind. (*C. D. F. P.*) [101]

HOOPER, BENJAMIN (1650–May 1715). **P.** Son of William Hooper, 'pleb.' of Exeter. Matric. at Lincoln Coll., Oxford, 15 Mar. 1666/7, aged 17. Minister of Bow Meeting, Exeter. Calamy preached on 7 May 1713 "to the Society of young Men at Mr Hooper's Meeting," Exeter. (*Cm. Em. F. Mh.*) [30]

HOPKINS, WILLIAM, B.A. (15 July 1629–March 1700). Born at Yeovilton, Som. Entered Oxford, 1647; matric. at Magdalen Coll., 'pleb,' 22 Jan. 1648/9; B.A., 1632; chorister, 1652–3. Taught school at Fifehead, Dors., 1653–5; preached for a year at Didcot; ordained at Wrington, Som., 12 N. 1656, as vicar of Milborne Port, Som.; ejected, 1662. The Episc. Returns, 1669, report him as preaching to 60 persons at Milborne Port. Licensed, June 1672, as "Pr. Teacher in his howse in Milborne Port." Opened a school, which was stopped owing to his excommunication (lasting till 1687) by Peter Mews (25 Mar. 1618/9–9 N. 1706), bishop of Bath and Wells (1672–84), whose niece he had married. Calamy says he died in his 70th year; according to the above dates it was at least his 71st year (his 72nd if he died before 25 March, in which case March 1700 would be 1700/1). (*C. F. P. T.*) [34, 92]

HOPPIN, or HOPPINGE, JOHN, M.A. (*d.* 8 Mar. 1704/5). **P.** Matric. at Exeter Coll., Oxford, as gent., 12 N. 1650; Fellow, 1652; B.A., 1654; M.A., 1657. Was episcopally ordained. Ejected from Fellowship, 1662. Licensed, 9 May and again 29 May 1672, being at Christon, Devon, to which place he moved in 1666 as "a Grãll Pr. Teacher." Signed the thanks of the Devon Ministers. Minister of Bow Meeting, Exeter, till 1704, in conjunction with Robert Gayhard [*q.v.*] and Robert Atkins [*q.v.*]. Rheumatism, the result of imprisonment, so crippled him that he was carried in a chair to the pulpit. (*C. Em. F. Mh. P. T.*) [30]

HOPTON HALL at Upper Hopton in Mirfield parish, Yorks. [130]

HORLEY. [110]

HORNCHURCH ('horn Church'). Ejected from this donative was . . . Wells. (*C.*) [1, 40, 43]

HORNE, . . . [27, 29]

HORRIGE. [62] *See* Lancashire

HORSHAM ('Horhsam'). The phonetic spelling in the Manuscript (in the Minutes, 'Horsam') shows the pronunciation. The modern tendency is to pronounce Evesham, Horsham, Masham (*see* Massums), etc., as if compounded with -sham instead of -ham. [114]

HORSHAM, WILLIAM (*d.* 1725). **P.** Probably related to John Horsham, ejected from the vicarage of Staverton, Devon, in 1662. Ordained (24 N. 1687) pastor of Topsham, where also Thomas Bernard Starre [*q.v.*] ministered. Stoake is perhaps Stoke Canon. Horsham was Minister at Topsham till his retirement in 1723. (*Ev. Mh.*) [31]

HORSLEY, in Ovingham parish. [80]

HORSMAN, JOHN, M.A. (*fl.* 1650–1695). 𝔓. Matric. 20 Mar. 1650/1 at Magdalen Coll., Oxford; demy, 1650–8; B.A., 1652; M.A., 1655. Ejected at Scilly island; well known at Plymouth; assistant (1695) to Richard Bures at Leather Lane, London. (*C. F. P. W.*) [2]

HORT, JOSIAH (1674 ?–14 Dec. 1751). Son of John Hort, of Marshfield, Glouc. Received grants, 1691/3, as student at Gloucester, under James Forbes, M.A. [*q.v.*]. Jeremy wrongly places him under Thomas Rowe [*q.v.*]. He appears to have preached as a Presbyterian at Soham, Cambs, and to have acted as assistant at Marshfield, Glou. In April 1704 he entered at Clare Hall, Cambridge, left in 1705 without a degree, took Anglican orders same year, was chaplain to John Hampden, M.P., and held in succession three livings in Buckinghamsh. In 1709 he went to Ireland as chaplain to Thomas, earl of Wharton, lord-lieutenant. His preferment was rapid: rector of Kilskyre; dean of Cloyne and rector of Louth; dean of Ardagh; bishop of Ferns and Leighlin (when Archbishop King refused to take part in his consecration because he was erroneously styled D.D.); bishop of Kilmore and Ardagh; finally (1742) archbishop of Tuam, retaining Ardagh *in commendam*. Failure of voice in 1738 had disabled him from preaching. Fenton John Anthony Hort (23 Apr. 1828—30 Nov. 1892), to whom the Greek text underlying the Revised Version of the New Testament (1881) is mainly due, was his great-grandson. (*Bu.*.*D. M.*) [182]

HORWICH. Chapelry in Deane parish, now vicarage. [62]

HOWARD, SAMUEL. [165]

HOWE, JOHN, M.A. (17 May 1630—2 Apr. 1705). 𝔓. Born at Loughborough, Leic.; son of John Howe, schoolmaster and curate at Loughborough, suspended; grandson of William Howe, vicar of Tattersall, Lincs. His father, suspended (1634) for Puritanism, took his family to Ireland in 1635, returning in 1641 to Lancashire. From the Winwick grammar school he entered Christ's Coll., Cambridge, 19 May 1647, as sizar. In 1648 he removed to Oxford, entering Brasenose Coll. as Bible clerk; B.A., 1649/50; Fellow of Magdalen Coll., 1652–5; M.A., 1652. The then president of Magdalen, Thomas Goodwin, D.D. [*q.v.*], had a gathered church among the scholars. This Howe "did not offer himself to join"; Goodwin, however, invited and admitted him "upon catholick terms." In 1652 he received Presbyterian ordination at Winwick. About 1654 he was appointed (in succession to Lewis Stuckley) perpetual curate of Great Torrington, Devon, a donative, from which the royalist, Theophilus Powell, M.A., had been extruded about 1646. In 1656, Cromwell made him his domestic chaplain, a position distasteful to him, though he retained the office under Richard Cromwell, of whose ability he had a high opinion. It is significant of his general temper of mind that he was present as a friendly outsider at the Savoy conference (Oct. 1658) in which the Westminster Confession was re-edited on Congregational principles. On the fall of Richard Cromwell (May 1659) he returned to Torrington, whence he was ejected in 1662. His latitude, he said, made him a Nonconformist. He took the Oxford oath (1665) to endeavour no alterations in Church or State. The Episc. Returns (1665) report him as living "peaceably" at Great Torrington. In Apr. 1670 he left for Ireland as chaplain to John, second viscount Massareene. At Antrim he officiated on Sunday afternoons at the parish church, of which Presbyterians had part use. He was a member of the ministerial conference known as the 'Antrim Meeting,' and took part (1675) in an Academy for training candidates for the Presbyterian ministry. In 1676 he became pastor of the Presbyterian congregation in Haberdashers' Hall, Staining Lane, Wood Street, Cheapside, London. He succeeded Thomas Manton, D.D. [*q.v.*], as a Pinners' Hall lecturer in 1677. Active persecution led him to embrace the offer of foreign travel with Philip, fourth baron Wharton. He settled at Utrecht (1686). James II.'s Declaration for Liberty of Conscience brought him back (May 1687) to his London flock, though he resolutely declined to sanction the claim to a dispensing power. The Toleration Act (1689) he greeted with a plea for mutual forbearance between Conformists and Dissenters. His work for the Common Fund and the Happy Union is detailed in the Introduction. He declined in

1694 to take part in a public ordination. In the same year he withdrew (Nov.) from the Pinners' Hall lectureship, and in the following month his congregation removed to a new Meeting-house in Silver Street, Wood Street. To the Socinian controversy he contributed (1694–5) two tracts, orthodox, but cautious. To the bill (1702) against occasional conformity he was strongly opposed. Just before his death he expressed entire concurrence in the scheme of non-synodical Presbyterianism developed in Calamy's "Defence of Moderate Nonconformity" (1704). (*C. D. F. P. T. W. Wc.*) [19, 31, 32, 86, 126, 127, 154, 155, 160, 164, 168, 181, 183, 189, 190]

HOWELL, or HOWEL, MORGAN (*fl.* 1654–94). C. Born at Bettwsbleddrws, near Lampeter, Card. He was a rich man and something of a poet. To frustrate the field-preaching of Walter Cradock (*d.* 14 D. 1659) he started a football game, sprained his ankle, listened to the sermon, and became Cradock's disciple. In Feb. 1654/5 he joined the Congregational church under Rees Powell at Lampeter, Card., and soon began to preach. Licensed, 28 (?) Oct. 1672, as "Congr̃ Teachr." at the house (still standing) of John Jones [*q.v.*] at Llanbadarn Odwyn, Card. The Common Fund gave him yearly grants of £3, 1691–3. He was a Teaching Elder in the churches at Cilgwyn, Caeronen, etc., Card., in 1694, and is supposed to have died soon after. (*M. Rj. Rw. T.*) [146]

HOXTON. [3]

HUBERT, or HUBBARD, FRANCIS, M.A. (1627—20 O. 1676). P. Son of Edward Hubbard, of Essex, afterwards of London. From Westminster school, matric. (as Francis Hubert, gent.) at Balliol Coll., Oxford, 9 N. 1650; B.A., 1653; M.A., 1655/6. Vicar of Winterbourne-Monkton and Berwick Basset, Wilts; ejected, 1662. Removed to Oxford, where his wife had relatives, and under stress of the Five Mile Act retired, 1666, to Witney, where he remained till death (save for six months' imprisonment at Oxford for conventicling). Licensed (as Francis Hubbard), 10 Aug. 1672, to be "Pr. Teach at his house" in Witney. (*C. F. P. Sb. T.*) [86]

HUBLAND, PETER. P. Elected a Manager, 8 Dec. 1690, replacing James Boddington, but attended no meeting. John Jurin [*q.v.*] was the intermediary with him, as with Boddington; he is therefore presumed to be of the same denomination. (*M.*) [162]

HUCHESON, GEORGE. Attended as Manager on 15 S. 1690; last attendance 20 Feb. 1692/3, when his name is given as Richard Hucheson in error. (*M.*) [162]

HUCKLOW. [26]

HUCKNALL TORKARD. Ejected here was John Leighton [*q.v.*]. [83]

HUDLESKEUGH ('Hudlesbough,' 'Hudlesbrough') in Kirkoswald parish. [21, 22]

HUGHES, JOHN (1665–1728/9), younger son of Obadiah Hughes [*q.v.*]. Educated at the Academy of Samuel Cradock [*q.v.*], also at Geneva and at Utrecht. Tutor in the Knightley family at Fawsley, Northants; travelling tutor with Sir J. Wentworth. Evening lecturer at Silver Street, London, and morning preacher at Hoxton Square. Minister at Ware, Herts, from about 1699 till death. (*Ev. Uh.*) [50]

HUGHES, OBADIAH, B.A. (1640—24 Jan. 1704/5). P. Son of George Hughes, M.A., B.D. (1603—4 July 1667); ejected from the vicarage of St. Andrew's, Plymouth. Matric. at Christ Church, Oxford, 23 July 1656; B.A., 1659; ejected from studentship, 1662. Ordained by presbyters at Plymouth, 9 Mar. 1670/1. Licensed, 11 Apr. 1672, as Presb. Teacher in any place licensed. Removed to London, Apr. 1674, ministering to a congregation there; and later, for 15 years, to a congregation at Enfield, Middx., where he died. (*C. D. F. P. T.*) [19, 32 166, 168]

HUGHES, STEPHEN (1622?–1688). C. Born at Carmarthen. Vicar of Meidrym, Carm.; ejected, 1660. Licensed, 17 Apr. 1672, as Congr. Teacher in Llanstephen parish and Pencader, Carm.; his house in Swansea was licensed, 20 Apr. 1672. Had a great reputation for making preachers. (*C. P. Rw.*) [28]

HUGHES, STEPHEN, *secundus* (*fl.* 1691–1693). Son of Stephen Hughes [*q.v.*], received grants, 1691–93, as student under Samuel Jones, M.A. [*q.v.*]. (*M.*) [28, 146]

HULL. Ejected here were (1) John Shawe (23 June 1608—19 Apr. 1678), son of John, of Sick-House, Bradfield chapelry, Ecclesfield parish, W.R.; of Christ's Coll., Cambridge; matric. pensioner, 1623; B.A., 1626/7; M.A., 1630; ord. episcopally, 1629; lecturer at Brampton chapelry, Derb., 1630–33; lecturer at Chumleigh, Der., 1633–6; lecturer at Allhallows-on-the-Pavement, York; vicar of Rotherham, 17 Apr. 1639; rector of Lymm, Ches., 1643; rector of Scrayingham, E.R.; lecturer at St. Mary's, Hull; at Holy Trinity, Hull; master of the Charter House, Hull, 1651–June 1662; royal chaplain, 25 July 1660; preached in Rotherham parish church from June 1662 alternately with Luke Clayton (*see* Rotherham); ejected, 1662; preached in 1663 at Beverley, in 1669 at Rotherham; *d.* 19 Apr. 1672. (*C. D. Rb. T. V. Wp.*) (2) Joseph Wilson (whom Calamy ejects from Beverley). [? Of Sidney Sussex Coll., Cambridge; matric. sizar, 1629; B.A., 1632/3; M.A., 1636], vicar of St. Mary's, Beverley, before 1645 till 1652; vicar of Hessle (a parish partly in Hull), where he founded a school; ejected, 1660; licensed, 20 June 1672, as Grāll Pr. Teacher, being of Newland near Hull; also, 25 July 1672, as Pr. Teacher in a house at Hull; on 10 Aug. 1672 was licensed "A new Meeting-house built by Presby att blackfriergate in Kingston upon Hull" (apparently the first built in Yorkshire); here he ministered till his death in Feb. 1678/9. (*C. T. V. Wp.*) [138]

HULNE ABBEY ('Hull Abby') in Alnwick parish, Northumb.

HUMPHRYES, JOHN. ["John Humpherys of Beckford in Glostersh," was licensed as "Presb.", also with his house, on 5 S. 1672. (*T.*)] [138]

HUNGERFORD. Ejected here was John Clark, much beloved. (*C. P.*) Grants were made to Hungerford of £2 a year from 1691. (*M.*) [6, 7, 123]

HUNNETT. [123] *See* Wiltshire

HUNSTON. Ejected here was James Waller, M.A. [*q.v.*]. [105]

HUNT, EDWARD (*fl.* 1643–90). **P.** Held (after 1643) the sequestered rectory of Dunchideock, Devon., which became legally his on the incumbent's death, 1645, aged 92; ejected, 1662. The Episc. Return, 1665, reports him as living at St. Thomas, near Exeter, "whether he hath taken any Degree he cannot learne. But is informed that he liveth peaceably." Licensed, 11 Apr. 1672, as "a Grāll Presb. Teacher." He removed to South Molton, and ministered there till death. (*C. P. T. Wc.*) [31]

HUNT, JOHN (*d.* 15 S. 1725). **C.** Second son of William Hunt, B.A., ejected from the vicarage of Sutton, Cambs. He was granted (1691–3) £10 a year as Student of university learning under his brother, William Hunt [*q.v.*], at Cambridge. Minister at Royston, Herts; Northampton (1698–1709); Newport Pagnell., Bucks, till 1721; and Tunstead, Norf. (1723–5).

His son, William (*d.* 20 May 1770), was Minister at Mattishall, Norf., Newport Pagnell, Bucks, from 1725, and Mare Street, Hackney, from Aug. 1738 till death. (*B. C. Cm. Ev. M. P. We.*) [14]

HUNT, WILLIAM (*fl.* 1691–92). **C.** Eldest son of William Hunt, B.A., ejected from the vicarage of Sutton, Cambs. The Common Fund made him (1691) a grant of £6 a year; on 11 Apr. 1692 it was reported that he had removed from Cambridge "to a place of £40 per annum and needs nothing." Happy man. Minister of Little Baddow, Essex. (*C. M. P.*) [12, 13, 14]

HUNTINGDON. [53]

HUNTINGDONSHIRE. [53, 168, 176] Only the headings "Huntingdon" are in the earliest handwriting, the rest in that of the Book-keeper. The returns are numbered 27 and 148.

Layton is Leighton Bromswold.

HUSSEY, JOSEPH (31 Mar. 1660—15 N. 1726). **C.** Born at Fordingbridge, Hants. Educated by Robert Whitaker [*q.v.*] and at Newington Green under Charles Morton. Chaplain (1681) to Lady Thompson, Clapham; chaplain (1683) to Sir Jonathan Keate, at the Hoo, Herts. Ordained by presbyters in London, 26 Oct. 1688. Removed (1688) to Sissiferns (parish of Codicote, Herts), and registered the place (Mids. 1689) under the Toleration Act. Preached also at the new Meeting-house (1690), Maiden Croft, Hitchin. Removed (1691) to Cambridge (where his Meeting-house was pillaged in 1716) and (1720) to Petticoat Lane, London. One of the witnesses against Richard Davis [*q.v.*] at Kettering in 1692, but subsequently published his regret at having opposed Davis. Originally Presbyterian, he became Congregational in 1699. He lived in Hoxton Square, and there died. (*Ev. Gl. Uh. W. We.*) [50]

HUSSIE, PETER. [166]

ICKLETON. [13]

ILFRACOMBE ('Ilfarcomb'). [32]

ILKESTON ('Ilston'). [27]

ILMINSTER. Ejected here in 1660 were (1) William Alsop [*q.v.*]. (2) James Strong, son of Thomas, of Chardstock, Dors.; of New Inn Hall, Oxford; matric. 8 Apr. 1636, aged 17; M.A., 1657; army chaplain; rector of Bettescombe, Dors., 1648; preaching at various places in Somerset in 1669; licensed, 8 May 1672, as Pr. Teacher in a house at Broadway, Som.; conformed; rector of Earnshill, and vicar of Curry Rivell, Som., 1686; *d.* 1694. (*C. F. T.*) [91]

ILSLEY ('Ilsly,' 'Ilseley'), EAST or MARKET. [7, 8]

ILSTON. [27] *See* Derbyshire

INGLESHOMBE. [92] *See* Somerset

IPSWICH. Ejected here were (1) Benjamin Browning or Brunning, of St. Catharine's Hall, Cambridge; matric. pensioner, 1644; B.A., 1644/5; rem. to Jesus Coll.; Fellow; M.A., 1648; lecturer at St. Clement's, Ipswich; *d.* Nov. 1688. (*B. C. V.*) (2) Robert Gouge [*q.v.*]. (3) Benjamin Stonham, of St. Catharine's Hall, Cambridge; matric. sizar, 1633; B.A., 1636/7; M.A., 1640; chaplain to Sir Anthony Irby [*see* Lady Irby]; pastor of a Congregational church in St. Peter's, Ipswich; silenced, 1662; removed to London, preaching in his lodging; a millenarian; *d.* 30 Mar. 1676, aged about 63. (*B. C. V.*) (4) Roger Young, of Jesus Coll., Cambridge, matric. pensioner, 1646; B.A., 1649/50; M.A., 1653; vicar of St. Nicholas, Ipswich; preaching at East Bergholt, Suff., 1669; afterwards conformed. (*B. C. T. V.*) [103, 105, 172]

IRBI, *i.e.* IRBY, LADY (*d.* 1695). **P.** Catherine (third daur. of William, Lord Paget of Beaudesert, Staff., by Frances, daur. of Henry Rich, earl of Holland, K.G.) became (1647) the fourth wife of Sir Anthony Irby (*d.* 2 Jan. 1691/2), of Whaplode, Linc., knighted 2 June 1624, recorder of Boston, and M.P. for Boston. He was on the royalist side during the Civil War, yet as chaplain in his house in Westminster he had (1662–5) Thomas Cawton, B.A. (1637?–1677), who ultimately founded the Presbyterian congregation in Westminster, which met first in his own house, St. Anne's Lane (licensed, 2 Apr. 1672), afterwards successively in a Meeting-house in Tothill Street, and a larger one in Long Ditch (now Prince's Street). Irby Hall still stands at Whaplode. Sir Anthony removed to Boston. By this his fourth wife he had five daughters and a son, Anthony, his heir. Joseph Hill [*q.v.*] was probably tutor to the latter's two sons, Lady Irby's grandsons, viz. Edward, created a baronet, 13 Apr. 1704 (his son William was created, 10 Apr. 1761, baron Boston of Boston, Linc.), and Anthony, who entered the army. (*C. F. P. Pe. S. T.* and documents lent by the kindness of Lord Boston.) [2]

IRLAM THOMAS (*d.* 1748). **C.** Entered Frankland's Academy, 20 Apr. 1687. As Minister of Congleton, he was a founder, 1691, of the Cheshire Classis (*see* p. 157), but ceased attendance after 1719 (with one exception, 1731). In the early part of his ministry, he preached also in Bosley Chapel. A new Meeting-house was built for him at Congleton (1733). On his first application (1691) to the Common Fund, the intended grant was deferred, pending a report from Daniel Williams [*q.v.*] "concerning y[e] circumstances of y[e] s[d] Irlam"; ultimately a grant of £8 a year was confirmed (4 Sept. 1691); reduced in 1695 to £6, and in 1723 to £5; continued to 1746. A special grant of £10 was made to him, 3 Mar. 1717/8, "in consideration of some late disturbances which have been given to the meeting-house there." In 1697 he obtained also a grant from the Congregational Fund of £5 a year, increased in 1701 to £6. Nevertheless, in 1729 he conveyed land to his son Thomas. His will (24 Jan. 1746/7) was proved, 19 Aug. 1748; he left a considerable landed estate. He married at Stockport, 17 Apr. 1688, Sarah Travis of Blackley, Lanc. Among his descendants were Thomas Wright, Minister of Lewin's Mead, Bristol; Josiah Wedgwood, the potter; and Charles Robert Darwin, the apostle of evolution. His name is sometimes incorrectly spelled Irelom. (*Cf. Dr. Ev. M. Pi. Uc. Ue.*) [16, 179]

ISLE OF WIGHT ('White'). [100]

ISSEB, *i.e.* ISSOT, JOHN, B.A. (*b.* 1628). **C.** Born in Yorkshire. Son of John Issot. Matric. pensioner at Clare Hall, Cambridge, 1646; B.A., 1649. Ejected from the rectory of Nun Monkton, West Riding. According to Calamy, he died about his 52nd year, though the Manuscript makes him 62 in 1690.

Licence was issued, 16 May 1672, to "John Issot, jun. to be a Congr. Teacher in his howse in Hasbery," *i.e.* Horbury in Wakefield parish, West Riding. The application, 11 May 1672, was for "a Lycence for M[r] J[no] Issett Jun[r] att his fath[r] M[r] J[no] Issetts house at Horbery in Yorkeshire of the Congregationall pswasion."

John Issot, *tertius*, son of Edward Issot of Horbury, entered Frankland's Academy on 20 Feb. 1673/4; he was ordained 10 July 1678, at Richard Mitchel's house in Craven; he lived with Frankland, assisting him both in his Academy and his congregation; later he was Minister in Craven; and died on 12 Jan. 1687/8.

Another "M[r] Issot" died at Fold in Northowram on 3 June 1729. (*C. Fr. Ho. Nk. Nr. P. T. V.*) [129]

ITINERANT PREACHERS. [24, 32, 33, 47, 79, 93, 94, 124, 137, 175]

JACKSON, JOHN (1622—26 D. 1696). C. Born at Oxton, Notts. Son of W. Jackson, a centenarian Puritan divine. [? Matric. pensioner at Trinity Coll., Cambridge, 1634; Scholar, 1634; did not graduate.] Vicar of Bleasby, Notts; ejected, 1662. Removed to Morton, Notts, and taught school. Licensed, June 1672, as "Congr. Teacher in his howse in Morton." Subsequently he kept school at Kneesall, Notts. The Common Fund granted him, 1690–96, £4 a year at Bleasby. (*C. M. P. T. Tc. V.*) [83]

JACKSON, JOHN, M.A. (*fl.* 1638–1690). P. Eldest son of Arthur Jackson (*d.* 5 Aug. 1666); ejected from St. Faith's, London, who married the eldest dau. of T. Bownert of Stonebury, Herts. Matric. pensioner at St. Catharine's Hall, Cambridge, 1638; B.A., 1642/3; migrated to Queens' Coll.; Fellow, 1644; M.A., 1646. Held, 1656–61, the sequestered rectory of St. Benet's, Paul's Wharf, London; and later the vicarage of Molesey (East and West), Surrey; ejected, 1662. Preached in London, 1663 and 1664. Lived by correcting the press. His father's guardian, Joseph Jackson, was of Edmonton, Middx., and in John Jackson's house at Edmonton the father died. Licensed, 30 Apr. 1672, as general Presb. Teacher at Brentford, Middx.; his house at Old Brentford licensed, 10 Aug. 1672. Published a sermon, a concordance, and memoir prefixed to his father's Annotations on Isaiah, 1682. (*C. Cc. D. P. T. V. Wc. We.*) [2, 72, 73]

JACOB, JOSEPH. (*D.*) [187]

JACOBSTOWE ('Jacobstow'). Ejected here was Peter Osborne [? of Oriel Coll., Oxford; matric. 23 Apr. 1619, aged 17; B.A., 1622/3]; rector of Jacobstowe, 1642; ejected, 1662. (*C. F.*) [31]

JAFFRAY, JAMES. On 22 D. 1690 the Common Fund made him a gift of £5, he being at Hexham. (*M.*) [79]

JAMES II. [118, 154, 188]

JAMES, JOHN, M.A. (1620–July 1694). P. Son of Philip James of Bicester, Oxfordsh. Matric. 8 Dec. 1637, aged 17, at St. Alban's Hall, Oxford; B.A., 1641; M.A., 1649. In Anglican orders. Incumbent of Brighton, Sussex (1649–56); rector of West Isley, Berks, from 1656; ejected, 1662. Offered canonry of Windsor. Harassed by Five Mile Act (1666). In Episcopal Returns (1669) "Mr James of Staynes" is reported as one of 13 Teachers of a Presbyterian conventicle at Wraysbury and Colebrooke, Bucks (*cf.* Vincent, Nathaniel); also as one of six Presbyterian Teachers at Newbury Berks; and as preaching to "above 100" Presbyterians "Att the house of John Tilly," Weybridge, Surrey. On 13 May 1672 he was licensed as Presb. Teacher in his house in the parish of Staines, Middx. He was nine years Minister at Staines, and removed to London. He is the Mr. James in the list of unplaced Ministers. (*C. F. P. T.*) [2]

JAMES, JOHN (1626 ?–1696). C. Son of Simon James of Woodstock, Oxfordsh., schoolmaster. Matric. 24 July 1642 at Exeter Coll., Oxford, aged 15. Vicar of Flintham-with-Sutton, Notts, and lecturer at Newark; ejected (1661 ?) and imprisoned in Nottingham gaol for 17 months; arrested again, he "lay in Newark gaol about six years." In the Episc. Returns, 1669, he is reported as "one Mr James" preaching to "about 12 or 20 persons" at the houses of Robert Walker and Mr Fillingham in Arnold, Notts; also as "John James, a Farmer & a Dangerous Seducer from the Church," one of two preachers to a "considerable" number of Independents or Anabaptists, "Att the houses of Mr John James & William Bradley & Anthony Marsh in Flintham"; he is probably also the "one James," an ejected Minister, one of the preachers to "about 20" of the "better sort" at Wanlip, Leic. On 16 May 1672, he was licensed as a Congr. Teacher in the house of Eliz. Reade in Bridlesmith Gate, Nottingham. On the withdrawal of Indulgence his goods were seized, and he fled to London. He became pastor of a Congregational church in Wapping. He joined the Happy Union, and was appointed (19 Dec. 1692) a Manager of the Common Fund. He was an original Manager of the Congregational Fund (1695). He died at Wapping. (*C. Co. F. M. P. T.*) [157, 161, 165]

JAMES, JOHN. C. The Common Fund voted him, 16 F. 1690/1, a gratuity of £2, he being at Criglas, otherwise Cricklas, in Abergwilly parish, Carm. (*M.*) [144]

JAMES, RICE. [146]

JAMES, STEPHEN (*d.* 1724/5). P. The Common Fund voted him (9 May 1692) £10 a year "when fixed with a Tutour." Studied, 1692–6, under Matthew Warren [*q.v.*]. Minister at Pitminster, Som. Succeeded (1706) Warren as divinity tutor in the Taunton Academy, having Henry Grove (4 Jan. 1684/5—27 F. 1737/8) as his coadjutor and successor. Died early in 1725 "almost in the midst of his days," after long illness. He could not be much short of fifty. The funeral sermon, by Grove, is void of particulars. (*D. Ev. M.*) [125, 172]

JAMES, THOMAS (*fl.* 1676–1718). **P.** Minister at Ashford, Kent, in 1676. On 4 May 1691 the Common Fund ordered "y[t] if hee please to accept of £5 :—towards defraying the charge hee has beene at or shall be at in repairing his meeting house, it shall be given him out of this Fond." He removed in 1718. (*Ev. M. W.*) [55]

JAQUES . . . Not at Rochester in 1715. (*Ev.*) [55]

JEAKES, . . . (*d.* 1691/2 ?). Query, identical with the foregoing. [A London Minister, named Jaque, is mentioned in the Fund Minutes on 16 Feb. 1690/1 and 7 Dec. 1691; Rodbard and Stretton are deputed to ask him to contribute to the Fund; hence he was probably a Presbyterian.] [116]

JENKYN, WILLIAM, M.A. (Dec. 1613–19 Jan. 1684/5). **P.** Born at Sudbury, Suff. Eldest son of William Jenkyn, vicar of All Saints', Sudbury. His father had been disinherited for his puritanism; his mother was granddaughter of John Rogers, the Marian proto-martyr. Matric., 3 July 1628, at St. John's Coll., Cambridge; B.A., 1632; M.A., 1635. Having held from 13 Feb. 1639/40 a lectureship at St. Nicholas Acons, London, he was presented (27 Jan. 1640/1) to the rectory of St. Leonard's, Colchester. Resigning from fear of the ague, he was admitted (1 Feb. 1642/3) to the vicarage of Christ Church, Newgate, holding in addition a lectureship at St. Anne's Blackfriars. A strong Presbyterian, he remonstrated against the trial of Charles I.; his attitude caused his suspension from the ministry (June 1650). Implicated in the plot (1651) of Christopher Love for the restoration of Charles II., he narrowly escaped execution. His suspension was removed, and in 1654 he became rector of St. Anne's Blackfriars; this he soon exchanged for his old position at Christ Church, Newgate. Welcoming the Restoration, he was ejected in 1662. In 1663/4 he was preaching at Mr. Clayton's in Wood Street, at "y[e] Angell" in Newgate Market, and at the Rose and Crown in Blowbladder Street. He was treasurer of a Fund "for the benefit of those ministers turned out in the city and country." In 1665 he was still preaching at various places in London; he retired to King's Langley, Herts, and preached there. The Episc. Returns, 1669, report him as one of the preachers to 100 Presbyterians at Mrs. Bachelor's, St. Albans, Herts, and also to a "considerable" congregation "of the middle and inferior sort," at the house of Mr. Roberts, Watford, Herts. His licences, 2 Apr. 1672, for his house or chamber in Horn Alley, Aldersgate Street, as a Meeting-place for Presbyterians, and for himself to teach in any other licensed place, were the very first issued under the Indulgence of 15 March 1671/2. He was one of the original six lecturers at Pinners' Hall, 1672. His congregation built for him a Meeting-house in Jewin Street, where his services were connived at till 1682. He still preached privately, till his arrest (2 Sept. 1684) at a prayer-meeting. Refusing the Oxford oath (1665) to endeavour no alterations in Church or State, he was committed to Newgate. A petition to the Crown, backed by medical certificates, evoked from Charles II. the reply: "Jenkyn shall be a prisoner as long as he lives." Four months of rigorous confinement killed him. A courtier told Charles, "Jenkyn has got his liberty." "Ay, who gave it him?" "A greater than your Majesty, the King of kings." Mourning rings, distributed at his funeral (attended by 150 coaches), bore the words "Murdered in Newgate." The epitaph (1715) on his tomb in Bunhill Fields describes him as a martyr. (*C. Cm. D. P. T. W.*) [154, 163, 188]

JENNINGS, JOHN, B.A. (1634–1701). **P.** Born in Oswestry parish, Shrops. Entered at Christ Church, Oxford, 2 O. 1652; B.A., 1655/6. Rector (1658) of Hartley Westpall, Hants; ejected, 1662. Tutor to Noyes, of Tuckwell; chaplain to Mrs. Phesant, of West Langton, near Kibworth, Leic., and preached to a congregation in her house. Licensed, Sept. 1672, being of West Langton, as "Pr. Teacher." Removed latterly to Kibworth, Leic., where he bought an estate, and there died.

His sons, John (*d.* 8 July 1723) and David, D.D. (18 May 1691—16 S. 1762), were tutors of notable Academies. (*C. D. F. P. T.*) [67]

JENNINGS, RICHARD, M.A. (1607?–12 Sept. 1709). **P.** Eldest son of Richard Jennings, portman of Ipswich, by Elizabeth, dau. of Edward Day, M.P. Matric. pensioner at St. Catharine's Hall, Cambridge, 1633; B.A., 1635/6; M.A., 1639. Was in New England, 1636–9. Returning, preached in Northants, Hunts, and Suffolk. Ordained,

18 Sept. 1645, in London. Rector of Coombs, Suffolk, 1647; ejected, 1662; but retained the parsonage till 1678, when he went to London. Licensed, 10 June 1672, as Presb. Teacher in his house at Coombs. Latterly, lived with "three pious widows at Clapham." Preached without notes at 92. He married Temperance Dandy. Published nothing. (*B. C. P. T. V.*) [2]

JERRETT, . . . 𝔓. Proposed as Manager by Thomas Cockerill [*q.v.*], 29 July 1690; attended no meeting. (*M.*) [162]

JEWIN STREET. This site, off Aldersgate Street, originally named Leyrestowe, was known as Jewen Garden, being assigned as a cemetery for Jews, long the only one in England. On the expulsion of the Jews by Edward I. he granted the ground to the Dean of St. Paul's. Stow speaks of it as "turned into faire garden plots and summer houses for pleasure." Strype calls it Jewen Street, "being a continued Street of contiguous Houses on each side of the way." Milton lived in the eastern part of Jewin Street from 1661 to 1663, and there wrote most of "Paradise Lost." (*Lo. Sl. St.*) [1]

JOHNSON, THOMAS, M.A. (1629–July 1707). 𝔓. Born at Painsthorpe, in Kirby-under-Dale parish, East Riding. Son of Edward Joynson, yeoman. From Crigglestone grammar school admitted pensioner at St. John's Coll., Cambridge, 8 June 1649, age 19; B.A., 1652/3; M.A., 1656. Ordained by Adel Presbytery on 31 Oct. 1655 as Minister of Great Houghton Chapel in Darfield parish. Ejected (1662) from the vicarage of Sherburn-in-Elmet, West Riding. Crigglestone is in Sandall Magna parish, West Riding. Licensed, 30 Sept. 1672, being of Sandall Magna, as "Pr. Teach at his house and elsewhere." He received Fund grants, 1691–1706; originally £5 a year for Crigglestone; from 1695, £8 for Flockton and Crigglestone. He seems to have removed to Painsthorpe, and died there "An ancient Dissenting min^r^." (*C. Jo. M. Nr. P. T. V. Y.*) [129]

JOLLEY, *i.e.* JOLLY, THOMAS (14 S. 1629—14 Mar. 1702/3). ℭ. Born at Droylsden, Lanc., son of Major James Jollie (1610–1666). Entered Trinity Coll., Cambridge, as subsizar, 28 Jan. 1645/6; matric. 1646, but did not graduate. Incumbent of Altham Chapel, parish of Whalley, Lanc., Sept. 1649; formed there a "gathered church"; was party to a projected "accommodation" (1659) between the Presbyterian and Congregational divines of Lancashire; ejected, 1662. Removed to Healey, near Burnley, Lanc. Five times imprisoned for conventicling. Bought (1667) the farmhouse of Wymondhouses, parish of Whalley, Lanc., and there preached. The Episc. Returns, 1669, report a conventicle of "Independents, and some seperatists" at Altham. On petition from ten dwellers in Blackburn hundred, and eight in Salford hundred, licence was asked for Jolly, "Of the Congregationall perswasion," to preach in the house of Richard Sagar, called Slade, that of Richard Cottham, called Sparth, that of Robert Whittaker, called Healy, and Jolly's own at Wymondhouses. These licences were all granted, 2 May 1672. In 1688 he built a Meeting-house at Wymondhouses; in 1689, the house at Sparth was certified for worship. He took up the case (1689) of Richard Dugdale, the supposed demoniac of Surey, near Clitheroe, which brought him no credit. He was a member of the Lancashire Provincial Meeting of United Ministers (1693). Buried at Altham Chapel. (*C. D. Nl. P. T. Tc. V. Y.*) [61, 64]

JOLLEY, *i.e.* JOLLIE, TIMOTHY (1659?–28 Mar. 1714). ℭ. Born at Altham, Lancs. Son of Thomas Jolly [*q.v.*]. Entered Frankland's Academy, 27 Aug. 1673; rem., Dec. 1675, to study in London. Called, 1679, to the Congregational church, meeting at the New Hall, Snig Hill, Sheffield; ordained by presbyters, 28 Apr. 1681. Imprisoned at York, 1683. A new Meeting-house (the Upper Chapel) was built for him about 1700. Frankland had removed his Academy from Attercliffe to Rathmell in July 1689. In 1691 Jollie opened another Academy at Attercliffe Hall (his residence) for training students for the ministry; his curriculum excluded mathematical studies as tending to scepticism. Among his students (about 100), several of whom had bursaries from the Fund up to 1696, was a larger proportion of distinguished men than in most Nonconformist Academies: the list includes John Bowes, Lord Chancellor of Ireland, Thomas Secker, archbishop of Canterbury, and Nicholas Saunderson, LL.D., the blind mathematician and numismatist. (*D. M. Ma. My.*) [130, 133]

JONES, DAVID (*d.* 1700). ℭ. Born in Cardiganshire. Matric. 'ser.', at Christ Church, Oxford, 10 Nov. 1654. Ordained by presbyters. Vicar of Llanbadarn-fawr, Card.; ejected (1660?), kept school, and continued preaching. Licensed, 28

Oct. 1672, as "Congr. genall Teach of Pencarreg in Cardigansh." The Common Fund granted him (22 June 1691) £4 a year for Pencarreg till 1693. He was pastor at Cilgwyn, Card., and preaching at various places in Cardiganshire as late as 1694. (*C. F. M. P. Rj. Rw. T.*) [145]

JONES, DAVID (*d.* 1718). **C.** Grant of £5 was made (1697) to "Mr David Jones of Salop" from the Congregational Fund. He was Minister at Shrewsbury till death. (*Cf. Ev. P.*) [15, 88, 89]

JONES, DAVID. **C.** A minister of these names was at Gellybion, Glam., and Pilton in Gower, in 1715. (*Ev.*) [146]

JONES, GAMALIEL (*d.* 1717). **C.** Son of John Jones, M.A. (*d.* July 1671), ejected from Marple chapelry in Stockport parish. Entered Frankland's Academy, 16 Apr. 1679. Ordained at Warrington, Jan. 1687/8. If he were "Att Congleton" it was for a short time between the ministry of Eliezer Birch [*q.v.*], ended in 1688, and that of Thomas Irlam [*q.v.*], begun before March 1691. In 1691 Jones was a founder of the Cheshire Classis (*see* p. 157) and its scribe, being Minister of Chadkirk Chapel; it is probable, as Chadkirk is not mentioned, that Congleton is a mistake for Chadkirk. Chadkirk Chapel was claimed by Episcopalians, and Jones removed his congregation (1706) to Hatherlow, where they built a chapel. He received, 1713–16, a yearly Fund grant of £4 at Bredbury, in Chadkirk parish. He was buried at Marple, 6 June 1717.

His second son, John Jones, succeeded him at Hatherlow. (*Ev. Fr. Ht. Nk. Uc.*) [15]

JONES, JOHN (1640—3 July 1722). **C.** Householder at Llwynrhys, a dwelling in Llanbadarn Odwyn parish, Card., still standing, and used as a place of worship till 19 Oct. 1735. Said to have been the earliest Nonconformist preacher in Cardiganshire after the Restoration. His house was licensed on 28 (?) Oct. 1672 (*see* Morgan Howell). By his wife Margaret, sister of David Edwards [*q.v.*], he had four sons and twelve daughters. Of his sons, Jenkin became a noted preacher, and John was the ancestor of Rev. Rees Jenkin Jones, Aberdare, by whom valuable information for these Notes has been most kindly furnished. (*M. Rj. T.*) [146]

JONES, MALACHI (*d.* 1728). **C.** Granted £3 by the Congregational Fund on 13 Apr. 1696, being then still "of Herefordshire." He emigrated to America, and at the time of his death had been long pastor of a congregation in Pennsylvania.

His son Samuel (1680 ?–1719) was the tutor of the Academy at Gloucester, afterwards at Tewkesbury, under whom Secker and Butler were students. (*Cf. D. Rj.*) [143, 145]

JONES, SAMUEL, M.A. (1628—7 S. 1697). **C.** Born near Chirk Castle, Denb. Son of John Roberts, of Corwen, Merion. Matric. pleb., at All Souls' Coll., Oxford, 2 Mar. 1646/7, aged 18; expelled, 15 May 1648, by the parliamentary visitors; admitted scholar of Jesus Coll., 2 Nov.; B.A., 1652; M.A., 1654; Fellow and Bursar. Ordained by presbyters at Taunton. Held (4 May 1657) the sequestered vicarage of Llangynwyd, Glam.; ejected, 1662. He lived at Brynllwarch, a farmhouse in Llangynwyd parish, and there (about 1672) established a famous Nonconformist Academy, the first in Wales, and the precursor of the Carmarthen (Presbyterian) College. Kildeudy, where his congregation met (the house of Rees Powell was licensed there as a Pr. Meeting Place on 18 Nov. 1672), is near Bridgend, Glam. He suffered imprisonment for Nonconformity. The Episc. Returns, 1669, report him as preaching at Bettws, Glam., "At the house of Mr Rees Powell in the late time of Rebellion a Sheriffe of the County, & a Justice of peace"; this was Rees Powell of Maesteg, parish of Llangynwyd, whose daughter Mary was Jones' first wife. Licensed, 30 Apr. 1672, as Pr. Teacher at his house in Llangynwyd, and elsewhere; also, 16 July 1672, as "Ind. to be a teacher at his howse in Margam Parish Glamorgan"; also, 30 S. 1672, as "Pr. Teacher at the house of Eve Christopher of Cowbridg in Glamorgansh." The Common Fund voted him (1690) £6 a year. He was a Welsh poet of distinction. (*C. D. F. M. P. Rj. Rw. T. Wc.*) [143, 146]

JONES, WATKIN (*fl.* 1662–1692). **C.** Curate to Henry Walter, B.C.L.; ejected (1662) from the vicarage of Newport, Monm., who served also the vicarage of Mynyddyslwyn and the rectory of Bedwas; and ejected with him. In 1668 he became pastor at Gellygrug, parish of Aberystwith, Monm., to a union of Congregationals and Baptists. The Baptists seceded, but (according to Rees) Jones, whom he places at Sychbant, parish of Mynyddyslwyn, was pastor to the residue till his death, after 1692. Licensed, June 1672, "to be a Pr. Teacher at his howse in Mynythysloy [*i.e.* Mynyddyslwyn] Parish, Monm." The Common Fund voted him (28 S. 1691) £4 a year;

on 27 June 1692, and 19 June 1693, he is paid this for Newport, Monm., apparently as assistant to Thomas Barnes [*q.v.*]. (*C. F. M. P. Rw. T.*) [143]

JOSSELYN, *i.e.* JOCELYN, SIR ROBERT (Jan. 1622/3–June 1712), created a baronet, 8 June 1665; sheriff of Herts, 1677–78; direct ancestor of the Earls of Roden (earldom, 1771). (*Ba.*) [51]

JURIN, JOHN. **P.** Citizen of London, and dyer, was of St. Dunstan's Hill, in 1677. He attended as Manager on 14 July 1690, when he was appointed one of the Treasurers, and a Correspondent for Dorsetshire, Hampshire, Middlesex, Suffolk, and Warwickshire. His last attendance was on 6 March 1692/3. On 19 June 1693 he was replaced as Correspondent for Warwickshire by Samuel Annesley [*q.v.*]. At Midsummer 1693 his subscription was in arrear. He was not a Manager of the reconstituted Fund (1695). (*Ld. M.*) [34, 35, 73, 101, 106, 119, 147, 162, 164, 168]

JUSTIFICATION CONTROVERSY. [156]

KANEDY. [144] *See* Llanedi

KAY, *i.e.* RAY, JOHN (1659—17 S. 1699). **P.** Entered Frankland's Academy, 30 Mar. 1676. Lived at Gomersal. Ordained at Alverthorpe, 4 Sept. 1689. At the time of his death was preaching alternately at Pudsey and Cleckheaton (*see* Holdsworth, John). Buried at Birstall, 20 S. 1699. (*Fr. Hh. Ht. My. Nk. Nr.*) [130]

KEELING, FRANCIS (*fl.* 1690–93). Elder son of Francis Keeling; B.A. (1632—14 Apr. 1690); ejected from the chapelry of Cogshot, Shropshire. He received, 1 Feb. 1691/2, a grant of £5 for his encouragement as itinerant Minister in Suffolk; renewed, 18 Jan. 1692/3; and increased, 20 March 1693, to a yearly grant of £10, which, however, ceased before June.

His younger brother, John, was granted £10 a year as student, on 1 Dec. 1690; confirmed, 12 Jan. 1690/1. He died Minister of Cirencester, Glou., in 1726. (*C. Ev. M. P.*) [2, 104]

KEITH, . . . (*fl.* 1690–96). **C.** Student, 1690, under Thomas Doolittle [*q.v.*]. Apparently a Londoner. The Minutes of the Congregational Fund Board show that on 13 April 1696 "Dr. Chancy gave his Oppinion concerning Mr Keath . . . for their being further instructed in their Studdies," and "That Mr Cross discourse with Mr Keath's mother about his maintenance"; further, on 11 May 1696, it was "Ordered that £10 be allowed unto young Mr Keith for his instruction for one yeare, leaveing the conduct of him to Mr Cross." Walter Cross, M.A. (*d.* 1701), was Minister of the Congregational church in Rope-makers' Alley, Moorfields. Keith was sent to study under Thomas Goodwin, *secundus* [*q.v.*], at Pinner. (*Cf. Co. W.*) [4]

KELLANS. [145] *See* Cardiganshire

KELLET, NETHER. Thomas Whitehead (1606–Feb. 1679/80), ejected from Dalton, Lancs, was licensed, 22 May 1672, as Pr. Teacher in James Dickenson's house here. (*C. T.*) A Fund grant of £10 a year for Kellet was made (4 July 1692) to Robert Waddington (**C.**), who was ordained April 1682, and succeeded George Benson [*q.v.*] at Kellet. Only £8 was paid in 1692 and 1693. Waddington removed (1700) to Tockholes; he received £5 a year for Tockholes (where he was succeeded (1715) by Peter Valentine. (*Ev. M. Nt.*) [23]

KELSEY, . . . **P.** Proposed as Manager by Samuel Powell [*q.v.*], 29 July 1690; attended no meeting. (*M.*) [162]

KEMPSTER, JOHN, M.A. (1630 ?–July 1692). **P.** Son of William Kempster, of Burford, Oxfordshire. Matric., 9 April 1647, at Christ Church, Oxford, aged 17; B.A., 1649/50; M.A., 1654; chaplain of his college. Held the sequestered vicarage of Brixham, Devon, 1659; ejected, 1662. Lived at Lupton, and remained there after ejection, removing to Dartmouth. The Episcopal Returns (1665) report him as living there "peaceably and quietly." Driven to London by the Five Mile Act (1666); but licensed, 11 Apr. 1672, as a general Presb. Teacher of Dartmouth. Signed the thanks from Devon Ministers. Returned to London, and preached occasionally. He married a Nicholls, of Liskeard, Cornwall. (*C. F. P. T. Wc.*) [2]

KENDAL ('Kendall'). Calamy gives John 'Wallis' as ejected here and scandalous; the reference is to John Wallace, M.A., vicar of Heversham, Westm., 1658; ejected, 1660; his conduct, as rector of Grasmere, 1653–8, had been scandalous in 1655; in 1664 he was imprisoned for Nonconformity. (*C. N.*) [121]

KENISTON. [26] *See* Kynaston

KENT. [51, 55, 56, 168, 176, 181] Only the headings "Kent" are in the earliest handwriting; the rest, with slight exception, in that of the Book-keeper. The returns are numbered from 60 to 125 (most of them 74), and in 1691 from 1 to 15.

Feversham, Fever, is Faversham [*q.v.*].
Leige Castle is Leeds Castle.
Westcum is Westerham [*q.v.*].

KENTISH, THOMAS (*d.* 1700). **P.** Son of Thomas Kentish, M.A. (*d.* 1695); ejected from the rectory of Overton, Hants. Grandson of Thomas Kentish, ejected from the rectory of Middleton, Durh. Probably studied (before 1685) in the Academy at Newington Green, of Charles Morton [*q.v.*]. Evening lecturer at Crosby Hall, Bishopsgate. Succeeded Nathaniel Oldfield (1674—31 D. 1696) as Minister of the Presbyterian Congregation in Globe Alley, Maid Lane, Southwark. (*W. We.*) [2, 166]

KENWYN ('Kenwin'). [19]

KER, JOHN, M.D. (1639–+1723). **P.** Born in Ireland. Possibly son of James Ker, Presbyterian Minister of Ballymoney, Co. Antrim (1646–60), who died in Scotland. Educated in Scotland, being probably the "Joannes Ker" who graduated at Edinburgh on 18 July 1664. He conducted an Academy in Dublin at which Ministers and laymen were educated. Two of his pupils, living in 1703, were Ministers of repute. In a return of Presbyterian Ministers and Probationers in Ireland, about the middle of March 1689, John Ker appears as one of the Probationers in and about Dublin. From Ireland he was driven, probably in that year, in consequence of the measures taken during the vice-royalty (1687–91) of Richard Talbot, earl of Tyrconnel. He became at once the chief instructor at the Academy in Bishop's Hall, Bethnal Green [*q.v.*], then under Thomas Brand [*q.v.*], on whose death (1 Dec. 1691) he conducted the Academy alone, for a year, when he was succeeded by John Short [*q.v.*]. From 1690 to 1692 the names of 21 of his divinity students are recorded. Probably he next opened an Academy of his own. On 3 March 1694 he became a student at the University of Leiden as "Johannes Ker, Hybernus," his age being 45, and his subject "Mathesis," which included Natural Philosophy. On 5 March 1696/7 he graduated M.D. at Leiden. Returning to London he resumed his Academy; the last grant to one of his students was in 1708. His forte was Latin: at prayers in his Academy he was more effective in Latin than in English. At this time he attended the ministry at Armourers' Hall, Coleman Street, of George Hamond, M.A. (1620–Oct. 1705); ejected (1662) from the united rectories of Trinity and St. Peter's, Dorchester. Nothing is said of his preaching anywhere. Of the conduct of his Academy and its studies a very full account (some of it reproduced by Jeremy) is given by Samuel Palmer (*d.* 1724), his pupil some time before 1698, who speaks of him as "the same Encourager of free and large thoughts in every part of our studies." He conducted his Academy at Highgate; afterwards, it is said, at St. John's Square, Clerkenwell. Calamy speaks of him as "critically disposed" and "very particular in his temper," yet ready to make ample amends for what he owned to be "a carping cavilling spirit." His publications are the following; if the latest is properly ascribed to him, he reached the age of 84.

1. "Disputatio de Secretionis Animalis efficiente Causa et Ordine," Lugd. Bat. 1697, 4to.
2. "Selectarum de Lingua Latina Libri duo," etc., 1708–9, 8vo.
3. "Quaternae Epistolae . . . ad R. Bentleium . . . ad E. Spanhemium . . . ad F. Bonetum, 1713, 8vo.
4. "Serenissimo . . . Principi Georgio . . . Regi . . . in illud Ciceronis 'O tempora! O mores!' Carmen." 1723 fol. anon. (Latin and English verse, addressed to George I.)

Ker is the spelling in his publications; the name is also spelled Kerr, Kir, Kirr, Karr, and Carr (the last two representing the Irish pronunciation). (*A. Cm. D.* (under O'Quinn) *Ed. Je. M. Pa. Re. Ri.*) [90, 166]

KERRING, . . . ? Nathaniel Kerridge (brother of John Kerridge of Colyton; *see* Ames Short), matric. at Magdalen Hall, Oxford, 16 July 1661, aged 18. (*F.*) [91]

KERSHAW, or KIRSHAW, NICHOLAS (*d.* Apr. 1707). **P.** Entered Frankland's Academy, 27 July 1680. Pasture House in Horton-in-Craven, parish of Gisburn, West Riding, misplaced in North Riding (p. 135), was the place of Nonconformist worship before 1689. Afterwards a Meeting-house in Horton was built by Richard Hargraves (*d.* 1718), a London merchant. Kershaw succeeded John Issot, *tertius* [*q.v.* under Isseb], as Minister in Craven, and was ordained at Rathmell, 8 Apr. 1691. He died in London, and was buried 18 Apr. 1707. The Fund gave yearly grants of £15, in favour of Kershaw and two others, for places in Craven, 1704–8. (*Fr. Hh. Ht. M. My. Nk. Nr.*) [130, 135]

KESWICK. [22, 23]

KETTERING. Ejected here was John Maydwell, M.A. [*q.v.*]. The Common

Fund in 1693 offered £5 to Kettering if a Minister were fixed there. (*M.*) [76, 186, 187]

KETTLEBASTON ('Kittle Barson'). [107]

KEY, THOMAS (*d.* Apr. 1698). **C.** Candidate for the ministry in 1662; silenced. Member of the church of Thomas Jolly [*q.v.*]. Ordained, 10 S. 1671, as Minister of the Nonconformists of Walmsley Chapel, Lanc. Application was made by ten dwellers within the hundred of Blackburn and eight within the hundred of Salford for licence to Key, and for licences for the houses of Francis Norbury, in Entwistle, John Wood, in Tottington, and John Harwood, in Hoddlesdon, as Meeting-places for him. Licence was given, 2 May 1672, to Key as "Congr. Teacher in the howse of Francis Norbury in the hundred of Salford," and at the same time the houses of Wood, Harwood, and Norbury were licensed as "Congr. Meeting Places." Entwistle and Walmsley are both in Bolton parish; Hoddlesdon, in Over Darwen, is in Jolly's district, and suggests that Key was to take part in Jolly's labours. He was one of those who conducted services at Hoghton Tower. The Common Fund granted him (1690) £5 a year for Walton Chapel, reduced (1695) to £4, ending 25 D. 1703; but this was one of the cases of continued payment of grant to the place though the Minister was dead. Key was buried at Walton, 22 Apr. 1698. (*C. M. Nl. P. T.*) [60]

KICKMANSWORTH. [51] *See* Hertfordshire

KIDDERMINSTER ('Kiderminster'). Ejected here in 1660 was Richard Baxter [*q.v.*]. [126, 127, 128]

KILDEUDY ('Kildeydy'), near Bridgend, Glam. [143]

KIMBOLTON ('Kimbleton'). [53]

KING, JOHN (*fl.* 1688–1746). **C.** Studied under Charles Morton [*q.v.*], at Newington Green. Assistant (1680–88) to John Collins in the Congregational church, Paved Alley, Lime Street, London; assistant (31 March 1688 + July 1690) to James Hannot in the Congregational church, Great Yarmouth; reported 1 Dec. 1690 as "now fixing at Wellingborough," and received a grant of £10. Minister of the Congregational church, Silver Street, Wellingborough, Northants, 1691, and removed it (1746) to a new Meeting-house in Cheese Lane. One of the witnesses against Richard Davis [*q.v.*] at Kettering in 1692 (*see* p. 186). He received grants from both Funds; the grant from the older Fund (ranging from £5 to £8) was paid to him up to 1745; thereafter, till 1750, a grant of £6 is paid to Wellingborough, without mention of Minister's name. (*B. Cf. Co. Gl. M. W.*) [75, 77, 186]

KING, JOHN (*d.* 1740 ?). **P.** Son of John King, "a poor Cutler of Sheffield." Received, 2 Mar. 1690/1, a yearly grant of £5 "towards his education." His name occurs at the end of a list of Yorkshire students, 1692. On 30 May 1692 a grant of £3, for books, was made to him as student under Vincent Alsop [*q.v.*]. He is probably the John King, ordained 21 O. 1707, Minister at Stone, Staff.; removed to Newport, Shrops., 1721; and received Fund grants yearly up to 1739. (*Ev. M.*) [134]

KING, SIMON, M.A. (1613–1693 ?). **P.** Son of Simon King of Woodhouse, Leic., pleb. Matric. at Balliol Coll., Oxford, 15 June 1632, aged 19; rem. to St. John's Coll.; B.A., 1633/4; returned to Balliol Coll.; M.A., 1638. Schoolmaster at Bridgnorth, Shrops., where he lived in the same house with Richard Baxter [*q.v.*]. Vicar of Holy Trinity, Coventry, 1642–5; rector of Botolph-Bridge, Hunts (now united with Orton Longueville); ejected, 1662. Licensed, July 1672, as "Pr. Teacher" in his house at Orton Longueville (burnt down in Aug. 1689). The Common Fund granted him (1690–93) £8 a year for Peterborough. (*C. F. M. P. T.*) [53, 76]

KING, WILLIAM (*d.* Sept. 1695). **P.** Brought up under the ministry of Vincent Alsop, M.A. [*q.v.*], who directed his studies in London. Minister at Romford, Essex. Ordained, 22 June 1694, with Thomas Reynolds [*q.v.*], and others. (*Cm.*) [2]

KING, WILLIAM (1638 ? – 1696 ?). **P.** [? Born in London. Son of William King. From Chelmsford grammar school admitted sizar at St. John's Coll., Cambridge, 8 June 1654, aged 16; B.A., 1657/8; rem. to King's Coll., M.A., 1661.] Place of ejection not known; Calamy ejects "Mr King" from somewhere in Dorset. Hutchins mentions "one George King" as "intruder" at Piddletown, Dors., to which the sequestered vicar, James Lukin, returned in 1660; but the holder of this sequestered cure was Simon Ford, who served it by supplies (*La.*); the strong probability is that the above "intruder" was George King, M.A., Oxon.; vicar of Frampton, Dors., 27 Apr. 1661; rector of Langton Matravers, Dors., 5 Dec. 1664, where he died, 1 June

1709, aged 83. William King was licensed, 10 June 1672, as " Pr. Teacher in the howse of Joane Troop in Newton," *i.e.* Maiden Newton, Dors. From 1692 to 1696 the Fund granted him £6 a year for Maiden Newton; reduced (1695) to £5. (*C. Hu. Jo. La. M. P. T. V.*) [34]

KING'S LYNN ('Lin'). Ejected here were: (1) John Dominick (C.). (2) . . . Fenwick. ? Edward Fenwick [*q.v.*]. (3) John Horne, of Trinity Coll., Cambridge; matric. sizar, 1633; B.A., 1636/7; preached first at Sutton St. James, Linc., near Long Sutton, his native place; also at Bolingbroke, Linc.; vicar of All Saints', King's Lynn, 1647; ejected 1662/3; preaching at Bradfield, Norf., and in his own house, King's Lynn, to 100 " Universallists," *i.e.* Arminians, in 1669; licensed, 5 Sept. 1672, as Congr. Teacher in King's Lynn; *d.* 14 Dec. 1676, aged 61. (*B. C. V.*) [71, 74]

KINGSBRIDGE. [31]

KINGSCLERE (' Kingscleere '). [102, 147]

KINGSTON UPON HULL. *See* Hull

KIRKBURTON. [132]

KIRKOSWALD (' Kirk Oswald,' ' Kirk oswald,' ' Hiellossould '). [21, 22]

KIRTLING (' Catlige '). Famous for the Synod of A.D. 977. The Common Fund granted (1691) £4 a year for Catlige. (*M.*) [13, 107]

KITTLE BARSON. [107] *See* Suffolk

KNIGHT, JOHN, M.A. (*d.* Aug. 1715). P. Matric. ' ser.' at Exeter Coll., Oxford, 28 Mar. 1653; B.A., 1656 (John Hoppin [*q.v.*] was his tutor); rem. to New Coll., M.A., 1659. Calamy connects him with the sequestered vicarage of Little Hempston, Devon, a living held during the whole time of sequestration by Thomas Friend, whom Palmer, following a misprint in Walker, places at the non-existent Little Kempston; while Calamy proposes (for Friend) the equally non-existent Little Yempston. It is possible that Knight acted as Friend's assistant at Little Hempston. The Episc. Returns, 1669, report him as one of the preachers at Cruwys-Morchard, Devon (*see* Saunders, Richard); also to " 2 or 300 " at Crediton " On Sundayes & other dayes." Licensed, 11 Apr. 1672, being of Crediton, as " a Grāll Pr. Teacher "; his house " in the West Town of Crediton " was licensed, 22 Apr. 1672, as " a Pr. Meeting Place." John Pope (*d.* 9 July 1689), licensed at Crediton on the same day and same terms, was pastor (1687) of the Crediton Presbyterians. Knight received, 23 Feb. 1691, a Fund grant of £3 and was advised " to settle with some people "; he was offered (18 May) £6 a year if he would fix at Bow, Devon; and was granted (1691–1714) £6 a year for Abbots-Kerswell, Dev., reduced (1695) to £4. His preaching was marred by an impediment in speech. The statement " Ancient and infirm not able to goe abroad to preach " must refer to James Burdwood [*q.v.*], though applied, in the first arrangement of material, to Knight. He appears to have been living in Exeter when he supplied Calamy with hints about Devon Ministers. (*C. Em. M. P. T. Wc.*) [31, 32]

KNIGHTLEY, LUCIE, or LUCY. P. Attended as Manager on 5 Jan. 1690/1 only. He died before 9 May 1692, when Christopher Fowler [*q.v.*] was appointed in his place. (*M.*) [162]

KNOWLE (' Knole '). [118, 119]

KNUTSFORD. Ejected here was Robert Hunter, who afterwards conformed and died in Liverpool. (*C.*) Here met the Cheshire Classis (*see* p. 157). The Meeting-house, built 1688 and still in use, is of an oblong architectural design, peculiar to this part of the country, of which samples remain also at Macclesfield and Dean Row. On either side of the front, external flights of steps, rising over the entrance doors, lead to the galleries; inside, the pulpit, crowned by a sounding board, was placed centrally between the entrance doors; fronting it was the long communion table, reaching (as in East Anglia) to near the back wall; the ground-floor seats, right and left, faced (not the pulpit, but) the table. [15]

KYLTLY, *i.e.* KEIGHLEY, EDWARD, M.A. (*d.* 1701). P. Born at Grays, Ess., seat of his family, whose name (pron. ' Kitely ') is variously spelled. Matric. ' arm ' at New Inn Hall, Oxford, 26 May 1651; B.A., 1654; M.A., 1657. Appointed to the chapelry of Aldborough Hatch, Ess., newly erected (1653) on property of his family; ejected, 1660. Licensed, 2 May 1672, as " Pr. Teacher " in his house at Aldborough Hatch; licensed also, 16 July 1672, as of Barking, Ess. He had been paid by the Pinners' Hall congregation for a Lecture at Romford, Ess. (where Edward Whiston [*q.v.*] was Minister); the Common Fund, from 18 May 1691 to 1693, undertook the payment of £10 a year for this Lecture. Later he preached at Billericay, Ess. He was buried at Barking on 3 July 1701. (*C. E. F. M. P. T.*) [38]

KYNNSTON, KENISTON, *i.e.* KYNASTON, THOMAS (1666—10 Jan. 1695/6). C. Son of Kynaston, the nonconforming, yet not ejected, Minister of Nether Whitley Chapel, in Great Budworth parish, Chesh. Entered Frankland's Academy, 12 Sept. 1681. Publicly ordained at Warrington, Jan. 1687/8. Minister at Knutsford, 1690 till death. He received, 10 N. 1690, £3 as share of an anonymous £50 donation made through Matthew Rapier. One of the founders of the Cheshire Classis (*see* p. 157). (*Ht. M. Nk. Uc.*) [15, 26]

LAMB, . . . [2]
LAMBROOK ('Lambrooke'), EAST. [93]
LANCACK. [20] *See* Cornwall
LANCASHIRE. [23, 58, 61, 63, 130, 131, 152, 155, 168, 171, 176, 177, 181, 186] Only the two headings "Lancaster" are in the earliest handwriting; the rest in that of the Book-keeper. The returns are numbered from 13 to 112.
Blakburne is Blackburn [*q.v.*].
Blakeley, Blakely is Blackley [*q.v.*].
Choleton, Choulton is Chorlton [*q.v.*].
Filde is Fylde [*q.v.*].
Fourness is Furness.
Horrige is Horwich.
Rachdale is Rochdale [*q.v.*].
St. Ellins is St. Helen's.
Teatham is Tatham [*q.v.*].
LANCAST ('Lancack'). [20]
LANCASTER. Ejected here was William Marshall, M.A. (1621–Dec. 1683). Born at Boroughbridge, Yorks, W.R. Son of Toby Marshall, porter, of St. Katharine Coleman's parish, London. From a London school, admitted sizar at St. John's Coll., Cambridge, 20 Sept. 1636, aet. 15; vicar of Lancaster in 1650; ejected, 1660; went about; settled in London as physician. Munk records the admission on 5 Apr. 1669, as Candidate of the College of Physicians, of William Marshall, of St. John's Coll., Cambridge; matric. sizar, Dec. 1637; B.A., 1640/1; M.D., 1652; the vicar of Lancaster is mentioned as "Mr of Arts" in the Parliamentary Survey of 1650. William Marshal (*sic*) in "Answers upon several heads in Philosophy," 1670, describes himself as "Dr. of Physick of the Colledge of Physicians, in London," where his study was "in Nags head Court in Gray's Church Street" (a Puritan evasion of the name Gracechurch). He was buried at Deptford, 21 Dec. 1683. (*C. Jo. Mu. Nl. V. Z.*) [58]
LANCASTON. [19] *See* Cornwall
LANDRAKE. [19] Ejected here was Gaspar Hickes, M.A. (1605–1677); born in Berks; son of a clergyman; matric. at Trinity Coll., Oxford, 26 O. 1621, aged 16; B.A., 1625; M.A., 1628; vicar of Launcelles, Corn., 1630–34; vicar of Landrake, 1632; ejected, 1662. Member of the Westminster Assembly, 1643. Licensed, 22 Apr. 1672, as "Grall Presb. Teacher" at Landrake. Signed the thanks of Cornish Ministers. (*C. F. P. T.*)
LANE, SIR THOMAS, of St. Laurence Lane, Cheapside; knighted, 30 July 1688. [? The Thomas Lane, civilian, who commanded a troop in King James' Army, 1689.] (*D. S.*) [164]
LANGPORT. Ejected here was John Bush [*q.v.*]. [91]
LANGSTON, JOHN (1640?–12 Jan. 1703/4). C. From the Worcester grammar school entered as servitor Pembroke Coll., Oxford, 7 N. 1655. Held the sequestered rectory of Ashchurch, Glou.; ejected, 1660. Removing to London, he taught a grammar school in Spitalfields. In 1662 went to Ireland as chaplain to Capt. Blackwell. Returning to London and his school, he assisted William Hook, M.A. (1601?—21 Mar. 1677/8), ejected from the mastership of the Savoy (*see* John Hook). On 20 Apr. 1672 he and Hook were licensed as Congr. Teachers "in the howse of Richard Loton in Spittle Yard." After 1679 he removed into Bedfordshire, where he ministered till 1686; invited then to Ipswich, he constituted (12 Oct.) the Congregational church which built (1687) a Meeting-house in Green Yard. He educated several students for the ministry. (*B. C. D. F. P. T.*) [103, 104, 108, 173]
LANGTON, EAST and WEST. Ejected from East or Church Langton were: (1) Samuel Blakesley or Blackerby, rector, 1656–59, afterwards conformed; but neither the date nor the fact of his alleged ejection has been ascertained (*C. Ln.*). (2) Richard Muston, of Christ's Coll., Cambridge; matric. pensioner, 1609; B.A., 1612/3; rector here in 1659; ejected, 1662; found a refuge in Coventry for his destitute old age; *d.* there, 1672/3; the funeral sermon, 1674, by John Bryan, D.D. (*see* John Bryan, M.A.), was rendered into verse, with title "Harvest-Home"; it contains three unique words, "aphthartal, amiantal, amarantall"; on its title-page Muston's name appears as "Ob. Musson"; Musson represents the pronunciation of Muston; the British Museum has two copies of "Harvest-Home," both corrected by Bryan himself; in each, "Ob." is corrected to "Rich." (*C. Ln. V.*) [67]
LANHAM. [107] *See* Suffolk
LARDNER. *See* Learner
LARKHAM, DELIVERANCE (9 July

1658–1723). ℭ. Born at Cockermouth. Eldest son of George Larkham, M.A. [*q.v.*]. Entered Frankland's Academy, 10 Jan. 1675/6. Went to London, 1677, for further training. Member of Congregational church at Cockermouth, 1681. Thence went to Launceston, Corn., as Minister. Ordained, 26 Aug. 1691. Invited to assist his father, 1694. Died Minister of Congregational church, Exeter. His address was Castle Street, Exeter. (*Em. Ev. Lc. N. Nk.*) [30]

LARKHAM, GEORGE, B.A. (20 Apr. 1630—26 D. 1700). ℭ. Born at Northam, Devon. Son of Thomas Larkham, M.A. (4 May 1601–1669); ejected from the vicarage of Tavistock. From Dorchester school went (according to Calamy) to Trinity Coll., Cambridge; did not matriculate. Matric. serv. at Exeter Coll., Oxford, 9 Apr. 1647, aged 17; B.A., 1650. Appointed, 1651, incumbent of the sequestered chapelry of Cockermouth; where a Congregational church was formed, 2 O. 1651; ordained by presbyters, 28 Jan. 1651/2, " for feare of offending the godly brethren of y^e^ Presbyteriall way "; joined the Associated Ministers of Cumberland; ejected, Nov. 1660. Continued to preach there and in the neighbourhood. The Episc. Returns, 1669, report him as preaching to 50 or 60 Independents, " meane for the most part," at Bridekirk, Cumb. Licensed, 8 May 1672, as " Pr. Teacher in his howse in Hameshill in the Parish of Bridekirke "; the house (which really belonged to Sister Hutton) was licensed, same date, and also 19 July. He was pastor of the Cockermouth Congregational church till death. Grant of £10 a year was made to him (1690) " on condition hee keep up y^e^ Lecture at Cockerm: ", and continued to 1693. From 1696 grants were made him from the Congregational Fund. (*C. Cf. F. Lc. M. N. P. T. Tc. Y.*) [21, 176]

LASLITHIEL ST. [19] *See* Cornwall

LATHAM, . . . ? Richard Latham, receiving Fund grants as Minister at Wem, Shrops., 1697–1710. (*M.*) [15]

LATIN. [181, 182]

LAUNCESTON (' Lancaston '). [19]

LAVENHAM (' Lanham '). [106, 180]

LAWRENCE, RICHARD, M.A. (1627–17 N. 1702). ℭ. Son of Francis Laurence, bricklayer, of Land-Beech, Cambs. Admitted sizar at St. John's Coll., Cambridge, 23 Feb. 1642/3, aet 14; then at Pembroke Coll., Oxford; M.A., 26 May 1659; incorp. at Cambridge, 1651. Rector of Trunch, Norf., 1651; ejected, 1662 (held also from 1654 the sequestered rectory of Stratton St. Michael's, Norf.; ejected, 1660). Pastor some time at Amsterdam to the Brownist congregation, whose Meeting-house, burnt in 1662, was rebuilt 1668. Assistant to Matthew Mead [*q.v.*]; declined calls to succeed John Owen [*q.v.*] in 1683, and to pastorate at Yarmouth in 1687. Disabled from work, from 1697.

A son of his was under education for the ministry in 1690, and is perhaps the Lawrence ministering at Wolverhampton, Staff., and from 1697 till after 1701 at Banbury, Oxon. (*B. C. F. Jo. M. P. Ss.*) [72]

LAWRENCE, SAMUEL (1661—24 Apr. 1712). 𝔓. Only son of William Lawrence, dyer, Wem, Shrops.; baptized, 5 N. 1661. Educated at the grammar schools of Wem and Newport, and at the Academy of Charles Morton [*q.v.*], Usher in Thomas Singleton's school, Bartholomew Close; chaplain to Lady Irby [*q.v.*]; assistant to Vincent Alsop [*q.v.*]. Minister at Nantwich from 1688 (ordained in Nov.) till death. One of the founders of the Cheshire Classis (*see* p. 157).

His son, Samuel Lawrence, D.D. (1693—1 O. 1760), was Minister at Newcastle-under-Lyme, 1714–28; Newcastle-on-Tyne, 1728–33; Monkwell Street, London, from 1733, and a Fund Manager from 1734. (*D. Ev. M. Uc.*) [15]

LAWTON, or LAUGHTON, JAMES (*fl.* 1660–90). Ejected from Dore (' Dower ') Chapelry in Dronfield parish, Derb. [Calamy identifies him with James Lawton (*d.* 1702), who in 1667 was living at Glodwick, near Oldham, where he had property. He was licensed, 10 Aug. 1672, as " Pr. Teacher " at a house in Stockport parish, Chesh.; was licensed schoolmaster at Oldham till 1702, having James Clegg as his pupil, 1689–94; and was ordained deacon, 11 June 1693; priest, 23 Sept. 1694, as curate at Milnrow, afterwards at Newton. The schoolmaster's name is sometimes given as " Loben " (a misreading of Loten = Lawton). No independent authority treats the Oldham man as Ejected; Clegg, his pupil (who does not give him a high character), speaks of him as having been " a Dissenting Minister in Derbyshire."] (*Ax. C. Nk. P. T.*) [53]

LAYTON. [2] *See* Leighton, John

LAYTON. [53] *See* Huntingdonshire

LEA, THOMAS (1656 ? – 17 May 1733). Entered Frankland's Academy, 11 May 1678. As minister of Upton in Wirral (properly Overchurch) was one of the founders (1691) of the Cheshire Classis (see p. 157). By 1709 "he labours under great discouragements at Upton," and accepted, on advice of the Classis, a call to Knutsford. The Upton congregation expired; Lea ministered at Knutsford till death. (*Fr. Uc.*) [15]

LEARNER, *i.e.* LARDNER, RICHARD (28 May 1653—17 Jan. 1739/40). C. Educated at the Academy of Charles Morton [*q.v.*]. Minister from 1673 at Deal, Kent; succeeded John Faldo [*q.v.*] at Plaisterers' Hall, London; ministered at Chelmsford, Ess., till 1718; retired from active duty, 1732. The name was pronounced, and often written, Larner.

His elder son was Nathaniel Lardner, D.D. (6 June 1684—24 July 1768), founder of the modern school of critical research in the field of early Christian literature. (*D. Ev. M.*) [55]

LECTURES. [154, 179, 180]

LEE, JOSEPH, B.A. (*b.* 1620). Son of Joseph Lee, M.A., rector of Catthorpe, Leic. Matric. at Oriel Coll., Oxford, 16 Mar. 1637/8, aged 17; B.A., 1641. Rector (1648) of Cotesbach, Leic.; ejected, 1662. The Episc. Returns, 1669, report him as preaching to "about 12 Presbyterians & Independ[ts] meaner sort" at Calthorpe, *i.e.* Catthorpe, Leic. The Common Fund granted him (1690–93) £8 a year for 'Calthrop.' (*C. F. M. P. T.*) [66, 67, 68]

LEE, THOMAS (*d.* 29 Sept. 1692). On 14 D. 1691 he was awarded a bursary of £8 a year from the Common Fund as a Student under Thomas Rowe [*q.v.*]. On 30 May 1692 this was continued to him as a Student under John Woodhouse [*q.v.*]. His death was reported on 2 Jan. 1692/3. (*M.*) [111]

LEE, *i.e.* LEIGH, WILLIAM (*fl.* 1687–1702). He wrote from London, 30 Apr. 1687, to Thomas Warren [*q.v.*] *re* James II.'s declaration (*P.* ii. 269). A letter from James Bristowe, dated Salisbury, 12 O. 1702, and addressed "To the rev. M[r] William Leigh, at Newport in the Isle of Wight," was delivered to an Anglican divine of the same name. This letter gave some account of Calamy's visit to Salisbury, including an interview with Bishop Burnet, in the course of which reference was made to a quarrel between two Nonconformist Ministers at Salisbury (Keeling and Squire), and the best way of composing it. The intercepted letter was made public by Francis Atterbury (afterwards bishop of Rochester), and was the occasion of injurious and ill-founded comment by Walker and others. (*Ac.* iv. 433. *Cd. Cm. Wc.*) [100]

LEEDS. Ejected here were: (1) Christopher Nesse (son of Thomas, farmer, North Cave, E.R.), of St. John's Coll., Cambridge; admitted sizar, 17 May 1638, age 16; matric., 1638; B.A., 1641/2; taught school at Beverley and preached about; rector of Cottingham, E.R., 1651; lecturer at Leeds, 1656; ejected, 1662; taught school at Hunslet and preached about; preaching at various places, 1669; licensed, 1 May 1672, as Congr. Teacher in Mainriding house, Leeds; this place licensed, same date as Congr. Meeting-place; Meeting-house at Hunslet opened by him, 3 June 1672; removed to London, 1674 (?), and preached in Salisbury Court, Fleet Street; *d.* 26 Dec. 1705, aged 84. (*C. D. Jo. T. V.*)

(2) James Sayle or Sale (*b.* at Pudsey), of Christ's Coll., Cambridge; matric. pensioner, 1636; B.A., 1639/40; incumbent of Thornton Chapel, in Bradford parish, W.R.; curate at Leeds, 1647; ejected, 1662; retired to Pudsey; licensed, 20 Apr. 1672, as Presb. Teacher in his house at Leeds; his house licensed, same date, as Presb. Meeting-place; request was made to alter Leeds to Pudsey (where Sale lived) and to license the Free School in Leeds for Sale as a preacher there; neither was done; *d.* 21 Apr. 1679. (*C. T. V.*)

(3) Robert Todd (1594–Jan. 1664/5), *b.* at South Cave, E.R.; of Jesus Coll., Cambridge; matric. sizar, 1614; B.A., 1617/8; M.A., 1627; ord. episcopally, 2 Sept. 1621; incumbent of Swinefleet Chapel in Whitgift parish, W.R.; vicar of Whitgift; vicar of Ledsham, W.R., 1625; vicar (1631?) of Leeds, where the parish church was rebuilt (1634) for him; ejected, 1662; *d.* 16 Jan. 1663/4, aet. 67. (*C. V.*) [129, 139]

LEEDS ('Leige') CASTLE, Kent. [55]

LEGG, TOBIAS, M.A. (1623–1700). Entered Glasgow University, 1644; matric., 31 Mar. 1645 (as Tobias Legge); M.A., 1646 (as Tobias Leggus); incorp. at Cambridge, 1652. Held, after 1644, the sequestered rectory of Hemingstone, Suff.; silenced, 1662. The Fund paid him (1691–1699) £5 a year (later £4) as Itinerant in Suffolk. He died at Ipswich, where he had assisted John Fairfax [*q.v.*]. (*B. C. Gm. M. P. V.*) [38, 105]

LEICESTER. Ejected here was William Simmes [? of Emmanuel Coll., Cambridge; matric. pensioner, 1619; B.A., 1622/3; M.A., 1626]. Confrater of Wigston Hospital, 1651; vicar of St. Margaret's;

ejected, 1662; *d.* 9 Aug. 1669. (*C. Ln. V.*) [66, 67]

LEICESTERSHIRE. [66, 68, 76, 168, 176, 181] Except the headings "Leicester" in the earliest handwriting, all is in the Book-keeper's hand. The returns are numbered from 25 to 176 (chiefly 35) and 17 in 1691.

Braddon is Bardon.

Calthorp is Catthorpe [*q.v.*], otherwise Calthorpe.

Harborow is Market Harborough [*q.v.*].

Swedeland is Swithland.

LEIDEN. [182]

LEIGE CASTLE. [55] *See* Kent

LEIGH IN LITTLE WOOLTON ('Wooton') is identical with Loe, The [*q.v.*]. [58, 59]

LEIGHTON ('Layton') BROMSWOLD. [53]

LEIGHTON, JOHN (1623 ?–1699 ?). 𝔓. [? Of Magdalene Coll., Cambridge; matric. sizar, 1651.] Calamy connects him with the rectory of Linby, Notts; if this is correct, he probably held it (a small living) along with the neighbouring vicarage of Hucknall Torkard. He was an active member of the Nottingham Classis. Ejected, 1662. The Episc. Returns, 1669, report him as one of three preachers at Basford, Notts, in the house of John Clark, M.A. (1630 ?–19 S. 1669); ejected, 1662, from the rectory of Cotgrave, Notts. Licensed, 17 Apr. 1672, as "Presb. Teacher in John Chamberlaines howse in Nottingham"; also, June 1672, being of Greasley, Notts, as "Grall Pr." The Common Fund granted him, 1690–99, £8 a year, at Adbolton, parish of Holme-Pierrepoint, Notts (reduced, 1695, to £6). (*C. M. No. P. T. V.*) [2, 83]

LEVER, or LEAVER, JOHN (Sept. 1631–4 July 1692). 𝔓. Born in Bolton. Baptized, 11 S. 1631. Son of Adam Leaver. Calamy says he was son of a Roman Catholic, and educated at Bolton grammar school and Brasenose Coll., Oxford; if so, he did not matriculate. Possibly he was John Leaver, 'ser.,' matric. at All Souls Coll., Oxford, 10 D. 1658; rem. to St. Mary Hall; B.A., 1659/60. He succeeded Peter Bradshaw (1660) at Cockey Chapel, parish of Middleton, Lanc.; ejected, 1662. He continued to preach at Cockey, where a Meeting-house was built for him (1672), known for distinction as Cockey Moor Chapel, so near to Cockey Chapel "yt yo Congregations may hear one another Sing Psalms," once a month, when the rector of Middleton preached at Cockey Chapel. Licensed, June 1672, as "Pr. Teacher in the howse of Widow Dickinson in Middleton, Lanc." On 5 Sept. 1672, and again 18 Nov., licence was given for "A new built house on Cockey More by Pr. of Middleton in Lancash." He left in 1689 for Bolton, Lanc. He has also been confused with John Lever, vicar of Bolton (1673–91). (*Bi. Br. C. F. Nl. P. T.*) [61]

LEVER, or LEAVER, ROBERT, B.A. (1625—1 July 1690). 𝔓. Born at York. Son of Robert Leaver, mercer there, who was grandson of Thomas Lever (1521–77), puritan master of St. John's Coll., Cambridge. From York grammar school, admitted to Sidney Sussex Coll., Cambridge, 21 June 1642; matric., 1642; rem. sizar to St. John's Coll., 24 Feb. 1644/5, aet. 19; M.A., 1645/6. Held, 1650, the sequestered vicarage of Bolam, Northum.; ejected, 1660. Retired to his estate at Scute house, parish of Brancepeth, Durh. Licensed, 10 June 1672, as Pr. Teacher in his house in Brancepeth. Preached also at Newcastle-on-Tyne and elsewhere. On the death (1683) of his first cousin, Ralph Wickliffe, ejected from the rectory of Whalton, Northumb., he took up his work as Minister to a congregation gathered from Whalton and neighbouring parishes. In Aug. 1684 he was committed to Durham gaol for conventicling at Milbourne Grange, Northumb.; here, after a division in his congregation, he continued to preach to the major portion. (*C. Jo. P. T. V. Wc. Y.*) [23, 80, 172]

LEWES ('Lewis'). Ejected here were (1) Edward Newton, M.A. [*q.v.*]; (2) Walter Postlethwaite (in preface to "A Voice from Heaven," 1655, he signs Gualter Postlethwaite), of Emmanuel Coll., Cambridge; matric. sizar, 1643; B.A., 1646; rector of St. Michael's, Lewes; Congregational, and a Fifth-Monarchy man, "his private Opinions affected not his Ordinary Preaching"; ejected, 1662; preaching at Lewes, 1669; he had gathered at Lewes, before 15 Apr. 1655, a Congregational church (in which he was succeeded as pastor by Joseph Whiston [*q.v.*]); *d.* 1671. (*C. Od. T. V.*) [112, 113, 114]

LEWIS, DAVID. [146]

LEWIS, or LEWES, JOHN (*d.* 1721 ?). ℭ. Received grants (1690–93) as Student, formerly with John Woodhouse [*q.v.*], then with James Owen [*q.v.*]; also studying under Matthew Henry [*q.v.*]. In 1695 he was studying under Stephen Lobb [*q.v.*]; in 1696 he became a Student under William Paine [*q.v.*]. The Fund granted him (1695–96) £4 a year as Itinerant in North Wales, where doubtless he preached in Welsh. The variety of his Academical studies, taken in combination with Itinerant effort, is somewhat remarkable. Minister (1698–1702) at Bethnal Green; removed (1702) to Ropemakers' Alley; dismissed, 1707, and became assistant to Samuel Harris [*q.v.*]. Minister, 1710, at Red Cross Street, Cripplegate, but not there in 1715. Perhaps removed to Clerkenwell Close. Subscriber at Salters' Hall, 1719. John Dunton gives him a high character. (*Cf. M. W. We.*) [17, 150]

LICHFIELD ('Litchfield'). Ejected here were: (1) John Butler, of St. Edmund Hall, Oxford; matric., 15 Dec. 1637, aged 16; B.A., 1641; rem. to University Coll.; M.A., 1648; vicar of St. Mary's; *d.* about 1670. (*C. F.*) (2) Thomas Miles [*q.v.*]. [96, 97, 180]

LIDGEK, LIDGET. [130, 132] *See* Yorks, W.R.

LIGHT, JOHN (*fl.* 1660–90). **C.** Curate or lecturer at Preston, Dors., where his wife, Mary, died on 4 Aug. 1660; ejected, 1660 or 1662. Agent (1672) for procuring licences (especially for Cambridgeshire and Canterbury); licensed, 13 Apr. 1672, as "Congr. Teacher in his own howse in Thames Street," London. (*C. Hu. P. T.*) [92, 93, 94]

LIME. [34] *See* Dorsetshire

LIMINGTON. [102] *See* Hampshire

LIMSTON. [30] *See* Devonshire

LIN. [71] *See* Norfolk

LINCOLN. Ejected here were: (1) James Abdy, of Lincoln Coll., Oxford; matric., 6 July 1638, aged 17; B.A., 1642; beneficed in Lincoln; ejected, 1662; licensed, 9 May 1672, as Pr. Teacher in a house at Lincoln; *d.* 1673? (*C. F. T.*)

(2) Edward Reyner (1600–1668), of St. John's Coll., Cambridge; B.A., 1620/1; M.A., 1624; schoolmaster at Asgarby, Linc., and at Market Rasen, Linc.; lecturer at Welton, Linc.; lecturer at St. Benedict's, Lincoln, 13 Aug. 1626; rector of St. Peter-at-Arches, Linc.; preacher at the Cathedral; prebendary of Lincoln, 10 Sept. 1635; ejected, 1662; remained at Lincoln; was dead at time of publication of his treatise of "Humane Learning," 1663. (*C. D. V.*)

(3) George Scortwreth, of Sidney Sussex Coll., Cambridge; matric. sizar, 1628; B.A., 1631/2; M.A., 1635; colleague of No. 2; ejected with him. (*C. V.*) [70]

LINCOLNSHIRE. [36, 70, 168, 176] Except the headings "Lincoln," and a marginal note, in the earliest handwriting, all is in the Book-keeper's hand. The returns are numbered from 65 to 175; and 8 to 29 in 1691.

Gedley is Gedney.

LINDFIELD. [112]

LINTON. [11]

LISKEARD ('Liskard'). Ejected here was Thomas Nichols, who afterwards conformed. (*C.*) [18]

LITCHFIELD. [96, 97, 180] *See* Lichfield

LITTLE HORN, in Bisley parish, Glou. In Evans' List the congregation appears as at Chalford Bottoms, same parish. [46]

LITTLE MOORFIELDS. [3]

LITTLE TOWER HILL. This name is retained by the street which runs north from Tower Bridge; but the original Little Tower Hill was the plot of high ground above this (now built over) lying north-east of the Tower, while Great Tower Hill was north-west of the Tower. (*Sl.*) [4]

LITTLEOVER. [26]

LIVERPOOL ('Liverpoole') was in the parish of Walton-on-the Hill. Ejected from its vicarage was Henry Finch [*q.v.*]; *see also* Robert Eaton, M.A. John Fogg (1622–1670), born at Darcy Lever in Bolton parish, Lanc., son of Laurence Fogg; matric. at Brasenose Coll., Oxford, 4 May 1638, aged 16; B.A., 1641/2; M.A., 1646/7; preached at Wigan, and was later appointed lecturer St. Nicholas Chapel, Liverpool; ejected or silenced in 1662; from 1666 lived with his father-in-law, John Glendole (*see* Chester), at Great Budworth, preaching on occasion. (*C. F.*) [58, 59, 177]

LIVINGSTONE, JOHN, M.A. (21 Jan. 1603—9 Aug. 1672). **P.** Born at Kilsyth, Stirl. Son of William Livingstone, M.A. (1576–1641), then Minister of the parish. Educ. at Stirling grammar school and Glasgow, graduating M.A. Licensed to preach, 1625. Ordained, 1630, as Minister of Killinchy, Co. Down. Deposed and excommunicated, he started for New England, Sept. 1636, but returned, storm-stayed. Inducted, July 1638, as Minister of Stranraer, Wigs.; translated, Aug. 1648, to Ancrum, Roxb. Banished at the Restoration, he spent the rest of his life at Rotterdam. (*D.*) [155]

LLANEDI ('Kanedy'). [144]

LLANGYFELACH ('Llangefelach'), Glam. [145]

LLOYD, WILLIAM. [146]

LOB, . . . ? Stephen Lobb, *secundus* (*d.* 1720); conformed and became chaplain of Penzance Chapel, Corn.; later (after

1716) vicar of Milton Abbot, Devon. (*Bo. D.*) [112]

LOBB, PETER (*d.* 1718). C. Son of Richard Lobb, high sheriff of Cornwall, 1652; M.P. for St. Michael's, Cornwall, 1659. Brother of Stephen Lobb [*q.v.*]. Place of education unknown. The Common Fund voted him (1690) £6 a year for Horley, Surr. The vote was reduced in 1695 to £5 and discontinued in 1696, when Lobb was voted (21 Sept.) £6 by the Congregational Fund. In 1697 Lobb was again on the original Fund, receiving £6 a year, from 1705, £5, and so continuing to 1718; he had grants also from the Congregational Fund. (*Bo. Cf. Ev. M. W.*) [110]

LOBB, STEPHEN (1647?–3 June 1699). C. Brother of Peter Lobb [*q.v.*]. Place of education unknown. His autograph signature is appended to an undated address to the Crown from Nonconforming Ministers in Cornwall, grateful for the 1672 Declaration of Indulgence; if at that time a regular Minister, he could hardly be less than 25. Contemporaneous is the following application in the handwriting of Francis Benson (chief clerk): "Stephen Lobb prisbiterion desires to have the Benefit of his Maiustey Decln to preach in Treworder house in Kenwyn [close to Truro] and fallmouth house in Mylor [near Falmouth] in the Countey of Cornewall the two houses being Mr Richard Lobbs." The licences asked for were issued on 16 Apr. 1672. Probably at one of the two houses above mentioned Stephen was born. In 1678 he was in London. After the death (1 Apr. 1681) of Thankful Owen, M.A., ejected from the Presidency of St. John's Coll., Oxford, he succeeded to the pastorate of a Congregational church, which met (1683) at "an ancient Meeting House near Swallow Street," and moved (1685) to the vacant Fetter Lane Meeting-house, now Moravian, and the oldest existing Nonconformist structure in London. His colleague in this ministry was Thomas Goodwin, *secundus* [*q.v.*]. In 1683 he was arrested in Essex by Capt. Henry Goring, on a charge of complicity with the Rye House Plot. In 1685, in conjunction with Francis Glascock [*q.v.*] and William Wickins [*q.v.*], he privately read lectures to former pupils of Charles Morton [*q.v.*]; ejected from the rectory of Blisland, Cornwall, and now gone to New England, in consequence of the prosecutions directed against his Academy in Newington Green. On the issue, 4 Apr. 1687, of James II.'s Declaration for Liberty of Conscience, Lobb took part in an Address of thanks to the King, and wrote in favour of the dispensing power. This gave him influence at court; he was denounced by Anglicans as "the Jacobite Independent," yet he simply repeated the action he had taken in regard to the previous Indulgence. As early as 1687 he was living at Hampstead, and afternoon preacher there. He joined the Happy Union in 1691, and afterwards wrote strongly on the Crispian side in the Crispian controversy. In May 1691 he is recorded by the Middlesex session as "preacher to a congregation of dissenting protestants at his house in Hampstead." On 10 May 1692, "the dwelling house of Isaack Honywood, Esquire, situated in Hampstead," was registered for the worship of Protestant Dissenters. It is possible that this was for a congregation in opposition to Lobb's; more probably, he had left Hampstead after his wife's death (1691). Early in 1692/3 William Nokes, who had returned from study at Utrecht, received a grant from the Common Fund as "at present with Mr Stephen Lobb" (*see also* John Lewis). On the retirement (1694) of Vincent Alsop [*q.v.*] from the Merchants' Lecture, Lobb was chosen in his stead. He died suddenly of apoplexy at the house of George Griffith [*q.v.*]. He married a daughter of Theophilus Polwheele, M.A. (*see* Tiverton), whose wife was a daughter of William Benn, M.A. (*see* Dorchester).

His son Stephen [*q.v.*] conformed. Another son, Theophilus, M.D., F.R.S. (17 Aug. 1678—19 May 1768), Minister at Guildford, 1702; Shaftesbury, 1706; Yeovil, 1713; Witham, Ess., 1722; Haberdashers' Hall, London, 1732; after leaving the Nonconformist ministry but remaining Congregational, became eminent as a London physician. Another son, Samuel, *d.* 1760, was rector of Farleigh Hungerford, Som. A daughter married John Greene, Cong. Min. at Great Baddow, Ess. (*Bo. D. Do. Ev. I. J. Je. L. Od. Ry. Sh. W.*) [1, 2, 3, 72, 158]

LOCK, ROGER. [166]

LOE, THE. Evidently synonymous with (perhaps a misreading of) Little Lee, in or near Gateacre, parish of Childwall, Lanc. *See* Leigh. [58, 59]

LOFTUS, THOMAS. One of the preachers sent out by Richard Davis (p. 185), his residence being at Thorpe Waterville, Northants. (*Gl.*) [78]

LOMAX, JOHN, M.A. (*d.* 1694?). C. Matric. sizar at Emmanuel Coll., Cambridge, 1650; B.A., 1643/4; M.A., 1657.

Leaving the University, he lived with his mother (*d.* 1689 ?), who had a jointure by Thomas Bonner (*d.* 1659), thrice mayor of Newcastle-on-Tyne. Held the sequestered vicarage of Wooler, Northum.; resigned, 1660. Removed to North Shields, and practised physic and surgery. Licensed, 18 N. 1672, as "Independt Teachr" in the bishopric of Durham. Received, 1690–93, £5 a year for Shields. (*C. Bn. M. P. T. V.*) [79]

LONDON. [1, 3, 21, 22, 28, 35, 39, 40, 41, 42, 48, 83, 85, 152, 155, 163, 169, 170, 175, 176, 177, 181, 184, 185, 186, 187, 189, 190]

LONG, or LONGE, GEORGE, M.A., M.D. (1628—26 D. 1712). **P.** Born in London. Subsizar at Trinity Coll., Cambridge, 2 June 1646; matric., 1646; Scholar, 1649; B.A., 1649/50; Fellow, 1650–60 (ejected); M.A., 1653. Supplied the vacant rectory of Newcastle-under-Lyme, Staff.; ejected, 1662. Graduated M.D. at Leiden,. 12 July 1668. Licensed, 22 July 1672, being of Leicester, as "Pr. Grall." Attempted to settle in Newcastle-under-Lyme and in Birmingham, but prosecuted in both places. Removed to Ireland, returning 1689; Calamy says to Newcastle-under-Lyme, labouring there "till his intellects failed." Evidently he was not the regular Minister of Darlington in 1690; and though in the Manuscript he is also entered as of Coventry, he was not the regular Minister there. He received, 10 Nov. 1690, £4 from an anonymous donation of £50 through Matthew Rapier [*q.v.*]. He probably left for Newcastle-under-Lyme in 1692, and certainly ministered there from 1700 till Midsummer 1705, as grants show. He then retired, the Fund granting him £4 a year to the end of his life. He died at Bristol.

His son Nathaniel (*d.* 14 July 1706), educated for the ministry by his father, and at Frankland's Academy (entered 12 Apr. 1692) with bursaries from the Common Fund, was Minister at Farnham, Surrey, removing thence to Wrexham, Denb., in 1705. (*Bw. C. M. P. T. V.*) [36, 117]

LONG LANE, from West Smithfield to Aldersgate Street, was noted for its traffic in clothing and upholstery, new and second-hand. (*Sl.*) [2]

LONG SANDALL, then a village in Doncaster parish, W.R. (misplaced in E.R.); now amalgamated with Kirk Sandall [*q.v.*]. [139]

LONGDOLES ('Longdales'), a hamlet in Ashbourne parish, Derb., very near the Staffordshire border. [27, 96]

LONGDON. [98]

LONGSTAFF, J. P. [171]

LONGTOWN ('Longtowne'). The Common Fund granted £5 a year from 1690 for work here. (*M.*) [48]

LOOE. [18]

LORD'S SUPPER. [141]

LORIMER, WILLIAM, M.A. (Jan. 1640/1–27 Oct. 1722). **P.** Born in Aberdeen; graduated at the Marischal Coll. and University there. Came to London, 1664, and lived with an uncle Lorimer. Took Anglican orders, was curate at the Charterhouse, and later held a vicarage in Sussex. Within a year, resigned through disapprobation of the Anglican canons, and travelled in France. Returning, he became chaplain to Squire Hall, at Harding, near Henley-on-Thames. Some time after 1689 he ministered for a few years at Lee, near Eltham, Kent. In 1695 he was invited to a chair of theology at St. Andrews; on his way there in 1696 he heard at Edinburgh of the plague at St. Andrews, and the closing of the University. He returned to London after taking part in the clerical outcry which brought about the execution of Thomas Aikenhead (8 Jan. 1696/7). In his "Two Discourses," 1713, Lorimer made a sufficiently lame defence of his action. From 1699 he for some years assisted Joshua Oldfield, D.D. [*q.v.*], in his Academy. He is the first trustee named in the will of Daniel Williams, D.D. In the division at Salters' Hall (1719), Oldfield, second on the list of Dr. Williams' trustees, was Moderator of the Non-subscribers; Lorimer was Moderator of the seceding Subscribers. He died unmarried at Hoxton, and was buried at St. Margaret Pattens, London. In his will, among many charities, he founded a bursary at Marischal Coll., and left bequests for the poor of the Scots churches at Founders' Hall and Swallow Street, London. His funeral sermon, "having been accidentally omitted," was preached 27 Oct. 1723, by James Anderson, M.A. (afterwards D.D.), Minister of Swallow Street, who gives a list of Lorimer's publications and manuscripts. (*C. Jc. Fun. Serm. by Anderson,* 1724.) [2]

LOSEBY. [66]

LOSTWITHIEL ('Laslithiel St'). [19]

LOUGHBOROUGH ('Loughborrow'). [67]

LOYD, *i.e.* LLOYD, J. **C.** He was a representative of the congregation of George Griffith [*q.v.*] on the Congregational Fund at its establishment, 17 Dec. 1695; and one of its correspondents for Essex,

Shropshire, Worcestershire, North Wales, and South Wales. (*Cf.*) [143]

LUCAS, JOHN, M.A. (1625—4 June 1703). **P.** Son of Richard Lucas, of Chelmsford, butcher. From Chelmsford school admitted pensioner at St. John's Coll., Cambridge, 2 June 1642, aet. 17; matric. 1642; rem. to Emmanuel Coll.; B.A., 1645/6; M.A., 1649. Vicar of Stalham, Norf.; ejected, 1662. The Episc. Returns, 1669, report him as one of the preachers to "Presbyterians & Independants 200 or thereabout most women" in St. Stephen's parish, Norwich, "Att the house of Mr John Willson Chimist once a weeke, if not twice"; also as one of the preachers to "Independants about 400" in Yarmouth "Att a house in the hoope Row, belonging to Mr Burton." He preached also at Tunstead, Bradfield, etc. Licensed, 29 May 1672, as "Pr. Teacher in the howse of John Munford in the Parish of St. Peters in the Markett [*i.e.* St. Peter's Mancroft] Norwich." Though a Presbyterian, he was evidently in strong accord with the union of the two denominations, and is buried (with a poetical epitaph, giving his age as 78) in the Old Meeting graveyard (Congregational), Norwich. (*B. C. Jo.* (gives him the fellowship which belongs to a namesake) *P. T. V.*) [74, 177]

LUDLOW. In 1676 there were 21 Nonconformists here. (*Ls.*) Ejected here in 1660 was Richard Sadler, born in Worcester [? matric. pensioner at Emmanuel Coll., Cambridge, 1637]; went to New England with his father; ord. by presbyters, 16 May 1648, as Minister of Whixhall, then a chapelry in Prees parish, Shrop.; removed to be Lecturer at Ludlow; preaching at Prees and Whitchurch, Shrop., in 1669; licensed, June 1672, as Pr. Teacher in a house at Prees; *d.* 1675, aet. 55. (*C. T. V.*) [89]

LUKIN, HENRY (1 Jan. 1627/8—17 S. 1719). **C.** Matric. pensioner at Christ's Coll., Cambridge, 1645/6; did not graduate. In 1662 he was in France with Sir William Masham, unbeneficed. He lived as chaplain to the Masham family at Matching Hall, Ess., preaching at Matching Green; licensed there, 1672, as Teacher of Congregationals. He was intimate with John Locke, and attended his death-bed. (*C. E. P. T. V.*) [40]

LULLINGTON. [115]

LUPTON. A manor in Brixham parish, Devon. [31]

LUTTERWORTH. Ejected here was John St. Nicholas [*q.v.*]. [66, 67, 68]

LYDGATE ('Lidget,' 'Lidgek'). Then a hamlet in Kirkburton parish, now in Holmfirth parish. It had a Fund grant of £2 a year from 1695. [130, 132, 180]

LYDIARD ('Lydyard'). [124] *See* Rashley, Jonathan

LYME REGIS ('Lime'). Ejected here was Ames Short, M.A. [*q.v.*]. [34]

LYMINGTON ('Limington'). [102]

LYMPSTONE ('Limston'). [30]

LYNN. [74] *See* Norfolk

MACCLESFIELD ('Mayfield'). Ejected here was James Bradshaw, M.A.; born at Darcy Lever, near Bolton, Lanc.; son of John Bradshaw of Bolton, pleb.; matric. at Brasenose Coll., Oxford, 9 D. 1631, aged 17; B.A., 1634; M.A., 1636/7; rector of Wigan, Lanc.; later vicar of Macclesfield, Ches.; ejected 1662; preached subsequently at Houghton Chapel, Lanc.; later at Bradshaw Chapel, Lanc., reading some of the Common Prayer; died May 1683. (*C. D. F. P.*) [15]

MACHIN. [40] *See* Essex

MAGDALENE COLL., Cambridge. [89]

MAID LANE, Southwark, is famous for its connection with the site of the Globe Theatre. Strype, who calls it Maiden Lane, describes it as "a long straggling Place with Ditches on each side, the Passage to the Houses being over little Bridges, with little Garden Plotts before them." It ran westward from Deadman's Place. (*Sl.*) [3]

MAIDENHEAD ('Maydenhead'). [7]

MAIDSTONE. Ejected here were (1) John Crump [? of Christ Church Coll., Oxford, 'cler fil.'; matric., 9 Dec. 1650], curate of Maidstone, 1651; ejected, 1662; preached often after ejection in Boxley church, by vicar's connivance. His "Parable of the Great Supper Opened," 1669, was posthumous. (*C. F. K.*) (2) Joseph Whiston [*q.v.*]

MALCOME, JOHN, M.A. (1652?–17 May 1729). **P.** Born in Scotland? Educ. at Glasgow, graduating M.A., 1674. Ordained, 5 D. 1687, as Minister of Lower Killead, Co. Antrim; transferred, 1699, to Dunmurry, Co. Antrim. He published "Personal Persuasion no Foundation for Religious Obedience" (1720); and "The Dangerous Principles . . . revived . . . by our Modern New Lights" (1726). (*D. Gm.*) [155]

MALDON ('Malden'). Ejected here was Thomas Horrox, or Horrocks, of St. John's Coll., Cambridge; matric. sizar, 1633; B.A., 1634/5; M.A., 1638; ord. by bishop of Durham; master of grammar school at Romford, Ess.; held the sequestered rectory of Stapleford Tawney, Ess., 1646; vicar of Maldon, 1650; ejected, 1662; preaching to Anabaptists at Hertford, 1664; *d.* at Battersea about 1687; bur. in the church there. (*C. E. T. V.*) [39]

MALMESBURY ('Malmsbury'). Ejected here was Simon Gawen (son of Simon, Tetbury, Glou.), of St. Edmund Hall, Oxford; matric., 13 July 1638, aged 18; vicar of Malmesbury; ejected, 1662; preaching at Bradford-on-Avon, Wilts, and Dunkerton, Som., in 1669. (*C. F. T.*) [44, 123]

MANCHESTER. Ejected here were (1) Henry Newcome, M.A. [*q.v.*]. (2) Edward Richardson (1632–1680), born in Lancashire; of Trinity Coll., Cambridge, subsizar, 17 Sept. 1652; matric., 1652; B.A., 1656; M.A., 1660; ord. by presbyters, 27 July 1658, as Minister at Stretford; morning preacher at Manchester Collegiate Church, 1661; ejected, 1662; licensed, 2 May 1672, as Pr. Teacher at Wharton Hall in Little Hulton, Lanc.; *d.* 1680. (*C. Sx. T. Tc. V.*) (3) Silenced here was John Wigan, Minister at Gorton Chapel; rem. to Birch Chapel, 1646; left about 1650, and became a major in the parliamentary army; a strong Congregational; preaching in Manchester at the building (his property) afterwards the Chetham School. (*C. Nl.*) [26, 59, 60, 174, 177]

MANCHESTER CLASSIS. [157]

MANLOVE, TIMOTHY, L.C.P. (*d.* 4 Aug. 1699). Born at Ashbourne, Derb. Ordained at Attercliffe, near Sheffield, 11 S. 1688. Minister, 1691, at Pontefract, Yorks. Admitted, 1 June 1694, an extra-licenciate of the Coll. of Physicians. Removed, 1694, to Mill Hill Chapel, Leeds; and, 1699, to Newcastle-on-Tyne, as assistant to Richard Gilpin [*q.v.*], dying of fever shortly after removal. (*D.* (errata) *Hh. Mu.*) [36]

MANNING, JOHN, M.A. (*d.* 1694). ℭ. Born at Cockfield, Suff. Son of William Manning, and younger brother of Samuel Manning [*q.v.*]. Entered Emmanuel Coll., Cambridge, in 1633; matric. sizar, 1634; B.A., 1637/8; M.A., 1641. In Jan. 1651/2 he was perpetual curate of Walpole with Cookley, Suff.; and at the same time pastor of the Congregational church at Walpole. In 1654 he became perpetual curate of Peasenhall, Suff., and pastor of the Congregational church there; ejected, 1662. He was many times imprisoned. Licensed, 13 May 1672, as "Congr. Teacher in his howse in Peasenhall." The Common Fund voted him (9 Mar. 1690/1 and 4 Jan. 1691/2) gifts of £5 for Sibton. Sibton, where he was living in 1690, is close to Peasenhall. The Meeting-place of his flock was transferred before his death to the parish of Swefling, and in 1750 to that of Rendham, where it now is. Manning was joint-editor with Samuel Petto [*q.v.*] of "Six Treatises," 1656, by John Tillinghast, the Fifth Monarchy man.

It is worthy of note that the Manuscript, while including John and Samuel Manning in its record, makes no reference to their brother William Manning, M.A. (1631?–13 F. 1710/11), of Christ's Coll., Cambridge, ejected from the perpetual curacy of Middleton, Suff., and licensed, 13 May 1672, as "Congr. Teacher in his howse in Peasenhall." Calamy describes him as "a man of great abilities and learning; but he fell into the Socinian principles, to which he adhered till his death." Among the Ejected he was one of two examples of this theological change, which affected no Presbyterian of their number. He continued to preach at Peasenhall (where he was buried) till deafness disabled him; this may explain John Manning's removals, noted above. (*B. C. Cp. D. M. P. T. V.*) The other example was that of John Cooper (1622–Mar. 1665), born at Worcester, son of John Cooper, pleb.; matric. at Balliol Coll., Oxford, 12 Sept. 1640, age 18; master of the Crypt School, Gloucester, 1647–1652; incumbent of Cheltenham in 1654; ejected; held there a Socinian conventicle, after 1662. (*C. F. La. Ug. State Papers, Dom.*, 1665.) [103, 106]

MANNING, SAMUEL, M.A. (*fl.* 1631–1690). ℭ. Born at Cockfield, Suff. Son of William Manning. Elder brother of John Manning [*q.v.*]. Matric. sizar at Emmanuel Coll., Cambridge, 1631; B.A., 1633/4; M.A., 1637. On 15 June 1654 (having then a wife and four children, and been seven years out of health) he succeeded his brother John [*q.v.*] as perpetual curate of Walpole, then united with Cookley, Suff., and was at the same time pastor of a Congregational church at Walpole; ejected, 1662. He suffered six months' imprisonment, which so enfeebled him that he was obliged to sit while preaching; the story ran that he had been bewitched, along with Thomas Spatchet (*see* Petto, Samuel). Licensed, 13 May 1672, as "Congr. Teacher in his howse in Walpool, Suffolke." His death probably took place before 1698. (*B. C. P. T. V.*) [103]

MANSFIELD. [83, 173]

MANSFIELD, LORD. [159]

MANSFIELD, NATHANIEL, M.A. (*fl.* 1651–1690). Matric. pleb. at Corpus Christi Coll., Oxford, 27 F. 1650/1; B.A., 6 Mar. 1560/1; admitted to Magdalene Coll., Cambridge, 18 May 1647; rem. to Peterhouse; B.A., 1654. Incumbent of Armitage Chapel, Staff.; ejected, 1662. The Episc. Returns, 1669, report him as one of two persons preaching to "few & Inconsiderable" persons at their own houses in Atherstone, Warw. Licensed, 10 June 1672, as "Pr. Teacher" in the "howse of Widow Thornton," Mancetter, Warw. He lived some time at Wolverhampton, and then at Walsall, where he died. (*C. F. P. T.*) [96]

MANTON, THOMAS, D.D. (March 1620–18 Oct. 1677). Ꝑ. Son of Thomas Manton of Whimple, Devon, pleb., was baptized at Lydyeard St. Lawrence, Somerset, on 31 March. From the Tiverton grammar school he entered Wadham Coll., Oxford; matric., 11 March 1635/6, aged 15; removed to Hart Hall; B.A., 1639; returned to Wadham, B.D., 1654. At the age of 20 he was ordained by Joseph Hall, bishop of Exeter, and preached his first sermon at Sowton, near Exeter. In Sept. 1643 he went to Lyme Regis, Dorset, and soon after became lecturer at Cullompton, Devon. In 1641 he was appointed to the sequestered rectory of Stoke Newington, Middx. He was one of the three scribes to the Westminster Assembly. Resigning Stoke Newington (1657), he became rector of St. Paul's, Covent Garden. In 1658 he was incorporated B.D. at Cambridge. He worked for the recall of Charles II., and was one of the deputation to Breda. His tenure of St. Paul's was invalidated at the Restoration, but on 19 Nov. 1660 he was created D.D., Oxon, and offered the deanery of Rochester; on 10 Jan. 1660/1 he was legally admitted to his rectory. He was a commissioner to the Savoy Conference (1661) for considering alterations in the Prayer-book. Ejected in 1662, he attended the ministry of Simon Patrick, his successor (afterwards bishop of Ely), till Patrick objected. He then preached in his own house, King Street, Covent Garden; arrested in 1670, he spent six months as a prisoner in the Gatehouse. On 2 Apr. 1672 he obtained a licence for his King Street house and a general licence as Presb. Teacher. He delivered the first lecture at Pinners' Hall (*see* p. 154). As his congregation grew he removed it to a Meeting-house in White Hart Yard, Brydges (now Catherine) Street. After his death the building was used by Baxter till 1682, and by Daniel Burgess [*q.v.*] from 1687. Manton excelled as a preacher, but did not study brevity. His published sermons fill six folio volumes. In the religious disputes of his time his constant aim was to make peace between parties. (*C.D.F.P.T.W.*) [154, 188]

MANUSCRIPT, THE. [170 *sqq.*]

MARAZION ('Mazarion') or MARKET JEW. [18, 19, 20]

MARCH. [13]

MARCHFIELD. [44] *See* Gloucestershire

MARKET HARBOROUGH. Ejected here was Thomas Laurie; M.A., Edin., 25 July 1635; held the sequestered rectory of Great Braxted, Ess., in 1642; appointed to the sequestered vicarage of Market Harborough, 24 F. 1648/9; declined lectureship at Maldon, Ess. (offered, 12 June 1649); ejected, 1662; preaching at Coggeshall, Ess., in 1669; licensed, 1 May 1672, as Congr. Teacher in his house at Coggeshall; his house licensed, same date, as Congr. Meeting-place; bur. there, 2 Apr. 1681. (*Bd. C. E. Ed. Ln. T.*) [66]

MARKET JEW (or Marazion). [18, 19, 20]

MARLBOROUGH ('Marlebrough,' 'Marlbrough'). Ejected here was William Hughes (*b.* at Bromham, Wilts; son of William, of Bedminster, Wilts), of New Inn Hall, Oxford; matric., 31 Oct. 1634, aged 16; B.A., 1638; M.A., 1640/1; vicar of St. Mary's, Marlborough; ejected, 1662; bought a house in Marlborough and kept school; preaching at Marlborough, 1669; licensed, 13 May 1672, as Congr. Teacher in his house at Marlborough; his house licensed, same date, as Congr. Meeting-place; signed the thanks of Wilts Ministers; *d.* 14 Feb. 1687/8, aged 68; for his descendants, see *P.* (*C. F. T.*) [123, 124, 125]

MARSHALL, JOHN. Though this young man's name is placed at the end of the alphabetical list of London Ministers, his position of "Reader" to John Quick [*q.v.*] can only mean that as a member of Quick's household he was employed in reading to him in his disablement. He received grants, 1691–2, as Student at Bishop's Hall, Bethnall Green; on 11 Apr. 1692 he is under John Ker, M.D. [*q.v.*]. (*M.*) [4]

MARSHALL, THOMAS (*d.* 1705 ?). Ꝑ. [? Matric. pleb. at Exeter Coll., Oxford, 10 Mar. 1656/7; B.A., 1660.] The Episc. Returns, 1669, report him as one of the preachers to 200 persons at White Lackington, Som.; also to 180 persons at

Broadway, Som.; also to 40 persons at Aisholt, Som. Licensed, 8 May 1672, as "Pr. Teacher in his howse in the Parish & Town of Ilminster, Somersett." Edmund Batson, whom Murch makes his predecessor, 1694–7, may have been his colleague for that period. Marshall (dying in 1705, according to Murch) was succeeded by his son Nicholas there in 1715 (*d.* 1725). (*Ev. F. Mh. T.*) [91]

MARSHFIELD ('Marchfield'). [44]

MARSTON, LONG, W.R. (misplaced in N.R.).

MARTELL, MADAM. **P.** Probably widow of Peter Martell. Her "gift" was through Samuel Powell [*q.v.*]. (*M.*) [166]

MARTELL, PETER. **P.** [165]

MARTHIR. [18, 19] *See* Cornwall

MARTIN, *i.e.* MARTYN, JOHN, M.A. (1620?–1692?). **C.** Born in Wiltshire. Son of John Martyn of Cockington, Devon, gent. Matric. at Exeter Coll., Oxford, 9 Mar. 1637/8, aged 18; B.A., 1642; Fellow, 1642–57; M.A., 1648. Student of Lincoln's Inn, 1641. Rector of Yarmouth, I. of Wight; ejected, 1662. Lived at Newport. Licensed, 13 May 1672, as "Ind. Teacher in Grace Byles howse in Yarmouth." Removed into Wiltshire, and there died. (*C. F. P. T.*) [100]

MARTOCK ('Martlock'). Ejected here in 1662 was James Stephenson, born in Scotland; Jacobus Steinsone, *major* and *minor*, entered Glasgow University together in 1621, and graduated M.A. together in 1624 (whether the Ejected was the *major* or the *minor*, there is nothing to show); repairing to Ireland, on 31 Mar. 1627 he was ord. deacon and priest by George Downham, the Calvinistic bishop of Derry; on 31 Oct. 1635 he was instituted to the vicarage of Kiltoghart, Co. Leitrim; in 1641 he fled to Bristol; he was rector of Tormarton, Glou., till 1649, removing thence to Holland, where he studied physic for two years; on 20 Oct. 1654 he was approved for the vicarage of Martock; in 1666 he removed to Crewkerne for two years; licensed, July 1672, as Pr. Teacher in a house at Martock; *d.* 15 July 1685. (*C. Gm. T.*) [92]

MARTYN, SAMUEL (*d.* 1692?). Son of Thomas Martyn, M.A., ejected from the vicarage of St. Andrew's, Plymouth. Occasional preacher at Plymouth till silenced, 1662. Imprisoned six months at Exeter for conventicling at Plymouth; gained absolution and release on communicating at church. (*C. P.*) [18]

MARY II., QUEEN. [137]

MASSUMS, *i.e.* MASHAM FAMILY. [40] *See* Lukin, Henry

MASTERS, *i.e.* MAISTERS, JOSEPH (13 N. 1640—6 Apr. 1717). **B.** Born at Kingsdown, near Ilchester, Som. Matric. 'pleb.' at Magdalen Hall, Oxford, 16 Mar. 1656/7; chorister, Magdalen Coll., 1659–60; ejected, 1660. Returned to Magdalen Hall, but was refused his B.A. for nonconformity; left Oxford, 1661. Ordained, 30 Oct. 1667, for Baptist ministry at Theobalds, in Cheshunt Parish, Herts. Licensed, 25 July 1672, being of Cheshunt, Herts, as "Bapt. Gr." At Theobalds his flock met in the Presbyterian Meeting-house, where he and the Presbyterian Minister, Archibald Hamilton [*q.v.*], preached on alternate Sundays. He probably preached at Enfield, Middx., in concert with Obadiah Hughes [*q.v.*]. About 1692 Maisters became pastor of the Particular Baptist congregation in Joiners' Hall, Thames Street (removed, 1708, to Pinners' Hall), but still ministered at Theobalds once a month. His London address was "at Mrs May's Brewer, in Longacre." By his request the pall-bearers at his funeral were two Baptist, two Congregational, and two Presbyterian Ministers. (*C. Ev. F. P. T. Uh. We.*) [50, 72, 189]

MATCHING ('Machin'). [40]

MATHER, NATHANIEL, M.A. (20 March 1630/1—26 July 1697). **C.** Born at Much Woolton, Lanc.; second son of Richard Mather (1596—22 Apr. 1669), Minister of the Ancient Chapel, Toxteth Park, Liverpool, from its erection in 1618. In 1635 his father took him to New England; he graduated B.A. at Harvard Coll., 1647; M.A., 1650; and returned for further study in England. He was curate to George Mortimer in the sequestered vicarage of Harberton, Devon, succeeding him there in 1655. In 1656 he was put into the sequestered vicarage of Barnstaple, Devon; ejected, 1660. Going over to Holland, he ministered for some years to the English church at Rotterdam. On the death of his elder brother, Samuel Mather, M.A. (13 May 1626—29 Oct. 1671), he succeeded him as pastor of the Congregational church in New Row, Dublin. Driven from Ireland in 1688, he was the successful candidate against Daniel Williams [*q.v.*] for the succession to John Collins, M.A. [*q.v.*], in the Congregational church, Paved Alley, Lime Street. Though an original Manager of the Common Fund, he did not join the 'Happy Union,' and was a leader in its disruption. He was chosen a Pinners' Hall lecturer on the withdrawal (1694) of William Bates, D.D. [*q.v.*]. The meeting by which the Congregational Fund was established was held on 17. Dec. 1695, at his Meeting-house, which continued to be the usual place of its Board meetings; he was one of the Fund's correspondents for Cheshire, Lancashire, and Nottinghamshire. (*C. D. P. Sg. Wc. We.*) [41, 156, 160, 164, 165, 166, 183]

MATHEWS, or MATTHEWS, MICHAYAH or MICAH or MICHAEL (*fl.* 1658–1729). **P.** Son of a clergyman. Matric. at Jesus Coll., Oxford, 21 Apr. 1658; B.A., 1658/9. He appears in 1715 as Minister (with a colleague) at Mount Soar Hill, Leic., and as taking a turn in preaching at Bardon, near Bosworth, Leic. In the Fund Minutes he appears as late as 1720 at Mount Sorrell, and was apparently there in 1729. (*Ev. F. M.*) [67]

MAUDUIT. *See* Modwit

MAURICE, MATTHIAS. [185]

MAVESYN RIDWARE ('Maves on Ridwar'). [96] Ejected here was Richard Swynfen ('Swinfyn'), B.A. [*q.v.*].

MAXFIELD. [15] *See* Cheshire

MAYDWELL, JOHN, M.A. (1612 ?–Jan. 1692/3). **C.** Born at Geddington, Northants. Matric. sizar, at Clare Hall, Cambridge, 1627, where he was chamber-fellow with Peter Gunning (16 Jan. 1613/4—6 July 1684), afterwards bishop of Ely; B.A., 1630/1; M.A., 1634. Rector of Simpson, Bucks. Leaving this to a curate, he went to London during the civil war, and at its close obtained the sequestered vicarage of Claybrooke, Leic., where he built a handsome parsonage. The question of his return to Simpson was left to four divines of the Westminster Assembly, who were equally divided in judgment, whereupon he returned to Simpson. About 1650, became rector of Kettering, Northants; ejected, 1662. Licensed, 1 May 1672, as "Congr. Teacher in the howse of Widow Cooper in Kettering"; on 16 May 1672, his own house in Kettering was licensed as "Presb. Meeting Place" (latterly Maydwell's church was Congregational). He subsequently opened a Meeting-house at Kettering, and there ministered till death. He was one of the witnesses against Richard Davis [*q.v.*] at Kettering in 1692. He was buried at Kettering on 4 Jan. 1692/3. Calamy gives his age as about 84; Coleman, with more probability, as "about 80." (*C. Cn. Gl. P. T. V.*) [76]

MAYFIELD, Staff. Ejected here was William Rock [*q.v.*]. [96]

MAYFIELD, Suss. *See* Becher, Mrs. Ejected here were (1) Paul D'Aranda (son of Elias, Minister of the French Church, Southampton), of Merton Coll., Oxford; matric., 10 Dec. 1641, aged 17; rem. to Pembroke Coll., Fellow and M.A., 1648; curate at Petworth [*q.v.*] to Francis Cheynell, D.D.; curate at Patcham, Suss.; curate at Mayfield to John Maynard, M.A. (*see* below), who gave him all the tithe; ejected, 1662; pastor of the French Church at Canterbury, 1664. (*C. D.* (under Maynard) *F.*) (2) John Maynard, born at Mayfield (*bapt.* 8 Mar. 1600/1); admitted, 21 June 1616, commoner at Queen's Coll., Oxford; B.A., 1619/20; rem. to Magdalen Hall; M.A., 1622; vicar of Mayfield (where he had property), 1624; member of the Westminster Assembly, 1643; ejected, 1662; *d.* at Mayfield, 7 June 1665. (*C. D. F.*) [112, 115]

MAYO, ISRAEL (1630—11 F. 1715/6). Son of John Mayo (1592—29 May 1675), of Bayford House, in the next parish to Little Berkhamstead, Herts. Kept meetings in his own house, temp. Charles II. His only son, George, was a pupil of Samuel Cradock [*q.v.*]. (*Uh.*) [50]

MAYO, RICHARD (1628—6 or 8 Sept. 1695). **P.** Son of Richard Mayo (*d.* 1660), St. Giles', Cripplegate, a man of some property. Came under the religious influence of Thomas Singleton, ejected for Puritan views from a mastership at Eton, and teaching in London from before 1647 till after 1660. Mayo "soon entered (tho' young)" on the ministry. On 17 Aug. 1652 he was appointed ship's chaplain on the 'Sovereign.' On 30 Nov. 1652, as "student in divinitie of Wadã Colledge in Oxford," he applied to the Fourth Presb. Classis of London for ordination as Lecturer in Whitechapel, and was ordained on 2 Dec. By 1654 he was curate to Edmund Staunton, D.D. (*d.* 14 July 1671), vicar of Kingston-on-Thames, Surrey (and a member, from 1647, of the Kingston Classis). Staunton resigned in his favour in 1659, but in 1662 he was ejected. In 1666 he took the Oxford oath against endeavouring alterations in Church or State. The Episc. Returns, 1669, report him as preaching occasionally to 100 "people of several opinions" in a house called Downhall at Kingston; also, with others, to "All other sorts of Sectaries [except Quakers] but chiefly Presbyterian" at Henley-on-Thames, Oxfordsh., "In the house of

Wm Craw, a London Vintner, once in three weeks, or oftener sometimes The principal Frequenters & promoters . . . are such as were Officers & Soldiers in ye Parliament Army"; also, with others, to "sometimes 100" Anabaptists at the house of John Clarke, Anabaptist, at Guildford, Surrey. On 13 Apr. 1672 he was licensed as a Presb. Teacher in John Pigot's house, Kingston. Towards the end of Charles II.'s reign, he became Minister of a Presbyterian congregation in Buckingham House, College-hill, Upper Thames Street, London, removing it after the Toleration Act (1689) to a new Meeting-house in Salters' Hall Court, Cannon Street. Here, after the exclusion (1694) of Daniel Williams, D.D. [*q.v.*], from the Pinners' Hall lectureship, a new Lecture was established, Mayo, who had co-operated in the Common Fund and the Happy Union, being among the first Lecturers. Dying in his 65th year, he was buried at Kingston (11 Sept. 1695).

His son Daniel (Jan. 1672/3—13 June 1733) was the first Minister (1715/6–1723) at the new-built Gravel Pit Meeting-house, Hackney. (*C. Cm. D. Fc. M. Ma. Mo. P. T. W.*) [35, 110, 124, 160, 164, 168, 181, 183]

MAZARION. [18, 19, 20] *See* Cornwall

MEAD, MATTHEW (1630?–16 Oct. 1699). **C.** Born at Leighton Buzzard, Beds; second son of Richard Mead, of Mursley, Bucks. Scholar of King's Coll., Cambridge, 1648; Fellow, 1649; resigned, 1651. Morning lecturer (1655) at St. Dunstan's, Stepney, and admitted (28 Dec. 1656) to membership in the Congregational church there. Appointed, 22 Jan. 1658, incumbent of the 'new chapel' at Shadwell (St. Paul's); ejected, 1660, but obtained a lectureship at St. Sepulchre's, Holborn; ejected, 1662. After 1663 he visited Holland. The Episc. Returns, 1669, report him as one of the preachers at Sibson, Leic., to a congregation of about 40, composed of Presbyterians, Independents and Anabaptists; also to Presbyterians at Woburn, Beds; also to Independents at the house of William Greenhill (the ejected vicar), next Stepney church; also to Anabaptists and Independents in Meeting-house Alley in Wapping "At ye Old Meeting house now made as big againe as in Cromwell's time." On 13 Oct. 1671 he was ordained pastor of Stepney Congregational church; its Meeting-house (opened, 13 Sept. 1674) had four pine pillars, presented by the 'States of Holland.' Over its ceiling was an attic designed as a hiding-place for the congregation in case of need; the Meeting-house was wrecked in Dec. 1682. He was arrested, 1683, on suspicion of complicity in the Rye House Plot, but at once discharged. In 1683 he succeeded John Owen, D.D. [*q.v.*], as Pinners' Hall lecturer. He was a leader both in the Common Fund and the Happy Union (inaugurated in his Meeting-house and by his sermon), but left both, and was an original Manager of the Congregational Fund, and one of its correspondents for Bedfordshire, Gloucestershire, Kent, Lancashire, Leicestershire, Middlesex, and Oxfordshire. His May Day sermon to the young, begun 1674, is still kept up.

Richard Mead, M.D. (11 Aug. 1673–16 Feb. 1754), his eleventh child, was the owner of one of the three extant copies of the original edition of Servetus' "Christianismi Restitutio," 1553; it is now in the Paris Bibliothèque Nationale. (*C. Co. D. M. P. T.*) [9, 10, 12, 45, 68, 72, 86, 110, 114, 156, 160, 163, 164, 167, 168, 189]

MEADOWES, MEADOWS, or MEADOWE, JOHN, M.A. (7 Apr. 1622–Feb. 1696/7). **P.** Born at Chattisham, Suff.; second son of Daniel Meadowe. Admitted at Emmanuel Coll., Cambridge, 26 F. 1639/40; B.A., 1643; rem. to Christ's College; Fellow, 1644; M.A., 1646. Rector of Ousden, Suff. (26 Aug. 1653); ordained by presbyters, 17 Apr. 1657; ejected, 1662 (but not till Michaelmas, obtaining the tithe). Removed to Ousden Hall; thence, in 1670, to Stowmarket. In Oct. 1672 was licensed "the house of John Meadowse of Stowmarket in Suffolk Pr." At the beginning of 1689 he removed to Bury St. Edmunds, where he had often preached. Here he died; he was buried at Stowmarket, 1 Mar. 1696/7. He was generous in his disposal of much wealth. He was thrice married, but the editor of *D.* thought this an extravagant allowance. (*B. C. D. P. Su.*) [104]

MEDDOWS, MR. **C.** [? John Meadows, clk. (1655–1715).] Received grant (1702) from the Congregational Fund for Reading. (*Cf. Su.*) [7]

MEDHURST. [113, 115] *See* Sussex

MEERBROOK ('Merbrock'), then a chapelry in Leek parish, now vicarage. [98]

MELBOURNE ('Melborne'). [25]

MELFORD, LONG. Ejected from this rectory was John Woods [? of St. John's Coll., Cambridge; matric. pensioner, from

Oxford, 1639; B.A., 1640/1]. (*B. C. Jo. V.*) [107]
MELTON MOWBRAY. [68]
MERBROCK. [98] *See* Staffordshire
MERCER, DANIEL. Attended as Manager on 9 Feb. 1690/1 only. He died before 23 May 1692, when Joseph Thomson [*q.v.*] was appointed in his place. (*M.*) [162, 165]
MERIONETHSHIRE. [141, 148, 149]
MERNER, or MARNER, SAMUEL (17 Sept. 1653–1691/2). C. Born at Midhurst; son of John Marner, clothier (*d.* Dec. 1693). The Episc. Returns, 1669, report him as one of many preachers to "great nūbers Some of them, Persons of good Quallity" at Midhurst, Suss. "at the houses of Robert Marner & Nicolas Brewer." Licensed, 8 May 1672, as "Congr. Teacher in the howse of Thomas Watersfield in Arundell, Sussex." The Common Fund voted him (1690) £4 a year for Midhurst; omitted, 27 June 1692. (*M. T.*) [113, 115]
MERRILL, *i.e.* MERREL, ZACHARY (*d.* 1730). P. Younger brother of Joshua Merrel; *see* Myrrald. Published a sermon (1709) before Societies for Reformation of Manners (no place stated). An original trustee of Dr. Williams' will (1711). In Evans' List (1715) appears as Minister at Hampstead, where he was succeeded (1730) by John Partington. He was a Subscriber at Salters' Hall, 1719. In the continuation of Matthew Henry's commentary he did 1 Peter. He was one of the original distributors (1723) of the English *regium donum*. (*Cm. Ev. Je.*) [2]
MERRIMAN, BENJAMIN (1662—22 Oct. 1734). C. Bapt., 9 Dec. 1662 (Newbury parish church register). Son of Thomas Merriman of Newbury. The Episc. Returns, 1669, report a small meeting of Anabaptists "At Thomas Merrimans," Newbury, adding, "These meetings consist of such as have been ingaged (as generally the whole towne was) in ye late warre agt the King; and their abettors are such as have been ejected upon ye Act for Regulating Corporacons." Matric., 30 Mar. 1677, at St. Alban Hall, Oxford, aged 15; remained at Oxford till 1680 (tombstone). Was some time at Dudley. Ordained publicly at Newbury, 1686, aged 24. Barn fitted up, 1687. The congregation had 172 church members, 1710; 400 attendants, 1715. Meeting-house built, 1716. Buried at Newbury; tombstone at Congregational Church. (*Ev. F. Sm. T.*) [6]
MERTHER. [18, 19]
MERTHYR TYDFIL. [143]
MESEBY, *i.e.* MOSELEY, ROBERT, M.A. (1622–1701). P. Son of John Moseley, D.D., of Newark on Trent, Notts. Matric. at Magdalen Hall, Oxford, 27 May 1636, aged 14; B.A., 1638; M.A., 1641; incorp. at Cambridge, 1654. Licensed, 25 July 1672, as "Pr. Teacher" in John Bonthame's barn, Cloughhead, Derb. [? Dane Head, above Cistern's Clough, in the Peak district.] For Gospel work in the High Peak Hundred, £18 a year was regularly voted by the Fund. One of the founders (1691) of the Cheshire Classis (*see* p. 157), being then Minister of Ringhay Chapel, Chesh., a building not consecrated till 1720. In 1692 he removed to Mellor Chapel, where he was buried, 5 N. 1701. He appears to have been one of the Nonconformist divines who escaped ejection. (*F. M. T. Uc.*) [15, 25]
MESSING. [42]
MIDDLESEX. [72, 73, 168, 176] Except the headings "Middlesex" in the earliest handwriting, all is in that of the Bookkeeper. With one exception (Webb, 135) all the returns are numbered 98.
Brainford is Brentford.
Colebrook is Colnbrook, partly in Middlesex, mostly in Buckinghamshire, being on the river Colne, here dividing the counties.
MIDDLETON. [26, 27]
MIDHURST ('Medhurst'). [113, 115]
MILBORNE ('Milborn') PORT. Ejected here was William Hopkins, B.A. [*q.v.*]. [34, 93]
MILBOURNE GRANGE ('Milborn Grang'). [23, 80]
MILES, THOMAS (*fl.* 1662–1690). P. Rector of St. Chad's, Lichfield; ejected, 1662. Remained in Lichfield till driven out by the Five Mile Act, 1666. The Episc. Returns, 1669, report him as one of the preachers to "above 300" persons at three houses in Walsall, Staff. Licensed, June 1672, being of Lichfield, as "Grāll Pr. Teacher." (*C. P. T.*) [96]
MILLS, GEORGE (1651—6 D. 1723). C. Had no regular education for the ministry. Ordained, 6 N. 1695, as pastor of the Congregational church at Guestwick, Norf. (on recommendation of London ministers), and remained there till death. (*B.*) [73]
MILLS, JOHN. [113]
MILNTHORPE ('Milthorp,' 'Milthrop'), now an ecclesiastical parish, was in Heversham parish. Thomas Bigge, the vicar, was sequestered in June 1644.

John Wallace, or Wallis, M.A. [? son of Richard Wallis, maltster, of Chesterton, Cambs; admitted sizar at St. John's Coll., Cambridge, 20 Sept. 1636, aet. 15; matric. 1637; B.A., 1640/1], who held the vicarage from 1658, and was ejected in 1660, was according to Calamy "of so scandalous a Life in several Respects, that his Memory is not worth preserving." Bigge was restored in 1660, and held the living till his death in March 1676/7. His successors were William Burrell, M.A., inst. 1677; Thomas Milner, inst. 1678; Thomas Ridley, inst. 1686; George Farmer, M.A., inst. 1691, *d.* Feb. 1723/4. The Common Fund granted (12 D. 1692) £8 a year for Milnthorpe, which was not paid after 1693. (*C. Jo. M. N. V.*) [121]

MILTON. [85, 86]

MILWAY, THOMAS (*d.* 1697). C. *See* p. 186. (*B. Cm. E. M. T.*) [103, 186]

MINISTER'S RESIDENCE. [178-9]

MINISTER'S SON. This was John Asty (1675?–20 Jan. 1729/30), born in Norwich, second son of Robert Asty (*d.* 14 Oct. 1681), Congregational Minister there; and grandson of Robert Asty, ejected from the rectory of one of the Stratfords, Suff. At eight years of age, two years after his father's death, he was, at the cost of Samuel Smith [*q.v.*], of Colkirk, Norf., taken into the family of John Collinges [*q.v.*], who (till his death) superintended his education. On 6 July 1691 the Common Fund voted him a bursary of £10 a year, and he was placed in the Academy of Thomas Rowe, M.A. [*q.v.*]; his bursary was paid till the end of 1692. Chaplain from 18 N. 1695 to Smith Fleetwood, Esq., of Armingland Hall, Norf., and Stoke Newington. From 1710 till death he was pastor of the Congregational church, Ropemakers' Alley, Moorfields, London (ordained, 4 Apr. 1711), and lived on the premises. He was a Subscriber at Salters' Hall (1719). He wrote the Life prefixed to the "Works" (1721) of John Owen, D.D. [*q.v.*]. The inscription on his tomb at Bunhill Fields (if rightly read) gives his age as 57; he could not have been above 54. (*B. C. Ev. P. W. We.*) [75]

MITCHILL, *i.e.* MITCHELL, JAMES (1672?–1712). Son of Richard Mitchell, of Marton Scar in Craven. Entered Frankland's Academy, 26 Aug. 1689. The Common Fund granted him, 1692–5, £6 a year. Ordained at Rathmell, 7 June 1693. He was probably the Cottingham man, preaching there as a Student, and succeeded by Abraham Dawson [*q.v.*]. From 1704 to 1711 he received Fund grants for Ravenstonedale. At the time of his death, "aged near 40," he is described as "Minr abt Rossendale." Buried there, 15 Sept. 1712. ["William Mitchell, the Antinomian Preacher near Bradford," who died in March 1705/6, is not likely to have been the Cottingham man.] (*Fr. Hh. Ht. M. Nk. Nr.*) [136, 138]

MODBURY. [32]

MODWITT, *i.e.* MAUDUIT, ISAAC (*d.* April 1718). P. Son of John Maudyt, M.A., ejected (1660) from the sequestered rectory of Penshurst, Kent. Succeeded at Stamford Edward Browne (*d.* Apr. 1682); ejected from the sequestered vicarage of All Saints, Stamford. Minister (1691–8) at Tooting, Surrey; next (1698) at Long Walk, Bermondsey, removing the congregation to a Meeting-house built for him (1690) at King John's Court, Bermondsey; he lived on the premises. Promoted (1715) the Horsleydown charity school. John Dunton [*q.v.*] commends him for modesty, learning, and wit. (*Ev. J. Rq. W. Wc.*) [70]

MOHUN, LADY. Philippa, fourth daughter of Arthur, first earl of Annesley, married Charles, third baron Mohun of Okehampton, who died in 1677. The widow remarried (1693) William Coward, serjeant-at-law, and died in 1714/5; buried at Lee, Kent. (*Pe.*) [56]

MONCKTON COMBE ('Coome'). [92]

MONMOUTH. Ejected from this vicarage was Nicholas Cary [? Nicholas Carey, of Corpus Christi Coll., Cambridge; matric., 1639; B.A., 1644/5]; after ejection, studied and practised medicine in London, with special success in diseases of eye and ear. (*C. V.*) [145]

MONMOUTHSHIRE ('Munmouthshire'). [143, 144]

MONTGOMERYSHIRE ('Mongomery,' 'Mountgomery,' 'Mount-Gomery'). [141, 148]

MOOR, *i.e.* MOORE, JOHN (1642—23 Aug. 1717). P. Born at Musbury, Devon. From Colyton grammar school, matric. pleb., at Brasenose Coll., Oxford, 13 July 1660. Vicar of Longburton, Dors., and curate at Holnest chapelry in that parish; resigned, 1667. Licensed, 18 Apr. 1672 ('John More'), being of Ottery St. Mary, Devon, where he had a small estate, as "Presb. Teacher in any licensed place." Signed the thanks of Devon Ministers. In 1676 became one of the Ministers of the congregation at Bridgwater (*see* Gardner, John), and laboured there for about thirty-six years. From 1688 he conducted an Academy of repute. He was one of the founders of the Somerset union, on the London model.

His son, John Moore, B.A. (1673–1747), succeeded him both in the congregation and the Academy. (*C. D. Ev. F. Mh. P. T.*) [91]

MOOR, SIMON. **C.** Chaplain in Lord Wharton's regiment, parliamentary army. Ejected from Worcester Cathedral (there in 1652) and retired to London. Baxter calls him an old Independent. [On 2 May 1672 Stephen More was licensed as an Indep. Teacher in the house of Barnabas Bloxon, Winchester Yard, Southwark. This is probably the same man.] (*C. P. T.*) [3]

MOOR, or MOORE, THOMAS (*d.* 1720). **P.** Son of John Moore (1642—23 Aug. 1717) [*q.v.*]. Educated in his father's Academy at Bridgwater, Som. Minister, 1701 till death, at Abingdon, where he kept school. Had, 1715, a congregation of 800. (*C. Ev. P. Sm.*) [7, 123]

MOOR, *i.e.* MORE, THOMAS, M.A. (*d.* Aug. 1699). **P.** Scholar of Trinity Coll., Oxford, 1648; B.A., 1651/2; M.A., 1654. Rector of Hammoon, Dorset; ejected, 1662. The Episc. Returns, 1665, report him as "now Resident at Milton Abbas." Licensed, 16 May 1672, as "Pr. Teacher in his howse in Milton Abbas, Dorset"; also, 30 S. and 28 Oct. 1672, as "Pr. Teacher att the house of Rob[t] Alford of Sturminster Newton," Dors.; signed the Address of thanks to the Crown from Dorset Ministers, 10 May 1672. The Common Fund granted him (1690) £10 a year for Milton Abbot, reduced (1695) to £5, raised again (1696) to £6, and paid to Midsummer 1697. (*C. F. Hu. M. P. T.*) [34]

MOORE, JOHN (*fl.* 1685–1729). **P.** Chaplain (1685–9) to Samuel Baker, Wattisfield Hall, Suff. On the death (10 July 1687) of Edmund Whincop, pastor of the Congregational church at Wattisfield, Moore filled the vacancy and was repeatedly asked to become pastor, but declined. In 1689 he removed to Tiverton, Devon (ordained, 29 July 1691). Here he conducted an Academy, which Roger Flexman entered in 1723. (*B. Ev. Mh.*) [30]

MOORE, or MORE, ROBERT (*d.* June 1704). **P.** Born at Nottingham. Matric. sizar, at Clare Hall, Cambridge, 1646; did not graduate. After ministering for a year at Belper, he obtained the perpetual curacy of Brampton, Derb., and was ordained by the Chesterfield Classis; ejected, 1662. Licensed, 25 July 1672, as Pr. Teacher in the house of Gabriel Wayne, Cutthorpe (in Brampton parish). He died Minister at Derby, having outlived the other Ejected Ministers of Derbyshire. (*C. P. T. V.*) [25]

MOORLANDS, THE. [98, 180]

MORCHARD. Either Morchard Bishop or Cruwys-Morchard. From Morchard Bishop was ejected Robert Snow, of Wadham Coll., Oxford; matric., 19 June 1629, aged 18; rem. to Exeter Coll.; B.A., 1631; Fellow, 1632–42; M.A., 1634; rector of Morchard Bishop, 1641; ejected, 1662; living in Exeter, 1665. (*C. F. T.*) [32]

MORELAND, *i.e.* MORLAND, MARTIN, M.A. (*b.* 1624?). **P.** Second son of Thomas Morland, rector of Bright Waltham and of Sulhampstead Abbas, Berks. Matric., 26 June 1644, at Wadham Coll., Oxford, aged 20; B.A., 1648; M.A., 1651, and Fellow; incorp. at Cambridge, 1652. Rector of Weld, Hants. Ejected, 1662. Licensed, 16 May 1672, as a Presb. Teacher at his house in Hackney. Spent there the latter part of his life. (*C. F. P. T.*) [3]

MORETON ('Moretown') HAMPSTEAD. Ejected here was Robert Wolcombe, of Oriel Coll., Oxford; matric., 22 Nov. 1650; B.A., 1652/3; Fellow, 1654/5; M.A., 1655; ord. by presbyters, 11 Nov. 1657; rector of Moreton Hampstead, 1657; ejected, 1662; disinherited by his father for nonconformity; licensed, 20 Apr. 1672, being of Chudleigh, Devon, as Pr. Teacher in any licensed place; obtained a licence, 1687, for worship at Moreton Hampstead; died at Chudleigh, 1692. (*C. F. Mh. T.*) [32]

MORLAND, THOMAS, B.A. (*b.* 1616). Eldest son of Thomas Morland, rector of Bright Waltham, etc. Brother of Martin Morland (*supra*). Matric. at Queen's Coll., Oxford, 9 Nov. 1632, aged 16; B.A., 1637, from New Inn Hall. He was probably the schoolmaster and 'companion.' For his youngest brother, Sir Samuel Morland, bart. (1625–1695), see *D.* (*F.*) [3]

MORLEY. Ejected here was . . . Etherington, who afterwards conformed. Originally a parish, it became soon after the Norman conquest a chapelry in Batley parish; the chapel was leased, temp. Charles I., by Thomas Savile, earl of Sussex, to trustees (Presbyterians) for 500 years. After many vicissitudes the building was replaced (1875–7) by St. Mary's Congregational church. (*C. Sq.*) [129, 131]

MORRIS, . . . [98]

MORTIMER, JOHN, B.A. (1633?–1696).

𝔓. Born at Exeter, son of a tradesman there who married a sister of Thomas Manton, D.D., ejected from St. Paul's, Covent Garden. Matric. at Exeter College, Oxford, 12 Nov. 1650; B.A., 1653/4. Vicar of Sowton St. Michael, *alias* Clyst St. Michael, Devon. Ejected, 1662. Reported in the Episcopal Returns (1665) as a peaceable liver at Totnes. Lost his books and papers in the fire of London (1666). Licensed, 11 Apr. 1672, as a general Presb. Teacher of Exeter. In great straits. Appears to have returned to Devonshire from London in 1691. He had been in receipt of £5 a year from Matthew Barker; this was granted him from the Common Fund, 12 O. 1691, and paid to Midsummer 1692, he being at Bow, Devon. He died at Exeter. He seems called a Scotchman through a confusion with Lorimer. (*C. F. M. P. T.*) [2, 33]

MORTIMER, . . . [112]

MORTLAKE ('Mortlack'). [2]

MORTON, CHARLES, M.A. (Feb. 1626/7–11 Apr. 1698). ℭ. Born at Pendavy, Egloshayle, Corn.; bapt. 15 Feb. 1626/7. Eldest son of Nicholas Morton (a descendant of Thomas Morton, secretary to Edward III.) by his wife Frances, only daughter of Thomas Kestell of Pendavy. Admitted scholar at Wadham Coll., Oxford, 7 Sept. 1649, aged 19 (really 22); B.A., 1649; M.A., 1652; incorp. at Cambridge, 1653. Originally a royalist, the lax character of that party at Oxford turned him to the other side. Rector of Blisland, Corn.; ejected, 1662. Retired to a small property at St. Ives, Corn. Lost much property through the fire of London, 1666, and came to London to make a livelihood. Licensed, 11 Apr. 1672, as "Presb. Teacher in his Howse in Kennington," Lambeth parish; his house there licensed, same date, as "a Presb. Meeting Place"; application also for his house at St. Ives, Corn., was not granted. Soon after he began at Stoke Newington what ranked as the chief Congregational Academy in London, as that of Thomas Doolittle [*q.v.*] was the leading Presbyterian Academy. John Dunton [*q.v.*] calls him "the very soul of philosophy." Defoe was one of Morton's Students. Samuel Wesley (father of the Evangelist), another Student, attacked the Nonconformist Academies in 1703, when a controversy followed with Samuel Palmer (*d.* 1724) which throws much light on the methods of the higher Nonconformist education, as well as the proclivities of Students in rival London Academies. Persecution drove Morton to New England; he reached Charlestown, Mass., in July 1686, and held the pastorate of the Congregational church there from 5 Nov. 1686 till death. His appointment as president of Harvard would have been obnoxious to the government, hence the office of vice-president was created for him. He died at Charlestown. (*Ap. C. D. F. P. T. V.*) [75]

MOSELEY, then chapelry in Bromsgrove parish, Worc. [120]

MOSELEY, ROBERT. *See* Meseby

MOTTERSHED, JOHN (1662—13 Oct. 1728). 𝔓. Son of a London tradesman; brought up under the ministry of Thomas Doolittle, M.A., and studied in Doolittle's Academy at Islington, where (in 1682) Calamy came to be a fellow-boarder. Went thence to Rotterdam, where he studied under Peter Bayle. Returning, he assisted Doolittle (1690 ?) at Monkwell Street; later, he assisted John Goffe at Kingston-on-Thames, gratuitously, being well off. From Kingston, in 1697, he moved to Queen Street, Ratcliffe Cross, in succession to George Day, ejected from Wivelscomb, Devon. There also he would have ministered gratuitously but for "his prudent father-in-law." His stipend, and much more, went in charity; he left for his Meeting-house an endowment of £500. His address was "in White-horse-street, Ratcliffe." (*Cm. Ev. W. We.; Fun. Serm. by Calamy*, 1729.) [2]

MYNYDDISLWYN. Ejected here was Henry Walter. (*B. C. L. See* Newport, Monm.) [143]

MYRRALD, *i.e.* MERREL, JOSHUA (*d.* 1716). 𝔓. [In 1665 John and Catherine Merrell, of Eyam, Derb., were presented and excommunicated as Anabaptists and for non-attendance at church.] Born in Cheshire; an eldest son; his parents members of the Knutsford congregation. Ordained in Derbyshire, 1687. The Common Fund voted him (1690) £10 a year "on condition hee keepe to the people att Longdoles" [*q.v.*]; in 1691–1692 it was for that place and Rosson (*see* Roston); it was continued, 1695–1703, for Uttoxeter. In 1704 he removed to the Great Meeting, Coventry (at a smaller stipend), as co-pastor with John Warren (*d.* 1742). The Fund Minutes call him John Merrill; Evans' List gives Joshua Merrell; Redfern's Uttoxeter has John Merret; the funeral sermon (3 July 1716) by John Warren gives Joshua Merrel. (*Ev. M. Si.*) [96, 97]

NABS, *i.e.* NABBS, EDWARD, B.A. (*fl.* 1638–93). Matric. sizar, at Magdalene Coll., Cambridge, 1636; migrated to St. Catharine's Hall, B.A., 1641/2. Curate at Dorking in 1659 to Samuel Cozens, B.D., the vicar, at whose death, 19 May 1661, his curacy ceased. Calamy (who calls him Samuel Nabbs) is misinformed; he was not ejected from Dorking; he was silenced in 1662, and may possibly have obtained some post after May 1661, and been ejected thence. The Book-keeper's entry probably means, not that he was ejected at Chester, but that he came thence to Binfield. The Common Fund granted him (1690–93) £5 a year for Binfield. Calamy reports him as living and dying "about London," "very Old and feeble," some years before 1713. (*C. M. P. V.; Surrey Archaeological Collections*, xxvii. 92.) [3, 7, 8]

NAILSWORTH. [44]

NANTWICH ('Nantwych'). [15]

NAWTON BUSHELL. [31] *See* Devonshire

NAYLAND ('Neiland'). [106, 107]

NAYLOR, JAMES (1664—12 Apr. 1710). **P.** Entered Frankland's Academy, 3 May 1684. Minister at St. Helen's Chapel, parish of Prescot, from 1688 (it was registered in his favour, 20 July 1696, by a majority of magistrates, which included Lord Willoughby and the Mayor of Liverpool) till his death, when it was recovered from the Presbyterians.

His son, Quintus Naylor, received a Fund bursary of £8, 1712–14, for his education for the ministry. (*M. Nk. Nl. X.*) [58]

NEEDHAM MARKET. Ejected from this vicarage was Thomas James; applied, 22 May 1672, for licence to preach in an outhouse at Needham, being "of the Congregationall pswasion"; the licence, through misreading of the application, was made out for him, 10 June 1672, as Pr. Teacher in a house at West Creeting, Suff. (*C. T.*) [103, 104]

NEGUS, STRICKLAND, *i.e.* STICKLAND, M.A. (1612–1693). **C.** Son of Thomas Negus of Shelton, Beds, pleb. Matric. at Lincoln Coll., Oxford, 25 N. 1631, aged 19; B.A., 1633; rem. to Sidney Sussex Coll., Cambridge, M.A., 1640. Vicar (1645) of Melchbourne, Beds; held some position at Irchester, Northants (a sequestered vicarage); Thursday lecturer at Oundle, Northants; ejected, 1662. Application was made twice in vain for licence for his preaching "in ye schoole house in Geddington." Licensed, 13 May 1672, as "Congr. Teacher in Rich: Barnes howse" at Wellingborough, Northants. The Common Fund granted him (1690) £5 a year at Geddington; on 1 May 1693 he was reported dead. He appears to have been a member of the Congregational church at Rothwell, Northants; he was one of the witnesses against Richard Davis [*q.v.*] at Kettering in 1692, and was then living at Stevington, Beds. (*C. F. Gl. M. P. T. Wc.*) [76, 77]

NEILAND. [106] *See* Suffolk

NELSON, GILBERT. [165]

NEONOMIAN. [156]

NESBET, *i.e.* NESBITT, JOHN, M.A. (6 Oct. 1661—22 Oct. 1727). **C.** Born in Northumberland. Entered Frankland's Academy, as John Nessbatt, 28 June 1674. Graduated at Edinburgh, as John Nisbett, 24 Mar. 1680. Coming to London from Edinburgh, he was usher at a school at Bishop's Hall, Bethnal Green [*q.v.*], kept by Walton, ejected from West Ham vicarage, Essex; after this, tutor in family of Matthew Richardson, Mile End. As he was leaving England in 1683 for study at Utrecht, he was arrested in Essex, on suspicion of complicity with the Rye House Plot. At Utrecht, where he occasionally preached in the English Church, he went by the name of White. Returning to London in 1689, he was Minister at Hare Court, Aldersgate Street, from 1691 till death. His having previously rendered ministerial assistance both to Williams and to Chauncy is interesting—the words (p. 3) referring to Chauncy are an addition to the original entry. As a Manager of the Common Fund he took part, till some time in 1692, in the Nonconformist survey, acting for Cumberland, Durham, Northumberland, and Westmorland, and joined the Happy Union. In the Congregational Fund he was a correspondent (1696) for Bucks, Cheshire, Cumberland, Dorset, Durham, Hunts, Northumberland, Sussex, and Yorkshire. He was elected a Pinners' Hall Lecturer in 1697, succeeding Nathanael Mather [*q.v.*]. He is referred to in Addison's "Spectator," 4 Mar. 1711/2, as Mr. Nisby, holding that "laced coffee is bad for the head." For the statistics known as Evans' List he supplied information for Cumberland, Northumberland, and Westmorland, and obtained the Staffordshire list. He married Elizabeth, daughter of Isaac Chauncy [*q.v.*]. In 1716 he was living "in Hare-Court, Aldersgate." (*Ad. Cm. Ed. Ev. Fr. Ha. M. R. Sg. W.*) [3, 23, 36, 80, 121, 161, 168, 186]

NETHERBURY. [34]

NEVIT, NEVITT, or NEVET, JOHN (*d.* 1696 ?). **P.** Son of Rowland Neavett, or Nevet, M.A., ejected from Oswestry [*q.v.*]. In 1692 a grant of £8 a year was made to him for Bridgnorth, reduced (1695) to £6, paid to 3 Nov. 1696, after which he disappears. (*M. P.*) [16, 83]

NEW LIGHTS. [155]

NEW STREET, now represented by Great New Street, ran behind the (now) Moravian Meeting-house on the east side of Fetter Lane. [2]

NEW WINDSOR. [6] *See* Windsor

NEWBURY. Ejected here in 1662 were (1) Benjamin Woodbridge, M.A., son of John Woodbridge, M.A., rector of Stanton Fitzwarren, Wilts; matric. at Magdalen Hall, Oxford, 9 N. 1638, aged 18; went to New England, 1639; B.A. at Harvard Coll., 1642 (being the first to graduate there); returning to England, preached in Salisbury; rector of Newbury, 18 May 1648; M.A., Oxford, Nov. 1648; chaplain to Charles II., 1660; offered a canonry at Windsor; commissioner at the Savoy Conference, 1661; preached at Newbury after ejection; thought of conforming, 1665; licensed, 9 Apr. 1672, as Teacher to Presbyterians in Town Hall, Newbury; preached at Highclere, Hants, 1678; at Englefield, Berks, 1683; died at Englefield, 1 Nov. 1684. Ejected with him was (2) his assistant, Henry Backaller (*see* Baikaller). (*C. D. F. P. T.*) [6, 102, 147]

NEWCASTLE-ON-TYNE ('new Castle'). Ejected here were (1) . . . Ashburnham, afterwards conformed; (2) . . . Cole, afterwards conformed; (3) William Durant (son of Thomas, of Bodmin), of Exeter Coll., Oxford; matric. 12 Sept. 1640, aged 16; no record of graduation; Friday afternoon lecturer at All Saints', Newcastle, 20 Feb. 1645/6; lecturer at St. Nicholas', Newcastle, 30 May; morning lecturer at All Saints', Newcastle, 5 July 1647; after ejection, preached privately; refused licence, 16 Apr. 1672, as Independent Teacher at Trinity House, Newcastle, but licensed, 13 May 1672, as Grāll Congregll Teacher, being of Newcastle; *d.* 1681, buried in his garden. (*C. F. P. T.*); (4) Samuel Hammond, of King's Coll., Cambridge; matric. sizar, 1638; B.A., 1641/2; M.A., 1645; Fellow of Magdalene Coll., 1645 (Calamy makes him B.D.; Palmer makes him D.D.; no record of either); preacher at St. Giles, Cambridge; chaplain to Sir Arthur Haselrig; preacher at Bishopwearmouth; preacher and lecturer at St. Nicholas', Newcastle, 5 Nov. 1652; ejected, 1660; preached at Hamburg, Stockholm and Danzig; returned to England, 1664/5, and died at Hackney; bur. 10 Dec. 1665. (*C. D. P. V.*); (5) John Knightbridge, of Wadham Coll., Oxford; matric. 8 Dec. 1637, aged 17; B.A., 1641; incorp. at Cambridge, 1645; Fellow of Peterhouse, and M.A., 1645; B.D., 1655; conformed; rector of Holy Trinity, Dorchester, 1663; D.D., 1673; founded chair of moral philosophy by will, 1683. (*C. F. V.*); (6) Henry Leaver, or Lever [? of Sidney Sussex Coll., Cambridge; matric sizar, 1624], son of Samson, grandson of Thomas, both of St. John's Coll., Cambridge; vicar of Alnwick, Northumb.; rector of Branspeth, Dur., 1644; commissioner for erecting a college at Durham; vicar of St. John's, Newcastle, 1659; ejected, 1662; removed to Shincliffe, Dur., till 1665; preaching at Newcastle in 1669; refused licence, 16 Apr. 1672, as Presb. Teacher at a Chapel adjoining the Magdalen Hospital, Newcastle, but licensed, 13 May 1672, as Grāll Pr. Teacher, being of Newcastle; bur. there 6 June 1673. (*C. P. T. V.*); (7) Richard Prideaux, of Exeter Coll., Oxford; matric. 2 Dec. 1631, aged 18; B.A., 1635; Fellow, 1635–43; M.A., 1638; vicar of Easton Neston, Northants, 1643; held the sequestered rectory of Greens Norton, 1645; after ejection conformed; *d.* at Newcastle, 1663. (*C. F.*) [22, 79, 80, 136]

NEWCASTLE ('New Castle') UNDER LYME. Ejected here was George Long, M.A., M.D. [*q.v.*]. [98]

NEWCOME ('Newcomen'), HENRY, M.A. (Nov. 1627—17 S. 1695). **P.** Born at Caldicote, Hunts; baptized 27 N. 1627; fourth son of Stephen Newcome (*d.* 1642), then rector. Educated by his brother Robert, who succeeded as rector. Admitted at St. John's Coll., Cambridge, 8 May 1644, aet. 16; precluded from study owing to the Civil War, till 10 May 1645; B.A., 1648/9; M.A., 1651. Schoolmaster (24 S. 1647) at Congleton, Ches., and began to preach. Ordained by presbyters, 22 Aug. 1648, at Sandbach, Ches.; perpetual curate, 23 N. 1648, of Goostrey, Ches.; admitted, 8 Apr. 1650, to the sequestered rectory of Gawsworth, Ches. Took the solemn league and covenant of 1643; also (reluctantly) the engagement (1649) of fidelity to the commonwealth without king or house of lords. Joined (Oct. 1653) in forming a clerical union for Cheshire, on Baxter's model. Elected (5 D. 1656) one of the preachers at Manchester Collegiate Church (now Cathedral); settled in Manchester, 23 Apr. 1657, and was member of the First Lancashire Classis, but warmly espoused the endeavours (1659) for an 'accommodation' with Congregationals. Involved in the royalist plans (1659) of Sir George Booth, and publicly prayed (6 May 1660) for the king "by periphrasis." New Fellows were installed (17 S. 1660) in the Collegiate Church; too late, Charles II. added his name (21 Sept.) to the list from which Fellows were to be chosen; the new Fellows having other preferments, he preached as their deputy till 31 Aug. 1662, when he was ejected, refusing episcopal ordination. Under the Five Mile Act he removed (1666) to Ellenbrook, now in Worsley parish, Lanc. Visiting Dublin, he declined a call (25 July 1670) to Wine Tavern Street Meeting-house. Licensed, 15 Apr. 1672, as "Presb. Teacher"; his house in Manchester being licensed, same day, as "a Presb. Meeting Place"; he preached later (till 1676) in "a howse near the Colledge" (licensed, 8 May 1672); also at a barn at Cold House, near Shude Hill, Manchester. Declined (1677) a chaplaincy to the widowed countess of Donegall. In 1687 he resumed public services, first in a vacant house, then in Thomas Stockton's barn (in Deansgate ?), with John Chorlton [*q.v.*] as assistant. He was one of the Monday lecturers at Bolton, Lanc. He was a member of the Lancashire Provincial Meeting of United Ministers (1693). Cross Street Chapel was built for him (1694). Buried in his Chapel. (*C. D. Jo. Nl. P. T. Wc.*) [26, 61]

NEWINGTON, *i.e.* STOKE NEWINGTON. Ejected here was Daniel Bull, M.A. [*q.v.*]. [4, 72]

NEWINGTON GREEN, in the parish of Stoke Newington, was a great resort of Nonconformists. The rector of Stoke Newington from 1665 till his death in 1704 was Sidrach Simpson, D.D., son of Sidrach Simpson (1600?–18 Apr. 1655), one of the Dissenting Brethren in the Westminster Assembly of Divines. The rector, a high churchman, is said to have been somewhat severe with Dissenters; though, as stated in his funeral sermon, "he did not go farther than the Assembly did with the Five Brethren." (*D.*) [4]

NEWMAN, WIDOW. ℭ. Her contribution was per Isaac Chauncey [*q.v.*]. (*M.*) [166]

NEWMARKET ('Newmarkett'). [107]

NEWPORT ('Nuport'), Isle of Wight. Ejected here was Robert Tutchin, father of John [*q.v.*], of Robert, ejected from Brokenhurst, Hants, and of Samuel, ejected from Odiham [*q.v.*]. [100]

NEWPORT, Monm. Ejected here were (1) Henry Walter (son of John, armiger, of Piersfield, Monm.) of Jesus Coll., Oxford; matric. 12 Apr. 1633, aged 22; B.C.L., 1633; an itinerating preacher; vicar of Newport; served also the vicarage of Mynyddyslwyn, Monm., and the rectory, of Bedwas, Monm.; ejected, 1660; preaching in his house, Park y Pill, at Caerleon, parish of Llangattoch (perhaps also at Horningsham, Wilts) in 1669; licensed, 10 June 1672, as Ind. Teacher at his house in Llanvihangel Llantarnam parish, Monm.; his house licensed, same date, Ind. (*C. F. T.*) Ejected with him was (2) his curate, Watkin Jones [*q.v.*]. [144, 179]

NEWTON, EDWARD, M.A. (1628–Jan. 1711/2). 𝔓. Born at Maidstone. Matric. pensioner, at Jesus Coll., Cambridge, 1645/6; B.A., 1647/8; Fellow of Balliol Coll., Oxford, 1649; incorp. B.A., 18 June 1650; M.A., 27 July 1650; incorp. at Cambridge, 1652. Ordained by presbyters at Salisbury, 1652. First ministered at Kingston, Suss. Succeeded his father-in-law, Benjamin Pickering, M.A., as rector of St. Peter's and St. Mary's Westout (later known as St. Anne's), Lewes, and rector of Southover, Lewes, Suss.; ejected, 1662. The Episc. Returns, 1669, report him as one of the preachers to "about 200" persons at Brighton, Suss.; also as one of two preachers to "Presbyterians At least 500 midle sort" at South Malling, Suss. Licensed, 15 May 1672, as Teacher in the house of Widow Swan, Lewes, "Presbyterian perswasion." Application was also made for two other licenses for houses in his favour. In 1687 the Westgate Meeting-house was fitted up for him in Lewes, where he officiated (with the assistance, 1695–1701, of Thomas Barnard [*q.v.*]) till in 1701 a new Meeting-house was built for him in Crown Lane. He retired in 1709. (*C. F. Lh. P. T. V.*) [112]

NEWTON ('Nawton') BUSHEL. [31]

NEWTON HEATH ('Newton'). Chapelry in Manchester parish (now rectory). Ejected here was John Walker, M.A. [*q.v.*]. [59, 61]

NICHOLAS, WILLIAM. 𝔓. Of Westminster. Elected a Manager, 9 May 1692, in room of Henry Coape [*q.v.*]; his appointment was conveyed to him by Vincent Alsop [*q.v.*], evidently his pastor. He was also a Manager (1695) of the reconstituted Fund. He appears as Alderman on 6 Feb. 1709/10. His last attendance was on 8 Dec. 1712. (*M.*) [162, 168]

NICHOLSON, GEORGE (1636—20 Aug. 1697). **C.** Born at Kirkoswald; bapt., 20 N. 1636; son of John Nicholson. Matric., 15 June 1657, as servitor at Magdalen Coll., Oxford; chorister, 1658–1661. In charge (1661) of the Congregational church at Melmerby, Cumb.; preached about a year, 1661–2, at Glassby, parish of Addingham, Cumb., and Kirkoswald; silenced, 1662. Preached in conventicles. The Episc. Returns, 1669, report him as one of the preachers to "Independents 60 or more" at Hesket, Lazonby, and Kirkoswald, Cumb. Licensed, 22 July 1672, as Giles Nicholson of Kirkoswald. Presented for Nonconformity, 1670–78. Pastor of Congregational church at Huddlesceugh, in Kirkoswald parish, till death. Grant of £6 was made to him (1697) from the Congregational Fund. (*C. Cf. N. P. T.*) [21, 22]

NICKOLSON, JOHN, M.A., M.D. (*fl.* 1651–1692). Admitted at Magdalene Coll., Cambridge, 24 May 1651; matric., 1651; B.A., 1654/5; rem. pensioner to St. John's Coll., 21 Feb. 1655/6; M.A., 1658; M.B., 1683; M.D., 1692. Licenciate of the Coll. of Physicians, 22 Dec. 1687. (*Jo. Mu. V.*) [37]

NICOLETTS, . . . [101]

NOBLE, DAVID, M.A. (*d.* 26 N. 1709). **C.** Born at Inverness. Put to the tailoring trade, but turned to study. Studied at Christ's College, Cambridge; did not matriculate. Schoolmaster at Morley and member (1670) of the Topcliffe congregation. Two sons of Oliver Heywood [*q.v.*] were his pupils. Minister of Morley, 1673–4. Chaplain (1678 ?) to Squire Thomas Woolhouse, of Glapwell, Derbs., preaching at Sutton. Ordained by presbyters, 1681. Pastor at Heckmondwike, Jan. 1686/7; a new Meeting-house was built for him in Chapel Fold, replaced by a larger one on 9 N. 1701. Died at Chapel Fold and was buried at Dewsbury. (*Hh. Ht. My. Tr.*) [130]

NOBLE, ISAAC (23 Jan. 1658/9–1726/7). **C.** Bapt., 30 Jan. 1658/9, at Greystoke, Cumb. Third son of John Noble (*d.* 1707/8) of Penruddock. Ordained, 28 May 1689, as Minister at Castle Green, Bristol. He gave great assistance to Calamy for his "Account," 1713. George Fownes, formerly Baptist Minister at Broadmead, Bristol, became Noble's colleague, 8 June 1708, removed (1715) to Andover, Hants, and thence to Nailsworth, Glou.; he was succeeded as Noble's colleague (1716–26) by John Alexander. (*C. Ci. Cm. Ev. N.*; Greystoke parish register.) [91]

NOBLE, JAMES, M.A. (1657—17 Aug. 1739). **P.** Educ. at Edinburgh; M.A., 5 Aug. 1679. Ordained, 1688, as Minister at Branton, Northum. Admitted, before 16 O. 1690, Minister of Yetholm, Roxburghsh.; translated to Eckford, Roxburghsh., 14 Apr. 1694. (*Ed. Sf.*) [80]

NONCONFORMITY ESTABLISHED. [159]

NORFOLK. [74, 75, 168, 172, 176, 177, 181] Except the names of Correspondents for the County, and two small notes, in the Book-keeper's hand, all is in the earliest handwriting. The returns are all numbered 2 (save a marginal addition).

Dereham, Derham, is East Dereham.

Lin, Lynn is King's Lynn [*q.v.*].

Telney is Tilney.

Watsam, North and South, is Walsham [*q.v.*].

Windham is Wymondham [*q.v.*].

NORTH CLAY, the, is the North Clay division of Nottinghamshire, in which East Retford lies. [84]

NORTH MOLTON ('Northmontton'). [32]

NORTHALLERTON ('North Alerton'). [135]

NORTHAMPTON. Ejected here was Jeremiah Lewis, of St. Catharine's Hall, Cambridge; matric. sizar, 1642; B.A., 1645/6; M.A., 1649; vicar of St. Giles', Northampton, 1650 (his father, also Jeremiah, was vicar there, 1616); ejected, 1662; died soon after. (*C. Np. V.*) [76, 178]

NORTHAMPTONSHIRE. [76, 77, 118, 168, 176, 181, 185] Except the headings "Northampton," and the Wellingborough entry, in the earliest handwriting, and two small notes in another hand, all is in the Book-keeper's handwriting. The returns are numbered 24 (with one exception, 27), and 8 in 1691.

Daintree is Daventry [*q.v.*].

Gilsborow is Guilsborough.

Okeley, Great, is Oakley, Great [*q.v.*].

Rowell is Rothwell.

Tocester is Towcester.

NORTHERN CLASSIS. [157]

NORTHERN COUNTIES. [137]

NORTHMONTTON. [32] *See* Devonshire

NORTHOWRAM ('Northouram'), then a village in Halifax parish, Yorks, now a vicarage. [129]

NORTHREPPS. Ejected from this rectory in 1662 was Edward Corbett; he was ejected also 1662/3, from the rectory of Sidestrand, Norf., to which he had been presented in 1661; he died soon after ejection. He was not Edward Corbet, D.D., of Merton Coll., Oxford, rector of Northrepps, 1636–43, who died rector of Great Haseley, Oxf., 5 Jan. 1657/8; nor was he his son. There was an Edward Corbett, of Christ's Coll., Cambridge; matric. pensioner, 1620; B.A., 1623; M.A., 1627. (*B. C. F. Nb. V.*) [74]

NORTHUMBERLAND. [23, 79, 80, 168, 176, 177, 181] Except the names of Correspondents for the County, six entries, and a marginal note, in the Book-keeper's hand, all is in the earliest handwriting. With three exceptions (numbered 60) all the returns are numbered 1.

Austin is Alston.

Eatall is Etal.

North Tine is North Tyne (a river).

Sheeles is North Shields.

NORWICH. Ejected here were (1) Thomas Allyn or Allen (1608—21 Sept. 1673), of Gonville and Caius Coll., Cambridge; matric. sizar, 1625; B.A., 1627/8; M.A., 1631; rector of St. Edmund's, Norwich; deprived, 1636; went to New England, 1638, and preached at Charlestown, Mass.; returned to Norwich as city preacher, 1651; also pastor of Congregational church, 12 Jan. 1656/7; ejected, 1661; preaching in St. Clement's parish, Norwich, in 1669; licensed, 10 June 1672, as Congr. Teacher in a house in St. Andrew's parish, Norwich. (*B. C. T. V.*) (2) John Collinges, D.D. [*q.v.*]. (3) Francis English, of Corpus Christi Coll., Cambridge; matric. sizar, 1645; B.A., 1648/9; M.A., 1655; rector of St. Lawrence's, Norwich, till 1654; perhaps held the rectory of St. Nicholas, Braconash; ejected; preaching in a house in the parish of St. Mary-in-the-Fields, Norwich. (*C. Nb. T. V.*) (4) John Hasbert, B.A. [*q.v.*]. (5) Benjamin Snowden, B.A. [*q.v.*]. (6) Thomas Windresse; born at Leeds, son of Richard Windresse, weaver; from Leeds grammar school admitted sizar at St. John's Coll., 14 June 1656, aged 18; B.A., 1659/60; ejected, 1662, from St. Faith's, Norwich. (St. Vedast's, corruptly called St Faith's, is united with St. Peter Parmentergate, Norwich.) (*C. Jo. V.*) (7) Enoch Woodward [*q.v.*]. [74, 177]

NOTT, JOHN, M.A. (1625 ?–28 D. 1702). **P.** Son of Charles Nott, rector of Shelsley, Worc. Matric. at Emmanuel Coll., Cambridge, 1642; pensioner at Trinity Coll., Cambridge, 29 May 1645; Scholar, 1646; B.A., 1646/7; Fellow, 1647; M.A., 1650. Curate at Wolverhampton to Ambrose Sparry (ejected from the rectory of Martley, Worc.). Vicar of Sheriffhales, Staff., 1650; ejected, 1662. Preached three or four years "at a chapel near Hadley" (? Hadley End, Staff.), then became chaplain to Richard Hampden [*q.v.*] till 1689, when Hampden removed to London. The reference, under Wendover, to Hampden's having "placed a public minister there" means that there had been an appointment to the vicarage. The Common Fund granted him, 1690–1702, £10 a year at Thame (reduced from 1695 to £8). (*C. M. P. Tc. V.*) [9, 10, 85]

NOTTINGHAM. Ejected here were (1) John Barrett, M.A. [*q.v.*]; (2) William Reynolds, M.A. [*q.v.*]; (3) John Whitlock, M.A. [*q.v.*]. [82, 178]

NOTTINGHAMSHIRE. [2, 82, 83, 84, 168, 173, 176] All is in the Book-keeper's handwriting, except the headings "Nottingham," the "East Ratford" entry, and two marginal notes, in the earliest handwriting. The returns are numbered 26, with three exceptions (63, 126, 173).

East Ratford is East Retford.

NUNEATON. [180]

NYE, PHILIP, M.A. (1596 ?–Sept. 1672). **C.** Born in Sussex, and described as gent. Entered, 21 July 1615, as commoner, at Brasenose Coll., Oxford; matric. 28 June 1616, aged 20; removed to Magdalen Hall, B.A., 1619; M.A., 1622. Began to preach, 1620; licensed, 9 Oct. 1627, to perpetual curacy of Allhallows, Staining; in 1630 he was lecturer at St. Michael's, Cornhill. Harassed for his nonconformity, he withdrew to Holland, 1633–40. On the presentation of Edward Montagu (afterwards second Earl of Manchester) he became vicar of Kimbolton, Hunts, and there organised (1643) a Congregational church. He was summoned (1643) to the Westminster Assembly of Divines, and was one of the Assembly's commissioners to Scotland. He delivered (25 Sept. 1643) the exhortation in St. Margaret's, Westminster, preliminary to the taking of the Solemn League and Covenant, showing that "the example of the best reformed churches" did not bind to the Scottish model. He received, 26 Oct. 1643, the sequestered rectory of Acton, Middlx., and was a leader of the "dissenting brethren" when the parliamentary Presbyterianism was debated in the Assembly. He was for toleration of all peaceable preachers. Besides his rectory he held a number of lectureships. He was one of

Cromwell's "triers" (20 March 1654), and "expurgators" (28 Aug. 1654). In 1655/6 he exchanged Acton for the sequestered rectory of St. Bartholomew's-by-the-Exchange. In Oct. 1658, he had a leading part at the Savoy, in the revision of the Westminster Confession for Congregational use. On the fall of Richard Cromwell (1659) he acted in the republican interest. Ejected in 1660, he obtained indemnity only on condition of never again holding civil or ecclesiastical office. In Jan. 1661 he signed the declaration of Congregational Ministers against the Fifth-monarchy rising under Venner. In 1666, after the Fire, he preached openly in London. In regard to Indulgence, he upheld the royal prerogative. On 15 Apr. 1672 he and John Loder (his former curate) were licensed as Congr. Teachers in Loder's house and garden, Cherry Tree alley, Bunhill, in Cripplegate parish. The congregation moved to Cutlers' Hall, Cloak Lane, Queen Street, but Nye can hardly have moved with it. He died at Brompton in the parish of Kensington, and was buried in St. Michael's, Cornhill, 27 Sept. 1672. (*C. D. F. He. P. T. W.*) [154, 188]

OAGLE, *i.e.* OGLE, LUKE, M.A. (1630–Apr. 1696). **P.** Rector of Ingram, Northumb.; held the sequestered vicarage of Berwick-on-Tweed; ejected, 1662. Preached for a time in the parish church of Ancroft, Northumb. Under the Five Mile Act, removed, 1666, to Bowsden, in Lowick parish, Northumb., where he had a small estate. After imprisonment he withdrew to Scotland, where he was inhibited by the Archbishop of St. Andrews, 19 S. 1671. Licensed, 2 May 1672, as "Grall Pr. Teacher," being of Berwick; but the "Schoole house" in Berwick for which he had desired licence was "not app." The Scottish Privy Council allowed him (20 S. 1679) to fill the vacant ministry of Langton, but he was replaced at the end of the following year. In 1685 he was imprisoned at Wooler, Northumb., on suspicion of complicity with Monmouth's rebellion. He returned to Berwick in 1687, and there remained, refusing calls to Kelso and Edinburgh. (*P. S. Sf. T. Wc.*) [79]

OAKHAM. Ejected here was Benjamin King, of Sidney Sussex Coll., Cambridge; matric. pensioner, 1628; B.A., 1630/1; M.A., 1634; rector of Flamstead, Herts, 1638–42; lecturer at Hitchin, 1642–49; held the sequestered vicarage of Oakham, Rut., 1649; ejected, 1660; licensed, 10 June 1672, as Pr. Teacher in a house at Oakham; one of his two daughters married Vincent Alsop, M.A. [*q.v.*]; the other married Robert Ekyns, B.A. [*q.v.*]. Andrew Kippie, D.D., the biographer, was his great-grandson. (*C. T. V.*) [87, 179]

OAKHAMPTON. [31] *See* Devonshire

OAKLEY. [110] *See* Surrey

OAKLEY, GREAT. Ejected here was Francis Dandy, M.A. [*q.v.*]. [76]

OAKS, . . . [14]

OCKINGHAM. [7] *See* Berkshire

OCKLEY. Ejected from this rectory was . . . Nowell. [109, 110]

ODIHAM ('Odiam'). Ejected from this vicarage in 1662 was Samuel Tutchin, third son of Robert Tutchin, ejected from the vicarage of Newport, Isle of Wight, of Wadham Coll., Oxford; matric. ser., 14 Nov. 1650; preaching at Gosport, Hants, 1669; went to the East Indies and *d.* chaplain to the Factory at Fort St. George, Madras. (*C. F. T.*) [102]

OGDEN, SAMUEL, B.A. (1627—25 May 1697). **P.** Born at Fowleach, parish of Oldham, Lanc. (his birthplace is entered at Cambridge as "Foulagii," misread in *Cp.* Fontagii). Son of John Ogden, yeoman. From Littleborough grammar school admitted sizar at Christ's Coll., Cambridge, 4 May 1648, age 20; matric. 1648; B.A., 1651. Master of Oldham grammar school; appointed, 1652, to the chapelry of Buxton, Derb.; ord., 27 S. 1653, by Wirksworth Classis; held, 1654, also the donative curacy of Fairfield; resigning these, he held, 1657, the vicarage of Mackworth, Derb.; ejected, 1662. He had kept a boarding school during the whole of his ministry, and continued it at Mackworth till compelled (1666) by the Five Mile Act to move it first to Yorkshire, then to Derby. Preaching at Little Ireton, Derb., in 1669. Licensed, 8 May 1672, as Pr. Teacher in house of Thomas Saunders, Little Ireton. His school was closed (1686) at the issue of a suit; Sir John Gell, of Hopton, at once made him master of Wirksworth grammar school, a post he held till death, preaching regularly from 1689 to nonconformist congregations.

His great-grandson, Samuel Ogden, D.D. (1716–1778), was author of sermons of high merit; also of the judgment that a goose was "too much for one, and not enough for two." (*C. Cp. D. P. T. V.*) [25]

OGLE, THOMAS, B.A. (1627–1703?) **C.** Son of Valentine Ogle, gent., of Pinchback, Linc. Admitted, 4 F. 1641/2, at Queens' Coll., Cambridge; sizar at St. John's Coll., 6 Aug. 1644, aet. 17; B.A., 1645/6. Vicar of Rolleston, Notts ; thence ejected. Licensed, 10 Aug. 1672, as "Congall Teach and for his house att Chesterfield, in Darbysh" ; also, 9 D. 1672, at the house of John Kendall at Tonge, parish of Breedon-on-the-Hill, Leic. Minister at Chesterfield, 1681–1703 ? to the congregation which built Elder Yard Chapel, 1694. (*C. Jo. P. T. V. Wa.*) [25]

OKEHAM. [87] *See* Rutland

OKEHAMPTON (' Oakhampton '). [31]

OKELEY, GREAT. [76] *See* Northamptonshire

OKLEY. [109] *See* Surrey

OLD FISH STREET. [2] *See* Dove Court

OLD STREET. [2] *See* Bartholomew Square

OLDBURY, formerly a chapelry in the Shropshire portion of Halesowen parish ; now a vicarage in Worcestershire. [89]

OLDENBURY INN; perhaps Hallingbury. [39]

OLDFIELD, JOHN (*b.* 1 Nov. 1654). Elder brother of Joshua Oldfield [*q.v.*]. He received Presbyterian ordination at Mansfield, 28 S. 1681, and afterwards conformed. (*D. Ht.*) [25, 29]

OLDFIELD, JOSHUA, D.D. (2 Dec. 1656–8 Nov. 1729). 𝔓. Born at Carsington, Derbs. Second son of John Oldfield or Otefield (1627 ?—5 June 1682) ; ejected (1662) from the rectory of Carsington. Studied at Lincoln Coll., Oxford, and Christ's Coll., Cambridge, but refused subscription, hence could not matriculate at Oxford. Studied also at the Academy of John Shuttlewood, B.A. (*see* John Shuttlewood). Chaplain at Hopton Hall, Derbs., to Sir Philip Gell, who offered him a good living if he conformed. Tutor to son of Paul Foley (afterwards Speaker). Chaplain in Pembrokeshire to Susan, widow of Sir John Lort. Assistant at Fetter Lane, London, to John Turner [*q.v.*]. Ordained at Mansfield, 18 Mar. 1681/2, as Minister at Tooting, Surr., whence he removed (1689 ?) to Oxford, where the Common Fund granted him (1690–93) £34 a year. At Oxford he was a shy man, but when Calamy got him to converse with scholars "they found he had a great deal more in him than they imagined." Calamy's first public sermon was at Oxford in Oldfield's absence. Removed to Coventry in 1694, and there maintained an Academy. Leaving in 1699 to Minister at Globe Alley, Maid Lane, Southwark, he continued his Academy there and at Hoxton, with the assistance of William Lorimer [*q.v.*]. Received D.D. from Edinburgh, 2 May 1709. Manager of the Fund from 7 Nov. 1709. An original trustee under the will of Daniel Williams [*q.v.*]. Living in 1716 "at Mrs Oldfield's in Red-Cross-street, Southwark." At Salters' Hall (1719) he was Moderator ; Lorimer was Moderator of the seceding Subscribers. In 1723 he was an original agent for distribution of the English *regium donum*. (*Cm. D. Ev. M.*) [85, 179]

OLDHAM (' Oldam '). Ejected here was Robert Constantine, M.A. [*q.v.*]. Respecting "Loben" (a misreading of Loten = Lawton) the schoolmaster who is said to have been ejected, *see* James Lawton. (*C.*) [59]

OLDHAM, JOHN (1630—5 Dec. 1716). 𝔓. Son of John Oldham, rector of Shipton Moigne, Glou. (? and of Easton Grey, Wilts). Curate (?) of Shipton Moigne ; perpetual curate of Newton South, Wilts ; ejected, 1662. Minister, till death, of a congregation at "Shipton or Wotton-under-edge." In 1708–9 the Fund gave him grants of £5 ; on 8 Mar. 1713/4, a grant of £8 ; in 1715, £10. Buried at Shipton. Father of the poet, John Oldham (9 Aug. 1653—9 Dec. 1683). *C. Ev. F. M. P. Rg.*) [44]

ONGAR (' Onger '), CHIPPING. Ejected here was John Larkin or Lorkin, of Clare Hall, Cambridge ; matric. pensioner, 1637 ; B.A., 1641 ; Fellow ; M.A., 1644 ; rector of Chipping Ongar, 1660 ; ejected, 1662. (*C. E. V.*) [39]

ONGAR (' Onger '), HIGH. Ejected here was John Lavender, of Queens' Coll., Cambridge ; matric. sizar, 1627 ; B.A., 1630/1 ; M.A., 1634 ; vicar of Kelvedon, Ess., in 1638 ; rector of High Ongar in 1647 ; member of the Sixth or Ongar Classis ; ejected, 1662 ; *d.* 23 Apr. 1670, aged 59. (*C. E. V.*) [39, 42]

ORLEBAR, or ORLIBEARE, MATTHEW, B.A. (*b.* 1640). 𝔓. Fifth son of George Orlebar, Esq. of Poddington Manor, Beds. Baptized, 16 Apr. 1640. Matric. pensioner, at Emmanuel Coll., Cambridge, 1657/8 ; B.A., 1661. Licensed, 16 May 1672, as "Pr. Teacher" at "his now dwelling house in Polebrook," Northants. ' Qualifying ' will mean that he had no regular charge. (*Hw. T.*) [78]

ORMSKIRK. Ejected here was Nathaniel Heywood [*q.v.*]. [58]

ORWELL. [13]

OSLAND, EDWARD (*d.* 1750 ?) 𝔓. Elder son of Henry Osland [*q.v.*]. Educ. at the Academy of John Woodhouse [*q.v.*]. Succeeded his father as Minister at Bewdley, Worc., and there died. (*C. Ev. M. P. To. Uw.*) [127]

OSLAND, HENRY, M.A. (1624 ?–19 Oct. 1703). **P.** Born at Rock, Worc. From Bewdley grammar school proceeded to Trinity Coll., Cambridge; subsizar, 22 Apr. 1646; matric., 1648/9; Scholar, 1649; B.A., 1649/50; M.A., 1653. Incumbent of Bewdley Chapel, Worc., 1650; ordained in London, 1651, without taking the covenant; member of Baxter's Worcestershire Association; ejected, 1662. Preached in the counties of Hereford, Leicester, Salop, Stafford, Warwick, and Worcester. The Episc. Returns, 1669, report him as one of the preachers to "2 or 300" persons "att the houses of Henry Hopkins & John Tunck" in Wednesbury, Staff.; also to "1 or 200" at houses in Darlaston, Staff.; also to "Presbyterians" at houses in Sedgeley, Staff.; also to "above 300" persons at houses in Walsall, Staff. Licensed, 25 July 1672, as "Pr. Teacher in his howse at Bawdley, Worc."; also, 30 Sept. 1672, as "Pr. Teacher at Oaken," in Codsall parish, Staff. The Common Fund granted him £6 a year as "near Bewdley," probably at Rock. He died Minister of Bewdley. (*C. M. P. T. Tc. Uw. V.*) [127]

OSWESTRY ('Oswestree'). Ejected here, in 1660, was Rowland Neavett, son of William Knyvett, of Henet, Shrop.; matric. at St. Edmund Hall, Oxford, 9 Mar. 1631/2, aged 17; B.A., 1633; M.A., 1635/6; vicar of Stanton, Shrop., 1636; held the sequestered vicarage of Oswestry, 1650; preaching at Oswestry, 1669; licensed (as Nevett), 25 July 1672, as Congr. Teacher in his house and another house at Weston, Shrop.; *d.* 8 Dec. 1675. John Nevit [*q.v.*] was his son. In 1676 there were 70 Nonconformists here. (*C. F. Ls. T.*) [16, 88, 90]

OTTERY ST. MARY ('St. Mary Ottery'). [30]

OTTWAY, . . . [50]

OUNDLE. Ejected here was Richard Resbury, of Sidney Sussex Coll., Cambridge; matric. sizar, 1625; B.A., 1629/30; M.A., 1633; vicar of Oundle; anticipated ejection by resigning in July, 1662; licensed, 10 Aug. 1672, as Cong. Teacher at Oundle; his house there licensed, same date, Con.; he practised medicine. (*C. T. V.*) [76]

OUSDEN. [13]

OWEN, CHARLES, D.D. (*d.* 17 Feb. 1746). **P.** Third son of John Owen, of Bryn, parish of Abernant, Carm., and brother of James Owen [*q.v.*]. Received grants, 1691–2, as Student with Thomas Brand [*q.v.*] at Bishop's Hall, Bethnal Green [*q.v.*], under the instruction of John Ker, M.D. [*q.v.*]. Received Fund grants, £6 yearly, for Wrexham, 1695–98. Succeeded (1699) Peter Aspinwall (*d.* June 1696) as Minister at Cairo Street Chapel, Warrington (registered, 10 Oct. 1698). His own dwelling-house at Warrington was registered for worship, Oct. 1697. Here the Fund made him no regular grant, but gave him between 1715 and 1741 sums amounting to £80. Held a small Academy of good repute. D.D., Edin. (1728). Was a pillar of the Hanoverian cause in the North of England.

His son John (*d.* 1775), educated (1726–7) under Thomas Dixon, M.D., at Bolton, Lanc., was Minister at Wharton, Lanc. (*D. M. X.*) [4, 90]

OWEN, HUGH (1639—15 Mar. 1699/1700). **C.** Born in Merionethshire. Son of Humphrey Owen. Matric. 'pleb.', at Jesus Coll., Oxford, 21 July 1660. Candidate for the ministry, silenced. Left Oxford, 1662, for London. Settled on his small estate of Bronycludwr, near Llanegryn, Merion., and preached gratis. He was once imprisoned in Powis Castle. Licensed, 22 May 1672, as "Congr. Teacher in his howse in Llanegryn." Succeeded Henry Williams [*q.v.*] as pastor at the Ysgafell, near Newtown, Montg., where the congregation was largely Baptist. The Common Fund granted him (1690–96) £8 a year, reduced (1695) to £4. Succeeded by his son John Owen [*q.v.*].

Hugh Farmer (20 Jan. 1713/4—5 F. 1787) of Walthamstow (famed for his works on the Temptation, miracles, and demoniacs) was Hugh Owen's grandson. (*C. D. M. P. Rw. T.*) [141, 148]

OWEN, JAMES (1 N. 1654—8 Apr. 1706). **C.** Born at Bryn, parish of Abernant, Carm., birthplace of James Howell, author of "Epistolae Ho-elianae," whose nephew, James Howell, a clergyman, was his godfather. Second son of John Owen, and brother of Charles Owen [*q.v.*]. His parents were Episcopalian royalists, but all their nine children became Nonconformists. Having been grounded in classics by James Picton, a Quaker, and at Carmarthen grammar school, he studied philosophy (1672) under Samuel Jones [*q.v.*]. After acting as tutor, he spent six months with his godfather, Howell, but, deciding on Nonconformity, he studied at Swansea under Stephen Hughes [*q.v.*]. His first settlement was at Bodwell, Carn.; his next as assistant to Hugh Owen [*q.v.*]. In Nov. 1676 he became chaplain to Mrs. Baker, Swinney, near Oswestry, and Minister of the Oswestry congregation founded by Roland Neavett (*see* Nevit, Thomas). From Oswestry he conducted a North Wales Mission, which led (1681) to a public discussion with William Lloyd, bishop of St. Asaph. In 1690 he opened an Academy for ministerial training. One of his Students was John Hardy, Minister at Nottingham (High Pavement), who afterwards conformed. The Common Fund granted him (1690–99) £8 a year for Oswestry; reduced (1695) to £5. He was twice invited to Cross Street, Manchester, as assistant. In 1700 he became colleague to Francis Tallents [*q.v.*], removing his Academy to Shrewsbury, and keeping up his preaching tours in Wales. He translated the Shorter Catechism into Welsh. 'Mr Owen' (p. 90), called his son, was Charles Owen [*q.v.*], his younger brother. (*Cm. D. Je. M. Rw.*) [16, 88, 90, 141, 148, 149, 150]

OWEN, JOHN, D.D. (1616—24 Aug. 1683). **C.** Second son of Henry Owen, vicar of Stadhampton, Oxfordsh., and born there. His descent is traced to Llewelyn ap Gwrgan, prince of Glamorgan. His schooling was at Oxford, under Edward Sylvester. Matric., 4 Nov. 1631, at Queen's Coll., Oxford, aged 16; B.A., 1632; M.A., 1635. Left Oxford (1637) through unwillingness to submit to Laud's new statutes. Chaplain to Sir Robert Dormer, Ascott, Oxfordsh.; afterwards to John, Lord Lovelace, at Hurley, Berks. On outbreak of Civil War, removed to Charterhouse Yard, London. In 1644 he obtained the sequestered rectory of Fordham, Essex, which he had to vacate in 1646, but was instituted by the House of Lords to the vicarage of Coggeshall, Essex. He had held Presbyterian views, but now (1646) adopted Congregational principles and modelled his church at Coggeshall accordingly. In 1649 he attended Cromwell as his chaplain in Ireland, and was instrumental in procuring (1650) the re-endowment of Trinity Coll., Dublin. On 8 March 1649/50 he was appointed preacher to the council of State. Having taken the engagement of allegiance to the government without king or house of lords, he was made (18 March 1650/1) dean of Christ Church, Oxford, preacher at St. Mary's, and (1652–8) vice-chancellor. As dean, he was most efficient, also tolerant, conniving at the public use of the Anglican prayer-book in a house close to the college. In 1653 he was created D.D., and in 1654–55 he was M.P. for the university. He took a leading part in the conference (Sept.–Oct. 1658) at the Savoy for revising the Westminster Confession to suit Congregationals, and wrote the preface. At the fall of Richard Cromwell he was in London, active on the republican side. Ejected from Christ Church (13 March 1659/60) he retired to Stadhampton. Clarendon, in 1664, offered him high preferment if he would conform. In 1664/5 he was indicted at Oxford for holding conventicles in his house. The Episc. Returns, 1669, report him as preaching in White's Alley, Moorfields, London. On 16 Apr. 1672 the London Leathersellers granted the use of their hall to Owen along with John Loder (*see* Nye, Philip), if they obtained licence for it; none is recorded. On the death (7 Feb. 1672/3) of Joseph Caryl, M.A., Owen was invited to succeed him in Leadenhall Street; he joined his own flock with Caryl's (5 June 1673). Charles II. in 1674 gave him 1000 guineas for sufferers under the penal laws. As a theological writer, Owen had no superiors in his time; but his objection (1659) to Walton's Polyglot, on the ground that it admitted various readings in the inspired text, was unfortunate. (*C. Cm. D. F. P. T. W. Wc.*) [154, 188]

OWEN, JOHN (1670—27 June 1700). **C.** Son of Hugh Owen [*q.v.*]. Entered Frankland's Academy, 23 Nov. 1689. Though his father was Congregational, his education had been financially assisted by the Presbyterians, Samuel Slater [*q.v.*] and Richard Stretton [*q.v.*]. The Common Fund granted him (1691–6) £14 a year. He became Frankland's assistant in the Academy, afterwards joining his father at Bronycludwr. Ultimately he succeeded his father as pastor at the Ysgafell (1699), but died in the following June, on a visit to Shrewsbury.

The entry "John Owen of Wrexham" (p. 141) is an error for John Evans [*q.v.*]. (*Fr. M. Rw.*) [136]

OWEN, THOMAS. **C.** Counsellor at Law. Member of the congregation of Stephen Lobb [*q.v.*]. Attended as Manager of the Common Fund, 18 Aug. 1690; last attendance, 8 May 1693. Manager (1695) of the Congregational Fund. (*Cf. Co. M.*) [162, 164]

OXFORD ('Oxon'). Ejected from the University (or disabled) were:

(1) Thomas Adams, of Brasenose Coll., matric., 5 Apr. 1650; Fellow, 1652; B.A., 1652/3; M.A., 1655; ejected, 1662; chaplain to Sir Samuel Jones; later, to

Dowager Countess of Clare; *d.* 11 Dec. 1670. (*C. F.*)

(2) James Allen, of New Coll.; chaplain, 1649; rem. to Magdalen Hall; matric., 1649/50; Fellow of New Coll., 1650; B.A., 1652; M.A., 1654; ejected, 1660; went to relatives in New England. (*C. F.*)

(3) Samuel Angier, born at Dedham, Ess.; from Westminster school elected, 1658, to Christ's Church Coll.; ejected from Studentship, 1662; licensed, 30 Sept. 1672, as Pr. Teacher in Hide Hall at Manchester; Minister at Dukinfield, Ches.; *d.* 8 Nov. 1713, aet. 75. (*C. F. Ga.*)

(4) James Ashurst, of Magdalen Hall, Fellow and M.A. [? of Queens' Coll., Cambridge, M.A., 1631]; after ejection, was pastor to a small congregation at Newington Green. (*C. F. V.*)

(5) Thomas Brace, of Magdalen Hall; matric., 9 Apr. 1647, aged 22; Fellow of St. John's Coll., 1648; M.A., 1648 (incorp. at Cambridge, 1652); B.D., 1660; ejected, 1662; preached privately at Westminster. (*C. F.*)

(6) Ralph Button, of Exeter Coll.; matric., 9 Dec. 1631, aged 19; B.A., 1632/3; Fellow of Merton Coll., 1633; incorp. at Cambridge, 1634; M.A., 1639/40; refused D.D.; Professor of geometry at Gresham College, 1643–8; Canon of Christ Church, 1648; ejected, 1660; kept school at Brentford; took pupils at Islington, 1672 (Sir Joseph Jekyll was one of them); *d.* there, Oct. 1680. (*C. D. F.*)

(7) Thomas Cawton, of Merton Coll. (son of Thomas Cawton, M.A., of Queens' Coll., Cambridge, rector of St. Bartholomew Exchange, who fled to Holland on the failure of Love's Plot, 1651); after three years at Utrecht university, matric. at Oxford, 31 Mar. 1660; B.A., 3 Apr. 1660; ord. episcopally; ejected, 1662; chaplain to Sir Anthony Irby (*see* Lady Irby); removed to Boston, 1665; chaplain to Lady Armyn; licensed, 2 Apr. 1672, as Presbyterian Teacher at his house in St. Anne's Lane, Westminster; the house licensed, same date; his new-built Meeting-house in New Way [Tothill Street], Westminster, licensed, Nov. 1672; *d.* 10 Apr. 1677, aged about 40. (*C. F. T. V. W.*)

(8) Thomas Cole, M.A. [*q.v.*].

(9) John Conant, of Exeter Coll.; matric., 18 Feb. 1626/7, aged 18; B.A., 1631; Fellow, 1632–4; M.A., 1634; ord. deacon, 1632; member of the Westminster Assembly, 1643; held the sequestered vicarage of St. Thomas, Salisbury, and the sequestered rectory of Whimple, Devon, 1645; rector of his college, 1649 (ejected, 1662); regius professor of divinity, and D.D., 1654 (ejected, 1660); vicar of Abergele, Denb., 1657 (resigned, 1660); rector of Kidlington, 1661; assistant commissioner at the Savoy Conference, 1661; conformed; ord. priest, 20 Sept. 1670; vicar of All Saints', Northampton, 1670/1; archdeacon of Norwich, 1676; canon of Worcester, 1681; *d.* 12 Mar. 1693/4, aged 86. (*C. D. F.*)

(10) William Conway [*q.v.*].

(11) Henry Cornish, D.D. [*q.v.*].

(12) George Cowper, of Pembroke Coll.; matric., 2 Apr. 1652; demy Magdalen Coll., 1654/5; B.A., 1655; Fellow, 1655; M.A., 1658; ejected, 1660. (*C. F.*)

(13) Joshua Cross, of Magdalen Hall; matric., 11 May 1632, aged 17; B.A., 1634; M.A., 1636/7; Fellow of Lincoln Coll., 1642; Fellow of Magdalen Coll., 1648; professor of natural philosophy, 1648; D.C.L., 1649/50; ejected, 1660; lived at Oxford; *d.* 9 May 1676, aged 62. (*C. F.*)

(14) Thomas Cruttenden, of Magdalen Coll.; matric., 19 Nov. 1650; B.A., 1651/2; M.A., and Fellow, 1654; ejected, 1662; assisted in Mrs. Salmon's boarding-school at Hackney, having married her daughter; preached occasionally; *d.* at Hackney. (*C. F.*)

(15) John Cudmore, of Magdalen Hall; matric., 21 July 1660; could not graduate, being Nonconformist; left with John Gay; licensed, 22 May 1672, as Grāll Presb. Teacher, being of Chard, Som.; Minister at Chumleigh, Dev., 1694, in succession to Thomas Hart [*q.v.*]; *d.* Oct. 1706. (*C. F. T.*)

(16) Richard Dyer, of Magdalen Hall; matric. 'serv.', 25 Jan. 1638/9, aged 16; B.A., 1642; ejected from Studentship at Christ Church, 1660; chaplain to three Lord Mayors; kept grammar school in London; *d.* 1695, aged 70. (*C. F.*)

(17) Theophilus Gale, M.A. [*q.v.*].

(18) John Gay (*bap.* 24 Nov. 1639–*bur.* 25 Jan. 1716/7), of Exeter Coll.; matric., 30 Apr. 1661, aged 20; B.A., 1664; left then as Nonconformist; licensed, 18 Apr. 1672, as Presb. Teacher in any licensed place, being of Barnstaple, Dev. (his native place); *d.* at Frithelstock, Dev. (his father's residence). (*C. F. T.*)

(19) John Gippes, first of Emmanuel Coll., Cambridge; next of Sidney Sussex Coll.; matric. pensioner, 1652; then of

Magdalen Hall; matric., 9 Dec. 1653; B.A., 1654; member of the Westminster Assembly; Clerk of Magdalen Coll., 1656–57; chaplain, 1657 (ejected, 1660); removed to London, then to Montpelier for health; *d.* in London, 1669. (*C. F. V.*)

(20) Jonathan Goddard (1617—24 Mar. 1674/5), of Magdalen Hall; son of Henry, shipbuilder; matric., 11 May 1632, aged 15; rem. 1637 to Christ's Coll., Cambridge; M.B., 1638; rem. to St. Catharine's Hall; M.D., 1642/3; incorp. at Oxford, 1651/2; Fellow of the College of Physicians, 4 Nov. 1646; army physician, 1649–51; Warden of Merton Coll., Oxford, 1651; incorp. M.D. at Oxford, 1651/2; M.P. for Oxford, 1653; Gresham professor of physic, 1655; ejected at Oxford, 1660, retaining his Gresham chair; one of the founders of the Royal Society, incorp., 1663; made with his own hands the first telescope constructed in this country. (*C. D. F. Mu. V.*)

(21) Thomas Goodwin, D.D. [*q.v.*]

(22) Daniel Greenwood, of Lincoln Coll.; matric., 30 Apr. 1624, aged 19; B.A., 1626/7; Fellow of Brasenose Coll.; M.A., 1629; rector of Chastleton, Oxf., 1640 (ejected, 1662); B.D., 1640/1; Principal of Brasenose, 1648 (ejected, 1660); D.D., 1649; rector of Steeple Aston (ejected, 1662); *d.* at Steeple Aston, Oxf., 29 Jan. 1673/4. (*C. F.*)

(23) Humphrey Gunter, M.A. [*q.v.*].

(24) Henry Hickman, of St. Catharine's Hall, Cambridge; matric. pensioner, 1647; B.A., 1647/8; Fellow, Magdalen Coll., Oxford, 1648 (ejected, 1660); M.A., 1649/50 (incorp. at Cambridge, 1651); rector of St. Aldate's, Oxford; vicar of Brackley, Northants, 1655 (ejected, 1662); B.D., 1658; Minister of the English church at Leiden; entered as medical student there, 18 Apr. 1675; *d.* at Utrecht (?) 1692. (*C. D. F. V.*)

(25) George Hitchcocke; Scholar of New Coll.; B.A., 1649; Fellow of Lincoln Coll.; M.A., 1652; ejected, 1662; meanwhile barrister at law of Gray's Inn, 1661; lived at Hackney. (*C. F.*)

(26) Francis Howell, of Exeter Coll.; matric., 24 July 1642, aged 17; M.A., 1648; Fellow, 1648–58; professor of moral philosophy, 1654–7, Principal of Jesus Coll., 1657; ejected, 1660; preached in and near London; colleague with John Collins (*d.* 3 Dec. 1687) at Paved Alley, Lime Street Congregational church; *d.* at Bethnal Green, 10 Mar. 1679/80. (*C. F. W.*)

(27) Richard Inglett, born near Chidley, Devon (*bap.* 30 Aug. 1632), of Exeter Coll.; matric., 12 Nov. 1650; Fellow, 1652; B.A., 1653/4; M.A., 1656; ejected, 1663; meanwhile admitted extra-licentiate of the College of Physicians, 22 Feb. 1660/1; practised at Plymouth. (*C. F. Mu.*)

(28) Francis Johnson, of Queen's Coll.; son of Francis, of Lilford, Northants; matric., 21 Nov. 1628, aged 17; B.A., 1630; M.A., 1633; Fellow of All Souls' Coll., 1648; chaplain to Cromwell; Master of University Coll., 1655; ejected, 1660; licensed, 10 Aug. 1672, as Indt Teach at his house in Gray's Inn Lane, London; his house licensed, same date, Indt; *d.* 9 Oct. 1677. (*C. F. T. V.* [the Cambridge references relate to another man].)

(29) John Johnson, of Emmanuel Coll., Cambridge; matric. pensioner, 1644; B.A., 1647/8; incorp. at Oxford, 1649; Fellow of St. John's Coll; Fellow of New Coll., 1650; M.A., 1650; incorp. at Cambridge, 1651; ejected [? licensed, 22 May 1672, as Pr. Teacher in his house at Barwell, Leic.]; *d.* in or near London, "where he affected to live retir'd." (*C. F. T. V.*)

(30) Thomas Kentish, of Pembroke Coll.; matric., 22 Feb. 1650/1; B.A., 1653/4; M.A., 1656; Clerk of Magdalen Coll., 1657–58; chaplain, 1658 (ejected, 1660); rector of Middleton, Dur. (ejected. 1660); rector of Overton, Hants (ejected, 1662); licensed, 11 Apr. 1672, being of Southwark parish, as Presb. teacher in any licensed place; he was Minister (1670 ?) of the congregation in Great Eastcheap, where Thomas Reynolds [*q.v.*] succeeded him; *d.* 1695; Thomas Kentish [*q.v.*] was his son. (*C. F. T. W.*)

(31) Henry Langley, of Pembroke Coll.; son of Thomas, shoemaker, Abingdon, Berks; matric., 6 Nov. 1629, aged 18; B.A., 1632; Fellow and M.A., 1635; at his ordination (1640) refused to answer questions concerning the Book of Sports, bowing to the altar, and the power of the Church; held the sequestered rectory of St. Mary, Newington, Surr., 1646; Master of Pembroke Coll., 1647; Canon of Christ Church, 1648; B.D., 1648; D.D., 1649; ejected, 1660; preaching at Tubney, Berks, 1669; had pupils in logic and philosophy; licensed, 16 Apr. 1672, as Presb. Teacher in his house at Tubney, Berks; his house licensed, same date, as Presb. Meeting-place; preached also at Abingdon; *d.* 10 Sept. 1679. (*C. D. F. T.*)

(32) Joseph Maisters ('Masters') [*q.v.*].

(33) John Milward, of New Inn Hall; matric., 16 Mar. 1637/8, aged 18; B.A., 1641; Fellow of Corpus (ejected, 1660); M.A., 1648; rector of Darfield, Yorks; ejected, 1662; licensed, 2 Apr. 1672, as Presbyterian Teacher in any place licensed; also, 2 May 1672, as Pr. Teacher at Farncombe, a hamlet in Doulting parish, Som. (near to Shepton Mallet, his native place), in the house of George Milward (his father's name); *d.* at Islington in 1683 or 1684. (*C. F. T.*)

(34) Thankful Owen, of Exeter Coll.; matric., 1 June 1636, aged 16; B.A., 1639/40; Fellow of Lincoln Coll., 1642; M.A., 1646; President of St. John's Coll., 1650; ejected, 1660; removed to London; assistant, and chosen (1681) successor to Thomas Goodwin, D.D. [*q.v.*]; *d.* in Hatton Garden, 1 Apr. 1681. (*C. F. W.*)

(35) John Panton, of All Souls' Coll.; matric., 20 Nov. 1650; B.A., 1651/2; M.A., 1654; Fellow, 1658; ejected, 1660, travelled in France, and practised physic in London. (*C. F.*)

(36) John Pointer, of Brasenose Coll.; matric., 28 Mar. 1617, aged 17; B.A., 1618; went to Leiden; lecturer at St. Mildred, Bread Street, 1629; at Wootton Wawen, War., 1630/1; at Huntingdon, 1632–43; vicar of Bures, Ess., 1646–55; Canon of Christ Church, 1655; ejected, 1662; never preached again; *d.* 2 Jan. 1683/4, in 84th or 85th year. (*C. F.*)

(37) George Porter, M.A. [*q.v.*].

(38) Thomas Risley, M.A. [*q.v.*].

(39) Christopher Rogers, of Lincoln Coll.; B.A., 17 July 1612; M.A., 1615; rector of St. Peter-le-Bailey, 1626; Principal of New Inn Hall, 1626–43, and 1646–62; D.D., 1648; Canon of Christ Church, 1648; one of the Parliamentary visitors; ejected, 1660; will proved at Oxford, 21 Aug. 1671. (*C. F.*)

(40) John Sayer, of Corpus Christi Coll.; matric., 20 Feb. 1648/9; B.A., 1649; rem. to Christ Church Coll.; M.A., 1652/3; ejected, 1662; chaplain to Sir William Waller; licensed, 5 Sept. 1672, as Pr. Teacher, being of Hagbourne, Berks; on 30 Sept. 1672 the house of Richard Sayer at Hagbourne was licensed Pr. (*C. F. T.*)

(41) William Segary, of Magdalen Hall; matric., 15 Nov. 1639, aged 17; M.A., 1648; ejected from Studentship; on 14 Sept. 1683 William Segary of Wokingham, Berks, clerk, was licensed to marry; if this is the same man, he was then aged 61. (*C. F.*)

(42) John Singleton, M.A. [*q.v.*].

(43) Robert Speare, of Lincoln Coll.; matric., 20 Mar. 1650/1; B.A., 1653; M.A., 1656; what he was ejected from is not clear; after ejectment, exercised his ministry at Port Royal, Jamaica; he is probably the Robert Speare, licensed, 10 June 1672, as Anab. Teacher in John Speare's house, Broomfield, Som. (*C. F. T.*)

(44) Richard Sprint, of Magdalen Coll.; matric. 'ser.', 25 Oct. 1659; ejected, 1660. (*C. F.*)

(45) Edmund Staunton (20 Oct. 1600–14 July 1671), son of Sir Francis Staunton, Knt., of Bletsoe, Beds; of Wadham Coll.; matric., 9 June 1615, aged 18; Scholar of Corpus Christi Coll., 1615; Fellow, 1616; B.A., 1619/20; Student of Gray's Inn, 1620; M.A., 1623 (incorp. at Cambridge, 1624); rector of Bushey, Herts, 1627; exchanged for vicarage of Kingston-on-Thames, 1631; B.D. and D.D., 1634; suspended, 1635, for not reading the Book of Sports; member of the Westminster Assembly, 1643; President of Corpus, 1648; ejected, 1660; retired to Rickmansworth, Herts, and preached about till silenced, 1662; thence to St. Alban's, Herts, where, and at other places, he was preaching in 1669; *d.* at Bovingdon, Herts, 14 July 1671. (*C. D. F. T.*)

(46) Philip Stephens, of St. Alban Hall; matric., 24 Mar. 1636/7, aged 17; B.A., 1640; rem. to Trinity Coll., Cambridge; M.A., 1645; Fellow of New Coll., Oxford, 1649; licensed to practise medicine, 1653; Principal of Hart Hall, 1653; M.D., 1655/6; admitted candidate College of Physicians, 30 Sept. 1659; ejected, 1660; *d.* in London, 4 Feb. 1679/80. (*C. F. Mu. V.*)

(47) William Stoughton, of Harvard Coll., New England, B.A., 1650; incorp. at Oxford, 1652; Fellow of New Coll., and M.A., 1653; ejected, 1660; returned to Boston, New England. (*C. F. Mc.*)

(48) John Thompson, of Christ Church Coll.; matric., 1656; B.A., 13 Oct. 1656; M.A., 1659; ejected from Studentship, 1662; pastor of Congr. church in Castle Street, Bristol, 1670; licensed, 16 Apr. 1672, as Congr. Teacher in Castle Street; *d.* there in gaol, 4 Mar. 1675/6. (*C. F. T.*)

(49) John Troughton, of St. John's Coll.; from Coventry Grammar School, matric., 28 Mar. 1655; Scholar, 1655; B.A., 1658/9; Fellow; ejected, 1660; preached at Oxford; licensed, 13 Apr. 1672, as Presb. Teacher in a house at Caversfield, Oxf.; also, June 1672, as Pr. Teacher in his house at Bicester, Oxf.;

his house licensed, same date, Pr.; blind; took pupils; *d.* at Oxford, 20 Aug. 1681, aged 44; father of John Troughton [*q.v.*]. (*C. D. F. T.*)

(50) Henry Wilkinson (4 Mar. 1609/10 –5 June 1675), son of Henry, of Waddesdon; of Magdalen Hall; matric., 14 Feb. 1622/3, aged 12; B.A., 1626; M.A., 1629; B.D., 1638; member of the Westminster Assembly, 1643; rector of St. Dunstan's-in-the-West, 1645; Canon of Christ Church, 1648; D.D., 1649; Margaret Professor of Divinity, 1652; ejected, 1660 (known as 'Long Harry'); licensed, 2 Apr. 1672, as Presbyterian Teacher in his house, or in the School House, at Clapham, Surrey; both these houses licensed, same date, as Places of Meeting of the Presbyterian way. (*C. D. F. T. Y.*)

(51) Henry Wilkinson, D.D. (known as 'Dean Harry') [*q.v.*].

(52) Richard Whiteway, of Exeter Coll.; matric., 1 June 1652; Fellow, 1654; B.A., 1657; M.A., 1659; ejected, 1662; chaplain to Sir John Maynard in Devonshire; *d.* soon after ejection. (*C. F.*)

(53) John Wightwick, or Whitwick, of Emmanuel Coll., Cambridge; matric. pensioner, 4 Apr. 1646; B.A., 1649; Fellow of St. John's Coll., Oxford, 1651; M.A., 1652; ejected, 1662; chaplain in private families. (*C. F. V.*)

(54) Robert Wood, son of Robert Wood (*d.* 1661), rector of Pepperharrow, Surr.; from Eton adm. at New Inn Hall; matric., 3 July 1640, aged 18; rem. to Merton Coll.; B.A., 1646/7; Fellow of Lincoln Coll., 1649; licensed to practise medicine, 1656; accompanied Henry Cromwell to Ireland; Fellow of Oliver Cromwell's College at Durham, 1657; ejected from Oxford Fellowship, 1660; teacher of mathematics and navigation in Christ Church Hospital, London; F.R.S.; accountant-general of the revenue in Ireland; *d.* in Dublin, 9 Apr. 1685, aged 63. (*C. F. Mn.*)

(55) William Woodward, M.A. [*q.v.*]

OXFORDSHIRE. [9, 85, 86, 138, 168, 176]. Except the headings "Oxford" in the earliest handwriting, all is in the Book-keeper's hand. The returns are numbered 20, with three exceptions (11, 30, 92).

Bisister is Bicester.
Coomb is Combe Longa.
Daddington, Dodington, is Deddington.
Tame is Thame

PADSTOW ('Pordstow,' 'Pudstow'). [19, 20]

PAGET, JOHN (*d.* 1723). **C.** There is no record of a grant for studies; but on 18 Jan. 1691/2, the Common Fund granted him £6 a year for Ongar, Ess.; it was paid to Midsummer, 1693. In 1696, the Congregational Fund granted him £3 for Ongar. The original Fund paid him various sums, 1718–22, amounting to £30, for Ockley, otherwise Stanstead, Surr. He was therein 1715. (*Cf. Ev. M.*) [33, 42]

PAINE, PAIN, or PAYN, WILLIAM (*fl.* 1690–96). **C.** Unless he is the Mr. Pain mentioned by Calamy as ejected from the vicarage of Kingsbury, Som., his previous history is not known. The Common Fund granted him (1691) £13 a year for Saffron Walden, but this was only paid for the first half-year. On 27 Apr. 1696, the Congregational Fund granted £10 to "Mr Paine, Senr at Saffron Walden"; in Oct. 1696 he had five Students in his charge. (*C. Co. M. P.*) [11]

PAINE, PAIN, PANE, or PAYN, WILLIAM, *secundus* (*fl.* 1690–1729). **C.** Son of William Paine [*q.v.*]. The Common Fund granted him (Midsummer, 1691 to 1693) £12 a year for Saffron Walden. On 4 May 1696 the Congregational Fund granted £5 to "Mr Paine, junr of Saffron Walden." He was there in 1716, receiving a grant from the Congregational Fund, and probably in 1729. (*Cf. Ev. M.*) [40, 41]

PAINSWICK. [44, 45]

PAKEMAN, THOMAS. (*See* Pateman)

PAL ('Pall'), near Llandilo, Carm. [143]

PALGRAVE. [107]

PALK, THOMAS, B.A. (1636—18 June 1693). **P.** Born at Staverton, Devon. Matric. 'serv.', at Exeter Coll., Oxford, 27 N. 1652; rem. to Newton Hall; B.A., 1658/9. Vicar of Woodland, Devon; ejected, 1662. Licensed, 11 Apr. 1672, being then of Ogwell, Devon, as "a Grāll Presb. Teacher"; signed the thanks of Devon Ministers. He endeavoured to maintain a school, but prosecutions in the spiritual court, followed by excommunication, deprived him of his livelihood and shortened his life. (*C. F. P. T.*) [31]

PALMER, ANTHONY, M.A. (1613–Sept. 1693). **P.** Son of William Palmer of Barnstaple, Devon, gent. Matric. at Exeter Coll., Oxford, 2 D. 1631, aged 18; B.A., 1634/5; M.A., 1637. Held the sequestered rectory of Bratton Fleming, Devon, 1645; ejected, 1662. Walker notes that he administered the communion but once in fourteen years;

similar instances (of less duration) testify to the fear to 'drink damnation,' if unworthy. Licensed, 18 Apr. 1672, as "Pr.", being of Barnstaple, where he had a good estate. (*C. F. P. T. Wc.*) [32]

PANE, *i.e.* PAYNE, JOHN, M.A. (*b.* 1616, living, 1691). 𝔓. Son of Robert Payne, of Berkhamstead, Herts, pleb. Matric. at New Inn Hall, Oxford, 20 June 1634, aged 18; B.A., 1636; M.A., 1638/9. Held (1643–7) the sequestered vicarage of Broxbourne, Herts; also (1646–1651) the sequestered vicarage of Sawbridgeworth, Herts; vicar (1651) of Bishops Stortford, Herts; ejected, 1662. Licensed, 1 May 1672, as "Teacher of Presbyterians in the House of George Holgate" at Bishops Stortford, where he still lived in 1684. He preached at Dunmow as well as at Thaxted, and other places in Essex. Calamy (followed by Davies) calls him Jonathan; he had a son Jonathan (*d.* 24 June 1681, aged 31 years). (*C. E. F. P. T. Uh.*) [39]

PANE, Juor. [40] *See* Paine, William, *secundus*

PAPIST. [41]

PARR, or PARRE, JOHN, B.A. (1633 ?–1716). ℭ. Probably related to Richard Parr or Parre (1592—24 Mar. 1644), bishop of Sodor and Man. Chaplain to John Bradshaw the regicide, who in a will of 1654 left him £24 a year for five years "to enable him in his studies" (revoked, 1655). Admitted subsizar at Trinity Coll., Cambridge, 24 May 1659; B.A., 1662/3. Preached at Preston and Walton. Licence noted, Dec. 1672, to John Parre as "Congr. Teachr at ffarington in Leicester," *i.e.* Farington, Lanc. Preached also at Darwen, Lanc., where the house of William and Henry Berry of Upper Darwen was licensed, "Pr.", 5 S. 1672. Farington is near Preston, so is Elswick, now in parish of Copp (Elswick Chapel was registered on his application, 18 July 1689); Euxton is near Chorley, Lanc. Probably Parr (ordained, 4 N. 1687) took part in the Preston Lecture (p. 64). He succeeded Thomas Key [*q.v.*] in 1698 at Walton Chapel, receiving from the Fund £4 a year till 1712, when he removed to Preston and was succeeded by John Turner. He also preached often at Hoghton Tower. He was a member of the Lancashire Provincial Meeting of United Ministers (1693). The Meeting-house at Preston was opened in the year of his death. (*C. D. Ev. M. Nl. P. T. Tc. V. X.*) [61]

PARROT. [55] *See* Perrot, Robert

PARSHOR. [126] *See* Worcestershire

PARSON, or PARSONS, . . . Probably a layman. ["Old Mr. Parsons" of Stoke-under-Hamdon, Som., received yearly grants of £5 from the Fund, 1703–16. (*M. Ev.*)] [1]

PASTON, EDWARD, M.A. (*b.* 1619 ?). Son of John Paston of King's Swinford, Staffs, pleb. Matric. at New Inn Hall, Oxford, 5 F. 1635/6, aged 17; B.A., 1639; M.A., 1642. Episcopally ordained. Rector of Solihull, Warw. (1646); vicar of Hales Owen, Shrops.; ejected, 1660. He preached occasionally by connivance in parish churches; also, in turn, to Nonconformists at Gornall, parish of Sedgley, Staff. He was for some time steward to Philip Foley [*q.v.*]. (*C. F. P.*) [89]

PASTURE HOUSE is in Horton-in-Craven, Gisburn parish, W.R. (misplaced in N.R.). The Meeting-house, on John Hey's ground, was opened by Oliver Heywood, 24 May 1682. [135]

PATEMAN, *i.e.* PAKEMAN, THOMAS, M.A. (1614–June 1691). 𝔓. Matric. sizar, at Trinity Coll., Cambridge, 1631; migrated to Clare Hall; B.A., 1633/4; M.A., 1637. Curate (1646) of Little Hadham, Herts; ejected, 1660 (with ten children); vicar of Harrow-on-the-Hill, Midx.; ejected, 1662; kept boarders there, and at Old Brentford; held chaplaincies at Brompton and London; removed (1687) to Stratford, Ess. (*C. P. Uh. V.*) [39]

PAYN, WILLIAM, father and son. *See* Paine

PEACH, JOHN (*d.* 1720). 𝔓. Entered Frankland's Academy, 12 June 1687. Minister at Uppingham, Rutl., 1701–3; Doddington, Oxon., 1705/6–1710; Ledbury, Heref., 1710–12; Oldbury, Shrop., 1716; Coseley, Staff., 1717–19; at these places he received a Fund grant of £6 annually. On 2 Jan. 1720/1 a grant of £10 was made to his widow for funeral charges. (*Fr. M.*) [27, 29]

PEACH, RICHARD (*fl.* 1690–93). Received grant, 23 Feb. 1690/1, of £6 (renewed, 1692) as Student under John Woodhouse [*q.v.*]. S. J. G., who had contributed to his schooling, is evidently Sir John Gell, Bart. (Oct. 1613—8 F. 1688/9), of Hopton, second baronet, who succeeded his father (also Sir John Gell, Bart.) on 26 Oct. 1671; and was Sheriff of Derbyshire, 1672–73. (*Ba. D. M.*) [29]

PEAK, THE. [98]

PEARD, OLIVER, B.A. (1636–Oct. 1696). ℭ. Born at Barnstaple. Matric. at Magdalen Hall, Oxford, 10 N. 1654; rem. to Magdalen Coll.; chorister, 1655;

B.A., 1657/8; clerk, 1658/9. He ministered at Ashford, near Barnstaple, and later at Barnstaple, where he had a good estate. He was not beneficed at the time of the Uniformity Act which silenced him; apparently he was not then ordained; at Bideford he was privately ordained. Under stress of the Five Mile Act he retired (1666) to Ilfracombe. Licensed, 20 Apr. 1672, as "Congr. Teacher in Joseph Andrews house in Barnestaple." Signed thanks from Devon Ministers. From 1689 he ministered, in conjunction with John Hanmer [*q.v.*], to a large congregation at Barnstaple. (*C. F. P. T.*) [30]

PEASENHALL ('Peasevall'). Ejected here was John Manning, M.A. [*q.v.*]. [103]

PEEVER. [15] *See* Cheshire

PEIRCE, *i.e.* PEARSE, WILLIAM (Jan. 1625/6—17 Mar. 1691/2). 𝔓. Son of Francis Pearse of Ermington, Devon, gent. Baptized, 26 Jan. 1625/6; educated at Exeter Coll., Oxford. Vicar of Dunsford, Devon., 25 Dec. 1655; ejected, 1662. Removed to Stretchleigh House in Ermington parish, and preached privately at Tavistock. Licensed, 11 Apr. 1672, being of Dunsford, as "a Presbyterien Teacher in any allowed place." Signed thanks of Devon Ministers. Persecution drove him to London, where he was imprisoned in 1683. In 1689 he settled as Minister at Ashburton, Devon. (*C. F. P. T.*) [31]

PELL, WILLIAM, M.A. (1634—2 D. 1698). 𝔓. Born at Sheffield. From the Rotherham grammar school, admitted sizar at Magdalene Coll., Cambridge, 29 Mar. 1651, aged 17; matric., 1651; B.A., 1654/5; Fellow; M.A., 1658. Ordained episcopally. Held the sequestered rectory of Easington, Durh.; ejected, 1660; also tutorship in Cromwell's Durham University, 1657, dropped, 1660. Rector of Great Stainton, Durh.; ejected, 1662. Imprisoned at Durham for Nonconformity. Practised medicine in the North Riding of Yorks. He was regarded (being, *inter alia*, a notable orientalist) as the right man to resume the teaching of "university learning" in the North, but had scruples based on his graduation oath; hence the work of a "Northern Academy" was begun by Richard Frankland [*q.v.*]. Licensed, 1 May 1672, "to be a Teacher of Presbyterians, and to teach in his own house in the City of Durham, or in any other place, etc." He next preached at Tattershall, Linc., and (1687–94) was Minister at Boston, Linc., removing to become assistant to Richard Gilpin [*q.v.*] at Newcastle-on-Tyne. (*C. D. P. T. V. Wc.*) [36, 37, 70]

PEMBERTON, MATTHIAS, M.A. (*d.* 1691?). 𝔓. Born in Essex. Subsizar at Trinity Coll., Cambridge, 8 May 1645; matric., 1645; Scholar, 1646; B.A., 1648/9; Fellow, 1649; M.A., 1652. Rector of Clayhidon, Devon; ejected, 1662. Removed to London. Licensed, 8 May 1672, being of Fenchurch Street, London, as "Grāll Pr. Teacher." Left London (1690) to be Minister at Marlborough, Wilts, and died soon after. (*C. P. T. Tc.*) [72, 123, 125]

PEMBROKESHIRE ('Pembrook'). [143, 144, 146]

PENCADAIR or PENCADER ('Penkader'), hamlet in Llanfihanget-ar-Arth parish, Carm. [144, 145]

PENCARREG ('Pen Carreg'), Carm., on the Cardiganshire border. [145]

PENDLEBURY, HENRY, M.A. (6 May 1626—18 June 1695). 𝔓. Born at Jowkin, parish of Bury, Lanc.; son of Henry Pendlebury. From Bury grammar school, proceeded to Christ's Coll., Cambridge, 1 May 1645; sizar; B.A., 1648; M.A. Began preaching (16 Aug. 1648) at Ashworth Chapel, parish of Middleton, Lanc., which he served as probationer. Ordained, 23 O. 1650, at Turton Chapel, by the Second Lancashire Classis, as incumbent of Horwich Chapel, parish of Deane, Lanc.; removed, 16 O. 1651, to the sequestered chapelry of Holcombe Chapel in Tottington township, parish of Bury, Lanc.; ejected, 1662. Licensed, 25 July 1672, being of Tottington, Lanc., as "Grāll Pr. Teacher"; on 5 S. 1672 the "Court house att Holcome" was licensed "Pr."; and on the same day Pendlebury "of Bury" was licensed as "Pr. Teacher." He ministered at Rochdale and Holcombe (Bass House) till death; buried at Bury. "One of the most learned Nonconformists of his day." His assistant was Joseph Whitworth [*q.v.*]. (*C. D. F. Nl. P. T.*) [59, 61]

PENRITH. Ejected here was Roger Baldwin [*q.v.*]. The first settled Nonconformist Minister was James Coningham, M.A. (1670—1 S. 1716). ℭ. Successively Minister at Penrith (1694–1700), Cross Street, Manchester (1700–1712), and Haberdashers' Hall, London (1712–16). Both at Penrith and Manchester (in conjunction, 1700–5, with John Chorlton) [*q.v.*] he carried on an Academy for university learning. In 1697 and 1698 he received grants of £5 from the Congregational Fund for Penrith. (*Cf. D.*) [22, 23]

PENRUDDOCK. [22]

PENRY, DAVID (*fl.* 1690–1715). 𝕮. Born in the parish of Llanedi, Carm. Intended for the Anglican ministry. Converted by the preaching of Stephen Hughes [*q.v.*]; by him trained as a preacher; and ordained (1688) as his successor at Llanedi. The Common Fund granted him (1690–93) £2 a year for Llanedi, where he was still ministering in 1715. (*Ev. M. Rw.*) [144]

PENRYN ('Penrin'). Ejected here was Joseph Allen; the Episc. Returns, 1665, report him as living and "peaceable" at Perran Arworthal, Corn.; licensed, 10 Aug. 1672, as "Pr. genall Teacher" at St. Michael Penkevel, Corn. (*C. P. T.*) [18, 19]

PENZANCE. Ejected here was Leonard Welstead, who afterwards conformed. [19, 180]

PEOVER. *See* Stringer, Josiah. Ejected at Upper Peover, 1662, was Robert Norbury, B.A., of Trinity Coll., Dublin; Fellow, 1659; ejected, 1660; preached afterwards at several places in Cheshire; after 1662 returned to Ireland and soon died. (*C. Dt. P.*) [15]

PEPYS, SAMUEL. [174]

PERKINS, . . . ? William Perkins (*d.* Nov. 1724), 𝕻., who entered Frankland's Academy, 10 Oct. 1697. The Academy closed in Oct. 1698. Fund grants were made to Fishlake from 1691, without Minister's name till 1705. In 1703 Perkins was granted £6 a year for Cotherstone, N.R., per John Shower [*q.v.*]; raised, 1705, to £10 for Hartforth (where a School-house, built by Sir Thomas Wharton, was used for public worship) and Cotherstone; reduced, 1706, to £4 for Hartforth; raised, 1707, to £7 for Swaledale, Hartforth and Cotherstone; reduced, 1709, to £6 for the same. In 1711–12 he was granted £6 a year for Elswick, Lanc. Between July and Sept. 1713 he settled at Dob Lane, near Manchester, and there received grants of £5 a year till his death. On 25 July 1715 his Meeting-house at Dob Lane was wrecked by a Jacobite mob; in Jan. 1718 his congregation numbered 375 adherents, including 23 county voters. The Minutes sometimes call him Parkin and Pickins. He was buried at Dob Lane on 4 Nov. 1724. (*Cu.* (26 Mar. 1904) *Ev. Fr. Gd. M.*) [136]

PERROT, ROBERT, M.B. (*fl.* 1642–91). 𝕻. Born at St. Ives, Hunts. Studied at Magdalene Coll., Cambridge; M.B., 1642. Vicar of Nether Dean, Beds, ejected, 1662. Practised physic at Kettering, Northants, and Nottingham. Preached in Huntingdonshire. Licensed, 13 May 1672, being of Grub Street, London, as "Gräll Pr. Teacher." Removed to Hackney and finally to Maidstone, where he practised physic and preached. Was 87 at death. His grandson was Thomas Cullen [*q.v.*]. (*C. Co. P. T. V.*) [55, 57]

PERSHORE ('Parshor,' the common pronunciation). John Knowles (*fl.* 1646–65), the Arian lay preacher, had resided here as "a professed Minister" for about fifteen years, when arrested here on 9 Apr. 1665. His papers (in the Record Office) throw much light on the Antitrinitarian movement originated by John Bidle. (*See* John Ward.) (*D.*) [126]

PETERBOROUGH. [76, 77]

PETERSFIELD ('Peterfield'). [101, 102]

PETHERTON, probably South Petherton. [93]

PETTO, PEYTO, or PETTAUGH, SAMUEL, B.A. (1624?–Sept. 1711). 𝕮. Entered St. Catharine's Hall, Cambridge, as sizar, 15 June 1644; matric., 1644; B.A., 1647. Held, 1648, the sequestered rectory of Sandcroft St. George (otherwise South Elmhall St. Cross), Suff.; vacated, 15 Jan. 1661/2. The Episc. Returns, 1669, report "Mr Petto of Alburgh" as preaching at Denton, Norf., to "40 Independts most women At the house of one widow Leman once a weake"; also, as "one Pettaugh," as one of the preachers at Gillingham, Norf., to "above 100" persons "Att the house of Mr Charles Fleetwood where one Shepheard now liveth." Licensed, 8 May 1672, as "Sam: Pettaugh to be a Congr. Teacher in his house in Wortwell cum Alburgh, Norf.; also, 10 June 1672, as "Sam: Petto to be a Congr. Teacher in the howse of John Wesgate in the Parish of Redenhall cũ Harlston, Norfolk." Before 1675 he removed to Sudbury, where he became pastor of the Friar's Street congregation. His son-in-law, Josiah Maultby, became his colleague in 1707. Petto was joint editor with John Manning [*q.v.*] of "Six Treatises," 1656, by John Tillinghast, the Fifth-Monarchy man; also one of three joint authors of "The Preacher Sent," 1657/8, a plea for lay preaching. His taste for the marvellous was shown in his account (1693) of the bewitchment of Thomas Spatchett, and his account (1698) of a parhelion, contributed to the "Philosophical Transactions." He was buried at All Saints',

Sudbury, 21 Sept. 1711. (*B. C. D. P. T. Wc.*) [103]

PETTY FRANCE, near Moorfields (which is probably meant), was rebuilt in 1730 as New Broad Street. Petty France, Westminster, is now York Street, so called in honour of John Sharp, archbishop of York, who had his town-house there in 1708. Milton, while Latin Secretary (1651–1660), lived in this street, in a house demolished in 1877. (*Lo.*) [1]

PETWORTH. Ejected here were (1) Francis Cheynell or Chennel (1608–1665), born at Oxford (son of John, M.D.), of Magdalen Hall, Oxford; matric., 2 July 1624, aged 16; rem. to Balliol Coll., B.A., 1626/7; rem. to Merton Coll., Fellow, 1629; M.A., 1633; B.D., 1648; D.D., 1649; vicar of Marston St. Lawrence, Northants, 1637; member of the Westminster Assembly, 1643; held the sequestered rectory of Petworth, 1643–1660; President of St. John's Coll., 1648–50; Margaret professor of Divinity, 1648–52; *d.* at Preston, near Brighton, Suss., Sept. 1665. Notorious as a Presbyterian polemic (subject to fits of derangement). His "Rise, Growth, and Danger of Socinianisme," 1643, contains a few valuable notices of contemporary English Socinians; his "Chillingworthi Novissima," 1643, gives an account of his persecution of William Chillingworth in his last days, excusable only as evidence of derangement. (*C. D.* (needs correction) *F.*) (2) Richard Stretton, M.A., [*q.v.*]. [112]

PEYTON, PETER (*fl.* 1690–1733). **P.** One Peyton was Minister of Uppingham, Rutl., with Fund grants (£6), 1697–9. Peter Peyton received, 8 Jan. 1732/3, a special grant of £5, being at Campden, Glou. (*M.*) [127]

PHILLIPS, DANIEL (*d.* 1722). Born in Carmarthenshire. Educ. in the Academy of Samuel Jones [*q.v.*]; hence described as "schr," *i.e.* scholar. Settled as pastor at Pwllheli, Carn., in 1684, living at Gwynfryn farmhouse; ordained, 1688. The Common Fund granted him (1690–1693) £4 a year as Itinerant; and (1711–1722) £6 a year for Carnarvon, doubled in 1722. He received also from the Congregational Fund. In 1715 he is described as ministering at Pwllheli and Carnarvon, and living "at Gunfryn near Poolhely." His two sons were in the ministry. (*Ev. M. Rw.*) [141, 148]

PHILLIPS, EVAN. [146]

PHILLIPS, HUMPHREY, M.A. (*d.* 27 Mar. 1707). **P.** Born at Somerton, Som. Matric. 'ser.', at Wadham Coll., Oxford, 14 N. 1650; Scholar, 1651; B.A., 1653/4; Fellow of Magdalen Coll., 1656; ordained by presbyters; incorp. at Cambridge, 1657; ejected, 1660. Curate at Sherborne, Dors., to Francis Bampfield, M.A. (whom he had already served as curate in 1658); ejected, 1662. He became chaplain to Thomas Bampfield at Dunkerton, Som.; after eleven months imprisonment he went to Holland, returning to Dunkerton to find both the Bampfields become Seventh-day Baptists. The Episc. Returns, 1669, report him as one of the preachers to 200 persons at White Lackington, Som.; also to 100 persons at Monckton Combe, Som.; also to 100 persons at Weston by Bath, Som.; also to 300 persons at Dunkerton, "Att the Sheepe-house of Willm Clement sen & Willm Clement Jun"; also to 200 persons "In the parish church" at Cameley, Som.; also to 300 persons at Glastonbury, Som. Licensed, June 1672, as "Pr. Teacher in the howse of Cath. Chafe," widow, of Sherborne, Dors.; also, 5 Sept. 1672, as Pr. of Priston, Som. He ultimately lived on his own estate at Beckington, Som., preaching at various places, particularly Frome Selwood, Som. (*C. D. F. P. T.*) [92]

PHILLIPS, PEREGRINE (1623—17 S. 1691). **C.** Born at Amroth, Pemb. Son of the vicar. From the Haverfordwest grammar school and other tuition, studied at Oxford, but did not matriculate. Curate to his uncle at Kidwelly, Carm. Held the sequestered rectory of Llangan and Freystrop, Pemb.; ejected, 1660. Retired to the farm of Dredgmanhill, parish of Haverfordwest, Pemb. Licensed, 30 Apr. 1672, as "Congr. Teacher in his own howse & Richard Maylors in Haverford West." Preached at Dredgmanhill (where a new Meeting-house was erected, 1691), morning, and Haverfordwest, afternoon. The Common Fund voted him (22 June 1691) £5 a year, but this was transferred (28 Sept.) to Thomas Davis, his successor at Dredgmanhill. (*C. M. P. Rw. T. Wc.*) [144]

PHILLIPS, PEREGRINE (*fl.* 1690–1743). **C.** Probably son of the foregoing. The Common Fund granted him (1690–93) £10 a year for Loseby, Leic. Special grants (£5) were made to Peregrine Phillips in 1742–43 (place not stated). (*M.*) [66]

PHILLIPS, SAMUEL (*d.* 1721). **P.** Died Minister of Bromyard, Heref., to which place the Common Fund voted £5 in 1693. (*Ev. M.*) [48]

PHILLIPS, . . . **C.** Proposed as

Manager by George Boddington [*q.v.*], 29 July 1690. Attended no meeting. (*M.*) [162]

PIGGHILL, near Billingsgate. Pig-Hill, described in Ned Ward's "London Spy," 1704, p. 53, as "resembling the Steep Descent down which *the Devil drove his Hogs to a Bad Market*," was the southern slope of the present Pudding Lane (so called from the entrails of hogs thrown out from the scalding-house there). (*Sl.*) [2]

PIGGOTT, *i.e.* PIGOT, JOHN (*fl.* 1686–1733). 𝔓. Entered Frankland's Academy, 21 Jan. 1686/7. In Evans' List (1715) he is Minister at Fishlake, W.R. He received from the Fund an extra grant of £6 for service at Fishlake, Oct. 1717 to Oct. 1718; also two extra grants of £5 for service at Bolsover, Derb., 1729 and 1733. (*Ev. Fr. M. Nk.*)

He has been wrongly identified with John Pigott who, in 1694, being then a member of the General Baptist church, Hart Street, Covent Garden, London, became its pastor, till a change in sentiment led him, at the end of 1699, to withdraw with a section of his flock to form a Particular Baptist church in Little Wild Street, Lincoln's Inn Fields; his funeral sermon (published with portrait) was preached by Joseph Stennett, Seventh Day Baptist, on 29 Mar. 1713. (*Co. W.*) [133]

PIKE, . . . [Joseph Pyke, 𝔓., was Minister at Blakeney, Glou., 1715; removed, 1719, to Warminster, Wilts, as C. (*Ev. M.*)] [66, 96]

PIKE, . . . [Samuel Pike (*d.* 1719), 𝔓., was Minister at Gravesend from 1716. (*Ev. M.*)] [4]

PINNER. Ejected from this chapelry in Harrow-on-the Hill parish was William (or John) Rolls; licensed, 30 Sept. 1672, as Congr. Teacher at Pinner; died at Harrow. [William Rolles was created M.A. from Exeter Coll., Oxford, 14 Apr. 1648. (*F.*)] One Rolles was ejected from Folkestone. (*C. T.*) [72]

PINNERS' ('Pinnars') HALL. The Glass House, which became the Hall of the (now extinct) Pinners' or Pinmakers' Guild, was in Old Broad Street at the corner of Great Winchester Street. Here the Merchants' Lecture was begun in 1672. The site was occupied by a Meeting-house having six galleries in two tiers, and here the Lecture was delivered till the lease expired in 1778. (*Lo. W. Trans. Baptist Hist. Soc.*, July 1916, p. 75.) [35, 66, 154, 157, 165]

PINNY or PINNEY, ROBERT (*d.* 1698 ?). 𝔓. [? of New Inn Hall, Oxford; matric. pleb., 1 Apr. 1656.] Ejected from the vicarage of Charlcombe, Som. The Episc. Returns, 1669, report him as one of the preachers at Crewkerne, Som., "At the house of Henry Ellyot called Tayle Mill"; also to 200 persons at Wayford, Som., "At the house of one Widow Darby"; also at houses in Chard, Som., to "oftentime 700" persons. Licensed, June 1672 ('Rob. Penny of Chard') as "Grāll Pr."; his house at Chard licensed Pr., 25 July 1672. 'Brookhorne' is Crewkerne; his settlement there is unknown to Murch. (*C. F. Mh. P. T.*) [91, 92, 93]

PITMINSTER. Ejected from this vicarage in 1662 was Thomas Forward, of New Inn Hall, Oxford; matric., 4 Nov. 1631, aged 21; B.A., 1631/2; curate at Broad Clyst, Dev.; vicar of Pitminster; preaching at West Monkton, Som., in 1669; licensed, 20 Apr. 1672, as Presb. Teacher in his house at Pitminster; his house licensed, same date, as Presb. Meeting-place; *d.* Dec. 1687. (*C. F. T.*) [93]

PITTS, AARON (*fl.* 1690–1715). 𝔓. Possibly a son of "Mr Pitts" ejected (1662) from curacy at Plympton St. Mary's, Devon. He preached at Chard out of charity to Henry Backaller (2) [*q.v.*], and was Minister at Chard in 1715. Probably father of Aaron Pitts (*d.* 1771), Minister at Topsham, Devon. (*C. Ev. Mh. P.*) [91]

PLIMPTON. [31] *See* Devonshire

PLUMSTED, or PLUMSTEAD, AUGUSTINE, B.A. (1634–1716). ℭ. Son of Augustine Plumsted of Beccles. *Bap.*, 23 Oct. 1634. From Westminster school elected King's scholar at Trinity Coll., Cambridge; matric. pensioner, 14 June 1654; B.A., 1657/8; Fellow, 1659; ejected, 1660; member of the Congregational church, Wrentham, 1661; licensed, 8 May 1672, as Grāll Pr. Teacher, "of Norfolk" (no denomination specified in the application); pastor at Wrentham, 1689, till death; *bur.* 10 Jan. 1715/6, aged 82. (*B. C. T. Tc. V.*) [105]

PLYMOUTH ('Plym,' 'Plimmouth'). Ejected here were (1) George Hughes, born in Southwark, 1603; of Corpus Christi Coll., Oxford; matric., 28 June 1620, aged 16; Fellow of Pembroke Coll.; M.A., 1625; incorp. at Cambridge, 1627; B.D., 1633; lecturer at All Hallows, Bread Street; vicar of St. Andrew's, Plymouth, 1644 (also of Tavistock, 1648); ejected, 1662; living at Plymouth, 1665; *d.* at Kingsbridge, Devon, 7 July 1667; Obadiah Hughes [q.v.] was his son. (C. D. F. T. V.) [20, 31]

(2) Thomas Martin, or Martyn, [? matric., Exeter Coll., Oxford, 12 July 1639, aged 16], from Oxford admitted pensioner at Queens' Coll., Cambridge, 1644; B.A., 1644; lecturer at St. Andrew's, Plymouth; ejected, 1662; living at Plymouth, 1665; licensed, 2 Apr. 1672, as Congr. Teacher in any licensed place, also, 11 Apr. 1672, as Pr. Teacher in Plymouth; his house in Plymouth was licensed, 13 May 1672, as a Pr. Meeting-place. (C. F. T. V.)

(3) Silenced here was his son, Samuel Martyn [q.v.]

PLYMPTON ST. MARY ('Plimpton'). Ejected here was John Searle, M.A. [q.v.]. [31]

POLEBROOK ('Polebrooke'). [78]

PONTEFRACT. Ejected from this vicarage in 1662 was Joshua Farrett; he preached in the house of one Ward, at Tanshelf in this parish; *d.* 1663, aged about 64. (C. My.) [130, 136]

POOL, . . . [4]

POOLE. Ejected here was Samuel Hardy, B.A. [q.v.]. [34, 35, 179]

POOLE, MATTHEW, M.A. (1624—12 O. 1679). **P.** Born at York; son of Francis Pole. Entered Emmanuel Coll., Cambridge, 2 July 1645; B.A., 1648/9; M.A., 1652; incorp. M.A. at Oxford, 1657. Obtained (1649) the sequestered rectory of St. Michael-le-Querne, and was a member of the Fifth Presbyterian Classis in the London province; ejected, 1662. He was the originator of a Fund (1658–1660) for maintaining students for the ministry; William Sherlock (1641 ?—19 June 1707), afterwards dean of St. Paul's, was one of its beneficiaries. He was among the first to write (1654) against John Bidle (14 Jan. 1615/6—22 S. 1662). His "Synopsis Criticorum," 1669–1676; is of permanent value. He was one of those who, in the year of Indulgence (1672), accepted a pension of £50 a year from the Crown. He took out no licence, but preached occasionally. He left England (1678) for Amsterdam, and died there. (Cm. D. Wc.) [188]

PORDSTOW. [19] *See* Cornwall

PORTER, GEORGE, M.A., B.D. (1623–July 1697). Born in Sussex. Demy of Magdalen Coll., Oxford, 1642–8; M.A., 1648; Fellow, 1649–60; Vice-president, 1658; Canon of Christ Church, 1658; ejected, 1662. He held Baxter's rectoral view of church-government. He lived some time in retirement at Lewes, Suss.; afterwards preached at Eastbourne, Suss.; lastly was pastor at Clare, Suff., in succession to Francis Crow [q.v.]. He was buried at Ovington, Ess. (C. E. F. P.) [39, 42]

PORTER, JOHN, *i.e.* JOSEPH (1659—24 Aug. 1721). **P.** Died Minister at Alcester, where he was living in 1715, and conducting an Academy for the training of Ministers and laymen. The mural tablet to his memory was removed (1901) from the dismantled Alcester Meeting-house, to the Oat Street Meeting-house, Evesham, Worc. The Minister of the Alcester Meeting-house (1834–64) was Thomas Warren, of Morton Hall (educ. at Manchester College, York), who conducted the service (which the present writer once attended in 1863) with Theophilus Lindsey's original Prayer-book, including the Apostles' Creed, and was the last Unitarian Minister to do so. (Bb. Ev. Si.) [117]

PORTER, . . . ? Samuel Porter (1659—16 Aug. 1706). **P.** Educated by Samuel Cradock [q.v.] before 1686; Minister of Nayland, Suff., from soon after the licensing of the Old Meeting-house on 19 Jan. 1690/1 till death. Buried at Nayland. (B. C. Cm. P.) [3, 39]

PORTSMOUTH. Ejected here were (1) Thomas Bragg; (2) Benjamin Burgess [? of Magdalen Hall, Oxford; matric., 31 Oct. 1623, aged 16; B.A., 1626], vicar of Portsmouth (St. Thomas à Becket), preaching at Gosport, Hants, 1669; licensed, Apr. 1672, as Teacher of Presbyterians in houses at Portsmouth and Gosport. (C. F. T.) [101]

POSTERN, THE, a lane running from Moor Lane to Moorfields; is now represented by the portion of Fore Street lying East of Moor Lane. Stow describes it as "a narrow lane called the Posterne, because it hath at eyther end a doore to be shut in the night season." (Sl. St.) [1]

POTTERSBURY ('Potters Perry,' 'Portersperry'). [76, 77]

POULTRY, THE. [24, 163]

POWDERHAM ('Powdram'). [31]

POWELL, JOHN, M.A. (1617—30 Apr. 1691). **C.** Son of Hoel Powell of Tythegston, Glam. Matric. 'pleb.' at St. Edmund's Hall, Oxford, on 8 May 1635, aged 18. Vicar of St. Lythans, Glam.; ejected, 1660. The Episc. Returns, 1669, report him as one of the preachers at Llanedern, Glam., "every other Sabath day" to "about 40 of meane Qualitie," "Entertained by Llewellin John"; at Eglwsilan, Glam., to an "uncertaine" number, "Their entertainers are: Willm John Thomas Jenkin Thomas & Willm Rees a mason"; and at Marshfield, Monm., to "100 Old Militiamen out of the severall counties of Monmouth and Glamorgan. At the house of Jane Reynold the relict of Henry William, a Leiutenant in the late Rebellion." Licensed, 10 June 1672, being of Newport, Monm., as "Grāll Ind." He continued to preach in the above and other places, and was Teaching Elder at Mynyddyslwyn in 1675. The Common Fund voted him £4 a year on 22 June 1691, not having heard of his death; on 28 Sept. the grant was transferred to Watkin Jones [*q.v.*]. (*C. F. M. P. Rw. T.*) [143, 144]

POWELL, SAMUEL (*d.* 1714). 𝔓. Elected a Treasurer, 14 July 1690. He was also a Manager of the reconstituted Fund (1695). Appears as Alderman, 3 May 1708. His last attendance was on 8 F. 1713/4. On 3 May 1714 it is mentioned that he left £100 to the Fund. (*M.*) [124, 162, 166, 168]

POWELL, THOMAS, M.A. (*fl.* 1648–92). ℭ. Matric. pensioner, at Jesus Coll., Cambridge, 1645; B.A., 1648/9; migrated to Pembroke Hall; M.A., 1657; incorp. at Oxford, 9 July 1657. Rector of St. Sidwell's, Exeter; ejected, 1662. The Episc. Returns, 1665, report him as residing at Exeter, an Independent and conventicler; those also of 1669 report "Powell, a very factious man" as preaching "In Cherry tree Alley, Bunhill," London, on 17 Oct. 1669; but this was probably Vavasor Powell (1617—27 Oct. 1670). Licensed, 9 D. 1672, as "Independ$^{t}$ Teach$^{r}$ of Exon in Devon." (*C. F. P. T. V.*) [33]

POWELL, THOMAS (1656?–Aug. 1716). 𝔓. Son of a Minister. Studied (1662–1664) at the grammar school in Houndsditch, of William Angel, M.A., ejected from the rectory of Merstham, Surrey. Began to preach before he was twenty; in 1675 was preaching in and about Hertfordshire, but in 1676 returned to London, ministering to a congregation in High Hall, Cow Lane, West Smithfield, removing it (1701) to a vacant Meeting-house in Jewin Street, and again to a Meeting-house in Red Cross Street.

His son William (1680—2 D. 1713) had a strange career. (*Ev. W. We.*) [166]

POWELL'S ALLEY, now Moor Lane, runs from the South side of Chiswell Street, at a point nearly opposite Bunhill Row. (*Sl.*) [3]

PREACHING FEES. [178]

PRESBYTERIAN. [158]

PRESBYTERIAN BOARD. [158, 171]

PRESBYTERIAN FUND. [184]

PRESBYTERIANISM. [151 *sqq.*]

PRESTON. [64, 65]

PRESTWICH. [59]

PRIESKLY, *i.e.* PRIESTLEY, NATHANIEL (*d.* 5 Sept. 1728). 𝔓. Son of Jonathan Priestley. Entered Frankland's Academy, 2 F. 1681/2. Ordained, 6 June 1694, at Little Horton, near Bradford, where he had been preaching from 1690. He was Minister at the same time at Halifax (where Northgate End Chapel was built in 1696), preaching there and at Little Horton, alternately with Eli Dawson (*d.* 1744), who succeeded him. For Little Horton he received Fund grants (from 1704) of £6. (*Ev. Fr. Hh. M. My.*) [130]

PRIG, *i.e.* PRIGG, NICHOLAS, M.A. (*fl.* 1662–1696). Matric. sizar, at Emmanuel Coll., Cambridge, 1634; B.A., 1637/8; M.A., 1641. Vicar of Ashford, Kent; ejected, 1662. A celebrated preacher. The portion of his wife (Scott), invested in land, was his maintenance after ejection. From the Common Fund he received (1690–1696) £6 a year. "After the death of his wife he was much better, and at length died in comfort." (*C. K. M. P. V.*) [56]

PRIME, RICHARD, *i.e.* EDWARD (1632—26 Apr. 1708). 𝔓. Born at Wheston in Tideswell parish, Derb. Son of John Prime. From Repton grammar school admitted sizar at Christ's Coll., Cambridge, 1 June 1649, age 17; matric., 1649; did not graduate. Tutor in family of Thomas Westby, Ravensfield, vicar of Baslow, Derb.; curate (1654) to James Fisher (*d.* Jan. 1665/6), vicar of Sheffield; both ejected, 1662. Remained in Sheffield. From 1662 till his death he maintained a lecture at Wheston. The Episc. Returns, 1669, report him as one of five preachers to "40 or 50 of the ordinary sort of people" every Sunday at Attercliffe, and every Thursday at Shiercliffe Hall, Sheffield, the residence of Rowland Hancock (*d.* 14 Apr. 1685); ejected from the vicarage of Ecclesfield. Licensed, 29 May 1672, as "Pr. Teacher in his howse in the Parish of Sheffield"; also, 10 June 1672, as "Pr. Teacher in the Malt-howse of Rob: Brilsworth in Sheffield." On 31 July 1689 his house in Sheffield was registered for worship. His daughter Hephzibah (1654–1735) married Christopher Richardson [*q.v.*] as her first husband. (*C. Cp. Ma. Nt. P. T. Y.*) [129, 131]

PRIMEROSE, EDWARD, *i.e.* PRIMROSE,

GEORGE, M.A. (*fl.* 1660–90). **P.** Educated in Scotland and at Saumur. Graduated M.A., Edin., 26 July 1634, as Georgius Prymrosius, *minister verbi*. One of four "joint pastors" in Hereford Cathedral; ejected, 1660. Licensed, 19 Apr. 1672, as "Presbyterian Teacher in his howse in Hereford." Retired to the country, but returned to Hereford, 1687; left again before his death. (*C. Ed. P. T.*) [48]

PRINCE, JAMES, M.A. (*fl.* 1652–96). **P.** A gentleman of good family, armiger. Matric. at Wadham Coll., Oxford, 2 Apr. 1652; B.A., 1654; M.A., 1657. Held the donative of Kingsbury, Midx.; ejected, 1662. Licensed, June 1672, as "Presb. Teacher" in house of Richard Whitehall or Withall "in Farnhã. Stafford," *i.e.* Farnham, Surrey. Subsequently Minister at Wokingham or Oakingham, Berks, till death. He is mentioned for a grant in 1692, but nothing was given. He preached a funeral sermon in 1696. (*C. F. M. P. Sm. T.*) [7]

PRINCES RISBOROUGH. [Calamy gives William Reeves, B.A., of Pembroke Coll., Oxford (not in Foster), as ejected from Resbury, Bucks (no such place). Palmer drops Oxford, and makes the place Risborough (quite wrong). William Reeve, B.A., matric. at Christ's Coll., Cambridge, Dec. 1607; B.A., 1610/1; held the sequestered vicarage of Wyrardisbury (Wraysbury), Bucks; ejected, 1660. (*C. Cp. P. V.*)] [9]

PRINCE'S STREET, near the Royal Exchange; it flanks the west side of the Bank of England. [2]

PROPAGATION OF THE GOSPEL. [179]

PROTESTANT DISSENTERS. [140, 188]

PROVINCIAL ASSEMBLY. [157]

PRYTHEROH, LEWIS. [146]

PRYTHRO, or PRYTHERCH, RICE (*d.* 25 Jan. 1698/9). An eminent schoolmaster, not a preacher, in 1662. Maintained his school for over forty years, living some time (perhaps always) at Ystradwalter, near Llandovery, Carm. Refused offers of preferment if he would conform, and became a Nonconformist Itinerant preacher. In 1675 became pastor to the Nonconformists in and about Llandovery. His congregation met for a time at Castellcraigwyddon, five miles from Llandovery. After 1682 he had, for some years, the pastoral charge of all the Nonconformist churches in Brecknockshire (yet he was not ordained till 25 Jan. 1688). This explains his connection with Aberllynfi, Brec., for which the Common Fund voted him (1690–93) £6 a year. He administered his various charges with the aid of a number of preaching elders. The year of his birth is not given, but he was 'born, ordained, and died on St. Paul's day.' (*C. M. P. Rw.*) [143]

PUCKERIDGE ('Puckerage,' 'Puckridge'), a village in the parishes of Braughing and Standon. [51, 52]

PUDSTOW. [20] *See* Cornwall

PUNCHION, *i.e.* PUNCHEON, TIMOTHY, M.A. (*d.* Dec. 1716). **C.** Born at Newcastle-on-Tyne. Graduated at Edinburgh ('Punshion'), Aug. 1686. Entered Frankland's Academy ('Punshon') on 19 Feb. 1687/8. Highly commended by Richard Gilpin [*q.v.*]. Lord Wharton [*q.v.*] was the patron of the perpetual curacy of Ravenstonedale. The Common Fund granted (15 June 1691) £10 a year to Puncheon for Ravenstonedale, paid to 1693. Later he ministered at Branton, Northumb.; Killingworth, Northumb.; and from 1715 or earlier at Riveley, Northumb. Buried at Alnwick, 29 Dec. 1716. (*Cm. Ed. Ev. Fr. M. N. Nk. Pe.*) [121]

PURITANISM. [188]

PURT, *i.e.* PORT, ROBERT, B.A. (*b.* 1624). **C.** Born at Ashbourne, Derb.; son of Francis Port, gent., of Ashby-de-la-Zouch, Leic.; from Repton school admitted pensioner at St. John's Coll., Cambridge, 11 June 1636, aet. 18; B.A., 1639/40. Rector of Barford, Norf.; held (1654) the sequestered rectory of Garveston, Norf.; ejected, 1662. The Episc. Returns, 1669, report him as preaching at Woodnorton, Oulton, and Lammas, Norf. (*see* Finch, Martin). Often imprisoned. Licensed, 23 D. 1672, as "... Dort Congr. Teach^r^ at his owne house att Barford in Norffolk." Succeeded (1689?) John Money (ejected from the rectory of Wymondham, Norf.) as pastor of the Congregational church at Wattlefield, a hamlet of Wymondham. He is mentioned in the Fund Minutes, 10 N. 1691. Died before the Meeting-house at Wymondham was built (1715). (*B. C. Jo. M. P. T. V. Wc.*) [74]

PYE ('Pie'), SIR ROBERT, Knt. (*d.* 1701), parliamentarian, married Anne, daur. of John Hampden. Henry James Pye, poet laureate, was his descendant. (*D.*) [6, 7]

PYKE, BENJAMIN. [Mr. Pyke or Pike received from the Fund £8 a year at Colebrooke, Bucks, 1706–9. (*M.*)] [4]

QUAKERS. [42, 152, 153, 187]

QUEEN CHARLTON ('Charleton'). [91]

QUICK, JOHN, B.A. (1636—29 Apr. 1706). **P.** Born at Plymouth. Entered at Exeter Coll., Oxford, about 1650; servitor, 1653; matric., 20 July 1654; B.A., 10 Oct. 1657. Preached at Ermington, Devon; ordained by presbyters, 2 Feb. 1659, at Plymouth; held the sequestered vicarage of Kingsbridge with Churchstow, Devon, whence ejected, 1660. Thereafter held the perpetual curacy of Brixton, Devon, and held on, nonconforming, till Sunday, 13 Dec. 1663, when he was arrested while preaching, and illegally committed to Exetor gaol; not liberated till March 1664. A prosecution for preaching to his fellow-prisoners failed. On 22 March 1671/2 he signed an Address to the Crown, of thanks from Nonconformist Ministers of Devon, for the Indulgence. He was licensed as a general Presb. Teacher on 11 Apr. 1672. After withdrawal of Indulgence he was committed to the Marshalsea, Plymouth. Released, he came to London. In 1679 he became Minister to the English church at Middelburg, Holland; but returned to London, 22 July 1681. Here he gathered a congregation (lasting till 1753) in a Meeting-house in Middlesex court, Bartholomew Close, Smithfield, which really formed part of the structure of St. Bartholomew's the Great. He favoured James II.'s Declaration for Liberty of Conscience (1687). He was active in relief of French Protestant refugees. On 22 Sept. 1690 he promised to help the Common Fund by "a more perfect account of Cornwall." His chief publication is the "Synodicon in Gallia Reformata," 1692, 2 vols. folio, containing the Acts and Canons of the French Reformed Church. His manuscript "Icones Sacrae," lives of 50 French and 20 English divines, fill three folio volumes in Dr. Williams' Library. In his latter years he was greatly disabled by internal ailments. (*C. D. F. M. P. T. W. Wc.*) [1, 4, 19, 164, 165, 180]

RACHDALE. [59] *See* Lancashire

RADBOR. *See* Rodbard

RADNORSHIRE. [143, 145]

RAINFORD. Ejected here was Roger Baldwin, M.A. [*q.v.*]

RAND, RICHARD, B.A. (*d.* 1692). **C.** Matric. sizar at Sidney Sussex Coll., Cambridge, 1645/6; B.A., 1647/8. First appears as rector of Easthorpe, Ess.; after 1650, rector of Mark's Tey, Ess.; ejected, 1662. The Episc. Returns, 1669, report him as one of two preachers at Mark's Tey. Licensed, 10 June 1672, as "Congr. Teacher in the howse of Rob. Maidston," at Boxted, Ess. Some one gave him the works of John Crell, the Socinian, "but he said he durst not read them." Died pastor at Little Baddow, Ess. His son died there about the same time. (*C. E. P. T.*) [38, 43]

RANGEWORTH ('Ranger'). [46]

RANT, . . . The family of Rant was important and numerous in Norfolk, but Rant of Swaffham has not been traced. [14]

RAPIER, MATTHEW. **C.** His surname is often written Raper, being doubtless so pronounced (*cf.* Napier, pronounced, in Scotland, Naper and Nepper). Member of the congregation of Thomas Cole [*q.v.*]. Attended as Manager of the Common Fund, 18 Aug. 1690; last attendance, 15 May 1693. Manager (1695) of the Congregational Fund, and one of its Correspondents for Norfolk and Northamptonshire. (*Cf. Co. M.*) [27, 63, 70, 77, 162, 164, 165, 166, 167, 168, 176, 186]

RASHLEY, JONATHAN (*fl.* 1670-1699). Calamy says that Thomas Rasley or Rashely, M.A., ejected from Salisbury [*q.v.*], lived at 'Abrey,' *i.e.* Avebury, near Marlborough, Wilts. 'Lydyard,' where Jonathan Rashley (perhaps son of Thomas) lived from about 1670, is either Lydiard Tregoze, or Lydiard Millicent (close together). The Common Fund granted him (30 May 1692) £6 a year, which was paid to 1699. (*C. M. P.*) [124]

RASTRICK, JOHN, M.A. (26 Mar. 1650–18 Aug. 1727). **P.** Born at Heckington, Linc.; son of John Raistrige. Graduated at Trinity Coll., Cambridge, B.A., 1660; M.A., 1674. Vicar of Kirton, Linc., 1674; resigned, 27 N. 1687. Preached as Nonconformist at Spalding, Linc., till 1694; then at Rotherham, Yorks (1694–1701); became (1701) colleague to Anthony Williamson [*q.v.*], in the ministry of the Presbyterian congregation in Spinner Lane, King's Lynn, Norf. Adopted the Christology of James Peirce. Refused a grant, 1690; received grant of £5, 1693, and from 1712 a grant of £10 a year.

His son William (*d.* Aug. 1752) succeeded him at Lynn. His manuscript "Index" of the Ejected (copy, dated 1734, is in St. Margaret's Library, Lynn) was of much service to Palmer for his "Nonconformist's Memorial." (*D. Ev. M. Tc. V.*) [70, 173]

RATFORD, EAST. [84] *See* Nottinghamshire

RATHBAND, WILLIAM, M.A. (1627–Oct. 1695). 𝔓. *Bap.* at Bolton, 30 Apr. 1627. Son of William Rathband, a Puritan divine, some time of Little Lever, Lancashire, writer against Brownists (1644). The son, as William Rathbone, was admitted sizar of Emmanuel Coll., Cambridge, 7 Apr. 1643; B.A., 1646/7. Incorp. at Oxford, as William Rathband, 10 Oct. 1648; Fellow of Wadham Coll., Oxford, 1648; M.A., 1649. He held the vicarage of South Weald, Essex, from 1658, in succession to Thomas Goodwin, and was ejected thence, as "Will. Rathbone," in 1662. In the applications for licences he is called Rathband and Rathbone (without Christian name); as Rathband he was licensed "to be a Presb. Teacher in the howse of Richard Day in Horsmonden, in Kent." After many removes he settled at Highgate. His funeral sermon, preached at Highgate, 13 Oct. 1695, by Samuel Slater, M.A., his fellow-student at Emmanuel, is dedicated to Sarah Rathband, the widow, but contributes nothing biographical, not even the date of death.

Rathband's brother, Nathaniel, M.A., Edin., was curate of Sowerby, 1635; preacher in York Minster 1645; rector of Prestwich, Lanc., 1652; rector of Ripley, W.R., 1657; resigned, 1660 (not in Calamy). (*C. E. F. Gd. P. Y.*) [3, 72]

RATHMELL ('Rawthmell'), then a village in Giggleswick parish, Yorks, now perpetual curacy. [129]

RAVENSTONEDALE ('Russendaile'; the common pronunciation). Calamy gives Thomas 'Dodgson' as ejected here and conforming afterwards. The reference is to Thomas Dodson [? of Christ's Coll., Cambridge; matric. sizar, 1623; B.A., 1626/7; M.A., 1630], who was ord. deacon, 23 May 1624, as 'literatus,' and appears as vicar of Ravenstonedale in 1628. Though his name figures in the list of the Presbyterian Classis (1645/6), he retained his cure (probably under the protection of Lord Wharton [*q.v.*]) till bis death in Jan. 1672/3. (*C. N. V.*) [121]

RAWLLINGSON, *i.e.* RAWLINSON, WILLIAM (*d.* 1693 ?). ℭ. The Common Fund granted (1691) £5 a year for work at Burnham, reduced in 1695 to £4. The Meeting-house in Moor Lane, Colchester, was conveyed to trustees, 14 Mar. 1691/2, by William Rawlinson, pastor of the church; he was succeeded in Dec. 1693 by John Gledhill (*see* Gleddall). (*E. M.*) [38, 41]

RAWTHMELL. [129] *See* Yorkshire, W.R.

RAY. *See* Kay

RAYLEIGH ('Reyleigh'). Ejected here was Abraham Caley, of St. John's Coll., Cambridge; matric. sizar, 1622; B.A., 1625/6; Fellow; M.A., 1629; B.D., 1637; ordained episcopally; rector of Rayleigh, 24 Jan. 1643/4; member of the Fourth Presb. Classis of Essex; ejected, 1662; offered lectureship at Gray's Inn, 13 Jan. 1662/3, but did not accept; lived with a married daughter in Suffolk; died, July 1672, on a visit to Stephen Bull, his nephew and successor at Rayleigh. (*C. E. V.*) The rector referred to was John Duffe, M.A., instituted 15 Jan. 1679/80; on 28 Aug. 1690, Hugh Pine, B.A., was instituted "per depr. Duffe." (*Nc.*) [41, 42]

READ, or READE, JOSEPH, B.A. (*d.* 1713). 𝔓. Born at Kidderminster. Sent to Cambridge by Richard Baxter [*q.v.*], whose assistant he became. Sizar at Trinity Coll., Cambridge, 18 June 1652; matric., 1652; B.A., 1655/6. Rector of Witley Magna, Worc. (in the patronage of the Foley family); ejected, 1662. In June 1672 he was licensed as a Presb. Teacher in his house, Stanbrook, Worc. In London he acted as reader and precentor when Baxter preached. A Meeting-house was built for him in Dyot Street, Great Russell Street; preaching there, 30 Apr. 1676, he was sent to prison. In his preaching he used the Common Prayer; hence a pamphleteer calls him "the Con-non-forming Mungril." From 1687 he ministered, undisturbed, till his retirement to Hampstead, where he died. He was specially interested in Deddington, Oxon, subscribing for it (1690–92) £10 a year. (*An. C. Ca. M. P. T. Tc. V. W.*) [165]

READING. Ejected here in 1662 was Christopher Fowler, M.A.; born at Marlborough, Wilts; son of John Fowler; entered Magdalen Coll., Oxford, 1627; matric., 14 Oct. 1631, aged 17; B.A., 1631/2; rem. to St. Edmund's Hall; M.A., 1634; rector of West Woodhey, Berks, 1640; vicar of St. Mary's, Reading, 1643; refused the engagement, 1649; lecturer at St. Margaret's, Lothbury, 1652; Fellow of Eton Coll. (ejected thence, 1660); licensed, 2 May 1672, as Congr. Teacher at Chesham, Herts; died in Southwark, 15 Jan. 1676/7. (*C. D. F. P.* (not in *Rr.*) *T.*) [6]

REDGWELL. [40] *See* Essex

REDRUTH. [19]

REHAKOSHT, P. [186]

REIGATE. [109]

REINOLDS, *i.e.* REYNOLDS, WILLIAM, M.A. (28 O. 1625—26 F. 1697/8). 𝔓. Son of William Reynolds, Abchurch Lane, London, citizen, clothworker, and Russia merchant. From the Charterhouse school he proceeded (1641) to Emmanuel Coll., Cambridge; B.A., 1644/5; M.A., 1648 (incorp. at Oxford, 10 Oct. 1649). After nearly two years in business in Russia as his father's agent, he joined John Whitlock [*q.v.*] at Leighton Buzzard, Beds, in Dec. 1646. Lecturer at St. Mary's, Nottingham, 1651, and active in the Nottingham Classis, 1656–60; ejected, 1662. Accompanied Whitlock in all his subsequent movements. Licensed, 1 May 1672, as "Pr. Teacher in the howse of Joseph James," Nottingham; an application for the County Hall was refused. His daughter married Samuel Coates [*q.v.*]. (*C. F. No. P. T. V.*) [82, 178]

REPTON. [25]

RETFORD ('Ratford'), EAST. For this place (with James Wright (1651–1694) [*q.v.*] as Minister) the Common Fund granted (1691) £10 a year; reduced (1695) to £6. (*M.*) [84]

REVELL, THEOPHILUS. 𝔓. Elected a Manager, 2 Mar. 1690/1, replacing Coward [*q.v.*]. His appointment was conveyed through John Jurin [*q.v.*]; hence he is presumed to be of the same denomination. His last attendance was on 15 May 1693. (*M.*) [162]

REYLEIGH. [41, 42] *See* Essex

REYNOLDS, JOHN (*d.* 25 D. 1692). 𝔓. Born at Winfarthing, Norf. Son of Cooper Reynolds, rector of Winfarthing. From the grammar schools of Shelfanger and Winfarthing admitted sizar at Gonville and Caius Coll., Cambridge, 26 S. 1646, age 16; matric., 1647; B.A., 1650/1; M.A., 1654. Ejected from the rectory of Roughton, Norf., apparently not till 6 F. 1662/3. Licensed, 25 July 1672, as a Presb. Teacher "in his howse in Bunhill fields, London." Colleague with Samuel Slater, M.A. [*q.v.*], at Crosby Hall, Bishopsgate. Joined in Address of thanks to James II., 1687 (*see* Alsop, Vincent). (*B. C. Gc. P. T. V. W.*) [165]

REYNOLDS, THOMAS (1668?–25 Aug. 1727). 𝔓. Born in London; brought up under ministry of John Howe. Meant first for the law. Entered Charles Morton's Academy, Newington Green (1683); proceeded to Geneva (1685), under Turretin, and to Utrecht (1686–9). Returned to London, 1689. Stephen Lobb and Stephen Ford, whom he assisted, were Congregational. He further assisted Howe, at Silver Street (City). He was one of seven (including Calamy) who were on 22 June 1694 "ordained minister of the catholic church," in Annesley's Meeting-house, Little St. Helen's; this being the first public ordination among London Dissenters since 1662. In 1695 succeeded Thomas Kentish (ejected from Middleton, Durham) at Great Eastcheap. Removed the congregation (1697) to a Meeting-house over the King's Weigh-house, where he preached till death. Elected a Fund Manager, 25 O. 1697. In 1719 he was strongly with the Subscribers at Salters' Hall. He lived "in Rood-lane, near Fanchurch-str^t." (*D. Ev. W. We.*) [3]

RHOSEYGWYLYN ('Rhoseygilwen'). [144]

RICH, LADY. Apparently this is Frances (1638—27 Jan. 1720/1), youngest daughter of Oliver Cromwell, married (1) on 11 N. 1657 to Hon. Robert Rich (*d.* 16 F. 1657/8, aged 23), grandson and heir of Robert, earl of Warwick; (2) on 7 May 1663 to Sir John Russell, bart. (1632–1669), of Chippenham, Cambs, by whom she had five children. The Rich family had estates in the Ongar neighbourhood. (*Pe.*) [39]

RICHARDS, DAVID (*d.* 1690?). [143]

RICHARDSON, CHRISTOPHER, M.A. (1618/9–Dec. 1698). 𝔓. Born in York; baptized, 17 Jan. 1618/9. Matric. sizar, at Trinity Coll., Cambridge, 1633; B.A., 1636/7; M.A., 1640. Held from 1646 the sequestered rectory of Kirkheaton, Yorks; ejected, 1660/1. Bought Lassell Hall in Kirkheaton parish and there preached. Licensed, 8 May 1672, as "Presb. Teacher" in the house of William [*i.e.* Thomas] Cotton, Denby Grange, Penistone, Yorks, whom he served as chaplain, preaching also at Sheffield and at Norton, Derb. On 30 Sept. 1672 licence was noted for "the house of Christopher Richardson in y^e Township Layton, Yorsh. Pr." Left Lassell Hall, 1687, for Liverpool, preaching there alternately with Toxteth Park (according to Calamy) till death, and assisted by Samuel Angier [*q.v.*]. Richardson appears to have been the first settled Nonconformist Minister in Liverpool, with a Meeting-house in Castle Hey, new in 1689. The Episc. Returns, 1669, report only Anabaptists. In Feb. 1672/3 licence was noted for "the house of Tho: Christian of Leverpoole in Lancash. Pr." Richardson was buried in Liverpool on 5 Dec. 1698.

His son Christopher, *bap.* at Kirkheaton, 15 June 1656, was educated at Bromsgrove under Henry Hickman, B.D. (*d.* 1692), ejected from the vicarage of Brackley, Northants. He entered Frankland's Academy, 3 June 1674, but was not ordained. He died at Lassell Hall and was *bur.* at Kirkheaton, 28 Aug. 1721. (*C. D. Fr. Nk. Nl. P. Rl. T. Tc. V. Wc. Y.*) [58]

RICHMOND, Yorks, N.R. (misplaced in E.R.) [139]

RICKMANSWORTH. [51]

RIDGE, JOHN, B.A. (1590 ?–1637 ?). Born at Oxford. Matric. at St. John's Coll., Oxford, 16 June 1610, aged 20; B.A., 1612. Ordained deacon by John Bridges, bishop of Oxford; presbyter (probably) by Robert Echlin, bishop of Down and Connor. Admitted by Echlin, 7 July 1619, to the vicarage of Antrim. Refusing to subscribe the new canons, he was licensed (not deprived) by Henry Leslie, Echlin's successor, on 12 Aug. 1636. He retired to Irvine, Ayrshire, and soon died. The Antrim Meeting, on the first Friday in each month, which he began in 1626, was originally designed to counteract fanatical excesses fostered by James Glendinning, vicar of Carnmoney, Co. Antrim, in connection with a revival meeting, held on the last Friday in each month, at the residence of Hugh Campbell, a layman from Ayrshire, at Oldstone, near Antrim. (*D.*) [155]

RIDGEWELL. Ejected here was Daniel Ray, born at Sudbury, Suff.; son of Ambrose Ray, mercer; from Sudbury school adm. sizar at St. John's Coll., Cambridge, 29 June 1652, aet. 16; matric., 1652; B.A., 1655/6; M.A., 1659; held the sequestered rectory of Debden, Ess., till 1660; vicar of Ridgewell; ejected, 1662; licensed, 22 July 1672, as Pr. Teacher in his house at Ridgewell; house licensed Pr. same date; removed, 1673, to Burshall, Suff. (a living held along with Bramford), where the vicar let him preach every other Sunday; *d.* 1677, in 42nd year. (*C. E. Jo. T. V.*) [40]

RIKAY, THOMAS. (*Bl.*) [180]

RILSTON, otherwise Rylstone ('Rulston'), W.R. (misplaced in N.R.) [136]

RINGHAY ('Rugeley') CHAPEL (*see* Cheshire) was in Nonconformist hands till the forcible ejection which led to the building of Hale Chapel, Chesh., in 1720. (*Ev. Uc.*) [15]

RINGWOOD. [102]

RISLEY, THOMAS, M.A. (27 Aug. 1630–1716). 𝔓. Born near Warrington. Second son of Thomas Risley (1588—14 O. 1670), of Newton-in-the-Willows, parish of Winwick. Matric. 'pleb.', at Pembroke Coll., Oxford, 9 D. 1650; B.A., 1652; Fellow, 1654; M.A., 1655. In 1662 he was given a year's grace to consider the terms of conformity; though ordained deacon and presbyter (10 N. 1662) by Edward Reynolds, bishop of Norwich, he resigned his fellowship. Four years later he declined an invitation to return to a better post in the University, but continued to preach to his neighbours at Croft, in the manor of Culcheth, parish of Winwick, where his barn was registered, July 1689, forming them (1689) into a congregation, and erecting (1707) a Meeting-house for them at Risley, near by. A grant of £5, made to him as "a present Supply," in 1706, was perhaps in view of the building. He received grants from the Congregational Fund. Buried at Risley Chapel. (*C. Ev. F. Nl. M. P. X.*) [59]

RIVINGTON. The election to the perpetual curacy (now vicarage) of Rivington Chapel was, and is, by the parishioners. Samuel Newton, son of John Newton, yarn-seller, of Ashton-under-Lyne, from a school at Newton Heath, Lanc., was admitted sizar, at St. John's Coll., Cambridge, 2 Aug. 1654, aet. 16; matric., 1654; B.A., 1658/9; appointed at Rivington, 1659 ?; ejected, 1660; but after preaching at Darwen, returned in 1669 or 1670, and was licensed as Gr̃all Pr. Teacher; the Meeting-place in Rivington, *i.e.* Rivington Chapel, was licensed, 16 July 1672, Pr.; here he preached till his death, 11 Mar. 1682/3; Calamy gives his age as "not above Forty"; it is usually given as 48, but was probably 44. He was succeeded by John Walker [*q.v.*]. (*C. Jo. Nl. Rt. T. V.*) [59]

ROBERTS, MARMADUKE. 𝔓. Assisted Thomas Rosewell, M.A., at Jamaica Row, Rotherhithe, chiefly at the Lord's Supper, for several years prior to 1692. Living in 1705. (*W. We.*) [3]

ROBINSON, ISAAC (*fl.* 1690–1723). 𝔓. Brother of Benjamin Robinson [*q.v.*]. Minister at Potterspury, Northants, 1704–1711; Chesham, Bucks, 1712–23. (*M.*) [26, 29]

ROBINSON, SIR LEONARD. Chamberlain of London. Knighted at the Guildhall, 29 Oct. 1692. From the Fund Minutes it appears that he was interested in Nonconformity at Stockton-on-Tees. His subscription was in arrear at Midsummer 1693. (*M. S.*) [164]

ROBINSON, . . . [21]

ROBISON, *i.e.* ROBINSON, BENJAMIN (1666—30 Apr. 1724). 𝕻. Born at Derby. Educated in the Academy of John Woodhouse [*q.v.*]. Chaplain to Sir John Gell, Hopton, Derb.; at Normanton to Samuel Saunders. Minister at Findern (ordained at Mansfield, 10 O. 1688); kept school there; removed, 1693, to Hungerford, Berks, where his school developed (1696) into an Academy for ministerial training; removed, 1700, to London as successor to Woodhouse; Fund Manager from 3 F. 1700/1; Salters' Hall lecturer, 1705; an original Trustee, 1711, of Daniel Williams' foundations; a subscriber at Salters' Hall, 1719. At that time he was living "in Spittle-Square, numb. 5, near Bishopsgate-Barr." (*D. Ev. M.*) [25]

ROBISON, *i.e.* ROBINSON, NATHANIEL (*d.* May 1696). 𝕮. He appears at Southampton in 1643, preaching, but not ordained. In Oct. 1648 he held the rectory of St. Lawrence, Southampton; before 1653 (probably by 1650) he was rector of All Saints', Southampton; ejected, 1662. He suffered imprisonment for conventicling. The Episc. Returns, 1669, report him as preaching at Southampton to a conventicle "of Independants greater than all the rest," viz. three of Presbyterians, three of Anabaptists, one of Quakers and one Fifth Monarchy. Licensed, 17 Apr. 1672, to preach "in the House of Anne Knight Widdow," Southampton; also, 30 Apr. 1672, as "Pr. Teacher in his howse in Southampton"; also, 22 July 1672, being "of the Congregationall perswasion to teach in the house of John Wheale," and in that of Thomas Phelps, both at Romsey, Hants. At Southampton he founded the Above Bar congregation, organised, 3 Aug. 1688, with ruling elders at the unanimous vote of the congregation, who hoped that "God shall persuade our said pastor," since Robinson himself was "not in all points satisfied concerning the office of ruling elders" (and therefore no Presbyterian in theory). In 1694 William Bolar became his assistant. The father of Isaac Watts [*q.v.*] was one of his deacons. He was buried at All Saints', Southampton, on 27 May 1696. (*As. C. Ds. P. T.*) [100]

ROCHDALE. Ejected here was Robert Bath or Booth, born in Kent; of Brasenose Coll., Oxford; matric., 6 Dec. 1622, aged 16; B.A., 1625/6; M.A., 1629; married a niece of Archbishop Laud, who sent him to Lancashire (his father, John, was a Manchester man); vicar of Rochdale, 2 Mar. 1635/6; member of the Bury Classis; ejected, 1662; preaching at Rochdale in 1669; licensed, 8 May 1672, as Pr. Teacher in a house called Underwood in Rochdale parish; *d.* 12 Mar. 1673/4. (*C. F. Nk. T.*) [59, 61]

ROCHESTER. Ejected here was Allyn Acworth (25 July 1613–1674) of Magdalen Hall, Oxford; matric., 4 Nov. 1631, aged 18; rem. to New Inn Hall; B.A., 1633; M.A., 1635/6; vicar of St. Nicholas', Rochester, 1649; ejected, 1660; vicar of Wandsworth, Surrey, 1661; apparently conformed. (*C. F. K.*) [55]

ROCK, WILLIAM (*b.* 1624?). [? Born at Shrewsbury. Son of Thomas Rocke, glover. From Shrewsbury grammar school admitted sizar at St. John's Coll., Cambridge, 9 Apr. 1640, aet. 16; matric., 1640, as "Knock"; did not graduate.] Ejected from the vicarage of Mayfield, Staff. (*C. Jo. P. V.*) [96]

RODBARD, THOMAS, Alderman. 𝕻. His surname is also spelled Rodberd and Radbor; he is probably identical with Thomas Robards, who in 1677 was a merchant in George Yard, Lombard Street. Chosen as a Correspondent for Somerset, 14 July 1690. First attended as Manager, 10 Nov. 1690. He was also a Manager of the reconstituted Fund (1695). His last attendance was on 8 June 1713. (*Ld. M.*) [92, 162, 168]

ROGERS, EDWARD (*d.* 1703?). 𝕻. Calamy makes him ejected from the rectory of Westcote, Glouc., and also from Medley, Heref., and thinks one of the two was a sequestered living. Edward Loggine, M.A., was rector of Westcote, 1630–72; Rogers may have been his curate, there is no evidence of sequestration. Medley is in Oxfordshire, but it is not a benefice, it is in the parish of Wolvercote. John Reeve, M.A., ejected, 1660, from the sequestered rectory of Springfield, Essex, was Presbyterian preacher at Chelmsford till his removal to London (1680); it is not known at what date Rogers succeeded him. (*C. E. P. Wc.*) [38]

ROGERS, TIMOTHY, M.A. (24 May 1658–Nov. 1728). 𝕻. Born at Barnard Castle, Durh. Son of John Rogers (21 Apr. 1610—28 N. 1680), ejected (1662) from the vicarage of Croglin, Cumb. Matric. at Glasgow, 1673, and graduated M.A., afterwards studying under Edward Veal [*q.v.*]. Evening Lecturer at Crosby Square, Bishopsgate. After 1682, prostrated by hereditary hypochondria. Recovering in 1690, he was evening Lecturer at Crosby Hall in conjunction with Thomas Kentish [*q.v.*]. In 1692 he became assistant to John Shower [*q.v.*]. Presented in 1692 two of his publications to Glasgow University "in token of his gratitude." Left the ministry in 1707, his hypochondria returning. Retired to Wantage, Berks, and there died; buried, 29 N. 1728. (*D. Gm. W.*) [3, 166]

ROKEBY, MADAM. Probably Elizabeth (*d.* 28 Jan. 1705/6), daughter of Thomas Bourchier, and widow of William Rokeby (1632—2 Feb. 1662/3) of Sandall. For another William Rokeby, *see* Shaw, Joseph. (*H.*) [139]

ROMAN CATHOLICISM. [188]

ROMFORD ('Rumford'). [40]

ROMSEY ('Rumsey'). Ejected here was John Warren; possibly related to Thomas Warren, M.A. [*q.v.*]. Presented, 1664, for not attending Romsey parish church. (*C.*) [101]

ROOD, *i.e.* ROODE, ONESIPHORUS, B.A. (1621–1712?). Son of Edward Roode, incumbent of Thame, Oxfordshire. Matric. at New Inn Hall, Oxford, 27 Oct. 1637, aged 16; B.A., 1641; incorp. at Cambridge, 1645. After the exclusion of the bishops (1642) he was chaplain to the House of Lords. In 1648 he succeeded Herbert Palmer as preacher in the New Chapel (now Christ Church), Westminster, from which he was ejected. Retiring to Hackney, he assisted William Bates, D.D., at Mare Street. He preached later (from 1685?) at Clapham. The allusion to services for the prisoners at the Compter [*q.v.*] is interesting. A "very strong healthy man," he lived to be upwards of ninety, but the date of death is not recorded. (*C. F. We.*) [3]

ROPE MAKERS ALLEY, starting westward just above the north-west end of the section known as Little Moorfields, is represented now by Ropemaker Street, Finsbury. Daniel Defoe died at his lodgings in this Alley. (*Lo. Sl.*) [3]

ROSE, THOMAS (*d.* 1697). **P.** Born near Sheffield. Educ. at Rotherham grammar school. With his schoolfellows did "great execution" on a detachment of the king's forces during the Civil War. Vicar of Blidworth, Notts; ejected, 1662. Removing to Nottingham, he was there imprisoned; he afterwards lived in the adjoining hamlet of Adbolton. The Episc. Returns, 1669, report him as preaching to "Presbyterians in great numbers Taylors, weavers, & poore Mechanicks. At the houses of William Marsh & Mordecai Shepheard, West Bridgeford," Notts; also to "about 30" persons in Wysall, Notts, "Att the house of John Cumberland on the Lords day both morning & evening in time of Divine Service"; also, as one of two preachers to 20 persons in Bradmore, Notts, "At the house of Mr Robert Kirkby on Sundayes, morning & evening, in time of Divine Service." Licensed, 2 May 1672, as "Pr. Teacher in his howse," Adbolton, Notts. Again imprisoned during the Monmouth rebellion, he resumed preaching, and died under excommunication. The Common Fund granted him, 1690, £6 a year at Adbolton (reduced from 1695 to £4). His death was reported by Dr. Bates on 10 May 1697.

His son Thomas was ordained by presbyters at Mansfield in 1681. (*C. M. P. T. Y.*) [83]

ROSS, Heref. [45, 48]

ROSSITER, . . . Rossiter (no Christian name) is given in Evans' List as one of three preachers at Westbury, Wilts, 1717; he is mentioned in the Fund Minutes, 7 Jan. 1716/7, at the head of a number of neighbouring Ministers testifying to a Student. He died before 1729. (*Ev. M.*) [92, 93]

ROSTON ('Rosson'), a hamlet in Norbury parish, Derb., not far from the Staffordshire border. [27]

ROTHERHAM ('Rotheram'), W.R. (misplaced in N.R.). Ejected here was Luke Clayton, *b.* at Rotherham, of Trinity Coll., Cambridge; matric. sizar, 1637; B.A., 1640/1; rem. to St. Catharine's Hall; M.A., 1644; vicar of Rotherham; held on there till Jan. 1662/3 and was imprisoned in consequence; preacher some years at Greasbrough Chapel, then in Rotherham parish; preaching at Rotherham and Swaith in 1669; licensed, 30 Apr. 1672, as Grāll Pr. Teacher; *d.* 13 June 1674, aged about 50. (*C. Rb. T. Tc. V.*) [136]

ROTHERHITHE ('Rotherith'). [3]

ROTHWELL ('Rowell'). [76, 184 *sqq.*]

ROUSE, LADY. Elizabeth (*d.* 1692), daughter of John Lisley, of Moxhall, War., married Sir Edward Rouse, bart. (*d.* 5 Nov. 1677), of Rouselench, Wor. (*Ba.*) [117]

ROW, *i.e.* ROWE, BENONI (1659—30 Mar. 1706). **C.** Born in London. Son of William Rowe by his wife Alice, daughter of Thomas Scott, the regicide. Educ. at Newington Green under Theophilus Gale, M.A. [*q.v.*]. Ministered at Epsom, Surr. (1690–99), and then succeeded Stephen Lobb [*q.v.*] at Fetter Lane. A Manager (1696) of the Congregational Fund. He married Sarah, only daughter of John

Rowe (1626—18 Oct. 1677), ejected (1660) from Westminster Abbey (who is often described as his father).

His eldest son, Thomas (1687–1715), was husband of Elizabeth Rowe, the poetess. (*Cf. Co. D. Nq.* (8 Nov. 1912) *W.*) [3]

ROWE, THOMAS, M.A. (1631—9 Oct. 1680). **P.** Born at North Petherwin, Devon. Son of Thomas Rowe, attorney. Matric. at Exeter Coll., Oxford, 17 Dec. 1650; B.A., 1654; rem. to Gloucester Hall, and thence to New Coll., M.A., 1657, and Chaplain. Rector of Lytchett Matravers, Dors., 1657; ejected, 1662. Preached some time as chaplain in house of Thomas Moore, at Spargrove, in Batcombe parish, Som. The Episc. Returns, 1665, report him as "Resident at Hampleston," *i.e.* Ham Preston, Dors. Preached at Little Canford, near Wimborne. Licensed, 8 May 1672, as "Pr. Teacher" in his house at Wimborne, Dors., also (same date) as "Grāll Pr. Teacher." A Meeting-house at Wimborne, the first in Dorset, was built in 1672. He died at Wimborne, and was buried at Lytchett, where he had married (1665) Sarah Conant. (*C. F. Od. P. T.*) [35]

ROWE, THOMAS (1657—18 Aug. 1705). **C.** Born in London. Elder son of John Rowe (1626—18 Oct. 1677), ejected (1660) from Westminster Abbey. Probably educ. at Newington Green under Theophilus Gale, M.A. [*q.v.*]. In 1678 he succeeded Gale both in his Academy and his ministry. The congregation he removed (1681) from Holborn to Girdlers' Hall, Basinghall Street. The Academy migrated, first to Clapham, next (1687 ?) to Little Britain. As a tutor, he made his mark in "free philosophy," untrammelled by the Aristotelian tradition; no tutor turned out more pupils of distinction; several had bursaries from the Fund. He was an original Manager (1695) of the Congregational Fund, and one of its correspondents for Cornwall, Devon, and Somerset. In 1699 he succeeded Stephen Lobb [*q.v.*] as a Pinners' Hall lecturer. (*Cf. Co. D. W.*) [35, 42, 110, 165, 183]

ROWE, THOMAS (*fl.* 1690–1735). **P.** Son of Thomas Rowe, M.A. (1631–1680) [*q.v.*]. He received from the Common Fund (1691) a bursary of £5, while under Thomas Rowe (1657–1705) [*q.v.*] (of a different family), and (1692) a bursary of £10 for study at Utrecht. He was Minister at Poole, Dors., in 1735. (*C. M. Mh. P.*) [35]

ROWLEY REGIS. Ejected here was William Turton, B.A. [*q.v.*]. [96]

ROYSTON. Ejected here was Nathaniel Ball (1623–July 1672), of King's Coll., Camb.; matric. sizar, 1644; B.A., 1647/8; ? M.A., 1660; held the sequestered rectory of Barley, Herts, 1652 (?); ejected, 1660; vicar of Royston, 1660; ejected, 1662; preaching at Thaxted, Ess., in 1669; licensed, 25 May 1672, as Grāll Pr. Teacher, being of Little Chishall, Ess.; licensed, July and 10 Aug. 1672, as Pr. Teacher in his house at Epping, Ess.; his house licensed, same dates, Pr. (*C. T. Uh. V.*) [51]

RUGBY. [119]

RUGELY CHAPPELL. [15] *See* Cheshire

RULSTON. [136] *See* Yorkshire, W.R.

RUMFORD. [40] *See* Essex

RUMSEY. [101] *See* Hampshire

RUSSENDAILE. [121] *See* Westmorland

RUSTON, EAST. Ejected here, in 1662, was John Elwood, who afterwards conformed [? of Sidney Sussex Coll., Cambridge; matric. sizar, 1648/9; B.A., 1652/3; M.A., 1656]; he was vicar of East Ruston, 1661; also vicar of Happisburgh, with Walcot, Norf., 1661; he again became vicar of Happisburgh, 1667, also rector of Ridlington, Norf., 1668. (*C. Nb. V.*) [74]

RUTHIN. Ejected here was Ellis or Elisha Rowland (son of Rowland Thomas, of Beaumaris, Anglesea), admitted ('Elizeus') sizar at St. John's Coll., Cambridge, 5 July 1639, aged 18; did not graduate; warden of Ruthin College; ejected, 1660 ?; his wife kept school; licensed ('Ellise'), Sept. 1672, as Pr., being of Carnarvon; his house there licensed, same time, Pr.; fled to Cheshire; *d.* there about 1683. (*C. Jo. T. V.*) [141, 149]

RUTLAND. [87, 168, 176] All is in the Book-keeper's hand, except the headings "Rutland" in the earliest handwriting. The returns are numbered 22, 82, and 110.

Okeham is Oakham [*q.v.*]

RYE. [116]

RYTHER, JOHN (*d.* 27 Jan. 1703/4). **C.** Son of John Ryther (1632–June 1681), son of a Quaker at York, ejected, 1662, from the vicarage of Ferryby, Yorks. Chaplain in merchant ships to the East and West Indies; pastor from 1686 of Bridlesmith Gate congregation, Nottingham, removed (3 O. 1689) to Castle Gate. His daughter Anne married Robert Kippis (*d.* 1730), and was mother of Andrew Kippis, D.D. (28 Mar. 1725—8 O. 1795), the biographer. (*C. D. No. P.*) [82, 84]

SACRAMENTAL COMMUNION. [156]

SAFFIELD, *i.e.* SUFFIELD, JOHN. The Suffield family was prominent in the early history of the Evesham congregation. Among the original trustees of the Oat Street Meeting-house (3 Oct. 1737) for "Protestant Dissenters commonly called Presbyterians" were Gerard Suffield, of London, gentleman, and Thomas Suffield, of Evesham, maltster. (*Cr.*, 1852.) [127]

SAFFORD, THOMAS, B.A. (*b.* 1621). **P.** Third son of Bartholomew Safford, rector of Enmore, Som. Matric. at New Inn Hall, Oxford, 26 Jan. 1637/8, aged 16; B.A., 1641. Appointed (1646) to rectory of Isfield, Suss.; ejected, 1660; held the chapelry of Bicknoller, Som., in succession to his brother, Bartholomew; ejected, 1662. The Episc. Returns, 1669, report him as one of the preachers at various houses in Bicknoller and Stogumber; also at houses in Crowcombe, Som.; also at the house of George Poole, Stringston, Som.; also to 40 persons at houses in Holford, Som.; also to 260 persons at various houses in Bridgwater, Som. Licensed, 8 May 1672, as "Pr. Teacher in the howses of Richard Gilling and Hannah Safford" in Bicknoller, Som. There he continued many years. (*C. F. P. T.*) [91]

SAFFRON WALDEN ('Waldon'). [40, 41]

SAGAR, CHARLES, B.A. (1636—13 F. 1697/8). **P.** Born at Ightenhill, parish of Whalley, Lanc. Son of Thomas Sagar, farmer. From Burnley grammar school admitted sizar at St. John's Coll., Cambridge, 28 May 1653, aet. 17; matric., 1653; B.A., 1657. Master (21 Jan. 1655/6) of Blackburn grammar school; ejected, 1660. Began to preach, 1660; left Blackburn (1666) owing to the Five Mile Act. The Episc. Returns, 1669, report at Blackburn "Severall Conventicles of Nonconformists, the hearers of them usually to the number of 100 of all sorts & condicons." Licence noted, Feb. 1672/3, to Charles Sagar, "Pr. Teacher of Blackborne Lancash." Imprisoned, 1683. Ministered at Walmsley (1686–7) and at Darwen, 1687 till death. Buried at Blackburn. (*C. Jo. Nl. P. T. V.*) [61, 64]

SAGAR, or SAGER, JOSHUA (1665/6?–28 Mar. 1710). **P.** Son of Charles Sagar [*q.v.*]. Entered Frankland's Academy, 9 June 1683. Preached at Alverthorpe (near Wakefield) and Pontefract, alternating at both places with Peter Naylor (1636–May 1690), ejected from Westhoughton Chapel, Lanc., and, after Naylor's death, with Jeremiah Gill [*q.v.*]. Ordained at Darwen, 20 Sept. 1693. Recognised pastor at Alverthorpe, 1693. The part of Lupset House in his possession was registered for worship, July 1696. His congregation removed to a new Meeting-house in Westgate, Wakefield, opened 29 Aug. 1697. He was buried at Tingley, in West Ardsley parish, W.R., on 31 Mar. 1710, being "about 44" at death. He married (18 May 1692) Baptista (*d.* 28 June 1739), daughter of Capt. Poole of Wakefield (cousin to Matthew Poole, M.A. [*q.v.*]). (*Fr. Ht. My. Nr. Ps. Sr. Wm.*)

He has been confused with another Joshua Sagar, baptized 6 Jan. 1655 (*Cp.*), in 16th year in 1680, *i.e.* born in 1665 (*Nk.*); son of John Sagar of Bradford, matric. sizar, at Christ's Coll., Cambridge, Dec. 1681; B.A., 1681/2; ord. deacon at York, Dec. 1690; priest, Sept. 1692. (*Cp. Nk.*) [130]

SALCALD, SASHIELD, *i.e.* SALKELD, JOHN (1622—26 D. 1699). Calamy makes him M.A. and Fellow of Queens' Coll., Cambridge; no trace of him at that University or at Oxford or Dublin. Rector of Worlington, Suff.; ejected, 16 Feb. 1662/3. Retired to his estate at Walsham-le-Willows, Suff. Imprisoned, 1670, for conventicling. Licensed, 30 Apr. 1672, as "Pr. Teacher" in his house at Walsham, house licensed Pr. same date. Preached also, by connivance, in Walsham parish church and in that of Badwell Ash, adjacent; imprisoned for this at Bury St. Edmunds, 1683–6. The Common Fund voted him, 9 N. 1691, £8 a year for Walsham, reduced (1695) to £6, and paid to 1699. His funeral sermon was preached in Walsham church by Josiah Chorley [*q.v.*]. (*B. C. M. P. T.*) [105]

SALISBURY. Ejected here were: (1) William Eyre (son of Giles, of Whiteparish, Wilts), of Magdalen Hall, Oxford; matric., 3 July 1629, aged 16; B.A., 1632; M.A., 1635; rector of Compton Bassett, Wilts, 1641; held the sequestered rectory of Odstock, Wilts, 1641; Lecturer at St. Edmund's, Salisbury, 1654; ejected, 1662; after a time retired to his estate at Melksham, Wilts; *d.* there, buried 30 Jan. 1669/70. (*C. F.*) (2) Thomas Rashley, or Rashely, of Trinity Coll., Cambridge; matric. pensioner, 1629; B.A., 1632/3; Fellow, 1633; M.A., 1636; one of the subscribers to the Wiltshire testimony, 1648; his position at Salisbury is not known; after ejection he lived at Avebury, Wilts. (*C. Tc. V.*) (3) John Strickland (from Westmorland), of Queen's Coll., Oxford; matric., 15 May 1618, aged 17; B.A., 1622; M.A., 1625; B.D., 1632; licensed to preach, 1633; chaplain to earl of Hertford; rector of Podymore Milton, Som., 1632; rector of St. Peter-the-Poor, London, 27 Oct. 1643; member of the Westminster Assembly; master of St. Nicholas' Hospital, East Harnham, Wilts, 1646; vicar of Lancaster, 12 Nov. 1647; rector of St. Edmund's, Salisbury, 1649 (his admission also to the vicarage of Kendal, 16 July 1656, seems to have been an accommodation, ended in 1659); ejected, 1662; preaching at Salisbury and Tisbury, Wilts, in 1669; buried in St. Edmund's churchyard, 25 Oct. 1670. (*C. F. N. Nk. T.*) (4) William Troughton [*q.v.*]. [123]

SALISBURY STREET is not in Rotherhithe, though very near it, but in Bermondsey; it runs northward towards the Thames from Jamaica Road to Bermondsey Wall. [3]

SALOP. *See* Shrewsbury or Shropshire

SALTASH. Ejected here was John Hickes, B.A. (1633—6 Oct. 1685); born in Yorkshire; elder son of William Hickes; educ. at Thirsk school and Trinity Coll., Dublin; B.A., 4 May 1655, and Fellow, rector of Stoke Damarel, Devon; perpetual curate of Saltash, 1660; ejected, 1662; the Episc. Returns, 1665, report him as living at Saltash, "notoriously disaffected"; removed to Kingsbridge, 1666; licensed, 2 Apr. 1672, as "Presbyt. Teacher in any licensed place"; also, 11 Apr. 1672, as "Pr. Teacher" in his house in Kingsbridge, Devon; his new-built Meeting-house at Kingsbridge licensed, Sept. 1672; his house in Hatton Garden, London, licensed, Dec. 1672; Minister at Portsmouth, 1675–81; removed to Keynsham, Som.; executed at Glastonbury for treason in the Monmouth rebellion; his younger brother was George Hickes, D.D., the Nonjuror. (*C. D. Db. P. T.*) [19, 20]

SALTERS' HALL. The Hall of the Salters' Guild is in St. Swithin's Lane, Cannon Street. Adjoining it was the Meeting-house, removed in the latter part of the last century for the enlargement of the Hall. (*Lo. W.*) [154]

SALVINGTON, hamlet in West Tarring parish, Suss. [113]

SAMPSON, HENRY, M.D. (1629?—23 July 1700). **P.** Born at South Leverton, Notts; eldest son of William Sampson (1590?–1636?), dramatist. His mother was remarried (1637) to Obadiah Grew, D.D. (*see* Grace), who taught his stepson at the Atherstone grammar school. From the Coventry grammar school he matric. (1646) at Pembroke Hall, Cambridge; B.A., 1649/50; Fellow, 1650; M.A., 1653. In 1650 his college placed him in the sequestered rectory of Framlingham, Suff., where, as at Coventry, he preached, though never ordained. Ejected, 1660, he continued to preach at Framlingham, and founded the Presbyterian congregation (now Unitarian). He studied medicine at Padua, graduated M.D. at Leiden (1668), and was made honorary fellow of the London College of Physicians (1680). He was a hearer of John Howe, M.A. [*q.v.*]. He was also a Manager (1695) of the reconstituted Fund. He had one son, Nathaniel (*d.* 18 Apr. 1669). He lived at Clapham; died on a visit to Clayworth, Notts, and was there buried, "next his Son." He projected a work to contain biographies of all the Ejected Ministers; his collections toward this were of use to Calamy in his Account, 1713; transcripts of some of his other papers are in the British Museum, and have been partly printed by Robert Brook Aspland in *Cr.*, 1862. (*C. D. Mu. P. V. Wc.*) [6, 7, 9, 10, 12, 41, 52, 56, 68, 70, 87, 106, 119, 162, 164, 167, 168]

SANDERS, HENRY (*fl.* 1690–1739). **P.** Calamy mentions "Mr Sanders" as "Minister at Oxford" in 1698. He appears in Evans' List as Minister (and resident) at Long Combe, Oxon, near Woodstock. The Fund voted him £8 a year on 6 May 1717; reduced, 1723, to £6, and paid to 1739; after which the congregation disappears. (*Cm. Ev. M.*) [85]

SANDERS, *i.e.* SAUNDERS, JULIUS (*fl.* 1680–1730). **C.** Born in Warwickshire; collateral descendant of Lawrence Saunders, the second of the Marian victims, burned at Coventry, 8 Feb. 1554/5. Went to Oxford; did not matric.; studied at the Academy of John Shuttlewood, B.A. (*see under* John Shuttlewood, his son), at Sulby, Northants. Imprisoned for two years at Warwick for preaching at Bedworth, Warw.; six months later was instrumental in founding (25 Jan. 1686/7) a Congregational church at Bedworth. He declined a call to Rothwell, Northants, and was ordained for Bedworth (16 N. 1687) in the house of John Bunn [*q.v.*] at Finham. For a time (before 10 Oct. 1693) he was under the influence of Richard Davis [*q.v.*]. From 1707 to 1720 he preached much at Coventry. A

Meeting-house was built for him at Bedworth in 1726. He was living in 1730. He educated for the ministry his sons John (1694—11 Apr. 1768) and Julius (*d.* 28 Jan. 1749/50) and his nephew Thomas (*d.* 21 July 1736). [The Book-keeper's entry "Sanders a junior" is clearly due to a misreading of the name Julius; there was no junior Saunders ministering at Bedworth in 1690.] (*B. Si. Uh.*) [117, 118]

SANDERS, or SAUNDERS, THOMAS (*fl.* 1682–1715). 𝔓. In 1682 was a student with Thomas Doolittle [*q.v.*]. Minister at Havant, Hants, in 1691–2; removed before 31 Oct. 1692. Minister at Wincanton, Som., Midsummer 1699–Midsummer 1712 (receiving £10 yearly from the Fund). Minister at Woodstock, Oxon, from Midsummer 1713 (receiving £6 from the Fund). On 7 F. 1714/5 a sum of £5 was voted him at "New Wodstock in Oxfordshr considering his Extreem Necessities." Nothing further is known of him. Evans' List gives no congregation at Woodstock. Henry Sanders [*q.v.*] was probably a relative. (*Du. Ev. M.*) [4]

SANDIACRE ('Sandyacre'). Ejected here was Joseph Moore, son of William Moore, tailor, of Nottingham; adm. sizar at St. John's Coll., Cambridge, 29 June 1655, aet. 17; matric., 1655; B.A., 1658/9; rector of Sandiacre; after ejectment he preached privately; licensed, June 1672, as Grāll Pr. Teacher, being of Hopton, Derb.; also, same month, as Pr. Teacher in his house at Hopton; his house licensed, same date, Pr.; also, 22 July 1672, Pr.; also, 10 Aug. 1672, Pr.; *d.* 25 Nov. 1684. (*C. Jo. T. V.*) [82]

SANDORS, or SAUNDORS, *i.e.* SANDERS, RICHARD (*d.* 12 July 1692). 𝔓. Born at Peyhembury, near Honiton; son of Lawrence Sanders. Younger brother of Humphrey Saunders, M.A., ejected from the rectory of Holsworthy, Devon, and of Major Saunders, a fierce parliamentarian. Went to Oxford at the age of 16, but did not matriculate; removed 1642, and committed to Exeter gaol. Held the sequestered rectory of Kentisbeare, Devon; ejected, 1660; rector of Loxbeare, Devon; ejected, 1662. Removed to Plymtree, afterwards to Honiton. The Episc. Returns, 1665, report him as "a lurking wanderer & seditious convent . . . sometymes lurkeing in Tiverton, sometymes in Loxbeare, & other places for the like ends." The Episc. Returns, 1669, report him as one of the preachers to 100 persons, "most of them Inconsiderable," at Cruwys-Morchard, Devon, "At ye house of one George Brooke an excom̄unicated person—every Sunday & Wednesday." Also as one of the preachers at Cullompton, "twice every Sunday," to "nigh 500" persons, "cheife Abbettors are: Willm Sumpter, a Capt under ye late Usurper, Christopher Clarke, merchant, James Hartnoll, Grocer, Anne Pulman. But most of ym are women & Children & men of noe esteeme." Also as one of two preachers at Uffculme to 300 persons "At ye house of Humphrey Boden, who entertaines the speakers—a constant Conventicle." Signed the thanks from Devon Ministers. Licensed, 11 Apr. 1672, as "neare Honiton, Devon̄. to be a Presbyt. Teacher in any allowed Place," also on 8 May 1672 as Pr. Teacher in a house at Tiverton. At this time he preached regularly at Tiverton, and again from 1687. His dwelling latterly was at Kentisbeare, Devon, and he was one of three preachers at Honiton, from 1687, in the back-house of William Clarke, chandler. He was the first Moderator of the Devon and Cornwall Assembly, at Tiverton, 17 and 18 Mar. 1691. In the Crispian controversy he was one of the "New Methodists," so called, and a strong approver of Daniel Williams' "Gospel Truth," 1692. (*C. Em. Mh. T. Wc.*) [30]

SANDWICH. Ejected here was Robert Webber [? of Wadham Coll., Oxford; matric., 20 Feb. 1648/9; Fellow, 1649; B.A., 1648 (*sic*); M.A., 1650], who held the sequestered vicarage of St. Clement's, 1650; ejected, 1660; some time after 1666 he was Master of Sandwich grammar school; *d.* 1671. (*C. F. K.*) [57]

SASHIELD. *See* Salcald

SAUNDERWICK, *i.e.* SANDERCOCK, JACOB (Sept. 1664–1729). 𝔓. Born in Cornwall. Educated at a grammar school and the Academy of Matthew Warren [*q.v.*]. Began his ministry at Tiverton. Ordained, 1 May 1688, and assisted Henry Flamank [*q.v.*] at Tavistock, where he succeeded him in 1692 as Minister of the Abbey Chapel, and opened a school. In theology he was a Baxterian. He is the subject of one of the character-sketches by John Fox (10 May 1693—3 S. 1747). From 1705 he received a grant of £6 a year for Tavistock; reduced, 1723, to £5. (*Ev. M. Mh.*) [30]

SAVOY CONFESSION. [156]

SAWRY, COL., *i.e.* ROGER SAWREY (*d.*

6 Aug. 1699). C. A Cromwellian soldier; member of the London flock of George Cokayne [*q.v.*]; living at Broughton Tower, and present at the formation (1669) of the Tottlebank congregation, which included Baptists. A chalice, paten, chair, table, etc., which belonged to him are preserved by this congregation. He had also an interest in Tatham Fells Chapel, and a knowledge of Bispham. The lost paper, No. 111, with information about these places, was doubtless written by him. (*Nl. Wn.*) [63]

SAY, GILES (1632—8 Apr. 1692). C. Born at Southampton; of Huguenot descent. Ordained by presbyters, at Bishopstoke, Hants, as vicar of St. Michael's Southampton, 1652; ejected, 1662. The Episc. Returns, 1669, report him as preaching at one of three Presbyterian conventicles in Southampton. Licensed, 2 May 1672, as "Congr. Teacher in his howse in Southampton." Pastor at Guestwick (on recommendation of London Ministers) from Nov. 1687 till death. (*B. C. P. T.*) [74]

SCANDARET, JOHN (*fl.* 1691–3). Son of Stephen Scandrett [*q.v.*]. Received (1691–3) £10 bursary as Student under John Ker [*q.v.*] and John Short [*q.v.*]. (*M.*) [43]

SCANDRETT, or SCANDARET, STEPHEN, M.A. (1631 ?—8 D. 1706). P. Son of a yeoman of the wardrobe to Charles I. Matric. as servitor at Wadham Coll., Oxford, 12 D. 1654; B.A., 1656/7; M.A., 1659; incorp. at Cambridge, 1659, and made chaplain of Trinity Coll.; ejected thence, 1660. He then became curate to Edward Eyres, vicar of Haverhill, Suff. Having received Presbyterian ordination, on the passing of the Uniformity Act (1662) he was prosecuted for preaching in the church and excommunicated for preaching in his own house. He preached for a while at Waterbeach, Cambs. The Episc. Returns, 1669, report him as preaching at Haverhill to "Presbyterians and Quakers" (he had two disputations with Friends); and at Thurlow Magna, Suff., to "60 sometimes 100" persons "At the house of one John Barnes & of Samuel Alison." Licensed, 13 May 1672, as Pr. Teacher in "an outhouse of Joseph Alders joining to his dwelling house in Haverill." He remained Minister at Haverhill till his death. He received, 1690–92, a grant of £6 for Haverhill from the Common Fund. His preaching extended over a wide area. 'Hannerick' is Haverhill. (*B. C. D. E. F. M. P. T. Tc.*) [11, 39, 43, 105]

SCHOLES, NATHANIEL (1665—2 Oct. 1702). P. Born in Salford, Lanc. Son of Jeremiah Scholes, M.A. (1629—27 Apr. 1685), ejected from the vicarage of Norton, Derb. Nephew of William Rathband [*q.v.*]. Entered Frankland's Academy along with John Chorlton [*q.v.*] on 4 Apr. 1682. Apparently he followed Thomas Lawton (*d.* 28 F. 1688/9), the Conforming but Puritan incumbent of Newton Heath Chapel, and had part use of the building till 1691, when his baptismal register begins. His separate services were apparently in a barn at Culcheth in Newton Heath. In 1698 a Meeting-house was built for him at Dob Lane, Failsworth. From 1697 he ministered also at Macclesfield, Ches., still living at Salford. From 1700, Joseph Heywood (*d.* Oct. 1729) was Scholes' assistant at Dob Lane, and became his successor, removing to Stand (1713). (*Gd.*) [61]

SCOFFIN, WILLIAM (1655 ?–Nov. 1732). P. Self-taught, and a good mathematician. Curate of Brothertoft, a chapelry in Kirton parish, Linc.; joined the Nonconformists, Aug. 1686. Minister at Sleaford, Linc., for over forty years. Very poor, but noted for his charities. For Sleaford (no Minister specified) the Common Fund granted £8 a year (1691); reduced in 1695 to £5 a year, and not paid after 1696. Special grants of £5 were voted to him, 9 N. 1730; and 5 Mar. 1732/3, in ignorance of his death; this was ordered, 4 June 1733, to be paid to his widow or his congregation as might be "most expedient." Buried, 12 N. 1732. (*D. Ev. M.*) [71]

SCOONES, JOHN. A grant of £20 "for perfecting his studies" was made by the Common Fund, 30 N. 1691. (*M.*) [57]

SCOTCHMAN. [2, 9, 22, 80]

SCOTLAND. [23, 80]

SEABRIDGE, township in Stoke-upon-Trent parish. [98]

SEAFORD. [115]

SEARLE, or SERLE, JOHN, M.A. (1613–Oct. 1699). P. Of Magdalen Coll., Oxford; M.A., 21 June 1634. Held (1656) the vicarage of Rattery, Devon.; sequestered from a pluralist; ejected, 1660; rector of Plympton St. Mary, 1660; ejected, 1662. Licensed, 30 Apr. 1672, as "Pr.", being of Plympton; his house there licensed, 30 Sept. 1672. Signed the thanks from Devon Ministers. The Fund granted him, 1690, £8 a year for Plympton; reduced to £6 in 1695, and paid to Midsummer, 1669. (*C. Em. F. M. P. T. Wc.*) [31]

SEDDON, ROBERT, M.A. (1630?—21 Mar. 1695/6). **P.** Born at Outwood, parish of Prestwich, Lanc. From Ringley school, proceeded to Christ's Coll., Cambridge; B.A., 1650/1; M.A., 1654; incorp. at Oxford, 11 July 1654. Lived in the family of John Angier (1605—1 S. 1677) of Denton, Lanc., till called to the ministry of Gorton Chapel, Lanc.; rector of Kirk Langley, Derb.; ejected, 1662. The Episc. Returns, 1669, report him as one of the preachers to 200 to 400 persons at Little Ireton, Derb., in the house of Col. Saunders; also to "70 or 80 ordinary sort of Tradesmen" at Basford, Notts, in the house of John Clark, M.A., ejected from the vicarage of Codgrave, Notts. Licensed, Nov. 1672, as "Pr. Teacher of Langley." From 1689 he preached at Derby. On the death (4 July 1692) of John Lever [*q.v.*], ejected from Cockey Chapel, Lanc., he succeeded him as Minister to Presbyterians of Bolton, Lanc. By deed of gift (17 F. 1695/6) he presented the land on which the present Bank Street Chapel stands. Buried 24 or 25 Mar. 1695/6; there is a discrepancy as to the exact date. (*Bb. C. Nr. P. T.*) [25, 138]

SEDGLEY. Ejected here was Joseph Eccleshall, B.A. [*q.v.*]. [97]

SEIMOURS COURT, Wilts. Seymour's Court is in Bucks. The reference here is to the seat of the Barons Seymour of Trowbridge, Wilts. [124]

SELBY, W.R. (misplaced in N.R.). [136]

SELLOM, THOMAS. (*Bl.*) [180]

SELSTON. Ejected from this vicarage was Charles Jackson? [son of George, merchant, of Buxton, Derb.; admitted sizar at St. John's Coll., Cambridge, 15 Nov. 1645, aet. 21; matric., 1645]; licensed, Dec. 1672, as Pr. Teacher in a house at Halsam, Notts; afterwards conformed. (*C. Jo. T. V.*) [83]

SEMPLE, GABRIEL, M.A. (1632?–Aug. 1706). **P.** Second son of Sir Bryce Semple, of Cathcart. Educ. Glasgow; M.A., 1653. Minister of Kirkpatrick-Durham, Kirkcudbrightsh., 1657; deprived, 1 O. 1662. He was the earliest of the field preachers, and engaged in several risings against the government in Scotland. Visited Ireland and the North of England. Occupied for some time the church of Ford, Northum. Etal is a chapelry in Ford parish. Declared a traitor, 1679. Arrested, July 1681, in Scotland; broke his bail, and withdrew to England. Reinstated at Kirkpatrick-Durham, 25 Apr. 1689; translated to Jedburgh, 29 O. 1690. (*Sf.*) [80]

SEVENOAKS ('Sevenock'). For this place with Westerham, five miles off, the Common Fund granted (1690) £5 a year; not renewed, 1695. [56]

SEYMONSFORD. [92] *See* Somerset

SHAFTESBURY ('Shaffton'). From the rectory of St. Peter's, Shaftesbury, which in 1654 had been long vacant (*La.*), was ejected (1660) one Hallett, who in 1663 was imprisoned at Dorchester (with four others) for preaching at Shaftesbury; and in the Episc. Returns, 1665, is described as late rector of St. Peter's and reported as "now Resident at Helton," *i.e.* Horton, Dors. This was probably (though the name has been given as Thomas) James Hallett, of neither university who in June 1672, being of Winterborne Kingston, was licensed as Pr. Teacher; a house at Winterborne Kingston and another at Cerne, Dors., having on 16 May been licensed for his services. (*C. La. Od. T.*) [34]

SHALLETT, ARTHUR. **C.** London merchant and M.P. In 1687 he co-operated with Samuel Warburton and Ferdinando Holland (all at that time members of the congregation of Nathaniel Vincent [*q.v.*]) in founding the Charity School in Gravel Lane, Southwark, for the free education of forty poor children. This was a counter-stroke to an offer of free education for the poor by the Jesuit Andrew Poulton (1654—5 Aug. 1710). The number of scholars was subsequently increased to 200. Elected a Treasurer of the Common Fund, 14 July 1690; after 1690, only attended the first meeting in each of the years 1691–2–3. Manager (1695) of the Congregational Fund, and one of its correspondents for Hampshire. Member of the Congregational church at Three Cranes, Fruiterers' Alley, Thames Street, under Thomas Gouge (*see* Gouge, Robert); he procured (1697) the dismissal of Joseph Jacob [*q.v.*] from a weekly lectureship in Gouge's Meeting-house.

His son, Arthur Shallett, **C.**, was assistant to Thomas Mitchell (*d.* 9 Jan. 1720/1) at Stepney from 5 N. 1708; on 4 D. 1718 he resigned, to take effect 25 Mar. 1719, and left the ministry. In 1715 he was living "at Mrs Shallet's in Clapham." (*Cf. Co. Ev. M. W. We.*) [162]

SHANGHBROOK. [33] *See* Devonshire

SHARP, THOMAS, M.A. (30 Oct. 1634–27 Aug. 1693). **P.** Born at Horton Hall, Little Horton, in Bradford parish,

W.R. Eldest son of John Sharp. Cousin to John Sharp (1646–1714), archbishop of York from 1691. Matric. sizar at Clare Hall, Cambridge, 1649; Tillotson was one of his tutors; B.A., 1653; Fellow; M.A., 1657; episcopally ordained, 1660. Began his ministry at Peterborough; returned to Yorkshire, 1660, and held for a short time the rectory (donative) of Adel, West Riding, sequestered from a pluralist; ejected, 1660. Retired to Little Horton for study. Licensed, 20 Apr. 1672, as "Presb. Teacher in his howse in Leeds"; corrected in another entry to Horton; he had asked for a licence to preach in the School-house in Leeds town-end. He preached also at Morley, West Riding, in 1673. In 1678 he succeeded Richard Stretton [*q.v.*] as Minister of Mill Hill Chapel, Leeds (erected 1672), but continued to reside at Horton Hall. [The Book-keeper's spelling of God, without a capital, is conformable to the usage of Philip Henry and Oliver Heywood in their diaries.] (*C. My. P. T. V. Wc. Wl. Y.*) [129]

SHAW, JOSEPH (*bur.* 3 Sept. 1691). **P.** Vicar of Worsbrough, West Riding; ejected. Tutor (till 1671) to William and Godfrey, sons of William Bosvile, J.P. of Gunthwaite, parish of Penistone, West Riding. Licensed, 9 D. 1672, as "Pr. Teacher at the house of Wm Kookby," *i.e.* Rookby, properly Rokeby, whose two houses were licensed, same date, for Presbyterian worship, one at Acknorth, *i.e.* Ackworth, West Riding, another at Shellore, *i.e.* Skellow Grange, West Riding. (William Rokeby's house, Skellow Grange, was certified for Nonconformist worship, April 1699.) He afterwards "preached at a place about six miles west of Hull," *i.e.* Swanland, East Riding. The Common Fund voted him £3 a year from Midsummer 1690. Oliver Heywood's Vellum Book enters his burial "at Woosper [*i.e.* Worsbrough] near Barnsly Sept. 3, '91, had preacht at —— near Hull." (*C. F. Ht. M. Nr. P. T. Y.*) [131, 138]

SHAW, SAMUEL, B.A. (1635—22 Jan. 1696/7). Born at Repton, Derb. Son of Thomas Shaw, blacksmith. From Repton grammar school admitted sizar at St. John's Coll., Cambridge, 23 D. 1650, aged 15; matric., 1651; B.A., 1655/6. Usher in Tamworth grammar school (1656); removed to Moseley, Worc. Ordained by Wirksworth Classis, 12 Jan. 1657/8, as rector of Long Whatton, Leic., a sequestered living; ejected, 1661. He had been a signatory (1659) of the protest against the royalist plans of Sir George Booth. Removed to Cotes-de-Val, near Loughborough, and preached in his own house. In 1666, removed to Ashby-de-la-Zouch, Leic., and became (1668) master of the grammar school. The Common Fund paid him (1690–91) £5 a year for Ashby-de-la-Zouch. (*C. Ds. Jo. M. P. V. Wc.*) [67]

SHEAL, *i.e.* SEAL or SEELE, GEORGE (*fl.* 1662–1715 ?). **C.** Schoolmaster at Cardiff, Glam., and preacher; ejected, 1662. Licensed, 22 July 1672, as "Pr. Teacher" in his house at Marshfield, Glou. Probably the influence of James Forbes [*q.v.*] made him Congregational. He remained Minister at Marshfield till his death (in or soon after 1715), but received (5 O. 1713) a grant of £10 from the Fund as being "past Service"; also (4 O. 1714) a grant of £10. One of his colleagues was Josiah Hort [*q.v.*], who had been a fellow-student with his son. (*C. Ev. M. Mh. P. T.*) [44]

SHEELES. [79] *See* Northumberland

SHEEPSTOR (' Shepistor '). [30]

SHEFFIELD (' Shefield '). [129, 130, 131, 134] Ejected here were (1) Matthew Bloome (*b.* at Brotherton, W.R.), of Magdalene Coll., Cambridge; matric. sizar, 1650; Minister of Attercliffe Chapel, near Sheffield; curate to James Fisher; ejected, 1662; became a maltster; preaching at two conventicles in Sheffield parish, 1669; licensed, 29 May 1672, as Pr. Teacher in a house at Attercliffe; his own house at Attercliffe licensed, Nov. 1672, Pr.; joined Rowland Hancock, 28 July 1676, in gathering a Congregational church, which broke in 1681; Bloome fitted a barn in Attercliffe as Meeting-place for his section; *d.* 13 Apr. 1686. (*C. Ma. T. V.*) (2) James Fisher, probably of Magdalene Coll., Cambridge; matric. sizar, 1622; B.A., 1625/6; M.A., 1629; ministered in London; vicar of Sheffield; ejected, 1662; Congregational; *d.* Jan. 1665/6. (*C. Ma. V.*) (3) Rowland Hancock; held the sequestered vicarage of Ecclesfield, W.R.; ejected, 1660; schoolmaster in Sheffield, 1661; curate to James Fisher, 22 Apr. 1661; ejected, 1662; preaching at Sheffield, 1669; licensed, June 1672, as Pr. Teacher in his own house, Shiercliffe Hall, Sheffield; his house licensed, same date, as Pr. Meeting-place; joined Matthew Bloome, as above, in gathering a Congregational church; when this broke in 1681, Hancock preached in a private house at Attercliffe; *d.* 14 Apr. 1685. (*C. Ma.*) (4) Edward Prime [*q.v.*]

SHEFFIELD, JOHN (1654?—24 Jan. 1725/6). 𝔓. Son of William Sheffield, M.A. (*d.* 1673), ejected (1662) from the rectory of Ibstock, Leic. Passed through Kibworth grammar school, and left business to enter the Academy at Sulby, Northants, of John Shuttlewood, B.A. (*see under* his son, John Shuttlewood). Ordained by presbyters, 27 S. 1682. Chaplain to Mrs Palmer at Temple Hall [*q.v.*], where a Meeting-house was built for him (1689?), since turned into cottages. A grant (1690) of £4 a year from the Common Fund was made to Sheffield for Appleby, Leic.; later (1691) a grant of £8 was made to the place. Sheffield, who preached there two Sundays in the month, was to have £4 of this so long as he did so. [This arrangement lasted till 1703; in 1704 Edward Boucher became Minister at Appleby.] Preached also at Atherstone, Warw. Succeeded (1697) Nathaniel Vincent [*q.v.*] at St. Thomas Street, Southwark. Elected a Fund Manager, 5 O. 1697. Friend of John Locke. Nonsubscriber at Salters' Hall (1719); a Baxterian in sentiment. (*D. Ev. M. W. We.*) [66, 67]

SHELMADINE, *i.e.* SHELMERDINE, DANIEL, M.A. (1 Jan. 1636/7—22 Oct. 1699). 𝔓. Born at Crich, Derb. Son of Thomas Shelmerdine, then its vicar; ejected afterwards from the rectory of Matlock, Derb. From Repton grammar school admitted pensioner at Christ's Coll., Cambridge, 22 May 1652, aged 16; matric., 1652; B.A., 1655/6; M.A., 1659. Ord., 20 May 1657, by Wirksworth Classis, of which his father was a member. Chaplain to Col. Grevis, of Moseley, Worc. Held the vicarage of Barrow-upon-Trent, Derb., with its chapelry of Twyford; ejected, 1662. He rented a farm at Twyford and was several times imprisoned for conventicling. The Episc. Returns, 1669, report him as preaching to Presbyterians at Matlock, Derb., in "the house of Robert Cliffe (a soldier under Lambert)"; also as one of the Lord's Day preachers at the house of Col. Saunders, Little Ireton; and as one of the preachers to a great Meeting of "Presbyterians & Anabaptists" at several houses in Burton-on-Trent, Staff. Licensed, 25 July 1672, as Pr. Teacher in his house at Twyford. Died at Findern, Derb. (*C. Cp. P. T. V.*) [25, 26]

SHELTON, THOMAS. [174]

SHENSTONE ('Shenston'). Ejected here were (1) Gamaliel Dunstall, who migrated from Oxford to Peterhouse, Cambridge, in 1651; B.A., 1653; he afterwards conformed. (*C. V.*) (2) William Grace, M.A. [*q.v.*]. [96, 97]

SHEPISTOR. [30] *See* Devonshire

SHEPPARD, *i.e.* SHEPHERD, WILLIAM (*d.* 1699). ℭ. [One of these names, M.A., Cantab, 1632; another, M.A., Cantab, 1656.] Rector of Tilbrook, Beds; conformed for many years. Resigning (1689?), he became pastor at Oundle, Northants. The Common Fund granted (1691–3) £6 a year for Huntingdon Lecture, not naming Shepherd. He was one of the witnesses against Richard Davis [*q.v.*] at Kettering in 1692. In 1695–6 he received £8 a year for Northampton. He succeeded Thomas Milway [*q.v.*] as Minister at Kettering (1697), and was buried there on 21 Mar. 1698/9. (*C. Cn. Gl. M. P. V.*) [53, 76]

SHEPTON MALLET. Ejected here was David Calderwood. [91]

SHERBORNE ('Sherbourn'). Ejected here were (1) Francis Bampfylde or Bampfield, of Wadham Coll., Oxford; matric., 16 May 1634, aged 18; B.A., 1635; M.A., 1638; rector of Rampisham, Dors., 1640; canon of Exeter, 1641–1646/7; vicar of Sherborne, 1653; ejected, 1662; he shares with Richard Baxter the distinction of being licensed (29 June 1672) simply as "a Nonconforming Minister to teach in any licensed place" (this licence is the only known one on parchment); after many changes he became a Seventh-Day Baptist; *d.* in Newgate prison, 16 Feb. 1683/4. (*C. D. F. T.*) (2) Humphrey Phillips, M.A. [*q.v.*]. [34]

SHERIFF HALES ('Sheriffhayles'), Shrop. and Staff. [16, 88]

SHERWILL, NICHOLAS, M.A. (*d.* 15 May 1696). 𝔓. Born at Plymouth; son of a clergyman. Matric. at Corpus Christi Coll., Oxford, 20 Mar. 1650/1; demy, Magdalen Coll., 1653–60; B.A., 1654; M.A., 1657; chaplain, 1660–61. Episcopally ordained. There is no statement of his ejection; he appears to have left Oxford (1661) for his estate at Plymouth, where he entered on a Nonconformist ministry; his register of baptisms and a few marriages begins in Sept. 1662, and extends to (at least) March 1686/7. The Episc. Returns, 1665, report him as a Nonconformist at Plymouth, "Episcopally Ordayned as he saith, But notoriously disaffected to ye Church of England in her discipline, and two years since endited at ye Towne Hall for a disturbance made by him at a funerall whiles the Comon Prayer was read." Hence he was arrested, 6 O. 1665, kept in close prison, and not released till 30 Mar. 1666 on his bond to leave Plymouth within 48 hours. Licensed, 11 Apr. 1672, as a "Presb. Grāll Teacher" at Plymouth. He maintained his Plymouth congregation till his death, assisted latterly by Byfield, and was succeeded (1698) by John Enty (1675?—26 N. 1743), for whom the Batter Street Meeting-house (subsequently Congregational) was built in 1708. (*D.* (under Enty) *F. Mh. P. T.*) [31]

SHERWOOD, JOSEPH, B.A. (1629?–1705?). Born at Truro. Son of Joseph Sherwood, M.A., vicar of St. Hilary, Corn., 1627. From Plymouth grammar school admitted pensioner at Christ's Coll., Cambridge, 6 July 1647, aged 18; matric., 1647; B.A., 1650. Ejected (1662) from the vicarage of St. Hilary, Corn. Resided at St. Ives till death, and preached regularly there and at Penzance alternately every Lord's-day, besides lectures on the weekdays. The Episc. Returns, 1665, report that "Mr Joseph Sheawood eiected out of St. Hilary for inconformity lives usually in ye parish of St. Earth [St. Erth] in ye Quality of a husbandman he was lately imprisoned for presuming to preach publiquely in ye Church there Contrary to ye Act of Uniformity." Erisey is a manor in the parish of Grade. (*C. Cp. F. P. T. V.*) [18]

SHIELDS, NORTH. [79]

SHIRE HEAD ('Skierstead') in Cleveley, chapelry in Cockerham parish, Lanc.; the Chapel, registered for Dissenting worship, 28 July 1698, was occupied by Nonconformists till about 1720. (*Nl. X.*) [58]

SHOBROOKE ('Shanghbrook'). [33]

SHOREHAM. [113]

SHORT, AMES, M.A. (1616—15 July 1697). **C.** Born at Ashwater, Devon. Third son of John Short of Newton St. Cyres, Devon, gent. Matric. at Exeter Coll., Oxford, 21 N. 1634, aged 18; B.A., 1639; M.A., 1641. Chaplain to Lady Clark, Suff. Minister for 5 years, from 1645, at Topsham, Dev., ordained by the Seventh London Classis, 2 Mar. 1646/7. Vicar of Lyme Regis, Dors., 1649/50; ejected, 1662. His father left him out of his will for his Nonconformity. The Episc. Returns, 1669, report him as one of the preachers to 300 persons "At the house of Thomas Moore Esqr" in Batcombe, Som.; also to 200 at houses in Winsham, Som.; further, at Colyton, Devon, "once a fortnight or 3 weeks, sometimes in one house, sometimes in another & in feilds and Orchards"; and to 200 or 300 at Lyme Regis "some of the towne returned to the Councill by Capt. Alford." Licensed, 13 Apr. 1672, as "Presb. Teacher at his howse in Lime"; this must be an error for Cong.; he certainly ministered to a gathered church of Independents. On 10 May 1672 he signed the Address of thanks to the Crown from Dorset Ministers. So likewise did John Kerridge, M.A., Oxon (*d.* 15 Apr. 1705), master of the grammar school at Abingdon, Berks, and afterwards of that at Lyme Regis (native place of his father, John Kerridge, M.A. (*d.* 1662?), ejected from the rectory of Wootton Fitzpaine, Dors.). Ejected from his school in 1662, Kerridge was licensed, 8 May 1672, being at Lyme, as "Grall Pr. Teacher"; he assisted Short at Lyme, and from about 1689 was Presbyterian Minister at Colyton, Devon. Both Short and Kerridge were molested on false suspicion of complicity in the Rye House Plot (1683). Short died on a visit to Exeter. (*C. F. Mh. Od. P. T.*)

His son, John Short (26 Mar. 1649–1716/7), is conjectured to have studied at Utrecht or Leiden; he is not in the "Album Studiosorum" of either university (but *see* p. 183). He probably got most of his education from his father and from John Kerridge, M.A. (*see* Ames Short). He taught a school at Lyme Regis where several Ministers received their early training, and later assisted Kerridge in the Presbyterian congregation at Colyton, possibly (but not probably) removing his school to that place. In Dec. 1692 he succeeded John Ker, M.D. [*q.v.*], as head of the Academy at Bishop's Hall, Bethnal Green [*q.v.*]; grants were made to his students till 1696. In 1696 he was one of the correspondents of the Congregational Fund for Devon, Dorset, and Somerset. In 1698 he succeeded Matthew Barker, M.A. [*q.v.*], as Minister of one of the two Congregational churches which then had joint occupancy of the Meeting-house in Miles' Lane, Cannon Street. An impediment in his speech marred his pulpit efforts; his congregation declined, removed to another Meeting-house in Maidenhead court, Great Eastcheap, and came to an end at his death. (*A. Co. J. Je. M. Mh. U. W.*) [34]

SHORTHAND. [173 *sq.*]

SHOWELL, or SHEWELL, THOMAS, M.A. (*d.* 19 Jan. 1693/4). **P.** Born at Coventry; son of a clothier. From Coventry grammar school, matric. ser. at Magdalen Hall, Oxford, 22 Feb. 1650/1; B.A., 18 Oct. 1654. Calamy makes him

M.A. of Cambridge; no trace of him there. Held the vicarage of Lenham, Kent (ejected, 1660 ?). Curate of Leeds, Kent; ejected, 1662. Kept school at Leeds. Returned to Coventry as assistant to Jarvis Bryan [q.v.]. Died of apoplexy during his Wednesday lecture. (C. F. P. Si.) [117, 118]

SHOWER, JOHN (May 1657—28 June 1715). **P.** Born at Exeter; second son of William Shower, merchant, and elder brother of Sir Bartholomew Shower (14 D. 1658—4 D. 1701), recorder of London, whose sympathy was with the Nonjurors. Educated at Exeter, Otterford (under Matthew Warren [q.v.]), the Academy at Newington Green of Charles Morton, M.A. [q.v.], and the Academy of Edward Veal, M.A. [q.v.]. Began to preach, 1677; held a lecture at Exchange Alley, 1679–83; ordained, 24 D. 1679, by presbyters, as assistant to Vincent Alsop, M.A. [q.v.]. In 1683, made the grand tour as one of three young ministerial companions of the nephew of Sir Samuel Barnardiston. Remained in Holland, 1684–6; returning to take up his Exchange Alley lecture, was driven back by persecution, and joined (1686) John Howe, M.A. [q.v.], at Utrecht. At end of 1687, became evening lecturer to the English Presbyterian congregation at Rotterdam. On 19 Jan. 1690/1 he was called to succeed Daniel Williams, D.D. [q.v.], as assistant to Howe. On 8 May 1691 he accepted the call of the Presbyterian congregation at Curriers' Hall, London Wall, which he removed to larger Meeting-houses in Jewin Street (1692) and Old Jewry (1701). Elected (1692) a Manager of the Common Fund, he was retained at its reconstitution (1695). He succeeded (1697) Samuel Annesley, D.C.L. [q.v.], as a Salters' Hall lecturer. Retiring from duty on 27 Mar. 1715, he died at Stoke Newington. (Cm. D. W.) [161, 166]

SHREWSBURY ('Salop'). Ejected here were (1) John Bryan, M.A. [q.v.]. (2) Richard Heath, B.A., born at Lilley, Herts; son of John Heath; admitted sizar at Christ's College, Cambridge, 17 June 1631, aged 20; B.A., 1634/5; rector of Hopesay, Shrop., 1645; vicar of St. Alkmund's, Shrewsbury, 1650; ejected, 1662; died at Wellington, Shrop., 28 May 1667. (C. P. Cp. V.) In 1676 there were 10 Nonconformists in St. Alkmund's parish; 40 in St. Chad's; 16 in St. Cross'; 6 in St. Julians. (Ls.) (3) . . . Lee; afterwards conformed. (C.) (4) Francis Tallents, M.A. [q.v.]. [15, 88, 89]

SHROPSHIRE ('Salop'). [16, 88, 89, 142, 148, 168, 176, 181] All is in the Book-keeper's hand, except the headings "Salop" and marginalia. The returns are numbered 6 to 158; and in 1691, 36, 37.

Acham is Atcham [q.v.]

SHUTTLEWOOD, JOHN (1667–1737). **C.** Only son of John Shuttlewood, B.A. (3 Jan. 1631/2—17 Mar. 1688/9); ejected (1662) from the rectory of Ravenstone and perpetual curacy of Hugglescote, Leic., who died at Creaton, Northants. Educ. at his father's Academy. Colleague in 1711 with Samuel Harris [q.v.], and Minister till 1727 of the Presbyterian congregation in Mill Yard, Goodman's Fields, London. (D. Ev. We.) [78]

SIBBERTOFT. [77]

SIBLE HEDINGHAM ('Sibbe Hedinghame'). The Common Fund granted (1691) £8 to Sible Hedingham "for one year only, on condition of having preaching there every Lord's Day." (M.) [42]

SIBTON. Ejected here was Thomas Danson, of New Inn Hall, Oxford; chaplain of Corpus Christi Coll., 1648; B.A., 1649/50; Fellow of Magdalen Coll. and M.A., 1652; preacher at Berwick-on-Tweed; rector of St. Peter's, Sandwich, Kent; ejected, 1660; vicar of Sibton and Peasenhall; ejected, 1663/4; removed to London; licensed, 22 Apr. 1672, as Pr. Teacher in his house in Spitalfields; his house licensed, same date, as Presb. Meeting-place; ministered at Abingdon, Berks, 1679–92; d. in London, 1694. (B. C. F. P. T.) [106]

SIMMONS, JOSEPH (fl. 1690–1730). Received £4 a year from the Fund, 1690–96, for Appledore, Devon. Joseph Simmons, or Simmonds, was Minister at Kingswood, Wilts, 1706–1716 (receiving Fund grants of £5 a year); and at Princes Risborough, Bucks, 1718–1721 (receiving Fund grants of £10 a year). A grant of £5 was made to him at Maiden Newton, Dors., 9 N. 1730. (Ev. M.) [31]

SIMONSBATH ('Seymonsford'). [92]

SINCLARE, i.e. SYNCLARE or SINCLAIR, ALEXANDER (1658 ?—1 Apr. 1722). **P.** Born and educated at Belfast. Licensed by Antrim Meeting (1680 ?). Chaplain in Dublin to two noble families. Sent on mission to Waterford, and (after persecution) ordained (1686) as first Presbyterian pastor there. Removed to Bristol as co-pastor with John Weekes [q.v.]. Settled in Dublin (1692) as colleague and successor to William Keyes, in Plunket Street congregation, and there remained till death. Moderator (1704) of the General Synod of Ulster. The year of his death is fixed by "Ane Elegy &c.", 1722. (*Am. Cm.*) [91]

SINGLETON, JOHN, M.A. (*d.* 18 Feb. 1705/6). **C.** Nephew of John Owen, D.D. [*q.v.*]. Entered at Christ Church, Oxford (1650), of which his uncle was then dean; matric. 'ser.', 18 O. 1654; B.A., 1655; M.A., 1658; ejected from Studentship, 1660. He studied medicine in Holland (Foster says, at Leiden; his name is not in the Album) but took no degree, though commonly styled Doctor. Chaplain to Lady Scot, in Hertfordshire, and preacher in Hertford. Applied for licences both for London and Oxford; licensed, 22 May 1672, as "Congr. Teacher in the howse of Thomas Cowdrey in Queenhithe, London"; the Oxford house was licensed same date. He preached a sermon at the Cripplegate Morning Exercise (1683). In or before 1687/8 he was, at his desire, dismissed from the pastorate of his flock, the members being received (1 March) into that of Thomas Cole [*q.v.*], then at Tallow Chandlers' Hall, Dowgate Hill. Singleton went into Warwickshire, and lived with his wife's brother, Timothy Gibbons, physician, preaching from 1687/8 at Stretton-under-Fosse, parish of Monks Kirby, Warw., where a thatched Meeting-house was built. From 1688 he preached also at Coventry, and succeeded (1690) John Bohun [*see* Bunn] as pastor of the Congregational church in Much Park Street, afterwards (1724) removed to Vicar Lane. This is probably the other "imploy" mentioned p. 118, since Singleton did not practise medicine save in the way of advice to particular friends. He was one of the witnesses against Richard Davis [*q.v.*] at Kettering in 1692. In March 1697/8 he returned to London, and practically to his old congregation, succeeding Thomas Cole at Pinners' Hall. He succeeded Cole also as Manager of the Congregational Fund, and as one of the Merchants' Tuesday Lecturers at Pinners' Hall. In 1704 he removed his congregation to Loriners' Hall, where Daniel Neal, M.A., the historian of New England and of the Puritans, became his assistant and ultimately his successor.

*N.B.*—He must be carefully distinguished from Thomas Singleton, tutor at Eton, and in London from before 1647 till after 1690. There is no evidence that John Singleton acted as tutor. (*C. F. Gl. P. Si. T. W.*) [118, 119]

SISSIFERNS ('Sissiphen'), or SISSEVERNES, a Manor in Codicote parish, Herts, then held by John Poyner (1662–1723), who sold it (1698) to Thomas Kentish, from whom it descended to John Kentish (26 June 1768—6 Mar. 1853), Minister of the New Meeting, Birmingham, by whom the present writer was baptized. (*Hc.*) [50]

SLAIDBURN ('Slait Burn'), W.R. (misplaced in N.R.). [136]

SLATER, SAMUEL, M.A. (*d.* 24 May 1704). **P.** Son of Samuel Slater (*d.* before 1671), ejected from St. Catherine's-in-the-Tower. Matric. pensioner or sizar, at Emmanuel Coll., Cambridge, 1644 or 1645; B.A., 1647 or 1647/8; M.A., 1658. Vicar some years of Nayland, Suff.; thereafter (before 1658) vicar of St. James', Bury St. Edmunds, Suff. Ejected, 1662. The Episc. Returns, 1669, report him as one of the preachers at Bradfield St. Clare, Suff., to "2 or 300" persons "att the houses of Robt Heyward, John Cooke, John Stannard, a wollen drap & sometimes in a barne of Mrs Adams's every Sunday." On 11 Apr. 1672 licence was issued to "Samuel Slater dwelling in Walthamstow of the Presbyterian Perswasion to teach in any allowed Place"; on 20 Apr. his house in Walthamstow was licensed. After the death (27 July 1680) of Stephen Charnock, B.D., he became joint pastor with Thomas Watson, M.A. [*q.v.*], at Crosby Hall, Bishopsgate. Daniel Alexander [*q.v.*] was one of his colleagues. Slater preached and published many funeral sermons, remarkable as giving no biographical particulars, rarely even the date of death, not always the full name. He produced a tiny volume of so-called "Poems," 1679. He had been "much taken" with Milton's "Paradise Lost," and "followed much in his method," but "used a more plain and familiar stile." He was a Manager (1695) of the reconstituted Fund. (*B. C. D. P. T. V. W.*) [164]

SLAUTER, *i.e.* SLAUGHTER, SAMUEL (*d.* 1706). **P.** Educ. for the Nonconformist ministry. Succeeded Richard Fincher (*d.* 10 F. 1692/3) [*q.v.*] as Minister at Unicorn Yard, Tooley Street, Southwark. The congregation ended with his death. (*W.*) [140]

SLEAFORD ('Sleeford'). Ejected here was George Bohemus or Boheme (1628—9 Sept. 1711), born at Colberg, Pomerania; of Queens' Coll., Cambridge; matric. sizar, 1647; vicar of Foxton, Leic., 14 Mar. 1651/2; vicar of Sleaford; ejected, 1662; kept school at Walcot,

Linc., where for some time his preaching in the church was connived at; rem. to his daughter's at Folkingham, 1704 ?, and there died. (*C. Ln. V.*) [70]

SLEIGH, ANTHONY, M.A. (1634—13 June 1702). Son of Anthony Slee of Penruddock, Cumb.; bapt. 3 S. 1634. From a school at Durham went to Edinburgh University, graduating, 19 July 1660. Preached in parish churches of Cumberland and Westmorland; from the end of 1660 ministered to the adherents of Richard Gilpin, M.A., M.D., at Greystoke, Cumb.; silenced, 1662. The Episc. Returns, 1669, report him as one of the preachers to "Independents 60 or more" at Hesket, Lazonby and Kirkoswald, Cumb. Licensed, June 1672, as Pr. Teacher in house of John Noble (*d.* 1708), Greystoke. Presented for nonconformity, 1675–7; thrice imprisoned. Received grants from the Common Fund (1690–3) of £8 a year, being then "att Threlkeld," Cumb. From 1696 received grants of £5 a year from the Congregational Fund, being then at Penruddock in the parish of Greystoke. (*C. M. N. P. T.*) [22, 178]

SMALL HEATH ('Smallheath'), Worc. [119]

SMALL, JAMES (*fl.* 1651–1704). **P.** Born at Sandford, Devon. At school there with Ezekiel Hopkins, afterwards bishop of Derry. Matric. 'pleb.' at New Inn Hall, Oxford, 23 Apr. 1651. Rector of Yaxley, Suff.; ejected, 1662. Chaplain to Davies, in West of England. Licensed, 11 Apr. 1672, being of Creedy near Crediton, Devon, as "Grāll Pr. Teacher." Signed the thanks of Devon Ministers. Chaplain (after 1675) to Lord Massarene at Antrim. Chaplain to Sir John and Lady Barrington at Hatfield Broad Oak, Ess., till 1690. Preached at Hatfield and at Bishops Stortford, Herts. Became pastor (1691) at Hatfield, on removal of John Warren [*q.v.*] to Bishop's Stortford; a Meeting-house was built for him. Left Hatfield, 1704. (*C. E. F. P. T.*) [39, 50]

SMITH, MATTHEW, M.A. (1650—29 Apr. 1736). **P.** Born at York, and there educ. for the ministry by Ralph Ward [*q.v.*]; rem. to Edinburgh University; M.A., 22 Mar. 1679/80. Minister at Kipping or Thornton, parish of Bradford, Yorks; soon divided his labours between this place and Mixenden, parish of Halifax, Yorks, to the dissatisfaction of Thornton. After ordination on 19 Aug. 1687, Smith settled at Mixenden, preaching alternately there and at Warley (where a Meeting-house was erected in 1705). He received, 1706–11, Fund grants of £6 a year for Mixenden; also a special grant of £5, 1728. The Mixenden Meeting-house (built 1689?) was replaced (1717) by a new one at Moor End, built on Smith's property and at his expense. Smith educated Students for the ministry; Students were sent to him by the Fund, 1703–16. Much controversy was raised by his "True Notion of Imputed Righteousness," 1700, which made the first inroad on the Calvinism of the North of England. Smith reduced 'election' to "God's purpose of saving every sinner, through Christ, who repents, believes and obeys."

His son and successor, John Smith (*d.* 1768), ultimately became an Arian, as Minister of Chapel Lane, Bradford, Yorks. (*Ev. Hh. M. My. Nr.*) [130]

SMITH, ROBERT, M.A. (*d.* Aug. 1705). **C.** [Three of these names graduated M.A. at Cambridge, 1643, 1655, 1660. (*V.*)] Ejected (unknown to Calamy) from the curacy or vicarage of Blythburgh, Suff. Licensed, 13 May 1672, as "Congr. Teacher in the howse of Joseph Gilder" at Westleton, Suff. On 17 N. 1672 he married Elizabeth (*d.* July 1679), daughter of William Ames, M.A. (1624—21 July 1689), ejected (1660) from the rectory of Wrentham; and thenceforth acted as coadjutor and successor to his father-in-law in the Congregational church at Wrentham. He was buried there on 24 Aug. 1705. (*B. T.*) [103]

SMITH, SAMUEL, M.A. (*d.* 1714). **P.** [? Matric. sizar at Magdalene Coll., Cambridge, 1634/5; B.A., 1637/8; M.A., 1641. (*V.*)] Held, 1643, the sequestered perpetual curacy of Maidstone, Kent; ejected, 1660, from the sequestered vicarage of Bodenham, Heref.; again ejected, 1662, from lectureship at St. Olave's, Southwark. Probably the Smith reported in Episc. Returns, 1669, as preaching to 200 persons "At ye Glasse house in Goswell Street"; also "At ye Artillery ground in Morefeilds," denomination not stated. He is perhaps the Smith at Town Malling, Kent (1690). He ministered to a Presb. congregation of 100 at New Windsor, Berks, and died there. (*C. Ev. F. P. Sm. T. Wc.*) [6, 9, 57]

SMITH, SAMUEL, the squire of Colkirk, Norf. *See* Minister's Son. (*B.*) [75]

SMITH, SAMUEL. [95]

SMITH, or SMYTH, WILLIAM (1624—20 Oct. 1686). **P.** Born in Worcestershire. Son of William Smyth of Evenlode, Worc., pleb. Matric. at New Inn Hall,

Oxford, 10 D. 1641, aged 17. Curate in the sequestered rectory of Church Langton, Leic.; vicar of Packington, Leic.; ejected, 1662. Removed to Diseworth Grange, Leic., and taught school. The Episc. Returns, 1669, report him as one of the preachers to about 40 Presbyterians at Hugglescote, Leic.; also, as one of the preachers to about 40 of the "meane sort," of "all sects," at Ibstock, Leic. Licensed, 13 May 1672, as Pr. Teacher at his house in Diseworth Grange; house licensed same date. (*C. F. P. T.*) [66]

SMITH. One of the widows of this name was widow of Jonathan Smith, jun., ejected from the rectory of Hempsted, Glou.; licensed, 10 June 1672, as "Congr. in his howse" in Rosse, Hereford, where he taught school. Licence was given, 29 May 1672, to another Jonathan Smith as "Congr. Teacher in his howse" at Tetbury, Glou. This may have been the father, and the elder Mrs. Smith his widow. (*C. P. T.*) [45]

SNOWDEN, BENJAMIN, B.A. (1626—28 Apr. 1696). **P.** Born at Norwich. Matric. sizar at Emmanuel Coll., Cambridge, 1642; B.A., 1645/6; episcopally ordained. Held the sequestered rectory of St. Clement's, Norwich (Calamy says of St. Giles'); ejected, 1662. The Episc. Returns, 1669, report him as preaching in Norwich with John Collinges [*q.v.*]. He applied for licence to preach in "A roome in y^e house late belonging to y^e Blackfryers in St. Andrews pish." This was the East Granary, and though the application was "not approved," the Presbyterians used it till 1689, under a corporation lease. Licensed, 29 June 1672, as "Pr. Teacher" in the house of John Barnham in St. Andrew's parish. (*B. C. P. T. V. Wc.*) [74, 177]

SOCIETY, meaning Congregation. [44] *See* Nailsworth

SOCINIANISING. [158]

SOHAM ('Soam,' 'Some'). *See* Fordham. [12, 14]

SOLESLEY. [6] *See* Berkshire

SOMERSET. [47, 91, 92, 155, 168, 176, 181] All is in the Book-keeper's hand, except the headings "Somerset" in the earliest handwriting. The returns are numbered 89 to 156 (nearly all, 90); and 12, in 1691.

Brookhorne is Crewkerne.

Charleton is probably Queen Charlton (sometimes spelled Charleton); Somerset also contains two Charltons, also Charlton Adam, Charlton Cross, Charlton Horethorne, Charlton Mackrell, and Charlton Musgrove.

Coome is Monckton Combe.

Frary is Witham Friary.

Gallington is Yarlington.

Hengrove is perhaps Henstridge.

Hillbishops is Bishop's Hull [*q.v.*].

Ingleshombe is Englishcombe.

Seymonsford is Simonsbath.

Stoackgursie is Stogursey.

Welleton is Wellington.

Wilscombe is Wiveliscombe.

SORETON, or SOURTON, FRANCIS, M.A. (1622–Aug. 1689). **P.** Son of Ellis Soorton of North Buckland, Devon, pleb. From Plymouth grammar school, matric. at Exeter Coll., Oxford, 12 May 1637, aged 15; B.A., 1641; Fellow, 1642–8; M.A., 1643/4. Held the sequestered rectory of Honiton, Devon, 1652; ejected, 1662. The patron of the living, Sir William Courtenay, of Powderham Castle, whose aunt he married, protected him. The Episc. Returns, 1665, report him as living at Honiton; hence, under the provisions of the Five Mile Act, he was imprisoned (1666) in Exeter gaol; but Courtenay, then high sheriff, procured his release and entertained him as his guest till his death. Licensed, 2 May 1672, being then of Powderham, as "Grāll Pr."; also, 5 Sept. 1672, as "Presb. tea." in Honiton, where he founded a congregation which endured till 1788; an unsigned, undated licence giving him the use of the schoolhouse, Honiton, is still among the State Papers. (*C. Em. F. Mh. P. T. Wc.*) [31]

SOUTH, COMPTON, M.A. (*d.* 22 July 1705). **P.** From Salisbury grammar school, matric. gent. at Wadham Coll., Oxford, 14 N. 1650; rem. to St. Alban's Hall, B.A., 1653; M.A., 1656. Calamy calls him B.D. Held the sequestered vicarage of Odiham, Hants; a year later held the sequestered rectory of Berwick St. John, Wilts; ejected, 1662. Much harassed for conventicling. The Episc. Returns, 1669, report him as one of five preachers at Donhead St. Andrew, Wilts, "At M^r Thomas Graves and his sonnes house" to "100 or 200" persons "of ordinary Ranke most foreigners." Licensed, 1 May 1672, as "Pr. Teacher in his howse at Dunhead in Wilts," *i.e.* Donhead St. Mary. Every week he went to preach at Ringwood, Hants (18 miles off), and was the guest of Lady Lisle, at Moyles Court (*see* Crofts, John). In 1687 he became Minister at Warminster to a large congregation, meeting in a barn till (8 Oct. 1704) the Old Meeting-house was opened by Dr. Cotton from Boston, who was pastor at Horningsham, Wilts.

By this time South was laid aside by infirmity; he died at Donhead St. Mary. 'Hunnett' appears to be the Book-keeper's misreading of Dunnett for Donhead. (*C. F. Mh. P. T. Wc.*) [123]

SOUTH-CAVE. *See* Cave

SOUTH MOLTON ('Southmorton'). [31, 95]

SOUTHAM ('Sowtham'). [119]

SOUTHAMPTON. Ejected here was Nathaniel Robinson ('Robison') [*q.v.*]. [100]

SOUTHAMPTON COUNTY. *See* Hampshire

SOUTHGATE. [72]

SOUTHMORTON. [31] *See* Devonshire

SOUTHWELL, or SOUTHALL, JOHN (*d.* 1694). **P.** Nephew of Richard Southwell [*q.v.*]. Educ. in the Academy of John Woodhouse [*q.v.*], and became his assistant. Minister at Dudley, Worc.; later at Newbury, Berks, till death. In each place he conducted an Academy on Woodhouse's model. (*Bb. C. Nm.*) [96, 126]

SOUTHWELL, or SOUTHALL, JOHN, *secundus* (*fl.* 1690–1703). Son of Richard Southwell [*q.v.*]. The Common Fund granted him (1690) £8 a year for Hinckley; reduced (1695) to £6, and paid to 1703. (*M.*) [66, 67]

SOUTHWELL, or SOUTHALL, RICHARD (*fl.* 1660–93). **P.** Ejected from the chapelry of Baswich, Staff. Removed to Dadlington, Leic. The Episc. Returns, 1669, report him as preaching at Fillongley, Warw., to "most women"; also as one of the preachers to about 200 Presbyterians at Great Bowden, Leic.; also as one of the preachers to about 200 "Presbyterians & Independents held together" at Kibworth, Leic.; also as one of the preachers to about 50 "Presbyterians & Independents" at Theddingworth, Leic.; also as one of the preachers to about 100 "Presbyterians & Independts" at Ashby Magna, Leic.; also as preaching to about 90 "Presbyterians Independents & Anabaptists" at Bitteswell, Leic. Licensed, 25 July 1672, as "Pr. Teacher att the house of Matthew Hubbard att Mitch Ashby," Leic. The Common Fund granted him (1690) £8 a year for "Hinckley" (in error? *see* Southwell, John, *secundus*), reducing it, same year, to £5, and continuing it till 1693, when he was still at Dadlington. (*C. M. P. T.*) [66, 67, 69]

SOUTHWICK. Ejected here was Symons [? Richard, of Emmanuel Coll., Cambridge; matric. pensioner, 1633]. (*C. V.*) [101]

SOUTHWOLD BY THE SEA. One Woodward, probably a lecturer, was ejected here in 1660. Davids identifies him with Woodward, who afterwards preached at Harlow, Ess., and founded the Baptist church there and a now extinct congregation at Little Parndon. (*B. C. E.*) [105, 107]

SOWTHAM. [119] *See* Warwickshire

SPALDING. [70, 173]

SPEN, hamlet in Birstal parish, W.R. [130]

SPENCER, EDMUND (*fl.* 1687–90). **P.** In 1687 he was of St. Martin's parish, Leicester, and about to marry Eliz. Kestins. (*Leicestershire Marriage Bonds.*) This was Elizabeth, only surviving child of Nicholas Kestian, M.A., of Christ's Coll., Cambridge (*d.* 1686), ejected (1662) from the rectory of Gumley, Leic., and afterwards (from 1680?) Congregational Minister in Leicester. The association of Congregational and Presbyterian preachers in founding and maintaining the congregation which built the Great Meeting, Leicester, was of many years duration. (*C. P. V.*)

SPILSBURY, JOHN, M.A. (1630—10 June 1699). **C.** Son of William Spilsbury, of Bewdley, Worc., pleb. Matric. at Magdalen Hall, Oxford, 20 Oct. 1646, aged 16; rem. to Magdalen Coll.; clerk, 1648–50; B.A., 1649; Fellow, 1650–60; M.A., 1652. Vicar (1657) of Bromsgrove, Worc.; ejected, 1660. Licensed, 19 Apr. 1672, as "Congreg. Teacher in his howse in Broomsgrove, Worcester." He suffered imprisonment for Nonconformity. He was warmly in favour of the Happy Union of 1691. He married a sister of John Hall, D.D., bishop of Bristol (born at Bromsgrove), who visited him every year, and left his property to Spilsbury's only son, John (*d.* 31 Jan. 1726/7), who succeeded Thomas Baldwin [*q.v.*] as Minister at Kidderminster. (*C. Ek. F. P. T.*) [126]

SPINK, WILLIAM (*fl.* 1689–90). Entered Frankland's Academy, 7 Mar. 1689/90. Died before 1702. (*Fr. Nk.*) [136]

SPITAL, THE. A part of the large grave-yard attached to the former priory of St. Mary Spital, and situated near the South-east end of Norton Folgate, was walled round, and known as the Spital, or Spital Yard (now Spital Square). Within it was a pulpit cross, from which (till destroyed by Puritans during the Civil War) the famous Spital sermons were originally delivered, in the open air. (*Lo. Sl.*) [2]

SPRATTON. [76]

SPRINT, JOHN (*d.* Jan. 1717/8). **P.** Son of Samuel Sprint [*q.v.*]. First settled at Wimborne, Dors. [1685?]; removed thence to Stalbridge, Dors. [1687 ?]; and thence to Milbourne Port, Som., about 1700. Died Minister of Milbourne Port, where he was succeeded (1718–26) by his son, John Sprint (who received £10 a year from the Fund). For his uncle, John Sprint, M.A., *see* Hampstead. [He has been confused with John Sprint, M.A. (*d.* 1693), ejected from the rectory of Portland, Dors.] (*Em. Ev. M. Od. P.* ii. 473.) [34]

SPRINT, or SPRINTE, SAMUEL (1624 ?–1695 ?) **P.** Born at Thornbury, Glou. Younger son of John Sprint, M.A. (*d.* 1623), vicar of Thornbury (author of "Cassander Anglicanus," 1615), and grandson of John Sprint, D.D. (*d.* 1590), dean of Bristol. Subsizar at Trinity Coll., Cambridge, 16 Jan. 1645/6; matric., 1647; did not graduate. Master of Newbury grammar school, Berks. Rector of South Tidworth, Hants; ejected, 1662. About 1665 he leased a small estate at Upper Clatford, near Andover, Hants. The Episc. Returns, 1669, report him as one of two preachers at Andover to "200 ordinary persons Presbyterians kept at one Feilders in a Malthouse." Repeated applications failed to obtain for him a licence to preach, as Presbyterian, in Andover Town Hall. After four applications, he was licensed, 29 June 1672, as "Congr. Teacher [an error] in his howse at Clatford"; on 25 July 1672 his house was licensed as "Pr." On 7 S. 1673 he was arrested along with Isaac Chauncy [*q.v.*] while preaching at a barn in New Street, Andover, which had been licensed (*see* a graphic account in *Dq.*) In 1691 the Andover Presbyterian Meeting-house was in the backyard of a substantial shopkeeper named Bradband. Till his last illness Sprint continued to preach on alternate Sundays at Andover and Winchester. He was reputed a Baxterian. (*C. Cm. D. Dq. P. T. Tc.*) [100]

SPURSTOWE, WILLIAM, D.D. (1605 ?–1666/7). **P.** Son of William Spurstowe, citizen and mercer of London. Admitted pensioner at Emmanuel Coll., Cambridge, 1623; matric., 1623; B.A., 1626/7; Fellow of St. Catharine's Hall (resigned, 1637); M.A., 1630; incorp. B.A., Oxford, 1628. Rector of Great Hampden, Bucks, 1638. One of the five divines who wrote (1641) as "Smectymnuus," the last three letters being his initials (VVS). Chaplain, 1642, to John Hampden's regiment. Original member (12 June 1643) of the Westminster Assembly, and took the covenant. Vicar of Hackney, Middx., 1643. Master of St. Catharine's Hall, 1645. Member of the Provincial Assembly of London (1647). Strongly opposed to judicial proceedings against Charles I. Ejected from his Mastership (1650) for refusing the engagement. Chaplain to Charles II., 1660. Ejected from his vicarage, 1662, but continued to live at Hackney, where he founded almshouses. Died suddenly, and was buried, 8 Feb. (*C. D. F. Sw. V.*) [188]

ST. ALBANS. Ejected here were (1) William Haworth, M.A. [*q.v.*]; (2) Nathaniel Partridge (1610—6 Aug. 1684), born at St. Albans; preacher at the Abbey Church, 1657; ord. by presbyters; ejected, 1662; preaching in Old Street, London, 1669; licensed, 10 June 1672, as Congr., for house in Old Street. (*C. T. Uh.*) [50]

ST. AUSTELL ('Tossell,' so pronounced). [19]

ST. COLUMB ('Colomb'). Ejected here was Thomas Travers, M.A., matric. sizar at Magdalene Coll., Cambridge, 1637; B.A., 1640/1; M.A., 1644 (no record of Fellowship); held the sequestered rectory of St. Columb Major; ejected; the Episc. Returns, 1665, report him as living at Saltash, Corn., "notoriously disaffected." (*C. P. T. V.*) [19]

ST. EBALL. [18] *See* Cornwall

ST. ELLINS. [58] *See* Lancashire

ST. ENODOR. [18, 19]

ST. EVAL ('Eball'). [18]

ST. GERMANS ('Germainės'). Ejected here was Solomon Carswell, B.A. (1601–1689 ?); born in Devon; matric. pleb. at Exeter Coll., Oxford, 3 May 1621, aged 20; B.A., 1623/4; held the sequestered rectory of Woodham Ferrers, Ess.; resigned, 1646; vicar of St. Germans, 1646; licensed, 22 Apr. 1672, as "Presb. Teacher" in his house at St. Germans; was about 89 years old at death. (*C. P. F. T.*) [19, 20]

ST. HELENS. [58]

ST. HELLENS. [18] *See* Cornwall

ST. INDOER, or ST. INODER. [18, 19] *See* Cornwall

ST. IVES, Corn. [19, 180]

ST. IVES, Hunts. [53, 54, 172]

ST. JOHN'S, *i.e.* ST. JOHN'S COURT, Clerkenwell, now represented by St. John's Square. (*Lo.*) [1]

ST. JOHN'S STREET is St. John's Street, Clerkenwell. [3]

ST. MARY OTTERY. [30] *See* Devonshire

ST. MARY OVERIES, or OVERY, was the church of the Priory of St. Mary Overy, but by Act of Parliament (1541) it was made the parish church of the united parishes of St. Margaret and St. Mary Magdalen, Southwark, to be called by the name of St. Saviour's; nevertheless the old name stuck. The building, restored, is now the cathedral of the Anglican diocese of Southwark. (*Lo.*) [3]

ST. MAWES ('Maws'). [20]

ST. NEOTS ('Neotts'). No grant was made to St. Neots till 4 April 1720. (*M.*) [5]

ST. NICHOLAS, JOHN (1604—27 May 1698). **P.** Birthplace and parentage unknown; of good estate; the family belonged to Ash-next-Ridley, Kent. Matric. pensioner at Emmanuel Coll., Cambridge (1619); did not graduate, but was an able scholar. Held the sequestered rectory of Lutterworth; ejected, 1660. In 1659 he had signed the protest against the royalist plans of Sir George Booth. Like Henry Sampson [*q.v.*] he probably was not ordained. On 22 Sept. 1660 "John St. Nicholas, Esq., late of Litterworth" was returned as holding property at Knowle, Warw., of the annual value of £34, but non-resident. In 1666 he had a residence at Knowle, where he sheltered ejected Ministers; among them, (1) James Wright (1610–91) [*q.v.*]; (2) John Gilpin, ejected (1660) from the sequestered rectory of Brinklow, Warw., "who to the very last preached in his ruff"; on 22 Sept. 1660, "John Gilpin, Clarke, late of Brinklow," was returned as holding property at Knowle of the annual value of £4, but non-resident; (3) Gilpin's son-in-law, Stokes. St. Nicholas was licensed, 22 July 1672, as "Pr. Teacher in his howse at Burbage Leic." He had married the daughter of Anthony Grey (1557—9 Nov. 1643), rector of Aston Flamville with Burbage from 1590, who succeeded (21 Nov. 1639) to the earldom of Kent. St. Nicholas, who in his later years was stone deaf, died at Burbage. (*C. Dk. Dw. P. Pe. T. V. Wc.*) [66, 68]

STACKHOUSE, JOHN (1648/9—14 Sept. 1707). **C.** Son of Roger Stackhouse, of London, gent. Matric., 25 May 1664, at New Inn Hall, Oxford, aged 15. Licensed, 16 Apr. 1672, "to teach in the house of James Hayes Merchant called Combe-Farm w[th] in y[e] Parish of Greenwich and County of Kent, Congregationall." In 1690/1 he became co-pastor at Norwich with Martin Finch [*q.v.*], on whose death (1697) he became sole pastor. In 1699 a dispute about an assistant led to Stackhouse's secession with the bulk of his flock to another place of worship. He died at Norwich, aged 59 years, having been 39 years in the ministry and 17 years pastor at Norwich. (*B. F. T.*) [4, 177]

STAFFORDSHIRE. [96, 97, 168, 176, 180] The headings "Stafford" and the marginal note are in the earliest handwriting; the rest in that of the Bookkeeper. The returns are numbered 53, except three (62, 71, 95).

Bromwich is West Bromwich [*q.v.*].

Merbrock is Meerbrook [*q.v.*].

Wassall is Walsall [*q.v.*]

STAINCLIFFE ('Stentliffe'), Yorks, W.R. (misplaced in E.R.) [139]

STAINES ('Stains'). Ejected here in 1660 was Gabriel Price, who held the sequestered vicarage; he is probably the Gabriel Price who became rector of Ashingdon, Ess., 17 Dec. 1613 till 1641; then vicar of North Shoebury, Ess., 20 Feb. 1640/1, being the last vicar recorded by Newcourt, who adds, "Note, that this Vicarage [North Shoebury] is so small, that it hath been held by Sequestration ever since 1660." (*C.*) [73]

STALBRIDGE ('Stawbridge'). [34]

STAMBOURNE ('Stamburn,' 'Stamborn,' 'Stanborn'). Ejected here was Henry Havers, B.A. [*q.v.*]. [39]

STAMFORD. Ejected here were (1) Edward Browne, of New Inn Hall, Oxford; matric., 22 Feb. 1638/9, aged 18; B.A., 1642; incorp. at Cambridge, 1642/3; rector of Buckland, Kent, 1642; rector of St. Peter with All Saints, Stamford, 1658; ejected, 1662; licensed, 10 June 1672, as Pr. Teacher in a house at Horbling, Linc.; *d.* Apr. 1682. (*C. T. V.*) (2) John Richardson, of Queens' Coll., Cambridge; matric. sizar, 1637; B.A., 1640/1; schoolmaster at St. Ives, Hunt.; rector of Botolph-Bridge, Hunt. (now incorp. in Orton-Longueville); rector of St. Michael's, Stamford; ejected, 1662; rem. (1666) to Stockerston, Leic.; thence to Uppingham, Rut.; licensed, 10 June 1672, as Pr. Teacher in his house at Uppingham; his house licensed, same date, as Pr. Meeting-place; *d.* May 1687. (*C. T. V.*) The Common Fund granted (1691) £10 a year for Stamford, reduced (1695) to £6. (*M.*) [70, 71]

STANCLIFF, or STANCLIFFE, SAMUEL, M.A. (1630—12 Dec. 1705). **P.** Born at Southowram, Yorks. Son of John Stancliffe, draper, of an old Halifax family. From Halifax grammar school, admitted sizar at St. John's Coll., Cambridge, 7 Apr. 1648, aet. 17; matric., 1648; B.A., 1651/2; M.A., 1655. Rector of Stanmore Magna, Middx.;

ejected, 1662. On the death (14 Feb. 1691/2) of Thomas Rosewell, M.A., ejected from the rectory of Sutton Mandevil, Wilts, Stancliff succeeded him as Minister at Jamaica Row, Rotherhithe. He was appointed a Manager of the Common Fund, 3 Apr. 1693. Resigning his pastorate (1705), he retired to Hoxton, and there died on 12 Dec. 1705. An inscription in the Halifax grammar school commemorates his gift of £100. To his family he left a good estate. He gave good help to Calamy in his biographies. (*C. Jo. M. P. V. W. Y.* Rosewell's Life, 1718.) [3, 161]

STANFORD. [6] *See* Berkshire

STANNINGTON, then hamlet in Ecclesfield parish, W.R., now vicarage. The Nonconformist Chapel was built, and endowed with land, by Richard Spoone in 1652. The Common Prayer was used in it till the Toleration Act. Calamy gives Isaac Darwen, appointed 1657, as ejected; but he preached till 1663, and held the Chapel land till 1665. (*C. My.*) [130]

STANTON DREW. [91]

STANTON HARCOURT. [7]

STAPLEHURST ('Stapleherst'). Ejected here was Daniel Pointell, born at Chislehurst, Kent; from Westminster school, Scholar of Trinity Coll., Cambridge; matric. pensioner, 1642; B.A., 1644/5; M.A., 1648; rector of Staplehurst (after 1646); ejected, 1662; licensed, 10 Aug. 1672, as Pr. Teacher in a house at Staplehurst; again, 30 Sept. 1672, as Pr. Teacher at Staplehurst; *d.* 1674. (*C. K. T. Tc. V. Wz.*) From 1691 the Common Fund granted £4 a year for Staplehurst. (*M.*) [55, 57]

STAPLETON ('Stappleton'), now in parliamentary borough of Bristol, North. [44]

STARBOTTOM, W.R. (misplaced in N.R.). [135]

STARKEY, JOHN, M.A. (1627–1692 ?). **P.** Born in Kent. From Tonbridge grammar school, admitted pensioner at Peterhouse, Cambridge, 7 June 1645, aged 18; matric., 1645/6; B.A., 1648/9; migrated to St. John's Coll.; Fellow; M.A., 1652. Lecturer at Grantham, Linc., 1655; ejected, 1660. Removed to Lancashire. Licensed, 29 June 1672, as "Pr. Teacher in the howse of Widow Ashurst in Ormskirk Parish, Lanc." Minister at Newington Green, 1686–92. (*C. Jo. P. Ph. T. V. We.*) [72]

STARR, COMFORT, M.A. (1625—30 Oct. 1711). **C.** Son of Comfort Starr (1589—2 Jan. 1659/60), surgeon, of Ashford, Kent. Went with his father to New England in the "Hercules," March 1634/5. Graduated at Harvard (B.A., 1647; M.A., 1650), and Fellow. Rector of St. Cuthbert's, Carlisle, 1656; thence ejected, 1660. Reported in the Episcopal Returns, 1669, as Nonconformist Minister at Cranbrook, Kent. Licensed, 17 Apr. 1672, as Congr. Teacher in his own house in Sandwich. He applied in vain (four times) for the use of the Old Chapel belonging to the Hospital of St. Bartholomew, near and without the walls of Sandwich. Elected, 12 Aug. 1687, pastor of the Congregational church, Dancing House Yard, Canterbury. He was not long in London without charge, for in 1690/1 he is at Dover, and in July 1691 Minister of Goudhurst, Kent (receiving £3 from the Common Fund). Subsequently he went to Lewes, Sussex, and there died. From 22 June 1696 he received a yearly grant of £6 from the Congregational Fund. (*C. Cf. M. N. P. Sg. T.*) [4, 55]

STARRE, THOMAS BERNARD (*d.* 28 Nov. 1700). Was at Topsham in 1687. Ordained, 25 Aug. 1687, at Lyme Regis, Dors. (*Em. Mh. N. W.*) [30]

STATISTICS, Orders for collecting. [169]

STAWBRIDGE. [34] *See* Dorsetshire

STEBBING. Ejected here was Samuel Bantoft, of Emmanuel Coll., Cambridge; matric. pensioner, 1638; B.A., 1642; Fellow of Jesus Coll.; M.A., 1645; sent out as preacher by the University, 1659; vicar of Stebbing; ejected, 1662; licensed, 5 Sept. 1672, as Pr. Teacher, being at Braintree, Ess.; went to London, excommunicated there; went to Ipswich; *d.* there, 21 Aug. 1692, aged 73. (*C. E. T. V.*) [39, 42]

STENNING. [115] *See* Sussex

STENTLIFFE. [139] *See* Yorkshire, W.R.

STEPHEN, SIR LESLIE (28 Nov. 1832—22 Feb. 1904). Born in London; youngest son of Sir James Stephen; educated at Eton, King's Coll., London, and Trinity Hall, Cambridge; B.A. and Goodbehere Fellow, 1854; M.A., 1854. Ordained deacon, 1855; priest, 1859; relinquished his orders, 25 Mar. 1875. First editor of the "Dict. Nat. Biog." (Nov. 1882–Apr. 1891), K.C.B., 1902. (*D. supp.* 2.) [182]

STEPNEY. Ejected here was William Greenhill, of Magdalen Coll., Oxford; matric., 8 June 1604, aged 13; demy, 1604/5; B.A., 1608/9; M.A., 1612; vicar of New Shoreham, Suss., 1615–33; afternoon preacher ("evening star") at Stepney Church, 1643, and member of the Westminster Assembly; founded the

Congregational church at Stepney, 1644; parliamentary chaplain to the royal dukes of York and Gloucester, and their sister Henrietta, 1649; vicar of Stepney, 1653; ejected, 1660; continued as Congregational pastor at Stepney; *d.* 27 Sept. 1671; succeeded by Matthew Mead [*q.v*]. (*C. D. F.*) [72, 156]

STERRY, PETER, M.A. (*d.* 19 Nov. 1672). **P.** Born in Surrey. Entered Emmanuel Coll., Cambridge, 21 Oct. 1629; B.A., 1633; Fellow, 1636; M.A., 1637. Preacher in London; nominated, May 1642, by House of Lords for Westminster Assembly of Divines. Chaplain to Elizabeth (1610–83), wife of Sir Robert Brooke, knight. Preacher to the Council of State, 16 Feb. 1648/9. One of Cromwell's Triers, 1653. A spiritually minded man, of soaring views, he had no love for the Presbyterian discipline, yet was not attracted to any other religious body. After Cromwell's death he took pupils in London. On 16 May 1672 he was licensed as Presb. Teacher in Edward Bushell's house, Hackney, and that of John Berry in Philpot Lane, London; a further licence for Bushell's house in Little St. Helen's does not seem to have been granted. On 22 July 1672 he was licensed as Presb. Teacher in the house of Richard Pemble, Little Berkhampstead, Herts. He had resorted thither in ill-health. F. D. Maurice signalises Sterry as the mystic of Puritanism. Baxter (in his "Reliquiae") couples him with his friend, Sir Henry Vane the younger, as "vanity and sterility" happily conjoined. (*D. T.*) [154]

STEWARD, THOMAS, D.D. (1668?—10 S. 1753). **P.** Born, probably at Norwich, of a family originally of Lackford, Suff. Educ. for the ministry by John Collinges [*q.v.*]. Pastor (1689) at Debenham, Suff. Succeeded (1706) Elias Travers as Presbyterian Minister at Cook Street, Dublin. He was an orthodox Non-subscriber in 1722. Removed (1724) to Bury St. Edmunds, Suff. Received D.D. from Aberdeen (1733). From 1739 he often received special grants of £5 from the Fund. Died at Bury St. Edmund's, aged 84. (*D. M.*) [75, 103]

STEYNING. [115]

STOACKGURSIE. [93] *See* Somerset

STOAKE, Devon. From Stoke Canon was ejected John Jordan, born in Exeter; of Emmanuel Coll., Cambridge; admitted pensioner, 1645/6; B.A., 1649; perpetual curate of Stoke Canon, 1655; ejected, 1662; living at Exeter, 1665; licensed, 11 Apr. 1672, as Grall Pr. Teacher near Newton, Devon; over 80 at death. (*C. T. V.*) From Stoke Damarel was ejected John Hicks (*see* Saltash). [31]

STOCKDEN, . . . [85]

STOCKPORT ('Stopford'). [15]

STOCKS MARKET. [163]

STOCKTON-ON-TEES. [36]

STOGURSEY. [93]

STOKE ('Stoak') GOLDING, originally a chapelry in Hinckley parish, Leic.; then a rectory attached to the vicarage of Hinckley. [66, 67, 69]

STONE, . . . [? John Stone. *See* Hellingly.] [34]

STONE, . . . Apothecary. [2]

STOPFORD. [15]. *See* Cheshire

STOPP, *i.e.* STOTT, DAVID (*d.* 1713). **P.** Not known as an Ejected Minister. After ministering at Harwich he removed, at the suggestion of the Fund Board, to Tunbridge Wells, Kent, where a gift of £5 was voted to him, 6 Oct. 1691. About 1700 he succeeded Joseph Hill at Swallow Street, Piccadilly; and was there succeeded (1710) by James Anderson, D.D., (ordained, 11 Dec. 1707), who converted a dying interest into a Scots Presbyterian congregation. Stott lived in Westminster. On 6 Apr. 1713 a gift of £8 was made to him from the Fund. On 7 Dec. 1713 his widow asked for a bursary for her son, a Student at Halle, Germany; £10 a year was given him till 1716. Stott's name is also wrongly given as Scott and Stort. (*E. M. We.*) [39]

STORY, . . . **C.** His "while" must have been some time between 1688 (when James Noble, M.A., was at Brampton) and 1690, when the "young man," John Kincaide (*d.* Oct. 1707) was presented "for preaching there unlysensed." Kincaide received grants of £3 from the Congregational Fund in 1696, and regularly from 1699. (*Cf. N.*) [23]

STRAND, THE. [2]

STRATFORD LE BOW ('Stratfor le bow'). [39]

STRATFORD-ON-AVON. Ejected here (1662) was Alexander Beane, born at Attleborough, Norf.; son of Daniel Beane, gent.; admitted, 5 June 1629, age 15, at Gonville and Caius Coll., Cambridge; matric. pensioner, 1630; B.A., 1632/3; M.A., 1636; vicar of Stratford, 1648; member of the Kenilworth Classis; soon after his ejection he died, overwrought, in his flight from persecution. (*C. Gc. Hn. Sa. V.*) In 1689, three dwelling-houses in Stratford were registered for Protestant Dissenting worship; viz. at Midsummer, those of Joseph Smith, ironmonger (afterwards of Birmingham), and

William Hunt, woollen-draper; at Michaelmas, that of Richard Bromley. The Meeting-house in the Rother Market "lately erected" was registered at Midsummer, 1714. (*Ab.*) [117, 119]

STRATTON. [20]

STRETHAM ('Strettam'). [13]

STRETTON, RICHARD, M.A. (1632?—3 July 1712). **P.** Born at Claybrook, Leic. Matric., 27 N. 1652 (signing Streaten) at New Coll., Oxford; B.A., 1655/6; M.A., 1658. Received Presbyterian ordination at Arundel, 26 Oct. 1658. Curate (1658–60) to Francis Cheynel, D.D., who held the sequestered rectory of Petworth, Sussex (which had been held *in commendam* by Henry King, bishop of Chichester); ejected, 1660. Chaplain in Yorkshire to Thomas, third Baron Fairfax (17 Jan. 1611/12—12 Nov. 1671) till his death. Licensed, 29 May 1672 as Presb. Teacher in house of Frances Richardson, Cawood, Yorks. Subsequently ministered in Leeds. Came to London, 1677, and ministered to a Presbyterian congregation at Haberdashers' Hall, Staining Lane, Wood Street, Cheapside. Imprisoned, 1683, for refusing the Oxford oath (1665) against endeavouring alteration in Church or State. Co-operated in the Common Fund and the Happy Union, of which he was an original Manager; a Manager also of the reconstituted Fund (1695); he was very generous in furnishing books to Students and to Academies. Stretton, who was one of the Lady Hewley Trustees, proposed (2 June 1712) to free the London Fund from its obligations in the counties of Cumberland, Durham, Northumberland, Westmorland, and York; his co-Trustees would not agree to this proposal.

His son Richard was Minister in 1688 of a Congregational church in York Buildings, Strand. (*C. F. M. P. T. W. Wc. Y.*) [23, 36, 80, 121, 129, 132, 135, 136, 138, 145, 160, 164, 165, 166, 168]

STRETTON-UNDER-FOSSE, in Monks Kirby parish. [118, 119]

STRINGER, JOSIAH. **C.** From the register book (at Somerset House) of the Congregational church at Allostock, Ches., it appears that "Mr Josiah Stringer" was an original member, probably ministering there at its formation on 2 Mar. 1689/90. Stringer was an original member of the Cheshire Classis (p. 157) attending twice, in March and April 1691, but not again. He is described in its Minutes (without Christian name) as "at New Chappel" *i.e.* Knutsford, then Congregational, where he probably was or had been a preacher in conjunction with Thomas Kynaston [*q.v.*]. "Peever" is probably Over Peover, chapelry in Rostherne parish, where the house of Philip Wright had been licensed for Presbyterian worship in Feb. 1672/3. Stringer is conjectured to have removed to Newcastle-under-Lyme. His daughter, Mary (*d.* 1766?), who had some property, married (1711?) Thomas Wedgwood (1685–1739), Master Potter, of the Churchyard, Burslem; the famous Josiah Wedgwood (*bapt.* 12 July 1730–3 Jan. 1795) was her youngest child, evidently named after her father. (*Ch. T. Uc. Wj.*) [15]

STROUD ('Strowd'). Ejected here was . . . Butt. [45]

STUBS, *i.e.* STUBBS, JOHN (*d.* 1740). **P.** Received grants, 1691–95, as Student under John Woodhouse [*q.v.*]. Minister at Wolverhampton, Staff., with grant of £6 a year from 1704 to 1739. Edward Elwall (1676–1744), afterwards Seventh Day Baptist, was a member of his flock, till Stubbs preached against him (about 1718) on account of Unitarian views, which subjected Elwall to a memorable but abortive prosecution. (*D.*) Stubbs' wife (Wilkes) was of the same family as John Wilkes, the politician.

His son, Samuel Stubbs (1715—13 May 1753), educ. under Ebenezer Latham, M.D., at Findern, Derb., was Minister at Lichfield and Longdon, Staff., from 1738 till death. His valuable collection of books, lent by his brother John (Minister at Wolverhampton, 1701–1740) to the Warrington Academy, formed the most important part of its Library; transferred, 8 July 1786, to the Manchester Academy (now Manchester Coll., Oxford), these books (95 volumes) were given, 16 Nov. 1787, by Samuel's widow, Elizabeth Stubbs, "for the use of the Academy at Manchester for ever"; they became (shortly before 1813) the property of that institution by gift of his niece, Miss Newnham. (*Ev. M. Mr.* (1813–14) *Sc.* Minutes of Manchester College.) [28]

STUDENTS. [163, 169, 170, 180-83]

STURMINSTER NEWTON. [35]

SUDBURY. Ejected here were (1) Samuel Crossman, of Pembroke Coll., Cambridge; matric. sizar, 1641; B.A., 1644/5; M.A., 1651; B.D., 1660; rector of Little Henny, Ess., where was no church; pastor of a Congregational church at Sudbury; ejected, 1662; afterwards conformed; prebendary of Bristol, 1667; dean of Bristol, 1683; *d.* 4 Feb.

1683/4, aet. 59. (*B. C. D. E. Le. V.*) (2) William Folkes, M.A. [*q.v.*]. [103]

SUFFIELD. *See* Saffield

SUFFOLK. [103, 106, 168, 172, 176, 181] All is in the Book-keeper's hand, except the headings "Suffolk" (and a marginal note) in the earliest handwriting. The returns are numbered 39 to 162; in 1691, 19, 35, 43; in 1692, 75.

Ai is Eye.
Deberham is Debenham.
E. Bregholt is East Bergholt.
Framlington is Framlingham.
Kittle Barson is Kettlebaston.
Lanham is Lavenham.
Neiland is Nayland.
Peasevall is Peasenhall.
Watsfield is Wattisfield

SUPERIORI, HONORATE. [4, 182]

SURREY. [70, 109, 110, 168, 176, 181] Except the headings "Surrey" in the earliest handwriting, and two entries in another hand, all is in the Book-keeper's hand. The returns are numbered 46 to 72; and 46 in 1691.

Billott is Byfleet [*q.v.*].
Darkinge is Dorking [*q.v.*].
Oakley, Okley is Ockley [*q.v.*].
Waltham on ye Thames is Walton on Thames [*q.v.*].

[It is to be noted that Ewell, where the Episc. Returns report in 1669 a congregation of 50 Nonconformists under Batho, ejected from Ewell rectory [to be distinguished from Thomas Balho, of Gonville and Caius Coll., Cambridge, ejected from Brampton, Suff.], is not mentioned in the Manuscript, though the existing congregation claims continuity from that date. (*C. Cp. T.*)]

SUSSEX. [112, 114, 116, 168, 176] The headings "Sussex," and a marginal note are in the earliest handwriting; the rest in that of the Book-keeper. The returns are numbered 29 to 174; 5, 46, in 1691; 72, in 1692.

Alsiston is Alciston [*q.v.*].
Bourne is Eastbourne.
East Greenstead is East Grinstead [*q.v.*].
Hapsfield is Hartfield.
Medhurst is Midhurst.
Stenning is Steyning.
Thaikham, Thecomb, Thacum is Thakeham.
Walldown is Waldron

SUTTON, Camb. Ejected here was William Hunt, M.A.; born in Hampshire; from Eton, matric. sizar at King's Coll., Cambridge, 1637; B.A., 1640/1; M.A., 1644; vicar of Sutton, July 1643; after ejection, had a dairy farm and taught school; licensed as Pr. Teacher in his house at Sutton, 29 May 1662; died at about 70 years old. His sons William [*q.v.*] and John [*q.v.*] and grandson William were in the Nonconformist ministry. (*C. P. T. V.*) [12]

SUTTON COLDFIELD ('Colefield'). Ejected here was Anthony Burgess (son of schoolmaster at Watford, Herts), of St. John's Coll., Cambridge; matric. sizar, 1623; B.A., 1626/7; rem. to Emmanuel Coll.; Fellow; M.A., 1630; vicar of Sutton Coldfield, 3 Nov. 1635; took refuge in Coventry in 1642, when his cure was filled by the royalist divine, James Fleetwood, D.D.; member of the Westminster Assembly, 1643; ejected, 1662; removed to Tamworth. (*C. Dw. V.*) [120]

SUTTON-IN-ASHFIELD. Ejected here was . . . Tuke, "an ancient blind Man; Congregational in his Judgment." (*C.*) [83]

SUTTON, LONG, Hants. [102]

SWAFFHAM. Ejected here was Jonathan Jephcot; son of John Jephcot of Anstey, Warw., pleb.; from Coventry grammar school matric. at New Inn Hall, Oxford, 20 Apr. 1627, aged 18; vicar of Shilton, Warw.; vicar of Swaffham St. Mary, 1633–62; and of the sequestered vicarage of Swaffham St. Ciric, 1647–61; ejected, 1661; master of Boston grammar school, 1661; ejected, 1662; after ejection, taught school; died Nov. 1673; aged about 65, though Calamy says 96. (*C. P. F.*) [12, 13, 14]

SWALEDALE, Yorks, N.R. (misplaced in E.R.). [139]

SWAN ALLEY was a continuation of Sutton Street, which ran eastward from the East side of St. John's Street, Clerkenwell. Great Sutton Street now covers Sutton Street and Swan Alley. Parallel to Swan Alley, on the north, was Little Swan Alley; this is now extended to John Street and called Little Sutton Street. (*Sl.*) [3]

SWANLAND. [138]

SWANSEA ('Swansey'). Ejected here was Marmaduke Matthews (son of Matthew, of Swansea), of All Souls' Coll., Oxford; matric., 20 Feb. 1623/4, aged 18; B.A., 1624/5; M.A., 1627; some time in New England; vicar of St. John's, Swansea; ejected, 1662; licensed, 12 Apr. 1672, as Independent Teacher in his own house at Swansea; his house in St. John's parish licensed, same date, as a Meeting-place of the Independent way; *d.* about 1683. (*C. F. T.*) [144]

SWEDELAND. [67] *See* Leicestershire

SWINFYN, *i.e.* SWYNFEN, RICHARD,

B.A. (1630–1691/2). ℗. Born at Swynfen, parish of Weeford, Staff. Younger son of John Swynfen, of Swynfen. After passing through schools at Tamworth, Sutton Coldfield and the Charterhouse, matric. at Pembroke Hall, Cambridge, 1650, and was chamber-fellow with Thomas Doolittle [*q.v.*]; B.A., 1653/4. Ordained, 18 Mar. 1655/6, as rector of Sandiacre, Derb. Held (1657) the sequestered rectory of Mavesyn Ridware, Staff.; ejected, 1660. Clarendon offered him high preferment. He remained in communion with the Anglican church, and though preaching as a Nonconformist held no pastorate. He took a farm at Pipe Ridware, Staff., but was driven by the Five Mile Act (1666) to Barton-under-Needwood, Staff. Licensed, June 1672, as "Pr. Teacher in his own house at Burton [*i.e.* Barton], Staff." Here he held a weekly lecture. Licensed, also, 22 July 1672, as "Pr. Teacher in the howse of Wm Palmer at Fish[er]wick, Staff." In 1685 he was imprisoned at Chester on suspicion of complicity with Monmouth's rebellion. Latterly he lived with his youngest son, a mercer at Burton-on-Trent. (*C. De. P. T. V.*) [96]

SWINHOW, GEORGE, M.A. (*fl.* 1631–91). ℗. Matric. pensioner, at Sidney Sussex Coll., 1631; B.A., 1634/5; M.A., 1638. Calamy ejects him from the cure of St. Leonard's Chapel in Aston Clinton, Bucks. The incumbent (1655–62) was George Swinnock (1627—10 N. 1673). Swinhow may have served the cure from 1661, when Swinnock obtained also the vicarage of Great Kimble, Bucks. Swinnock was ejected from both livings in 1662. The Episc. Returns, 1669, report Swinhow as preaching, with Swinnock, at High Wycombe, Bucks, to a meeting "of Presbyterians & Independents very great, & y^e persons very insolent Att the house of M^r William Guy (formerly a Justice of Peace) where is a Pulpit"; also as preaching to about 100 Presbyterians in his own house at Woodrow, Amersham, Bucks, and he was licensed, 11 Apr. 1672, as Presb. Teacher in this house. Removed later to Princes Risborough, Bucks. He "held on his work till age disabled him." The Fund made him (Apr. 1691) a grant of £6 a year for Princes Risborough, but he is not included in the list for June of that year, having removed to Barnet, Herts. (*C. D. M. P. Sm. T. V.*) [9, 10]

SWITHLAND ('Swedeland'). [67]

SYLEHAM. Ejected here was Samuel Habergam, of Emmanuel Coll., Cambridge; matric. sizar, 1641; B.A., 1644/5; M.A., 1648; pastor of the Congregational church of Heveningham, Cookley and Walpole, Suff., before 1650; pastor of the Congregational church of Syleham and Wingfield, 1651/2; vicar of Syleham, ejected, 1662; he was a contributor to the preface (1656) to Tillinghast's treatises (*see* Petto, Samuel); *d.* 1665. (*B. C. V.*) [107]

SYLVESTER, MATTHEW, B.A. (1637?—25 Jan. 1707/8). ℗. Born at Southwell, Notts. Son of Robert Sylvester, mercer. From Southwell grammar-school he entered St. John's Coll., Cambridge, as pensioner on 4 May 1654, aged 17; matric., 1654; B.A., 1658. Vicar of Great Gonerby, Linc., 1659; ejected, 1662; the bishop of Lincoln, Robert Sanderson (1587–1663), his distant relative, in vain offered him further preferment. He became chaplain successively to Sir John Bright, and to John White. From Mansfield (where he lived with Joseph Truman, M.A. (2 Feb. 1630/1—19 July 1671), ejected from the rectory of Cromwell, Notts) he came in 1667 to London. On 13 Apr. 1672, being of Coleman Street, he was licensed as "Presb. Teacher in any allowed place." His congregation met in Rutland House, Charterhouse Yard, but moved in 1692 to a Meeting-house in a court off Knightrider Street. Richard Baxter [*q.v.*], who made him his literary executor, was his unpaid assistant (1687–91); Edmund Calamy, D.D. [*q.v.*], was his assistant (1692–3). His chief work was his ill-edited "Reliquiae Baxterianae," 1696, a work of prime importance. (*D. Jo. T. V.*) [165]

TAFT. [13] *See* Cambridgeshire

TALLENT, *i.e.* TALLENTS, FRANCIS, M.A. (Nov. 1619—11 Apr. 1708). ℗. Born at Pilsley, parish of North Wingfield, Derb. Eldest son of Philip Tallents, whose father was a Frenchman. From the grammar schools of Mansfield and Newark he was admitted sizar at Peterhouse, Cambridge, 14 May 1636; matric., 1637; migrated to Magdalene Coll.; B.A., 1640; Fellow; M.A., 1645. He travelled abroad (1642) with pupils, including a son of the earl of Suffolk. Ordained (1648) by presbyters in London. Lecturer and curate (1653) at St. Mary's, Shrewsbury; ejected, 1662. He was much in London in 1663 and 1664. The Episc. Returns, 1669, report him as preaching at Wirksworth, Derb., in "the house of John Gell, Esq^r. of Hopton, who comes to church to Divine service and sermon constantly & his family: but noe other Conventicle in the countrey observes this Decorum." In 1671-4 he was in France with his pupil, John Hampden, the younger. Returning, he became colleague with John Bryan, M.A. [*q.v.*], in the ministry at High Street, Shrewsbury. The building was known as Oliver Chapel, hence the inscription placed upon it by Tallents, stating that it was "not built for a faction or party, but for promoting repentance and faith, in communion with all that love our Lord Jesus Christ, in sincerity." He joined in thanks to James II. for his liberty of conscience declaration. (*C. Cm. D. P. Ph. T. V.*) [15, 88, 89]

TAME. [85, 86] *See* Oxfordshire

TAMWORTH. [98]

TAPPER, SAMUEL, B.A. (1636—3 Mar. 1709/10). **P.** Second son of Oliver Tapper, gent., of Exeter. Entered Exeter Coll., Oxford, aged 15; matric., 27 N. 1652; B.A., 1655/6. Left Oxford on grounds of health, and preached at Exeter. Ordained by presbyters, 5 Aug. 1657, as curate to Humphrey Saunders, M.A., rector of Holsworthy, Devon (ejected, 1662). Held the sequestered vicarage of St. Merran, Corn.; ejected, 1660. Chaplain to R. Erisey of Erisey, parish of Glade, Corn. Removed to Exeter, where the Episc. Returns, 1665, report him as a Presbyterian, not conventicling. Not licensed (yet signed the thanks from Devon Ministers), but preached some time (the liturgy being read by another) by connivance of the Bishop (Seth Ward), who valued him for his learning and moderation. In 1687 became Minister of "the people commonly called Presbyterians" at Lympstone, Devon, where a Meeting-house was built for him (1689). He resigned, 1708, in favour of Joseph Manston, his assistant from 1703. (*C. F. Mh. P. T. Wc.*) [30]

TARRANT, W. G. [171]

TARYSTOCK. [30] *See* Devonshire

TATHAM. Ejected from this rectory was Nicholas Smith, who was Minister at Tatham before 1646. (*C. Sy.*) The Common Fund granted (1691) £5 a year for work at Tatham [*i.e.* Tatham Fell] Chapel; this was dropped in 1695. (*M.*) [63, 64]

TAUNTON. Ejected here were (1) Joseph Alleine (1634—17 Nov. 1668) of Lincoln Coll., Oxford; rem. to Corpus Christi Coll.; matric., 14 Nov. 1651; Scholar, 1651; chaplain, 1653; B.A., 1653; curate to George Newton, 1655; ejected, 1662; *d.* at Taunton. His posthumous "Alarme to Unconverted Sinners" is a classic among religious tracts. (*C. D. F. P.*) (2) George Newton, cler. fil., of Exeter Coll., Oxford; matric., 17 Dec. 1619, aged 17; B.A., 1621; M.A., 1624; curate in charge of Bishop's Hull, Som.; vicar of St. Mary Magdalen, Taunton, 1631; ejected, 1662; preaching at Taunton and West Monkton, Som., in 1669; licensed, 2 May 1672, as Pr. Teacher in a house at Taunton; *d.* 12 June 1681, aged 79. (*C. D. F. T.*) [91, 92, 172]

TAVERTON. [31]. *See* Devonshire

TAVISTOCK ('Tarystock'). Ejected here was Thomas Larkham (4 May 1601-1669), **P.**, of Trinity Coll., Cambridge; admitted sizar, 1619; M.A., 1626; preached first at Northam, Dev.; driven by persecution to New England, vicar of Tavistock; ejected, 1662; living at Tavistock, 1665; founded congregation there. (*C. N. T. V.*) [30]

TAYLER, *i.e.* TAYLOR, JOHN (*fl.* 1690-1729). **C.** Entered Frankland's Academy, 11 Apr. 1690. "John Tayler of Fournace ffells," student under Frankland, received Fund grants of £10 a year from 26 Jan. 1690/1. Minister in 1694 at the Meeting-house near Smarber Hall, Swaledale, W.R. Ordained at Rathmell, 26 May 1698, along with James Taylor [*q.v.*] and seven others. Minister at Swarsdale, W.R., in 1715, and apparently in 1729. Received grants from the Congregational Fund. (*Cf. Ev. Fr. Hh. M. My. Nk.*) [136]

TAYLER, . . . [9]. *See* Archibald Hamilton

TAYLOR, CHRISTOPHER (*d.* 26 O. 1723). **P.** Born at Taunton. Educ. in the Academy of Matthew Warren [*q.v.*]. Ordained, 25 Aug. 1687, at Lyme, Dorset. Minister (1692 ?) at Frog Lane, Bath; succeeded Richard Bures (*d.* 7 May 1697) at Leather Lane, London. He was elected a Fund Manager, 25 O. 1697. He lived in 1715 "in Eagle-street, near Redlion-square," removing to "Clerkenwell-green, over agt ye Church." Taylor was sent by the Government to Scotland in 1706, along with John Barrington Shute (afterwards Viscount Barrington) a Congregational, to plead the cause of the Union, which English Nonconformists desired as a security for the Protestant succession. Shute was to deal with nobility and gentry, Taylor with the Ministers. He was disabled for a considerable time before his death; his last attendance as Manager of the Fund was on May 1722. (*Cm. Ev. M. Mh. W.*) [93, 94]

TAYLOR, EDMUND, M.A. (*fl.* 1647–1715 ?). **P.** Educated at Emmanuel Coll., Cambridge, B.A., 1647/8; M.A., 1651; incorp. at Oxford, 1657. Held 1655, the sequestered rectory of Littleton, Middx.; ejected, 1660. Licensed, 29 May 1672, as "Pr. Teacher in his howse in Wittham, Essex." Imprisoned in Tilbury Fort during the Monmouth rebellion. He was of Ledbury, Heref., 1705–9 (receiving £8 a year from the Fund); removing to Alton, Hants, where £10 was voted to him on 3 May 1714. He received also from the Congregational Fund. He died in or soon after 1715. (*C. Ev. F. Lz. M. P. T.*) [41]

TAYLOR, JAMES (1670—11 Feb. 1743/4). His first year with Frankland was, apparently, not as a regular Student; his entrance in the Academy is dated 9 Mar. 1691/2. Received (23 Feb. 1690/1) a grant of £4 a year; increased (6 June 1692) to £8; ended June 1696. Ordained, 26 May 1698, as Rathmell along with John Taylor (*see* Tayler) and seven others. Minister at Ellenthorp, N.R., where he died. Received special Fund grants of £5, 1732–36–42. [Since his father was of Preston there is no reason for mixing him up with John Taylor.] (*Ev. Fr. Hh. M. My. Nk.*) [64]

TAYLOR, MICHAEL, B.A. (*d.* 26 May 1705). **P.** Born at Silverton, Devon. Matric. pensioner, at Sidney Sussex Coll., Cambridge, 1647; B.A., 1650/1. Ordained by presbyters. Assistant to Humphrey Saunders, M.A., ejected from the rectory of Holsworthy, Devon; held the sequestered rectory of Pyworthy, Devon; ejected, 1660; "but would have conformed on the *Restoration*, could he have kept the *Living*" (Walker); his widow, Mary Taylor (a relative of Saunders) denied, by letter of 12 F. 1717/8 that her husband had "any Inclination to Conformity." The Episc. Returns, 1665, report him as living "quietly" at Holsworthy. Licensed, 1 May 1672, as "John Taylour of Pyworthy" to be "a Grāll Pr. Teacher; also, 8 May 1672, as "Michael Taylour of Holsworthy" to be "a Grāll Pr. Teacher." Also, 10 June 1672, as Michael Taylor of Tavistock, to be Grāll Pr. Teacher. From 1687 he had a Meeting-house in Holsworthy. The Fund granted him, 1690–1704, £5 a year for Holsworthy (increased to £6). (*C. M. P. T. V. Wc.*) [31]

TAYLOR, RICHARD, M.A. (*d.* 12 Aug. 1697). **C.** Matric., 9 Dec. 1653, at Jesus Coll., Oxford, as 'gent'; his tutor was Samuel Jones, M.A. [*q.v.*]; B.A., 1657; M.A., 1659. Perpetual curate of Holt, Denbighsh., 1659; ejected, 1662. Before 1683 became Congregational Minister at Barking, Essex. Apparently he assisted Richard Wavell [*q.v.*] at Pinners' Hall. Unlike Wavell, he did not join the Happy Union; though elected (3 Apr. 1693) a Manager of the Common Fund, he never attended. He was an original Manager (1695) of the Congregational Fund, and one of its correspondents for Bedfordshire, Buckinghamshire, Cambridgeshire, Northumberland, Westmorland, and Yorkshire.

He must be distinguished from a contemporary Richard Taylor, also Congregational, who lived "in Chiswell Street, near Finsbury," whose Meeting-house was in Little Moorfields, London, and who died in 1717. In his Meeting-house in 1694 Calamy preached the funeral sermon of a Student, Samuel Stephens, and had the coffin brought into the Meeting-house during the service; this he records as a novelty. (*C. Cm. Co. E. Ev. F. M. P.*) [35, 38, 156, 161, 165]

TAYLOR, RICHARD (1649—20 Apr. 1699), only child of Samuel Taylor (1624—29 Mar. 1679), who was major in the Parliamentary army, governor of Tangier, temp. Charles II., and settled at Wallingwell Hall, near Carlton in Lindrick, Notts, worth £5000 a year. Richard, his heir, was sheriff of Nottinghamshire and M.P. for Retford. He was buried at Carlton. His only daughter and heiress, Bridget, married Thomas White, of Tuxford, Notts, from whom descends the present Sir Archibald Woollaston White, Bart., of Wallingwells Hall. (*Bu. H.*) [83]

TAYLOR ('Tayler'), SAMUEL, B.A. (1627—26 June 1695). **P.** Matric. pensioner, at Magdalene Coll., Cambridge, 1645; B.A., 1648/9. Curate of Edstaston, then a chapelry in the parish Wem, Shrops.; ejected, 1662. Lived at Wem, where his house was burnt down (1676). Licensed, 8 May 1672, as Pr. Teacher in his house at Wem. He received, from 1690, a yearly grant of £6 (reduced in 1695 to £5) for Wem. (*C. M. P. T. V.*) [16, 89]

TAYLOR, THOMAS, B.A. (Nov. 1625–Nov. 1700). **C.** Born at Sheringham, Norf., son of Stephen Tailor, gent., of Kimberley, Norf. From Wymondham grammar school admitted sizar at Gonville and Caius Coll., Cambridge, 23 Oct. 1641, age 16; matric., 1642; B.A.,

1645/6. His father, a cavalier, fearing roundhead influence, removed him to a private school at Matteshall. Embracing puritan sentiments, he preached in and about Norwich, and became master of the Swaffham grammar school, and lecturer, 1653 (ordained, 3 Jan. 1655/6) to a gathered church at Bury St. Edmunds, meeting in the Shire House, and (from 1659 ?) in the chancel of St. Mary's. Ejected in 1662, and imprisoned for over a year, he became a tobacco merchant in London, still preaching there and at Croydon. The Episc. Returns, 1669, report him as one of the preachers to 2 or 300 persons in St. Mary's parish, Bury St. Edmunds "att the houses of Robt Heyward, John Cooke, John Stannard, a wollen drap & sometimes in a barne of Mrs Adams's every Sunday." He was an agent for procuring licences, and obtained the licence (9 May 1672) for John Bunyan. His own licence, 25 July 1672, was as Congr. Teacher in his house in Gracechurch Street, London. About 1689 he succeeded Francis Holcroft [*q.v.*] at Green Street Meeting-house, Cambridge, and held this pastorate till his death. He was one of the witnesses against Richard Davis [*q.v.*] at Kettering in 1692. (*B. C. D. Gc. Gl. P. T. V.*) [11, 14, 117]

TAYLOR, THOMAS (*fl.* 1684–90). Entered Frankland's Academy, 6 Feb. 1684/5. [On 15 July 1690 the house of Esther Leigh in Newton was registered for worship, the Minister being Thomas Taylor.] (*Fr. X.*) [63, 64]

TEATHAM. [63, 64] *See* Lancashire

TELNEY. [71] *See* Norfolk

TEMPLE HALL, hamlet in Sibson parish, Leic. Here (in a small Meeting-house, still standing, though converted into a dwelling) in conjunction with Atherstone, Warw., ministered (1765–1794) the present writer's great-grandfather, Richard Wright, an Arian divine and schoolmaster, grandson of Thomas Irlam [*q.v.*], and here he found his wife, Mary Hall. Some years ago, in the company of the late Charles Henry Butcher, dean of Cairo, it was mentioned that the only likeness of Richard Wright is in a pen-and-ink sketch by his pupil, Edmund Butcher, the dean's grandfather. The Temple Hall small endowment, on the failure of the congregation, was assigned to the Great Meeting, Leicester (*see* John Sheffield). [66, 67]

TERRY, EDWARD, M.A. (*d.* 7 Mar. 1715/6). **C.** Younger son of Edward Terry, rector of Greenford Magna, Middx. Matric. at Christ Church, Oxford, 5 April 1650; migrated to University Coll., B.A., 17 Dec. 1650; Fellow, 1650–60; M.A., 1653. Rector of Agmondesham, Bucks, 1657–60. Succeeded his father as rector of Greenford Magna, 27 Feb. 1661. Ejected, 1662.

In the Episcopal Returns (1669) "Mr Terry" is recorded as one of the preachers to Presbyterians at Chalfont St. Giles, Bucks. On 16 May 1672 Edward Terry was licensed as a Congr. Teacher in the house of Anne Fleetwood, widow, at Chalfont St. Giles. In 1689 he was assisting Isaac Chauncy, M.A., in Mark Lane. Some years before his death he became blind.

His elder brother, James Terry (1609–1680), was ejected from the sequestered rectory of Michelmersh, Hants. (*C. F. P. T. W. Wc.*) [4]

TETNEY. Ejected here was Martin Finch [*q.v.*]. The Common Fund offered (1691) £8 to Tetney for one year "on condition they fix a minister"; but "none fixed" (1692). (*M.*) [71]

TEWKESBURY (' Tuexbery '). The Common Fund granted (1691) £10 a year for Tewkesbury, reduced (1695) to £8; the Minister was Mr. Sloane. [46]

THAKEHAM ('Thaikham,' 'Thacum,' 'Thecomb'). [115]

THAME. [85, 86]

THAMES STREET. Old Swan Lane still runs from the South side of Upper Thames Street, between Nos. 100 and 101. [2]

THAXTED (' Thackstead '). Ejected here was James Parkin, of Emmanuel Coll., Cambridge; matric. sizar, 1631; B.A., 1633/4; M.A., 1637; vicar of Thaxted, 1648; ejected, 1662. (*C. E. V.*) [39]

THECOMB. [115] *See* Sussex

THELKELD. [22] *See* Cumberland

THEOBALDS. [50]

THIRTY-NINE ARTICLES. [156]

THOMAS, ANTHONY. [146]

THOMAS, JENKIN (*d.* 1711). **C.** Minister at Wrexham, Denb. (*Rj.*) [145, 146]

THOMAS, JOHN (*d.* 1748 ?). **P.** Apparently it was while ministering at Rhoseygwylyn that he entered the Carmarthen College, studying under Thomas Perrot, tutor there, 1719–33. He succeeded Daniel Phillips [*q.v.*] at Pwllheli and Carnarvon, and married his widow soon after his ordination (21 June 1723). Received Fund grants, £5 a year, 1723–1748. His "orthodoxy" was doubted. He died in 1748 or soon after. (*Ev. Je. M. Rj.*) [144]

THOMAS, ROBERT (*d.* 1690 ?). 𝕮. Matric. pleb. at Jesus Coll., Oxford, 9 Aug. 1658. Preaching at Baglan, Glam., as Nonconforming candidate for the ministry in 1662. The Episc. Returns, 1669, report him as preaching at Baglan to "About 20 Catabaptists, Anabaptists, Independents entertained by" him. Licensed, 16 July 1672, as "Congr. in his howse at Bagland." Baglan parish is near Neath, and Thomas became pastor of the Congregational churches at Neath, Llangyfelach, Blaengwrach, etc. (*C. F. P. Rj. Rw. T.*) [145]

THOMAS, WILLIAM, B.A. (*d.* 1693). 𝕮. Born in Wales. Matric. pleb. at Gloucester Hall, Oxford, 24 June 1653; B.A., 30 Jan. 1655/6. Minister and schoolmaster at Bristol "in Oliver's time." Had offers of good preferment in Wales if he would conform. Taught many Students for the ministry. Died in Bristol. (*C. Cm. F. P.*) [91]

THOMPSON, JOHN, *i.e.* THOMAS (23 July 1661—7 Apr. 1729). 𝕻. Entered Frankland's Academy, 27 April 1681. Ordained, 11 July 1688, as Minister of Stockton-on-Tees. From a room in Bolton House Yard the congregation moved (1699) to a Meeting-house in Mill Garth, where Thompson ministered till death. He was succeeded by his youngest son, John (1702—23 F. 1753). (*Ev. Nr. Rs.*) [36]

THOMPSON, *i.e.* THOMSONE, or THOMSON, WILLIAM, M.A. (*fl.* 1671–1716). 𝕻. Educ. at Edinburgh; M.A., 20 Mar. 1671. Minister of Douglas, Lanarksh., 20 S. 1682; translated to Borrowstounness, 1685; deprived, 12 S. 1689. Ordained Minister of Lochmaben, Dumfriessh., 27 May 1691; demitted, 1716. (*Ed. Sf.*) [80]

THOMSON, JAMES (*fl.* 1690–93). Entered the Academy of John Woodhouse [*q.v.*]. The Fund made him (Feb. 1691) a gift of £4, and (1692–3) a bursary of £4 a year. (*M.*) [17]

THOMSON, *i.e.* THOMPSON, SIR JOHN (1648 ?—1 N. 1710) of Haversham, Bucks; baronet, 1673; created Baron Haversham, 1696. (*Ba. Pe.*) [58]

THOMSON, JOSEPH. Elected a Manager, 23 May 1692, replacing Daniel Mercer, [*q.v.*]. His last attendance was on 19 June 1693. Not a Manager (1695) of the reconstituted Fund. Capt. Wm. Thompson was a Manager (1695) of the Congregational Fund, and one of its correspondents for Cumberland. (*Co. M.*) [162, 166]

THORNEY LANE ('Thorny Lanes') is a hamlet about 3 miles S.E. of Uttoxeter. [98]

THORNLY, . . . [4] [John Thornly or Thorley. 𝕻. Minister of Chipping Norton, Oxon; received Fund grants of £5, raised to £10, 1701–1751; living in 1759. (*Ev. M.*)]

THOROWGOOD, NICHOLAS, M.A. (1620—17 Nov. 1691). 𝕻. Born at Deal. While at grammar school learnt also modern languages. Engaged in foreign trade (1636), travelled in Spain and Italy, studied at Padua. Resolved on the ministry, he entered at New Hall Inn, Cambridge; and migrated to Corpus Christi Coll.; B.A., 1644/5. After graduation he became chaplain, on the ship Happy Entrance, to Robert Rich, earl of Warwick, lord high admiral. On 12 Dec. 1644 he obtained the rectory of Hawkhurst, Kent (ordained in London by presbyters, 20 June 1645), but lost it (30 Apr. 1651) through not taking the engagement (allegiance to government without king or house of lords). From 13 June 1651 he held the vicarage of Monkton, Kent; ejected, 1662. He removed to Stockbury, and (1667) to Canterbury, where (1668) he preached publicly and got into prison; in 1669 he also preached at Sandwich. On 13 Apr. 1672 he was licensed as Presb. Teacher in his own house, Canterbury. He removed to Rochester, and on 10 June 1672 was licensed as Presb. Teacher in house of William Buck. He left Rochester, owing to "unkindness of some people." Apart from this Manuscript there is no reference to his ministry at Woolwich, which probably followed immediately upon that of David Evans, who left in 1689. His last move was to Godalming, Surrey, not long before his death. The Common Fund offered him (28 S. 1691) £10 a year "if he fix at Town Malling, Kent." (*C. M. P. T. V.*) [4, 57]

THORP, RICHARD, M.A. (*d.* 6 Jan. 1716). 𝕻. Matric. pensioner at Sidney Sussex Coll., Cambridge, 1654; B.A., 1657/8; M.A., 1661. Though included (as Thorpe and Thorps) in Calamy's list as ejected from Hopton, Yorks, there is no evidence that Thorp ever held any preferment; nor, in 1660, was there any place of worship at Hopton. Becoming a Nonconformist at the Restoration, Thorp held services and administered the Lord's Supper at his residence, Hopton Hall, in Upper Hopton, a village in Mirfield parish, W.R. (having now a church, built 1846, and made an ecclesiastical parish in 1860). In 1667 "Richard Thorpe, of Hopton, Gent," founded in Mirfield a school (still maintained) for the education of fifteen poor children. The Episc. Returns, 1669, report him as preaching, along with Oliver Heywood [*q.v.*], to "a great number many people of good estates at the house of Thomas Webster of Dewisbury." Licensed, 30 Sept. 1672, as "Pr. Teacher at his owne house at Hopton in Yorksh." He died at Lees Hall, near Thornhill, West Riding, which he had bought a few months previously for about £1800.

His son, Daniel (buried at Mirfield, 11 Mar. 1718/9), continued to conduct services at Hopton Hall, but did not administer the sacrament. Richard Thorp's wife, Madam Thorp, died, 8 May 1725, at the house of her son-in-law, Richard Hutton of Pudsey; she had been preceded by her daughter, Madam Hutton (*d.* Dec. 1723), who left £5 a year to maintain services at Hopton. (*Ay. C. My. Nr. P. T. V. Y.*) [130]

THORPE MALSOR. Ejected here was John Courtman, M.A., B.D. [*q.v.*]. [76]

THORPE WATERVILLE ('Waterfield'). Manor in Achurch parish, Northants. [77, 78]

THORVERTON, or THAVERTON ('Daverton,' 'Taverton'). [30, 31]

THREE DENOMINATIONS. [189]

THRELKELD ('Thelkeld'). [22, 178]

THRIPLOW ('Thriplo'). [13]

TIDCOMBE, TOBIAS, M.A. (*fl.* 1647–90). Of St. Edmund Hall, Oxford, B.A., 3 June 1647; rem. to New Inn Hall, M.A., 1648; Fellow of Corpus Christi Coll., 1648. Held (1656) the sequestered rectory of Ditcheat, Som.; ejected, 1660. [Probably father of Jeremiah Tidcombe (*d.* 1717), Minister of Beckington, Som., in 1703, and grandfather of Jeremiah Tidcombe (*d.* 1740), Minister at Gloucester, 1722; Ratcliffe Cross, 1729, also from 1735 afternoon preacher at Salters' Hall.] (*C. Ev. F. M. Mh. P. W. Wc.*) [92, 93]

TIDESWELL ('Tidswell'). [26]

TILNEY. [71]

TINE, NORTH. [80] *See* Northumberland

TINGCOMB, THEOPHILUS, B.A. (*d.* 1719). **P.** Matric. at Pembroke Hall, Cambridge, 1654; B.A., 1658. Not beneficed, but preached occasionally before 1662, then silenced; licensed, 29 May 1672, as Pr. Teacher in his house at Lostwithiel, Corn., where also the house of William Elliott was licensed, 22 July. Signed the thanks from Cornish Ministers. Minister at Callington, Corn., 1689. He received special Fund grants of £6 and £12, between 1713 and 1717; he is described as "an Aged Ejected Ministr." In May 1718 he was still preaching to 60 people at Talvaus, near St. Germans, Corn., and living "at Metherel in Calstock-Parish [on ye Borders of Devonshire]," not far from Callington, but a dozen miles from St. Germans. On 5 O. 1719 a grant of £10 was voted to, but not received by him; his death was reported on 7 D. 1719. (*C. Ev. M. P. T.*) [18]

TINTAGEL ('Tintagoll'). Ejected here was Thomas Hearne, vicar or curate. [19]

TIPPETT, ANDREW (*fl.* 1690–93). The Common Fund granted him (1691) £6 a year for Painswick; not renewed, 1695. (*M.*) [44, 45]

TIPTREE ('Tiptry') HEATH, partly in Messing parish. [42]

TIRREY, or TERRY, WILLIAM (*fl.* 1690–1699). **C.** The Common Fund voted (1691) £10 a year for Hastings "on condition Mr Terry fix there"; by 18 Apr. 1692 he had removed. From 1694 to 1699 he was pastor at Back Street, Hitchin, Herts. The Congregational Fund voted him (1 June 1696) £5. He removed to Kettering, Northants, and was pastor for a short time there, going thence to London. He "had travelled in Holland and Germany, and did not seem inclined to settle long in any place." (*Cf. Cn. M. Uh.*) [113]

TIVERTON. Ejected here were (1) Theophilus Polwheele, born in Cornwall; of Emmanuel Coll., Cambridge; admitted sizar, 1644; M.A., 1651; preached in Cumberland at Egremont, Kirkbampton, Carlisle (1651–55); vicar of Tiverton, 1655; ejected, 1660; living and preaching at Tiverton, 1665; preaching at Cruwys Morchard, 1669; licensed, 2 Apr. 1672, as Teacher, Congregational, in Tiverton; bur. 3 Apr. 1689; father-in-law of Stephen Lobb [*q.v.*]. (*C. D. N. T. V.*) (2) John Chishull [? of Christ's Coll., Cambridge; admitted sizar, 1640; B.A., 1643/4], from keeping a boarding school at Enfield, Middx., came as preacher to Tiverton, and here silenced [not identical with John Chiswell, B.A., preaching at his house in London, 1669]; licensed, 20 Apr. 1672, as Presb. Teacher at his house in Enfield; house licensed same date as Presb. Meeting-place; *d.* about 1674. (*C. T. V.* not in *F.*) [30]

TOCESTER. [77] *See* Northamptonshire

TOD, *i.e.* TODD, CORNELIUS, M.A. (July 1631—29 June 1696). **P.** Born at Ledsham, West Riding; baptized, 28 July 1631. Eldest son of Robert Todd, M.A. (1594—16 Jan. 1664/5), then vicar, ejected (1662) from the vicarage of St. John's, Leeds. From Leeds grammar school he proceeded to Clare Hall, Cambridge; matric. sizar, 1647; B.A., 1650; M.A., 1654. Chaplain to Mrs. Leighton, and afterwards to Lord Fairfax. Ordained by presbyters at Adel, West Riding, 31 Oct. 1655. Rector of Bilborough, Notts; four years later vicar of Bilton, West Riding; ejected, 1662. Lord Wharton gave him a pension of £8 a year and a residence at Healaugh Manor, West Riding. On the Indulgence of 1672 he was chosen one of four Nonconformist Ministers to preach at the new Meeting-house, Mill Hill, Leeds. Accordingly application was made by J. Acklam, alderman of Hull, for a general licence "for Cornelius Todd of Healey Mannor in Yorkeshire a Master of Arts to preach in or nigh ye Towne of Leedes in the same County or elsewhere in any Licensed Towne of England." Licensed, 16 May 1672, as "Grāll Pr. Teacher." His Leeds ministry ended in 1674, and soon after he was employed as one of the preachers at a Chapel erected (1658) by the Brookes family near Ellenthorpe Hall, parish of Aldborough, North Riding. This Chapel was endowed with £20 a year by Lady Brook, or Brookes [*q.v.*]. Todd ultimately was in sole charge at Ellenthorpe. An imprisonment at Pontefract injured his health. He was buried at Alne, North Riding. (*Ba. C. My. Nr. P. T. V. Wl.*) [131, 135]

TOFT ('Taft'). [13]

TOKENS. [178]

TOLAND, JOHN, M.A. (30 N. 1670—11 Mar. 1721/2). Born at Inishowen, Co. Derry. Died at Putney. His first book, "Christianity not Mysterious," 1696 (anonymous; written at Oxford, 1694–5), "struck the keynote of the long discussion as to the relation between the religion of nature and the accepted doctrines" (Leslie Stephen). Calamy, who rejected overtures from him in 1705, speaks of him as "a very pushing man," with "a strange inclination to unbeaten and untrodden paths." (*Cm. D. M.*) [182, 183]

TOLERATION ACT. [154, 188]

TOLLAND. [91]

TOMLYNS, JOHN (*d.* 1693?). ℭ. Probably son of Samuel Tomlyns, M.A. [*q.v.*]. The Common Fund voted him in 1690 £6 a year for Alton, on 20 Mar. 1693 an additional sum of £4 was voted, but as nothing was paid after 19 June 1693, his death probably occurred in that year. (*M.*) [101]

TOMLYNS, or TOMLINS, SAMUEL, M.A. (1633—18 June 1700). ℭ. Born at Newbury, Berks. Pensioner at Trinity Coll., Cambridge, 9 N. 1647; matric., 1647; B.A., 1651; migrated to Corpus Christi Coll.; M.A., 1655. After a chaplaincy, became (1655) rector of Crawley, Hants; ejected, 1662. The Episc. Returns, 1669, report him as one of the preachers to "Presbyterians Att the house of one Jones St Michaels in the Soke at Winton." Excommunicated, 1 July 1671. Licensed, 13 Apr. 1672, as "Presb. Teacher in ye howse of Ann Complin in Wintoñ & over the Markett place of that Citty." He was nine years Minister at Winchester; imprisoned there in 1679; and removed thence to Hilcott, Wilts. In 1687 he became Minister at Andover, Hants (he was there in 1692, teaching as well as preaching); he removed thence to Marlborough, Wilts, where he died. On 16 Feb. 1690/1 Matthew Mead handed to the Fund Board a certificate signed by Samuel Tomlyns and John Tomlyns [*q.v.*] in favour of Joseph Standen, a Student in Alton parish, Hants, who received a grant of £10 a year, 1691–3, for study under a Tutor to be fixed by Mead, who placed him with Samuel Tomlyns. (*C. M. P. T. Tc. V.*) [100]

TOOELL, RICHARD (*fl.* 1687–90). Ordained, 25 Aug. 1687, at Lyme, Dorset, being then of Dulverton, Som. (where Joseph Chadwick [*q.v.*] was Minister in 1690). [Arthur Towel (*d.* 1729) was Minister at Minehead, Som., from 1722.] (*Ev. M. W.*) [93, 94, 95]

TOOGOOD, *i.e.* TOWGOOD, STEPHEN (*d.* 1722). ℭ. Elder son of Matthew Towgood (*d.* 1669?), ejected (1660) from the sequestered rectory of Hilperton, Wilts, and (1662) from the rectory of Semley, Wilts. From Axminster, Devon (there in 1715), he removed in 1721 to Newport, I.W. (*D. Ev. Wc.*) [30]

TOOTING. [70]

TOOZER, *i.e.* TOZER, EDMUND. [31] [Giles and Peter Tozer were members, in April 1672, of the congregation of John Flavell [*q.v.*] at Dartmouth. Abraham Tozer was Minister of Bow Meeting, Exeter, 1755–94. (*Mh. T.*)]

TOPCLIFFE ('Topliff'), a Hall and hamlet in West Ardsley (otherwise Woodkirk) parish, W.R. (*My.*) There is another Topcliffe in N.R.; from its vicarage was ejected in 1662 James Calvert (son of Robert, grocer, York) of Clare Hall, Cambridge; matric. pensioner, 1646; B.A., 1649/50; M.A., 1653; after ejection removed to York; licensed 25 July

1672, as Pr. Teacher in his house at York; his house licensed, same date, Pr.; chaplain to Sir W. Strickland of Boynton; chaplain to Sir W. Middleton; *d.* 1698. (*C. T. V.*) [129, 132]

TOPSHAM. [30]

TORRINGTON, GREAT. Ejected here was John Howe, M.A. [*q.v.*] [30, 31]

TOSSELL. [19] *See* Cornwall

TOSSIDE. [135]

TOTNES ('Tottnas'). Ejected here was Francis Whiddon, of Wadham Coll., Oxford; matric., 2 Apr. 1652; B.A., 1654/5; M.A., 1657. Ordained by presbyters; rector of Moreton Hampstead, Devon, 1656; resigned this for the vicarage of Totnes; ejected, 1662. Living peaceably at Totnes, 1665; licensed, 11 Apr. 1672, as Presb. Teacher in his house at Totnes. Died, 21 Sept. 1679. (*C. F. P. T.*) [31]

TOTTENHAM ('Totnam'). Ejected here was Thomas Sympson [? M.A., Edinburgh, 30 July 1646; incorp. at Cambridge, 1653], vicar of Tottenham, 1655; ejected, 1660?; living in 1662. (*Ed. P. V.*) [72]

TOTTLEBANK HOUSE, in the parish of Colton-in-Furness, or West Colton. The Common Fund voted (19 Jan. 1690/1) £6 a year for work at Tottlebank and Broughton Tower (dropped, 1695). (*M.*) [63]

TOW-CESTER. [77]

TOWN MALLING. Ejected here was Samuel French [*q.v.*]. The Common Fund granted (1692) £10 a year for Town Malling; reduced (1695) to £4. The vicar in 1690 was Abraham Lord. (*M.*) [57]

TOXTETH PARK. No ejection here; *see* Thomas Crompton, M.A. [58, 59, 177]

TRAIL, ROBERT, M.A. (May 1642–May 1716). **C.** Born at Elie, Fife. Second son of Robert Trail, M.A. (1606—12 July 1678), then Minister of Elie (afterwards of first charge, Greyfriars, Edinburgh), by his wife, Jean Annan. Graduated at Edinburgh, 14 July 1659. In 1667, owing to persecutions, joined his father in Holland. Received Presbyterian ordination in London, 1670. Licensed, 16 May 1672, as Presb. Teacher in house of William Love, at Cranbrook, Kent. Returned to preach in Scotland. Arrested, 19 July 1677, on charge of field-conventicling, and committed to the Bass Rock. Appears as preacher in London, 1682, at which time Thomas Cole [*q.v.*] was Congregational Minister at Tallow-chandlers' Hall, Dowgate Hill. Assisted Nathaniel Mather [*q.v.*] at Paved Alley, Lime Street, till Mather's death (26 July 1697). Became a Manager of the Congregational Fund. Afterwards "gathered a separate congregation, of which he was pastor several years." Trail took an active part in the Crispian controversy, defending the positions of Crisp. It is pleasant to note that a special grant of £5 from the older Fund was voted to him on 4 Jan. 1713/4. (*Ed. M. Sf. T. W.*) [4, 183]

TREVETHICK, 'THOMAS,' *i.e.* WILLIAM, M.A. (1613?–July 1693). **P.** Son of Thomas Trevethick, of St. Eval, Corn. Matric., 11 May 1632, at Magdalen Hall, Oxford, aged 16; B.A., 1634; M.A., 1636/7. Held the sequestered rectory of Petrockstow, Devon, 1656; ejected, 1660, though the death of the old rector gave him a legal title. Went abroad as tutor to Samuel, son of his patron, Col. Robert Rolle (*d.* 1661), of Heanton Satchville, Devon. Licensed, June 1672, as Pr. Teacher in his house at St. Eval. Signed the thanks of Cornish Ministers. (*C. Em. P. T. Wc.* Fun. Serm. *for Rolle.*) [18]

TROSSE, GEORGE (25 O. 1631—11 Jan. 1712/3). **P.** Born at Exeter; younger son of Henry Trosse, counsellor at law. Educated at Exeter grammar school; spent ten years (1646–57) in foreign trade and self-indulgence. Entered Pembroke Coll., Oxford, May 1657; matric., 6 Aug. 1658; his tutor was Thomas Cheesman [*q.v.*]; took no degree, refusing subscription; left, 1664. Preached privately at Exeter; ordained by presbyters, 1666. Licensed, 30 Apr. 1672, as "Thomas Tross of Exoñ Pr." Imprisoned, 1685. Succeeded Joseph Hallett (1628?—14 Mar. 1688/9) as Minister of James' Meeting, Exeter (built, 1687). His assistant from 1690 was the younger Joseph Hallett [*q.v.*]. Trosse's autobiography (1714), rare in its original form, is a very striking work, unique in its amazing story of dissipation and consequent delirium tremens, and valuable for its details of Oxford discipline and early dissenting usage. (*C. D. F. P. T.*) [30]

TROUGHTON, JOHN (1666—3 D. 1739). **P.** Born at Bicester, Oxf. Son of John Troughton, B.A. (1637?—20 Aug. 1681, son of Nathaniel, clothier, Coventry), ejected from Fellowship at St. John's Coll., Oxford. Probably educ. by his father (blind from infancy), who removed to Oxford in 1672, and had pupils. Assistant at Bicester to Henry Cornish [*q.v.*], whom he followed as Pastor from 1698, and author of several sermons.

Received Fund grants, £6, raised to £7, 1718–39. (*C. D. Dn. F. M.*) [112]

TROUGHTON, WILLIAM (*b.* 1614). C. Son of William Troughton, rector of Waberthwaite, Cumberland. Matric. at Queen's Coll., Oxford, 24 Oct. 1634, aged 20. Chaplain to Col. Robert Hammond, governor of the Isle of Wight, 1647; rector of Wanlip, Leicestershire, 1651; rector of St. Martin's, Salisbury, 1652?; ejected thence, 1662. Preached privately in Salisbury. The Episc. Returns, 1665, report him as living in Bristol. Licensed, 30 Sept. 1672, as "Congr. Teacher" in his own house, St. Philip Street, Bristol. After some years, he removed (1674?) to London. (*C. F. P. T.*) [4]

TRURO. Ejected here was John Tingcombe, B.A.; son of Philip Tingcombe, M.A., rector of Lansallos, Corn.; matric. at Exeter Coll., Oxford, 17 Mar. 1636/7, aged 18; B.A., 1640; rector of Truro; ejected, 1662. (*C. F. P.*) [19]

TUCKNEY, ANTHONY, D.D. (1599–Feb. 1669/70). P. Born (bapt. 22 S.) at Kirton, Linc., where William Tuckney, his father, was vicar. Admitted pensioner at Emmanuel Coll., Cambridge, 4 June 1613; B.A., 1616/7; Fellow, 1619; M.A., 1620; B.D., 1627. Chaplain to Theophilus Clinton, fourth earl of Lincoln. Returning to Cambridge, he was ten years tutor. Elected (1629) town preacher at Lincoln; succeeded John Cotton (1584–1652), his cousin, as vicar (1633). Original member of the Westminster Assembly, and rector of St. Michael-le-Querne, Cheapside (1643). "In the assemblie," he wrote (1651), "I gave my vote with others that the Confession of Faith, putt-out by Authoritie, shoulde not bee required to bee eyther sworne or subscribed-too; we having bin burnt in the hand in that kind before; but so as not to be publickly preached or written against." Appointed (1645) Master of Emmanuel; resigned (1648) his London rectory; made D.D., 1649. Admitted (1653) Master of St. John's Coll. One of Cromwell's Triers, 1654. Regius professor of Divinity (1656), to which pertained the rectory of Somersham, Hunts. In examinations for Fellowships at St. John's, he was particular about grammar in addition to grace; "they may deceive me in their godliness, they cannot in their scholarship." He took great interest in the conversion of American Indians. Resigned his Boston vicarage, 1660. Though appointed on the Savoy commission (1661) for revision of the Prayer-book, he did not attend. Ejected from his mastership and chair, June 1661; but received a life pension of £100 from the profits of Somersham. After this, he moved about a good deal, and died in Spital Yard, London.

His son, Jonathan (1639?–1693), was ejected from a Fellowship at St. John's, 1662, and licensed, 1 May 1672, as "Pr. Teacher in his howse in Hackney." (*D. T.*) [188]

TUEXBERY. [46] *See* Gloucestershire

TULLER. *See* Fuller

TUNBRIDGE ('Tunbridg.') WELLS. The Common Fund offered a gratuity of £5 to David Stott (*see* Stopp), of Harwich, Ess., "if he remove to Tunbridge Wells," which he did in 1691. (*M.*) [55]

TUNSTEAD. Ejected here was John Green, B.A. [*q.v.*]. [74]

TURNER, JOHN (1629?–1692?). P. [? Son of John Turner of Oxenparke, parish of Colton, Lanc., near Ulverston. From Sedbergh grammar school admitted pensioner at St. John's Coll., Cambridge, 6 N. 1649, aet. 20; did not graduate. Four of these names matric. at Cambridge, 1646–54, without graduation.] Ejected from the vicarage or perhaps from a curacy at Sunbury, Middx., in 1662. (Richard Hill was appointed vicar in 1655.) He was an active preacher in London during the plague year. The Episc. Returns, 1669, report him as preaching to 300 persons "at his owne house at Hatton Wall," London. On 17 Apr. 1672 he was licensed as a Presb. Teacher in his "owne howse near Fetter Lane." This Meeting-house, built in 1666, consisted of four rooms opening into each other, with benches and seventeen pews; it had been seized for Anglican use. Rebuilt by Turner, it was occupied (1685) by Stephen Lobb [*q.v.*], Turner removing to a new Meeting-house in Leather Lane, Hatton Garden, where he preached, with assistance, till death. (*C. Jo. Lz. P. T. V. W.*) [1, 165]

TURNER, or TORNER, JOHN, B.A. (1616–1700?). Son of Ralph Turner, rector of Cricket Malherbie, Som. Matric. at New Inn Hall, Oxford, 20 Mar. 1634/5, aged 18; B.A., 1638. Rector of Cricket Malherbie, 1641; ejected, 1662. The Episc. Returns, 1669, report him as one of the preachers to 200 persons at houses in Winsham, Som.; also to 200 persons at White Lackington, Som.; also to 300 persons at Martock, Som.; and to the same number at Kingsbury, and at Wayford. Licensed, July 1672, as "Presb. Teacher" at his own house in Cricket. The Common Fund granted him (1690) £5 a year, for Cricket, reduced from 1695 to £4, and continued to 1700. (*C. F. M. P. T.*) [92]

TURNER, LEWIS (*fl.* 1669–90). **C.** The Episc. Returns, 1669, report Lewis Turner, parish of Aberhafesp, Montg., as an abettor, along with Rhinald Wilson [*q.v.*], of conventicles in that county. (*T.*) [148]

TURNER, SAMUEL. Apparently the Mr Turner of North Wales who received £4 a year from the Common Fund as Itinerant, 1690–93. (*M.*) [148]

TURTON, WILLIAM, B.A. (*d.* 1716). **P.** Matric. 'ser.' at Brasenose Coll., Oxford, 26 May 1653; B.A., 1656/7. Vicar of Rowley Regis, Staff.; ejected, 1662. The Episc. Returns, 1669, report him as one of the preachers to "2 or 300" persons at two houses in Wednesbury, Staff.; also to "1 or 200" persons at various houses in Darlaston, Staff.; also to "above 300" persons at various houses in Walsall, Staff. Licensed, 1 May 1672, as "Pr. Teacher in Wm Keeling's howse," Darlaston; also, 13 May 1672, as "Pr. Teacher in the howse of Joseph Wade in Stafford." In 1688 he was preaching at Nantwich, but soon became Minister in Birmingham, first as colleague to William Fincher [*q.v.*], later as sole Minister in the Old Meeting-house, built in 1689. In 1702 Daniel Greenwood [*q.v.*] became his colleague. On 17 July 1715 the Old Meeting-house was wrecked by a Jacobite mob. Turton retired from active duty at Birmingham (perhaps in 1712); he preached also at Oldbury (now in Staff.) for which he received from the Fund £4 a year (1706–11). £6 a year was paid for Turton at Oldbury, 1712–22, but this Turton must have been his son, Samuel, Minister at Kenilworth, 1700–1728. (*Bm. C. Ev. F. M. P. Si. T. Wb.*) [96, 117]

TUTCHING, *i.e.* TUTCHIN, JOHN, B.A. (1623?–1697?). **P.** Eldest son of Robert Tutchin, ejected (1662) from the vicarage of Newport, I. of Wight. From Dorchester grammar school he matric. sizar at St. Catharine's Hall, Cambridge, 1637, aged 14; B.A., 1641; no record of M.A. Tutor to earl of Kent's son. Vicar of Fowey, Corn.; ejected, 1662. His brothers, Robert (vicar of Brockenhurst, Hants) and Samuel (vicar of Odiham, Hants, a sequestered living), were also ejected in 1662. The Episc. Returns, 1665, report that he "now liveth in the towne of Fowey." Licensed, 8 May 1672, being of Fowey, as a general Pr. Teacher. Signed the thanks of Cornish Ministers. Grant of £6 a year was made to him (1690) for Fowey "on condition hee fix there," and continued till Midsummer, 1697. (*C. M. P. T. V. Wc.*) [18]

TUTORS. [182]

TWEEDMOUTH ('Twedmouth'). Ejected from this chapelry, and that of Spittall, in Berwick parish (now vicarages), was William Mein, M.A., Edinburgh, 23 May 1655, as Gulielmus Minaeus, *minister verbi*; ord. Minister at Tweedmouth, 28 Feb. 1659/60; ejected, 1660; Minister of Lochrutton, Kirkcudbrightshire, 19 Feb. 1660/1; deprived, 1662; he is probably the "Scotch man, returned"; he had declined a call to Dunlop in 1672, but on 7 July 1691 he was admitted Minister of Dalkeith, Edinburghshire; *d.* 11 Jan. 1698/9, aged 64. (*C. Ed. Sf.*) [23, 80]

TYNE, NORTH, the river. [80]

TYRER, PETER (*fl.* 1690–1707). The Common Fund granted him (1690–1702) £6 a year for "about Heywood in Bury parish, on condition that he stay there." From 1703 to Midsummer, 1705, he had the same grant for Lincolnshire; in 1706, £3 as "a present supply"; in 1707, "no more . . . till he hath given satisfaction that he needs it." (*M.*) [60]

TYRO, . . . He received £3 from the anonymous donation brought in, 10 Nov. 1690, by Matthew Rapier. (*M.*) [39]

UNDERHILL, EDWARD. **C.** Alderman of London. Member of the congregation of John Nesbitt [*q.v.*]. Elected a Manager of the Common Fund, 14 Dec. 1691; first attendance, 18 Apr. 1692; last attendance, 26 June 1693 (his Christian name is sometimes given in the Minutes as Richard); he was interested in the cases of Hungerford, Berks, and Holbeach, Linc. Manager (1695) of the Congregational Fund. (*Cf. Co. M.*) [162]

UNICK, UNIK. [472] *See* Vinke

UNIONS IN COUNTIES. [157]

UNITARIANS. [158]

UNITED BRETHREN. [155-7, 185]

UNITED MINISTERS. [158, 184-7]

UNIVERSITY LEARNING. [90, 139]

UPTON-IN-WORRAL, or UPTON-BY BIRKENHEAD; properly, Overchurch. [15]

UPTON-ON-SEVERN. Ejected from this sequestered rectory was Benjamin Baxter (son of George, M.A., rector of Little Wenlock, Shrop.), of St. John's Coll., Cambridge; matric. sizar, 1628; B.A.,

1631/2; *d.* in 57th year. His younger brother, Stephen, M.A., was ejected from Harvington, Worc., in 1662. (*C. V.*) [127]

USSHER, JAMES, D.D. (4 Jan. 1580/1—21 Mar. 1655/6). Born at Dublin. Son of Arland Ussher, clerk of the Irish Court of Chancery. One of the original Scholars (1594) of Trinity Coll., Dublin; B.A., 1597; Fellow, 1599; M.A., 1600/1; B.D., 1607; D.D., 1614. Chancellor of St. Patrick's, Dublin, and rector of Finglas, 1605; professor of divinity, 1607; rector of Assey, 1611; rector of Trim, 1620; bishop of Meath, 1621; archbishop of Armagh, 1625; held the see of Carlisle *in commendam*, 1641/2. Died at Reigate. This great scholar's "Reduction of Episcopacie unto the form of Synodical Government received in the Ancient Church," played a great part in the discussions on church government both in 1641 and in 1660. After the issue of several surreptitious editions, it was published (1656) from Ussher's autograph, with his last corrections, by his chaplain, Nicholas Bernard, D.D. Ussher's plan differs from the Presbyterian ideal mainly in this cardinal point, that his synods were purely clerical, 'admitting no lay representation except in the meeting of parochial officers, which had no jurisdiction. (*D.*) [154]

UTKINTON. [17]

UTRECHT. [182, 183]

UTTOXETER ('Utoxcester'). [90, 97, 98]

UXBRIDGE. Ejected from this chapelry in Hillingdon parish was . . . Godbolt, an aged divine [? John Godbould, of Pembroke Hall, Cambridge, matric., 1599]. (*C. V.*) [73]

VALE, THE, OF BELVOIR. [84]

VALENTINE, . . . (*d.* 1703 ?). The Common Fund granted him (1690) £4 a year for Blackley, near Manchester, ending 25 Dec. 1703. Mrs. Valentine of Salford, widow, was buried, 4 Apr. 1704. He was probably related to Thomas Valentine, who entered Frankland's Academy, 1 May 1690, and is marked as dead in Oliver Heywood's list, *i.e.* dead before 1702 if the marking is Heywood's own. (*C. M. Nl. Nr. P.*) [60]

VEAL, EDWARD, M.A. (1632 ?—6 June 1708). **P.** Matric. (as Veel), 27 F. 1650/1 at Christ Church, Oxford, as 'gent.'; B.A., 1651/2; M.A., 1653/4. Fellow of Trinity Coll., Dublin, 1654. Ordained at Winwick, Lanc., 14 Aug. 1657. Deprived of his fellowship, 1660. Chaplain to Sir William Waller (1597 ?–1668) of Brenchly, Kent. The Episc. Returns, 1669, report that "one Mr Veale, an Independt hath lately set up a Meeting in this [Stepney] parish, And first solicited for Subscriptions, before he would come." In his application for licence he describes himself as "Edward Veal Presbyt:"; on 13 Apr. 1672 licence was issued to "Edmund Veale to be a Pr. Teacher in ye howse known by all in Globe Alley, Wapping." His ministry at Wapping where he also conducted an Academy (receiving Students with bursaries from the Fund), lasted till his death. (*C. Db. F. P. T.*) [165]

VINCENT, NATHANIEL, M.A. (1638 ?—21 June 1697). **P.** Third son of John Vincent (1591–1646), who held from 1644 the sequestered rectory of Sedgefield, Durh. Entered Corpus Christi Coll., Oxford, as chorister, 18 Oct. 1648, aged 10; matric. 28 Mar. 1655; removed to Christ Church, B.A., 1655/6; M.A., 1657; chaplain of Corpus Christi Coll.; and appointed Fellow of Cromwell's abortive Durham University (1656). On 5 May 1659 he was ordained by the Fourth London Classis, on a call to the sequestered rectory of Langley Marish, Bucks. Ejected, 1662, he was chaplain for three years to Sir Henry Blount, Tittenhanger, Herts. He appears to have come to London with other Nonconformists as preachers after the Fire (1666). The Episc. Returns, 1669, report him as one of the preachers at Wraysbury and Colebrooke, Bucks, to "Presbyterians 2 or 300 none of any Qualitie the most considerable is one Slowcomb a mercer They say they will uphold their Conventicle in spight of the King or Bp"; also to "5 or 600 some people of good fashion, the rest servants & streete walkers" at Farthing Alley, parish of St. Olave's, Southwark, "in a house built on purpose"; he "Chatechiseth the people and baptiseth Children some privately some publickly in his Conventicle." In July 1670 he was arrested and suffered six months' imprisonment. On 2 Apr. 1672 he was licensed as "a Teacher of the Presbyterian way" at "a certaine Howse or Roome in Farthing Alley." He was again arrested and imprisoned, 1682 and 1686. In 1692 some sixty members of his congregation left him for the ministry of Richard Fincher [*q.v.*]. He joined the Happy Union, but declined (1693) to act as Manager of the Common Fund, nor was he appointed a Manager when the Fund was reconstituted (1695). (*C. D. F. Fc. M. P. Q. T. W.*) [161]

VINCENT, . . . [117]

VINKE, PETER, M.A., B.D. (1625 ?—6 Sept. 1702). **P.** Son of a Norwich citizen of Flemish ancestry. Matric., pensioner, at Corpus Christi Coll., Cambridge, 1641; B.A., 1643/4; migrated to Pembroke Coll.; Fellow; M.A., 1647; B.D., 1654. On 29 N. 1649 he was ordained by the Fourth London Classis on a call to the sequestered rectory of St. Michael's, Cornhill; ejected, 1660; curate of St. Catherine, Cree; ejected, 1662. On 11 Apr. 1672, licence was granted "to Peter Winke of Augustine Friers, London, to be a Presbyterian Teacher in any allowed place." He constantly preached, usually in his own house. Latterly he lived at Dalston in Hackney parish, where he died. (*C. Fc. P. T. V. Wc.*) [4, 72]

VIVENHO. [42] *See* Essex

VORTIER, VOLIER, *i.e.* VOTIER, JAMES (*b.* 1622). **P.** Born in Surrey. Son of Daniel Votier, M.A., rector of St. Petercheap, London (sequestered in 1645). Matric. at New Inn Hall, Oxford, 28 June 1639, aged 17. His first ministry was at Ilketshall St. Margaret, Suff. In 1658, when he published his "Vox Dei & Hominis," he was rector of Heveningham, Suff.; ejected, 1662. Licensed, 29 June 1672, as Pr. Teacher in house of Widow Craine at Spexhall, Suff. His age in 1690 was 68. [Calamy and Foster give his Christian name as James; he was licensed as Jacob; his sole publication has only the initial J.] (*C. F. P. T.*) [104]

WAITE, JOHN (*fl.* 1690–93). **C.** The Common Fund granted him, 1691–3 (calling him Thomas in 1693), £5 a year for Cheshunt, Herts; he had previously received the same from Matthew Barker [*q.v.*]. He may be John Wayt, yeoman, reported in the Episc. Returns, 1669, as preaching in his barn at Toft, Camb. More probably he is Calamy's Joseph Wait [? Joseph Waight, matric. sizar, at St. Catharine's Hall, Cambridge, 1637/8; B.A., 1641/2; Fellow; M.A., 1645], ejected from the rectory of Sproughton, Suff.; elder (1662) in the church of Francis Holcroft [*q.v.*]; imprisoned at Cambridge; removed to Bedford; preaching (before 1669) at Hitchin and elsewhere; preaching in London (1681); he began his Sabbath on Saturday evening. (*C. M. P. T. Uh. V.*) [50]

WAKEFIELD. Ejected here was Joshua Kirby (son of Francis, London), of Merchant Taylors' School, 1628; of New Inn Hall, matric. 20 June 1634, aged 17; B.A., 1637; M.A., 1640; held the sequestered rectory of Eastwick, Herts, Oct. 1645; vicar of Roade, Northants, May 1646; curate at Putney, 1648; lecturer at Wakefield, 1650; ejected, 1662; preaching at Swaith, W.R., 1669; licensed, 8 May 1672, as Pr. Teacher in his house at Wakefield; his house licensed, same date, as Pr. Meeting-place; *d.* 12 June 1676, aet. 59; bur. in his garden. (*C. T.*) [129, 139]

WAKERHOUSE, *i.e.* WATERHOUSE, JONAS, M.A. (1628—13 Feb. 1716/7). Born at Tooting, Surr. Son of Henry Waterhouse, gent. From Halifax grammar school, admitted sizar at St. John's Coll., Cambridge, 23 June 1645, aet. 17; matric., 1645; B.A., 1648/9; Fellow; M.A., 1652. Ejected from the vicarage of Bradford, W.R. Attended the parish church, but usually preached on Sunday evenings at his own house. (*C. Jo. My. Nr. P. V. Y.*) [129]

WALDRON ('Walldown'). [112]

WALES, NORTH. [141, 142, 148, 168, 177, 181] The headings "North Wales," etc., pp. 92, 93 of the Manuscript are in the earliest handwriting; the rest is in that of the Book-keeper. The returns are numbered 6. Pages 98, 99 are entirely in the Book-keeper's hand, except four names and a place name, not in the earliest hand. The returns are numbered 6 to 66

WALES, SOUTH. [28, 127, 143, 145, 168, 177, 181] The headings "South Wales," etc., are in the earliest handwriting; so are a few additions and marginalia. The rest is in the Book-keeper's hand. The returns are numbered 42 (mostly) and 102.

WALKER, JOHN (*d.* 1703). **P.** There is a confusion in the Manuscript (as elsewhere) between father and son. John Walker, born in England; educated at Glasgow; M.A., 1647; was called to Rivington Chapel, Lanc., in 1648, but the Second Lancashire Classis refused ordination, as the Rivington parishioners would not adopt the Presbyterian church order. He was ordained to Newton Heath Chapel, Lanc., 9 Jan. 1650, by First Lancashire Classis; ejected, 1662; in the will (11 June 1672) of James Holland of Holme Hall in Newton, he is referred to as John Walker of Rivington, clerk; licensed, 25 July 1672, as "Pr. Teacher in the howse of James Holland at Newton"; also, 18 N. 1672, as "Pr. Teacher at the house of y[e] widd: [Jane] Eckersall" of Rochdale. He appears to have preached occasionally at Rivington, but Newton Heath was the place of his ministry. He died, 8 Feb. 1684/5, aged about 60.

John Walker, *secundus*, son of the above, is the person to whom the Manuscript really refers. He succeeded in 1683, Samuel Newton, at Rivington [*q.v.*], preaching in the parochial chapel, from which Nonconformists were not yet dispossessed. His "plentiful estate" was at Heath Charnock, Lanc. In his time the present Nonconformist chapel at Rivington was projected and perhaps built. He died in 1703. (*C. Gd. Nl. P. Rt.*) [59]

WALLDOWN. [112] *See* Sussex

WALLER, JAMES, M.A. (1635–Mar. 1697). **P.** Admitted from Suffolk, 1652, at Corpus Christi Coll., Cambridge; matric. pensioner, 1654; B.A., 1655/6; M.A., 1659. Curate or vicar (1658) of Hunston, Suff.; ejected, 1662. Removed to Rattlesden, Suff., in consequence of the Five Mile Act, but met his former flock, somewhere, every week. Licensed, 13 May 1672, as Pr. Teacher in "the howse of Ed[mund] Frost in Hunston." The Common Fund voted him (1690) £5 a year for Hunston; reduced (1695) to £4 a year as Itinerant, and paid to 1696. Died at Rattlesden. (*B. C. Lm. M. P. T. V.*) [105]

WALPOLE ('Wallpoole'). Ejected here was Samuel Manning, M.A. [*q.v.*]. [103]

WALSALL. Reckoned by Calamy with the Silenced was Thomas Burdall or Byrdall, of Emmanuel Coll., Cambridge; matric. pensioner, 1626; B.A., 1628/9; M.A., 1632; vicar of Walsall, who died in April 1662 before the Bartholomew Act received the royal assent (19 May). Apparently he had taken the covenant; whether he used the prayer-book, after the Restoration, is not known. (*C. V. Wg.*) [96]

WALSHAM-LE-WILLOWS. [105]

WALSHAM, NORTH. Ejected here was Nathaniel Michel or Mitchell, of St. Catharine's Hall, Cambridge; matric. sizar, 1634/5; B.A., 1639/40; M.A., 1643; vicar of Edingthorp, Norf., in 1647; vicar of North Walsham in 1656/7; ejected, 1662; preaching at Catton, Norf., in 1669; licensed, 25 July 1672, as Pr. Teacher in a house at Norwich; his own house at Norwich licensed, 28 Oct. 1672, Pr.; licensed, 13 Jan. 1672/3, as Pr. Teach[r] at another house in Norwich; married a sister of John Collinges, D.D. [*q.v.*]. (*B. C. T. V.*) [75]

WALSHAM, SOUTH. Ejected here was John Baker. (*C.*) In 1631 Thomas Baker was rector of St. Lawrence's, South Walsham. If John Baker is a different person, he may have been ejected from St. Mary's, South Walsham. (*Nb.*) [75]

WALTHAMSTOW ('Waltham Stow,' 'Withamstow'). [39, 42]

WALTON LE DALE, chapelry in Blackburn parish. [60]

WALTON ('Waltham') ON THAMES. Ejected from this vicarage was David Anderson (*d.* Mar. 1697/8). He left for Zealand and settled at Middleburgh, where, being in straits, he was befriended in 1681 by John Quick [*q.v.*]. Later, he succeeded William Spang as Minister of the English church at Middleburgh. Calamy (copied by Palmer) places his death in March 1677; probably an erratum for 1697. (*C. P.*) [110]

WANTAGE. Ejected here was William Lee, who afterwards conformed. (*C.*) [6, 7, 8]

WAPPING. [1]

WARBLETON. [112]

WARD, JOHN (*fl.* 1654–96). **C.** [? Matric. pensioner at St. Catharine's Hall, Cambridge, 1648; B.A., 1651/2; M.A., 1655.] Held (after Nov. 1654) the sequestered rectory of Harvington, Worc.; ejected, 1660. Licensed, July 1672, as "Congr. Teacher in the howse of Widow Rickett at Elington, Gloc," *i.e.* Eckington, Worc. The Common Fund granted him (1690–96) £5 a year for Pershore, Worc. (*C. M. P. T. V. Wc.*) [126]

WARD, SIR PATIENCE (7 D. 1629—10 July 1696). Born at Tanshelf, Yorks; son of Thomas Ward (*d.* 1635), who named him Patience, as he was hoping for a daughter. After a university education, became merchant-tailor in London; knighted, 29 O. 1675; Lord Mayor, 1680–81; to his mayoralty was due the inscription on the Monument, stating that the Great Fire was the work of Papists; F.R.S., 1682; convicted on a charge of perjury (1683) and fled to Holland till 1688; M.P. for London, 1689. (*D.*) [166]

WARD, RALPH, M.A. (1630—13 Mar. 1691/2). **C.** Born at Denby in Penistone parish, West Riding. Educ. at Sidney Sussex Coll., Cambridge; B.A., 1650/1; M.A., 1654; incorp. at Oxford, 11 July 1654. Began to preach at Denby chapel in Penistone parish. Chaplain to Col. Fenwick, to whose regiment he preached at Leith in August 1651. Rector (1653) of Wolsingham, Durh.; ordained at St. John's, Newcastle-on-Tyne, 14 S. 1653; held the sequestered vicarage of Hartburn, Northumb.; ejected, 1660. Retired to Newcastle-on-Tyne and kept school. Chaplain to Sir John Hewley (1619—24 Aug. 1697) of York; preaching in the house of Lady Watson (1599—4 Oct. 1679; *née* Nelson and widow of Stephen Watson, Lord Mayor of York) alternately with Peter Williams (1625—26 Mar. 1680), ejected from a lectureship at York. He left York under the operation (1666) of the Five Mile Act, but returned. Licensed, 10 June 1672, as "Ind. Teacher in the howse of Brian Dawson in Outgate, York"; on the same date, the "howse of the Lady Watson in Saviour Gate, York," was licensed as an "Ind. Meeting-place"; and the house of Andrew Taylor in Micklegate was licensed for the same purpose; ou 25 July 1672 Peter Williams was licensed as "Grāll Pr. Teacher"; on same date his house in York was licensed for "Pr." worship. In 1684 Ward and Andrew Taylor (a merchant) were imprisoned for many months in Ousebridge gaol. He lived either at East or West Askham, near York. He was assisted by Noah Ward (1640–1699; no relative). (*C. F. Ht. My. Nr. P. T. Wc. Y.*) [130, 135, 136]

WARE. Ejected here was John Young, M.A. (university not known); vicar of Kimpton, Herts, 1650–54; lecturer at Hitchin, 1642; vicar of Ware, 1656; ejected, 1661. (*C. Uh.*) [50]

WAREHAM ('Warham'). Ejected here was Thomas Chaplin, of St. Catharine's Hall, Cambridge; matric. sizar, 1639; B.A., 1642/3; M.A., 1646; held, with assistants, the four sequestered rectories of Wareham; St. Martin's, from about 1643; Holy Trinity from 1648; ejected, 1660; returned to Cambridge; *d.* 31 Aug. 1667, aet. 46; monument in St. Benet's Church, Cambridge. His widow dying excommunicated, her body was twice exhumed before final interment. (*C. H. V.*) [34, 35]

WARMINGTON. Perhaps ejected from this vicarage was . . . Gascoyn, who certainly ended as a conformist. [? George Gascoigne, vicar of St. John's, Peterborough, in 1667; bur. 14 July 1680.] (*C. Np.*) [77]

WARMINSTER. [124]

WARREN, JOHN, M.A. (29 S. 1621–July 1696). **C.** [? Matric., pensioner, at Sidney Sussex Coll., Cambridge; B.A., 1644/5; M.A., 1648.] Calamy makes him a graduate of Oxford (not in Foster). Lecturer (1643) at Hatfield Broad Oak, Ess., held the sequestered rectory, 1646; ejected, 1662 (?). The Episc. Returns, 1669, report him as preaching at Hatfield, where he had founded (1665) a Congregational church. Licensed, 11 Apr. 1672, to be "a Teacher of the congregation . . . in . . . Hatfield . . . commonly called Congregationall." In 1690 he removed to Bishops Stortford, Herts, but still visited Hatfield. Buried, 3 Aug. 1696. (*C. E. P. T. V.*) [39, 50, 51]

WARREN, JOHN. (*M.*) [184]

WARREN, MATTHEW (1642—14 June 1706). **P.** Younger son of John Warren of Otterford, Som. From Crewkerne grammar school, matric. at St. John's Coll., Oxford, 3 July 1658; left 1660. Began ministry at Otterford, 1661; held no benefice. From 1662, employed himself in teaching. His earliest known pupil, John Shower [*q.v.*], entered in 1671. Licensed, 10 June 1672, as "Pr. Teacher in the howse of John Hill," Withypool, Som. In 1687 he became co-pastor with Emanuel Harford [*q.v.*] at Paul's Meeting, Taunton, Som. Here he conducted his Academy with much repute; conservative himself, he encouraged in his Students the resort to modern books and promoted "free and critical study of the Scriptures, as the best system of theology." He had several Students with bursaries from the Fund. (*C. D. F. J. M. P. T. Tt.*) [91, 93, 172]

WARREN, THOMAS, M.A. (1616?—27 Jan. 1693/4). **P.** Matric. sizar, either at Emmanuel Coll., Cambridge, 1632, or at St. Catharine's Hall, 1634; B.A., 1635/6 or 1637/8; M.A., 1639 or 1641. Held (6 F. 1650/1) the sequestered rectory of Houghton, Hants; ordained (22 D. 1660) deacon and priest (without subscription) by Thomas Sydserff, then bishop of Galloway; instituted to his rectory, 1 F. 1660/1; ejected, 1662. After ejectment he was offered a choice of the bishoprics of Salisbury and Winchester. Licensed, 1 July 1672, as Presbyterian Teacher in the house of Thomas Burbanck, Romsey, Hants; also, 25 July 1672, as "Pr. Teacher in the howse of Clem: Warren in Romsey." He continued to preach at Romsey for eighteen years. The Common Fund granted him £6 a year (1690–1693). According to his tombstone, his age at death was 77; if so, it is understated by the Book-keeper's informant. (*C. D. M. P. T. V. Wc.*) [101]

WARRINGTON. Ejected here was Robert Yates (1611–1678). **P.** Matric.

at Merton Coll., Oxford, 9 May 1628, aged 17. [F. Nicholson (a descendant) and E. Axon, in "Robert Yates, Rector of Warrington," 1915, suggest that he was born about 1612, son of John Yate or Yates, of Blackburn, and never at a University.] Preacher at Preston, 1646; rector of Warrington, 1647; ejected, 1662; licensed, 25 July 1672, as Grall Pr. Teacher; his house at Warrington licensed, same date, Pr.; the Court Howse and other houses at Warrington licensed, 5 Sept. 1672, Pr. (the Court House licence, preserved at Cairo Street Chapel, bears date 30 Sept.); bur. 28 Oct. 1678. His son Samuel succeeded him at Warrington. (*C. F. Nl.*) [58]

WARRINGTON CLASSIS. [157]

WARWICK. Ejected from the vicarage of St. Nicholas was Henry Butler [? of Peterhouse, Cambridge, matric. pensioner, 1626]. (*C. V.*) [119]

WARWICKSHIRE. [76, 117, 118, 119, 168, 179] The headings "Warwick" are in the earliest handwriting; the rest is in that of the Book-keeper. The returns are numbered 34 to 149 (mostly 50); 34, 53, 62, in 1691.

Ashton is Aston-juxta-Birmingham.

Sowtham is Southam

WASSALL. [96] *See* Staffordshire

WATERHOUSE. *See* Wakerhouse

WATERS, JAMES (26 Mar. 1661—5 May 1725). **P.** Born at Bath. Educ. in the Academy of Henry Langley, D.D. (1611—10 Sept. 1679), ejected from the Mastership of Pembroke Coll., Oxford, at Tubney, near Abingdon, Berks; and (1682) in that of Thomas Doolittle [*q.v.*]. Tutor in the family of Francis, second Baron Holles (*d.* 1 Mar. 1689/90) at Aldenham, Herts; thereafter (in 1685) chaplain and tutor in the family of George Evelyn, M.P., of Nutfield, Surrey, till 1689, when he entered on the public ministry at Reigate. The Common Fund voted him (1690) £10 a year for Reigate, which place he left, May 1692, for Uxbridge, Middx., where latterly he was assisted by Thomas Mole, his successor. (*Bg. Cm. Ev. M. Mw. Pe. Ws.*) [109, 110]

WATFORD. Ejected here was Philip Goodwin, of St. John's Coll., Cambridge; matric. sizar, 1623; B.A., 1626/7; M.A., 1630; curate at St. Andrew's, Hertford, 1633; curate at Watford, 1638; vicar of Watford, 1643; ejected, 1661; conformed; rector of Liston, Ess., 1673; *d.* 1699. (*C. D. Uh. V.*)

The Episc. Returns, 1669, report two conventicles here: (1) "Mixt of Presbyterians Anabaptists &c. In the house of John Ovey Fellmonger The same Ovey is a notorious Ringleader And the same is for the most the Speaker." (2) "Sabbatarians who observe Saturday In the house of Mary East, Wid., & sometimes of Gregory West, Weaver." (*T.*) [51]

WATSAM, NORTH and SOUTH. [75] *See* Norfolk

WATSFIELD. [106] *See* Suffolk

WATSON, THOMAS, M.A. (*d.* July 1686). **P.** Matric. pensioner, at Emmanuel Coll., Cambridge, 1635; B.A., 1638/9; M.A., 1642. Chaplain to Mary, widow of Sir Horace Vere, Baron Tilbury. Appointed (1647) to the sequestered rectory of St. Stephen's, Walbrook; joined the Presbyterian remonstrance against the death of Charles I. Imprisoned, 1651, for his share in Christopher Love's plot to restore Charles II. Reinstated, 30 June 1652, as rector of St. Stephen's, Walbrook. In 1652 he was Scribe of the Third London Classis. Ejected, 1662. Reported by informers as conventicling, in 1664–5, at various places, including "his own house in the Minories." Reported in Episc. Returns, 1669, as preaching in Devonshire House, Bishopsgate (otherwise known as Fisher's Folly, having been built by Jasper Fisher, clerk in Chancery). Here Watson had constructed (1666) a Meeting-house, which as "a convenient place, with two galleries, pews, and seats" was seized for Anglican use in 1671. On 19 Apr. 1672 he was licensed as Presb. Teacher in his own house, in Dowgate. Later, his congregation moved to Crosby Hall, Bishopsgate, then the property of Sir John Langham. His health giving way, he retired to Burnham, Essex, where he was buried, 28 July 1686. (*Be. C. D. Fc. P. Q. T. Th. V. W.*) [154]

WATTISFIELD ('Watsfield'). [106]

WATTS, HENRY, M.A. (1629—2 Feb. 1690/1). **P.** Matric. pensioner, at Sidney Sussex Coll., Cambridge; 1645; B.A., 1647/8; M.A., 1651. Held the sequestered rectory of Swepston, Leic.; ejected, 1662. He had signed (1659) the protest against the royalist plans of Sir George Booth. Removed to Weddington, Warw. Licensed, 5 S. 1672, as "Pr. Teacher" in his house at Weddington. Removed (after 1682) to Barwell, Leic. From 1689 till death, preached at Hinckley, Leic., on Sunday afternoons. Buried in Barwell church. (*C. P. T. V. Wc.*) [68]

WATTS, ISAAC, D.D. (17 July 1674—25 N. 1748). **C.** Born at Southampton; eldest son of Isaac Watts, clothier and schoolmaster. From Southampton grammar school he proceeded (1690) to the Academy of Thomas Rowe [*q.v.*]; receiving (16 O. 1693) a bursary of £8 from the Common Fund through Arthur Shallett [*q.v.*]. Became tutor (Oct. 1696) to the son of Sir John Hartopp, bart., Stoke Newington. Began to preach, 1698; chosen (1699) assistant to Isaac Chauncy [*q.v.*] whom he succeeded at Mark Lane; the congregation removed to Pinners' Hall (1704) and Duke's Place, Bury Street, St. Mary Axe (1708). From 1712 he was the permanent guest of Sir Thomas Abney [*q.v.*] at Theobalds, and (after 1722) of Lady Abney at Theobalds and Stoke Newington. He was D.D., Edinburgh, 8 Nov. 1728. His educational manuals were of great service, but his fame rests on his "Horae Lyricae" (1706), "Hymns" (1707), "Divine Songs" (1715) and "Psalms" (1719). His latest thoughts were far from being Trinitarian. (*D. Ed. M.*) [183]

WAVELL, RICHARD, B.A. (3 Apr. 1633—19 D. 1705). **C.** Youngest son of Major Wavell, of Lemerston, I.W., a cavalier. Matric., 9 D. 1653, at Wadham Coll., Oxford, as gent.; B.A., 1657/8. Studied divinity under William Reyner, B.D., ejected from the vicarage of Egham, Surrey, whose curate he became till 1662. Declining preferment, he preached privately at Egham and taught school till prevented. On the death of Anthony Palmer, M.A. (1618 ?—26 Jan. 1678/9), ejected from the rectory of Bourton-on-the-Water, Glouc., he succeeded him as Minister of the Congregational church at Pinners' Hall. He was much molested, but had a friend in his kinsman, Sir Henry Tulse, Lord Mayor. He joined the Happy Union. He was an original Manager (1695) of the Congregational Fund, and one of its correspondents (1696) for Berkshire. (*C. Cf. Co. F. P.*) [165]

WAYTE, ROBERT. (*Bl.*) [180]

WAYTE, THOMAS, M.A. (*fl.* 1631–93). Born at York. Admitted sizar at Peterhouse, Cambridge, 21 June 1631; matric., 1632; B.A., 1634/5; M.A., 1638. Ejected from the vicarage of Wetwang, E.R., where his long sermons had gained him "the Name of a *Burn Roast*." Continued there, preaching publicly in his own house, and farming, his wife keeping school. Lady Norcliffe allowed him £5 a year. The Common Fund granted him £3 a year (1691–93) for Yorkshire. (*C. M. P. Ph.*) [131]

WAYTES, . . . **P.** Appears to have been elected a Manager, but did not act, and was replaced, 2 Mar. 1690/1, by Sir Thomas Abney [*q.v.*]. (*M.*) [162]

WEAVER, HUMFREY, B.A. (1620–1696). **P.** Son of Allan Weaver, of Wokingham, Berks, pleb. Matric. at Magdalen Hall, Oxford, 31 Mar. 1637, aged 17; B.A., 1640. Vicar of Crondall, Hants; ejected, 1662. The Episc. Returns, 1669, report him as preaching in his house at Crondall "ever since the 24th of Aug$^{t}$ 1662," to "Presbyterians very numerous, most of them of the parish, the rest from the Adjoyning townes The Principall persons of good estates & Quality." Licensed, 16 May 1672, as "Pr. Teacher in his howse in Crundall." He preached till the last Sunday of his life. (*C. F. P. T.*) [100]

WEAVER, JOHN (1632 ?–1712). Born in or near Ludlow. [? Matric., 'pleb.', at St. John's Coll., Oxford, 10 April 1652.] Held the sequestered living of Old Radnor, 1653; ejected, 1660; rector of Knill, Heref.; ejected, 1662. Succeeded George Primrose [*q.v.*] as Minister "to a small handful" at Hereford. He was useful at Abergavenny on the defection of Roger Griffith [*q.v.*]. Samuel Jones (1680 ?–1719), the conductor of the Academy at Gloucester (removed (1712) to Tewkesbury), had been his pupil at Knill, and married his daughter Judith (*d.* 25 Jan. 1746), who, by a second marriage, to Edward Godwin, was grandmother of the author of "Political Justice." (*C. D. F. P. Wc.*) [48]

WEBB, . . . [? Stephen Webb, cler. fil., matric. at Exeter Coll., Oxford, 2 May 1659. The Episcopal Returns, 1669, give Stephen Webb as one of seven preachers to a congregation of Presbyterians at Romesbury, Wilts. Licence was issued, 30 Apr. 1672, to Stephen Webb, as Presb. Teacher in house of Mrs. Bradshaw, Farnborough, Hants. A similar licence (denomination not stated), for Stephen Webb to teach in the house of Mr. Bradshaw (place not stated), and a general licence for Stephen Webb, were received, 15 May 1672.] To "Mr Webb" £3 was granted (10 Nov. 1690) from an anonymous donation per Matthew Rapier [*q.v.*]. (*F. M. T.*) [4, 72]

WEDMORE. [93]

WEDNESBURY. Ejected here was William Fincher [*q.v.*]. [96]

WEEFORD. Ejected here was Richard Chantry, B.A. [*q.v.*]. [96]

WEEKDAY SERVICES. [178]

WEEKES, JOHN (1633—22 Nov. 1698). **P.** Nephew of Samuel Hardy, rector of Poole, Dors. Vicar of Buckland Newton,

Dors. (there in 1660); ejected, 1662. Came to Bristol soon after; twice imprisoned for conventicling. The Episc. Returns, 1669, report him as one of the preachers to 200 persons at North Cheriton, Som.; also to 300 persons at Dunkerton, Som.; also at North Cadbury, Som.; also to "about 200 Presbyterians" at Bradford, Wilts; also to "6 or 700 Presbyterians" every week, at Horningsham, Wilts; also to "about 200 or 300 Presbyterians Independents Anabaptists promiscuously" at Warminster, Wilts. Licensed, 19 Apr. 1672, as "Pr. Teacher in the howse of John Loyde," St. James's Back, Bristol. A Meeting-house in Lewin's Mead was built for him in 1693–4. He then had "an unwieldy body" but a "mighty voice" and spirit. (*C. Cm. Hu. Mh. Od. P. T.*) [91]

WEEKS, . . . ["Mr Weeks of Exeter" is mentioned in the Fund Minutes, 8 Mar. 1708/9.] (*M.*) [4]

WELFORD ('Wellford"). [77, 78]

WELLASTON. [17] *See* Cheshire

WELLETON. [91] *See* Somerset

WELLINGBOROUGH ('Wellingborow'). Ejected here was Thomas Andrews, of Cambridge University [either of Clare Hall, matric. sizar, 1629; B.A., 1633/4; M.A., 1637; or of Trinity Coll., B.A., 1657]; vicar of Wellingborough; ejected, 1662; retired to Mears Ashby, Northants; took the Oxford oath; preaching at Nuneaton, Warw., in 1669; licensed, 25 May 1672, as Pr. Teacher in his house at Mears Ashby; his house licensed, same date, as Pr. Meeting-place. (*C. T. V.*) [77]

WELLINGTON. [91, 93]

WELLS, MARTIN, B.A. (*fl.* 1650–92). **P.** Matric. at Queen's Coll., Oxford, 'ser.', 18 N. 1650; B.A., 1653. Rector of Yaverland, I. of Wight; ejected, 1662. Licensed, 16 Apr. 1672, "to teach at the house of W^m Slater in the Towne of Newport & Isle of Wight. Presbyterians." (*C. F. P. T.*) [100]

WELSH LANGUAGE. [16, 17, 48, 88]

WEM. Ejected here in 1660 was Andrew Parsons, M.A., son of John Parsons, of Milton, Som., pleb.; matric. at Christ Church Coll., Oxford, 20 June 1634, aged 18; B.A., 1635; M.A., 1638; held the sequestered rectory of Wem, 1647; conventicling in London, 1664; licensed, 2 Apr. 1672, as Presbyterian Teacher in Deadman's Place, Southwark, or any other licensed place; his house in Deadman's Place licensed, same date; *d.* in London about the end of 1684. (*C. F. P.*) [16, 89]

From Edstaston chapelry in Wem parish was ejected Samuel Taylor [*q.v.*]

WENDOVER. [10]

WESLEY, JOHN [Benjamin], M.A. (17 June 1703—2 March 1791). Born at Epworth rectory, Linc.; fifteenth child of Samuel Wesley, the rector (son of John Wesley, M.A., ejected from the vicarage of Winterborn-Whitchurch, Dors., and grandson of Bartholomew Wesley, ejected from the sequestered rectories of Charmouth and Catherston, Dors.), and Susanna, his wife, youngest daughter of Samuel Annesley (*q.v.*). From the Charterhouse School, London, he was elected scholar (1720) of Christ Church, Oxford; B.A., 1724; Fellow of Lincoln College, 1726; M.A., 1727. Ordained deacon, 1725; priest, 1728. He resigned his Fellowship, his only promotion, on his marriage in 1751. The name Methodist was first applied to his brother Charles, in 1729. It was adopted by John Wesley as the badge of that marvellous movement of religious evangelism combined with constant efforts for the educational and social welfare of the people, the details of which are beyond the scope of the present publication. They may be read, in a condensed form, in *D.* [178, 187]

WEST BROMWICH. Ejected here was Richard Hilton, B.A. [*q.v.*]. [96]

WESTERHAM ('Westcum'; in *M.*, Westrum). *See* Sevenoaks. [56]

WESTMACOTT, THEODORE (*d.* 31 Aug. 1728). **P.** Son of the ejected (1660) vicar of Cropthorn, Worc., whom Calamy calls William Westmacott; he was licensed, July 1672, as John Westmakote; he had "Eight or Nine Children" when ejected. Theodore was later born, or began his study for the ministry very late; he received, 1691–93, a bursary of £10 from the Common Fund as Student under John Woodhouse [*q.v.*]. He received Fund grants (1703–23) of £5 a year, increased (1720) to £10, as Minister at Chalford Bottoms, Glou. On 3 Oct. 1720 he is called "Dr. Westmacott." (*C. Ev. M. P. T.*) [90]

WESTMINSTER. [2, 4]

WESTMINSTER CONFESSION AND CATECHISMS. [156]

WESTMORLAND. [121, 168, 177] The names of Managers for the County, an entry of 1691, and the marginal note are in the Book-keeper's hand; the remainder is in the earliest handwriting. The returns are numbered 1 to 3; and 2, in 1691.

Russendaile is Ravenstonedale [*q.v.*].

The place "5 Miles W. of Kendall" is probably Crosthwaite, where the house of James Garnett, called Moss Side, was registered for worship, 15 Jan. 1691/2. "Crosthwaite may have been a forerunner of Crook," where Samuel Bourn, *secundus* (1689—22 Mar. 1754), began his ministry in 1711. (*Nk.*) [121]

WETHERSFIELD. Ejected here was John Cole, of Cambridge University, M.A. [his tombstone in *C.* makes him Fellow of Jesus Coll.; *V.* gives no John Cole at Jesus Coll., or as Fellow of any Coll.; John Coale, of Christ's Coll., matric. pensioner, 1637/8; B.A., 1641/2; M.A., 1645]. Held the sequestered vicarage of Burwell, Camb.; removed to the sequestered vicarage of Wethersfield, 1655; ejected, 1660; preaching at Nayland, Suff., Bury St. Edmunds, and Wethersfield, and imprisoned at Chelmsford, 1669; licensed (Coale), 11 Apr. 1672, as Presbyt. Teacher in his house at Wethersfield; his house licensed, same date, as Pr. Meeting-place; *d.* 11 Apr. 1673, aged about 52. (*C. E. T. V.*) [40]

WEYMOUTH. Ejected here was George Thorne [? of Sidney Sussex Coll., Cambridge, matric. sizar, 1640; B.A., 1643/4; Fellow; M.A., 1647]; held the sequestered rectory of Weymouth, 1641; ejected, 1662; fled to Rotterdam (1663–1664); living at Compton Valence, 1665; licensed, 1 May 1672, as Congr. Teacher in James Bud's house at Weymouth. (*C. F. Od. T.*) [34]

WHALEY, or WHALLEY, THOMAS (*d.* 1706). **P.** Probably son or grandson of Thomas Whalley of Rishton, gent. (*d.* Jan. 1672/3), elder of the Second Lancashire Classis. Entered Frankland's Academy, 27 Aug. or 3 Oct. 1679. In 1689 was Minister in Chipping, Lanc. Minister (1690) of Hindley Chapel, parish of Wigan (built, 1641, by Puritans, and unconsecrated), till its consecration in 1698; afterwards at Hindley New Chapel, built, 1700, for Nonconformists, by Richard Crook, of Abram. He appears to have lived at Blackburn, where he was buried, 3 July 1706. (*Nl. Nk.*) [62, 64, 136]

WHARTON, LORD. Philip Wharton (8 Apr. 1613—5 Feb. 1695/6), fourth Baron Wharton. **P.** Lay member of the Westminster Assembly, 1643. Thrice married, the Wooburn House estate came to him by his second wife, Jane, daur. and heiress of Col. Arthur Goodwin, M.P., of Winchenden and Wooburn, Bucks. By deed of 1692 Lord Wharton founded a Charity for distributing (in four counties) Bibles and Puritan Catechisms, those by Thomas Lye and Joseph Alleine [*q.v.*]; the trustees, becoming Anglican, substituted for these catechisms the Church Catechism and the Book of Common Prayer. Under a scheme (1898) approved by the Chancery Court, the charity is now administered by nine trustees, five being Anglican and four Nonconformist. The Anglican trustees give Bibles and Prayer-books in the counties of Bucks, York, Westmorland, and Cumberland. The Nonconformist trustees give Bibles and Westminster Shorter Catechisms in the same counties, and in others when funds permit. (*D. Wk.*) [9, 121]

WHEATLEY, WHATELEY, or WHATELY, THOMAS, B.A. (1620–Jan. 1698/9). **P.** Second son of William Wheatley or Whately (1583—10 May 1639), vicar of Banbury, Oxf. Baptized, 10 S. 1620. Matric. at New Inn Hall, Oxford, 2 N. 1638, aged 18; B.A., 1642. Rector of St. Mary Woolchurch Haw, London, 1646–49. Ejected from the [sequestered ?] vicarage of Sutton-under-Brailes, Warw. The Episc. Returns, 1669, report him as preacher at Deddington, Oxf., to "Presbyterians About 40 In y^e^ houses of Timothy Bicknell, Widd. Wyer. But most frequently in M^r^ Whateley's Barne at Hampton [*i.e.* Hempton, hamlet and chapelry in Deddington parish] on Sundays"; also as one of the preachers at Adderbury, Oxf., to "Sometimes 200 Sometimes Quakers, sometimes Presbyterians & Anabaptists In the houses of M^r^ Bray Doyley, sometimes of William Gardener, sometimes of Widow Swift. Weekly"; also as one of the preachers at Bicester to "100 or 200 Separatists of all sorts In y^e^ house or Barne of Thomas Harriss Baker In this Place they have a Pulpit, Seats & Galleries erected: & are said by reason of their impunity to increase"; also as one of the preachers at Burton Dassett, Warw., "Att the houses of James Wagstaffe, Richard Brookes & Nathaniel Lidbrooke." Licensed, June 1672, as "Pr. Teacher in his howse in Dedington Parish, Oxoñ. He preached also at Milton, Woodstock, and Combe Longa. The Common Fund gave him (11 May 1691), he being then of Milton, a gratuity of £5. He was buried at Banbury, 27 Jan. 1698/9. (*C. D. F. M. P. T. Wc.*) [85, 86]

WHISTON, JOSEPH (1628–Jan. 1690/1). **C.** Youngest brother of Edward Whiston (*see* Whitston). Chaplain to Col. Thomas Harrison (1606—26 Oct. 1660), the regicide.

Ejected from curacy or lectureship at Maidstone, a sequestered (1643) perpetual curacy. Removed to succeed Walter Postlethwaite (*d.* 1671) in the pastoral charge at Lewes, Suss., which he held "near twenty years" till his death. Left "what he had" to the children of his elder brother, Josiah (1625–Jan. 1685/6), rector of Norton-juxta-Twycross, Leic.; one of these children being William Whiston, M.A. (9 Dec. 1667—22 Aug. 1752), the translator of Josephus, and champion of "primitive Christianity." (*C. P. Ww.*) [112, 113]

WHITAKER. *See* Whitekar

WHITAKER, THOMAS, M.A. (1651—19 N. 1710). C. Born at Healey, parish of Rochdale, Lanc. Son of Robert Whitaker, M.D. Educ. at grammar schools of Burnley, Blackburn, and Manchester. Entered Frankland's Academy 6 July 1670; rem. to Edinburgh University; M.A., 1674. Preached in Lancashire under the auspices of Thomas Jolly [*q.v.*]. Succeeded, at Leeds (1675), Christopher Nesse, M.A. (26 D. 1621—26 D. 1705); ejected (1662) from Leeds parish church, and founder of the Congregational church in the Main Riding-house, Leeds. Imprisoned, eighteen months, from 16 July 1683, in York Castle, with Oliver Heywood [*q.v.*], for Nonconformity, he regularly ministered to his flock by written sermons. In 1691 a Meeting-house was built for him in Call Lane, Leeds. For some time Thomas Bradbury (1677—9 S. 1759), the leader of the Subscribers at Salters' Hall in 1719, lived under his roof. Whitaker, who lost his first wife while a prisoner at York, was succeeded at Call Lane (after William Moult, *d.* 17 S. 1727) by his son Thomas (by his third wife), whose son William assisted him. (*Ed. Fr. My. Nk. Nr. Ps. Wl. Wm.*) [129]

WHITCHURCH, Hants. Calamy preached here for several Sundays in 1691, as guest of Pointer, a layman. (*Cm.*) [100, 102]

WHITCHURCH ('Whittchurch') (Shrops., and partly Chesh.). Ejected here in 1660 was Thomas Porter, M.A., born in Northants; matric. sizar at Christ's Coll., Cambridge, July 1616; B.A., 1619/20; M.A., 1623; episcopally ordained deacon and priest, 21 and 22 Sept. 1623; vicar of Hanmer, Flint., 15 Mar. 1625/6; one of the lecturers for Chester, 4 May 1642; held the sequestered rectory of Whitchurch, 1645; member of the Fourth Presbyterian Classis of Salop; died at Shrewsbury, 19 June 1667. His son, Thomas Porter, M.A., ordained by his father's Classis as preacher at Tilstock chapel in Whitchurch parish, afterwards conformed, was reordained, and held the perpetual curacy of Bunbury, Chesh. (*C. Cp. P. V.*) [15]

WHITE COLNE. John Bigley held this donative in 1662, and kept it without conforming; in 1669 he was preaching at Marks Tey, Ess., and Stoke-by-Nayland, Suff.; licensed, 13 May 1672, being of White Colne. (*C. T.*) [39]

WHITE CROSS, the, in the Poultry. [2]

WHITE FRIARS. Now represented by Whitefriars Street (which runs southward from Fleet Street between Nos. 67 and 68), and by its continuation, Carmelite Street. The White Friars were Friars of our Lady of Mount Carmel. Till 1697 the precinct of White Friars was a sanctuary by royal charter, and hence was colonised by a lawless community of ruffians, who gave to their quarters the name Alsatia. (*Lo. Sl.*) [1]

WHITE, JEREMIAH, M.A. (1629–1707). C. Cromwell's famous and witty chaplain, tricked into a marriage with the waiting-woman when he aspired to the hand of Cromwell's youngest daughter, Frances (*see* Rich, Lady). Admitted subsizar at Trinity Coll., Cambridge, 7 Apr. 1646; matric., 1646; B.A., 1649/50; M.A., 1653; no record of Fellowship. Held no ecclesiastical preferment. Congregational in judgment, he was politically a zealous Independent, an ardent member of the Calf's Head Club (held a dinner each 30 Jan. to gloat over the execution of Charles I.). After 1688 he preached occasionally at a Meeting-house (with no settled ministry) in Queen Street, Lower Rotherhithe. He is reported to have said grace at the dinners of the Calf's Head Club, 1693–99. Preached also for Robert Bragge [*q.v.*]. His posthumous work, "The Restoration of All Things," 1712 (often reprinted), is an able plea for Universalism. This hardly explains his connection with Bragge; it may be taken as a set-off against the proceedings of the Calf's Head Club, seeing that it implies the salvation of the decapitated monarch. (*C. Cm. D. P. Tc. V. W.*) [4]

WHITE, JOHN. (*M.*) [182]

WHITEHAVEN. The first Minister was Roger Anderton, who entered Frankland's Academy, 3 May 1684. Ordained at Rathmell in 1693, he was at that time Minister at Whitehaven, and probably was so from 1690. On 29 D. 1690 a grant of £10 a year was made from the Common Fund "towards the propagation of the Gospell at Whitehaven." He was one of the original trustees of the Whitehaven Meeting-house, for the use of Presbyterians and Congregationals. He removed to Newcastle-on-Tyne in 1704/5, and died in April 1705. (*Fr. Hh. M. Nk. Nr.*) [23]

WHITEHURST, RICHARD (1637—5 Sept. 1697). C. Ejected from the vicarage of Laughton-en-le-Morthen, West Riding. He remained there, despite the Five Mile Act, protected by Anthony Hatfield of Westhall. Licensed, 1 May 1672, as "Congr. Teacher at Westhall in Hatfield," West Riding; this was at the house of John Rooke. Later, he ministered (before 1678) at Lydgate, parish of Kirkburton, in Bradford Dale. The Common Fund granted him (1690–93) £4 a year for Lydgate. Before 1695 he had removed to Bridlington, East Riding, where he died. He was a Fifth Monarchy man, holding the thousand years' reign of our Lord after the Second Advent. (*C. Ht. M. My. Nr. P. T. Y.*) [130]

WHITEKAR, *i.e.* WHITAKER, ROBERT, B.A. (*d.* Jan. 1717/8). P. Born in Lancashire. Admitted at Magdalene Coll., Cambridge, 1656; matric. sizar, 1658; B.A., 1661; no record of Fellowship, from which Calamy says he was ejected in 1662. Licensed, Apr. 1672, as "Presb." in "the house of William Bulkley Esq^r at Burgate in the parish of Fordingbridg in Southamptonshire." He died at Fordingbridge where he had begun his ministry almost fifty years before (Fun. Sermon by Edward Warren, 17 Jan. 1718); but he is not given in Evans' List as ministering there in 1715.

"Mr. Whitaker of Fordingbridge," who received a Fund gift of £5 in 1732, may have been his son. (*C. Ev. M. P. T. V. W.*) [101]

WHITEMARSH, GEORGE (*fl.* 1654–1705). C. Held (after 1654) the sequestered rectory of Rowner, Hants; ejected, 1662 (?). The Episc. Returns, 1669, report "M^r Whitmarsh formerly a Taylor in Sarum" as one of three preachers to "Presbyterians some hundreds of all sorts Tradesmen in Portsmouth, seamen & workmen in His Ma^ties yard w^th their wives & children" at a conventicle "kept in a Malthouse" at Gosport, Hants. Licensed, 10 June 1672, as "Congr. Teacher in his howse at Gosport." The Common Fund voted him (1690) £10 a year for Brighton, reduced (1695) to £4 for Lindfield, withdrawn, 1696, but renewed, 1697, and paid to 1705. The Congregational Fund voted him £5 on 20 Apr. 1696. (*C. Cf. M. P. T. Wc.* [113]

WHITLEY ('Whitly') CHAPEL (in Nether Whitley township, parish of Great Budworth, Chesh.). Ejected here was John Machin, M.A., P., born at Seabridge, parish of Stoke-upon-Trent, Staff., 2 Oct. 1624; son of John Machin; entered Jesus Coll., Cambridge, Dec. 1645; B.A., 1649; M.A., 1653; ord. by presbyters, 1649; lecturer at Ashborne, Derb., 1650; lecturer at Atherstone, Warw., 1652; lecturer at Astbury, Chesh., 1653; perpetual curate of Whitley Chapel, 17 May 1661; ejected, 1662; remained at Whitley; died at Seabridge, 6 S. 1664. (*C. D. P.*) [15]

WHITLOCK, JOHN, M.A. (1625—4 Dec. 1708). P. Son of Richard Whitlock, merchant of London. Matric. pensioner, at Emmanuel Coll., Cambridge, 1642; B.A., 1645/6; M.A., 1649. Vicar of Leighton Buzzard, Beds, 1646; joined there by William Reynolds (*see* Reinolds), who lived under the same roof with him till Reynolds died; they supplied also Wokingham, Berks (1647), and Aylesbury, Bucks (1649–50). Appointed to the (sequestered ?) vicarage of St. Mary's, Nottingham, 1651; ordained, Oct. 1651, in London; the parish was at once organised on the Presbyterian model; the Nottingham Classis was not duly formed till 1656, and continued till 6 June 1660. Whitlock was ejected 6 July 1662, and removed in October to Colwich Hall, Notts; removing in 1666, under stress of the Five Mile Act, to Shirebrook, Derbs., and in 1668 to Mansfield, Notts. The Episc. Returns, 1669, report him as one of five preachers at Mansfield to "not 20, on the weeke days but on Sundayes 40 or 50 Presbyterians" of "better qualitie" than the Papists or Quakers. Licensed, 17 Apr. 1672, as "Presb. Teacher in his howse in Mansfield"; also, 2 May 1672, as "Pr. Teacher in the howse of Thomas Lupton," Nottingham; an application for the Town Hall was refused. Settled as Minister in St. Mary's Gate, Nottingham, 14 Oct. 1687; the High Pavement Meeting-house was built 1690–91. He married the daughter of Anthony Tuckney, D.D. [*q.v.*]. (*C. No. P. T. V. Wc.*) [82, 178]

WHITLOCK, JOHN, *junior* (1663?—17 Mar. 1723/4). P. Son of John Whitlock [*q.v.*]. It is interesting to notice that while preaching two Sundays in twelve at the Presbyterian Meeting, he preached one Sunday in twelve at the Congregational Meeting. On the death of his father, whom he assisted, he became colleague to John Barrett [*q.v.*], at the High Pavement, Nottingham; on Barrett's death (1713) he had John Hardy as colleague. In addition to his High Pavement ministry, he preached also, in turns, at Cole Orton, Leic., East Leake and Normanton, Notts. His son, Nathaneal Whitlock (*d.* June 1749), was assistant to Hardy (1727), and co-pastor at the High Pavement from 1729 till death. (*Ev. No.*) [82, 178]

WHITSTON, *i.e.* WHISTON, EDWARD, M.A. (*d.* 1697). **P.** Eldest brother of Joseph Whiston [*q.v.*]. Graduated at Trinity Coll., Cambridge; B.A., 1634/5; M.A., 1638; Lic. Med., 1639. Vicar in 1647 of Norton Mandeville, Ess., and member of the Sixth or Ongar Classis; rector (before 1656) of Little Laver, Ess.; ejected, 1662. Application for licence to "Mr. Wiston Presbiterion Minister" in Essex was unsuccessful. He was owner of the Meeting-place in East Smithfield, licensed, 8 May 1672, for Baptist worship under the ministry of Samuel Loveday. He was at Romford, Essex, in 1684. The Common Fund granted him, 1690–93, £4 a year for Romford; not renewed, 1695. He is said to have preached at Aldborough Hatch, Ess., when nearly ninety. He was buried at Romford, in 1697. (*C. E. Lr. M. P. T. Tc. V.*) [40]

WHITWORTH, JOSEPH (1655—13 Feb. 1721/2). **P.** Entered Frankland's Academy, 17 Aug. 1676. On leaving the Academy (20 Jan. 1679/80) he taught school at Falinge, Rochdale. He assisted Henry Pendlebury [*q.v.*] for a short time, afterwards assisting John Crompton [*q.v.*] from 1687. An inscription (seemingly recut) on his tombstone in Cockey Moor Meeting-house describes him as "minister att Cockey neare 25 yeares"; this should probably be 35. The existing Meeting-house was registered in 1714; Cockey Chapel having been taken from Nonconformists. He was succeeded by Peter Seddon (1689–1731). [A Joseph Whitworth appears in Evans' List as ministering at Oswestry, Shrops., from 1718; but this Joseph Whitworth of Oswestry was dead before Oct. 1720.] (*D. Ev. M. Nk. Nl. X.*) [61]

WICKENS, *i.e.* WICKINS, WILLIAM (Sept. 1614–Sept. 1699). **P.** Born in London. Matric. pensioner, at St. Catharine's Hall, Cambridge, 1631; B.A., 1634/5; M.A., 1638. Chaplain to Sir Edward Scott, Scot's Hall, Kent. Held the sequestered rectory of St. Andrew's Hubbard, London, allowing the use of the house to former rector. Was the scribe to the Fourth London Classis. Removed (after 1657) to the sequestered living of St. George's, Southwark, which he ceded, 1660. Preacher at the Poultry Compter, whence ejected, 1662. Licensed, 16 May 1672, as Presb. Teacher in house of Alderman John Forth, Hackney, with whom he resided as chaplain. Was one of those who read lectures privately to pupils of Charles Morton, M.A., after Morton's removal to New England, 1685. One of the ordainers of Matthew Henry [*q.v.*]. At this time he was assisting John Starkey [*q.v.*] at Newington Green; he continued his assistance to Starkey's successor, Joseph Bennet, ejected from Brightling, Sussex. He was buried in Bunhill Fields, 21 Sept. 1699, aged 85. (*C. Fc. P. T. V. W. Wc.*) [4]

WICKLIFFE. *See* Wycliffe

WIDOWS' FUND. [157]

WIGHT, DANIEL, senior. Of Southwark. Attended as Manager, 3 Oct. 1692, only; his subscription was in arrear at Midsummer 1693. (*M.*) [162, 166]

WILBRAHAM, SIR THOMAS, Bart. (1630?–Aug. 1692), succeeded as third and last baronet of Woodhey, Chesh., on 31 O. 1660. His seat, Woodhey Hall, was in Acton parish, Chesh.; here his widow built Woodhey Chapel, about 1700. (*Ba.*) [88, 90]

WILKINSON, HENRY, D.D. (1616—13 May 1690). **P.** Son of William Wilkinson, rector of Adwick-le-Street, Yorks. From an Oxford grammar school he matric. at Magdalen Hall, Oxford, 10 O. 1634, aged 17; B.A., 1635; M.A., 1638. Vicar of Buckminster, Leic., 1642; held the sequestered vicarage of Epping, Ess., 1643–60. Member of the Westminster Assembly, 1643. Fellow and vice-president of Magdalen Coll., 1648; B.D., 1648; Principal of Magdalen Hall, 1648; Whyte's professor of moral philosophy, 1649–54; D.D., 1652; to distinguish him from his first cousin of the same names (*see* Oxford) he was known as 'Dean Harry'; ejected, 1662. As a Nonconformist he preached first at Buckminster. Licensed, 16 May 1672, as "Pr. Teacher in his house in Gosfield, Ess."; his house licensed, same date, as Pr. Meeting-place; also, 5 S. 1672, for the same place. He removed, later, to Sible Hedingham, Ess., and ultimately to Great Cornard, Suff., where he died. The date of his death accounts for the erasure of his name by the Book-keeper. (*C. D. E. F. P. T. Wc. Y.*) [40]

WILKINSON, . . . Dunton mentions

"Wilkinson," in verse, as a London Minister. "Mr Wilkinson" of Goudhurst, Kent, received a Fund grant of £4 in 1704. (*Du. M.*) [3]

WILLASTON, in Wirral. [17]

WILLETTS, WILLIAM (1664 ?—9 Mar. 1699/70). **C.** Educ. at the Academy of John Woodhouse [*q.v.*]. Minister at Dudley, Worc., and died of decline, aet. 36. (*Td. To.*) [128]

WILLIAM III. [137, 154]

WILLIAMS, BENJAMIN (*fl.* 1690–92), Minister at Guildford, Surr. (*M.*) [166]

WILLIAMS, DANIEL, D.D. (1643 ?—26 Jan. 1715/6). **P.** Born at or near Wrexham, Denbighshire. Admitted preacher, by Independents, before he was nineteen. Chaplain (1665 ?) to Mary, Countess of Meath, and regular preacher to Congregational church in Drogheda. Colleague (1667) and successor to Samuel Marsden (*d.* 1677), a moderate Congregational, at Wood Street, Dublin. [If the licences, 10 Aug. and 5 Sept. 1672, for "Daniel Williams to be a Pr. Teacher in Wrexham" refer to him, it may mean that he was there, or expected there, on a visit; but he was not then a Presbyterian.] From 1682 to 1687, Gilbert Rule, M.D. (1629 ?–1701), afterwards Principal of Edinburgh University, was his colleague at Wood Street; from Rule he got his (theoretical) admiration of the Presbyterian system and of the Scottish universities. Removing to London in Sept. 1687, he became assistant to John Howe, M.A. [*q.v.*], and led the successful opposition to a united Address of thanks from London Nonconformist Ministers for James II.'s Declaration for Liberty of Conscience. On the death (3 Dec. 1687) of John Collins, Congregational Minister at Paved Alley, Lime Street, he was a candidate for that post, but Nathaniel Mather [*q.v.*] was elected. John Oakes, ejected from the vicarage of Boreham, Essex, Presbyterian Minister at Hand Alley, Bishopsgate Street (reported in 1669 as "new built," and when seized for Anglican use, 1671, described as "a large room, purposely built for a Meeting-house, with three galleries, thirty large pews, and many benches and forms"), died in Dec. 1688. Williams succeeded him in 1689, and remained in this charge till death. His part in the Crispian controversy is detailed in the Commentary. In March 1701/2 he headed the Address to Queen Anne from the London Nonconformist Ministers, this being the first occasion on which the Three Denominations acted together. He was made D.D. of Edinburgh and of Glasgow in May 1709. His will (26 June 1711; codicil, 22 Aug. 1712) put some £50,000 in trust for purposes of education and religion; the trusts took effect, 26 July 1721. John Dunton says of Williams, defending him from some aspersions, "his very complexion and his countenance have nothing but good humour in them." Compare his portrait. He lived in Hoxton Square. (*Be. C. D. Du. Je. P. T. W.*) [3, 15, 16, 53, 63, 89, 97, 141, 142, 145, 152, 154, 156, 160, 161, 164, 165, 168, 184, 186, 187, 189]

WILLIAMS, FRANCIS. [12]

WILLIAMS, HENRY (1622 ?–1685 ?). **B.** Son of Reginald Williams of Uske, Monm., gent.; matric. at Pembroke Coll., Oxford, 28 May 1639, aged 17. He was a public preacher before 1662; thereafter, living on his small estate of Ysgafell, near Newtown, Montg., he preached much, without fee, and ultimately became pastor of the church at Newtown, founded by Vavasor Powell (1617—27 O. 1670). The Episc. Returns, 1669, report him as "a great Conventicle holdr" at Llanllwchaiarn, Montg. He was ordained on 28 Aug. 1672 at Gwynle, near Newtown. For his preaching he suffered much imprisonment. He was a Baptist, and most of his church members were likewise, but Congregationals were not excluded. As pastor at Newtown he was succeeded by Hugh Owen [*q.v.*]. His daughter Rosamond married Richard Davis [*q.v.*]. Calamy says he died "about 1685," "aged about 60." (*C. F. P. Rj. Rw. T.*) [141, 148, 189]

WILLIAMS, JOHN (*fl.* 1650–90). **C.** A man of means. Called Captain, having been in the Parliamentary army. Itinerant preacher in the counties of Montgomery, Radnor, and Denbigh; an active supporter of Vavasor Powell (1617—27 Oct. 1670) in carrying out the provisions of the Ordinance (22 Feb. 1650) "for the better propagation and preaching of the Gospel in Wales." He was one of the sixteen members sent from Wales to the Parliament which met on 4 July 1653, called 'Barebone's Parliament,' from Praisegod Barbon (1596 ?–Jan. 1679/80). Latterly he lived at Llangollen, Denb., and was there buried in the churchyard, but his body was exhumed by opponents, and ultimately interred in his own garden.

His son, John Williams (1662—5 Oct. 1725) (**C.**), was educated at some Academy, as Evans' List calls him "scholar." The Common Fund granted him (1690–93) £4 a year as Itinerant. He became Pastor at Wrexham, Denb., on the death (1711) of Jenkin Thomas [*q.v.*]. He received no stipend; his flock lent him (from a charity) £20, and later £40, for both which he paid 6 % interest; the loans were repaid some time after his death. About 1715 he became a Baptist; this increased his flock, though some of its members joined the Presbyterian congregation. He lived at Rhual, Flint., and was buried in Rhosddu graveyard, near Wrexham (inscription). (*M. Pw. Rj. Rw.*) [148]

WILLIAMS, MORGAN. [143, 146]

WILLIAMS, ROGER (1667—25 May 1730). **C.** Probably educated by Rice Prythro [*q.v.*]. Ordained (1698) as Pastor jointly of Cwm-y-Glo (near Merthyr Tydfil, Glam.) and of Cefnarthen (near Llandovery, Carm.), places nearly 30 miles apart. He was particularly cautious in the reception of candidates for church membership. His theology was Arminian, but his flock, divided in sentiment, was kept together by the appointment of James Davies, of Llanwrtyd, Brecon, an extreme Calvinist, as co-pastor.

After the death of Williams, Richard Rees was chosen (1723) co-pastor with Davies; in 1747 Rees, with a section of the flock, seceded to form a new congregation (now Unitarian) at Cefn-Coed-y-Cymmer, Brecon, two miles from Merthyr. Rees was replaced by the son of Davies, who, however, left his father's position for views akin to those of Rees. (*Rj.*) [143]

WILLIAMSON, ANTHONY (*fl.* 1690–1701). **P.** The first known Minister at Spinner Lane, King's Lynn; in 1701 John Rastrick [*q.v.*] became his colleague. It is not probable (or his full name would have appeared in William Rastrick's "Index") that he was Calamy's "Mr Williamson," ejected from the rectory of Washington, Durh. (*B.*) [74]

WILLIAMSON, HENRY (*d.* 1727 ?). **C.** The Common Fund made him (4 Jan. 1691/2) a gift of £5 for Southwold. About 1698 he became Minister of Palgrave, Suff., and received grants from the Congregational Fund. There was no Communion Service at Palgrave till the ministry of Rochemont Barbauld in 1774, the church members communicating at Denton and Wattisfield. (*B. M.*) [105, 106, 107]

WILLINGHAM. Ejected here was Nathanael Bradshaw, M.A. [*q.v.*] [12, 172]

WILLS, *i.e.* WILLES, JOHN, M.A. (*d.* 1703 ?). **P.** Matric. 'ser.' at Magdalen Hall, Oxford, 28 Mar. 1655; M.A., 1661. Rector of Faxton, Northants; ejected, 1662. Licensed, 13 May 1672, as "Pr. Teacher in the howse of John Morton in Ringstead," Northants. Buried at Spratton, Northants, soon after his wife, who died in 1703. (*C. F. P. T.*) [76]

WILLS, JONATHAN (*d.* 1691). Eldest son of John Wills, B.A. (1582—20 F. 1654/5), vicar of Morval, Corn. Matric., 13 Feb. 1648/9, at Exeter Coll., Oxford; Fellow, 1648–52. Held the sequestered rectory of St. Mabyn, Corn., 1652–5; later, from 1655, the sequestered rectory of Lanteglos (now called Camelford), Corn; ejected, 1662. The Episc. Returns, 1665, report "There is one Jonathan Wills who never took any degree in the Schooles yet in ye tyme of sequestracōn intruded himself into ye Rectory of Mabyn, and from thence removed to ye Rectory of Lanteglos neare Camelford, from whence being eiected he returnes to the house of Anne Silly in St. Mabyn, where he still shelters himselfe, where as is strongly reported, he keepes great & frequent Conventicles." Licence was given, 22 Apr. 1672, to "Jonathan Wills of Helligan neare Bodmine" as general Pr. Teacher; at same date the house of Mrs. Anne Silly, "called Helligan," near Bodmin, was licensed as a Presb. Meeting place. Heligan (seat of the Tremaynes) is in the parish of St. Ewe, far from Bodmin; Haligan or Helligon is a manor in St. Mabyn parish, seat of the family of Silly. Wills was buried at St. Mabyn, 11 S. 1691. (*C. F. P. T.*) [18]

WILLSON, *i.e.* WILSON, ROBERT, M.A. (1634 ?—5 Mar. 1713). **P.** Educ. at Edinburgh; M.A., 13 June 1651. Admitted Minister of Melrose, Roxburghsh., 9 S. 1690. (*Ed. Sf.*)

WILSCOMBE. [93, 94] *See* Somerset

WILSON, AGNES. Widow, sister or daughter of Richard Wilson; *see* Davice. [80]

WILSON, JOHN (1662—8 Apr. 1695). **P.** Son of John Wilson, M.A. (*d.* 1672 ?); ejected from the vicarage of Backford, Chesh. Educated in the Academy of Thomas Rowe [*q.v.*], and further instructed by Philip Henry [*q.v.*]. Minister at Bromborough, Cheshire, and member (1691) of the Cheshire Classis (*see* p. 157). Removed to Warwick (1691), and died there. (*Uc.*) [17]

WILSON, JOHN (*fl.* 1669–1717). **B.** The Episc. Returns, 1669, report "John Wilson, a Taylor," as one of five preachers to "about 30 Anabaptists of the meaner sort of comon people" at houses in Bakewell, etc., Derb. On 29 Mar. 1677 John Wilson was transferred from Bedford to Hitchin and became pastor, 1 Oct. 1677 (set apart 28 Apr. 1678). In 1692 the Tile-House Street Chapel was built. In 1697 Wilson was assisted by his son Ebenezer. He was living in 1717. His congregation included Congregationals. (*T. Uh.*) [51, 189]

WILSON, RYND, *i.e.* REYNOLD (*d.* 1720). **B.** The Episc. Returns, 1669, report "Rhinald Wilson a Scholmaster," parish of Aberhafesp, Montg., as an abettor of conventicles in that county. His education had been with a view to the Anglican ministry, but he became a member of the Baptist church under Henry Williams [*q.v.*], and preached much at Llanbrynmair, Montg., and elsewhere. Like Williams and some others he admitted to church membership Congregationals as well as Baptists. The Common Fund granted him, as Reynold Wilson (called also "Mr Itinerant Willson"), £4 a year, 1690–93. Ultimately he became Pastor at Isgafell, near Newtown, Montg. (*see* Hugh Owen). He kept up his school, and had many pupils of note; one of them, Francis Turner (1654—16 S. 1727) became his co-pastor, but left in 1696, and was Pastor of the ancient Baptist church at Hill Cliffe, near Warrington. He died shortly before the beginning of 1720, *i.e.* in Feb. or March 1720, present reckoning. (*Ev. M. T. Rj.*) [148, 189]

WILSON, THOMAS (*fl.* 1651–93). **P.** Son of Thomas Wilson, B.A. (1601–1651/2), who died holding the sequestered perpetual curacy of Maidstone, Kent, leaving ten children. Vicar of Lamesley, Durh.; ejected. Licensed, 10 June 1672, as "Pr. Teacher" in his house at Lamesley. Preached there for two years in conjunction with Robert Lever [*q.v.*]. "Utterly disabled" in his latter years. Received from the Common Fund, 1690–93, £5 a year, being "near Newcastle." (*C. Cl. M. P. T.*) [79]

WILSON, . . . [27, 29]

WILTSHIRE. [47, 123, 124, 155, 168, 177, 181] The headings "Wilts" are in the earliest handwriting; the names Bourne and Conway are in another hand; the rest is in that of the Book-keeper. The returns are numbered 5 to 90 (mostly 19); and 71, in 1692.

Alton is Allington in South Wilts [*q.v.*].

Causam is Corsham.

Chepenham is Chippenham.

Colne is Calne [*q.v.*].

Hunnett is Donhead St. Mary (*see* Compton South).

It may be noted that no mention is made of Horningsham, as the locality of a Meeting-house or congregation. The existing Meeting-house has a stone inserted with the date 1566; the local legend maintains that a congregation, founded by Scottish Presbyterian masons, has worshipped in the building ever since that date (it is now Congregational). There is good evidence of conventicling at Horningsham in 1669 and 1672, but none of the present Meeting-house till its registration in 1704. Evans' List for Wilts (13 Dec. 1717) mentions the place, but gives no particulars of congregation, and is silent as to Minister and denomination (*see* Clifford, S.; Flower, B.; South, C.; and Weekes, J.). (*Ev. Jp. T.*)

WIMBLETON, *i.e.* WIMBLEDON, LADY. **C.** Edward Cecil (29 Feb. 1571/2—16 Nov. 1638), naval and military commander, created, 9 Nov. 1625, Baron Cecil of Putney and Viscount Wimbledon of Wimbledon, married (Nov. 1632) as his third wife, Sophia, daughter of Sir Edward Zouche, of Woking, Surrey. John Finet writes (16 Oct. 1635): "My Lord of Wimbledon (of whose valor, I think, no man ever doubted in his youth) hath now in his age [60½] also showed himself no less valiant and venturous, having lately marryed the young daughter (of 17 years old) of Sir Edward Zouche deceased." By this marriage he had an only son, Algernon, who predeceased him. The Dowager Viscountess became the second wife of Sir Robert King, of Boyle, Co. Roscommon, who died (1657) at Cecil House in the Strand. Lady Wimbledon's house in Nether Whitacre parish, Warw., was licensed, 30 Apr. 1672, as a Congr. Meeting-place. She died, 16 Nov. 1691, at Ketton, Suffolk, seat of her son-in-law, Sir Thomas Barnardiston, bart., who had married (1670) Elizabeth (*d.* 1707), her daughter by Sir Robert King. (*Ba. D. Pe. T.*) [2]

WIMBORNE ('Winbourn'). Ejected here was Baldwin Deacon [*q.v.*]. [35]

WINCANTON. Ejected here in 1662 was John Sacheverell, son of John Cheverell, rector of East Stoke, Dors., who took the name Sacheverell. Of New Inn Hall, Oxford; matric., 1 Feb. 1632/3, aged 18; B.A., 1636; rector of Langton Matravers, 1646; rector of Rimpton, Som., 1653; held the donative of Wincanton; retired to Stalbridge, Dors., his wife's property; *d.* in Dorchester gaol. His son Joshua, vicar of Marlborough, Wilts, was father of Henry Sacheverell, D.D., the high-church firebrand. (*C. F.*) [92]

WINCHCOMBE ('Winchomb'). Ejected here was Carnsew Helme [q.v.]. The Common Fund granted (1690) £10 a year for Winchcombe with Bishop's Cleave (*M.*) [45, 46]

WINCHESTER ('Winton'). Ejected here were (1) . . . Cook. (2) Humphrey Ellis, who afterwards conformed. (3) Theophilus Gale, M.A. [q.v.]. (4) Faithfull Teate, D.D., of Trinity Coll., Dublin; B.A., 1621; M.A., 1624; father of Nahum Tate, the versifier. (*C. Db.*) If he were ejected from Winchester, his position cannot have been more than that of a lecturer for a short time; in 1654–58 he describes himself in published sermons as preacher of the Gospel at Sudbury, Suff.; in 1660 he held the living of St. Werburgh's, Dublin. There was, however, another Faithfull Teate, of Pembroke Coll., Cambridge; matric. pensioner, 1646; B.A., 1646/7; M.A., 1650. (*D. V.*) [100, 102]

WINDHAM. [74] *See* Norfolk

WINDSOR. Most of Windsor borough is in the parish of New Windsor [q.v.]; the Windsor Castle tract is extra-parochial. [9]

WINFRITH NEWBRUGH ('Winfruit'). [35]

WINNY, *i.e.* WINNEY, SAMUEL (1627 ?–1700). **P.** Born at Kingswood, Wilts. Son of William Winney. From Wotton-under-Edge school, admitted sizar at Christ's Coll., Cambridge, 26 Mar. 1645, age 17; matric., 1645; did not graduate. Began his ministry in Gloucestershire. Vicar of Glastonbury, Som.; ejected, 1662. The Episc. Returns, 1669, report him as one of the preachers to 260 persons at various houses in Bridgwater, Som.; also to 300 persons at Glastonbury " In a Barne, belonging to John Austin, where a Pulpitt and seats are built." Licensed, 10 June 1672, as "Pr. Teacher in his howse at Glastry, Bristoll." He had a small congregation there, and taught school. In 1692 Calamy found him "almost superannuated." (*C. Cm. Cp. P. T. V.*) [91]

WINSHAM. [92]

WINSLOW. [10]

WINTERBURN ('Winterburne'), W.R. (misplaced in N.R.). [135]

WINTON. [100, 102] *See* Hampshire

WINWICK. [59]

WISBECH ('Wisbich'). Ejected here was John Sheldreck. (**C.**) — The Congregational Fund made a gift (1696) of £5 to "Mr Borroughs of Wishbytch in Lincolnshire," *i.e.* Ishmael Burroughs, who preached at various places in Lincolnshire and was given £8 from the Common Fund, 23 May 1692 "for his encouragement to settle at Holebeach." This he did not do. From 1717 to 1722 he received £5 a year from the Fund for Wisbech, Camb. In 1724 he removed to London. (*Cf. Ev. M.*) [13]

WITHAM. Ejected here was John Ludgates, of Edmund Hall, Oxford; matric., 31 Jan. 1633/4, aged 19; did not graduate; held the sequestered rectory of Great Birch, Ess., 21 May 1643; member of the Twelfth Presb. Classis of Essex; held the sequestered vicarage of Witham in 1656; ejected, 1660. (*C. E. F.*) [41, 42]

WITHAM FRIARY ('Frary'). [91]

WITHAMSTOW. [42] *See* Sussex

WITHER, ANTHONY. Attended as Manager, 15 Sept. 1690; last attendance, 18 Apr. 1692. (*M.*) [162]

WITHERS, JOHN (26 Mar. 1669 – 1729). **P.** Ordained 26 Aug. 1691. Ministered in the private chapel at Lupton House, in Brixham parish, seat of the Upton family. Succeeded John Hoppin [q.v.] in 1705 as a Minister of Bow Meeting, Exeter. He was a strong writer against the Anglican polity, and on the Whig side against Jacobite movements. In the Exeter controversy he was personally against tests, but at length secured his position by offering (5 Mar. 1718/9) to subscribe the Nicene Creed. He lived "near John's Bow." (*D* (under Peirce). *Em. Ev. M. Po. T.*) [31]

WITNEY. Ejected here in 1662 from lectureship was William Gilbert [? of Wadham Coll., Oxford; matric., 2 Mar. 1652/3; rem. to Magdalen Coll.; M.A., 1657]; licensed, 17 Apr. 1672, being of Stanton Harcourt, Oxf., as Presb. Teacher in any allowed place. (*C. F. T.*) [86]

WIVELISCOMBE. [93, 94]

WIVENHOE ('Vivenho'). A congregation here was founded by John Argor, ejected from Braintree [q.v.]. The Common Fund granted (1691) £5 a year for Wivenhoe; reduced (1695) to £4. (*M.*) [42]

WIVLINGHAM. [12] *See* Willingham

WOBURNE. [9] *See* Buckinghamshire

WOKINGHAM ('Ockingham'). Ejected here in 1662 was Rowland Stedman; born (1630 ?) at Corfton in Diddlebury parish, Shrop.; son of Henry Stedman, pleb.; matric. at Balliol Coll., Oxford, 12 Mar. 1648/9; Scholar, 1648; Scholar, University Coll., 1649; B.A., 1651; M.A., 1655/6; rector of Hanwell, Midx., 1657–60; rector of Wokingham, 1660; after ejection, chaplain to Lord Wharton [*q.v.*] at Wooburn, Bucks; *d.* there, 14 Sept. 1673. His descendant, Thomas Stedman, clergyman at Shrewsbury, published the first collection of Doddridge's letters (1790). (*C. D. F. P.*) [7]

WOLVERHAMPTON. Ejected in 1661 from the Collegiate church here was John Reynolds [either of Balliol Coll., Oxford, B.A., 1652/3, or of Pembroke Coll., Oxford, B.A., 1653/4]; preached in parish churches till silenced, 1662; removed to his patrimony at King's Norton; thence to Stourbridge; besides preaching, practised physic and obtained somewhere the degree of M.D.; rem. to London, Aug. 1683, and *d.* there Dec. 1683. (*C. F.*) [77, 98]

WOMBRIDGE. [90]

WOOBURN ('Woburne'). [9]

WOOD, JAMES (*d.* 1695). **P.** Son of James Wood (*d.* 10 Feb. 1666/7), ejected (1662) from the perpetual curacy of Ashton-in-Makerfield, Lanc. Succeeded James Livesey (1657) as perpetual curate of Atherton Chapel, Lanc. (built, 1648, and not consecrated), which he held till 1670. After imprisonment he preached at Wharton Hall, seat of Robert Mort. Recovered Atherton Chapel, 1676; in 1689 he is returned as "conformable"; assisted latterly by his son and successor, James Wood (1672—20 F. 1759), known as 'General' Wood, who held Atherton Chapel till 1721, and for whom the existing Chowbent Chapel in Atherton was built (1722). (*D.*) [61]

WOOD, JAMES (*d.* Jan. 1698/9). **C.** Subscribed a petition (1672) from "a Church of Christ in Tiverton." From 1695 to 1699 received from the Fund £4 a year for North Molton. (*Em. M. T.*) [30, 33]

WOOD, JOHN, M.A. (1631 ?–1690). **P.** Born at Chesterfield, Derb. Son of Richard Wood, druggist. From Chesterfield School, admitted pensioner at St. John's Coll., Cambridge, 30 May 1651, aged 18; matric., 1651; B.A., 1654/5; Fellow; M.A., 1658; ejected, 1662. Remained at Cambridge till excluded by the Five Mile Act, 1666. Licensed, 29 May 1672, as "Pr. Teacher in his howse in the Parish of Norton," Derb. Died at Norton. (*C. Jo. P. T. V.*) [98]

WOOD, JOHN, D.D.? (1622—19 Sept. 1692). From the Charterhouse school, matric. pensioner, at Magdalene Coll., Cambridge, 1639; B.A., 1642/3; Fellow; M.A., 1646; President (before 1654); ejected, 1660; [? D.D. by royal letters, 1666]. The Common Fund granted him (1690-92) £6 a year "on condition that he give vp himselfe to the Ministry." Calamy calls him a learned but shiftless man. He died at Minton, parish of Church Stretton, Shrops. (*C. Jo. M. P. V.*) [89]

WOOD, JOHN (1617 ?–1695). **P.** [? Matric. pensioner at Emmanuel Coll., Cambridge, 1637; did not graduate.] Held the sequestered rectory of Northchapel, Suss.; ejected, 1662. Retired to his small estate at Westgate, *i.e.* Westcott, a chapelry in the parish of Dorking, Surr. The Episc. Returns, 1669, report him as one of two preachers to "about 300 Presbyterians" in his house at Dorking. Licensed, 11 Apr. 1672, as "Pr. Teacher" in the said house; this may have been his dwelling-house, where he preached for some time, or the barn which he subsequently fitted up. (*C. P. T. V.*) [109]

WOODBRIDGE. Ejected here were (1) Robert Cade [? of Emmanuel Coll., Cambridge, M.A., 1618; or of Jesus Coll., Cambridge, matric., 1644. (*C. V.*)] (2) Frederick Woodall, of St. Catharine's Hall, Cambridge; matric. sizar, 1632; B.A., 1636/7; M.A., 1640; rector of Brome, Suff., 1645–7; pastor of a Congregational church at Woodbridge, and exercised his ministry in the parish church; ejected, 1660; preaching at Woodbridge, 1669; licensed, 1 May 1672, as Congr. Teacher in a house at Woodbridge; a Fifth Monarchy man; *d.* 1 Dec. 1681. (*B. C. T. V.*) [103]

WOODCOCK, JOSIAH (*b.* 1665). Son of Josias Woodcock of Taunton, Som. Matric. at Balliol Coll., Oxford, 18 Mar. 1685/6, aged 20. Ordained, 25 Aug. 1687, at Lyme, Dorset, being then of Oxford. (*F. W.*) [93, 94]

WOODCOCK, THOMAS, M.A., B.D. (*d.* 1695). **P.** Came of a Rutland family of good estate. Matric. pensioner at St. Catharine's Hall, Cambridge, 1641; B.A., 1644/5; migrated to Jesus Coll.; Fellow; M.A., 1648; B.D., 1655. Lecturer (unpaid) at Allhallows', Cambridge. Held the sequestered rectory of St. Andrew Undershaft, London; ejected, 1660. He and Anthony Tuckney, D.D. [*q.v.*], lived together in the country. By 1686 he had removed to Leiden and Utrecht, for the education of his sons. Returning, he settled at Hackney, preaching in his own house, and (later) assisting William Bates, D.D. [*q.v.*], at Mare Street (always gratis). Extracts from his papers (often racy) were edited by Prof. George C. Moore Smith, in the Camden Miscellany, vol. xi. 1907.

His son Thomas (at Utrecht in 1686) was Minister at Hampstead before Zachary Merrel [q.v.]. (*C. Cc. P. V. Wc.*) [4, 72, 87, 168, 176]

WOODHOUSE, JOHN (1627—Oct. 1700). **P.** Third son of John Woodhouse of Wombourn Woodhouse, Staff. Fellow-commoner at Trinity Coll., Cambridge, 1655; did not matriculate. In 1662, when silenced, was chaplain to Lady Grantham, in Nottinghamshire, unordained. The Episc. Returns, 1669, report John Woodhouse, gent., as preaching at Saxelby, Leic., to "about 50 ordinary" persons, denomination "not knowne." Had a large fortune by his wife, Mary Hubbert, of Reresby, Leic. Conducted at Sheriff Hales an Academy of note; many Students went to him with bursaries from the Fund; Robert Harley, first earl of Oxford, was among his pupils. In 1697 he succeeded Samuel Annesley, D.D. [*q.v.*], as Minister of Little St. Helen's, London, still continuing to train Ministers. His successor, Benjamin Robinson [*q.v.*], had been his pupil. Buried at Reresby, 17 Oct. 1700. (*Bc. C. H. J. P. T. Tc. To. W.*) [16, 28, 69, 88, 90, 175]

WOODHOUSE, JOHN, M.D. (12 Jan. 1676/7—28 May 1733). Third and youngest son of John Woodhouse [*q.v.*]. Entered, 11. Feb. 1699/1700, as medical student at Leiden, and graduated M.D. Practised at Nottingham. Buried at Reresby, Leic. (*A. H.*) [66]

WOODHOUSE, WILLIAM (11 Aug. 1669—24 Feb. 1742/3). Eldest son of John Woodhouse [*q.v.*]. Buried at Reresby, Leic. (*H.*) [25]

WOODWARD, WILLIAM, M.A. (1627–1691/2). **P.** Son of Thomas Woodward of Woodstock, Oxf., gent. Matric. at University Coll., Oxford, 1 July 1642, aged 15; B.A., 1646; Fellow, 1648–50; M.A., 1649/50; John Flavell [*q.v.*] was his pupil. Held the sequestered rectory of Richard's Castle, Heref., 1658; ejected, 1662. Travelled in the East. Licensed, 17 Apr. 1672, as "Presb. Teacher in the howse of John Yapps, in Orleton, Heref." Minister at Leominster, Heref., till death. (*C. F. P. T. Wc.*) [48]

WOODYARD, *i.e.* WOODWARD, ENOCH (*b.* 1634). **C.** Born at Norwich. Son of John Woodward. From Norwich grammar school admitted sizar at St. John's Coll., Cambridge, 22 May 1651, aet. 17. Held some position at one of the Norwich churches dedicated to St. George (probably St. George's Tombland), and thence ejected. The Episc. Returns, 1669, report him ('Woodyard') as preaching to Independents at John Toft's house in St. Clement's parish, Norwich (*see* Martin Finch). Licensed, 10 June 1672, as Enock Woodward, to be Congr. Teacher "in the howse of John Toft in S^t Clement's Parish." An "old difference" between him and the Norwich Congregational church was made up in 1675, but apparently renewed in 1680. According to tradition he was "a very worthy good man, but not a popular preacher." (*B. C. Jo. P. T.*) [74]

WOOLHOUSE, ANTHONY. Younger son of Thomas Woolhouse, gent., of Glapwell, Derb. Lived in Ireland. Had issue, by his wife (Edwards), Thomas, Anthony, Richard, Chaworth, and Mary. (*H.*) [133]

WOOLHOUSE, RICHARD. Son of above. (*H.*) [133]

WOOLWICH. [4]

WOOTON UNDER HEDGE. [44, 45, 46] *See* Gloucestershire

WORCESTER. Ejected here were (1) Joseph Baker, first of St. Catharine's Hall, then of Emmanuel Coll., Cambridge; matric. pensioner, 1647; B.A., 1647/8; M.A., 1651; from a better living in Kent, came at Richard Baxter's instance, to be rector of St. Andrew's, Worcester; ejected, 1662. (*C. P. V.*) (2) Richard Fincher, B.A. [*q.v.*]. (3) Thomas Duce, B.A. [*q.v.*]. (4) Simon Moor [*q.v.*]. [126, 127]

WORCESTERSHIRE. [67, 126, 127, 144, 152, 155, 168, 177] The headings "Worcester" are in the earliest handwriting; the name, "M^r Ward," is in another hand; the remainder is in that of the Book-keeper. The returns are numbered 21; except one, 100; and 170, in 1691. Parshor is Pershore [*q.v.*]

WORDEN, THOMAS (*fl.* 1669–96). **C.** The Episc. Returns, 1669, report "one Worden" as one of three preachers to "20 or 30 Anabaptists & oth^r Sects" at Whichford, War.; they report also a conventicle of "20 or 30 Independents" at Chipping Norton, Oxf., "In y^e house of Josiah Lilson, on Sundays Monthly Their Teacher not certaine, but often one Worden, formerly a Shoemaker." Licensed, 10 June 1672, as "Congr. Teacher" in the house of William Brockman, Hinton Waldrist, Berks; also, July 1672, as "Congr. Teacher in his howse at Broadway Worc."; application was also made for a licence for him at Chipping Campden, Glou. On 29 D. 1690 the Common Fund "ordered that £5:—per aunum be allowed to M^r Thomas

Worden att Nailsworth in Glocestershire and yt hee now receive halfe a yeares allowance ending the 25° Instant"; but there is no record of any payment, probably because he did not remain at Nailsworth. He was one of the witnesses against Richard Davis [*q.v.*] at Kettering in 1692, being then of Willingham, Camb. On 28 S. 1696 the Congregational Fund "Order'd That Mr Tho. Worden in Oxfordshire be allowed 4£ as a present gifft beeing in necessity." The use of the term "Society" for the Nailsworth congregation seems an early instance of a term greatly in vogue among Liberal Dissenters from about the middle of the eighteenth century. (*Co. Gl. M. T.*) [44]

WORKSOP. [84]

WORTH, JOHN (*fl.* 1654–99). Born at Wolston, Warw. Matric. ser. at Magdalen Hall, Oxford, 10 N. 1654. Held (1657) the sequestered rectory of Bourton-on-Dunsmoor, Warw.; ejected, 1660; vicar of Kilsby, Northants; ejected, 1662. Licensed, 10 June 1672, as "Pr. Teacher in the howse of John Billing" at Weedon Beck, Northants. He received £2 (10 N. 1690) from a donation received through Matthew Rapier [*q.v.*]. The Common Fund granted him (1692–99) £10 a year, first at Daventry, then in Oxfordshire (Chipping Norton).

He had three sons in the ministry, John, L.C.P. [*q.v.*]; William (at St. Ives, Cornw.), and Stephen (educ. under John Woodhouse [*q.v.*], and Minister at Cirencester, Glouc., in succession to William Beebie [*q.v.*]). (*C. F. M. P. T.*) [76, 118]

WORTH, JOHN, L.C.P. (*fl.* 1690–1706). Born in Oxfordshire. Educ. by his father, John Worth [*q.v.*]. The Common Fund granted him (1692–93) £6 a year, as his father's coadjutor in itinerant preaching from Daventry, Northants, and Chipping Norton, Oxf. He was admitted an extra-licentiate of the College of Physicians, 7 May 1697. In 1703 he was at Ramsbury, Wilts (grant of £3); in 1706 he was at Marlborough, Wilts (grant of £5). Neither he nor his brothers are in Evans' List. (*C. M. Mu. P.*) [76, 118]

WORTH, *i.e.* WORTS, THOMAS (*d.* 1697?). **P.** Rector of one of the Barninghams, Norf.; ejected thence. Afterwards pastor at Guestwick. The Episc. Returns, 1669, report him as one of the preachers at Trunch, Norf. (*see* Amirant, Christopher). His house "in Norfolk" was licensed, 10 June 1672, and, same day, he was licensed as "Congr. Teacher in the howse of Rob: Geel in Inghã"; in the same month a licence is noted for him as "Pr. Teacher in the howse of Thomas Brady in Cawston, Norfolk." The Common Fund granted to Thomas Woorts, East Rushton [*i.e.* Ruston], £8 a year in 1692, reduced in 1695–96 to £6. (*B. C. M. P. T.*) [74]

WOTTON UNDER EDGE ('Wootton under hedge'). Ejected here was . . . Bodin, who, after ejectment, preached privately at Bath, and is probably the Bowden reported as preaching "Att a Publiqe Inne" at Bath (and elsewhere), 1669. (*C. T.*) [44, 45, 46]

WRENTHAM. Ejected here were (1) William Ames (of the family of the puritan, William Ames, D.D.); matric. pensioner, at Emmanuel Coll., Cambridge, 1638; B.A., 1641/2; rem. to Queens' Coll.; Fellow; M.A., 1645; 'curate to his uncle at Wrentham, 1645; serving also Frostenden, Suff.; ejected, 1660; 'doctor' in the Congregational church at Wrentham, till death; on the petition, 29 Apr. 1672, "of the Congregation and Nonconformist in and about the parish of Wrentham" (21 names), he was licensed, 13 May 1672, as "Pr. Teacher in the Meeting-howse in Wrentham," and the Meeting-house licensed, same date, Presb. (doubtless because the petition had specified no denomination); *d.* 21 July 1689, aged 65. (*B. C. Mc. T. V.*) (2) Thomas King; rector of Wrentham, 1660; ejected, 1662; bur. there, 18 Nov. 1683. (*B. C.*) [For Augustine Plumsted, *see* Cambridge.] [103, 105]

WREXHAM. Ejected here was Ambrose Mostom (son of Henry, LL.D., of Calcott, Flint, canon of Bangor); of Brasenose Coll., Oxford; matric., 15 Jan. 1629/30, aged 19; B.A., 28 Jan. 1629/30; after preaching in Montgomery, he held the vicarage of Holt, Denb., till in 1659 he removed to the sequestered vicarage of Wrexham; ejected, 1660; chaplain to William, Lord Saye and Sele (*d.* 14 Apr. 1662), at Broughton Castle, Oxf.; removed to London; *d.* there "not long after the Fire" (1666). (*C. F. Pe.*) [141, 148]

WRIGHT, DANIEL (*d.* 1729). **P.** Not educated for the Ministry. Ordained, 1689, by Samuel Cradock [*q.v.*], John Fairfax [*q.v.*], John Meadows [*q.v.*], and John Salkeld [*q.v.*]. Preached first at Ousden, Suff. Succeeded John Salkeld [*q.v.*] at Walsham in 1700. His uncle, Captain Roper, left him a small estate at Walsham; hence the congregation raised no funds, and died with him. The Fund, however, supported a Lecture at

Walsham for many years. (*B. Ev. M.*) [13, 104, 107]

WRIGHT, JAMES, M.A. (1610–Dec. 1691). **P.** Younger son of an emigrant to New England. Matric. sizar, at Jesus Coll., Cambridge, 1635; B.A., 1638/9; M.A., 1642. Ejected from the vicarage of Wootton Wawen, Warw., in 1662 (*Co.* May 1916). Remained at Wootton after ejectment till the operation (1666) of the Five Mile Act, when John St. Nicholas [*q.v.*] welcomed him to his house at Knowle, Warw. After a time, Wright preached at his own house in Knowle parish (perhaps Blewlake, now Bluelake House) to "as many hearers as two rooms would hold." The Episc. Returns, 1669, report him as preaching to "100 & more" persons at the house of Thomas Worrall of Bordesley in the parish of Aston-juxta-Birmingham, and also at his own house at Knowle. He taught school and kept boarders. In 1685 Wright was imprisoned, in the scare due to the Monmouth rebellion. In 1686 Mary Eades was indentured "to James Wright of Chesset Wood in the said Manner of Knoll gent . . . for & in Consideration of Seuerall goods in hand delivered unto the Said James Wright to about the value of twenty shillings to teach and Instruct or cause to be taught and instructed by Katherine his Wife the calling or art of huswifery." The Common Fund granted him (1690) £8 a year; by the end of the year he was reported dead. Calamy, who calls Wootton Wawen 'Witton,' places his death in 1692, "aged eighty-one, or eighty-two." He was buried at Knowle, on 12 Dec. 1691; his wife, Catherine, was buried there on 17 Dec. 1702; his son James, on 8 Feb. 1722. In the Fund Minutes, Wright's Christian name is wrongly given as Abraham, probably from confusion with Abraham Wright, M.A., ejected (1660) from the sequestered rectory of Cheveley, Camb., buried at Wimbish, Ess., on 20 Aug. 1684 (parish register), "aged 80 or upwards." (*C.*) With John Wilkinson (ejected, 1660, from the sequestered vicarage of Ansley, Warw., but conforming later), who became vicar of Knowle (27 Sept. 1673), Wright and other Nonconformists were on terms of communion. After Wilkinson's death (*bur.* 20 Sept. 1695) Lord's Day services by Nonconformists were resumed at Blewlake, with help from the Fund. The Ministers were:

Charles Clemenson, Midsummer, 1696–1706; educ. 1691–3, under John Woodhouse [*q.v.*]. He received grants also, 1704–1706, for services at Moseley Chapel, registered (1689) for Dissenting worship.

John Nettleton, 1707–1708 (removed). He was also in charge of Southam. He married Elizabeth, sister of Philip Doddridge, D.D.

Samuel Knight, 1709–1712 (removed).

John Sparrey, 1713–1715. He had been at Uttoxeter, 1705–1709.

John Tonks, 1716–1734. He lectured also at Kingswood, Worc. At Midsummer, 1735, Blewlake was reported "dropped." (*C. Dk. Dw. M. P. T. Wc.*) [118]

WRIGHT, JAMES, M.A. (1651–1694). Son of John Wright (*d.* 1 Feb. 1684/5), ejected (1660) from the chapelry of Billinge, parish of Wigan. Matric. at Lincoln Coll., Oxford, 2 Mar. 1665/6, aged 14; B.A., 1669; rem. to Magdalene Coll., Cambridge; M.A., 1673. Became Nonconformist through the influence of William Cotton, ironmaster, of Wortley, near Sheffield, whose daughter Elinor (*d.* 1695) he married. The Common Fund voted him (1690) £6 a year for Attercliffe; but by June 1691 he had removed to East Retford, Notts, to which place, not to Wright personally, £10 a year was paid.

His eldest son, Samuel Wright, D.D. (20 Jan. 1682/3—3 Apr. 1746), was Minister at Carter Lane, London. (*D. F. M.*) [130, 131]

WRIGHT, JONATHAN (1659—25 June 1727). Bapt. 18 Dec. 1659. Son of Joseph Wright, of Hipperholme. Entered Frankland's Academy on 13 Apr. 1680. Applied in vain (19 July 1689) for registration of Idle Chapel, parish of Calverley, West Riding, for Nonconformist worship. Preached at Idle till 1691 or later; also at Little Horton near Bradford. Ordained, 6 June 1694, at Little Horton. Settled, same year, at Hove Edge, Lightcliffe, in Halifax parish; and received Fund grants (£5 yearly) for Lightcliffe till 1713, but was still preaching there in 1715 and later, according to Evans' List. He was buried at Halifax. Famous for a marvellous memory was his wife, Dorothy (*d.* 3 Jan. 1719/20), daughter of Bryan Dixon, of Hunslet, first married to William Courlass, rector of Long Marston, West Riding. (*Ev. Fr. Hh. M. My. Nk. Nr. Ti.*) [130]

WRIGHT, SAMUEL (*fl.* 1690–1727). **C.** Became assistant, July 1690, to James Hannot [*q.v.*] at Yarmouth, and continued in this office till 1 June 1709, when he became assistant to Augustine Plumsted [*q.v.*] at Wrentham, Suff.; removed

(1719) to the pastorate at Southwold, Suff.; resigned, 1727. (*B. J.*) [74, 177]

WYCLIFFE, JOHN, D.D. (1324?—31 Dec. 1384). Born at Hipswell, Yorks. Master of Balliol Coll., Oxford, in 1361; rector of Fillingham, Linc., May 1361; exchanged it for the rectory of Ludgershall, Bucks, 1368, with two years' licence of non-residence for study at Oxford; D.D., 1372; resigned Ludgershall for the rectory of Lutterworth, 1372 (?); condemned by Archbishop William Courtenay in council, 1382; translator of the Bible; died at Lutterworth. In 1428 his remains were disinterred, burnt, and the ashes thrown into the river Swift, by order of the Council of Constance. (*D.*) [68]

WYCOMBE (High or Market). Resigned here in 1660, before the Restoration, anticipating ejection, George Towner, M.A.; born in Shropshire; from Shrewsbury grammar school, matric. at Emmanuel Coll., Cambridge, 1651; B.A., 1654/5; M.A., 1659; held the vicarage of Wycombe several years; preached there after resignation; removing to London, assisted Anthony Palmer, M.A., at Pinners' Hall; licensed, with Palmer, 19 Apr. 1672, as Congr. Teacher in John Savage's house, London Bridge; in 1679 became pastor to Baptists in Broad Street, Bristol; died in Gloucester gaol, 29 Nov. 1685, after two and a half years' cruel incarceration. (*C. P. T. W.*) [9]

WYKES, THOMAS. [78]

WYMONDHAM. Ejected here was John Money [? of Queens' Coll., Cambridge; matric. pensioner, 1625; B.A., 1628/9; M.A., 1632]; rector of Mannington, Norf., 1633; preaching at Wymondham, 1646; pastor of Congregational church there, 1655; later, held the vicarage of Wymondham; ejected, 1660?; preaching at Bunwell in 1669; licensed, 10 June 1672, being at Wymondham, as Grāll Ind. Teacher. (*C. Nb. T. V.*) [74]

YARLINGTON ('Gallington'). [92]

YARMOUTH, GREAT. Ejected here were (1) John Allen; held some position at Mettingham, Suff.; lecturer at Yarmouth, 1650; ejected, 1660; lived and preached at Gorleston, Suff., as Presbyterian; *d.* 1665, aged over 50. (*B. C.*) (2) William Bridge, M.A. [*q.v.*]. (3) John Brinsley (1600—22 Jan. 1664/5); son of John, of Emmanuel Coll., Cambridge; matric. sizar, 1615; B.A., 1619/20; M.A., 1623; amanuensis to his maternal uncle, Joseph Hall, D.D. (afterwards bishop of Norwich), at the Synod of Dort, 1618; preached (apparently as chaplain) at Preston, an estate in South Hanningfield parish, Ess.; presented as parish Minister of Yarmouth, 4 Apr. 1625; dismissed, Midsummer, 1627; preached in the Dutch Church; rector of Somerleyton, 1632; town-preacher at Yarmouth, 1644; ejected, 1662; Presbyterian; *d.* 22 Jan. 1664/5, aged 64. (*B. C. V.*) (4) Job Tookie or Tookey (11 Dec. 1616—20 Nov. 1670), of Emmanuel Coll., Cambridge; matric. sizar, 1631; B.A., 1634/5; M.A., 1638; chaplain to Lady Westmorland; rector of St. Martin, Vintry, London; preacher at St. Alban's Abbey, where he gathered a Congregational church; preacher at Yarmouth, where Bridge was pastor and Tookie teacher of a Congregational church; ejected, 1661; removed to London, 1665. (*B. C.*) [74, 177]

YEA, *i.e.* YEO, WILLIAM, M.A. (1618–Nov. 1699). **P.** Born at Totnes, Devon; son of George Yeo. From Exeter grammar school, matric. at New Inn Hall, Oxford, 26 S. 1634, aged 16; B.A., 1637/8; rem. to Emmanuel Coll., Cambridge; M.A., 1641. Chaplain in Col. Gold's regiment; ministered at Brighton, Sussex; rector (1646) of Woolborough, Devon (having a chapel of ease at Newton Abbot); lost augmentation by refusing the engagement (1649) of loyalty to government without king or house of lords; ejected, 1662. Signed the thanks of Devon Ministers. Licensed, 11 Apr. 1672, being of Newton Bushel, Devon, as "a Grāll Presb. Teacher"; also, 30 Apr. 1672, his house "in the Parish of Woolbrough"; and, 13 May 1672, his house "in Newton Abbott Devon Presb. Meeting-place." Here he ministered till death. (*C. Em. F. P. T.*) [31]

YELDHAM ('Yeldam'), LITTLE. [41]

YEO, BARTHOLOMEW, M.A. (1617–Feb. 1692/3). Son of John Yeo, of Hatherleigh, Devon. Matric. at Corpus Christi Coll., Oxford, 28 Aug. 1634, aged 17; rem. to New Inn Hall; B.A., 1637/8; M.A., 1640. Rector of Exton, Som., 1643; held the sequestered rectory of Frittenden, Kent, 1644–6; rector of Merton, Devon; ejected, 1662. Signed the thanks of Devon Ministers. Licensed 11 Apr. 1672, being of Hatherleigh, as "a Grāll Pr. Teacher." He died in the neighbouring parish of Jacobstowe, in the house of a kinsman. For Jacobstowe he received, 1690–92, a grant of £4 a year from the Common Fund. (*C. Em. F. M. P. T.*) [31]

YEO. *See* Yea.

YEOVIL ('Yeovill'). Ejected here were (1) Henry Butler, M.A. [q.v.]. (2) Dr. Martin (?), who afterwards conformed. (C.) [91]

YORK. Ejected here were (1) usually included is Edward Bowles (Feb. 1613/4–Aug. 1662), son of Oliver, B.D., rector of Sutton, Beds; of St. Catharine's Hall, Cambridge; matric. sizar, 1628; B.A., 1632/3; M.A., 1636; chaplain to the second earl of Manchester; appointed, July 1644, one of the four city Ministers, officiating alternately at the Minster and Allhallows-on-the-Pavement; "he ruled all York"; his "Catechism" was prominent in the Lady Hewley case; refused the deanery of York; *d.* just before the Act came into force; bur. 23 Aug. 1662. (*C. D. V.*) (2) Thomas Calvert, of Magdalene Coll., Cambridge; matric. sizar, 1622; rem. to Sidney Sussex Coll.; B.A., 1625/6; M.A., 1629; ord. episcopally; chaplain to Sir T. Burdet; vicar of Holy Trinity, King's Court, York; one of the four city Ministers, 1644 (*see* above); ejected, 1662; remained at York till 1666; chaplain to Lady Berwick, near Tadcaster; licensed, 25 July 1672, as Pr. Teacher in his house at York; his house licensed, same date, Pr.; *d.* Mar. 1679, aged 73. (*C. D. T. V.*) (3) . . . Lamb; who afterwards conformed. (*C.*) (4) Richard Perrot, son of Richard, vicar of Hessle, E.R.; *b.* 1629; of Sidney Sussex Coll., Cambridge; matric. pensioner, 1645; B.A., 1648/9; M.A., 1652; Fellow; B.D., 1659; one of the four city Ministers (*see* above), 1658; ejected, 1662; studied and practised medicine; extra-licenciate of the College of Physicians, 18 May 1670; *d.* at York, 1671, aged 41. (*C. Mu. V.*) (5) Peter Williams [? of Emmanuel Coll., Cambridge; matric. pensioner, 1645/6]; tutor to (Sir) John Brookes (*see* Lady Priscilla Brookes) at York; one of the four city Ministers (*see* above); ejected, 1662; preached a week-day lecture at Lady Lister's; after her death, at Lady Watson's, who left him her house by will; licensed, 25 July 1672, as Grãll Pr. Teacher; his house at York licensed, same date, Pr.; *d.* 26 Mar. 1680, aged 55. (*C. T. V.*) [135, 136]

YORKSHIRE. [71, 152, 168]

YORKSHIRE, EAST RIDING. [138, 177] Mostly in the earliest handwriting; the Book-keeper has added only the name of the Manager for the County, and the 1691 entries. The returns are numbered 4; and 20 to 41, in 1691.

YORKSHIRE, NORTH RIDING. [135, 177] Except the name of the Manager for the County, and the entries, Selby to Fishlake, in the Book-keeper's hand, all is in the earliest handwriting. The returns in this hand are all numbered 3; the others, 12 to 167; but none of the places named are really in the North Riding.

Hawton is probably Haughton-le-Skerne, Durh.; or may be Long Marston, W.R.

YORKSHIRE, WEST RIDING. [129, 132, 177, 181] Except the headings "Yorkesheir West Riding" and "Yorkesheire," in the earliest handwriting, all is in the Book-keeper's hand. The returns are numbered 9 (mostly) to 138; 49, in 1691.

Alverthorp, Aterthorp, Atterthorp is Alverthorpe.

Betley is Batley [q.v.].

Bradsworth is Brodsworth [q.v.].

Burham is Byram [q.v.].

Ealand is Elland.

Gummershall is Gomersal [q.v.].

Lidget, Lidgek is Lydgate [q.v.].

Rawthmell is Rathmell [q.v.].

Rulston is Rilston, otherwise Rylstone.

Stentliffe is Staincliffe (misplaced in E.R.)

YOUNG, RICHARD (*fl.* 1669–90). **B.** The Episc. Returns, 1669, report him as preacher to Anabaptists in his house at Edlesborough, Bucks; also as an abettor of Anabaptists at Redbourne, Herts. (*T.*) [9]

YOUNG, . . . ? Samuel Young, M.A. (1648–1707). Son of John Young, of Plymouth, Dev. pleb. Matric. at Lincoln Coll., Oxford, 15 Mar. 1666/7, aged 18. Palmer places him as "an ejected Minister" in Devonshire; but in 1662 he was not above 14 years old. Succeeded Ralph Sprake, M.A., 1 Jan. 1627/8—13 Jan. 1681/2, as Nonconformist Minister at South Molton, Dev. Removed to London to take part in the Crispian controversy; wrote against Baxter in 1696. Wrote also much against Quakers, 1696–1700, under the pseudonyms *Trepidantium Malleus* and Calvin Philanax. A good classic, of strange temper, who "died before he was quite mad." (*F. P.*) [91]

# CONTENTS


| | PAGE |
|---|---|
| Preface | v |
| Typography | vii |
| The Manuscript | 1–150 |
| Commentary | 151–190 |
| The Happy Union | 151 |
| Breach of the Union | 156 |
| The Common Fund | 158 |
| Managers of the Fund | 160 |
| Meetings of the Fund | 163 |
| Contributions to the Fund | 163 |
| Subscribers to the Fund | 164 |
| Survey of Counties | 167 |
| Collection of Statistics | 169 |
| The Manuscript | 170 |
| Condition of the Manuscript | 171 |
| Date of the Manuscript | 171 |
| The Shorthand Notes | 173 |
| Use of the Manuscript | 175 |
| Grants to Ministers | 175 |
| Grants to Congregations | 179 |
| Grants to Students | 180 |
| Two Funds | 183 |

PAGE

COMMENTARY (*continued*)—

RICHARD DAVIS . . . . . . . . 184

CONCLUSION . . . . . . . . 188

INDEX . . . . . . . . . . 191–393

AUTHORITIES . . . . . . . . 192

CONTENTS . . . . . . . . . 395

*Printed by* R. & R. CLARK, LIMITED, *Edinburgh*.

# Manchester University Historical Series.

No. I. **MEDIÆVAL MANCHESTER AND THE BEGINNINGS OF LANCASHIRE.** By JAMES TAIT, M.A., Professor of Ancient and Mediæval History in the University of Manchester. With 3 Illustrations. 8vo, gilt top, 7*s*. 6*d*. net.

No. II. **INITIA OPERUM LATINORUM QUAE SAECULIS XIII., XIV., XV. ATTRIBUUNTUR.** By A. G. LITTLE, M.A., Lecturer in Palæography in the University of Manchester. 8vo. (*Out of Print.*)

No. III. **THE OLD COLONIAL SYSTEM.** By GERALD BERKELEY HURST, M.A., B.C.L., Lecturer in Colonial History in the University of Manchester. 8vo, gilt top, 6*s*. net.

No. IV. **STUDIES OF ROMAN IMPERIALISM.** By W. T. ARNOLD, M.A. Edited by EDWARD FIDDES, M.A., Lecturer in Ancient History in the University of Manchester. With Memoir of the Author by Mrs. HUMPHRY WARD and C. E. MONTAGUE, and a Photogravure portrait of W. T. Arnold. 8vo, gilt top, 7*s*. 6*d*. net.

*** *The Memoir may be had separately. 8vo, gilt top, 2s. 6d. net.*

No. V. **CANON PIETRO CASOLA'S PILGRIMAGE TO JERUSALEM IN THE YEAR 1494.** By M. MARGARET NEWETT, B.A., formerly Jones Fellow of the University of Manchester. With 3 Illustrations. 8vo, gilt top, 7*s*. 6*d*. net.

No. VI. **HISTORICAL ESSAYS.** Published in 1902 in Commemoration of the Jubilee of The Owens College, Manchester. Edited by T. F. TOUT, M.A., F.B.A., Bishop Fraser Professor of Mediæval and Ecclesiastical History in the University of Manchester, and JAMES TAIT, M.A. Re-issue with Index and new Preface. 8vo, gilt top, 7*s*. 6*d*. net.

****The Index can be purchased separately, 6d. net.*

No. VII. **STUDIES AND NOTES SUPPLEMENTARY TO STUBBS' CONSTITUTIONAL HISTORY DOWN TO THE GREAT CHARTER.** Vol. I. By CHARLES PETIT-DUTAILLIS, Litt.D., Rector of the University of Grenoble. Translated by W. E. RHODES, M.A., formerly Jones Fellow of the University of Manchester, and edited by JAMES TAIT, M.A. 8vo, gilt top, 5*s*. net.

No. VIII. **MALARIA AND GREEK HISTORY.** By W. H. S. JONES, M.A., Fellow of St. Catharine's College, Cambridge. To which is added The History of Greek Therapeutics and the Malaria Theory by E. T. WITHINGTON, M.A., M.B., Balliol College, Oxford. 8vo, gilt top, 6*s*. net.

No. IX. **THE HISTORY OF GRUFFYDD AP CYNAN.** The Welsh Text with Translation, Introduction, and Notes by ARTHUR JONES, M.A., Lecturer in Modern History in Birkbeck College, University of London, and late Assistant Lecturer in History in the University of Manchester. With 3 Illustrations. 8vo, gilt top, 6*s*. net.

No. X. **THE GREAT CIVIL WAR IN LANCASHIRE, 1642-1651.** By ERNEST BROXAP, M.A. With Map and 6 Plates. 8vo, gilt top, 7*s*. 6*d*. net.

No. XI. **A BIOGRAPHY OF THOMAS DEACON, THE MANCHESTER NON-JUROR.** By HENRY BROXAP, M.A. With 2 Illustrations. 8vo, gilt top, 7*s*. 6*d*. net.

No. XII. **THE EJECTED OF 1662:** In Cumberland and Westmorland. Their Predecessors and Successors. By B. NIGHTINGALE, M.A., Litt.D. 2 vols. 8vo, gilt top, 28*s*. net.

No. XIII. **GERMANY IN THE NINETEENTH CENTURY.** Edited by C. H. HERFORD, Litt.D. - Lectures by J. HOLLAND ROSE, Litt.D., on the Political History, C. H. HERFORD, Litt.D., on the Intellectual and Literary History, E. C. K. GONNER, M.A., on the Economic History, and M. E. SADLER, M.A., C.B., LL.D., on the History of Education. With a Prefatory Note by T. F. TOUT, M.A., F.B.A. 8vo, 3*s*. 6*d*. net.

No. XIV. **A HISTORY OF PRESTON IN AMOUNDERNESS.** By H. W. Clemesha, M.A. With 5 Maps. 8vo, gilt top, 7*s.* 6*d.* net.

No. XV. **A SHORT HISTORY OF TODMORDEN.** With some Account of the Geology and Natural History of the Neighbourhood. By Joshua Holden, M.A. With 25 Illustrations. Crown 8vo, cloth, 2*s.* net; cloth, gilt top, 2*s.* 6*d.* net.

No. XVI. **THE LOSS OF NORMANDY, 1189-1204.** Studies in the History of the Angevin Empire. By F. M. Powicke, M.A., Fellow of Merton College, Oxford, Professor of Modern History in the Queen's University, Belfast, and late Langton Fellow and Lecturer in History in the University of Manchester. With 6 Maps. 8vo, gilt top, 15*s.* net.

Nos. XVII. and XVIII. **IRELAND UNDER THE COMMONWEALTH,** Being a Selection of Documents relating to the Government of Ireland from 1651-1659. Edited, with Historical Introduction and Notes, by Robert Dunlop, M.A., Lecturer in Irish History in the University of Manchester. 2 vols. 8vo, gilt top, 25*s.* net.

No. XIX. **THE NAVAL MUTINIES OF 1797.** By Conrad Gill, M.A., Lecturer in Economic History in the University of Belfast, late Assistant Lecturer in History in the University of Manchester. With 2 Maps. 8vo, gilt top, 10*s.* 6*d.* net.

No. XX. **CHRONICA JOHANNIS DE READING ET ANONYMI CANTUARIENSIS.** Edited with Introduction and Notes by James Tait, M.A., Professor of Ancient and Mediæval History in the University of Manchester. 8vo, gilt top, 10*s.* 6*d.* net.

No. XXI. **THE PLACE OF THE REIGN OF EDWARD II. IN ENGLISH HISTORY.** Based upon the Ford Lectures delivered in the University of Oxford. By T. F. Tout, M.A., F.B.A., Bishop Fraser Professor of Mediæval and Ecclesiastical History in the University of Manchester. 8vo, 10*s.* 6*d.* net.

No. XXII. **STUDIES AND NOTES SUPPLEMENTARY TO STUBBS' CONSTITUTIONAL HISTORY.** Vol. II. By Charles Petit-Dutaillis, Litt.D., Rector of the University of Grenoble. Translated by W. T. Waugh, M.A., Lecturer in History in the University of Manchester, and edited by James Tait, M.A. 8vo, 5*s.* net.

No. XXIII. **STUDIES AND NOTES SUPPLEMENTARY TO STUBBS' CONSTITUTIONAL HISTORY.** Vols. I. and II., Consisting of Nos. VII. and XXII. of the Historical Series in 1 vol. 8vo, 9*s.* net.

No. XXIV. **GERMANY IN THE NINETEENTH CENTURY.** Edited by C. H. Herford, Litt.D. A Second Series of Lectures containing contributions by Professor A S. Peake on Theology, Dr. Bernard Bosanquet on Philosophy, and F. Bonavia on Music. With a Prefatory Note by T. F. Tout, M.A., F.B.A. 8vo, 3*s.* 6*d.* net.

No. XXV. **GERMANY IN THE NINETEENTH CENTURY.** Edited by C. H. Herford, Litt.D. Consisting of Nos. XIII. and XXIV. of the Historical Series in 1 vol. 8vo, 6*s.* net.

No. XXVI. **THE INCENDIUM AMORIS OF RICHARD ROLLE OF HAMPOLE.** Edited with Introduction and Notes by Margaret Deanesly, Research Student in History, late Assistant Mistress at the Manchester High School for Girls. With 2 Illustrations. 8vo, 10*s.* 6*d.* net.

No. XXVII. **BELGIAN DEMOCRACY, ITS EARLY HISTORY.** By Henri Pirenne, Professor of Mediæval and Belgian History in the University of Ghent. Translated by J. V. Saunders, M.A., Second Master at Hymer's College, Hull. Crown 8vo, 4*s.* 6*d.* net.

No. XXVIII. **THE MAKING OF BRITISH INDIA, 1756-1858.** Described in a Series of Dispatches, Treaties, Statutes, and other Documents. Selected and Edited, with Introductions and Notes, by Ramsay Muir, M.A., Professor of Modern History in the University of Manchester. Crown 8vo, 6*s.* net.

## Manchester University Historical Series—*continued.*

No. XXIX. **STUDIES IN ENGLISH FRANCISCAN HISTORY.** The Ford Lectures delivered in the University of Oxford during 1916. With Appendices. By A. G. LITTLE, M.A., Lecturer in Palæography in the University of Manchester. 8vo, 8*s*. 6*d*. net.

No. XXX. **FREEDOM AFTER EJECTION.** A Review (1690-1692) of Presbyterian and Congregational Nonconformity in England and Wales. Edited by ALEXANDER GORDON, M.A., sometime Lecturer in Ecclesiastical History in the University of Manchester. Fcap. 4to, 15*s*. net.

No. XXXI. **THE CHARTIST MOVEMENT.** By MARK HOVELL, M.A., late Assistant Lecturer in History in the University of Manchester. Edited and completed, with a Memoir, by T. F. TOUT, M.A., F.B.A. Crown 8vo. [*In the Press.*

No. XXXII. **STUDIES IN FOURTEENTH CENTURY ECONOMIC HISTORY BY MEMBERS OF THE HISTORY SCHOOL.** Edited by G. UNWIN, Professor of Economic History in the University of Manchester. 8vo. [*In the Press.*

No. XXXIII. **A SHORT HISTORY OF MANCHESTER.** By F. A. BRUTON, M.A., of the Manchester Grammar School. Crown 8vo. [*In Preparation.*

PUBLISHED AT

THE UNIVERSITY PRESS

12 LIME GROVE, OXFORD ROAD, MANCHESTER

LONGMANS, GREEN AND CO.

39 PATERNOSTER ROW, LONDON, E.C.

443-449 FOURTH AVENUE AND THIRTIETH STREET, NEW YORK

PRAIRIE AVENUE AND TWENTY-FIFTH STREET, CHICAGO

BOMBAY, CALCUTTA, MADRAS

Lightning Source UK Ltd.
Milton Keynes UK
UKHW020613240719
346734UK00011B/1083/P

9 781313 541275